READINGS IN AMERICAN VALUES

*. . . there exist no sources of historical information in a free and enlightened country, so rich and so valuable, as its publick journals, and the proceedings and debates of its publick bodies and associations.*

(from the Preface to Volume I of *American Archives*
published in 1837 by Peter Force)

**PRENTICE-HALL, INC.**     Englewood Cliffs, New Jersey

I N

*William Miller*

# READINGS

# AMERICAN VALUES

Selected and Edited from Public Documents of the American Past

For

*Patricia, Gregory, Jill, Laurence, Sonya, Laura, Arthur, Warren, Lauraine, and Nicky*

PRENTICE-HALL INTERNATIONAL, INC., *London*

PRENTICE-HALL OF AUSTRALIA, PTY., *Sydney*

PRENTICE-HALL OF CANADA, LTD., *Toronto*

PRENTICE-HALL OF INDIA PVT., LTD., *New Delhi*

PRENTICE-HALL OF JAPAN, INC., *Tokyo*

*Library of Congress*
*Catalogue Card No. 64-10870*
*Printed in the United States*
*of America.*

*Designed by Walter Behnke*

Current printing (last digit):

11   10   9   8   7   6   5

READINGS IN AMERICAN VALUES
*William Miller*

C-75546

# PREFACE

Although this is a book of public documents, each a unit, it is designed in content and layout as a book to be read. Although it is a short book which nevertheless aims at offering a meaningful variety of public documents, it also has a theme—the elaboration of the *values* by which Americans have conducted their public affairs.

By public documents I simply mean more or less formal statements of public officials or public bodies, temporary or permanent—for example, presidents, legislatures, administrators and judges; congresses, committees, and courts of law. By values I simply mean beliefs that condition policies or positions—for example, Jefferson's assertion toward the end of the Declaration of Independence, "That these United Colonies are, *and of Right ought to be* Free and Independent States."

Since American values are most evident in the rightly most famous documents of the American past, there has been no problem of selection on that account. The inevitable documents are here, and in most instances here in full. I hope that such familiarity as we may have with their names—Mayflower Compact, Declaration of Independence, Constitution of the United States, Monroe Doctrine,

Emancipation Proclamation, Fourteen Points, Marshall Plan, *Brown v. Board of Education of Topeka*—does not deter us from looking closely into their matter.

The problem of selection becomes acute once we pass such great milestones on the American way. In attempting to meet this problem in the short compass of this book I have sternly refrained, except in the opening document, in one or two other early ones, and in the United Nations Charter, from using material not wholly of American origin. I have also chosen those documents which I hope underscore the continuing tradition, or at least those values which were long-lived.

For illumination and impact more than for reasons of space I frequently have combined a number of related items in one unit, such as Document No. 6 on the evolution of "slavery" in the laws of Virginia, or No. 21 on the significance of the Louisiana Purchase, or No. 51 on New Deal legislation. Since I have found books of this sort, even when oriented to a theme, most useful for reference and most flexible for teaching when the selections were arranged chronologically, I have followed that practice almost without exception.

At the head of each document I have placed a single quotation from it illustrating its major theme. I hope these quotations will engage the interest of the reader in the whole selection. The introductions following these quotations attempt to place each document in its historical setting and to evoke its value content. In many of these introductions I have deliberately quoted passages that occur in the document itself. I believe that the familiarity thus afforded with portions of the material just ahead will help make its meaning more readily available when encountered a second time. Many of these documents, in any case, bear rereading in full.

In certain early documents I have modernized spelling and punctuation to the extent that in my judgment ease of reading required it. I have also broken interminable paragraphs into parts. The case for these practices is well made by Samuel Eliot Morison in the Preface to his excellent modern edition of William Bradford, *Of Plymouth Plantation 1620-1647* (New York, Alfred A. Knopf, 1952). But I have not gone as far as Professor Morison in eliminating those unobtrusive reminders in the early documents themselves that they are of another age when the English language as well as English rights and privileges were undergoing revolutionary changes.

I wish here to express my appreciation to my friend, Professor Henry Bamford Parkes, for his critical and most helpful reading of the manuscript of this book; to the administrators of the great Yale University Library for silent service of the most liberal and scholarly sort; to Dr. Albert H. Leisinger, Jr., of the National Archives for the facsimile of the document reproduced on the cover from the original in the Archives and for other assistance; to my typist, Mrs. Christine G. Valentine, for the prompt and painstaking work which I may seem to take for granted, but which I would not like to be without; and to Wilbur Mangas and Edgar P. Thomas of Prentice-Hall, whose unusual professional accomplishments and unfailing personal consideration have gone far toward making this a better book.

WILLIAM MILLER

*West Redding, Connecticut*
*June 20, 1964*

# CONTENTS

INTRODUCTION    *page 1*

**1**    *page 7*

Virginia,    *April 25, 1609*

**2**    *page 12*

The Foundations of Colonial Government in Virginia,    *1606-1658*

**3**    *page 18*

The Mayflower Compact,    *November 11, 1620*

4    *page 19*

The Book of the General Lawes and Libertyes
concerning the Inhabitants of the Massachusets,    1648

5    *page 26*

The Spirit of the Colonial Franchise,    1623-1736

6    *page 30*

The Institution of Slavery in the Laws of Virginia,    1630-1691

7    *page 34*

The Navigation System Opposed,    1698, 1701

8    *page 37*

Andrew Hamilton's Defense of John Peter Zenger,    August 4, 1735

9    *page 41*

Indian Relations on the Imperial Frontier,    1756, 1768

10    *page 46*

The Declarations of the Stamp Act Congress,    October 19, 1765

11    *page 48*

The Association,    October 20, 1774

# 12 *page 53*

The Declaration of Independence,   *July 4, 1776*

# 13 *page 57*

Articles of Confederation and Perpetual Union,   *May 1, 1781*

# 14 *page 66*

James Madison:
A Memorial and Remonstrance Against Religious Assessments,   *1785*

# 15 *page 70*

An Ordinance for the Government of the Territory
of the United States Northwest of the River Ohio,   *July 13, 1787*

# 16 *page 75*

The Constitution of the United States of America,   *September 17, 1787*

# 17 *page 91*

Alexander Hamilton to President Washington
on the Constitutionality of a National Bank,   *February 23, 1791*

# 18 *page 95*

Washington's Farewell Address,   *September 17, 1796*

**19** *page* 100

Thomas Jefferson: The Kentucky Resolutions,   *November 10, 1798*

**20** *page* 106

Thomas Jefferson: First Inaugural Address,   *March 4, 1801*

**21** *page* 111

The Louisiana Purchase in the Empire of Liberty,   *1801-1803*

**22** *page* 120

John Marshall and the Constitution,   *1803, 1819*

**23** *page* 129

The Monroe Doctrine,   *December 2, 1823*

**24** *page* 134

The Spirit of the Jacksonian Franchise,   *1818-1848*

**25** *page* 141

Henry Clay: The "American System,"   *March 30-31, 1824*

**26** *page* 147

Andrew Jackson: The Maysville Veto and Bank Veto,   *May 27, 1830   July 10, 1832*

27 *page 156*

Horace Mann's Fifth Annual Report
to the Massachusetts Board of Education, *January 1, 1842*


28 *page 164*

Asa Whitney's Memorial
for a Land Grant for a Pacific Railroad, *January 28, 1845*


29 *page 169*

Manifest Destiny and Disunion, *1844-1850*


30 *page 180*

Abraham Lincoln:
Speech at Peoria, Illinois, in Reply to Senator Douglas, *October 16, 1854*


31 *page 190*

Dred Scott *v.* Sandford, *March 6, 1857*


32 *page 198*

Abraham Lincoln: First Inaugural Address, *March 4, 1861*


33 *page 205*

The Homestead Act, the Pacific Railroad Act, and the Morrill Act, *1862*

34 *page 211*

The Emancipation Proclamation,    *January 1, 1863*

35 *page 214*

Lincoln's Gettysburg Address,    *November 19, 1863*

36 *page 216*

The Black Code of Mississippi,    *1865*

37 *page 223*

Annual Report of the Commissioner of Indian Affairs,    *November 1, 1872*

38 *page 229*

Simon Sterne Interrogates William K. Vanderbilt
for the Hepburn Committee,    *August 29, 1879*

39 *page 233*

Report of the Committee on Interstate Commerce,
Senator Shelby M. Cullom, Chairman,    *January 18, 1886*

40 *page 241*

President Cleveland and Congressman Reed
on the Protective Tariff,    *1887, 1888*

41 *page 248*

The Labor Injunction in the Pullman Strike,    *1894, 1895*

42 *page 258*

The Spirit of the Southern Franchise, *1890-1901*

43 *page 267*

McKinley's War Message and Congress's Joint Resolution
on Cuban Independence, *April, 1898*

44 *page 274*

Senator Albert J. Beveridge's Speech
on Retaining the Philippine Islands, *January 9, 1900*

45 *page 280*

The Platt Amendment and the Roosevelt Corollary, *1901, 1904, 1905*

46 *page 287*

Muller *v.* Oregon, *February 24, 1908*

47 *page 292*

Theodore Roosevelt on Liberty and Property
in an Industrial Society, *December 8, 1908*

48 *page 300*

Regulating Trusts and Monopolies, *1914*

49 *page 311*

Woodrow Wilson: The Fourteen Points, *January 8, 1918*

50 *page 318*

Franklin D. Roosevelt: First Inaugural Address,    *March 4, 1933*

51 *page 324*

General Welfare Legislation under the New Deal,    *1933, 1935*

52 *page 336*

Franklin D. Roosevelt and the End of Isolation,    *January 6, 1941*

53 *page 343*

The Charter of the United Nations,    *June 26, 1945*

54 *page 350*

The Marshall Plan and the Alliance for Progress,    *1947, 1961*

55 *page 358*

The Desegregation Decision and the Civil Rights Act,    *1954, 1964*

Selections and Sources,    *page 368*

# INTRODUCTION

Of all the proud lands of the western world, the United States was among the last to establish a National Archives for the collection, preservation, and public examination of its historic records. The National Archives building in Washington, D.C., begun in 1931 and completed in 1935, capped more than half a century of resolute promotion by scholars and librarians led by John Franklin Jameson. The story of their long and usually discouraging campaign is well told in *An Historian's World, Selections from the Correspondence of John Franklin Jameson*, edited by Elizabeth Donnan and Leo F. Stock (Philadelphia, 1956).

Earlier Thomas Jefferson, who for fifty years "spared no pains, opportunity, or expense," as he said in 1814, to collect the seven thousand books that were to form the nucleus of the Library of Congress, had also made characteristically strenuous efforts to assemble the principal public documents of his day. "His indefatigable labors," writes Julian P. Boyd, the able editor of the

Jefferson papers, "reveal the consciousness of his effort to preserve for posterity a full account of the major events through which the country passed in its formative years and his own part in those events." Jefferson's inexhaustible motivation for such documentary work lay in his grasp of the lasting meaning of the American Revolution for mankind, as disclosed in his letter to John Dickinson from the White House, March 6, 1801, reproduced below in Document No. 21. But Jefferson was a singular figure, and for a long time there was little building upon the foundation he so jealously laid.

In the Jacksonian era Peter Force, a Whig printer in Washington, launched a monumental enterprise looking to the publication of at least twenty volumes of "Authentick Records, State Papers, Debates, and Letters and Other Notices of Publick Affairs" covering the "Origin and Progress of the North American Colonies" to the "Final Ratification" of the Constitution. In the Preface to his first volume, published in 1837, Force wrote:

> If in Europe there exist sufficient motives to prompt such undertakings, how infinitely more weighty and more efficient ought they to be among us. These inquiries, originating in the liberal and inquisitive character of the age, may be expected to be most zealously pursued in those countries where freedom prevails. Designed, as they are, to exhibit the fundamental principles of government, they might naturally be expected to be most warmly cherished, where free institutions exist. Independently of this, all our historical memorials are of comparatively recent date, they are written in a language familiar to all, they tend to illustrate existing institutions, and a history which still retains all its personal interest.

Force's work was to be paid for by the State Department; but when Secretary of State William L. Marcy cut off the funds in 1853 the project died. By then Force had published only the nine volumes of *American Archives* covering the years 1774-1776.

A third pioneering effort to keep the official record straight was that of General Adolphus Washington Greely, the self-taught engineer and Arctic explorer who in the 1890's began to put the War Department's library in order. His work here led him eventually to the publication of his bibliography, "Public Documents of the First Fourteen Congresses 1789-1817," still the best in its field. Until Greely's work was issued in 1900 as *Senate Document 428, 56th Congress 1st Session*, there was not even a "detailed list," as he himself said, let alone a complete collection of the documents, of the transactions of this momentous period of "the making of the nation."

The work of Jefferson, Force, and Greely, of course, does not exhaust the pioneer efforts to assemble the basic public documents of the American past. One of the most notable collections, made under the direction of General William Hickey, is the 38 volumes of *American State Papers* from the period 1789-1833, published between 1832 and 1861. But J. H. Powell discloses the characteristic inadequacy of such early efforts when he observes in his illuminating work, *The Books of a New Nation, United States Government Publications 1774-1814*

(Philadelphia, 1957): "The *American State Papers* had contained 2,464 documents for . . . [Greely's] period. He had listed and identified upwards of 5,000." Similarly slipshod is an even better known monument to this epoch, James D. Richardson, *A Compilation of the Messages and Papers of the Presidents 1789-1897* (10 volumes, Washington, D.C., 1897).

Most Americans, perhaps, have been too full of life to worry excessively about the documentary record of the past. And yet the hopes and fears, aspirations and responsibilities of the most ignorant as well as of the best informed rest upon it all the same. When Henry Ford was challenged in 1916 with having made the thoughtless remark that "History is more or less bunk," he defended his statement with honest ingenuousness: "I did not say it was bunk. It was bunk to me . . . but I did not need it very bad." He did not need it because unbeknown to him others had subscribed to the covenants, made the declarations, framed the constitutions, and written the laws which, as a member of his own family said, assured him of "the sense of freedom, the feeling of independence, the opportunity to meet the necessities with all . . . [his] natural resourcefulness."

No one, moreover, had sought to deprive Ford of his liberties as Charles I, for example, had sought to deprive Englishmen of theirs in 1628 by taxing them without their consent. This royal pretension to absolutism sent its intended victims hastily enough back to "a statute made in the time of the reign of King Edward the First" in the thirteenth century, and to "other good laws and statutes of this realm," by which "your subjects have inherited this freedom, that they should not be compelled to contribute to any tax . . . not set by common consent in Parliament." These statutes on taxation, and on other subjects comprising the cherished "privileges and immunities" of Englishmen, Puritan leaders in particular reviewed in their famous "Petition of Right." When King Charles, having conceded the lawfulness of this Petition, promptly ignored it, certain Puritans hastened their departure for a freer land. Once here, they pressed for and soon completed the first legal code in the English-speaking world, "whereby," as they said, "we may manifest our utter disaffection to arbitrary government."

Their English legal heritage, in so far as they understood it, furnished useful precedents for the first lawmakers in America. But the Puritans had a second recourse closer to their hearts and minds. This was the Mosaic code of ancient Israel, which provided moral underpinning as well as written substance for the rule of law. In Document No. 4, I quote the "Epistle" of 1648, "To Our Beloved Brethren and Neighbours, the Inhabitants of the Massachusets," in which the committee of magistrates and deputies named "to satisfie your longing expectation" to see "in print" the statutes of the colony, commend their code to the people. This Epistle begins:

> So soon as God had set up Politicall Government among his people Israel hee gave them a body of lawes for judgement both in civil and criminal causes.

These were breif and fundamental principles, yet withall so full and comprehensive as out of them clear deductions were to be drawn to all particular cases in future times. For a Common-wealth without lawes is like a Ship without rigging and steeradge.

When the Massachusetts code of 1648 was "in a manner agreed upon," the General Court ordered that in printing the laws "there be larg margents left," for "any references, scriptures, or the like." That Scripture was often followed is plainly evident from the "Capital Lawes" in this code, also reproduced below with chapter and verse in Document No. 4. The capital laws of England at this time invoked the death penalty for hundreds of infractions, most of them petty crimes against the property of the mighty. Those of Massachusetts named only the fifteen offences, for murder, personal defilement, idolatry, witchcraft, and blasphemy, found in the Old Testament.

Human life (Christian more than heathen, of course) was precious in America. John Cotton, probably the most influential preacher in early New England and not the gentlest, gave it as "a Rule without Exception, . . . That no human law can justly take away the life of a man for any offence, without a general or particular warrant from God's word; because man's life is onely at God's disposing."

Human life was precious in America for less transcendent reasons as well. Men were urgently needed to defend the wilderness Zions against the Indians, to clear and cultivate the land, to "farm the sea" for fish, to build the houses and the ships, the churches and the schools. Thus they could not as freely be executed here for venial trespasses, as they could be everywhere at home. In this respect, and eventually in many others, American law was forced to bend with the environment, as the colonial charters, the third written recourse of the pioneers, foresaw. The Massachusetts charter of 1629, for example, required only that New World legislation be "not contrairie to the Lawes of this our Realme of England." This limitation being met, it was "lawfull . . . for the Governor . . . and . . . Assistants and Freemen . . . to make, ordeine, and establishe all Manner of wholesome and reasonable Orders, Lawes, Statutes, and Ordinances, Directions, and Instructions . . . fitt and necessary for the said Plantation and the Inhabitants there," and these shall be "published in Writing, under their common Seale."

It is impossible to read very far in the proceedings of any of the early legislative bodies in America (see, for example, the record of the Virginia House of Burgesses reproduced below in Document No. 2) without being impressed by the speed with which the members, distant from the authority of king and parliament, grasped the reins of government thus innocently offered to them, and by the boldness with which they reached out for power beyond their charter rights to make a written record of their own. The overweening spirit of independence manifest in these actions gradually became ingrained in the American character, and when, in the middle of the eighteenth century, governors and kings were to grow careless of American sensibilities, they were promptly rebuked with stern reminders of the legal rights of British subjects and the natural rights of God-fearing men (Documents No. 10, 11, and 12).

Rebukes unheeded soon led to rebellion, and successful rebellion to a new sense of responsibility. As Charles A. Beard wrote of the founding fathers in *The American Spirit*:

> Reflective thinkers in the United States meditated upon their heritage, the place of the recent revolutionary act in the long drama of mankind, and its significance for the future of the continent. . . . They bent their minds to charting a course for the realization in practice, public and private, of the humane principles to which Americans were committed in great official documents—republican ideals, self-government for the people, rights to life, liberty and the pursuit of happiness, and administration for the general welfare.

The American Constitution of 1787 grew out of the meditations of these men. This great document (No. 16) may be called the first modern written constitution, to be sure. But its larger importance lies elsewhere. The Constitution gave orderliness and the open stamp of authority to the "humane principles" of which Beard wrote, and which themselves derived from ancient Holy Writ, modern English law, liberal colonial charters, and above all from the few short decades of American experience. After 1787, the spread of these humane principles became identified with nothing less than the progress of "civilization," a word that entered the language only late in the eighteenth century and then only in connection with the American republican "experiment." When, in 1863, Abraham Lincoln spoke at the cemetery in Gettysburg (Document No. 35) of "the unfinished work which they who fought here have thus far so nobly advanced," it was these principles of "government of the people, by the people, for the people," that he held foremost in view.

And yet as Lincoln's phrase, "unfinished work," forcibly reminds us, we cannot blink the uses made of certain other principles that were also operative in America with the sanction of official documents; for example, the justification found in "Manifest Destiny" for the systematic destruction of the Indians; or the justification found in "the sanctity of private property" for the degradation of the African in slavery; or the justification found in "individualism" for the brutalization of industrial workers. Each of these *inhumane* principles, as documents presented in this book make clear, also had its warrant in solemn treaties, statutes, and decisions of the courts.

But if some public documents disclose the harshness of American values, others, it must be added promptly, reveal the deep American concern for tempering the harsh effects—by broadening educational opportunities (Documents No. 4, 27, 33, 55), unlocking economic opportunities (Documents No. 7, 25, 33, 48), and by otherwise advancing the general welfare even when it meant going beyond the powers implied in the supreme law of the land as the pioneers went beyond their charters (Documents No. 30, 47, 50, 51). Americans have been quick to excuse many vices by invoking the "higher law" of their destiny as the Chosen People in the Promised Land—a destiny strongly impressed upon them from the very start of their New World adventure (Document No. 1). But they have been no less quick to enlarge many virtues by invoking the "higher law" of Humanity. For, as the Massachusetts Epistle of 1648 said, "nor is it enough to have lawes except they be also just."

In recent years American values have been challenged as sternly as English values were in the 1620's and 1630's, as sternly as colonial values were in the 1760's and 1770's. In part as a response to this challenge, the United States has recently taken long strides forward in assembling, organizing, and publishing its historic documents, and in some respects has taken world leadership in such work. It is one of the ironies of our great tradition of insistence upon written law, written constitutions, written interpretations of our rights and duties, that we should have been so late in opening up our public archives and the private archives of our public men. But this delay itself illuminates our vast confidence in our heritage and the extent to which, as free men, we have taken its privileges for granted. No longer may we do so with the aplomb of a Henry Ford. We need our history, warts and all, and especially a knowledge of its documentary foundations. This book offers an introduction to this knowledge, highly selective as such a short work needs be, and yet one that I trust supplies the elements which larger works must themselves confront.

# 1

## "Get thee out of thy Countrey, . . . unto the land that I will shew thee"

In England early in the seventeenth century the Established Church was a tool of the Crown, and sermons preached by Church of England ministers in praise of Crown enterprises thereby took on the character of official as well as clerical acts. In its most bedeviled early years, even so materialistic a Crown enterprise as that of the "Adventurers and Planters for Virginia" won favorable notice in a number of Church of England sermons, some of which were preached explicitly to promote the fortunes of the initial English settlement in the New World. Probably the first of such promotional sermons to be printed for wide distribution was that delivered by the Reverend William Symonds at "White-Chappel" in London, April 25, 1609. Running to no less than 20,000 words and never reissued in full, it is reproduced in part in this Document.

In exhorting his countrymen, in defiance of the claims of papist Spain, to "get thee out of thy Countrey, . . . unto the land that I will shew thee," Symonds promised them the same bright future in "Virginea Britannia" as the Lord promised the seed of Abraham in the land of Canaan, and in the selfsame words: "And I will make thee a great nation, and will blesse thee, and make thy name great." More than that, in his powerful importunings and his proffered rewards, Symonds thus early marshaled the authority of Scripture behind many of what were to become the most enduring impulses in American life: the "calling to seeke for roome"; the injunction to "till the earth"; the propriety of expelling by force the wastrel savages who "live but like Deer in herds and . . . know no God but the divell," so that "Thy dominion should be from sea to sea, and from the river to the end of the land." And what a dominion it would be: "Wherefore seeing we are contented, when the King doth press us out to war, to go we know not whither, nor under whom, and can propose no thing unto us but to fight with a mightie enemie: Let us be cheerful to go to the place that God will shew us to possess in peace and plentie, a Land more like the Garden of Eden . . . than any part else of all the earth."

*April 25, 1609*

# Virginia

*(A Sermon Preached at White-Chappel in the Presence of many, Honour-*
*able and Worshipfull, the Adventurers and Planters for Virginia.)*

EPISTLE DEDICATORIE

To the Right Noble and Worthie Advancers of The Standard of Christ, among the Gentiles, The Adventurers for the Plantation of Virginia, W[illiam] S[ymonds] prayeth that Nations may blesse them, and be blessed by them.

Right Noble and Worthy, such as do prayse the worthies do cloth them with the robes of others that have gone before them in vertues of like nature. A thing which I cannot doe of your Plantation, seeing neither Testament (that I can find) dooth afford us a Parallel in men of like qualities. . . .

This land was of Old time offered to Our Kings. Our late Soveraigne Q. Elizabeth (whose storie hath no peere among Princes of her sexe) being a pure Virgin, found it, set foot in it, and called it Virginia. Our most sacred Soveraigne, in whom is the spirit of his great Ancestor, Constantine the pacifier of the World, and planter of the Gospell in places most remote, desireth to present this land a pure Virgine to Christ. Such as do manage the expedition, are carefull to carry thither no traitors, nor Papists that depend on the Great Whore. Lord finish this Good worke thou hast begun; and marry this land, a pure Virgine to thy Kingly son Christ Jesus; so shall thy name be magnified; and we shall have a Virgin or Maiden Britaine, a comfortable addition to our Great Britaine. . . .

VIRGINEA BRITANNIA

For the Lord had said unto Abram, get thee out of thy Countrey, and from thy Kindred, and from thy father's house, unto the land that I will shew thee.

And I will make thee a great nation, and will blesse thee, and make thy name great, and thou shalt be a blessing.

I will blesse them also that blesse thee, and curse them that curse thee, and in thee shall all the families of the earth be blessed (*Genesis* 12.1.2.3.)

This Book of Genesis containeth the story of the Creation and Plantation of heaven and earth with convenient inhabitants. The heaven hath Angels, the skie starres, the aire fowles, the water fishes, the earth (furnished with plants and herbes and beasts) was provided for man a while to inhabite, who after was to be received into Glory, *like unto the Angels* (Matth. 22.30.) Hereupon the Lord . . . did make man both male and female, *After his owne image*, that is *Jesus Christ* (2. Cor. 4.4.), and gave them this blessing, *Bring forth fruit and multiplie, and fill the earth, and subdue it*, &c. (Gen. 1.26.27.28.). And howsoever this precept might seeme to find interruption by the sinne of man, that had incurred the curse *to die the death* (Gen. 2.17 & 3.3): yet we see that God would not, for any thing, *alter his oath and word, that was gone out of his mouth* (Isai. 45.23.); for unto *Noah* he revived this precept after the flood. . . .

Now if it be demaunded how *Abraham* was called, to go into another Countrey: the answer is, both ordinarily and extraordinarily. It was a knowne rule of the word of God, concluded, and pronounced before the Creation, and often repeated afterwards, that man should spread abroad, &c. *and inhabite the earth, and fill it* (Gen. 9.12.). Hitherto belongeth that, which God said: *Let us make man in our image, and let them rule over the Fish of the Sea, and over the Fowles of Heaven, and over the Beastes, and over ALL the earth* (Gen. 1.26.). Then must he replenish the earth, else can he not rule over ALL. To the same effect is that spoken of *Adam*, after his fall, that *God sent him forth of the Garden of Eden to till the earth* (Gen. 3.23.): so that the fall of *Adam* did not, in the least thing, cause the Lord to alter his first decree. So to *Noah* after the flood; *Bring forth fruite, and multiply, grow plentifully in the earth, and encrease therein, and replenish the earth* (Gen. 9.2.7.). By all this it doth appeare, that God did call *Abraham* abroade, by a general Vocation. But when he is called to a certaine place, and under certaine conditions, it is also plaine he had a special and extradordinary calling, . . . Yet still we must remember that this special calling was subject to the general law of replenishing the earth. For although God called him to one land; yet to upholde the general rule, God often laide a necessitie upon him to spread further: . . .

The reason why God will have his to fill the earth is, because the Lord would have his workes to be knowne. . . . When *David* saith, *All thy workes praise thee, O God, and thy Saints blesse thee; they shew the glory of thy kingdome, and speake of thy power* (Psal. 145. 10.12.): the implication is manifest, that his Saints must be witnesses of all his workes, in all Climates; for else they cannot blesse him in all his workes. Another reason is, that one that hath the knowledge of the feare of God, should communicate it to others. . . . Marke this, that he biddeth us to pray, *God be mercifull unto us*; The meanes how, is this: *That they may know thy way upon earth, and thy saving health among all nations* (Psal. 67.2.); whereby he doth imply, that God hath with-held some mercy from us, till all nations have the means of salvation. . . .

Then here must we know that what inducement *Abraham* had to go out of his Countrey by a generall calling, the same doth binde all his sonnes, according to the faith, to go likewise abroad, when God doth not otherwise call them to some special affaires . . .: *Go teach* (saith he) *all nations, and baptize them in the name of the Father, the Sonne, and the holy Ghost* (Matth. 28.19.). Gave he this Commandment to his Apostles only? have not also the labours of godly Preachers, which they have spread over the face of the whole earth, been bestowed by the power of this Commandment? And though the words, as they lie, do bind the Ministers of the Word, to endeavour the propagation of the Gospell, with all their power; yet not only them: For we reade, that poor Tentmakers and others have done much good in spreading the Gospell, according to their vocations (Acts 18.3.26.); they also satisfying thus much of Christ's precept. Neither can there be any doubt, but that the Lord that called *Abraham* into another Countrey doeth also by the same holy hand call you to go and carry the Gospell to a Nation that never heard of Christ. The prophet *Zachary*, speaking of the days of the Gospell, doth shew, that it is a good Vocation for men to go abroad when the number of the children of God do exceede. . . . Unto whom agreeth the Prophet Isaiah: *The children of thy barrennesse shall say againe, in thine eares, the place is too strait for me, give me place, that I may dwell* (Isai. 49.20.). Wherefore seeing that, thanks be to God, we are thronged with multitudes; the Lord of hostes himselfe hath given us the calling of his children to seeke for roome, and place to dwell in.

And heer might we have proceeded to the next point were it not for one scruple which some that think themselves to be very wise do cast in our way; which is this in effect. The countrey, they say, is possessed by owners, that rule, and governe it in their own right: then with what conscience, and equitie can we offer to thrust them, by violence, out of their inheritances?

For answer to this objection: first it

is plain, that the objector supposeth it not lawfull to invade the territories of other princes, by force of sword. . . . Come forth ye great Princes and Monarches of Assyria, Persia, Media, Greece and Rome with your gravest counsellours, and answer for your facts in conquering and subduing nations. For your stories, that were wont to be read with singular admiration of your fortitude, your wisdom, your magnificence, and your great justice, are now araigned and must bee found guiltie, that through your sides an action of truer honour than ever you attempted may bee wounded. Your strong title of the sword, heretofore magnified by Historians, Politicians, and Civilians, is to our objector, but a spiders web, or the hatching of a Cockatrice his egge. But whatsoever the rest can say for their own defence, the Lord himself doth say thus much for *Cyrus: Thus saith the Lord unto Cyrus, his anointed: whose right hand I have holden to subdue nations before him: therefore will I weaken the loynes of Kings, and open the doores before him, and the gates shall not be shut: I will goe before thee, and make the crooked straight: I will breake the brasen doores, and burst the iron barres. And I will give thee the treasures of darkenesse, and the things hid in secret places; that thou maist know, that I am the Lord, which call thee by thy name, even the God of Israell* . . . (Isai. 45.1.2.3.). Then who can blame *Cyrus*, and keep himself from blaspheming the almightie.

Nay, that which is more to be trembled at, we must also to summon up and call to the bar the most holy worthies of the Scripture: and see if man, or God, hath any thing to be said for them, why they should not be condemned as injust, cruell, and bloudy. O *Jacob*, thy blessed bow and sword, with the fruit whereof thou blessedest thy son *Joseph*, the staff of thy gray head and feeble knees must be broken and burnt: and thou must be condemned for thy unlawful conquest (Gen. 48.22.). Worthy *Joshuah*, & most worthy *David* with thy cloud of worthies, who hanged up so many shields in the house of God, and who sweetly singeth that *God was his fortitude and buckler* (Psal. 18.2; Josh. 10.14.) must incurre the note of injustice. . . . Nay thou glory of men and true type of Christ, King *Solomon*, whose wisdome was like unto the wisedome of God: teach us to say somewhat in thy defence. . . . Give an account of his innocence that said unto thee: *Girde thee with thy sworde upon thy thigh, O thou most mightie,—Thy right hand shall teach thee terrible things,—The people shall fall under thee* (Psal. 45.3.4.5.). Thy father, the son of Ishai, made a sinfull prayer for thee (as our objectors blaspheme) when he said, thou shouldest so enlarge thy borders, that *Thy dominion should be from sea to sea, and from the river to the end of the land.* He would have thee too rigid when he saith, *That thine enemies should lick the dust.* . . .

I know that the divell himselfe, with all his distinctions that ever he made, which are recorded in Scripture, or which he left in hell, in his cabinet of *Abstruse Studies*, (locked safe till he found out the Jesuits, his trustie secretaries, to keepe them) I say none of them all can arm a subject against his prince without sin. But he that will set open his school . . . and take upon him to nurture princes as petties telling them that they must not make offensive warres, if it were to gaine the whole world to Christ, shall never be bidders of guests to *the marriage of the kings sonne* (Matth. 22.2.), who are required to compell them to *come in* (Luke 14.23.). And if I might be so bold, I would faine aske one question of these objectors, that come dropping out of some Anabaptist Spicery: whether (if it be unlawfull to conquer) the crowne sit well on the head of our most sacred soveraigne? For by this objection they shew, that had they power to untwist that, which in so many ages hath been well spun, they would write him crownless, as far as he hath his title from the conqueror.

O but God forbid, saith the objector,

that wee should doe any wrong at all, no not to the divell . . . What wrong, I pray you, did the Apostles in going about to alter the lawes of nations, even against the expresse commandement of the princes, and to set up the throne of Christ. If your mouth be so foul to charge them with wrong, *as the Gentiles did*, we have more need to provide you a medicine for a cankred mouth, and a stincking breath, then to make you any answer at all.

O but, in entering of other countries, there must needs be much lamentable effusion of bloud. Certainly our objector was hatched of some popish egge; & it may be in a JESUITS vault, where they feed themselves fat with tormenting innocents. . . . And if these objectors had any braines in their head but those which are sick, they could easily finde a difference between a bloudy invasion and the planting of a peaceable Colony in a waste country where the people do live but like Deer in herds and have not as yet attained unto the first modestie that was in *Adam*, that knew he was naked, where they know no God but the divell, nor sacrifice, but to offer their men and children unto *Moloch*. . . .

The children of Israel that were in the wilderness, readie to perish if God withdrew his miraculous hand, like a stiffnecked people as they were, refused to goe, fell into a mutiny, and made a commotion, upon the newes that the *Land had fenced cities, and walled townes exceeding great. And because there were the sonnes of Anak* (Num. 13:29.): mightie Giants that were armed in Brasse, & their speare like a Weavers cloth beam. For they forgat the God that brought them out of Egypt, and that made the raging waves of the sea to stand in heaps and take the office of strong walls, that they might easily march through upon drie land. They forgat that God was the creator of the mountains, whereof one of the least is stronger than all the sons of *Anak*. They forgat that God putteth away all the ungodly of the earth like drosse. But we should be worse than mad to be discouraged by any such imaginations of this place. There are but poore Arbors for Castles, base and homely sheds for walled townes. A Mat is their strongest Portcullis, a naked brest their Target of best proofe, an arrow of reade, on which is no iron, their most fearful weapon of offence, here is no feare of nine hundred iron chariots. . . . Wherefore, seeing we are contented when the King doth press us out to war, to go we know not whither, nor under whom, and can propose no thing unto us but to fight with a mightie enemie: Let us be cheerfull to go to the place that God will shew us to possess in peace and plentie, a Land more like the Garden of Eden, which the Lord planted, then any part else of all the earth.

## 2

*"Such a form of government . . . as may be to the greatest benefit and comfort of the people"*

The first charter of the Virginia enterprise, April 10, 1606, in effect created a trading company under the personal rule of his "divine Majesty," James I. James claimed to be an absolute monarch "by the grace of God," but even he felt obliged to give lip service, at least, to those "liberties, franchises, and immunities" which Englishmen asserted as their legal rights (item "a" below). That these rights did not yet extend to religious freedom such as might weaken "the obedience of us, our heires, and successors" is clear from the "Instructions . . . for the good Order and Government of Virginia" which James issued on November 20, 1606 (item "b"). These instructions especially stressed the conversion of the "salvages" to the Church of England so that they too might more readily be brought under royal sway for "sociable traffique and dealing" (item "c").

By 1609 it had become clear that trade was not easily to be developed in the American wilderness and that if the Virginia "plantation" were to survive, the company must be transformed into a "Body Politic" with an authoritative governor resident in the New World. To effect this transformation James issued a new charter, May 23, 1609. When this step, after a test of almost ten years, brought little improvement in conditions, the company itself, in the form of instructions to Governor George Yeardley, November 18, 1618, undertook "to lay the foundation whereon A flourishing State might in process of time by the blessing of Almighty God be raised." Yeardley's instructions were the first to provide for the use of America's vast land resources for the support of public functions (item "d"). They also provided the first opportunity for settlers not themselves members of the company to acquire private land-holdings. Presumably other instructions accompanied those of November, 1618, enjoining the governor to permit the settlers to "have a hand in the governing of themselves" by electing "burgesses" to the second of "two supreme councils." In any case, although the creation of the Virginia House of Burgesses was not confirmed until the Ordinance and Constitution of July 24, 1621 (item "e"), it actually held its first session, the momentous first meetings of any legislative body in the colonies, July 30 to August 4, 1619.

Even this step could not reverse Virginia's ill fortunes. These became so menacing by 1624 that James terminated the rule of the company and resumed royal command. Meetings of the House of Burgesses itself now lapsed for five years. But in 1629 the House began to convene once more and, as England's domestic difficulties deepened in the Cromwellian era (1650-1660), the members gradually asserted that independence and authority which became the most portenous feature of Virginia's political development (items "f" to "i").

*1606-1658*

# The Foundations
# of Colonial Government in Virginia

(a) *The "liberties, franchises and immunities" of Englishmen*

(from the first Virginia charter, April 10, 1606)

XV. Also we do, for us, our heirs, and successors, declare, by these presents, that all and every the persons, being our subjects, which shall dwell and inhabit within every or any of the said colonies and plantations, and every of their children which shall happen to be born within any of the limits and precincts of the said several colonies and plantations, shall have and enjoy all liberties, franchises, and immunities, within any of our other dominions, to all intents and purposes as if they had been abiding and born within this our realm of England, or any other of our said dominions.

(b) *"Service of God" limited "to the doctrine . . .*
*now professed" in England*

(from James I's Instructions for the Government of Virginia, November 20, 1606)

. . . And we do specially ordaine, charge, and require, the said presidents and councells, and the ministers of the said several colonies respectively, . . . that they, with all diligence, care and respect, do provide, that the true word, and service of God and Christian faith be preached, planted and used, not only within every of the said colonies, and plantations, but also as much as they may amongst the salvage people which do or shall adjoin unto them, or border upon them, according to the doctrine, rights, and religion now professed and established within our realme of England, and that they shall not suffer any person, or persons to withdrawe any of the subjects or people inhabiting, or which shall inhabit within any of the said several colonies and plantations from the same, or from their due allegiance, unto us, our heirs and successors, as their immediate soveraigne under God; and if they shall find within any of the said colonies and plantations, any person or persons so seeking to withdrawe any of the subects of us, our heirs or successors, or any of the people of those lands or territories, within the precincts aforesaid, they shall with all diligence, him or them so offending cause to be apprehended, arrested, and imprisoned, until he shall fully and throughly reform himself, or otherwise, when the cause so requireth, that he shall, with all convenient speed be sent into our realme of England, here to receive condigne punishment for his or their said offence or offences.

(c)  *"All just kind and charitable courses shall" be followed toward the Indians*

(from James I's Instructions for the Government of Virginia, November 20, 1606)

Furthermore, our will and pleasure is, . . . that every person and persons being our subjects of every the said colonies and plantations shall . . . use all good means to draw the salvages and heathen people of the said several places, and of the territories and countries adjoining, to the true service and knowledge of God, and that all just, kind and charitable courses, shall be holden with such of them as shall conforme themselves to any good and sociable traffique and dealing with the subjects of us, our heirs and successors, which shall be planted there, whereby they may be the sooner drawne to the true knowledge of God, and the obedience of us.

(d)  *Land grants "to Ease all the Inhabitants of Virginia forever of all taxes and public burthens"*

(from Instructions from the Virginia Company in London to George Yeardley, November 18, 1618)

And because our intent is to Ease all the Inhabitants of Virginia forever of all taxes and public burthens as much as may be and to take away all occasion of oppression and corruption we have thought fit to begin . . . to alot and lay out a convenient portion of public lands for the maintenance and support as well of Magistracy and officers as of other public charges. . . . We therefore . . . require you the said Governor and Council of Estate to put in execution with all convenient speed a former order . . . for the laying and seting out of bounds and metes of three thousand acres of land in the best and most convenient place . . . to be the seat and land of the Governor of Virginia for the time being and his Successors, and to be called by the name of the Governors Land. . . . In like sort we require you to set and lay out by bounds and Metes other three thousand Acres of good land . . . which . . . shall be called the Companies Land. . . .

We further will and ordain that in every of those Cities or Burroughs the several quantity of one hundred acres of land be set out . . . toward the maintenance of the several Ministers of the parishes . . . And Whereas by a special grant and license from his Majesty a general contribution over this realm hath been made for the building and planting of a college for the training up of the Children of those Infidels in true Religion, moral virtue, and Civility and for other godly uses, We do therefore . . . ordain that . . . ten thousand acres . . . be alotted and set out for the endowing of the said . . . College with convenient possessions.

## (e)  *The establishment of the Virginia House of Burgesses*

(from the Ordinance and Constitution
of the Treasurer, Council, and Company in England, July 24, 1621)

I. . . . Know ye, that we, . . . taking into our careful consideration the present state of the said colony of Virginia, and intending by the divine assistance, to settle such a form of government there, as may be to the greatest benefit and comfort of the people, . . . have thought fit to make our entrance by ordering and establishing such supreme councils as may not only be assisting to the governor for the time being, in the administration of justice, and the executing of other duties to this office belonging, but also, by their vigilant care and prudence, may provide . . . for advancing of increase, strength, stability, and prosperity of the said colony:

II. We therefore, . . . by authority directed to us from his majesty . . . do hereby order and declare, that, from hence forward, there shall be two supreme councils in Virginia, for the better government of the said colony aforesaid.

III. The one of which councils, to be called the council of state, . . . shall be chosen, nominated, placed, and displaced, from time to time, by us the said treasurer, council and company, and our successors: . . . Which said . . . council we earnestly pray and desire, and in his majesty's name strictly charge and command, that (all factions, partialities, and sinister respect laid aside) they bend their care and endeavours to assist the said governor; first and principally, in the advancement of the honour and service of God, and the enlargement of his kingdom against the heathen people: and next, in erecting of the said colony in due obedience to his majesty, and all lawful authority from his majesty's directions; and lastly, in maintaining the said people in justice and christian conversation amongst themselves, and in strength and ability to withstand their enemies. And this council, to be always, or for the most part, residing about or near the governor.

IV. The other council, more generally to be called by the governor, once yearly, and no oftener, but for very extraordinary and important occasions, shall consist for the present, of the said council of state, and of two burgesses out of every town, hundred, or other particular plantation, to be respectively chosen by the inhabitants: which council shall be called The General Assembly, wherein (as also in the said council of state) all matters shall be decided, determined, and ordered by the greater part of the voices then present; reserving to the governor always a negative voice. And this general assembly shall have free power, to treat, consult, and conclude, as well of all emergent occasions concerning the publick weal of the said colony and every part thereof, as also to make, ordain, and enact such general laws and orders, for the behoof of the said colony, and the good government thereof, as shall, from time to time, appear necessary or requisite;

V. Whereas in all other things, we require the said general assembly, as also the said council of state, to imitate and follow the policy of the form of government, laws, customs, and manner of trial, and other administration of justice, used in the realm of England, as near as may be even as ourselves, by his majesty's letters patent, are required.

VI. Provided, that no law or ordinance, made in the said general assembly, shall be or continue in force or validity, unless the same shall be solemnly ratified and confirmed, in a general quarter court of the said company here in England, and so ratified, to be returned to them under our seal; it being our intent to afford the like measure also unto the said colony, that after the government of the said colony shall once have been well framed, and settled accordingly, . . . no orders of court afterwards, shall bind the said colony, unless they be ratified in like manner in the general assemblies.

## (f)    No taxation without representation
### (from Acts of the Grand General Assembly, 1646)

Act XXI. Be it enacted by this present Grand Assembly . . . and further . . . confirmed that no leavies be raised within the colony but by a General Grand Assembly.

## (g)    No executive power except as granted by the General Assembly
### (from the Journal of the Grand Assembly, April 30, 1652)

After long and serious debate and advice taken for the settleing and governing of Virginia, It was unanimously voted and concluded, by the commissioners appointed here by authority of parliament and by all the Burgesses of the severall countys and plantations, . . . That . . . the said Governour, Secretary and Council of State are to have such power and authorities and to act from time to time, as by the Grand Assembly shall be appointed and granted to their several places respectively.

## (h)    Burgesses to elect all executive officers
### (from the Journal of the Grand Assembly, May 5, 1652)

It is agreed and thought best for the government of this country by the Governor, Council and Burgesses that the right of election of all officers of this colony be and appertain to the Burgesses, the representative of the people.

## (i)    "Not dissolvable by any power . . . but our own"
### (from the Journal of the Assembly, April 1-2, 1658)

The Governor and Council for many important causes do think fitt hereby to declare, That they do now dissolve this present Assembly, And that the Speaker accordingly do dismiss the Burgesses.

SAMUEL MATHEWES, Gov.

WM. CLAIBORNE, Sec.

THE ANSWER OF THE BURGESSES
TO THE DECLARATION
OF THE HONOURABLE
GOVERNOUR AND COUNCIL.

THE House humbly present, That the said dissolution as the case now standeth is not precedentall, neither legal according to the lawes now in force; Therefore we humbly desire a revocation of the said declaration, especially seeing we doubt not but speedily to finish the present affaires to the satisfaction of your honour and the whole country.

*Subscribed,*

JOHN SMITH, *Speaker.*

THE REPLY OF THE HONOURABLE
THE GOVERNOUR AND COUNCIL.

UPON your assurance of a speedy issue to conclude the acts so near brought to a confirmation in this Assembly, we are willing to come to a speedy conclusion, And to refer the dispute of the power of dissolving and the legality thereof to his Highness the Lord Protector:

*Subscribed,*

SAMUEL MATHEWES, *Gov.*

WM. CLAIBORNE, *Sec.*

THE House, unsatisfied with these answers, appointed a committee to draw up a report for manifestation and vindication of the Assembly's power which after presentation to the House to be sent to the Governour and Council.

THE REPORT OF THE COMMITTEE
NOMINATED FOR VINDICATION
AND MANIFESTATION
OF THE ASSEMBLYES POWER.

WE have considered the present constitution of the government of Virginia and do propose, That we find by the records, The present power of government to reside in such persons as shall be impowered by the Burgesses (the representatives of the people), who are not dissolvable by any power now extant in Virginia, but the House of Burgesses. . . .

UPON WHICH REPORT WAS
DRAWNE UP THIS DECLARATION.

THE Burgesses taking into consideration the many letts and obstructions in the affaires of this Assembly and conceiveing that some persons of the present councell endeavour by setting up their own power to destroy the apparent power resident only in the burgesses, representatives of the people, as is manifest by the records of the Assembly:

We, the said Burgesses do declare, That we have in our selves the full power of the election and appointment of all offices in this country until such time as we shall have order to the contrary from the supreme power in England, All which is evident upon the Assembly records.

And for the better manifestation thereof and the present dispatch of the affaires of this countrey we declare as followeth:

That we are not dissolvable by any power yet extant in Virginia but our own. That all former elections of Governour and Council be void and null; That the power of governour for the future shall be conferred on Coll. Samuel Mathewes, Esq. who by us shall be invested with all the just rights and priviledges belonging to the Governour and Capt. General of Virginia, and that a council shall be nominated, appointed and confirmed, by the present burgesses convened (with the advice of the Governour, for his assistance,); And that for the future none be admitted a councellor but such who shall be nominated, appointed and confirmed by the house of Burgesses as aforesaid, until further order from the supreme power in England.

*Subscribed,*

JOHN SMITH, *Speaker*

# 3

*"Do covenant & combine our selves togeather*
*. . . to enacte . . . such just & equal lawes"*

The head of the Virginia Company
in London at the time of the creation of the House of Burgesses in America was
Sir Edwin Sandys whose brother, Samuel, landlord of Scrooby Manor in Notting-
hamshire, had been among the first to befriend the Nonconformist congregation
that gathered in Scrooby village early in 1607, in defiance of the law prohibiting
meetings of Dissenters. Sir Samuel's liberal stand did not deter less tolerant
Anglicans in the neighborhood from so persecuting the members of this congregation that before the end of 1607 many of them "were faine to flie & leave
their howses and habitations, and the means of their livelehood." Ten years
of exile in Holland followed, during which the Pilgrims, as these wanderers
came to call themselves, grew only the more disenchanted with the alien Dutch.
Although some of them argued that on English territory in the New World,
"it might be worse," the leaders concluded by 1617 that their best hope "was to
live as a distinct body by themselves under the general government of Virginia."
On the part of the "best sort" in the Virginia Company, in turn, Sir Edwin
Sandys, who was as liberal as his brother, assured the Pilgrims' agents in November, 1617, that "all forwardness to set you forward shall be found."

Difficulties, nevertheless, piled up, and no less than three years went by before
*Mayflower* completed her woeful voyage, only to land a mixed lot of Pilgrims and
strangers well outside Virginia's limits, on Cape Cod. There, on November 11,
1620, the leaders of the Scrooby group formed the first voluntary association in
the colonies, modeled on the covenant with God which was the foundation of
their own Separatist or Congregational church. Why they took this step is
told by the first governor, William Bradford, in his *Of Plimouth Plantation*,
in the following paragraph introducing the "Mayflower Compact" which (with
the manuscript lost) now appears in Bradford's eloquent book in its most au-
thentic form: "I shall a litle return back and begin with a combination made by
them before they came ashore, being the first foundation of their govermente in
this place; occasioned partly by the discontented & mutinous speeches that some
of the strangers amongst them had let fall from them in the ship—That when
they came ashore they would use their own libertie; for none had power to command them, the patent they had being for Virginia, and not for New-england,

18

which belonged to another Government, with which the Virginia Company had nothing to do. And partly that such an act by them done (this their condition considered) might be as firm as any patent, and in some respects more sure. "The forme was as followeth."

*November 11, 1620*

# The Mayflower Compact

In the name of God, Amen. We whose names are underwritten, the loyall subjects of our dread Soveraigne Lord KING JAMES by the grace of God, of great Britaine, Franc, & Ireland king, defender of the faith, &c.

Haveing undertaken, for the glorie of God, and advancement of the christian faith and honour of our king & countrie, a voyage to plant the first colonie in the Northern parts of Virginia, doe by these presents solemnly & mutually in the presence of God, and one of another, covenant, & combine our selves togeather into a Civill body politick; for our better ordering, and preservation and furtherance of the ends aforesaid; and by Vertue hearof to enacte, constitute, and frame such just & equal lawes, ordinances, Acts, constitutions, & offices, from time to time as shall be thought most meete & convenient for the general good of the Colonie: unto which we promise all due submission and obedience. In witness whereof we have hereunder subscribed our names at Cap-Codd the 11 of November in the year of the raigne of our soveraigne Lord King James of England, France, & Ireland the eighteenth and of Scotland the fiftie fourth. Anno: Dom. 1620.

**4**

*"To satisfie your longing expectation" to "see the rule which you ought to walke by"*

The first "patent" of Massachusetts Bay was similar to that of Virginia in that it chartered a company, not a "body politic." Virginia was transformed into a colony with political rights by order of the company's General Assembly sitting at home in London. The dramatic difference in the transformation of Massachusetts Bay was the removal, virtually at the start of the enterprise in 1629 and 1630, of the entire company and *its* General Court to New England, where, as Cotton Mather later explained, "we would have our posterity settled under the pure and full dispensation of the gospel; defended by rulers who should be ourselves." These rulers, according to the Massachusetts patent, made up a self-perpetuating body with the same absolute authority as *company* directors usually have. They were wise enough, however, at the very first meeting of the General Court in America in October, 1630, to seek "the generall vote of the people" by "ereccion of hands" for "the establishinge of the government" which the people themselves would be expected to obey.

Once having earned the endorsement of the faithful, the Massachusetts authorities clung to their conviction that they were answerable only to God for the administration of Christian justice. As in Virginia, however, the people of Massachusetts needed little more than a taste of power to acquire a hunger for it. As early as May, 1635, they began to press for the preparation and publication of an explicit code of laws for the colony, "whereby," as the General Court later put it, "we may manifest our utter disaffection to arbitrary government." By November, 1646, little headway had been made against the obstructive tactics of Governor John Winthrop in particular, but two years later the momentous first legal code of any English-speaking land was published in Massachusetts Bay.

Winthrop had lost the battle to control, under his own discretion, what he called "that wild beast" in man, "which all the ordinances of God are bent against." And yet in their Epistle printed here, recommending their work to "Our Beloved Brethren and Neighbours," (item "a"), the General Court committee charged with the task of codification showed that Winthrop had not in fact lost the war for a Godly commonwealth. The public laws made by self-governing freemen, to be sure, as the resounding opening of the code itself sets forth, were to take precedence over the laws of God. But where men's lives were at stake, as in the "Capital Lawes," and yet not only there, "we . . . had opportunitie put into our hands . . . to frame our civil Polities, and Laws according to the rules of his most holy word whereby each do help and strengthen other (the Churches the civil Authoritie, and the civil Authoritie the Churches)," and the "opportunitie" was not missed.

The Massachusetts code was more humane as well as more righteous than other laws of the time, and it was submitted to the people with the recommendation that it be observed in the generous spirit with which it was formulated. When other northern colonies undertook to draw up codes of their own, they looked to the Massachusetts code for guidance. The opening of the Massachusetts code and selections from it, including the "Capital Lawes" in their appropriate alphabetical place, are presented in item "b."

*1648*

# The Book of the General Lawes
# and Libertyes concerning
# the Inhabitants of the Massachusets

(a)  *The Introductory Epistle*

TO OUR BELOVED BRETHREN AND
NEIGHBOURS

the Inhabitants of the Massachusets, the Governour, Assistants and Deputies assembled in the Generall Court of that Jurisdiction wish grace and peace in our Lord Jesus Christ.

So soon as God had set up Politicall Government among his people Israel he gave them a body of lawes for judgement both in civil and criminal causes. These were breif and fundamental principles, yet withall so full and comprehensive as out of them clear deductions were to be drawn to all particular cases in future times. For a Common-wealth without lawes is like a Ship without rigging and steeradge. Nor is it sufficient to have principles of fundamentalls, but these are to be drawn out into so many of their deductions as the time and condition of that people may have use of. And it is very unsafe & injurious to the body of the people to put them to learn their duty and libertie from generall rules, nor is it enough to have lawes except they be also just. Therefore among other priviledges which the Lord bestowed upon his peculiar people, these he calls them specially to consider of, that God was neerer to them and their lawes were more righteous then other nations. God was sayd to be amongst them or neer to them because of his Ordnances established by himselfe, and their lawes

righteous because himselfe was their Law-giver: yet in the comparison are implyed two things, first that other nations had something of Gods presence amongst them. Secondly that there was also somewhat of equitie in their lawes, for it pleased the Father (upon the Covenant of Redemption with his Son) to restore so much of his Image to lost man as whereby all nations are disposed to worship God, and to advance righteousness. . . .

But the nations corrupting his Ordinances (both of Religion, and Justice), God withdrew his presence from them proportionably whereby they were given up to abominable lusts Rom. 2.2. Wheras if they had walked according to that light & law of nature they might have been preserved from such moral evils and might have enjoyed a common blessing in all their natural and civil Ordinances.

Now, if it might have been so with the nations who were so much strangers to the Covenant of Grace, what advantages have they who have interest in this Covenant, and may enjoye the special presence of God in the puritie and native simplicitie of all his Ordinances by which he is so neer to his own people. This hath been no small priviledge, and advantage to us in New-England that our Churches, and civil State have been planted, and grown up (like two twins) together like that of Israel in the wilderness by which we were put in mind (and had opportunitie put into our hands) not only to gather our Churches, and set up the Ordinances of Christ Jesus in them according to the Apostolick pattern by such light as the Lord graciously afforded us: but also withall to frame our civil Politie, and Lawes according to the rules of his most holy word whereby each do help and strengthen other (the Churches the civil Authoritie, and the civil Authoritie the Churches) and so both prosper the better without such emulation, and contention for priviledges or priority as have proved the misery (if not ruine) of both in some other places.

For this end about nine years since we used the help of some of the Elders of our Churches to compose a model of the Judiciall lawes of Moses with such other cases as might be referred to them, with intent to make use of them in composing our lawes, . . . and accordingly we have inserted them into this volume under the several heads to which they belong yet not as fundamentalls, for divers of them have since ben repealed, or altered, and more may justly be (at least) amended heereafter as further experience shall discover defects or inconveniences for *Nihil simul natum et perfectum.* The same must we say of this present Volume, we have not published it as a perfect body of laws sufficient to carry on the Government established for future times, nor could it be expected that we should promise such a thing. For if it be no disparagement to the wisdom of that High Court of Parliament in England that in four hundred years they could not so compile their lawes, and regulate proceedings in Courts of justice &c: but that they had still new work to do of the same kind almost every Parliament: there can be no just cause to blame a poor Colonie (being unfurnished of Lawyers and Statesmen) that in eighteen years hath produced no more, nor better rules for a good, and setled Government then this Book holds forth. . . .

These Lawes which were made successively in divers former years, we have reduced under several heads in an alphabetical method, that so they might the more readily be found, & that the divers lawes concerning one matter being placed together the scope and intent of the whole and of every of them might the more easily be apprehended: we must confesse we have not been so exact in placing every law under its most proper title as we might, and would have been: the reason was our hasty endeavour to satisfie your longing expectation, and frequent complaints for want of such a volume to be published in print: wherin (upon every occasion) you might readily see the rule which you ought to walke by. . . .

You have called us from amongst the rest of our Bretheren and given us power to make these lawes: we must now call upon you to see them executed: remembring that old & true proverb, *The execution of the law is the life of the law.* If one sort of you *viz:* non-Freemen should object that you had no hand in calling us to this work, and therfore think yourselvs not bound to obedience &c. We answer that a subsequent, or implicit consent is of like force in this case, as an express precedent power: for in putting your persons and estates into the protection and way of subsistance held forth and exercised within this Jurisdiction, you do tacitly submit to this Government and to all the wholesome lawes thereof, and so is the common repute in all nations. . . .

If any of you meet with some law that seemes not to tend to your particular benefit, you must consider that lawes are made with respect to the whole people, and not to each particular person: and obedience to them must be yeilded with respect to the common welfare, not to thy private advantage, and as thou yeildest obedience to the law for common good, but to thy disadvantage: so another must observe some other law for thy good, though to his own damage; thus must we be content to bear one anothers burden and so fulfill the Law of Christ.

That distinction which is put between the Lawes of God and the lawes of men, becomes a snare to many as it is mis-applyed in the ordering of their obedience to civil Authorities; for when the Authoritie is of God and that in way of an Ordinance *Rom. 13.1.*, and when the administration of it is according to deductions, and rules gathered from the word of God, and the clear light of nature in civil nations, surely there is no human law that tendeth to common good (according to these principles) but the same is mediately a law of God, and that in way of an Ordinance which all are to submit unto and that for conscience sake. Rom. 13.5.

## (b) Selections, alphabetically, from the Code of 1648

### THE OPENING

Forasmuch as the free fruition of such Liberties, Immunities, priviledges as humanitie, civilitie & christianity call for as due to everie man in his place, & proportion, without impeachment & infringement hath ever been & ever will be the tranquillity & stability of Churches & Comon-wealths; & the deniall or deprivall thereof the disturbance, if not ruine of both:

It is therefore ordered by this Court, & Authority thereof, That no mans life shall be taken a way; no mans honour or good name shall be stayned; no mans person shall be arrested, restrained, bannished, dismembred nor any wayes punished; no man shall be deprived of his wife or children; no mans goods or estate shall be taken away from him; nor any wayes indamaged under colour of Law or countenance of Authoritie unless it be by vertue or equity of some expresse law of the Country warranting the same established by a General Court & sufficiently published; or in case of the defect of a law in any particular case by the word of God. And in capital cases, or in cases concerning dismembring or banishment, according to that word to be judged by the General Court.

### ARRESTS

No mans person shall be arrested or imprisoned for any debt or fine if the law can finde any competent meanes of satisfaction otherwise from his estate. And if not his person may be arrested and imprisoned, where he shall be kept at his own charge, not the Plaintiffs, till satisfaction be made; . . . provided neverthelesse that no mans person shall be kept in prison for debt but when there appears some estate which he will not produce, . . .

### BOND-SLAVERY

There shall never be any bondslavery, villenage or captivitie amongst us; unlesse it be lawfull captives, taken in just warrs, and such strangers as willingly sell themselves, or are solde to us; and such shall have the libertyes and christian usages which the law of God established in Israell concerning such persons doth morally require, provided, this exempts none from servitude who shall be judged thereto by Authoritie.

### CAPITAL LAWES

If any man after legal conviction shall HAVE or WORSHIP any other God, but the LORD GOD: he shall be put to death. (Exod. 22.20. Deut. 13.6, & 10. Deut. 17.2.6.)

2. If any man or woman be a WITCH, that is, hath or consulteth with a familiar spirit, they shall be put to death. (Exod. 22.18. Levit. 20.27. Deut. 18.10.11.)

3. If any person within this Juris-

diction whether Christian or Pagan shall wittingly and willing presume to BLASPHEME the holy Name of God, Father, Son or Holy-Ghost, with direct, expresse, presumptuous, or high-handed blasphemy, either by wilfull or obstinate denying the true God, or his Creation or Government of the world: or shall curse God in like manner or reproach the holy Religion of God as if it were but a politick device to keep ignorant men in awe; or shall utter any other kind of Blasphemy of the like nature & degree they shall be put to death. (Levit. 24.15.16.)

4. If any person shall commit any wilfull MURDER, which is Man slaughter, committed upon premeditate malice, hatred, or crueltie not in a mans necessary and just defence, nor by meer casualty against his will, he shall be put to death. (Exod. 21.12.13. Numb. 35.31.)

5. If any person slayeth another suddenly in his ANGER, or CRUELTY of passion, he shall be put to death. (Levit. 24.17. Numb. 35.20.21.)

6. If any person shall slay another through guile, either by POYSON-ING, or other such devilish practice, he shall be put to death. (Exod. 21.14.)

7. If any man or woman shall LYE WITH ANY BEAST, or bruit creature, by carnall copulation; they shall surely be put to death: and the beast shall be slain, & buried, and not eaten. (Lev. 20.15.16.)

8. If any man LYETH WITH MAN-KINDE as he lieth with a woman, both of them have committed abomination, they both shall surely be put to death; unles the one partie were forced (or be under fourteen years of age in which case he shall be seveerly punished) (Levit. 20.13.)

9. If any person commit ADUL-TERIE with a married, or espoused wife; the Adulterer & Adulteresse shall surely be put to death. (Lev. 20.19. & 18.20. Deu. 22.23.27.)

10. If any man STEALETH A MAN, or Man-kinde, he shall surely be put to death. (Exodus 21.16.)

11. If any man rise up by FALSE-WITNES wittingly, and of purpose to take away any mans life; he shall be put to death. (Deut. 19.16.18.16.)

12. If any man shall CONSPIRE, and attempt any Invasion, Insurrection, or publick Rebellion against our Common-Wealth: or shall endeavour to surprize any Town, or Townes, Fort, or Forts therin; or shall treacherously, & perfidiously attempt the Alteration and Subversion of our Frame of Politie, or Government fundamentally he shall be put to death. (Numb. 16.2. Sam. 3.2. Sam. 18.2. Sam. 20.)

13. If any child, or children, above sixteen years old, and of sufficient understanding, shall CURSE, or SMITE their natural FATHER, or MOTHER; he or they shall be put to death: unless it can be sufficiently testified that the Parents have been very unchristianly negligent in the education of such children; or so provoked them by extream, and cruel correction; that they have been forced therunto to preserve themselves from death or maiming. (Exod. 21.17. Lev. 20.9. Exod. 21.15.)

14. If a man have a stubborn or REBELLIOUS SON, of sufficient years & understanding (viz) sixteen years of age, which will not obey the voice of his Father, or the voice of his Mother, and that when they have chastened him will not harken unto them: then shall his Father & Mother being his natural parents, lay hold on him, & bring him to the Magistrates assembled in Court & testifie unto them, that their Son is stubborn & rebellious & will not obey their voice and chastisement, but lives in sundry notorious crimes, such a son shall be put to death. (Deut. 21.20.21.)

15. If any man shall RAVISH any maid or single woman, committing carnal copulation with her by force, against her own will; that is above the age of ten years he shall be punished either with death, or with some other greivous punishment according to circumstances as the Judges, or General court shall determine.

CHILDREN

*Forasmuch as the good education of children is of singular behoof and benefit to any Common-wealth; and where as many parents & masters are too indulgent and negligent of their duty in that kinde.* It is therefore ordered that the Select men of everie town, in the severall precincts and quarters where they dwell, shall have a vigilant eye over their brethren & neighbours, to see, first that none of them shall suffer so much barbarism in any of their families as not to endeavour to teach by themselves or others, their children & apprentices so much learning as may inable them perfectly to read the englishtongue & knowledge of the Capital lawes: upon penaltie of twentie shillings for each neglect therin. Also that all masters of families doe once a week (at the least) catechize their children and servants in the grounds & principles of Religion, & if any be unable to doe so much: that then at the least they procure such children or apprentices to learn some short orthodox catechism without book, that they may be able to answer unto the questions that shall be propounded to them out of such catechism by their parents or masters or any of the Select men when they shall call them to a tryall of what they have learned in this kinde. And further that all parents and masters do breed & bring up their children & apprentices in some honest lawful calling, labour or imployment, either in husbandry, or some other trade profitable for themselves, and the Common-wealth if they will not or cannot train them up in learning to fit them for higher imployments. . . .

IMPRESSES

No man shall be compelled to any publick work, or service, unlesse the Presse be grounded upon some act of the General Court; and have reasonable allowance therfore. . . . Nor shall any man be compelled to go out of this Jurisdiction upon any offensive wars, which this Common-wealth, or any of our freinds or confoederates shall voluntarily undertake; but only upon such vindictive and defensive wars, in our own behalf, or the behalf of our freinds and confederates; as shall be enterprized by the counsell, and consent of a General Court, or by Authoritie derived from the same. . . .

IMPRISONMENT

No mans person shall be restreined or imprisoned by any authoritie whatsoever before the Law hath sentenced him thereto: if he can put in sufficieint securitie, *Bayle* or *Mainprize* for his appearance, and good behaviour in the mean time; unles it be in crimes Capital, and contempt in open Court, and in such cases where some expresse Act of Court doth allow it.

MASTERS, SERVANTS, LABOURERS

When any servants shall run from their masters, or any other Inhabitants shall privily goe away with suspicion of ill intentions, it shall be lawful for the next Magistrate, or the Constable and two of the chief Inhabitants where no Magistrate is, to presse men and boats or pinnaces at the publick charge to pursue such persons by Sea or Land and bring them back by force of Arms.

MONOPOLIES

There shall be no *Monopolies* graunted or allowed amongst us, but of such new inventions that are profitable for the Countrie, and that for a short time.

TORTURE

No man shall be forced by torture to confesse any crime against himselfe or any other, unles it be in some Capital case, where he is first fully convicted by clear and sufficient evidence to be guilty. After which, if the Case be of that nature that it is very apparent there be other Conspirators or Confoederates with him; then he may be tortured, yet not with such tortures as be barbarous or inhumane.

*"The Government hath some shew of a Demo-craticall forme which is . . . the most just and most profitable"*

The early assertion of the principles of the rule of law in the colonies and of the sovereignty of elected assemblies in making the laws leads naturally to the question of the standards by which the assemblies themselves were to be constituted. Perhaps the most significant part of this question, and the subject of this Document, is, who ought to exercise the privilege and indeed perform the duty of electing "the representatives of the people."

In the very first election in America, that of the Virginia burgesses in 1619, apparently all of the "inhabitants" of the colony had been permitted by the Virginia Company to vote (see Document No. 2, above). One of the accusations made in 1623 by the enemies of the Sandys regime in Virginia, which led King James to dissolve the Company the next year and make Virginia a royal colony, was that by such an indiscriminate extension of "freedom," the "Government, as it now stands, is Democraticall and tumultuous." This, the regime replied, was "a bold censure" to lay before such a pillar of monarchy as James I. "Their allegacion is a slaunder for the Government is not Democraticall," said the Company, for it derives its power directly from "your majesty." And yet the Company felt obliged out of conscience to acknowledge that "the Government hath some shew of a Democraticall forme" after all. The engaging terms of this acknowledgement are presented here as item "a."

Once the population of the American colonies became large and stratified, both a continued yearning for democracy and a fearful backing away from it (with the justifications of Mother Country precedents) became manifest. These tendencies are best illustrated in the subsequent history of the franchise in Virginia itself, the largest and perhaps the most sharply stratified of the English settlements. The Virginia franchise stipulations, well into the eighteenth century, are presented below in item "b."

One's attention must be called to the complexities of the terms, "freeman" and "freeholder," even though it would take a book to clarify them. In Virginia, "freeman" became such an exceedingly liberal designation that, as in the statute of 1646 below, it seems to have included even "covenanted" or indentured servants. "Freeholder" was a much more restrictive term, meaning a freeman with at least a lifetime land-holding above a certain minimum value or size.

# The Spirit of the Colonial Franchise

(a) *The Virginia Company's defense of the "Democraticall forme"*

(from the Company's Court Records, April 12, 1623)

That Government cannot be termed Democraticall where the King only hath absolute power and where the people swear alleagiance only to him, but is truly Monarchy called. . . .

[But] it is true that according to your Majesty's Institution in their Letters Patente the Government hath some shew of a Democraticall form which is in this case the most just and most profitable and the most apt means to work the ends and effect desired by your Majesty for the benifit, encrease and wealth of these Plantations, by which the profit of your Majesty and the Adventurer and Planter will rise together.

Most just because these plantations, though furthered much by your Majesty's grace yet being not made at your Majesty's charge or expence but cheifly by the private purses of the Adventurers, they would never have Adventured in such an Action wherein they interest their own fortunes if in the regulating and governing of their business their own votes had been excluded.

And most profitable for the advancing of the Plantation because of the great supplies which the necessities of the people there often require and cannot be sent but by the purses of many, who if a few had the managing of the business would and that not without reason leave them unsupplyed: And whereas they cry out against Democracie and call for Oligarchie they make not the Government thereby either of better form or more Monarchicall.

And to discern what is the judgement of a Company if there be not unanimity, there is no way but by pluralitie of voyces; and if plurallytie of voyces were not, there would scarce at any time in any poynte be unanimity in any Assembly [but] that unanimity that is proceeding for the most part from Despair of prevailing in their pryvate opinions or from shame to discover opposition to publique good.

(b) *Virginia statutes on the election of burgesses*

*1639*

No sheriff to compell any man to go off the plantation where he lives to choose burgesses.

*1646*

Whereas divers inconveniences are likely to ensue by disorderly and illegal election of Burgesses, . . . by which

means it also happeneth that few or none do appear personally according to summons, *Be it therefore enacted,* That no election shall be made of any Burgess or Burgesses but by plurality of voices, and that no hand writing shall be admitted: Be it also further enacted that what freemen so ever, having lawful summons of the time and place for election of Burgesses, that shall not make repair accordingly, Such person or persons unless there be lawful cause for absenting himself shall forfeit 100 lbs. of tobacco for his non appearance, freemen being covenanted servants being exempted from the said fine.

### 1654

All Burgesses shall be sumoned and elected in manner hereafter expressed, That is to say, that the several and respective sherriffs shall within ten days after the receipt of . . . writs . . . to that purpose cause to be published, and by giving notice of the same from house to house, . . . the certain day of the week and month for choosing Burgesses to serve in the Assembly for all accustomed places in the several counties and parishes respectively. . . .

All house keepers whether freeholders, lease holders, or otherwise tenants, shall only be capeable to elect Burgesses, and none hereby made uncapable shall give his subscription to elect a Burgess upon the pennalty of four hundred pounds of tobacco and cask . . . : Provided that this word house keepers repeated in this act extend no further than to one person in a family.

### 1655

WHEREAS we conceive it something hard and unagreeable to reason that any persons shall pay equall [poll] taxes and yet have no voice in elections [because they are not at least householders], *Therefore it is enacted by this present Grand Assembly*, That so much of the act for choosing Burgesses be repealed as excludes freemen from votes, Provided allways that they fairly give their votes by subscription [of hands] and not in a tumultous way.

### 1670

WHEREAS the usual way of chuseing burgesses by the votes of all persons who having served their time are freemen of this country who having little interest in the country do oftener make

tumults at the election to the disturbance of his majesties peace, than by their discretions in their votes provide for the conservation thereof by making choyce of persons fitly qualifyed for the discharge of so great a trust, And whereas the lawes of England grant a voyce in such election only to such as by their estates real or personal have interest enough to tie them to the endeavour of the publique good; *It is hereby enacted*, that none but freeholders and housekeepers who only are answerable to the publique for the levies shall hereafter have a voice in the election of any burgesses in this country; and that the election be at the courthouse.

### 1676

"BACON'S LAWS"

BE *it enacted* . . . that the act of assembly made in the 22nd year of his majesties reigne that now is, which forbids freemen to have votes in the election of burgesses be repealed, and that they may be admitted together with the freeholders and housekeepers to vote as formerly in such elections.

### 1676

WHEREAS Nathaniell Bacon the younger, in the month of June, 1676, . . . did enter James Citty in a rebellious manner with a considerable number of armed men, to the number of six hundred or thereabouts, environing and beseigeing the governour and counsell and burgesses, and offering force and violence to them, and every of them, threatening them with sudden death if they would not grant his unreasonable, unlawfull, rebellious and treasonable demands, and by his threats and offered violence did obteine to himself whatsoever he so unlawfully demanded; *And whereas* the kings most excellent majestie . . . hath long since declared all the proceedings of the said assembly to be voyd in law: *Bee it therefore enacted by this present grand assembly* . . . that all acts, orders and proceedings of the said grand assembly be repealed and made null and voyd.

1676

CHARLES REX. *Additional instructions for our trusty and welbeloved* SIR WILLIAM BERKELEY, *Knt. our governour of our colony of Virginia.*

1. You shalbe no more obliged to call an assembly once every year, but only once in two years. . . . Also whensoever the assembly is called fourteen dayes shalbe the time prefixed for their sitting and no longer, unless you find good cause to continue it beyond that time.

2. You shall take care that the members of the assembly be elected only by *freeholders*, as being more agreeable to the custom of England, to which you are as nigh as conveniently you can to conform yourself.

1699

No person or persons shall be enabled to give a vote for the election of a burgess or burgeses to serve in the general assembly . . . but those who are freeholders in the respective county or town for which the said burgess shall be elected. . . . *Provided always*, . . . that no woman, . . . infants under the age of twenty-one years, or recusant convict, [although] being freeholders, shall be enabled to give a vote or have a voice in the election of burgeses. . . .

No person or persons hereafter to be elected as a burgess shall . . . before his or their election give, present or allow, to any person or persons having voice or vote in such election any money, meat, drink or provision, or make any present, gift, reward or entertainment or any promise, engagement or obligation to give or allow any money, meat, drink or provision, present, reward or entertainment in order to procure the vote or votes of such person or persons; and every person or persons so giving, presenting, or allowing, making, promising or engaging any money, meat, drink or provision, . . . being elected, shall be disabled and incapable to sit and act as a burgess.

1705

No freeholder being a feme-sole, or feme-covert, infant, under age, or recusant convict, shall be obliged to appear, and give his or her vote in any of the said elections; neither, if they do appear, shall they have liberty to vote, but shall be excluded therefrom, as though they were not freeholders. . . .

Every person who hath an estate real for his own life, or the life of another, or any estate of any greater dignity, shall be accounted a freeholder, within the meaning of this act.

1723

No free negro, mullatto, or indian whatsoever, shall hereafter have any vote at the election of burgesses, or any other election whatsoever.

1736

I. WHEREAS, divers frauds have of late been practised to create and multiply votes in elections of members to serve in the general assembly by making leases of small and inconsiderable parcels of land, upon feigned considerations, and by sub-dividing lots of ground in towns, in prejudice of the rights of the true freeholders, and contrary to the true intent and meaning of the laws in that behalf:

II. *Be it therefore enacted*, . . . That no person . . . shall hereafter have a right to vote at any election of members to serve in the general assembly, for any county, who hath not an estate of freehold, or other greater estate, in one hundred acres of land, at least, if no settlement be made upon it; or twenty five acres with a house and plantation, in his possession, or in the possession of his tenant or tenants, for term of years, in the same county where he gives such vote. . . .

III. *And be it further enacted,* That all estates and conveyances whatsoever, heretofore or hereafter to be made to any person or persons, in any fraudulent or collusive manner, on purpose to qualify him or them to give his or their vote or votes at such elections, shall be null and void.

6

## *"Children . . . shalbe bond or free only according to the condition of the mother"*

Slavery is at least as old as warfare itself, and the buying and selling of captured Africans, specifically, had been practiced by European overseas traders for almost two hundred years before a Dutch privateer, "about the latter end of August," 1619, brought to Virginia (as the Company's records say) "not any thing but 20 odd Negroes, which the Governor and Cape Marchant bought for victualls . . . at the best and easiest rate they could." Thereafter, for half a century, the Virginia Negro population grew slowly. By 1670, Negroes numbered about 2,000 in a colony of 40,000, at least three-fourths of whom had started life in the New World as white indentured servants. Bonded Negroes at first came naturally under the general laws of the servant class. Not until 1656 does the term, "slave," appear in Virginia law, and then only parenthetically in connection with Indians; and not until 1661 is servitude for life even obliquely acknowledged. As W. F. Craven writes, however, "it is a mistake to make too much of this delay in the enactment of a full-fledged slave code."

In this Document we trace the development of legal distinctions between white and colored, beginning in 1630. Many Virginia white servants, at the end of their usual seven-year indentures, rose to the ranks of freeholders and even of burgesses and higher officers. But the Negro was pushed only the more distinctly outside the pale of Christian humanity and democratic aspiration, until by 1671 he was lumped with "sheep, horses and cattle" as properly part of orphans' estates.

*1630-1691*

# The Institution of Slavery
# in the Laws of Virginia

*1630*

Hugh Davis to be soundly whipped, before an assembly of Negroes and others for abusing himself to the dishonor of God and shame of Christians, by defiling his body in lying with a negro; which fault he is to acknowledge next Sabbath day.

*1639*

All persons except negroes to be provided with arms and amunition or be fined at pleasure of the Governour and Council.

*1661*

In case any English servant shall run away in company with any negroes who are incapable of making satisfaction by addition of time, [because they are already servants for life] *Be it enacted* that the English so running away in company with them shall serve for the time of the said negroes absence as they are to do for their own by a former act.

*1662*

WHEREAS some doubts have arisen whether children got by any Englishman upon a negro woman should be slave or free, *Be it therefore enacted* . . . [thus legalizing the hereditary status of slaves], that all children borne in this country shalbe held bond or free only according to the condition of the mother, *And* that if any christian shall commit fornication with a negro man or woman, he or she so

offending shall pay double the fines imposed by the former act.

*1667*

WHEREAS some doubts have risen whether children that are slaves by birth, and by the charity and piety of their owners made pertakers of the blessed sacrament of baptism, should by vertue of their baptism be made free; *It is enacted* . . . that the conferring of baptism doth not alter the condition of the person as to his bondage or freedom; that divers masters, freed from this doubt, may more carefully endeavour the propagation of christianity by permitting children, though slaves, or those of greater growth if capable, to be admitted to that sacrament.

*1669*

WHEREAS the only law in force for the punishment of refractory servants resisting their master, mistris or overseer cannot be inflicted upon negroes, [because servitude for life forestalled punishment by extension of the service period], nor the obstinacy of many of them by other than violent means supprest, *Be it enacted* if any slave resist his master (or other by his masters order correcting him) and by the extremity of the correction should chance to die, that his death shall not be accompted felony, but the master (or that other person appointed by the master to punish him) be acquit from molestation, since it cannot be presumed that prepensed malice (which alone makes murder felony) should induce any man to destroy his own estate.

### 1670

WHEREAS some dispute have arisen whether Indians taken in war by other nation, and by that nation that taketh them sold to the English, are servants for life or term of years, *It is resolved and enacted* that all servants not being christians imported into this colony by shipping shalbe slaves for their lives; but what shall come by land to serve, if boys or girls, until thirty years of age, if men or women twelve years and no longer.

### 1671

WHEREAS in the former act concerning the estates of persons dying intestate, it is provided that sheep, horses, and cattle should be delivered in kind to the orphant, when they came of age, according to the several ages the said cattle were of when the guardian took them into his possession, to which some have desired that negroes may be added; this assembly considering the difficulty of procuring negroes in kind, as also the value and hazard of their lives, have doubted whether any sufficient men would be found who would engage themselves to deliver negroes of equal ages if the specificall negroes should dye, or become by age or accident unserviceable; *Be it therefore enacted* . . . that the consideration of this be referred to the county courts who are hereby authorized and empowered either to cause such negroes to be duly apprized, sold at an outcry, or preserved in kind, as they then find it most expedient for preservation, improvement or advancement of the estate and interest of such orphants.

### 1680

WHEREAS the frequent meeting of considerable numbers of negro slaves under pretence of feasts and burials is judged of dangerous consequence; for prevention whereof for the future, *Be it enacted* . . . that from and after the publication of this law, it shall not be lawfull for any negroe or other slave to carry or arm himself with any club, staff, gun, sword, or any other weapon of defence or offence, nor to go or depart from of his masters ground without a certificate from his master, mistris or overseer, and such permission not to be granted but upon perticuler and necessary occasions; and every negroe or slave so offending not haveing a certificate as aforesaid shalbe sent to the next constable, who is hereby enjoyned and required to give the said negroe twenty lashes on his bare back well layd on, and so sent home to his master, mistris or overseer. *And it is further enacted* . . . that if any negroe or other slave shall presume to lift up his hand in opposition against any christian, shall for every such offence, upon due proof made thereof by the oath of the party before a magistrate, have and receive thirty lashes on his bare back well laid on. *And it is hereby further enacted* . . . that if any negroe or other slave shall absent himself from his masters service and lye hid and lurking in obscure places, committing injuries to the inhabitants, and shall resist any person or persons that shalby any lawfull authority be employed to apprehend and take the said negroe, that then in case of such resistance, it shalbe lawfull for such person or persons to kill the said negroe or slave so lying out and resisting, and that this law be once every six months published at the respective county courts and parish churches within this colony.

### 1691

WHEREAS many times negroes, mulattoes, and other slaves unlawfully absent themselves from their masters and mistresses service, and lie hid and lurk in obscure places killing hogs and committing other injuries to the inhabitants of this dominion, for remedy whereof for the future, *Be it enacted* that in all such cases . . . two of their majesties justices of the peace . . . are hereby empowered and commanded to issue out their warrants directed to the sheriff, . . . which said sheriff is hereby likewise required upon all such occasions to raise such and so many forces from time to time as he shall think convenient and necessary for the effectual apprehending such negroes, mulattoes and other slaves, and in case any negroes, mulattoes or other slave or slaves lying out as aforesaid shall resist, runaway, or refuse to deliver and surrender him or themselves to any person or persons that shall be by lawfull authority employed to apprehend and take such negroes, mulattoes or other slaves that in such cases it shall and may be lawfull for such person and persons to kill and distroy such negroes, mulattoes, and other slave or slaves by gun or any otherwise whatsoever.

*Provided* that where any negroe or malattoe slave or slaves shall be killed in pursuance of this act, the owner or owners of such negro or mulatto slave shall be paid for such negro or mulatto slave four thousand pounds of tobacco by the publique.

### 1691

And for prevention of that abominable mixture and spurious issue which hereafter may increase in this dominion, as well by negroes, mulattoes, and Indians intermarrying with English, or other white women, as by their unlawfull accompanying with one another, *Be it enacted* . . . that for the time to come, whatsoever English or other white man or woman being free shall intermarry with a negroe, mulatto, or Indian man or woman bond or free, shall within three months after such marriage be banished and removed from this dominion forever.

### 1691

And forasmuch as great inconveniences may happen to this country by the setting of negroes and mulattoes free, by their either entertaining negro slaves from their masters service, or receiving stolen goods, or being grown old bringing a charge upon the country; for prevention thereof, *Be it enacted* . . . That no negro or mulatto be after the end of this present session of assembly set free by any person or persons whatsoever, unless such person or persons, their heirs, executors or administrators pay for the transportation of such negro or negroes out of the countrey within six months after such setting them free, upon penalty of paying of ten pounds sterling to the Church wardens of the parish where such person shall dwell, with which money . . . the said Church wardens are to cause the said negro or mullato to be transported out of the countrey.

# 7

## *"In defiance of the authority of the Court of Admiralty there erected"*

The tumultuous reign of the later Stuarts in England, culminating in the parliamentary invitation to William of Orange to become king in 1687 and in the flight of James II to France a year later, was tumultuous in America as well. One source of trouble in England was the Stuarts' determination to crush Nonconformity in religion and thereby rebuild widespread loyalty to the Crown. In this they failed. A second source of trouble was their determination to extend the reach of the Crown all the more firmly to the New World, and particularly to those northern mainland colonies where both Nonconformity and independence flowered. This ambition clashed with that of English merchants, who resented royal interference with their American trade, however well meant. When such interference became excessive under James II, these merchants gladly helped harry the last of the Stuarts from the throne.

But Dutch William scarcely improved matters either in England or America. With him across the Channel he brought his traditional continental rivalry with the Catholic French, which hardly was mitigated by Louis XIV's hospitality to James. As early as 1689 this rivalry flared up in the War for the League of Augsburg. In America it was more appropriately known as King William's War, the first of the long series between the French and the English which ended with the expulsion of the French from North America in 1763. The better to fight these wars in Europe, William buttressed the hegemony of the Anglican Church at home. The better to fight them in the New World, he promptly revamped the entire colonial administration. His pet targets were the old charter colonies in New England and the newer proprietary colonies such as Pennsylvania, where royal authority was weak.

Pennsylvania, a creation of James himself, and yet Quaker, pacifist, and heavily non-English in population, became a favorite butt of Edward Randolph, the most tireless of English officials in searching out American infractions. One of the boldest "infractions" was the Pennsylvania law of 1698 "For Preventing Frauds & Regulating Abuses in Trade"—that "shamm Law," as Randolph called it for its pretense of assisting the king in implementing the new navigation laws (item "a," below). Because it provided for jury trials in customs cases in defiance of the English stipulation that such cases be tried in new admiralty courts without juries, and because it excused Quakers from taking the stipulated oaths, this law, at Randolph's urging, was disallowed in England as early as August, 1699. In items "b" and "c" we present Randolph's official strictures on these provisions and his indictment, in 1701, of the conduct of other colonies as well, reflecting the persistent American response to the whole Navigation System once the English became serious about enforcement.

**1698   1701**

# The Navigation System Opposed

(a)  *An Act for Preventing Frauds & Regulating*
     *Abuses in Trade, Within . . . Pennsylvania*

(from The Laws of Pennsylvania, 1698)

*And whereas* . . . there was sent to the government an Act of parliament made in the 7th and 8th year of the King entitled, An Act for preventing frauds & regulating abuses in the plantation trade, whereby it is amongst other things Enacted, That from and after the 25th day of May 1698, No ship or vessel whatsoever should be deemed or pass as a ship of the built of England, Ireland, Wales, Berwick, Guernsey, Jersey or any of his Majesties plantations in America, so as to be qualified to trade to, from or in any of the said plantations until the person or persons claiming propertie in such ship or vessel should Register the same by proof upon oath of one or more of the owners of such ship or vessel, as by the said act is Directed.

Now forasmuch as most part of the merchants, traders & owners of ships or vessels within this government being of ye people called quakers, who, for Conscience sake cannot take an Oath upon any acct. whatsoever; In which respect It will be very prejudicial to the Kings interest, Destructive to trade and a ruin to many families to Lay up their vessels and be deprived of the Liberties and priveledges of English subjects, as must unavoidably follow, if their Solemn affirmat'n. or attestat'n. be not accepted here instead of an Oath, as it is in the like Case and upon ye Same and other occasions very favourably allowed to be in England. . . .

Therefore *It is enacted* . . . that all & every person or persons . . . who Cannot for Conscience sake take an oath and shall be required to take the oath in the said act of Parliament mentioned, or any other oath in that or in any other Case relating to the acts of trade & navigation whatsoever & wheresoever, . . . shall, instead of an oath be permitted to make his or her Solemn Affirma'n. Attesta'n. or Declara'n, . . . which . . . shall be adjudged . . . to be binding and most available in Law and shall be accepted instead of an Oath in all Courts and other places within this government. . . .

*And it is further Enacted* . . . , that when any Bill, plaint or information shall be Exhibited or Commenced against any person in any Court to be held within This Province or territories, for or upon breach or Non-observance of any of the Acts of trade or Navigation in any Case Whatsoever, The mean or manner of trial shall be according to the course of the Common Law, known practice of the Courts of record within this government by twelve Lawful men of the neighborhood, where the offence is Committed.

## (b)   *Edward Randolph to the Board of Trade, August 25, 1698*

I went to Phyladelphia and discoursed Mr. Markham [the deputy governor] about his Law and told him that he had therein acted Expressly against the 10th Article of his Instructions . . . which he had taken an Oath to observe in passing a law repugnant to the Act for preventing Frauds etc. . . .

But so long as the Colonies of Road Island and Connecticott, the Province of East and West new Jerseys of Pensilvania and Counties annexed, and North Carolina [are] adjoyning to and intermixt among . . . His Majestys Plantations, tis Impossible that their Respective Governors can suppresse the Scotch and Other illegal trade. . . .

The Inhabitants of the Province of Pensilvania have already by their shamm Law utterly destroyd the design & Intent of the Act for preventing Frauds &c. and they question not but by Mr. Penns prevailing Interest to get that Law passed in their Favour, which if so will be an admirable precedent for all the other Governors in the Propriety to pass the like law, and then they will be soon peopled, for many more of the Inhabitants [of the royal colonies] of New York, Mary-land & Virginia will settle amongst them, where all goods and Commodities are Exported and Imported Duty Free: And their laws like those in Pensilvania as favourable as they please to make them.

## (c)   *Edward Randolph to the Board of Trade, March 24, 1701*

ARTICLES OF HIGH CRIMES;
MISDEMEANOURS CHARGED
UPON THE GOVERNOURS
IN THE SEVERALL PROPERTIES,
ON THE CONTINENT OF AMERICA,
AND ISLANDS ADJACENT.

*Bahama Islands.* Pirates entertained there, and illegal Trade maintained, and carryed on by the Inhabitants.

Every the Pirate, and his men were entertain'd when Collonell Trott was Governor of Providence. . . . Read Elding the present Governour, stands charged with Piracy lately committed upon a New England Vessell richly Loaden, bound from Jamaica to Boston. He Tyrannically beat and Wounded Mr. Thomas Gower, the Present Secretary, and Soon after kept him in Prison 17 daies.

*South Carolina*— . . . Mr. Archdale the late Governour Harboured Pirates, . . .

Mr. Joseph Blake late Governour Deceased, . . . , caus'd Some Vessells, and their Loading to be Seized and Condemned upon pretence of the Acts of Trade, and getting them to be apprized at half ye vallue, he and his Accomplices gott them into their Hands, denying to ye Owner's appeals to his Majestie in Councill.

He caused other Vessells to be seiz'd upon the same pretence and upon Private Contract with the Masters to pay him half ye Vallue of their Vessells (which they did) he discharged their Vessells. . . .

*Mary-land*—His Majestie took the Government of That Province out of the Hands of the Lord Baltimore the Proprietor, because Colonell Talbott his Governour murder'd the Collector of his Majesties Customes in Cool Blood.

*The Three Lower Counties on Delaware Bay*— . . . There were not Long Since Two persons Try'd & Condemned, the Judges and Juries not being Sworn, and afterwards executed in those Counties.

*Pensilvania*—Another person was

Try'd, Condemned, and Executed in Mr. Penn's own Province, the Judge and Jury not being Sworn.

It has been, and still is ye only receptacle for Pirates & illegal Traders.

Mr. Penn in Defyance of ye Authority of ye Court of Admiralty there erected, Has appointed a person to Execute ye office of Marshall by Warrant under his hand and Seal. . . .

*Colony of Connecticut.* Receive and countenance illegall Traders and Lately intended to Oppose with Force persons Legally impowr'd to Seize, & Carry away Prohibited Goods in Order to be Try'd in his Majesties Court of Admiralty at New York.

*Road Island.* They have all along Harboured Pirates. Walter Clarke, the late Governour, refused to Take ye Oath enjoyn'd by the Acts of Trade to be taken by all Governours &c.

Samuell Cranston the present Governor openly opposed the Authority of the Court of Admiralty, Order'd by Act of Parliament to be There erected.

*Province of Massachusetts Bay—* . . . They enrich themselves by their continued breach of the Acts of Trade. Some of the members of ye Council being illegal Traders, sitt Judges in ye Courts upon Tryall of Seizures for his Majestie, . . . .

They have likewise Turn'd out Mr. Byfield a man zealous for haveing the Acts of Trade duly executed, who . . . was Judge of the Court of Admiralty in That Province. And made Mr. Waite Winthrop (a small Practitioner in Physick) to be Judge of That Court Tho' in no Sort qualifyed for ye Office. . . . Some of the First Pirates I ever heard of in the Northern Plantations were sett out from Boston who brought in a Great Deal of Riches from the Spanish Plantations.

# 8

*"And all the high things that are said . . . upon the side of power will not be able to stop the people's mouths"*

New York, a proprietary possession of James Stuart until he became king of England in 1685, and firmly established as a royal colony by Dutch William in 1691, ranked notoriously among the worst governed of all the mainland settlements. And among the worst of New York's governors stood William Cosby, who arrived with all his "God damn ye" manners to take command in 1732. One prompt error Cosby made was to offend certain grandees in the Hudson Valley by suing one of them, his interim predecessor, for that part of his salary earned during Cosby's passage overseas. Foiled here, he plunged blindly on to question the very validity of these grandees' land titles, the better to carve out vast estates for himself. Cosby so wilfully trespassed on the legislature's prerogatives that the Secretary of the Board of Trade in London had to read him the terms of his royal commission. Reprimanded, he continued to find it so difficult to play anything but king among the colonials that the populace as well as the patroons soon turned against him.

In November, 1733, with grandee backing, the young immigrant printer, John Peter Zenger, started the New York *Weekly Journal.* In less than two months, he was charged before a grand jury by Cosby's Chief Justice with "seditious Libels" which, "with the utmost Virulency have endeavoured to asperse his Excellency and villify his Administration." When on this and later charges the grand jury refused to indict Zenger, Cosby, in November, 1734, took the extraordinary step of having him arrested under an "information" of the kind once used in Star Chamber proceedings by the early Stuarts before the Long Parliament abolished that secret and arbitrary tribunal in 1641. Bail was placed so onerously high that Zenger languished in jail for nine months before being brought to trial early in August, 1735.

Zenger's New York attorneys so boldly challenged the right of the Chief Justice himself to sit on the case that they were disbarred virtually at the start of the proceedings. His friends thereupon briefed Andrew Hamilton of Philadelphia, one of the giants of the American bar. Hamilton's charge to the trial jury, reproduced in part in this Document, won him immediate international fame. By insisting, over the adamant stand of the court itself, that the jury must find published statements false as well as scandalous before branding them seditious libels, he carried the day for his client and for the future freedom of the press. Hamilton's principle was not to become statutory law for more than half a century. But as a correspondent said in Ben Franklin's *Pennsylvania Gazette,* "If it is not law, it is better than law, it ought to be law, and will always be law wherever justice prevails."

*August 4, 1735*

# Andrew Hamilton's Defense
# of John Peter Zenger

*Mr. Attorney.* Indeed, Sir, as Mr. Hamilton has confessed the printing and publishing these libels, I think the jury must find a verdict for the king; for supposing they were true, the law says that they are not the less libellous for that; nay indeed, the law says their being true is an aggravation of the crime.

*Mr. Hamilton.* Not so neither, Mr. Attorney, there are two words to that bargain. I hope it is not our bare printing and publishing a paper, that will make it a libel: you will have something more to do, before you make my client a libeller; for the words themselves must be libellous, that is, "false, scandalous, and seditious," or else we are not guilty. . . . I observed just now, that Mr. Attorney, in defining a libel, made use of the words, scandalous, seditious, and tend to disquiet the people; but (whether with design or not I will not say) he omitted the word false.

*Mr. Attorney.* I think I did not omit the word false: but it has been said already, that it may be a libel, notwithstanding it may be true.

*Mr. Hamilton.* In this I must still differ with Mr. Attorney. . . . This word False must have some meaning, or else how came it there? I hope Mr. Attorney will not say, he put it there by chance, and I am of opinion his information would not be good without it. But to shew that it is the principal thing which, in my opinion, makes a libel, I put the case, the information had been for printing and publishing a certain true libel, would that be the same thing? or could Mr. Attorney support such an information by any precedent in the English law? No; the falsehood makes the scandal, and both make the libel. . . .

*Mr. Ch. Justice.* Mr. Attorney, you have heard what Mr. Hamilton has said, and the cases he has cited, for having his witnesses examined, to prove the truth of the several facts contained in the paper set forth in the information. What do you say to it?

*Mr. Attorney.* The law, in my opinion, is very clear; they cannot be admitted to justify a libel; for, by the authorities I have already read to the court, it is not the less a libel because it is true. . . .

*Mr. Ch. Justice.* Mr. Hamilton, the court is of opinion, you ought not to be permitted to prove the facts in the papers: these are the words of the book, "It is far from being a justification of a libel, that the contents thereof is true, or that the person upon whom it is made had a bad reputation, since the greater appearance there is of truth in any malicious invective, so much the more provoking it is."

*Mr. Hamilton.* These are Star-chamber cases, and I was in hopes, that practice had been dead with the court.

*Mr. Ch. Justice.* Mr. Hamilton, the court have delivered their opinion, and we expect you will use us with good manners. . . .

*Mr. Hamilton.* I thank your honour. Then, gentlemen of the jury, it is to you we must now appeal. . . . And were you to find a verdict against my client, you must take upon you to say, the papers referred to in the information, and which we acknowledge we printed and published, are false, scandalous, and seditious; but of this I can have no apprehension. You are witnesses of New-York; you are really what the law supposes you to be, honest and lawful men; and, according to my brief, the facts which we offer to prove were not committed in a corner; they are notoriouslly known to be true; and therefore in your justice lies our safety. And as we are denied the liberty of giving evidence, to prove the truth of what we have published, I will beg leave to lay it down as a standing rule in such cases, That the suppressing of evidence ought always to be taken for the strongest evidence: and I hope it will have that weight with you. . . .

*Mr. Ch. Justice.* No, Mr. Hamilton; the jury may find that Zenger printed and published those papers, and leave it to the court to judge whether they are libellous; you know this is very common; it is in the nature of a special verdict, where the jury leave the matter of law to the court.

*Mr. Hamilton.* I know, may it please your honour, the jury may do so; but I do likewise know, they may do otherwise. I know they have a right beyond all dispute, to determine both the law and the fact, and where they do not doubt of the law, they ought to do so. This of leaving it to the judgment of the court, whether the words are libellous or not, in effect renders juries useless (to say no worse) in many cases; . . . and I must insist upon saying, That according as this case seems to be understood by the court and Mr. Attorney, it is not law at this day: . . . and I will go so far into Mr. Attorney's doctrine, as to agree, that if the faults, mistakes, nay even the vices of such a [public] person be private and personal, and do not affect the peace of the public, or the liberty or property of our neighbour, it is unmanly and unmannerly to expose them either by word or writing. But when a ruler of a people brings his personal failings, but much more his vices, into his administration, and the people find themselves affected by them, either in their liberties or properties, that will alter the case mightily, and all the high things that are said in favour of rulers, and of dignities, and upon the side of power, will not be able to stop people's mouths when they feel themselves oppressed, I mean in a free government.

It is true in times past it was a crime to speak truth, and in that terrible court of star-chamber, many worthy and brave men suffered for so doing; and yet even in that court, and in those bad times, a great and good man durst say, what I hope will not be taken amiss of me to say in this place, to wit, "The practice of informations for libels, is a sword in the hands of a wicked king, and an arrand coward, to cut down and destroy the innocent . . .".

*Mr. Attorney.* Pray, Mr. Hamilton, have a care what you say, do not go too far neither; I do not like those liberties.

*Mr. Hamilton.* Sure, Mr. Attorney, you won't make any applications; all men agree, that we are governed by the best of kings, and I cannot see the meaning of Mr. Attorney's caution: . . . but when a governor departs from the duty enjoined him by his sovereign, and acts as if he was less accountable than the royal hand that gave him all that power and honour which he is possessed of; this sets people upon examining and enquiring into the power, authority, and duty, of such a magistrate, and to compare those with his conduct; and just as far as they find he exceeds the bounds of his authority, or falls short of doing impartial justice to the people under his administration, so far they very often, in return, come short in their duty to such a governor. . . . I beg leave to insist, that the right of complaining or remonstrating is natural; and the restraint upon this natural right is the law only, and that those restraints can only extend to what is false. . . .

I think it will be agreed, That ever since the time of the star-chamber, where the most arbitrary and destructive judgments and opinions were given, that ever an Englishman heard of, at least in his own country; I say, prosecutions for libels since the time of that arbitrary court, and until the glorious revolution, have generally been set on foot at the instance of the crown or its ministers; and it is no small reproach to the law, that these prosecutions were too often and too much countenanced by the judges, who held their places at pleasure, (a disagreeable tenure to any officer, but a dangerous one in the case of a judge.) To say more to this point may not be proper. And yet I cannot think it unwarrantable, to shew the unhappy influence that a sovereign has sometimes had, not only upon judges, but even upon parliaments themselves.

It has already been shewn, how the judges differed in their opinions about the nature of a libel, in the case of the seven bishops. There you see three judges of one opinion, that is, of a wrong opinion, in the judgment of the best men in England, and one judge of a right opinion. How unhappy might it have been for all of us at this day, if that jury had understood the words in that information as the court did? Or if they had left it to the court, to judge whether the petition of the bishops was or was not a libel? No! they took upon them, to their immortal honour, to determine both law and fact, and to understand the petition of the bishops to be no libel, that is, to contain no falsehood nor sedition, and therefore found them not guilty. . . . [In still another case the jury] took upon them to judge both the law and the fact; at which the court (being themselves true courtiers) were so much offended, that they fined the jury forty marks a-piece, and committed them till paid. But Mr. Bushel, who valued the right of a jury-man and the liberty of his country more than his own, refused to pay the fine; and was resolved (though at a great expence and trouble too) to bring, and did bring, his *habeas corpus*, to be relieved from his fine and imprisonment, and he was released accordingly; and this being the judgment in his case, it is established for law, "That the judges, how great soever they be, have no right to fine, imprison, or punish a jury, for not finding a verdict according to the direction of the court." And this I hope is sufficient to prove, That jurymen are to see with their own eyes, to hear with their own ears, and to make use of their own consciences and understandings, in judging of the lives, liberties or estates of their fellow-subjects. And so I have done with this point. . . .

Gentlemen, the danger is great, in proportion to the mischief that may happen, through our too great credulity. A proper confidence in a court is commendable; but as the verdict (whatever it is) will be yours, you ought to refer no part of your duty to the discretion of other persons. If you should be of opinion, that there is no falsehood in Mr. Zenger's papers, you will, nay (pardon me for the expression) you ought to say so; because you do not know, whether others (I mean the court) may be of that opinion. It is your right to do so, and there is much depending upon your resolution, as well as upon your integrity.

[The jury found John Peter Zenger, "Not Guilty."]

9

## *"An unaccountable thirst for large Tracts of Land . . . hath prevailed with a singular rage"*

In 1748, "inasmuch," as they said, "as nothing can more effectively tend to defeat the dangerous designs of the French" in the Ohio Valley, George II and his Council approved a princely grant of 200,000 acres beyond the Allegheny Mountains to the Ohio Company of Virginia, a private land company organized the year before by Thomas Lee, head of the Virginia Council of State. This step did not sit at all well with other proud Virginia councilors who knew from the charter of 1609 that only the Old Dominion itself, and not the Crown, had the disposition of its western lands "from Sea to Sea, West and Northwest." These councilors promptly formed the Loyal Company, significantly named, and began to make even more princely grants to *its* members without consultation with any "foreign power."

The French response to these and similar activities elsewhere in the landed colonies was to build and man the line of log forts in the West that would serve them so well in the early stages of the French and Indian War, which began in America in 1754. An even more important phase of French policy was the wooing of the Indians whose land it was, after all, for which the white men were contending. When the French defeated General Edward Braddock's redcoat regulars and killed the General himself near Fort Duquesne in July, 1755, the Indians of the Northwest, many of them their friends of long standing, went over to them in a body. Of still graver concern to the British was the wavering of *their* ancient allies, the Six Iroquois Nations, whose power extended great distances from their heartland in the strategic Mohawk Valley of New York.

The Six Nations supported the British throughout the French and Indian War largely because of the work of General William Johnson, New York's veteran Superintendent of Indian Affairs, and of Peter Wraxall, his secretary and aide. Why the red men first wavered is set forth in "Some Thoughts Upon The British Indian Interest in North America," Wraxall's report to the Board of Trade in London, January 9, 1756. This report is characterized by C. W. Alvord in his classic work, *The Mississippi Valley in British Politics* (2 vols., Russell and Russell New York, 1959) as, "unquestionably the ablest paper on the Indian question" at this time; "its influence," he adds, "may be traced in all later communications and in the final construction of a definite [Indian] policy." It is printed here in part as item "a."

In so far as Wraxall stressed the Indians' "complaint about their land," and urged great care and moderation in its alienation to white speculators and settlers alike, his recommendations directly confronted the ungovernable land hunger of the Americans—the "calling to seeke for roome" that William Symonds preached back in 1609 (Document No. 1, above)—and helped bring on the Revolution. The great problem, as Wraxall said, was the "singular rage" among the grandees for "large Tracts of land" in the wilderness, "without the design of cultivation." But poor immigrant settlers were no less hungry for more modest holdings to farm for a livelihood. As disclosed in item "b" on the Indian issue in Pennsylvania in 1768, five years after the King's Proclamation of 1763 had nominally closed much of the West to settlement, the poor were no less determined than the grandees to appease their appetite for space, and for independence, if need be, to insure its attainment.

*1756  1768*

# Indian Relations
# on the Imperial Frontier

(a)  *From Peter Wraxall's, "Some Thoughts*
*Upon the British Indian Interest in North America,*
*More Particularly as it Relates to the Northern Confederacy*
*commonly called The Six Nations" 1756.*

One of the most fatal Causes of the decrease of our Indian Interest & influence, and which hath not only weakened their good opinion and affection towards us, but has made numbers of them our enemies, sown a gloomy discontent and suspicion of our Intentions amongst the whole confederacy, hath been very near loosing us their Alliance, and will in all probability wholly do it, if proper measures are not fallen on to give them satisfaction & security: This Cause is relating to their Lands.

An unaccountable thirst for large Tracts of Land without the design of cultivation, hath prevailed over the inhabitants of this and the neighbouring Provinces with a singular rage. Patents have been lavishly granted (to give it no worse term) upon the pretence of fair Indian purchases, some of which the Indians have alledged were never made but forged—Others bought of Indians who were no Proprietors some by making two or three Indians Drunk and giving them a trivial consideration —They say also the Surveyors have frequently run Patents vastly beyond even the pretended conditions or limits of sale. . . .

The vast Grant of Land to the Ohio company is an other and one of the most material articles of discontent & Jealousy to the confederate Nations and their allies, aggravated by many other Patents granted by the Governors of Virginia and Maryland.

There is reason to believe the last Pensilvania Purchase, tho' agreed to at a publick meeting, is a matter of no small Grievance to many of the six Nations, and so disgusting to the Delaware & Shawanese Indians, as hath probably occasioned those Indians now ravageing our back Settlements.

That memorable and important act by which the Indians put their Patrimonial and conquered Lands under the Protection of the King of Great Britain their Father against the incroachments or Invasions of the French is not understood by them as a cession or Surrender as it seems to have been ignorantly or willfully supposed by some. They intended and look upon it as reserving the Property and Possession of the Soil to themselves and their Heirs. . . . These are their hunting Grounds, by the profits of which they are to maintain themselves and their Families, they are therefore against any settlements there because the consequence would be the driving away Game & destroying their Livelyhood and Riches. . . .

Our Six Nations and their Allies at least the Polititians amongst them look upon the present disputes between the English and French in this part of the world notwithstanding our plausible pretences of rescuing their Lands, and some such pretences the French plead on their side, as a point of selfish Ambition in us both and are apprehensive that which ever Nation gains their Point will become their Masters not their deliverers—They dread the success of either and their ablest Politicians would very probably rather wish us to continue destroying each other than that either should be absolute conquerors. . . .

In June, 1754, A meeting was appointed at Albany by the Lᵗ Govʳ of New York, at which the Indians were informed that Commissioners from most of the Colonies would be present and that very considerable Presents would be given. Yet such was the discontented cold disposition of the Indians toward us, that tho' they were very uneasy & much alarmed at the Proceedings of the French upon the Ohio & well knew how important a Crisis it was, Yet maugre all these temptations & motives, never were so few Indians seen at any public meeting. Those who did come appeared to be very much out of humor, and before they would proceed to the public Conferences remonstrated to the Lt. Gov of New York upon the injustice done them with regard to their Lands, complained bitterly, that tho a Deputation had gone down to New York the year before to Govʳ Clinton with these complaints, yet no redress had been granted. At this meeting they (the Indians)

accused the Albany Commissioners in their public speech to their Faces, of the neglect & contempt with which they had treated the six Nations, [and] . . . bid them take notice that the fire of friendship between the six Nations & Albany was burnt out. . . .

I will beg leave to offer some Hints in the shape of a Plan for such an administration of Indian affairs . . . as I humbly apprehend may best tend to secure, extend and apply the British Indian Interest for the welfare of these His Majestys Colonies. . . .

7. That the Indians be remedied and satisfied with regard to their complaints about their Lands particularly those Grants & Patents mentioned in the former part of these Papers, and that no Patents for Lands be hereafter Granted but for such as shall be bought in the presence of the superintendent at public meetings & the sale recorded by His Majesty's Secretary for Indian affairs.

No one point will be of more beneficial consequence than this and unless it be put upon some satisfactory footing, it will be utterly impossible to establish the confidence of the Indians, to defeat the measures of the French and to secure these colonies from the ravages to which they are and will be subjected. If this is not done, we shall vainnly project Expedients, waste our Treasure and the Indians will infallibly quit our Alliance. . . .

(b) *Governor John Penn to the Pennsylvania Assembly, January 5, 1768, and the Assembly's reply, January 13, 1768.*

Gentlemen: You will perceive by a Letter from his Excellency General Gage, herewith laid before you, that, from accounts received from all Quarters (particularly from Sir William Johnson), of the dissatisfaction of the Indians, and their ill disposition towards us, there is great reason to apprehend an immediate Rupture with them, unless some effectual Means are fallen upon to Pacify them; and that the In-

sults and Injuries they have received from the Frontier Inhabitants, chiefly of Virginia, and the perverse and obstinate disposition of a Number of People, who, contrary to his Majesty's Proclamation, and the Principles of Justice, have settled, and are daily Settling upon their unpurchased Lands, are the principal Causes of their complaints. . . .

As nothing can be of more Importance to this Province than preventing the Calamitous effects of an Indian War, of which we have had the most melancholy Experience; And the Principles both of Justice and Policy call for a speedy Redress of the Grievances complained of by the Indians, I . . . most earnestly recommend to you the framing of a Law not only to remedy the present Evil, but to punish future Delinquencies of the same kind. . . .

JOHN PENN.

A MESSAGE TO THE GOVERNOR
FROM THE ASSEMBLY

May it please Your Honour: We find from his Excellency's Letter, and our own Enquiry, that the Causes of the present ill Temper of the Indians are the audacious Encroachments made by a Number of People who have settled on their Lands, on Red Stone Creek and Cheat River, within the Bounds of this Province, and the Murders committed on a number of Seneca and other Indians, by Persons who have hitherto bid Defiance to the Laws and Eluded the hands of Justice. These Offences, so injurious to the Rights of the Natives and the security of their Persons, in violation of the solemn Treaties of Peace and Friendship established with them, . . . cannot fail to create in their Minds the most dangerous Jealousies of our publick Faith and Integrity, and are probably motives to their design of forming a powerful Confederacy in the Spring. . . .

And as in all Probability those People will not distinguish between the Publick Acts of Government and the wicked Conduct of Lawless Men, they must in the End bring on a Savage War, attended with an immense Expence to Great Britain and her Colonies, in which the Innocent will be involved with the Guilty, and neither Age nor Sex find Compassion or Mercy. . . . In order to remove those lawless Intruders on the Indian Lands, and to

prevent any future Settlements thereon, we are preparing a Bill which we hope will be effectual. . . .

But may it please your Honour, should the Effects of this Law answer our Expectation of removing those Lawless People from the Indian Lands, we fear that there will still remain a principal Cause of their Dissatisfaction. We have received information that a Number of Senecas has been lately killed on the Frontiers of this and the neighbouring Provinces, and we can never forget those flagrant Breaches of the Laws of Hospitality, and the horrid Acts of Barbarity committed in the Year 1763, on the Remains of a Tribe of the same Indians and others, at Conestogo and Lancaster, which must also be remembered by your Honour. If murders will admit of Aggravation, the Circumstances attending the last mentioned of those impious Transactions, would greatly enhance the Guilt of the Offenders. The Forefathers of those innocent Victims, were received into an Alliance of Friendship by our first honourable Proprietary. Their Posterity were settled by the Government on a Tract of Land at Conestogo, and remained there Peaceably until part of them were inhumanly massacred.

The rest, reposing the firmest Confidence in the Faith of the Government, were taken in their distress under its more immediate Protection in the Work-house at Lancaster, where Men, Women, and helpless Infants, alike became a Sacrifice to the Frantic Rage and relentless Cruelty of a sett of Men equally regardless of the Dictates of Humanity, Religion, and the Laws of their Country.

These Murders we find have reached the Ears of the Indians, and . . . are undoubtedly one of the Causes of their present discontent, and will, we fear, be made use of to excite the Resentment of the Natives against this Province in a particular Manner, should a Rupture with them unhappily take place. . . . We are pressed, . . . therefore, . . . by the Strongest Motives to

take this opportunity of earnestly in-
treating your Honour that diligent and
Speedy Inquisition be made after those
attrocious offenders who have stained
the Land with innocent Blood and bid

defiance to the Laws of their Country,
to effect which, no Assistance in our
Power shall be wanting that the importance of the Occasion requires.

# 10

## "It is unreasonable . . . for the People of Great Britain to grant to his Majesty the Property of the Colonists"

Forewarned though they were that it
would be hazardous for "the Parliament of *Great Britain* to impose Taxes upon
the Subjects *here,* by Laws to be passed *there,*" (to quote the New York
Assembly's pithy definition of the issue in 1764), Parliament on March 22,
1765, did adopt the fatal meaure known as the Stamp Act. This was the second
of two revenue acts designed to raise money in America "toward defraying the
expences of defending, protecting, and securing" the massive new North American possessions won from the French and the Indians in 1763, and which the
French and their red allies were expected soon to make efforts to retrieve.

News of the Stamp Act's passage reached America late in April, 1765, and a
few weeks later the Massachusetts General Court proposed that delegates from
all the colonies meet in New York City in October to petition for its repeal.
This meeting of the Stamp Act Congress, attended by twenty-seven delegates
from nine colonies, was the first intercolonial assembly convened on American
initiative. On October 19, although some of the delegates refused to sign even
so mild a statement, the Stamp Act Congress issued its famous fourteen "declarations" printed here in full. Humble as it was, this petition did go beyond the
critical revenue issue to oppose the extension of the jurisdiction of the admiralty
courts, institutions which Americans then considered among the most offensive
engines of tyranny.

*October 19, 1765*

# The Declarations
# of the Stamp Act Congress

The Members of this Congress, sincerely devoted, with the warmest Sentiments of Affection and Duty to his Majesty's Person and Government, inviolably attached to the present happy establishment of the Protestant Succession, and with Minds deeply impressed by a Sense of the present and impending Misfortunes of the *British* Colonies on this Continent; having considered as maturely as Time will permit, the Circumstances of the said Colonies, esteem it our indispensable Duty, to make the following Declarations of our humble Opinion, respecting the most Essential Rights and Liberties of the Colonists, and of the Grievances under which they labour, by Reason of several late Acts of Parliament.

I.   That his Majesty's Subjects in these Colonies, owe the same Allegiance to the Crown of *Great-Britain*, that is owing from his Subjects born within the Realm, and all due Subordination to that August Body the Parliament of *Great-Britain*.

II.   That his Majesty's Liege Subjects in these Colonies, are entitled to all the inherent Rights and Liberties of his Natural born Subjects, within the Kingdom of *Great-Britain*.

III.   That it is inseparably essential to the Freedom of a People, and the undoubted Right of *Englishmen*, that no Taxes be imposed on them, but with their own Consent, given personally, or by their Representatives.

IV.   That the People of these Colonies are not, and from their local Circumstances cannot be, Represented in the House of Commons in *Great-Britain*.

V.   That the only Representatives of the People of these Colonies, are Persons chosen therein by themselves, and that no Taxes ever have been, or can be Constitutionally imposed on them, but by their respective Legislature.

VI.   That all Supplies to the Crown, being free Gifts of the People, it is unreasonable and inconsistent with the Principles and Spirit of the *British* Constitution, for the People of *Great-Britain* to grant to his Majesty the Property of the Colonists.

VII.   That Trial by Jury, is the inherent and invaluable Right of every *British* Subject in these Colonies.

VIII.   That the late Act of Parliament, entitled, *An Act for granting and appyling certain Stamp Duties, and other Duties, in the* British *Colonies and Plantations in* America, *&c.* by imposing Taxes on the Inhabitants of these Colonies, and the said Act, and several other Acts, by extending the Jurisdiction of the Courts of Admiralty beyond its ancient Limits, have a manifest Tendency to subvert the Rights and Liberties of the Colonists.

IX.   That the Duties imposed by several late Acts of Parliament, from the peculiar Circumstances of these Colonies, will be extremely Burthensome and Grievous; and from the scarcity of Specie, the Payment of them absolutely impracticable.

X.   That as the Profits of the Trade of these Colonies ultimately center in *Great-Britain*, to pay for the Manufactures which they are obliged to take from thence, they eventually contribute very largely to all Supplies granted there to the Crown.

XI.   That the Restrictions imposed

by several late Acts of Parliament, on the Trade of these Colonies, will render them unable to purchase the Manufactures of *Great-Britain.*

XII.    That the Increase, Prosperity, and Happiness of these Colonies, depend on the full and free Enjoyment of their Rights and Liberties, and an Intercourse with *Great-Britain* mutually Affectionate and Advantageous.

XIII.    That it is the Right of the *British* Subjects in these Colonies, to Petition the King, or either House of Parliament.

*Lastly,* That it is the indispensable Duty of these Colonies, to the best of Sovereigns, to the Mother Country, and to themselves, to endeavour by a loyal and dutiful Address to his Majesty, and humble Applications to both Houses of Parliament, to procure the Repeal of the Act for granting and applying certain Stamp Duties, of all Clauses of any other Acts of Parliament, whereby the Jurisdiction of the Admiralty is extended as aforesaid, and of the other late Acts for the Restriction of *American* Commerce.

# 11

## *"To the end that all such foes to the rights of British America may be publickly known, and universally contemned"*

Parliament thought so little of American opinion in 1765 that it refused even to receive the Declarations of the Stamp Act Congress sent to it late that year. Other petitions addressed by this Congress to the King, the Lords, and the Commons fared little better. But the British could not ignore the more ominous news that soon reached them. Violent action by the Sons of Liberty throughout the colonies saw to it that not a shilling was ever collected in stamp taxes in America before repeal of the act on March 18, 1766. Repeal itself was effected by the cries of *British* merchants made to squeal by the American boycott of their goods while the Stamp Act was in force.

Repeal, however, was simply an expedient, not a shift in policy. On the very day that Parliament repealed the Stamp Act it passed the Declaratory Act:

> The said colonies and plantations in America have been, are, and of right ought to be, subordinate unto, and dependent upon the imperial Crown and Parliament of Great Britain . . . in all cases whatsoever. . . . All . . . proceedings in any of the said colonies or plantations whereby the power and authority of the Parliament of Great Britain . . . is denied, or drawn into question, are hereby declared to be utterly null and void.

Henceforth, militancy in America drew heedless retribution from Britain until, as Thomas Jefferson wrote in July, 1774, "Scarcely have our minds been able to emerge from the astonishment into which one stroke of Parliamentary thunder has involved us, before another more heavy and more alarming is fallen on us." Jefferson went on to draw the moral: "Single acts of tyranny may be ascribed to the accidental opinion of a day; but a series of oppressions, begun at a distinguished period, and pursued unalterably through every change of ministers, too plainly prove a . . . systematical plan of reducing us to slavery."

The climax of this "systematical plan" had come a few months earlier when Parliament, in retaliation for the Boston Tea Party (December 16, 1773), adopted the "Intolerable Acts" closing the port of Boston and putting Massachusetts squarely under the royal thumb. Further measures so heightened the anxiety of the other colonies that when in June, 1774, Massachusetts called for a new continental meeting in Philadelphia to consider the American predicament, all but Georgia sent delegates. The assemblage at Philadelphia in September, 1774, The First Continental Congress, may rightly be considered the first national government in America. "By assuming the powers of legislation," wrote a Tory critic at the time, "the Congress have not only superseded our provincial legislatures, but have excluded every idea of monarchy; and not content with the havock already made in our constitution, in the plentitude of their power have appointed another Congress to be held in May."

The most remarkable "legislation" by the First Continental Congress was the "Association," adopted on October 20, 1774, and here printed in full. The Association reflected almost a decade of American commercial pressure on Great Britain. But it took a bold step beyond the past by authorizing, in paragraph 11, the selection of governing committees "in every county, city, and town" in America not only for enforcing the non-importation, non-consumption, non-exportation policy and the other sumptuary prohibitions (especially as in paragraph 8), but also for publishing as "the enemies of *American* liberty," and thereby exposing to public attack, the names of all violators.

*October 20, 1774*

# The Association

We, his Majesty's most loyal subjects, the Delegates of the several Colonies of *New-Hampshire, Massachusetts Bay, Rhode-Island, Connecticut, New-York, New-Jersey, Pennsylvania,* the three Lower Counties of *New-Castle, Kent,* and *Sussex,* on *Delaware, Maryland, Virginia, North Carolina* and *South Carolina,* deputed to represent them in a Continental Congress, held in the City of *Philadelphia* on the fifth day of *September,* 1774, avowing our allegiance to his Majesty; our affection and regard for our fellow-subjects in *Great Britain* and elsewhere; affected with the deepest anxiety and most alarming apprehensions at those grievances and distresses with which his

Majesty's *American* subjects are oppressed; and having taken under our most serious deliberation the state of the whole Continent, find that the present unhappy situation of our affairs is occasioned by a ruinous system of Colony Administration, adopted by the *British* Ministry about the year 1763, evidently calculated for enslaving these Colonies, and, with them, the *British Empire*. In prosecution of which system, various Acts of Parliament have been passed, for raising a Revenue in *America*, for depriving the *American* subjects, in many instances, of the constitutional Trial by Jury, exposing their lives to danger by directing a new and illegal trial beyond the seas for crimes alleged to have been committed in *America*; and in prosecution of the same system, several late, cruel, and oppressive Acts have been passed, respecting the Town of *Boston* and the *Massachusetts-Bay*, and also an Act for extending the Province of *Quebec*, so as to border on the Western Frontiers of these Colonies, establishing an arbitrary Government therein, and discouraging the settlement of *British* subjects in that wide extended country; thus, by the influence of civil principles and ancient prejudices, to dispose the inhabitants to act with hostility against the free Protestant Colonies, whenever a wicked Ministry shall choose so to direct them.

To obtain redress of these Grievances, which threaten destruction to the Lives, Liberty, and Property of his Majesty's subjects in *North America*, we are of opinion, that a Non-Importation, Non-Consumption, and Non-Exportation Agreement, faithfully adhered to, will prove the most speedy, effectual, and peaceable measure; and, therefore, we do, for ourselves, and the inhabitants of the several Colonies, whom we represent, firmly agree and associate, under the sacred ties of Virtue, Honour and Love of our Country, as follows:

1. That from and after the first day of *December* next, we will not import into *British America*, from *Great Brit-ain* or *Ireland*, any Goods, Wares, or Merchandises whatsoever, or from any other place, any such Goods, Wares or Merchandises as shall have been exported from *Great Britain* or *Ireland*; nor will we, after that day, import any *East India* Tea from any part of the World; nor any Molasses, Syrups, Paneles, Coffee, or Pimento, from the *British* Plantations or from *Dominica*; nor Wines from *Madeira*, or the *Western Islands*; nor Foreign Indigo.

2. That 'we will neither import nor purchase, any Slave imported after the first day of *December* next; after which time, we will wholly discontinue the Slave Trade, and will neither be concerned in it ourselves, nor will we hire our vessels, nor sell our Commodities or Manufactures to those who are concerned in it.

3. As a Non-Consumption Agreement, strictly adhered to, will be an effectual security for the observation of the Non-Importation, we, as above, solemnly agree and associate, that from this day we will not purchase or use any Tea imported on account of the *East India Company*, or any on which a Duty hath been or shall be paid; and from and after the first day of *March* next, we will not purchase or use any East India Tea whatsoever; nor will we, nor shall any person for or under us, purchase or use any of those Goods, Wares, or Merchandises, we have agreed not to import, which we shall know, or have cause to suspect, were imported after the first day of *December*, except such as come under the rules and directions of the tenth Article hereafter mentioned.

4. The earnest desire we have not to injure our fellow-subjects in *Great Britain*, *Ireland*, or the *West Indies*, induces us to suspend a Non-Exportation, until the tenth day of *September*, 1775; at which time, if the said Acts and parts of Acts of the *British* Parliament herein after mentioned, are not repealed, we will not directly or indirectly, export any merchandize or commodity whatsoever to *Great Britain*, *Ireland*,

or the *West Indies*, except Rice to *Europe*.

5. Such as are Merchants, and use the *British* and *Irish* Trade, will give orders, as soon as possible, to their Factors, Agents, and Correspondents, in *Great Britain* and *Ireland*, not to ship any Goods to them, on any pretence whatsoever, as they cannot be received in *America*; and if any Merchant, residing in *Great Britain* or *Ireland*, shall directly or indirectly ship any Goods, Wares or Merchandises, for America, in order to break the said Non-Importation Agreement, or in any manner contravene the same, on such unworthy conduct being well attested, it ought to be made publick; and, on the same being so done, we will not from thenceforth have any commercial connection with such Merchant.

6. That such as are Owners of vessels will give positive orders to their Captains, or Masters, not to receive on board their vessels any goods prohibited by the said Non-Importation Agreement, on pain of immediate dismission from their service.

7. We will use our utmost endeavours to improve the breed of Sheep, and increase their number to the greatest extent; and to that end, we will kill them as sparingly as may be, especially those of the most profitable kind; nor will we export any to the *West Indies* or elsewhere; and those of us who are or may become overstocked with, or can conveniently spare any Sheep, will dispose of them to our neighbours, especially to the poorer sort, upon moderate terms.

8. That we will, in our several stations, encourage Frugality, Economy, and Industry, and promote Agriculture, Arts and the Manufactures of this Country, especially that of Wool; and will discountenance and discourage every species of extravagance and dissipation, especially all horse-racing, and all kinds of gaming, cock fighting, exhibitions of plays, shews, and other expensive diversions and entertainments; and on the death of any relation or friend, none of us, or any of our families, will go into any further mourning-dress, than a black crape or ribbon on the arm or hat for gentlemen, and a black ribbon and necklace for ladies, and we will discontinue the giving of gloves and scarves at funerals.

9. That such as are venders of Goods or Merchandises will not take advantage of the scarcity of Goods that may be occasioned by this Association, but will sell the same at the rates we have been respectively accustomed to do, for twelve months last past. And if any vender of Goods or merchandises shall sell any such Goods on higher terms, or shall, in any manner, or by any device whatsoever, violate or depart from this Agreement, no person ought, nor will any of us deal with any such person, or his or her Factor or Agent, at any time thereafter for any commodity whatever.

10. In case any Merchant, Trader, or other person, shall import any Goods or merchandise, after the first day of *December*, and before the first day of *February* next, the same ought forthwith, at the election of the owner, to be either re-shipped or delivered up to the Committee of the County or Town wherein they shall be imported, to be stored at the risk of the importer, until the Non-Importation Agreement shall cease, or be sold under the direction of the Committee aforesaid; and in the last mentioned case, the owner or owners of such Goods shall be reimbursed out of the sales the first cost and charges; the profit, if any, to be applied towards relieving and employing such poor inhabitants of the Town of *Boston* as are immediate sufferers by the *Boston* Port Bill; and a particular account of all Goods so returned, stored, or sold, to be inserted in the publick papers; and if any Goods or Merchandises shall be imported after the said first day of *February*, the same ought forthwith to be sent back again, without breaking any of the packages thereof.

11. That a committee be chosen in every County, City, and Town, by those

who are qualified to vote for Representatives in the Legislature, whose business it shall be attentively to observe the conduct of all persons touching this Association; and when it shall be made to appear to the satisfaction of a majority of any such Committee, that any person within the limits of their appointment has violated this Association, that such majority do forthwith cause the truth of the case to be published in the Gazette; to the end that all such foes to the rights of *British America* may be publickly known, and universally contemned as the enemies of *American* liberty; and thenceforth we respectively will break off all dealings with him or her.

12. That the Committee of Correspondence, in the respective Colonies, do frequently inspect the Entries of their Custom Houses, and inform each other, from time to time, of the true state thereof, and of every other material circumstance that may occur relative to this Association.

13. That all Manufactures of this country be sold at reasonable prices, so that no undue advantage be taken of a future scarcity of Goods.

14. And we do further agree and resolve that we will have no Trade, Commerce, Dealings or Intercourse whatsoever with any Colony or Province, in North America, which shall not accede to, or which shall hereafter violate this Association, but will hold them as unworthy of the rights of freemen, and as inimical to the liberties of this country.

And we do solemnly bind ourselves and our constituents, under the ties aforesaid, to adhere to this Association until such parts of the several Acts of Parliament passed since the close of the last war, as impose or continue Duties on Tea, Wine, Molasses, Syrups, Paneles, Coffee, Sugar, Pimento, Indigo, Foreign Paper, Glass, and Painters' Colours, imported into *America,* and extend the powers of the Admiralty Courts beyond their ancient limits, deprive the *American* subject of Trial by Jury, authorize the judge's certificate to indemnify the prosecutor from damages that he might otherwise be liable to from a trial by his peers, require oppressive security from a claimant of Ships or Goods seized, before he shall be allowed to defend his property, are repealed.—And until that part of the Act of the 12th *George III.* ch. 24, entitled "An Act for the better securing his Majesty's Dock-yards, Magazines, Ships, Ammunition, and Stores," by which any person charged with committing any of the offences therein described, in *America,* may be tried in any Shire or County within the Realm, is repealed—and until the four Acts, passed the last session of Parliament, viz: that for stopping the Port and blocking up the Harbour of *Boston*— that for altering the Charter and Government of the *Massachusetts-Bay*— and that which is entitled "An Act for the better Administration of Justice, &c."—and that "for extending the Limits of *Quebec,* &c." are repealed. And we recommend it to the Provincial Conventions, and to the Committees in the respective Colonies, to establish such farther Regulations as they may think proper for carrying into execution this Association.

# 12

## *"We hold these truths to be self-evident"*

On May 10, 1776, just one year after it had hastily convened in Philadelphia following the battle of Lexington and Concord, the Second Continental Congress adopted John Adams's resolution advising those provinces that had not yet established "such government as shall best conduce to the happiness and safety of their constituents in particular, and America in general," to get on with this task. "I thought it was independence itself," Adams wrote of this resolution in later years, "but we must have it with more formality yet." On June 7, 1776, on behalf of the Virginia delegation, Richard Henry Lee submitted three resolutions to Congress. The first of these, the decisive "Resolution of Independence," was formally adopted on July 2, but only after nine hours of uninterrupted debate the day before had helped swing certain laggard delegates into line. Lee's measure stated

> RESOLVED, That these United Colonies are, and of right ought to be, free and independent States, that they are absolved from all allegiance to the British Crown, and that all political connection between them and the State of Great Britain is, and ought to be, totally dissolved.

Independence was in fact decreed by this act. Yet consideration of Lee's second resolution—"That it is expedient forthwith to take the most effectual measures for forming foreign alliances"—made it appear especially desirable to certain delegates that one further step still be taken. As Jefferson put it in his characteristically general vein, "a decent respect to the opinions of mankind requires that they should declare the causes which impel them to the separation." On June 11 Congress had named a Committee of Five—Jefferson, John Adams, Benjamin Franklin, Roger Sherman, and Robert R. Livingston—to draw up this declaration of causes. The Committee report was debated just after Lee's Resolution of Independence was adopted on July 2; and on the evening of July 4, having made numerous alterations in Jefferson's initial draft, Congress ordered,

> That the declaration be authenticated and printed. That the committee appointed to prepare the declaration superintent and correct the press. That copies of the declaration be sent to the several assemblies, conventions & committees or councils of safety and to the several commanding officers of the continental troops, that it be proclaimed in each of the united states & at the head of the army.

53

Unanimity before the world was one of the great objects of the Congress. But not until July 9 did New York permit its delegates to vote for independence; and not until July 19, when the parchment copy to be signed by the members was ordered, did the great declaration bear its lasting title: "The Unanimous Declaration of the Thirteen United States of America." Even so, unanimity was gained only after painful compromise, especially over the issue of the slave trade, which was to become such a stern testing ground of American values. What John Adams called Jefferson's "vehement philippic against negro slavery" had survived in successive drafts of the declaration until near the end of the debate. Then, as Jefferson said in notes made at the time, "it was struck out in complaisance to South Carolina and Georgia. . . . Our northern brethren also I believe felt a little tender under these censures; for tho' their people have very few slaves themselves, yet they have been pretty considerable carriers of them to others." But virtually all the delegates willingly subscribed to the ringing opening phrases of the declaration, those "self-evident truths" set forth, as Jefferson wrote years later, "in terms so plain and firm as to command their assent, and to justify ourselves in the independent stand we are compelled to take."

In the 1820's an argument broke out over the authorship and originality of the great declaration. John Adams wrote querulously, "There is not an idea in it, but what had been hackneyed in Congress for two years before." But Adams underestimated the time by a century and more, as the evidence so far offered in the present book makes plain. The declaration was a summing up of the experience of Americans in the New World, without neglecting their debt to the liberties won by generations of Englishmen at home. The manifesto of a newly independent nation, the declaration was also a manifesto of the independent spirit—the self-reliance, and the determination to retain self-government—of this nation's people. "It was intended," Jefferson said, "to be an expression of the American mind, and to give that expression the proper tone and spirit called for by the occasion. All its authority rests then on the harmonizing sentiments of the day."

*July 4, 1776*

# The Declaration of Independence

THE UNANIMOUS DECLARATION
OF THE THIRTEEN
UNITED STATES OF AMERICA

When in the Course of human events, it becomes necessary for one people to dissolve the political bands, which have connected them with an-

other, and to assume among the powers of the earth, the separate and equal station to which the Laws of Nature and of Nature's God entitle them, a decent respect to the opinions of mankind requires that they should declare the causes which impel them to the separation.—We hold these truths to be self-evident, that all men are created equal, that they are endowed by their Creator with certain unalienable Rights, that among these are Life, Liberty and the pursuit of Happiness.—That to secure these rights, Governments are instituted among Men, deriving their just powers from the consent of the governed,—That whenever any Form of Government becomes destructive of these ends, it is the Right of the People to alter or to abolish it, and to institute new Government, laying its foundation on such principles and organizing its powers in such form, as to them shall seem most likely to effect their Safety and Happiness. Prudence, indeed, will dictate that Governments long established should not be changed for light and transient causes; and accordingly all experience hath shewn, that mankind are more disposed to suffer, while evils are sufferable, than to right themselves by abolishing the forms to which they are accustomed. But when a long train of abuses and usurpations, pursuing invariably the same Object evinces a design to reduce them under absolute Despotism, it is their right, it is their duty, to throw off such Government, and to provide new Guards for their future security.—Such has been the patient sufferance of these Colonies; and such is now the necessity which constrains them to alter their former Systems of Government. The history of the present King of Great Britain is a history of repeated injuries and usurpations, all having in direct object the establishment of an absolute Tyranny over these States. To prove this, let Facts be submitted to a candid world. —He has refused his Assent to Laws, the most wholesome and necessary for the public good.—He has forbidden his Governors to pass Laws of immediate and pressing importance, unless suspended in their operation till his Assent should be obtained; and when so suspended, he has utterly neglected to attend to them.—He has refused to pass other Laws for the accommodation of large districts of people, unless those people would relinquish the right of Representation in the Legislature, a right inestimable to them and formidable to tyrants only.—He has called together legislative bodies at places unusual, uncomfortable, and distant from the depository of their public Records, for the sole purpose of fatiguing them into compliance with his measures.— He has dissolved Representative Houses repeatedly, for opposing with manly firmness his invasions on the rights of the people.—He has refused for a long time, after such dissolutions, to cause others to be elected; whereby the Legislative powers, incapable of Annihilation, have returned to the People at large for their exercise; the State remaining in the meantime exposed to all the dangers of invasion from without, and convulsions within.—He has endeavoured to prevent the population of these States; for that purpose obstructing the Laws for Naturalization of Foreigners; refusing to pass others to encourage their migrations hither, and raising the conditions of new Appropriations of Lands.—He has obstructed the Administration of Justice, by refusing his Assent to Laws for establishing Judiciary powers.—He has made Judges dependent on his Will alone, for the tenure of their offices, and the amount and payment of their salaries.—He has erected a multitude of New Offices, and sent hither swarms of Officers to harrass our people, and eat out their substance. —He has kept among us, in times of peace, Standing Armies without the Consent of our legislatures.—He has affected to render the Military independent of and superior to the Civil power.—He has combined with others to subject us to a jurisdiction foreign to our constitution, and unacknowledged by our Laws, giving his Assent to their Acts of pretended Legislation.— For quartering large bodies of armed troops among us.—For protecting them, by a mock Trial, from punishment for any Murders which they should commit on the Inhabitants of these States:—

For cutting off our Trade with all parts of the world:—For imposing Taxes on us without our Consent:—For depriving us in many cases, of the benefits of Trial by Jury:—For transporting us beyond Seas to be tried for pretended offenses:—For abolishing the free System of English Laws in a neighboring Province, establishing therein an Arbitrary government, and enlarging its Boundaries so as to render it at once an example and fit instrument for introducing the same absolute rule into these Colonies:—For taking away our Charters, abolishing our most valuable Laws, and altering fundamentally the Forms of our Governments:—For suspending our own Legislatures, and declaring themselves invested with power to legislate for us in all cases whatsoever.—He has abdicated Government here, by declaring us out of his Protection and waging War against us.—He has plundered our seas, ravaged our Coasts, burnt our towns, and destroyed the lives of our people.—He is at this time transporting large Armies of foreign Mercenaries to compleat the works of death, desolation and tyranny, already begun with circumstances of Cruelty & perfidy scarcely paralleled in the most barbarous ages, and totally unworthy the Head of a civilized nation.—He has constrained our fellow Citizens taken Captive on the high Seas to bear Arms against their Country, to become the executioners of their friends and Brethren, or to fall themselves by their hands.—He has excited domestic insurrections amongst us, and has endeavoured to bring on the inhabitants of our frontiers, the merciless Indian Savages, whose known rule of warfare, is an undistinguished destruction of all ages, sexes and conditions. In every stage of these Oppressions We have Petitioned for Redress in the most humble terms: Our repeated Petitions have been answered only by repeated injury. A Prince whose character is thus marked by every act which may define a Tyrant, is unfit to be the ruler of a free people. Nor have We been wanting in attentions to our British brethren. We have warned them from time to time of attempts by their legislature to extend an unwarrantable jurisdiction over us. We have reminded them of the circumstances of our emigration and settlement here. We have appealed to their native justice and magnanimity, and we have conjured them by the ties of our common kindred to disavow these usurpations, which would inevitably interrupt our connections and correspondence. They too have been deaf to the voice of justice and of consanguinity. We must, therefore, acquiesce in the necessity, which denounces our Separation, and hold them, as we hold the rest of mankind, Enemies in War, in Peace Friends.—

We, therefore, the Representatives of the united States of America, in General Congress Assembled, appealing to the Supreme Judge of the world for the rectitude of our intentions do, in the Name, and by the Authority of the good People of these Colonies, solemnly publish and declare, That these United Colonies are, and of Right out to be Free and Independent States; that they are Absolved from all Allegiance to the British Crown, and that all political connection between them and the State of Great Britain, is and ought to be totally dissolved; and that as Free and Independent States, they have full Power to levy War, conclude Peace, contract Alliances, establish Commerce, and to do all other Acts and Things which Independent States may of right do.—And for the support of this Declaration, with a firm reliance on the protection of divine Providence, we mutually pledge to each other our Lives, our Fortunes and our sacred Honor.

# 13

*"The said states hereby severally enter into
a firm league of friendship with each other"*

The third of the three resolutions submitted to the Second Continental Congress by Richard Henry Lee on June 7, 1776, stated: "RESOLVED . . . That a plan of confederation be prepared and transmitted to the respective Colonies for their consideration and approbation." This was not the first the delegates had heard on the subject of establishing a permanent central government the better to conduct the war in America and to win allies abroad. In June, 1775, Benjamin Franklin had informally disclosed a draft of "Articles of Confederation and Perpetual Union," as he called it, to certain members in his confidence. They, in turn, were asked to canvass the opinions of others whose discretion they could trust. Many delegates told Franklin's emissaries they "were revolted" by the proposal that Congress set up a separate sovereign government while a glimmer of hope remained for reconciliation with George III. "We found that it could not be passed," Jefferson said of Franklin's trial balloon, and they laid it aside.

On January 9, 1776, Thomas Paine published *Common Sense,* that meteoric pamphlet for the promotion of American independence. "Nothing but . . . a Continental form of government," said Paine, "can keep the peace of the Continent and preserve it inviolate from civil wars." Paine proceeded to sketch in a "Continental form" similar in some respects to Franklin's, but even with such backing the friends of confederation in Congress could not yet muster a majority even on the noncommittal question, "Whether a Day shall be fixed for considering the Instrument of Confederation."

When John Adams first encountered *Common Sense* in February, 1776, he had a mixed reaction, which he recorded in his *Autobiography* as follows:

> In the Course of this Winter appeared a Phenomenon in Philadelphia, *a Star of Disaster.* I mean Thomas Paine. . . . [His] Arguments in favor of Independence I liked very well. . . . The part relative to a form of Government I considered as flowing from simple ignorance. . . . His plan was so democratical, without any restraint or even an Attempt at any equilibrium or Counterpoise that it must produce confusion and every Evil Work.

Because he "dreaded the Effect so popular a pamphlet might have among the people," Adams, in April, published his own pamphlet, *Thoughts on Govern-*

57

*ment: Applicable to the Present State of the American Colonies,* which he had written originally at the request of those preparing to frame new state constitutions. Franklin and Paine proposed a popularly elected one-house legislature where all power, executive and judiciary as well as legislative, was indiscriminately lumped. Adams stressed the values of legislative bicameralism, of independent executives and judiciaries, and of checks and balances among the three ruling parts—"all established modes to which the people have been familiarized by habit." Adams went farther. "The blessings of society," he asserted, "depend entirely on the constitutions of government." His constitutional plan would not only insure the health of the state; it would also nourish the spirit of its citizens: "The elevation of sentiment inspired by such a government makes the common people brave and enterprising. That ambition which is inspired by it makes them sober, industrious, and frugal." Adams's *Thoughts* reflect what he called his own "research after the best," in "the divine science of politics," and are reproduced in part below as item "a."

The most enduring monument to Adams's precepts is the Massachusetts Constitution of 1780, a model in many respects for the great Constitution of 1787, and still in force to this day, although much amended. Many earlier state constitutions shaped from Adams's mold lasted from half to three-quarters of a century. Their success makes all the more remarkable the form of the first *federal* constitution, which owed more than its name to Franklin's unfortunate original draft, and which Congress at last completed and submitted to the states on November 17, 1777.

Congress was fully aware of the difficulties and defects of its work. In its official letter to the states it apologized for the "uncommon embarrassment and delay" in framing the Articles, and begged the most generous consideration of their form, "as that alone which affords any tolerable prospect of general ratification." Still one more divisive issue, moreover, remained to be faced—the disposition of the lands of those states claiming territory beyond the mountains, and even to the "South Sea." The delegates had managed to evade this issue until the last moment, when Virginia, one of the seven "landed" states, carried the proviso in Article IX, "that no state shall be deprived of territory for the benefit of the United States." The landless commonwealths found this proviso so offensive that they succeeded in postponing ratification until Virginia (following the lead of New York in 1780) reversed her stand in January, 1781. The Articles of Confederation (reproduced in full in item "b" below) went into effect March 1, 1781. By then, the movement to supplant them with "a more perfect union" conforming closely to Adams's *Thoughts* was already well under way.

*March 1, 1781*

# Articles of Confederation
# and Perpetual Union

### (a)  *From John Adams, Thoughts on Government Applicable to the Present State of the American Colonies, April, 1776*

If I was equal to the task of forming a plan for the government of a colony, I should be flattered with your request, and very happy to comply with it; because, as the divine science of politics is the science of social happiness, and the blessings of society depend entirely on the constitutions of government, which are generally institutions that last for many generations, there can be no employment more agreeable to a benevolent mind than a research after the best. . . .

We ought to consider what is the end of government, before we determine which is the best form. Upon this point all speculative politicians will agree that the happiness of society is the end of government, as all divines and moral philosophers will agree that the happiness of the individual is the end of man. From this principle it will follow that the form of government which communicates ease, comfort, security, or, in one word, happiness, to the greatest number of persons, and in the greatest degree, is the best. . . .

Fear is the foundation of most governments; but it is so sordid and brutal a passion, and renders men in whose breasts it predominates so stupid and miserable, that Americans will not be likely to approve of any political institution which is founded on it. . . . The noblest principles and most generous affections in our nature, then, have the fairest chance to support the noblest and most generous models of government. . . .

There is no good government but what is republican. . . . As good government is an empire of laws, how shall your laws be made. In a large society inhabiting an extensive country, it is impossible that the whole should assemble to make laws. The first necessary step, then, is to depute power from the many to a few of the most wise and good. . . . The principal difficulty lies, and the greatest care should be employed in constituting this representative assembly. . . . Equal interests among the people should have equal interests in it. Great care should be taken to effect this, and to prevent unfair, partial and corrupt election. . . .

A representation of the people in one assembly being obtained, a question arises whether all the powers of government, legislative, executive, and judicial, shall be left in this body? I think a people cannot be long free, nor ever happy, whose government is in one assembly. My reasons for this opinion are as follow:

1. A single assembly is liable to all the vices, follies, and frailties of an individual; . . . and all these errors ought to be corrected and defects supplied by some controlling power.

2. A single assembly is apt to be avaricious, and in time will not scruple to exempt itself from burdens, which it will lay, without compunction, on its constituents.

3. A single assembly is apt to grow ambitious, and after a time will not hesitate to vote itself perpetual. . . .

4. A representative assembly . . . is unfit to exercise the executive power,

for want of two essential properties, secrecy and despatch.

5. A representative assembly is still less qualified for the judicial power, because it is too numerous, too slow, and too little skilled in the laws. . . .

But shall the whole power of legislation rest in one assembly? Most of the foregoing reasons apply equally to prove that the legislative power ought to be more complex. . . .

Let the representative assembly then elect by ballot, from among themselves or their constituents, or both, a distinct assembly, which . . . we will call a council. . . . It should have a free and independent exercise of its judgement, and consequently a negative voice in the legislature.

These two bodies, thus constituted, and made integral parts of the legislature, let them unite, and by joint ballot choose a governor, who, after being stripped of most of those badges of domination called prerogatives, should have free and independent exercise of his judgement, and be made also an integral part of the legislature. . . . If he is annually elective, as he ought to be, he will always have so much reverence and affection for the people, their representatives and counsellors, that although you give him an independent exercise of his judgement, he will seldom use it in opposition to the two houses. . . .

The dignity and stability of government in all its branches, the morals of the people, and every blessing of society depends so much upon an upright and skilful administration of justice that the judicial power ought to be distinct from both the legislative and executive, and independent upon both, that so it may be a check upon both, as both should be checks upon that. . . .

Laws for the liberal education of youth, especially of the lower class of people, are so extremely wise and useful, that, to a humane and generous mind, no expense for this purpose would be thought extravagant. . . .

A constitution founded on these principles introduces knowledge among the people, and inspires them with a conscious dignity becoming freemen; a general emulation takes place, which causes good humor, sociability, good manners, and good morals to be general. The elevation of sentiment inspired by such a government makes the common people brave and enterprising. That ambition which is inspired by it makes them sober, industrious, and frugal. You will find among them some elegance, perhaps, but more solidity; a little pleasure, but a great deal of business; some politeness, but more civility. If you compare such a country with the regions of domination, whether monarchical or aristocratical, you will fancy yourself in Arcadia or Elysium.

## (b)  Articles of Confederation and Perpetual Union, March 1, 1781

TO ALL TO WHOM these Presents shall come, we the undersigned Delegates of the States affixed to our Names send greeting. Whereas the Delegates of the United States of America in Congress assembled did on the fifteenth day of November in the Year of our Lord One Thousand Seven Hundred and Seventy seven, and in the Second Year of the Independence of America agree to certain articles of Confederation and perpetual Union between the States of Newhampshire, Massachusetts-bay, Rhodeisland and Providence Plantations, Connecticut, New York, New Jersey, Pennsylvania, Delaware, Maryland, Virginia, North-Carolina, South-Carolina and Georgia in the Words following, viz. "Articles of Confederation and perpetual Union between the states of Newhampshire, Massachusetts-bay, Rhodeisland and Providence Plantations, Connecticut, New-York, New-Jersey, Pennsylvania, Delaware, Maryland, Virginia, North-Carolina, South-Carolina and Georgia.

*Art. I.* The Stile of this confederacy shall be "The United States of America."

*Art. II.* Each state retains its sovereignty, freedom and independence, and every Power, Jurisdiction and right, which is not by this confederation expressly delegated to the United States, in Congress assembled.

*Art. III.* The said states hereby severally enter into a firm league of friendship with each other, for their common defence, the security of their Liberties, and their mutual and general welfare, binding themselves to assist each other, against all force offered to, or attacks made upon them, or any of them, on account of religion, sovereignty, trade, or any other pretence whatever.

*Art. IV.* The better to secure and perpetuate mutual friendship and intercourse among the people of the different states in this union, the free inhabitants of each of these states, paupers, vagabonds and fugitives from Justice excepted, shall be entitled to all privileges and immunities of free citizens in the several states; and the people of each state shall have free ingress and regress to and from any other state, and shall enjoy therein all the privileges of trade and commerce, subject to the same duties, impositions and restrictions as the inhabitants thereof respectively, provided that such restriction shall not extend so far as to prevent the removal of property imported into any state, to any other state of which the Owner is an inhabitant; provided also that no imposition, duties or restriction shall be laid by any state, on the property of the united states, or either of them.

If any Person guilty of, or charged with treason, felony, or other high misdemeanor in any state, shall flee from Justice, and be found in any of the united states, he shall upon demand of the Governor or executive power, of the state from which he fled, be delivered up and removed to the state having jurisdiction of his offence.

Full faith and credit shall be given in each of these states to the records, acts and judicial proceedings of the courts and magistrates of every other state.

*Art. V.* For the more convenient management of the general interests of the united states, delegates shall be annually appointed in such manner as the legislature of each state shall direct, to meet in Congress on the first Monday in November, in every year, with a power reserved to each state, to recal its delegates, or any of them, at any time within the year, and to send others in their stead, for the remainder of the Year.

No state shall be represented in Congress by less than two, nor by more than seven Members; and no person shall be capable of being a delegate for more than three years in any term of six years; nor shall any person, being a delegate, be capable of holding any office under the united states, for which he, or another for his benefit receives any salary, fees or emolument of any kind.

Each state shall maintain its own delegates in a meeting of the states, and while they act as members of the committee of the states.

In determining questions in the united states, in Congress assembled, each state shall have one vote.

Freedom of speech and debate in Congress shall not be impeached or questioned in any Court, or place out of Congress, and the members of congress shall be protected in their persons from arrests and imprisonments, during the time of their going to and from, and attendance on congress, except for treason, felony, or breach of the peace.

*Art. VI.* No state without the Consent of the united states in congress assembled, shall send any embassy to, or receive any embassy from, or enter into any conference, agreement, or alliance or treaty with any King, prince or state; nor shall any person holding any office of profit or trust under the united states, or any of them, accept of any present, emolument, office or title of any kind whatever from any king, prince or foreign state; nor shall the united states in congress assembled, or any of them, grant any title of nobility.

No two or more states shall enter into any treaty, confederation or alliance whatever between them, without the consent of the united states in congress assembled, specifying accurately the purposes for which the same is to be entered into, and how long it shall continue.

No state shall lay any imposts or duties, which may interfere with any stipulations in treaties, entered into by the united states in congress assembled, with any king, prince or state, in pursuance of any treaties already proposed by congress, to the courts of France and Spain.

No vessels of war shall be kept up in time of peace by any state, except such number only, as shall be deemed necessary by the united states in congress assembled, for the defence of such state, or its trade; nor shall any body of forces be kept up by any state, in time of peace, except such number only, as in the judgment of the united states, in congress assembled, shall be deemed requisite to garrison the forts necessary for the defence of such state; but every state shall always keep up a well regulated and disciplined militia, sufficiently armed and accoutred, and shall provide and constantly have ready for use, in public stores, a due number of field pieces and tents, and a proper quantity of arms, ammunition and camp equipage.

No state shall engage in any war without the consent of the united states in congress assembled, unless such state be actually invaded by enemies, or shall have received certain advice of a resolution being formed by some nation of Indians to invade such state, and the danger is so imminent as not to admit of a delay, till the united states in congress assembled can be consulted: nor shall any state grant commissions to any ships or vessels of war, nor letters of marque or reprisal,

except it be after a declaration of war by the united states in congress assembled, and then only against the kingdom or state and the subjects thereof, against which war has been so declared, and under such regulations as shall be established by the united states in congress assembled, unless such state be infested by pirates, in which case vessels of war may be fitted out for that occasion, and kept so long as the danger shall continue, or until the united states in congress assembled shall determine otherwise.

*Art. VII.* When land-forces are raised by any state for the common defence, all officers of or under the rank of colonel, shall be appointed by the legislature of each state respectively by whom such forces shall be raised, or in such manner as such state shall direct, and all vacancies shall be filled up by the state which first made the appointment.

*Art. VIII.* All charges of war, and all other expences that shall be incurred for the common defence or general welfare, and allowed by the united states in congress assembled, shall be defrayed out of a common treasury, which shall be supplied by the several states, in proportion to the value of all land within each state, granted to or surveyed for any Person, as such land and the buildings and improvements thereon shall be estimated according to such mode as the united states in congress assembled, shall from time to time direct and appoint. The taxes for paying that proportion shall be laid and levied by the authority and direction of the legislatures of the several states within the time agreed upon by the united states in congress assembled.

*Art. IX.* The united states in congress assembled, shall have the sole and exclusive right and power of determining on peace and war, except in the cases mentioned in the sixth article—of sending and receiving ambassadors—entering into treaties and alliances, provided that no treaty of commerce shall be made whereby the legislative power of the respective states shall be restrained from imposing such imposts and duties on foreigners, as their own people are subjected to, or from prohibiting the exportation or importation of any species of goods or commodities whatsoever—of establishing rules for deciding in all cases, what captures on land or water shall be legal, and in what manner prizes taken by land or naval forces in the service of the united states shall be divided or appropriated—of granting letters of marque and reprisal in times of peace—appointing courts for the trial of piracies and felonies committed on the high seas and establishing courts for receiving and determining finally appeals in all cases of captures, provided that no member of congress shall be appointed a judge of any of the said courts.

The united states in congress assembled shall also be the last resort on appeal in all disputes and differences now subsisting or that hereafter may arise between two or more states concerning boundary, jurisdiction or any other cause whatever; which authority shall always be exercised in the manner following. Whenever the legislative or executive authority or lawful agent of any state in controversy with another shall present a petition to congress, stating the matter in question and praying for a hearing, notice thereof shall be given by order of congress to the legislative or executive authority of the other state in controversy, and a day assigned for the appearance of the parties by their lawful agents, who shall then be directed to appoint by joint consent, commissioners or judges to constitute a court for hearing and determining the matter in question: but if they cannot agree, congress shall name three persons out of each of the united states, and from the list of such persons each party shall alternately strike out one, the petitioners beginning, until the number shall be reduced to thirteen; and from that number not less than seven, nor more than nine names as congress shall direct, shall in the presence of congress be drawn out by lot, and the persons whose names shall be so drawn or any five of them, shall be commissioners or judges, to hear and finally determine the controversy, so always as a major part of the judges who shall hear the cause shall agree in the determination; and if either party shall neglect to attend at the day appointed, without shewing reasons, which congress shall judge sufficient, or being present shall refuse to strike, the congress shall proceed to nominate three persons out of each state, and the secretary of congress shall strike in behalf of such party absent or refusing; and the judgment and sentence of the court to be appointed, in the manner before prescribed, shall be final and conclusive; and if any of the parties shall refuse to submit to the authority of such court, or to appear to defend their claim or cause, the court shall nevertheless proceed to pronounce sentence, or judgment, which shall in like manner be final and decisive, the judgment or sentence and other proceedings being in either case transmitted to congress, and lodged among the acts of congress for the security of the parties concerned: provided that every commissioner, before he sits in judgment, shall take an oath to be administered by one of the judges of the supreme or superior court of the state, where the cause shall be tried, "well and truly to hear and determine the matter in question, according to the best of his judgment, without favour, affection or hope of reward:" provided also that no state shall be deprived of territory for the benefit of the united states.

All controversies concerning the private right of soil claimed under different grants of two or more states, whose jurisdictions as they may respect such lands, and the states which passed such grants are adjusted, the said grants or either of them being at the same time claimed to have originated antecedent to such settlement of jurisdiction, shall on the petition of either party to the congress of the united states, be finally determined as near as may be in the same manner as is before prescribed for deciding disputes respecting territorial jurisdiction between different states.

The united states in congress assembled shall also have the sole and exclusive right and power of regulating the alloy and value of coin struck by their own authority, or by that of the respective states—fixing the standard of weights and measures throughout the united states.—regulating the trade and managing all affairs with the Indians, not members of any of the states, provided that the legislative right of any state within its own limits be not infringed or violated—establishing and regulating post-offices from one state to another, throughout all the united states, and exacting such postage on the papers passing thro' the same as may be requisite to defray the expences of the said office—appointing all officers of the land forces, in the service of the united states, excepting regimental officers.—appointing all the officers of the naval forces, and commissioning all officers whatever in the service of the united states—making rules for the government and regulation of the said land and naval forces, and directing their operations.

The united states in congress assembled shall have authority to appoint a committee, to sit in the recess of congress, to be denominated "A Committee of the States," and to consist of one delegate from each state; and to appoint such other committees and civil officers as may be necessary for managing the general affairs of the united states under their direction—to appoint one of their number to preside, provided that no person be allowed to serve in the office of president more than one year in any term of three years; to ascertain the necessary sums of Money to be raised for the service of the united states, and to appropriate and apply the same for defraying the public expences—to borrow money,

or emit bills on the credit of the united states, transmitting every half year to the respective states an account of the sums of money so borrowed or emitted,—to build and equip a navy— to agree upon the number of land forces, and to make requisitions from each state for its quota, in proportion to the number of white inhabitants in such state; which requisition shall be binding, and thereupon the legislature of each state shall appoint the regimental officers, raise the men and cloath, arm and equip them in a soldier like manner, at the expence of the united states, and the officers and men so cloathed, armed and equipped shall march to the place appointed, and within the time agreed on by the united states in congress assembled: But if the united states in congress assembled shall, on consideration of circumstances judge proper that any state should not raise men, or should raise a smaller number than its quota, and that any other state should raise a greater number of men than the quota thereof, such extra number shall be raised, officered, cloathed, armed and equipped in the same manner as the quota of such state, unless the legislature of such state shall judge that such extra number cannot be safely spared out of the same, in which case they shall raise officer, cloath, arm and equip as many of such extra number as they judge can be safely spared. And the officers and men so cloathed, armed and equipped, shall march to the place appointed, and within the time agreed on by the united states in congress assembled.

The united states in congress assembled shall never engage in a war, nor grant letters of marque and reprisal in time of peace, nor enter into any treaties or alliances, nor coin money, nor regulate the value thereof, nor acertain the sums and expenses necessary for the defence and welfare of the united states, or any of them, nor emit bills, nor borrow money on the credit of the united states, nor appropriate money, nor agree upon the number of vessels of war, to be built or purchased, or the number of land or sea forces to be raised, nor appoint a commander in chief of the army or navy, unless nine states assent to the same: nor shall a question on any other point, except for adjourning from day to day be determined, unless by the votes of a majority of the united states in congress assembled.

The congress of the united states shall have power to adjourn to any time within the year, and to any place within the united states, so that no period of adjournment be for a longer duration than the space of six Months, and shall publish the Journal of their proceedings monthly, except such parts thereof relating to treaties, alliances or military operations as in their judgment require secrecy; and the yeas and nays of the delegates of each state on any question shall be entered on the Journal, when it is desired by any delegate; and the delegates of a state, or any of them, at his or their request shall be furnished with a transcript of the said Journal, except such parts as are above excepted, to lay before the legislatures of the several states.

*Art. X.* The committee of the states, or any nine of them, shall be authorised to execute, in the recess of congress, such of the powers of congress as the united states in congress assembled, by the consent of nine states, shall from time to time think expedient to vest them with; provided that no power be delegated to the said committee, for the exercise of which, by the articles of confederation, the voice of nine states in the congress of the united states assembled is requisite.

*Art. XI.* Canada acceding to this confederation, and joining in the measures of the united states, shall be admitted into, and entitled to all the advantages of this union: but no other colony shall be admitted into the same, unless such admission be agreed to by nine states.

*Art. XII.* All bills of credit emitted, monies borrowed and debts contracted by, or under the authority of congress, before the assembling of the united states, in pursuance of the present confederation, shall be deemed and considered as a charge against the united states, for payment and satisfaction whereof the said united states, and the public faith are hereby solemnly pledged.

*Art. XIII.* Every state shall abide by the determinations of the united states in congress assembled, on all questions which by this confederation are submitted to them. And the Articles of this confederation shall be inviolably observed by every state, and the union shall be perpetual; nor shall any alteration at any time hereafter be made in any of them; unless such alteration be agreed to in a congress of the united states, and be afterwards confirmed by the legislatures of every state.

AND WHEREAS it hath pleased the Great Governor of the World to incline the hearts of the legislatures we respectively represent in congress, to approve of, and to authorize us to ratify the said articles of confederation and perpetual union. KNOW YE that we the under-signed delegates, by virtue of the power and authority to us given for that purpose, do by these presents, in the name and in behalf of our respective constituents fully and entirely ratify and confirm each and every of the said articles of confederation and perpetual union, and all and singular the matters and things therein contained: And we do further solemnly plight and engage the faith of our respective constituents, that they shall abide by the determinations of the united states in congress assembled, on all questions, which by the said confederation are submitted to them. And that the articles thereof shall be inviolably observed by the states we respectively represent, and that the union shall be perpetual. In Witness whereof we have hereunto set our hands in Congress.

## 14

*"If religion be not within the cognizance of civil government, how can its legal establishment be necessary to civil government?"*

When John Locke died on October 28, 1704, he went, according to his last recorded words, "in perfect charity with all men, and in sincere communion with the whole church of Christ, by whatever names Christ's followers call themselves." Locke's life spanned the two great English revolutions, the Puritan revolution of the middle of the seventeenth century, and the Glorious Revolution near that century's end. The onset of the first had precipitated the "great migration" which secured the permanent settlement of North America by Englishmen. Locke's justification of the second supplied the philosophical foundation for America's own rebellion against the Crown.

Both the Puritan revolution and the Glorious Revolution were religious revolutions, the one against the authoritarianism of the Established Church of England, the second against the renewed threat of Catholicism to Protestantism. Both were also political revolutions in which religious liberty was only the fundamental one among the many other liberties that were asserted. And both revolutions soon displeased John Locke. The fanaticism of the Puritans led him to the discovery in his youth that "the popular assertors of liberty were the greatest engrossers of it too, and not unfitly called its *keepers.*" The opportunism of the Anglicans under William III, in turn, in employing the established religion to sanctify the sorriest policies of the reign, soured his old age.

Locke's "sincere communion with the whole church of Christ" was as far in religious latitude as even the most nearly libertarian promoters of English settlement in America, such as Roger Williams and William Penn, would go. Williams would have no one "accounted a Delinquent for *Doctrine,*" as his Rhode Island General Court said in 1641, "Provided, it be not directly repugnant to ye Government or Lawes established." The "Lawes established" required all government officers to make "an Ingagement by oath," wherein "I judge myself bound before God to walk faithfully." According to Penn's "Charter of Privileges" of 1701, only "persons who . . . profess to believe in Jesus Christ the Saviour of the world shall be capable . . . to serve this government in any capacity." After the American Revolution, moreover, most Americans continued to find the only reliable keepers of political liberty in particular religious denominations.

There were exceptions, however. As loyalism spread among the Anglican clergy during the Revolution, especially in the South where the Anglican was the established church, the more independent American sects, notably the southern Baptists and Presbyterians, used their own conspicuous patriotism to promote political equality for all dissenting groups. Occasionally they included Catholics, Jews, and Mohammedans among the beneficiaries of their program. In Virginia, the largely Anglican legislature had proved peculiarly harsh on Dissenters, who themselves made up a majority of the population by the time of the Revolution. Virginia thus became the prime target of the reformers' campaign, and in the Bill of Rights in the Old Dominion's revolutionary constitution of 1776 they won the famous Article 16, which said: "Religion . . . can be directed only by reason and conviction, and not by force or violence; and therefore all men are equally entitled to the free exercise of religion, according to the dictates of conscience."

This article was a signal victory. But it only opened what Jefferson in his *Autobiography* recalled as "the severest contests in which I have been engaged." These contests developed over the successive pieces of legislation now required to "put down" the special privileges which the Anglican Church still held by law. By 1779, the Anglican Church in Virginia had been disestablished. But more yet was wanted. In his *Letter Concerning Toleration*, published in 1689, "The Great Mr. Locke," as Americans had come to call the beloved philosopher of revolution, wrote as follows: "Promises, covenants, and oaths, which are the bonds of human society, can have no hold upon an atheist. The taking away of God, though but even in thought, dissolves all." Jefferson and his friends were of an age that had less fear of atheists, more confidence in the *natural* goodness of mankind, a horror, above all else, of thought control. Religious *toleration*, implying a superior political authority, had for them become incompatible with liberty of conscience, one of Locke's own "unalienable rights" with which legislation itself could not rightfully tamper. Their goal was the utter divorce of religion from authority, political equality as well as religious freedom for the subscribers to all faiths or none.

In 1784, in a bid to revive their fortunes, Virginia Anglicans had a bill introduced in the legislature "establishing a provision for Teachers of the Christian Religion." Certain Dissenters, once liberal but grown fearful for morality under the strains of the late war, rallied to the Anglicans' side. With the watchful Jefferson out of the country, young James Madison rallied the opposition. They were willing to leave the nurture of morality to free public schools, which they also sponsored. The Anglican's mild proposal they saw only as an opening wedge for the revival of sectarian privilege and the resumption of religious persecution. Late in 1785 they succeeded in defeating this proposal in the legislature. On the momentum of this victory they were able to pass the following year Virginia's famous "Statute of Religious Liberty" which Jefferson had first submitted seven years before. This statute opens with the resounding proposition that, "Almighty God hath created the mind free." And it goes on to prescribe "that all men shall be free to profess, and by argument to maintain their opinion in matters of religion, and . . . the same shall in no wise diminish, enlarge, or affect their civil capacities."

The turning point in the defeat of the Anglican resolution of 1784 and in the enactment of the "Statute of Religious Liberty" in 1786 was the publication late in 1785 of Madison's "Memorial and Remonstrance" to the legislature, "to declare the reasons by which we are determined." This document, the most conclusive argument for what would soon become the American policy of separation of church and state, is reproduced in part below.

*1785*

# James Madison: A Memorial and Remonstrance

## Against Religious Assessments

TO THE HONORABLE
THE GENERAL ASSEMBLY OF THE
COMMONWEALTH OF VIRGINIA:

We, the subscribers, citizens of the said commonwealth, having taken into serious consideration a bill printed by order of the last session of General Assembly, entitled "A Bill establishing a provision for Teachers of the Christian Religion," and conceiving that the same, if finally armed with the sanctions of a law, will be a dangerous abuse of power, are bound as faithful members of a free state to remonstrate against it, and to declare the reasons by which we are determined. We remonstrate against the said bill—

1. Because we hold it for a fundamental and undeniable truth that . . . the religion . . . of every man must be left to the conviction and conscience of every man; and it is the right of every man to exercise it as these may dictate. This right is in its nature an unalienable right. . . .

2. Because, if religion be exempt from the authority of the Society at large, still less can it be subject to that of the Legislative Body. . . . The pres-

ervation of free government requires not merely, that the metes and bounds which separate each department of power may be invariably maintained; but more especially, that neither of them be suffered to overleap the great Barrier which defends the rights of the people. . . .

3. Because it is proper to take alarm at the first experiment on our liberties. We hold this prudent jealousy to be the first duty of citizens, and one of the noblest characteristics of the late Revolution. The freedom of America did not wait till usurped power had strengthened itself by exercise and entangled the question in precedents. They saw all the consequences in the principle, and they avoided the consequences by denying the principle. We revere this lesson too much soon to forget it. Who does not see that the same authority which can establish Christianity, in exclusion of other Religions, may establish with the same ease any particular sect of Christians, in exclusion of all other Sects? . . .

4. Because the law violates that equality which ought to be the basis of

every law. . . . Whilst we assert for ourselves a freedom to embrace, to profess, and to observe the Religion which we believe to be of divine origin, we cannot deny an equal freedom to them whose minds have not yet yielded to the evidence which has convinced us. . . .

5. Because the bill implies either that the Civil Magistrate is a competent Judge of Religious truths or that he may employ Religion as an engine of Civil policy. The first is an arrogant pretension, falsified by the contradictory opinions of Rulers in all ages, and throughout the world; the second, an unhallowed perversion of the means of salvation.

6. Because the establishment proposed by the Bill is not requisite for the support of the Christian Religion. To say that it is, is a contradiction to the Christian Religion itself; for every page of it disavows a dependence on the powers of this world; it is a contradiction to fact; for it is known that this Religion both existed and flourished, not only without the support of human laws, but in spite of every opposition from them. . . .

7. Because experience witnesseth that ecclesiastical establishments, instead of maintaining the purity and efficacy of Religion, have had a contrary operation. During almost fifteen centuries has the legal establishment of Christianity been on trial. What have been its fruits? More or less in all places, pride and indolence in the clergy; ignorance and servility in the laity; in both, superstition, bigotry, and persecution. . . .

8. Because the establishment in question is not necessary for the support of Civil Government. . . . If Religion be not within the cognizance of civil government, how can its legal establishment be necessary to civil government? What influence in fact have ecclesiastical establishments had on Civil Society? In some instances they have been seen to erect a spiritual tyranny on the ruins of Civil authority;

in many instances they have been seen upholding the thrones of political tyranny; in no instance have they been seen the guardians of the liberties of the people. Rulers who wished to subvert the public liberty, may have found an established clergy convenient auxiliaries. A just government, instituted to secure & perpetuate it, needs them not.

9. Because the proposed establishment is a departure from that generous policy, which, offering an asylum to the persecuted and oppressed of every nation and religion, promised a luster to our country, and an accession to the number of its citizens. What a melancholy mark is the bill of sudden degeneracy! Instead of holding forth an asylum to the persecuted, it is itself a signal of persecution. . . . The magnanimous sufferer under this last cruel scourge in foreign regions must view the bill as a beacon on our coast warning him to seek some other haven, where liberty and philanthropy, in their due extent, may offer a more certain repose from his troubles.

10. Because it will have a like tendency to banish our citizens. The allurements presented by other situations are every day thinning their number. To superadd a fresh motive to emigration, by revoking the liberty which they now enjoy, would be the same species of folly which has dishonoured and depopulated flourishing kingdoms.

11. Because it will destroy that moderation and harmony which the forbearance of our laws to intermeddle with Religion has produced among its several sects. . . . The very appearance of the bill has transformed "that Christian forbearance, love and charity" which of late mutually prevailed, into animosities and jealousies which may not soon be appeased. What mischiefs may not be dreaded, should this enemy to the public quiet be armed with the force of a law? . . .

12. Because the policy of the bill is adverse to diffusion of the light of Christianity. . . . Instead of levelling as far as possible, every obstacle to the

victorious progress of truth, the Bill, with an ignoble and unchristian timidity, would circumscribe it, with a wall of defense, against the encroachments of error.

13. Because attempts to enforce by legal sanctions, acts obnoxious to so great a proportion of Citizens, tend to enervate the laws in general, and to slacken the bands of society. . . .

14. Because a measure of such singular magnitude and delicacy ought not to be imposed, without the clearest evidence that it is called for by a majority of citizens; and no satisfactory method is yet proposed by which the voice of the majority in this case may be determined, or its influence secured. . . .

15. Because, finally, "the equal right of every citizen to the free exercise of his Religion, according to the dictates of conscience," is held by the same tenure with all our other rights. . . .

Either then, we must say, that the will of the Legislature is the only measure of their authority; and that in the plenitude of that authority, they may sweep away all our fundamental rights; or, that they are bound to leave this particular right untouched and sacred: Either we must say, that they may control the freedom of the press, may abolish the trial by jury, may swallow up the Executive and Judiciary Powers of the State; nay that they may despoil us of our very right of suffrage, and erect themselves into an independent and hereditary Assembly; or we must say, that they have no authority to enact into a law the bill under consideration. We the subscribers say that the General Assembly of this commonwealth have no such authority; And that no effort may be omitted on our part against so dangerous an usurpation, we oppose to it this remonstrance.

# 15

*"For the establishment of States . . . and for their admission . . . on an equal footing with the original states"*

In 1772, Lord Dunmore, Governor of Virginia, wrote home to his chief in the colonial office: "I have learnt from experience that . . . the Americans acquire no attachment to Place: But wandering about seems engrafted in their Nature; and it is a weakness incident to it, that they Should forever immagine the Lands further off, are Still better than those upon which they are already settled." In another letter in 1774, Dunmore advised, "that seeing there is no possibility of setting bounds to the settlements of the Americans, . . . His Majesty should indulge . . . adventurers who willingly conform to government." His Majesty, however, was indulging no Americans at all at that time, and it soon fell to the government of Congress to make "adventurers" conform if it could.

In its constant need for revenue, Congress had an overwhelming incentive to organize the vast trans-Appalachian West on a financially rewarding basis. Not until New York ceded her western claims in March, 1781, however, did Congress gain formal title to any part of the Northwest Territory. Other cessions soon followed; but Congress had still to win the war with Britain to make good its right of possession. Even then, there remained the problem of "quieting" the Indians' title before revenue-producing sales could be made. By 1785, though with certain stipulations, the landed states had virtually completed their cessions north of the Ohio River; the Treaty of Paris ending the Revolutionary War had confirmed the new nation's title all the way to the Mississippi; and the ceremony of purchase by various treaties with the Indians had sanctified, or so it seemed to white men, the Americans' full right to settlement on much of the territory involved.

Thus armed, Congress, on May 20, 1785, adopted its famous ordinance establishing "the mode of disposing of Lands in the Western Territory." So much of this land had already been staked out by absentee speculators under the southern mode of "indiscriminate location," that Washington, after a trip west in the fall of 1784, had warned Congress, "that scarce a valuable spot within a tolerable distance of [the Ohio River] . . . is left without a claimant." He urged the condemnation of all such holdings beyond the river and the forcible removal of intruders there, a policy Congress was to follow later on. In the Land Ordinance of 1785, Congress prescribed a variation of the New England system of "township planting," under which town surveys preceded sales. Sales themselves were to be made under what Washington called "progressive seating" to settlers obliged promptly to clear and improve their homesteads. Under these terms, as a member of Congress wrote to Washington, "all those inducements to emigration which are derived from friendship, religion and relative connections" are fortified, whereas under "indiscriminate location" they would be destroyed.

The Land Ordinance of 1785 reserved no less than one-seventh of the Northwest Territory "for the use of the late continental army." It also reserved four lots in each township for the United States, and one "for the maintenance of public schools." The rest of the land was to be sold at auction at stated times and places within the territory, with bidding to start at $1.00 per acre. Congress quickly learned, however, that this minimum price was far too high for most potential settlers. When the longed-for revenue failed to materialize from the first seven ranges of townships surveyed, the delegates, early in July, 1787, yielded to the blandishments of speculators who offered ready money, at far less than the minimum, for millions of acres beyond these ranges and who agreed to settle the land under Ordinance conditions other than price. Later in July, after dallying for three years over the mode of governing the territory, Congress adopted the Northwest Ordinance of 1787.

The Land Ordinance of 1785 provided a durable pattern of survey and settlement for the orderly occupation of the beckoning West. The Northwest Ordinance of 1787 guaranteed that the land so occupied—and eventually the whole continental range—would be peaceably encompassed within the humane system of government for the establishment of which the delegates of the original thirteen states had pledged "to each other our Lives, our Fortunes, and our sacred Honor." The linchpin of this guarantee was derived from the stipulation in the very first tender of western claims, that of New York in 1780, which required that her cession "shall be formed into distinct republican States, which shall become members of the Federal Union, and have the same rights of sovereignty, freedom, and independence as the other states." The Northwest Ordinance set forth how this should be done. Lest time and circumstance erode the attachment of such new states, moreover, to the "unalienable rights" for which the old contended, the Northwest Ordinance further required that "the people and states in the said territory" adopt "articles of compact" with the "original states" which shall "forever remain unalterable, unless by common consent." These articles in effect spelled out the first *federal* bill of rights, with the momentous addition of the very last item: "There shall be neither slavery nor involuntary servitude in the said territory." The Northwest Ordinance, Congress's crowning achievement, is reproduced below with only technical deletions.

*July 13, 1787*

# An Ordinance for the Government
# of the Territory of the United States
# Northwest of the River Ohio

Sec. 1. *Be it ordained by the United States in Congress assembled,* That the Said Territory, for the purpose of temporary government, be one district, subject, however, to be divided into two districts, as future circumstances may, in the opinion of Congress, make it expedient. . . .

Sec. 3. . . . There shall be appointed, from time to time, by Congress, a governor, whose commission shall continue in force for the term of three years, unless sooner revoked by Congress; he shall reside in the district, and have a freehold estate therein, in one thousand acres of land, while in the exercise of his office.

Sec. 4. There shall be appointed from time to time, by Congress, a secretary, whose commission shall continue in force for four years, unless sooner revoked; he shall reside in the district, and have a freehold estate therein, in five hundred acres of land, while in the exercise of his office. . . . There shall also be appointed a court, to consist of three judges, any two of whom to form a court, who shall have a common-law jurisdiction and reside in the district, and have each therein a freehold estate, in five hundred acres of land, while in the exercise of their offices; and their commissions shall continue in force during good behavior.

Sec. 5. The governor and judges, or a majority of them, shall adopt and publish in the district such laws of the original States, criminal and civil, as may be necessary, and best suited to the circumstances of the district, and report them to Congress from time to time, which laws shall be in force in the district until the organization of the general assembly therein, unless disapproved of by Congress; but afterwards the legislature shall have authority to alter them as they shall think fit. . . .

Sec. 9. So soon as there shall be five thousand free male inhabitants, of full age, in the district, upon giving proof thereof to the governor, they shall receive authority, with time and place, to elect representatives from their counties or townships, to represent them in the general assembly:

*Provided,* That for every five hundred free male inhabitants there shall be one representative, and so on, progressively, with the number of free male inhabitants, shall the right of representation increase, until the number of representatives shall amount to twenty-five; after which the number and proportion of representatives shall be regulated by the legislature:

*Provided,* That no person be eligible or qualified to act as a representative, unless he shall have been a citizen of one of the United States three years, and be a resident in the district, or unless he shall have resided in the district three years; and, in either case, shall likewise hold in his own right, in fee-simple, two hundred acres of land within the same:

*Provided* also, That a freehold in fifty acres of land in the district, having been a citizen of one of the States, and being resident in the district, or the like freehold and two years' residence in the district, shall be necessary to qualify a man as an elector of a representative.

Sec. 10. The representatives thus elected shall serve for the term of two years; . . .

Sec. 11. The general assembly, or legislature, shall consist of the governor, legislative council, and a house of representatives. The legislative council shall consist of five members, to continue in office five years, unless sooner removed by Congress; any three of whom to be a quorum; and the members of the council shall be nominated and appointed in the following manner, to wit: As soon as representatives shall be elected the governor shall appoint a time and place for them to meet together, and when met they shall nominate ten persons, resident in the district, and each possessed of a freehold in five hundred acres of land, and return their names to Congress, five of whom Congress shall appoint and commission to serve as aforesaid; . . . and every five years, four months at least before the expiration of the time of service of the members of the council, the said house shall nominate ten persons, qualified as aforesaid, and return their names to Congress, five of whom Congress shall appoint and commission to serve as members of the council five years, unless sooner removed. And the governor, legislative council, and house of representatives shall have authority to make laws in all cases for the good government of the district, not repugnant to the principles and articles in this ordinance established and declared. And all bills, having been passed by a majority in the house, and by a majority in the council, shall be referred to the governor for his assent; but no bill, or legislative act whatever, shall be of any force without his assent. The governor shall have power to convene, prorogue, and dissolve the general assembly when, in his opinion, it shall be expedient.

Sec. 12. . . . As soon as a legislature shall be formed in the district, the council and house assembled, in one room, shall have authority, by joint ballot, to elect a delegate to Congress, who shall have a seat in Congress, with a right of debating, but not of voting, during this temporary government.

Sec. 13. And for extending the fundamental principles of civil and religious liberty, which form the basis whereon these republics, their laws and constitutions, are erected; to fix and establish those principles as the basis of all laws, constitutions, and governments, which forever hereafter shall be formed in the said territory; to provide, also, for the establishment of States, and permanent government therein, and for their admission to a share in the Federal councils on an equal footing with the original States, at as early periods as may be consistent with the general interest:

Sec. 14. It is hereby ordained and declared, by the authority aforesaid, that the following articles shall be considered as articles of compact, between the original States and the people and States in the said territory, and forever remain unalterable, unless by common consent, to wit:

ART. I. No person, demeaning himself in a peaceable and orderly manner, shall ever be molested on account of his mode of worship, or religious sentiments, in the said territory.

ART. II. The inhabitants of the said territory shall always be entitled to the benefits of the writs of *habeas corpus*, and of the trial by jury; of a proportionate representation of the people in the legislature, and of judicial proceedings according to the course of the common law. All persons shall be bailable, unless for capital offences, where the proof shall be evident, or the presumption great. All fines shall be moderate; and no cruel or unusual punishment shall be inflicted. No man shall be deprived of his liberty or property, but by the judgment of his peers, or the law of the land, and should the public exigencies make it necessary, for the common preservation, to take any person's property, or to demand his particular services, full compensation shall be made for the same. And, in the just preservation of rights and property, it is understood and declared, that no law ought ever to be made or have force in the said territory, that shall, in any manner whatever, interfere with or affect private contracts, or engagements, *bona fide*, and without fraud previously formed.

ART. III. Religion, morality, and knowledge being necessary to good government and the happiness of mankind, schools and the means of education shall forever be encouraged. The utmost good faith shall always be observed towards the Indians; their lands and property shall never be taken from them without their consent; and in their property, rights, and liberty they never shall be invaded or disturbed unless in just and lawful wars authorized by Congress; but laws founded in justice and humanity shall, from time to time, be made, for preventing wrongs being done to them, and for preserving peace and friendship with them.

ART. IV. The said territory, and the States which may be formed therein, shall forever remain a part of this confederacy of the United States of America, subject to the articles of Confederation, and to such alterations therein as shall be constitutionally made; and to all the acts and ordinances of the United States in Congress assembled, conformable thereto. The inhabitants and settlers in the said territory shall be subject to pay a part of the Federal debts, contracted, or to be contracted, and a proportional part of the expenses of government to be apportioned on them by Congress, according to the same common rule and measure by which apportionments thereof shall be made on the other States; and the taxes for paying their proportion shall be laid and levied by the authority and direction of the legislatures of the district, or districts, or new States, as in the original States, within the time agreed upon by the United States in Congress assembled. The legislatures of those districts, or new States, shall never interfere with the primary disposal of the soil by the United States in Congress assembled, nor with any regulations Congress may find necessary for securing the title in such soil to the *bona-fide* purchasers. No tax shall be imposed on lands the property of the United States; and in no case shall non-resident proprietors be taxed higher than residents. The navigable waters leading into the Mississippi and Saint Lawrence, and the carrying places between the same, shall be common highways, and forever free, as well to the inhabitants of the said territory as to the citizens of the United States, and those of any other State that may be admitted into the confederacy, without any tax, impost, or duty therefor.

ART. V.   There shall be formed in the said territory not less than three nor more than five States; . . . And whenever any of the said States [within boundaries fixed by Congress] shall have sixty thousand free inhabitants therein, such State shall be admitted by its delegates, into the Congress of the United States, on an equal footing with the original States, in all respects whatever; and shall be at liberty to form a permanent constitution and State government: *Provided,* The constitution and government, so to be formed, shall be republican, and in conformity to the principles contained in these articles, and, so far as it can be consistent with the general interest of the confederacy, such admission shall be allowed at an earlier period, and when there may be a less number of free inhabitants in the State than sixty thousand.

ART. VI.   There shall be neither slavery nor involuntary servitude in the said territory, otherwise than in the punishment of crimes, whereof the party shall have been duly convicted: *Provided always,* That any person escaping into the same, from whom labor or service is lawfully claimed in any one of the original States, such fugitive may be lawfully reclaimed, and conveyed to the person claiming his or her labor or service as aforesaid.

# 16

*"We the people . . . do ordain and establish this Constitution for the United States of America"*

On February 21, 1787, the Second Continental Congress, on the motion of the members for Massachusetts, resolved that "on the second Monday in May next, a convention of delegates . . . be held in Philadelphia, for the sole and express purpose of revising the Articles of Confederation." Delegates were duly elected under the terms of this resolution. Following the leisurely fashion of the age, representatives from a majority of the states failed to reach Philadelphia before May 25, but thereafter they lost little time in getting down to business. On May 30, Edmund Randolph of Virginia disclosed something of the revolutionary temper of the leaders by offering the following propositions:

1. That a union of the states merely federal will not accomplish the objects proposed by the Articles of Confederation—namely common defence, security of liberty, and general welfare.
2. That no treaty or treaties among the whole or part of the states, as individual sovereignties, would be sufficient.
3. That a *national* government ought to be established, consisting of a *supreme* legislative, executive, and judiciary.

The Convention, that same day, agreed to postpone debate on propositions 1 and 2; but sitting as the *"Committee of the Whole* on the state of the Union" —and not on the state of the Articles—it directly applied itself to the summer-long task of shaping a framework of government conforming to proposition 3. Randolph, the day before, had submitted the so-called Virginia Plan for such a government, which the Convention now adopted as its point of departure. By June 19, the Committee of the Whole had reduced this plan to nineteen resolutions from which the great Constitution grew.

The Articles of Confederation disallowed any "alteration" unless agreed to by Congress and "afterwards confirmed by the legislatures of every state." When the Convention completed its work on September 17, 1787, it courteously sent Congress a copy of the Constitution, but with a letter that did not mince words. "In all our deliberations on this subject," said the delegates, "we kept steadily in our view that which appeared to us the greatest interest of every true American—the consolidation of the Union—in which is involved our prosperity, felicity, safety, perhaps our national existence." They petitioned Congress for no vote, no approval. Nor would they apply to state legislatures for confirmation. Instead, in keeping with their revulsion from existing governments, in the Constitution itself they asked only the assent of nine special conventions like their own, and laggards beware: "The ratification of the conventions of nine States shall be sufficient for the establishment of this Constitution between the States so ratifying the same."

By June 21, 1788, nine states had ratified. Largely because union itself was now the issue, Virginia came in on June 25, New York on July 26. Only after the first Congress, in September, 1789, adopted the ten amendments comprising the federal "Bill of Rights," promised during the ratification debates, did North Carolina rejoin the nation in November. Rhode Island delayed until May, 1790, when Congress had in view a bill placing her on the footing of a foreign nation.

Neither in the Great Convention, where the Constitution's every phrase received minute scrutiny, nor in the major ratifying conventions, where its every implication was sifted "clause by clause," did any one rally to the defense of the Articles of Confederation. Yet the embarrassments of the "half-starved, limping government" of the time did not arise entirely from the failure of the Articles to endow Congress with elementary powers. Congress did have numerous and important ones. The difficulty arose because the Articles left Congress at the mercy of the states for the means of putting these powers into execution. Even this defect would not have become so weighty if many state governments had not been lax instrumentalities unwilling or unable to tax or otherwise constrain their citizens. That was the rub. Many Americans preferred the states to be weak; on such weakness individual liberty seemed to them to rest. It was because he feared government and treasured its weakness that Patrick Henry roused himself to lead the assault in the Virginia ratifying convention on "the great consolidated government" the Constitution openly promised. "Who authorized them to speak the language of *We, the People,* instead of *We, the States?*" cried Henry. "States are the characteristics and the soul of a confederation." Edmund Pendleton, speaking for the Constitution, and for those who carried the day, replied:

> What was it that brought us from a state of nature to society, but to secure happiness? And can society be formed without government? . . . There is no quarrel between government and liberty; the former is the shield and protector of the latter. . . . Where is the cause of alarm? We, the people, possessing all power, form a government, such as we think will secure happiness. . . . In the same plan we point out an easy and quiet method of reforming what may be found amiss. . . . Permit me to ask the gentleman who made this objection, who but the people can delegate powers? Who but the people have a right to form a government?

It is true that many ambiguities swarm around such constitutional terms as "the people," "delegated powers," "supreme law," "the general welfare." The Constitution itself, amendments and all, covers 13 pages in this book. The annotated edition, published by the United States Government in 1953, contains more than 1,350 pages, largely judicial commentary on these ambiguities. The Constitution is a living document, to which we will have further occasion to refer. That it well answered the material needs of well-to-do special pleaders— public creditors and contractors, merchants, money-lenders and land speculators —who spent almost a decade promoting the type of strong central government it afforded, is obvious even from a cursory reading. Nor need it be denied that the Constitution also served "property" in succeeding generations. To eighteenth-century political thinkers, property still seemed to be the well-spring of public responsibility as well as of private reward, and merited protection. In the nineteenth century, property became the transcendent value in American life, its easy accumulation the proof of the vitality of the higher ideals. "Each man is born to be rich," said Emerson in 1860. "Poverty demoralizes." Property was the proof of open opportunity, the gauge of progress. And yet, were the Constitution a cynically economic and not a humane political document, the government it established could hardly have outlasted the new monarchies, plain and mixed, or the new aristocracies, landed and mercantile, which, in Europe in the middle of the eighteenth century, were also confronting the fundamental issue of personal liberty in powerful, competitive states.

For all its stress on property, the Constitution required no property qualifications for office, not even for the Presidency. It forbade religious tests for any federal position. It stipulated "a compensation—to be ascertained by law, and paid out of the Treasury of the United States" for all elective posts, so that the poor as well as the rich might seek them. It provided that "for any speech or debate in either House," Senators and Representatives "shall not be questioned in any other place," thereby assuring their fullest freedom of expression. It guaranteed trial by jury for all crimes," except in cases of impeachment"; and forbade suspension of "the privilege of the writ of habeas corpus," except at times of invasion or rebellion. Other engaging details may be cited wherein the life and the liberty of those without property, equally with those well-endowed, also became the concern of the state. But the greatness of the Constitution, in the eyes of the self-conscious framers, lay in the wholeness and unity of the overarching system itself, founded, as John Adams put it, "on the natural authority of the people alone," and "contrived" from there "merely by the use of reason and the senses."

*September 17, 1787*

# The Constitution
## of the United States of America

We the people of the United States, in order to form a more perfect Union, establish justice, insure domestic tranquility, provide for the common defence, promote the general welfare, and secure the blessings of liberty to ourselves and our posterity, do ordain and establish this Constitution for the United States of America.

ARTICLE I

Section 1. All legislative powers herein granted shall be vested in a Congress of the United States, which shall consist of a Senate and House of Representatives.

Section 2. (1) The House of Representatives shall be composed of members chosen every second year by the people of all the several States, and the Electors in each State shall have the qualifications requisite for electors of the most numerous branch of the State Legislature.

(2) No person shall be a representative who shall not have attained to the age of twenty-five years, and been seven years a citizen of the United States, and who shall not, when elected, be an inhabitant of that State in which he shall be chosen.

(3) Representatives and direct taxes * shall be apportioned among the several States which may be included within this Union, according to their respective numbers, which shall be determined by adding to the whole number of free persons, including those bound to service for a term of years, and excluding Indians not taxed, three fifths of all other persons.† The actual enumeration shall be made within three

* See Amendment 16.
† See Amendment 14.

years after the first meeting of the Congress of the United States, and within every subsequent term of ten years, in such manner as they shall by law direct. The number of representatives shall not exceed one for every thirty thousand, but each State shall have at least one representative, and until such enumeration shall be made, the State of New Hampshire shall be entitled to chuse three, Massachusetts eight, Rhode-Island and Providence Plantations one, Connecticut five, New-York six, New Jersey four, Pennsylvania eight, Delaware one, Maryland six, Virginia ten, North Carolina five, South Carolina five, and Georgia three.

(4) When vacancies happen in the representation from any State, the executive authority thereof shall issue writs of election to fill such vacancies.

(5) The House of Representatives shall chuse their speaker and other officers; and shall have the sole power of impeachment.

Section 3. (1) The Senate of the United States shall be composed of two senators from each State, chosen by the legislature thereof,* for six years; and each senator shall have one vote.

(2) Immediately after they shall be assembled in consequence of the first election, they shall be divided as equally as may be into three classes. The seats of the senators of the first class shall be vacated at the expiration of the second year, of the second class at the expiration of the fourth year, and of the third class at the expiration of the sixth year, so that one third may be chosen every second year; and if vacancies happen by resignation, or otherwise, during the recess of the legislature of any State, the executive thereof may make temporary appointments until the next meeting of the legislature, which shall then fill such vacancies.†

(3) No person shall be a senator who shall not have attained to the age of thirty years, and been nine years a citizen of the United States, and who shall not, when elected be an inhabitant of that State for which he shall be chosen.

(4) The Vice President of the United States shall be President of the Senate, but shall have no vote, unless they be equally divided.

(5) The Senate shall chuse their other officers and also a president pro tempore, in the absence of the Vice President, or when he shall exercise the office of President of the United States.

(6) The Senate shall have the sole power to try all impeachments. When sitting for that purpose, they shall be on oath or affirmation. When the President of the United States is tried, the chief justice shall preside: and no person shall be convicted without the concurrence of two thirds of the members present.

(7) Judgment in cases of impeachment shall not extend further than to removal from office, and disqualifications to hold and enjoy any office of honor, trust or profit under the United States: but the party convicted shall nevertheless be liable and subject to indictment, trial, judgment and punishment according to law.

Section 4 (1) The times, places, and manner of holding elections for senators and representatives, shall be prescribed in each State by the legislature thereof; but the Congress may at any time by law make or alter such regulations, except as to the places of chusing senators.

(2) The Congress shall assemble at least once in every year, and such meeting shall be on the first Monday in December, unless they shall by law appoint a different day.*

Section 5. (1) Each House shall be the judge of the elections, returns and qualifications of its own members, and a majority of each shall constitute a quorum to do business; but a smaller number may adjourn from day to day,

* See Amendment 17.
† See Amendment 17.

* See Amendment 20.

and may be authorized to compel the attendance of absent members, in such manner, and under such penalties as each House may provide.

(2) Each House may determine the rules of its proceedings, punish its members for disorderly behaviour, and, with the concurrence of two thirds, expel a member.

(3) Each House shall keep a journal of its proceedings, and from time to time publish the same, excepting such parts as may in their judgment require secrecy; and the yeas and nays of the members of either House on any question shall, at the desire of one fifth of those present, be entered on the journal.

(4) Neither House, during the session of Congress, shall, without the consent of the other, adjourn for more than three days, nor to any other place than that in which the two Houses shall be sitting.

Section 6. (1) The senators and representatives shall receive a compensation for their services to be ascertained by law, and paid out of the Treasury of the United States. They shall in all cases, except treason, felony, and breach of the peace, be privileged from arrest during their attendance at the session of their respective Houses, and in going to and returning from the same; and for any speech or debate in either House, they shall not be questioned in any other place.

(2) No senator or representative shall, during the time for which he was elected, be appointed to any civil office under the authority of the United States, which shall have been created, or the emoluments whereof shall have been increased, during such time; and no person holding any office under the United States shall be a member of either House during his continuance in office.

Section 7. (1) All bills for raising revenue shall originate in the House of Representatives, but the Senate may propose or concur with amendments as on other bills.

(2) Every bill which shall have passed the House of Representatives and the Senate, shall, before it become a law, be presented to the President of the United States; if he approves he shall sign it, but if not he shall return it, with his objections to that House in which it shall have originated, who shall enter the objections at large on their journal, and proceed to reconsider it. If after such reconsideration two thirds of that House shall agree to pass the bill, it shall be sent, together with the objections, to the other House, by which it shall likewise be reconsidered, and if approved by two thirds of that House, it shall become a law. But in all such cases the votes of both Houses shall be determined by yeas and nays, and the names of the persons voting for and against the bill shall be entered on the journal of each House respectively. If any bill shall not be returned by the President within ten days (Sundays excepted) after it shall have been presented to him, the same shall be a law, in like manner as if he had signed it, unless the Congress by their adjournment prevent its return, in which case it shall not be a law.

(3) Every order, resolution, or vote to which the concurrence of the Senate and the House of Representatives may be necessary (except on a question of adjournment) shall be presented to the President of the United States; and before the same shall take effect, shall be approved by him, or being disapproved by him, shall be repassed by two thirds of the Senate and House of Representatives, according to the rules and limitations prescribed in the case of a bill.

Section 8. The Congress shall have the power

(1) To lay and collect taxes, duties, imposts, and excises, to pay the debts and provide for the common defence and general welfare of the United States; but all duties, imposts, and excises shall be uniform throughout the United States;

(2) To borrow money on the credit of the United States;

(3) To regulate commerce with foreign nations, and among the several States, and with the Indian tribes;

(4) To establish an uniform rule of naturalization, and uniform laws on the subject of bankruptcies throughout the United States;

(5) To coin money, regulate the value thereof, and of foreign coin, and fix the standard of weights and measures;

(6) To provide for the punishment of counterfeiting the securities and current coin of the United States;

(7) To establish post offices and post roads;

(8) To promote the progress of science and useful arts, by securing for limited times to authors and inventors the exclusive right to their respective writings and discoveries;

(9) To constitute tribunals inferior to the Supreme Court;

(10) To define and punish piracies and felonies committed on the high seas, and offences against the law of nations;

(11) To declare war, grant letters of marque and reprisal, and make rules concerning captures on land and water;

(12) To raise and support armies, but no appropriation of money to that use shall be for a longer term than two years;

(13) To provide and maintain a navy;

(14) To make rules for the government and regulation of the land and naval forces;

(15) To provide for calling forth the militia to execute the laws of the Union, suppress insurrections and repel invasions;

(16) To provide for organizing, arming, and disciplining the militia, and for governing such part of them as may be employed in the service of the United States, reserving to the States respectively, the appointment of the officers, and the authority of training the militia according to the discipline prescribed by Congress;

(17) To exercise exclusive legislation in all cases whatsoever, over such district (not exceeding ten miles square) as may, by cession of particular States, and the acceptance of Congress, become the seat of the government of the United States, and to exercise like authority over all places purchased by the consent of the legislature of the State in which the same shall be, for the erection of forts, magazines, arsenals, dock-yards, and other needful buildings, and

(18) To make all laws which shall be necessary and proper for carrying into execution the foregoing powers, and all other powers vested by this Constitution in the government of the United States, or in any department or officer thereof.

*Section 9.* (1) The migration or importation of such persons as any of the States now existing shall think proper to admit, shall not be prohibited by the Congress prior to the year one thousand eight hundred and eight, but a tax or duty may be imposed on such importation, not exceeding ten dollars for each person.

(2) The privilege of the writ of habeas corpus shall not be suspended, unless when in cases of rebellion or invasion the public safety may require it.

(3) No bill of attainder or ex post facto law shall be passed.

(4) No capitation, or other direct, tax shall be laid, unless in proportion to the census or enumeration hereinbefore directed to be taken.*

(5) No tax or duty shall be laid on articles exported from any State.

(6) No preference shall be given by any regulation of commerce or revenue to the ports of one State over those of another, nor shall vessels bound to, or from, one State be obliged to enter, clear, or pay duties in another.

(7) No money shall be drawn from the treasury, but in consequence of ap-

* See Amendment 16.

propriations made by law; and a regular statement and account of the receipts and expenditures of all public money shall be published from time to time.

(8) No title of nobility shall be granted by the United States; and no person holding any office of profit or trust under them, shall, within the consent of the Congress, accept of any present, emolument, office, or title, of any kind whatever, from any king, prince, or foreign State.

*Section* 10. (1) No State shall enter into any treaty, alliance, or confederation; grant letters of marque and reprisal; coin money; emit bills of credit; make any thing but gold and silver coin a tender in payment of debts; pass any bill of attainder, ex post facto law, or law impairing the obligation of contracts, or grant any title of nobility.

(2) No State shall, without the consent of the Congress, lay any imposts or duties on imports or exports, except what may be absolutely necessary for executing its inspection laws; and the net produce of all duties and imposts laid by any State on imports or exports, shall be for the use of the treasury of the United States; and all such laws shall be subject to the revision and control of the Congress.

(3) No State shall, without the consent of the Congress, lay any duty of tonnage, keep troops, or ships of war in time of peace, enter into any agreement or compact with another State, or with a foreign power, or engage in war, unless actually invaded, or in such imminent danger as will not admit of delay.

ARTICLE II

*Section* 1. (1) The executive power shall be vested in a President of the United States of America. He shall hold his office during the term of four years, and together with the Vice President, chosen for the same term, be elected, as follows:*

(2) Each State shall appoint, in
* See Amendment 22.

such manner as the legislature thereof may direct, a number of electors, equal to the whole number of senators and representatives to which the State may be entitled in the Congress: but no senator or representative, or person holding an office of trust or profit under the United States, shall be appointed an elector.

The electors shall meet in their respective States, and vote by ballot for two persons, of whom one at least shall not be an inhabitant of the same State with themselves. And they shall make a list of all the persons voted for, and of the number of votes for each; which list they shall sign and certify, and transmit sealed to the seat of the government of the United States, directed to the president of the Senate. The president of the Senate shall, in the presence of the Senate and House of Representatives, open all the certificates, and the votes shall then be counted. The person having the greatest number of votes shall be the President, if such number be a majority of the whole number of electors appointed; and if there be more than one who have such majority, and have an equal number of votes, then the House of Representatives shall immediately chuse by ballot one of them for President; and if no person have a majority, then from the five highest on the list the said House shall in like manner chuse the President. But in chusing the President, the votes shall be taken by States, the representation from each State having one vote; a quorum for this purpose shall consist of a member or members from two thirds of the States, and a majority of all the States shall be necessary to a choice. In every case, after the choice of the President, the person having the greatest number of votes of the electors shall be the Vice President. But if there should remain two or more who have equal votes, the Senate shall chuse from them by ballot the Vice President.*

(3) The Congress may determine
* Superseded by Amendment 12.

the time of chusing the electors, and the day on which they shall give their votes; which day shall be the same throughout the United States.

(4) No person except a natural born citizen, or a citizen of the United States, at the time of the adoption of this Constitution, shall be eligible to the office of President; neither shall any person be eligible to that office who shall not have attained to the age of thirty five years, and been fourteen years a resident within the United States.

(5) In case of the removal of the President from office, or of his death, resignation, or inability to discharge the powers and duties of the said office, the same shall devolve on the Vice President, and the Congress may by law provide for the case of removal, death, resignation or inability, both of the President and Vice President, declaring what officer shall then act as President, and such officer shall act accordingly, until the disability be removed, or a President shall be elected.*

(6) The President shall, at stated times, receive for his services a compensation, which shall neither be increased nor diminished during the period for which he shall have been elected, and he shall not receive within that period any other emolument from the United States, or any of them.

(7) Before he enter on the execution of his office, he shall take the following oath of affirmation:—"I do solemnly swear (or affirm) that I will faithfully execute the office of President of the United States, and will to the best of my ability, preserve, protect and defend the Constitution of the United States."

Section 2. (1) The President shall be commander in chief of the army and navy of the United States, and of the militia of the several States, when called into the actual service of the United States; he may require the opinion, in writing, of the principal officer in each of the executive depart-

* See Amendment 20.

ments, upon any subject relating to the duties of their respective offices, and he shall have power to grant reprieves and pardons for offenses against the United States, except in cases of impeachment.

(2) He shall have power, by and with the advice and consent of the Senate, to make treaties, provided two thirds of the senators present concur; and he shall nominate, and by and with the advice and consent of the Senate, shall appoint ambassadors, other public ministers and consuls, judges of the Supreme Court, and all other officers of the United States, whose appointments are not herein otherwise provided for, and which shall be established by law: but the Congress may by law vest the appointment of such inferior officers, as they think proper, in the President alone, in the courts of law, or in the heads of departments.

(3) The President shall have power to fill up all vacancies that may happen during the recess of the Senate, by granting commissions which shall expire at the end of their next session.

Section 3. He shall from time to time give to the Congress information of the state of the Union, and recommend to their consideration such measures as he shall judge necessary and expedient; he may, on extraordinary occasions, convene both Houses, or either of them, and in case of disagreement between them with respect to the time of adjournment, he may adjourn them to such time as he shall think proper; he shall receive ambassadors and other public ministers; he shall take care that the laws be faithfully executed, and shall commission all the officers of the United States.

Section 4. The President, Vice President, and all civil officers of the United States, shall be removed from office on impeachment for, and conviction of, treason, bribery, or other high crimes and misdemeanors.

ARTICLE III

Section 1. The judicial power of the United States shall be vested in one

Supreme Court, and in such inferior courts as the Congress may from time to time ordain and establish. The judges, both of the supreme and inferior courts, shall hold their offices during good behavior, and shall, at stated times, receive for their services, a compensation, which shall not be diminished during their continuance in office.

Section 2. (1) The judicial power shall extend to all cases, in law and equity, arising under this Constitution, the laws of the United States, and treaties made, or which shall be made, under their authority;—to all cases affecting ambassadors, other public ministers and consuls;—to all cases of admiralty and maritime jurisdiction;—to controversies to which the United States shall be a party;—to controversies between two or more States;—between a State and citizens of another State; *—between citizens of different States;—between citizens of the same State claiming lands under grants of different States, and between a State, or the citizens thereof, and foreign States, citizens or subjects.

(2) In all cases affecting ambassadors, other public ministers and consuls, and those in which a State shall be party, the Supreme Court shall have original jurisdiction. In all the other cases before mentioned, the Supreme Court shall have appellate jurisdiction, both as to law and fact, with such exceptions, and under such regulations as the Congress shall make.

(3) The trial of all crimes, except in cases of impeachment, shall be by jury; and such trial shall be held in the State where the said crimes shall have been committed; but when not committed within any State, the trial shall be at such place or places as the Congress may by law have directed.

Section 3. (1) Treason against the United States shall consist only in levying war against them, or in adhering to their enemies, giving them aid and comfort. No person shall be convicted

* See Amendment 11.

of treason unless on the testimony of two witnesses to the same overt act, or on confession in open court.

(2) The Congress shall have power to declare the punishment of treason, but no attainder of treason shall work corruption of blood, or foreiture except during the life of the person attainted.

ARTICLE IV

Section 1. Full faith and credit shall be given in each State to the public acts, records, and judicial proceedings of every other State. And the Congress may by general laws prescribe the manner in which such acts, records and proceedings shall be proved, and the effect thereof.*

Section 2. (1) The citizens of each State shall be entitled to all privileges and immunities of citizens in the several States.

(2) A person charged in any State with treason, felony, or other crime, who shall flee from justice, and be found in another State, shall on demand of the executive authority of the State from which he fled, be delivered up to be removed to the State having jurisdiction of the crime.

(3) No person held to service or labour in one State under the laws thereof, escaping into another, shall, in consequence of any law or regulation therein, be discharged from such service or labour, but shall be delivered up on claim of the party to whom such service or labour may be due.†

Section 3. (1) New States may be admitted by the Congress into this Union; but no new State shall be formed or erected within the jurisdiction of any other State; nor any State be formed by the junction of two or more States, or parts of States, without the consent of the legislatures of the States concerned as well as of Congress.

(2) The Congress shall have power to dispose of and make all needful rules and regulations respecting the territory

* See Amendment 14, Section 1.
† See Amendment 13.

or other property belonging to the United States; and nothing in this Constitution shall be so construed as to prejudice any claims of the United States, or of any particular State.

*Section 4.* The United States shall guarantee to every State in this Union a republican form of government, and shall protect each of them against invasion; and on application of the legislature, or of the executive (when the legislature cannot be convened) against domestic violence.

ARTICLE V

The Congress, whenever two thirds of both Houses shall deem it necessary, shall propose amendments to this Constitution, or, on the application of the legislatures of two thirds of the several States, shall call a convention for proposing amendments, which in either case, shall be valid to all intents and purposes, as part of this Constitution, when ratified by the legislatures of three fourths of the several States, or by conventions in three fourths thereof, as the one or the other mode of ratification may be proposed by the Congress; Provided that no amendment which may be made prior to the year one thousand eight hundred and eight shall in any manner affect the first and fourth clauses in the ninth section of the first article; and that no State, without its consent, shall be deprived of its equal suffrage in the Senate.

ARTICLE VI

(1) All debts contracted and engagements entered into, before the adoption of this Constitution, shall be as valid against the United States under this Constitution, as under the Confederation.*

(2) This Constitution, and the laws of the United States which shall be made in pursuance thereof; and all treaties made, or which shall be made, under the authority of the United States, shall be the supreme law of the land; and the Judges in every State shall be

* See Amendment 14, Section 4.

bound thereby, any thing in the Constitution or laws of any State to the contrary notwithstanding.

(3) The senators and representatives before mentioned, and the members of the several State legislatures, and all executive and judicial officers, both of the United States and of the several States, shall be bound by oath or affirmation to support this Constitution; but no religious test shall ever be required as a qualification to any office or public trust under the United States.

ARTICLE VII

The ratification of the conventions of nine States shall be sufficient for the establishment of this Constitution between the States so ratifying the same.

Done in Convention by the unanimous consent of the States present the seventeenth day of September in the year of our Lord one thousand seven hundred and eighty seven, and of the independence of the United States of America the twelfth. In witness whereof we have hereunto subscribed our names.

*Articles in addition to, and amendment of the Constitution of the United States of America, proposed by Congress, and ratified by the legislatures of the several States, pursuant to the fifth article of the original Constitution.*

AMENDMENTS

*First Ten Amendments Passed by Congress September 25, 1789. Ratified by Three-fourths of the States December 15, 1791.*

AMENDMENT I

Congress shall make no law respecting an establishment of religion, or prohibiting the free exercise thereof; or abridging the freedom of speech, or of the press; or the right of the people peaceably to assemble, and to petition the government for a redress of grievances.

AMENDMENT II

A well regulated militia, being necessary to the security of a free State, the right of the people to keep and bear arms, shall not be infringed.

AMENDMENT III

No soldier shall, in time of peace be quartered in any house, without the consent of the owner, nor in time of war, but in a manner to be prescribed by law.

AMENDMENT IV

The right of the people to be secure in their persons, houses, papers, and effects, against unreasonable searches and seizures, shall not be violated, and no warrants shall issue, but upon probable cause, supported by oath or affirmation, and particularly describing the place to be searched, and the persons or things to be seized.

AMENDMENT V

No person shall be held to answer for a capital, or otherwise infamous crime, unless on a presentment or indictment of a grand jury, except in cases arising in the land or naval forces, or in the militia, when in actual service in time of war or public danger; nor shall any person be subject for the same offence to be twice put in jeopardy of life or limb; nor shall be compelled in any criminal case to be a witness against himself, nor be deprived of life, liberty, or property, without due process of law; nor shall private property be taken for public use, without just compensation.

AMENDMENT VI

In all criminal prosecutions, the accused shall enjoy the right to a speedy and public trial, by an impartial jury of the State and district wherein the crime shall have been committed, which district shall have been previously ascertained by law, and to be informed of the nature and cause of the accusation; to be confronted with the witnesses against him; to have compulsory process for obtaining witnesses in his favor, and to have the assistance of counsel for his defence.

AMENDMENT VII

In suits at common law, where the value in controversy shall exceed twenty dollars, the right of trial by jury shall be preserved, and no fact tried by a jury shall be otherwise reëxamined in any court of the United States, than according to the rules of the common law.

AMENDMENT VIII

Excessive bail shall not be required, nor excessive fines imposed, nor cruel and unusual punishments inflicted.

AMENDMENT IX

The enumeration in the Constitution of certain rights shall not be construed to deny or disparage others retained by the people.

AMENDMENT X

The powers not delegated to the United States by the Constitution, nor prohibited by it to the States, are reserved to the States respectively, or to the people.

AMENDMENT XI

*Passed by Congress March 5, 1794.*
*Ratified January 8, 1798.*

The judicial power of the United States shall not be construed to extend to any suit in law or equity, commenced or prosecuted against one of the United States by citizens of another State, or by citizens or subjects of any foreign State.

AMENDMENT XII

*Passed by Congress December 9, 1803.*
*Ratified September 25, 1804.*

The electors shall meet in their respective States, and vote by ballot for

President and Vice President, one of whom, at least, shall not be an inhabitant of the same State with themselves; they shall name in their ballots the person voted for as President, and in distinct ballots, the person voted for as Vice President, and they shall make distinct lists of all persons voted for as President and of all persons voted for as Vice President, and of the number of votes for each, which lists they shall sign and certify, and transmit sealed to the seat of the government of the United States, directed to the President of the Senate;—The President of the Senate shall, in the presence of the Senate and House of Representatives, open all certificates and the votes shall then be counted;—The person having the greatest number of votes for President, shall be the President, if such number be a majority of the whole number of electors appointed; and if no person have such majority, then from the persons having the highest numbers not exceding three on the list of those voted for as President, the House of Representatives shall choose immediately, by ballot, the President. But in choosing the President, the votes shall be taken by States, the representation from each State having one vote; a quorum for this purpose shall consist of a member or members from two thirds of the States, and a majority of all the States shall be necessary to a choice. And if the House of Representatives shall not choose a President whenever the right of choice shall devolve upon them, before the fourth day of March next following, then the Vice President shall act as President, as in the case of the death or other constitutional disability of the President. The person having the greatest number of votes as Vice President shall be the Vice President, if such number be a majority of the whole number of electors appointed, and if no person have a majority, then from the two highest numbers on the list, the Senate shall choose the Vice President; a quorum for the purpose shall consist of two

thirds of the whole number of Senators, and a majority of the whole number shall be necessary to a choice. But no person constitutionally ineligible to the office of President shall be eligible to that of Vice President of the United States.

AMENDMENT XIII

*Passed by Congress February 1, 1865.*
*Ratified December 18, 1865.*

Section 1. Neither slavery nor involuntary servitude, except as a punishment for crime whereof the party shall have been duly convicted, shall exist within the United States, or any place subject to their jurisdiction.

Section 2. Congress shall have power to enforce this article by appropriate legislation.

AMENDMENT XIV

*Passed by Congress June 16, 1866.*
*Ratified July 28, 1868.*

Section 1. All persons born or naturalized in the United States, and subject to the jurisdiction thereof, are citizens of the United States and of the State wherein they reside. No State shall make or enforce any law which shall abridge the privileges or immunities of citizens of the United States, nor shall any State deprive any person of life, liberty or property, without due process of law, nor deny to any person within its jurisdiction the equal protection of the laws.

Section 2. Representatives shall be apportioned among the several States according to their respective numbers, counting the whole number of persons in each State, excluding Indians not taxed. But when the right to vote at any election for the choice of electors for President and Vice President of the United States, representatives in Congress, the executive and judicial officers of a State, or the members of the legislature thereof, is denied to any of the male inhabitants of such State, being twenty-one years of age, and citizens of the United States, or in any way abridged, except for participating in rebellion, or other crime, the basis of representation therein shall be reduced in the proportion which the number of such male citizens shall bear to the whole number of male citizens twenty-one years of age in such State.

*Section* 3. No person shall be a senator or representative in Congress, or elector of President and Vice President, or hold any office, civil or military, under the United States, or under any State, who having previously taken an oath, as a member of Congress, or as an officer of the United States, or as a member of any State legislature, or as an executive or judicial officer of any State, to support the Constitution of the United States, shall have engaged in insurrection or rebellion against the same, or given aid or comfort to the enemies thereof. But Congress may by a vote of two thirds of each House, remove such disability.

*Section* 4. The validity of the public debt of the United States, authorized by law, including debts incurred for payment of pensions and bounties for services in suppressing insurrection or rebellion, shall not be questioned. But neither the United States nor any State shall assume or pay any debt or obligation incurred in aid of insurrection or rebellion against the United States, or any claim for the loss or emancipation of any slave; but all such debts, obligations, and claims shall be held illegal and void.

*Section* 5. The Congress shall have power to enforce, by appropriate legislation, the provisions of this article.

### AMENDMENT XV

*Passed by Congress February 27, 1869.*
*Ratified March 30, 1870.*

*Section* 1. The right of citizens of the United States to vote shall not be denied or abridged by the United States or by any State on account of race, color, or previous condition of servitude.

*Section* 2. The Congress shall have power to enforce this article by appropriate legislation.

### AMENDMENT XVI

*Passed by Congress July 12, 1909.*
*Ratified February 25, 1913.*

The Congress shall have power to lay and collect taxes on incomes, from whatever source derived, without apportionment among the several States, and without regard to any census or enumeration.

### AMENDMENT XVII

*Passed by Congress May 16, 1912.*
*Ratified May 31, 1913.*

The Senate of the United States shall be composed of two senators from each State, elected by the people thereof, for six years, and each senator shall have one vote. The electors in each State shall have the qualifications requisite for electors of the most numerous branch of the State legislature.

When vacancies happen in the representation of any State in the Senate, the executive authority of such State shall issue writs of election to fill such vacancies: *Provided,* That the legislature of any State may empower the executive thereof to make temporary appointments until the people fill the vacancies by election as the legislature may direct.

This amendment shall not be so construed as to affect the election or term of any senator chosen before it becomes valid as part of the Constitution.

### AMENDMENT XVIII

*Passed by Congress December 17, 1917.*
*Ratified January 29, 1919.*

After one year from the ratification of this article, the manufacture, sale, or transportation of intoxicating liquors within, the importation thereof into, or the exportation thereof from the

United States and all territory subject to the jurisdiction thereof for beverage purposes is hereby prohibited.

The Congress and the several States shall have concurrent power to enforce this article by appropriate legislation.

This article shall be inoperative unless it shall have been ratified as an amendment to the Constitution by the legislatures of the several States, as provided in the Constitution, within seven years from the date of the submission hereof to the States by Congress.*

AMENDMENT XIX

*Passed by Congress June 5, 1919.*
*Ratified August 26, 1920.*

The right of citizens of the United States to vote shall not be denied or abridged by the United States or by any State on account of sex.

Congress shall have power to enforce this article by appropriate legislation.

AMENDMENT XX

*Passed by Congress March 3, 1932.*
*Ratified January 23, 1933.*

*Section 1.* The terms of the President and Vice President shall end at noon on the 20th day of January, and the terms of Senators and Representatives at noon on the 3d day of January, of the years in which such terms would have ended if this article had not been ratified; and the terms of their successors shall then begin.

*Section 2.* The Congress shall assemble at least once in every year, and such meeting shall begin at noon on the 3d day of January, unless they shall by law appoint a different day.

*Section 3.* If, at the time fixed for the beginning of the term of the President, the President elect shall have died, the Vice President elect shall become President. If a President shall not have been chosen before the time fixed for the beginning of his term, or if the President elect shall have failed to

* Repealed by Amendment 21.

qualify, then the Vice President elect shall act as President until a President shall have qualified; and the Congress may by law provide for the case wherein neither a President elect nor a Vice President elect shall have qualified, declaring who shall then act as President, or the manner in which one who is to act shall be selected, and such person shall act accordingly until a President or Vice President shall have qualified.

*Section 4.* The Congress may by law provide for the case of the death of any of the persons from whom the House of Representatives may choose a President whenever the right of choice shall have devolved upon them, and for the case of the death of any of the persons from whom the Senate may choose a Vice President whenever the right of choice shall have devolved upon them.

*Section 5.* Sections 1 and 2 shall take effect on the 15th day of October following the ratification of this article.

*Section 6.* This article shall be inoperative unless it shall have been ratified as an amendment to the Constitution by the legislatures of three-fourths of the several States within seven years from the date of its submission.

AMENDMENT XXI

*Passed by Congress February 20, 1933.*
*Ratified December 5, 1933.*

*Section 1.* The Eighteenth Article of amendment to the Constitution of the United States is hereby repealed.

*Section 2.* The transportation or importation into any State, Territory, or possession of the United States for delivery or use therein of intoxicating liquors in violation of the laws thereof, is hereby prohibited.

*Section 3.* This article shall be inoperative unless it shall have been ratified as an amendment to the Constitution by conventions in the several States, as provided in the Constitution, within seven years from the date of the submission thereof to the States by the Congress.

AMENDMENT XXII

*Passed by Congress March 12, 1947.*
*Ratified March 1, 1951.*

No person shall be elected to the office of the President more than twice, and no person who has held the office of President, or acted as President, for more than two years of a term to which some other person was elected President shall be elected to the office of the President more than once.

But this article shall not apply to any person holding the office of President when this article was proposed by the Congress, and shall not prevent any person who may be holding the office of President, or acting as President, during the term within which this article becomes operative from holding the office of President or acting as President during the remainder of such term.

This article shall be inoperative unless it shall have been ratified as an amendment to the Constitution by the legislatures of three-fourths of the several States within seven years from the date of its submission to the States by the Congress.

AMENDMENT XXIII

*Passed by Congress June 16, 1960.*
*Ratified March 29, 1961.*

*Section 1.* The District constituting the seat of Government of the United States shall appoint in such manner as the Congress shall direct:

A number of electors of President and Vice President equal to the whole number of Senators and Representatives in Congress to which the District would be entitled if it were a State, but in no event more than the least populous State; they shall be in addition to those appointed by the States, but they shall be considered, for the purposes of the election of President and Vice President, to be electors appointed by a State; and they shall meet in the District and perform such duties as provided by the twelfth article of amendment.

*Section 2.* The Congress shall have power to enforce this article by appropriate legislation.

AMENDMENT XXIV

*Passed by Congress August 27, 1962.*
*Ratified January 23, 1964.*

*Section 1.* The right of citizens of the United States to vote in any primary or other election for President or Vice President, for electors for President or Vice President, or for Senator or Representative in Congress, shall not be denied or abridged by the United States or any state by reason of failure to pay any poll tax or other tax.

*Section 2.* The Congress shall have the power to enforce this article by appropriate legislation.

# 17

*"Implied powers are to be considered as dele-
gated equally with express ones"*

In his major work, *A Defence of the
Constitutions of Government of the United States of America*, published in
three volumes in 1787 and 1788, John Adams made the interesting point that
in bicameral legislatures, the Senate, "to all honest and useful intents," was a
place of "ostracism." It served to remove from the House of Representatives
persons "of immense wealth, the most respected birth, and transcendent abilities," who in the nature of things would otherwise be "too much for simple
honesty and plain sense" to contend with. The representatives thereby would
be left freer to perform their fundamental role in the scheme of government
as the unintimidated spokesmen of the "sense of the people" with whom they
shared their humble endowments. It was on the success of such ingenious
political arrangements that Adams staked "the greatest trust . . . that Providence
ever committed to so small a number [as the framers of American constitutions]
since the transgression of the first pair." To him and to many of his colleagues
in what was to become the Federalist party, America represented above all a
"great experiment" in political management, with "happiness" as the goal.

Others who shared Adams's devotion to political contrivances, and who also
became Federalists, saw "happiness" as a philosophical snare. Their passion was
for the means of action, and especially for the means of power. None was more
ardent in this pursuit than Alexander Hamilton, who in Number 11 of the
*Federalist Papers* long anticipated Henry Clay (see Document No. 25, below)
in calling for the erection of "one great American system . . . able to dictate
the terms of the connection between the old and the new world."

Hamilton accepted with what good grace he could muster that degree of
popular participation in government that the Adamsites esteemed as the crowning glory of the Constitution. Once in office as Secretary of the Treasury in
September, 1789, he lost no time in thrusting the "executive impulse" to the
forefront of government, ahead of the popular legislature which he hoped to
make his creature. Late in 1789, the House of Representatives asked the new
Secretary for reports on the nation's finances. In January, 1790, Hamilton presented the first of these reports, and others soon followed. Since there were in
America, as his friend and successor, Oliver Wolcott, put it, no "clergy, nobility
and armies . . . interested in the support of the government," Hamilton used

his reports to array the moneyed elite behind his "engine of government." He also "spent most of his time running from place to place among the members" in Congress (as one of these members recalled) personally shepherding to safe passage the bills called for by his reports.

One of Hamilton's bills, proposing the incorporation of a national bank, was passed by Congress in February, 1791. James Madison had bitterly opposed the measure in the House as going beyond the powers expressly delegated to Congress by the Constitution. When the bill came before President Washington for his signature, he asked the opinions of his Cabinet on Madison's stand. Jefferson, as Secretary of State, supported Madison's "strict interpretation" of the supreme law. Hamilton argued that "principles of construction like those espoused by the Secretary of State . . . would be fatal to the just and indispensable authority of the United States." Jefferson conceded that there were "implied" as well as "express" constitutional powers. He urged that implied powers be reserved for situations of dire necessity. Hamilton, taking the position accepted by Washington, would use implied powers as freely as any others.

The bank issue was the first over which the framers of the Constitution themselves clearly split on its interpretation. This issue widened rifts already apparent in the Federalist party and inspired Madison and Jefferson to begin the organization of a "legal opposition," which would soon become the Republican party. Although Hamilton's project for consolidating the Union into a "leviathan state" failed, the "broad construction" of the Constitution, upon which this project rested, may be said to have become the traditional one. His powerful argument for it in his bank opinion is presented in part below.

*February 23, 1791*

# Alexander Hamilton to President Washington
## on the Constitutionality of a National Bank

The Secretary of the Treasury having perused with attention the papers containing the opinions of the Secretary of State and the Attorney-General, concerning the constitutionality of the bill for establishing a national bank, proceeds, according to the order of the President, to submit the reasons which have induced him to entertain a different opinion.

It will naturally have been antici-pated, that in performing this task he would feel uncommon solicitude. Personal considerations alone, arising from the reflection that the measure originated with him, would be sufficient to produce it. The sense which he has manifested of the great importance of such an institution to the successful administration of the department under his particular care, and an expectation of serious ill consequences to result from a failure of the measure, do not permit him to be without anxiety on public accounts. But the chief solicitude arises from a firm persuasion, that principles of construction like those espoused by the Secretary of State and the Attorney-General would be fatal to the just and indispensable authority of the United States.

In entering upon the argument, it ought to be premised that the objections of the Secretary of State and the Attorney-General are founded on a general denial of the authority of the United States to erect corporations. . . .

Now it appears to the Secretary of the Treasury that this *general principle* is *inherent* in the very *definition* of government, and *essential* to every step of the progress to be made by that of the United States, namely: That every power vested in a government is in its nature *sovereign*, and includes, by *force* of the *term*, a right to employ all the *means* requisite and fairly applicable to the attainment of the *ends* of such power, and which are not precluded by restrictions and exceptions specified in the Constitution, or are not immoral, or not contrary to the *essential ends* of political society.

This principle, in its application to government in general, would be admitted as an axiom; and it will be incumbent upon those who may incline to deny it, to prove a distinction, and to show that a rule which, in the general system of things, is essential to the preservation of the social order, is inapplicable to the United States.

The circumstance that the powers of sovereignty are in this country divided between the National and State governments, does not afford the distinction required. It does not follow from this, that each of the portion of *powers* delegated to the one or to the other, is not sovereign with *regard to its proper objects*. It will only *follow* from it, that each has sovereign power as to *certain things*, and not as to *other things*. To deny that the Government of the United States has sovereign power, as

to its declared purposes and trusts, because its power does not extend to all cases, would be equally to deny that the State governments have sovereign power in any case, because their power does not extend to every case. The tenth section of the first article of the Constitution exhibits a long list of very important things which they may not do. And thus the United States would furnish the singular spectacle of a *political society* without *sovereignty*, or of a *people governed*, without *government*.

If it would be necessary to bring proof to a proposition so clear, as that which affirms that the powers of the Federal Government, as to *its objects*, were sovereign, there is a clause of its Constitution which would be decisive. It is that which declares that the Constitution, and the laws of the United States made in pursuance of it, and all treaties made, or which shall be made, under their authority, shall be the *supreme law of the land*. The power which can create the *supreme law of the land* in *any case*, is doubtless sovereign as to such case.

This general and indisputable principle puts at once an end to the *abstract* question, whether the United States have power to erect a corporation; that is to say, to give a *legal* or *artificial capacity* to one or more persons, distinct from the *natural*. For it is unquestionably incident to *sovereign power* to erect corporations, and consequently to *that* of the United States, in *relation* to the *objects* intrusted to the management of the government. The difference is this: where the authority of the government is general, it can create corporations in *all cases*; where it is confined to certain branches of legislation, it can create corporations *only* in those cases.

Here, then, as far as concerns the reasonings of the Secretary of State and the Attorney-General, the affirmative of the constitutionality of the bill might be permitted to rest. It will occur to the President, that the principle here advanced has been untouched by either of them.

For a more complete elucidation of the point, nevertheless, the arguments which they had used against the power of the government to erect corporations, however foreign they are to the great and fundamental rule which has been stated, shall be particularly examined. And after showing that they do not tend to impair its force, it shall also be shown that the power of incorporation, incident to the government in certain cases, does fairly extend to the particular case which is the object of the bill.

The first of these arguments is, that the foundation of the Constitution is laid on this ground: "That all powers not delegated to the United States by the Constitution, nor prohibited by it to the States, are reserved to the States, or to the people." Whence it is meant to be inferred, that Congress can in no case exercise any power not included in those enumerated in the Constitution. And it is affirmed, that the power of erecting a corporation is not included in any of the enumerated powers.

The main proposition here laid down, in its true signification, is not to be questioned. It is nothing more than a consequence of this republican maxim, that all government is a delegation of power. But how much is delegated in each case is a question of fact, to be made out by fair reasoning and construction, upon the particular provisions of the Constitution, taking as guides the general principles and general ends of governments.

It is not denied that there are *implied*, as well as *express powers*, and that the *former* are as effectually delegated as the *latter*. And for the sake of accuracy it shall be mentioned that there is another class of powers, which may be properly denominated *resulting powers*. It will not be doubted that if the United States should make a conquest of any of the territories of its neighbors, they would possess sovereign jurisdiction over the conquered territory. This would be rather a result from the whole mass of the powers of the government, and from the nature of political society, than a consequence of either of the powers specially enumerated.

But be this as it may, it furnishes a striking illustration of the general doctrine contended for; it shows an extensive case, in which a power of erecting corporations is either implied in, or would result from, some or all of the powers vested in the National Government. The jurisdiction acquired over such conquered country would certainly be competent to any species of legislation.

To return:—It is conceded that *implied powers* are to be considered as delegated equally with *express ones*. Then it follows, that as a power of erecting a corporation may as well be implied as any other thing, it may as well be employed as an *instrument* or *means* of carrying into execution any of the specified powers, as any other *instrument* or *means* whatever. The only question must be in this, as in every other case, whether the means to be employed, or, in this instance, the corporation to be erected, has a natural relation to any of the acknowledged objects or lawful ends of the government. Thus a corporation may not be erected by Congress for superintending the police of the city of Philadelphia, because they are not authorized to *regulate* the *police* of that city. But one may be erected in relation to the collection of taxes, or to the trade with foreign countries, or to the trade between the States, or with the Indian tribes; because it is the province of the Federal Government to *regulate* those objects, and because it is incident to a general *sovereign* or *legislative* power to *regulate* a thing, to employ all the means which relate to its regulation to the best and greatest advantage. . . .

# 18

*"Discountenancing whatever may suggest even*
*a suspicion that your . . . national union . . .*
*can in any event be abandoned"*

Writing to his recently retired Secretary of War, General Henry Knox, in September, 1795, President Washington remarked on his own public conduct: "As I have found no better guide hitherto than upright intentions, and close investigation, I shall adhere to these maxims while I keep watch; leaving it to those who will come after me to explore new ways, if they like; or think them better." The new ways the aging President disdained were those offered by political parties, their caucuses and kept press.

During Washington's first administration, domestic issues arising largely from Hamilton's financial schemes had divided the country seemingly irreconcilably over "construction" of the Constitution itself. Moreover, ground had been furnished by these schemes, as Washington said, "for characterizing parties by *geographical* discriminations," thereby suggesting to "designing men" that the Union may yet be broken into rival, warring sections. By 1792 the President had become so impressed with this menace that he proposed to deliver a "valedictory address" to the wayward people before retiring from office that year, admonishing them never to forget "that we are *all* children of the same country." The rival party leaders themselves reminded Washington that his own august presence remained the one rallying point of unity, and on their pleas he agreed at the last moment to pigeonhole his admonitions and to postpone for another four years his gnawing wish to retreat to Mount Vernon.

As Washington's second term neared its end in 1796 he felt a more compelling urgency than ever to offer the witness of his own experience in support of the proposition that "every portion of our country finds the most commanding motives for carefully guarding and preserving the union of the whole." Washington's stronger impulse now was well justified by the events of his second administration, which only broadened party rifts along sectional lines. The most ominous of these events occurred in foreign affairs, and the most divisive of them arose from the wars of the French Revolution which opened in Europe in February, 1793.

The rising Republican party, its strength still largely in the South, embraced revolutionary France as a worthy follower of revolutionary America in the universal struggle for the rights of man. The Republicans' commitment to France

95

grew all the stronger because the Federalists, whom they believed would destroy the country by domestic policies dictated by the mercantile North, appeared to favor England, their most active trading partner. The Federalists' leaning toward England was confirmed for many by Jay's Treaty, completed by the Anglo-American negotiators in November, 1794, but not fully accepted by the United States Congress until April, 1796. This long time gap accurately measures the widespread American resistance to the pro-British treaty terms; and only the knowledge that Washington himself favored the treaty as in the general interests of the country narrowly carried the day for it.

Washington's own popularity was so damaged by the controversies over foreign issues that he felt impelled from time to time privately, as in his letter to General Knox in September, 1795, quoted above, and publicly, as in his Farewell Address of September, 1796, to offer fulsome self-vindications. In the interests of space I have deleted these from the Farewell Address as presented in this document. The most influential sections of the Farewell Address concern themselves with "the great rule of conduct for us in regard to foreign nations." This rule was, to have as little *political* connection with them as possible, and no permanent connection. But Washington's emphasis on aloofness toward foreign connections was most closely related to their likely evil consequences for domestic unity. This unity he valued highest, and for its preservation he offered arguments based on sectional "interest" as well as "sympathy," which were to become a resource for spokesmen of succeeding decades when union was indeed to be more sorely tried (see especially Documents No. 25 and No. 29, below).

*September 17, 1796*

# Washington's Farewell Address

(*As published in* The American Daily Advertiser.)

*Friends and Fellow-Citizens:* The period for a new election of a citizen to administer the Executive Government of the United States being not far distant, . . . it appears to me proper, especially as it may conduce to a more distinct expression of the public voice, that I should now apprise you of the resolution I have formed to decline being considered among the number of those out of whom a choice is to be made. . . .

The impressions with which I first undertook the arduous trust were explained on the proper occasion. . . . A solicitude for your welfare which cannot end with my life, and the apprehension of danger natural to that solicitude, urge me on an occasion like the present to offer to your solemn contemplation and to recommend to your frequent review some sentiments which are the result of much reflection, of no inconsiderable observation, and which appear to me all important to the permanency of your felicity as a people. These will be offered to you with the more freedom as you can only see in them the disinterested warnings of a parting friend. . . .

Interwoven as is the love of liberty with every ligament of your hearts, no recommendation of mine is necessary to fortify or confirm the attachment.

The unity of government which constitutes you one people is also now dear to you. It is justly so, for it is a main pillar in the edifice of your real independence, the support of your tranquillity at home, your peace abroad, of your safety, of your prosperity, of that very liberty which you so highly prize. But as it is easy to foresee that from different causes and from different quarters much pains will be taken, many artifices employed, to weaken in your minds the conviction of this truth, as this is the point in your political fortress against which the batteries of internal and external enemies will be most constantly and actively (though often covertly and insidiously) directed, it is of infinite moment that you should properly estimate the immense value of your national union to your collective and individual happiness; that you should cherish a cordial, habitual, and immovable attachment to it; accustoming yourselves to think and speak of it as of the palladium of your political safety and prosperity; watching for its preservation with jealous anxiety; discountenancing whatever may suggest even a suspicion that it can in any event be abandoned, and indignantly frowning upon the first dawning of every attempt to alienate any portion of our country from the rest or to enfeeble the sacred ties which now link together the various parts.

For this you have every inducement of sympathy and interest. . . . With slight shades of difference, you have the same religion, manners, habits, and political principles. You have in a common cause fought and triumphed together. The independence and liberty you possess are the work of joint councils and joint efforts, of common dangers, sufferings, and successes.

But these considerations, however powerfully they address themselves to your sensibility, are greatly outweighed by those which apply more immediately to your interest. Here every portion of our country finds the most commanding motives for carefully guarding and preserving the union of the whole.

The *North*, in an unrestrained intercourse with the *South*, protected by the equal laws of a common government, finds in the productions of the latter great additional resources of maritime and commercial enterprise and precious materials of manufacturing industry. The *South*, in the same intercourse, benefiting by the same agency of the *North*, sees its agriculture grow and its commerce expand. . . . The *East*, in a like intercourse with the *West*, already finds, and in the progressive improvement of interior communications by land and water will more and more find, a valuable vent for the commodities which it brings from abroad or manufactures at home. The *West* derives from the *East* supplies requisite to its growth and comfort, and what is perhaps of still greater consequence, it must of necessity owe the *secure* enjoyment of indispensable *outlets* for its own productions to the weight, influence, and the future maritime strength of the Atlantic side of the Union, directed by an indissoluble community of interest as *one nation*. Any other tenure by which the *West* can hold this essential advantage, whether derived from its own separate strength or from an apostate and unnatural connection with any foreign power, must be intrinsically precarious.

While, then, every part of our country thus feels an immediate and particular interest in union, all the parts combined can not fail to find in the united mass of means and efforts greater strength, greater resource, proportionably greater security from external danger, a less frequent interruption of their peace by foreign nations, and what is of inestimable value, they must derive from union an exemption from those broils and wars between themselves which so frequently afflict neighboring countries not tied together by the same governments, which their own rivalships alone would be sufficient to produce, but which opposite foreign alliances, attachments, and intrigues would stimulate and imbitter. Hence, likewise, they will avoid the necessity of those overgrown military establishments which, under any form of government, are inauspicious to liberty, and which are to be regarded as particularly hostile to republican liberty. . . .

In contemplating the causes which may disturb our union it occurs as matter of serious concern that any ground should have been furnished for characterizing parties by *geographical* discriminations—*Northern* and *Southern*, *Atlantic* and *Western*—whence designing men may endeavor to excite a belief that there is a real difference of local interests and views. . . . To the efficacy and permanency of your union a government for the whole is indispensable. No alliances, however strict, between the parts can be an adequate substitute. . . . Sensible of this momentous truth, you have improved upon your first essay by the adoption of a Constitution of Government better calculated than your former for an intimate union and for the efficacious management of your common concerns. This Government, the offspring of your own choice, uninfluenced and unawed, adopted upon full investigation and mature deliberation, completely free in its principles, in the distribution of its powers, uniting security with energy, and containing within itself a provision for its own amendment, has a just claim to your confidence and your support. . . .

Toward the preservation of your Government and the permanency of your present happy state, it is requisite not only that you steadily discountenance irregular oppositions to its ac-

knowledged authority, but also that you resist with care the spirit of innovation upon its principles, however specious the pretexts. One method of assault may be to effect in the forms of the Constitution alterations which will impair the energy of the system, and thus to undermine what can not be directly overthrown. In all the changes to which you may be invited remember . . . that facility in changes upon the credit of mere hypothesis and opinion exposes to perpetual change, from the endless variety of hypothesis and opinion; and remember especially that for the efficient management of your common interests in a country so extensive as ours a government of as much vigor as is consistent with the perfect security of liberty is indispensable. Liberty itself will find in such a government, with powers properly distributed and adjusted, its surest guardian. . . .

I have already intimated to you the danger of parties in the State, with particular reference to the founding of them on geographical discriminations. Let me now take a more comprehensive view, and warn you in the most solemn manner against the baneful effects of the spirit of party generally.

This spirit, unfortunately, is inseparable from our nature, having its root in the strongest passions of the human mind. It exists under different shapes in all governments, more or less stifled, controlled, or repressed; but in those of the popular form it is seen in its greatest rankness and is truly their worst enemy. . . . It agitates the community with ill-founded jealousies and false alarms; kindles the animosity of one part against another; foments occasionally riot and insurrection. It opens the door to foreign influence and corruption, which find a facilitated access to the government itself through the channels of party passion. Thus the policy and the will of one country are subjected to the policy and will of another. . . .

Of all the dispositions and habits which lead to political prosperity, religion and morality are indispensable supports. . . . Let it simply be asked, Where is the security for property, for reputation, for life, if the sense of religious obligation *desert* the oaths which are the instruments of investigation in courts of justice? And let us with caution indulge the supposition that morality can be maintained without religion. . . .

Observe good faith and justice toward all nations. Cultivate peace and harmony with all. Religion and morality enjoin this conduct. And can it be that good policy does not equally enjoin it? . . . In the execution of such a plan nothing is more essential than that permanent, inveterate antipathies against particular nations and passionate attachments for others should be excluded. . . . The nation which indulges toward another an habitual hatred or an habitual fondness is in some degree a slave. . . . Sympathy for the favorite nation, facilitating the illusion of an imaginary common interest in cases where no real common interest exists, and infusing into one the enmities of the other, betrays the former into a participation in the quarrels and wars of the latter without adequate inducement or justification. It leads also to concessions to the favorite nation of privileges denied to others, which is apt doubly to injure the nation making the concessions by unnecessarily parting with what ought to have been retained, and by exciting jealousy, ill will, and a disposition to retaliate in the parties from whom equal privileges are withheld; and it gives to ambitious, corrupted, or deluded citizens (who devote themselves to the favorite nation) facility to betray or sacrifice the interests of their own country without odium, sometimes even with popularity, gilding with the appearances of a virtual sense of obligation, a commendable deference for public opinion, or a laudable zeal for public good the base or foolish compliances of ambition, corruption, or infatuation. . . .

The great rule of conduct for us in regard to foreign nations is, in extending our commercial relations to have with them as little *political* connection as possible. So far as we have already formed engagements let them be fulfilled with perfect good faith. Here let us stop.

Europe has a set of primary interests which to us have none or a very remote relation. Hence she must be engaged in frequent controversies, the causes of which are essentially foreign to our concerns. Hence, therefore, it must be unwise in us to implicate ourselves by artificial ties in the ordinary vicissitudes of her politics or the ordinary combinations and collisions of her friendships or enmities.

Our detached and distant situation invites and enables us to pursue a different course. If we remain one people, under an efficient government, the period is not far off when we may defy material injury from external annoyance; when we may take such an attitude as will cause the neutrality we may at any time resolve upon to be scrupulously respected; when belligerent nations, under the impossibility of making acquisitions upon us, will not lightly hazard the giving us provocation; when we may choose peace or war, as our interest, guided by justice, shall counsel.

Why forego the advantages of so peculiar a situation? Why quit our own to stand upon foreign ground? Why, by interweaving our destiny with that of any part of Europe, entangle our peace and prosperity in the toils of European ambition, rivalship, interest, humor, or caprice?

It is our true policy to steer clear of permanent alliances with any portion of the foreign world, so far, I mean, as we are now at liberty to do it; for let me not be understood as capable of patronizing infidelity to existing engagements. . . . But in my opinion it is unnecessary and would be unwise to extend them. Taking care always to keep ourselves by suitable establishments on a respectable defensive posture, we may safely trust to temporary alliances for extraordinary emergencies.

Harmony, liberal intercourse with all nations are recommended by policy, humanity, and interest. But even our commercial policy should hold an equal and impartial hand, neither seeking nor granting exclusive favors or preferences; consulting the natural course of things; diffusing and diversifying by gentle means the streams of commerce, but forcing nothing; establishing with powers so disposed, in order to give trade a stable course, to define the rights of our merchants, and to enable the Government to support them, conventional rules of intercourse, the best that present circumstances and mutual opinion will permit, but temporary and liable to be from time to time abandoned or varied as experience and circumstances shall dictate; constantly keeping in view that it is folly in one nation to look for disinterested favors from another; . . . There can be no greater error than to expect or calculate upon real favors from nation to nation. It is an illusion which experience must cure, which a just pride ought to discard.

In offering to you, my countrymen, these counsels of an old and affectionate friend I dare not hope they will make the strong and lasting impression I could wish. . . . But if I may even flatter myself . . . that they may now and then recur to moderate the fury of party spirit, to warn against the mischiefs of foreign intrigue, to guard against the impostures of pretended patriotism—this hope will be full recompense for the solicitude for your welfare by which they have been dictated.

# 19

*"These and successive acts of the same character, . . . may tend to drive these States into revolution and blood"*

Washington was hardly wrong, during his years as president, in his estimate of the fragility of the American union. When the time came, in 1797, to hand over his "arduous trust" to John Adams, the second President, he thus felt a swelling pride in having survived long enough to be able to demonstrate before the world how a republic could peacefully effect a change in its head of state in compliance with the voice of the people. Adams himself said of his inauguration, "All agree that . . . it was the sublimest thing ever exhibited in America."

Yet Washington and his successor both knew that the future of the union then hung more precariously than ever on the shifting tides of the wars of the French Revolution in Europe, and more immediately on the party struggle over that war at home.

To the Federalists, by 1797, France had become "the terrible Republic," a bloody reproof to all democratic aspirations. When after learning of Jay's Treaty with Britain, France recklessly stepped up her assault on neutral American ocean craft, the so-called High (or Hamiltonian) Federalists openly demanded a declaration of war against her the easier to crush the "tools of France," the apostles of democracy, at home. Early in 1798, in the notorious X.Y.Z. encounter, France added insult to injury by demanding bribes of the emissaries President Adams had sent to Paris in an effort to avert war. On receiving the news of this latest affront, many moderates joined the High Federalists in calling for satisfaction on the battlefield. Mrs. Adams, moreover, now decided that the Republican partisans of France were "very wicked men" who would be "adjudged traitors to their country."

The Republicans did not lag in uncovering traitors themselves. As Jefferson put it in 1795, he and his party looked on Jay's Treaty as "acquiescence under insult." They deemed the attempted rapprochement with Britain a betrayal of the Revolution by men who had never really lost their affection for the Mother Country; and worse, a betrayal of the Constitution by those whose love for kingship, in prayerful anticipation of a better day, had only from expediency been kept under wraps in 1787.

Unfortunately for themselves, the Republicans harbored in their ranks certain Frenchmen who no doubt had come to spy, to prey with their inscrutable diplomatic wiles, as Federalist leaders complained, on the simple minds of the people's representatives, mistakenly admitted to the realms of power. But many legitimate refugees from the Terror in France also filled out Republican ranks. Besides the Frenchmen there were, in the words of Federalist Congressman Harrison Gray Otis, the "hordes of wild Irishmen" who fled to America in 1798 from certain death on the gallows at home after Lord Cornwallis had smashed their projected revolution against the British Crown. Many of these foreigners quickly rose to political and journalistic leadership in the Republicans' broad offensive against king worshippers and Anglophiles. More than that, they promised, as soon as the law allowed, to help vote the Federalists out.

Such was the confrontation of forces as the election of 1800 loomed. To thwart the Republicans, the Federalists in June and July, 1798, pushed through Congress a series of four acts popularly known as the Alien and Sedition Acts. The first of these, actually a naturalization act, so extended the period before an alien could become a citizen that it virtually disfranchised for life many of the new arrivals. The second and third acts gave the president extraordinary power over the imprisonment or deportation of aliens in peace or war. The fourth, the sedition act, provided fines and jail sentences for anyone, citizen and alien alike, speaking, writing, or publishing, "with intent to defame . . . or bring into contempt or disrepute," the government or any of its officers. By these repressive measures, many foreigners were dissuaded from seeking asylum in the land of liberty; many aliens were persuaded to flee the country; and many Republican editors were jailed, their newspapers silenced.

Republican leaders, notably Madison and Vice President Jefferson, lost no time in picking up the challenge in the party duel. Their most elaborate publications were the Kentucky and Virginia Resolutions, the first secretly the work of Jefferson and adopted by the Kentucky Legislature in November, 1798; the second secretly the work of Madison and adopted by the Virginia Legislature in December. The Kentucky Resolutions, written in Jefferson's usual resounding phrases that fully bear rereading, are reproduced in full below in the form in which they were presented to the Kentucky Legislature by John Breckinridge, November 10, 1798.

The importance of the Kentucky Resolutions, like that of the less comprehensive ones in Virginia, goes well beyond their critical role in defining the issues of the 1800 election. These resolutions made state rights their central theme, and thereby supplied the broadest philosophical underpinning for later disunion campaigns culminating in the Civil War. Jefferson and Madison, nevertheless, developed this philosophy in a characteristically expansive spirit alien to later state rights movements. What they were most expansive about was the meaning of the first amendment to the Constitution; specifically, the permissible scope of freedom of expression in a government where the people themselves were sovereign. To the Republican leaders, the Alien and Sedition Acts intolerably circumscribed this freedom, and for mean and partisan purposes. By employing the loosest construction of the Constitution to impose the tightest tyranny, they soured, Jefferson said in the Kentucky Resolutions, "the mild spirit of our country and its laws." Rightfully men feared, and feared for, such a Union.

*November 10, 1798*

# Thomas Jefferson:
# The Kentucky Resolutions

1. *Resolved*, that the several States composing the United States of America, are not united on the principle of unlimited submission to their general government; but that by compact under the style and title of a Constitution for the United States and of amendments thereto, they constituted a general government for special purposes, delegated to that government certain definite powers, reserving each State to itself, the residuary mass of right to their own self-government; and that whensoever the general government assumes undelegated powers, its acts are unauthoritative, void, and of no force: That to this compact each State acceded as a State, and is an integral party, its co-

States forming, as to itself, the other party: That the government created by this compact was not made the exclusive or final judge of the extent of the powers delegated to itself; since that would have made its discretion, and not the Constitution, the measure of its powers; but that as in all other cases of compact among parties having no common Judge, *each party has an equal right to judge for itself, as well of infractions as of the mode and measure of redress.*

2. *Resolved,* that the Constitution of the United States having delegated to Congress a power to punish treason, counterfeiting the securities and current coin of the United States, piracies and felonies committed on the high seas, and offenses against the laws of nations, and no other crimes whatever, and it being true as a general principle, and one of the amendments to the Constitution having also declared "that the powers not delegated to the United States by the Constitution, nor prohibited by it to the States, are reserved to the States respectively, or to the people," therefore also [the Sedition Act] passed on the 14th day of July, 1798; as also the act passed by them on the 27th day of June, 1798, entitled "An act to punish frauds committed on the Bank of the United States" (and all other their acts which assume to create, define, or punish crimes other than those enumerated in the Constitution), are altogether void and of no force, and that the power to create, define, and punish such other crimes is reserved, and of right appertains solely and exclusively to the respective States, each within its own Territory.

3. *Resolved,* that it is true as a general principle, and is also expressly declared by one of the amendments to the Constitution that "the powers not delegated to the United States by the Constitution, nor prohibited by it to the States, are reserved to the States respectively or to the people;" and that no power over the freedom of religion, freedom of speech, or freedom of the press being delegated to the United States by the Constitution, nor prohibited by it to the States, all lawful powers respecting the same did of right remain, and were reserved to the States, or to the people: That thus was manifested their determination to retain to themselves the right of judging how far the licentiousness of speech and of the press may be abridged without lessening their useful freedom, and how far those abuses which cannot be separated from their use should be tolerated rather than the use be destroyed; and thus also they guarded against all abridgment by the United States of the freedom of religious opinions and exercises, and retained to themselves the right of protecting the same, as this State, by a law passed on the general demand of its citizens, had already protected them from all human restraint or interference: And that in addition to this general principle and express declaration, another and more special provision has been made by one of the amendments to the Constitution which expressly declares, that "Congress shall make no law respecting an establishment of religion, or prohibiting the free exercise thereof, or abridging the freedom of speech, or of the press," thereby guarding in the same sentence, and under the same words, the freedom of religion, of speech, and of the press, insomuch, that whatever violates either, throws down the sanctuary which covers the others, and that libels, falsehoods, defamation equally with heresy and false religion, are withheld from the cognizance of Federal tribunals. That therefore [the Sedition Act], which does abridge the freedom of the press, is not law, but is altogether void and of no effect.

4. *Resolved,* that alien friends are under the jurisdiction and protection of the laws of the State wherein they are; that no power over them has been delegated to the United States, nor prohibited to the individual States distinct from their power over citizens; and it being true as a general principle, and

one of the amendments to the Constitution having also declared that "the powers not delegated to the United States by the Constitution, nor prohibited by it to the States, are reserved to the States respectively, or to the people," the act of the Congress of the United States, passed on the 22d of June, 1798, entitled "An Act concerning Aliens," which assumes power over alien friends not delegated by the Constitution, is not law, but is altogether void and of no force.

5. *Resolved,* that in addition to the general principle as well as the express declaration, that powers not delegated are reserved, another and more special provision inserted in the Constitution from abundant caution has declared, "that the migration or importation of such persons as any of the States now existing shall think proper to admit, shall not be prohibited by the Congress prior to the year 1808." That this Commonwealth does admit the migration of alien friends described as the subject of the said act concerning aliens; that a provision against prohibiting their migration is a provision against all acts equivalent thereto, or it would be nugatory; that to remove them when migrated is equivalent to a prohibition of their migration, and is therefore contrary to the said provision of the Constitution, and void.

6. *Resolved,* that the imprisonment of a person under the protection of the laws of this Commonwealth on his failure to obey the simple order of the President to depart out of the United States, as is undertaken by the said act entitled "An act concerning aliens," is contrary to the Constitution, one amendment to which has provided, that "no person shall be deprived of liberty without due process of law," and that another having provided "that in all criminal prosecutions, the accused shall enjoy the right to a public trial by an impartial jury, to be informed of the nature and cause of the accusation, to be confronted with the witnesses against him, to have compulsory process for obtaining witnesses in his favour, and to have the assistance of counsel for his defense," the same act undertaking to authorize the President to remove a person out of the United States who is under the protection of the law, on his own suspicion, without accusation, without jury, without public trial, without confrontation of the witnesses against him, without having witnesses in his favour, without defense, without counsel, is contrary to these provisions also of the Constitution, is therefore not law, but utterly void and of no force. That transferring the power of judging any person who is under the protection of the laws, from the courts to the President of the United States, as is undertaken by the same act concerning aliens, is against the article of the Constitution which provides, that "the judicial power of the United States shall be vested in courts, the judges of which shall hold their offices during good behavior," and that the said act is void for that reason also; and it is further to be noted, that this transfer of judiciary power is to that magistrate of the general government who already possesses all the executive, and a qualified negative in all the legislative powers.

7. *Resolved,* that the construction applied by the general government (as is evinced by sundry of their proceedings) to those parts of the Constitution of the United States which delegate to Congress a power to lay and collect taxes, duties, imposts, and excises; to pay the debts, and provide for the common defense, and general welfare of the United States, and to make all laws which shall be necessary and proper for carrying into execution the powers vested by the Constitution in the government of the United States, or any department thereof, goes to the destruction of all the limits prescribed to their power by the Constitution: That words meant by that instrument to be subsidiary only to the execution of the limited powers ought not to be so construed as themselves to give unlimited

powers, nor a part so to be taken as to destroy the whole residue of the instrument: That the proceedings of the general government under color of these articles will be a fit and necessary subject for revisal and correction at a time of greater tranquillity, while those specified in the preceding resolutions call for immediate redress.

8. *Resolved,* that the preceding Resolutions be transmitted to the Senators and Representatives in Congress from this Commonwealth, who are hereby enjoined to present the same to their respective Houses, and to use their best endeavors to procure, at the next session of Congress, a repeal of the aforesaid unconstitutional and obnoxious acts.

9. *Resolved,* lastly, that the Governor of this Commonwealth be, and is hereby authorized and requested to communicate the preceding Resolutions to the Legislatures of the several States, to assure them that this Commonwealth considers Union for specified National purposes, and particularly for those specified in their late Federal Compact, to be friendly to the peace, happiness, and prosperity of all the States: that faithful to that compact according to the plain intent and meaning which it was understood and acceded to by the several parties, it is sincerely anxious for its preservation: that it does also believe, that to take from the States all the powers of self-government, and transfer them to a general and consolidated government, without regard to the special delegations and reservations solemnly agreed to in that compact, is not for the peace, happiness, or prosperity of these States: And that, therefore, this Commonwealth is determined, as it doubts not its co-States are, tamely to submit to undelegated and consequently unlimited powers in no man or body of men on earth: that if the acts before specified should stand, these conclusions would flow from them; that the general government may place any act they think proper on the list of crimes and

punish it themselves, whether enumerated or not enumerated by the Constitution as cognizable by them: that they may transfer its cognizance to the President or any other person, who may himself be the accuser, counsel, judge, and jury, whose suspicions may be the evidence, his order the sentence, his officer the executioner, and his breast the sole record of the transaction: that a very numerous and valuable description of the inhabitants of these States being by this precedent reduced as outlaws to the absolute dominion of one man, and the barrier of the Constitution thus swept away from us all, no rampart now remains against the passions and the powers of a majority of Congress, to protect from a like exportation or other more grievous punishment the minority of the same body, the legislatures, judges, governors, and counselors of the States, nor their other peaceable inhabitants who may venture to reclaim the constitutional rights and liberties of the State and people, or who for other causes, good or bad, may be obnoxious to the views or marked by the suspicions of the President, or be thought dangerous to his or their elections or other interests, public or personal: that the friendless alien has indeed been selected as the safest subject of a first experiment, but the citizen will soon follow, or rather has already followed: for, already has a sedition act marked him as its prey: that these and successive acts of the same character, unless arrested on the threshold, may tend to drive these States into revolution and blood, and will furnish new calumnies against Republican governments, and new pretexts for those who wish it to be believed, that man cannot be governed but by a rod of iron: that it would be a dangerous delusion were a confidence in the men of our choice to silence our fears for the safety of our rights: that confidence is everywhere the parent of despotism:

Free government is founded in jealousy and not in confidence; it is jealousy and not confidence which prescribes limited Constitutions to bind down those whom we are obliged to trust with power: that our Constitution has accordingly fixed the limits to which and no further our confidence may go; and let the honest advocate of confidence read the alien and sedition acts, and say if the Constitution has not been wise in fixing limits to the government it created, and whether we should be wise in destroying those limits; let him say what the government is if it be not a tyranny, which the men of our choice have conferred on the President, and the President of our choice has assented to and accepted over the friendly strangers, to whom the mild spirit of our country and its laws had pledged hospitality and protection: that the men of our choice have more respected the bare suspicions of the President than the solid rights of innocence, the claims of justification, the sacred force of truth, and the forms and substance of law and justice.

In questions of power then let no more be heard of confidence in man, but bind him down from mischief by the claims of the Constitution. That this Commonwealth does therefore call on its co-States for an expression of their sentiments on the acts concerning aliens, and for the punishment of certain crimes herein before specified, plainly declaring whether these acts are or are not authorized by the Federal Compact. And it doubts not that their sense will be so announced as to prove their attachment unaltered to limited government, whether general or particular, and that the rights and liberties of their co-States will be exposed to no dangers by remaining embarked on a common bottom with their own: That they will concur with this Commonwealth in considering the said acts so palpably against the Constitution as to amount to an undisguised declaration, that the compact is not meant to be the measure of the powers of the general government, but that it will proceed in the exercise over these States of all powers whatsoever: That they will view this as seizing the rights of the States and consolidating them in the hands of the general government with a power to bind the States (not merely in cases made Federal) but in all cases whatsoever, by laws made, not with their consent, but by others against their consent: That this would be to surrender the form of government we have chosen, and to live under one deriving its powers from its own will, and not from our authority; and that the co-States, recurring to their natural right in cases not made Federal, will concur in declaring these acts void and of no force, and will each unite with this Commonwealth in requesting their repeal at the next session of Congress.

20

*"This Government, the world's best hope"*

In his first inaugural address, March 4, 1801 (here reproduced in full) Jefferson said that in the Alien and Sedition Acts the Republicans had confronted "a political intolerance as despotic, as wicked, and capable of as bitter and bloody persecutions" as "that religious intolerance" which we had "banished from our land." By withstanding such political intolerance, the Republicans felt they had confirmed the right of a loyal opposition to seek power in the United States by all the means of persuasion. On attaining power, in an election contest that made the impending change in national leadership far more foreboding than in 1797, they themselves would countenance no backsliding: "If there be any among us who would wish to dissolve this Union or to change its republican form, let them stand undisturbed as monuments of the safety with which error of opinion may be tolerated where reason is left free to combat it."

Jefferson's inaugural address is usually thought of as a bid for conciliation with the enemy: "Let us, then fellow-citizens, unite with one heart and one mind. . . . Every difference of opinion is not a difference in principle. . . . We are all Republicans, we are all Federalists." And yet his epochal tolerance of minority rights did not for a moment delay his joining battle with Federalist irreconcilables. "Possessing a chosen country, with room enough for our descendants to the thousandth and thousandth generation," the people, Jefferson said, required neither the elaborate contrivances of Adam's "divine science of politics" to protect them from themselves, nor Hamilton's rod of iron to curb their unseemly aspirations. "Kindly separated by nature and a wide ocean from the exterminating havoc of one quarter of the globe; too high-minded to endure the degradations of the others," all that we needed "to close the circle of our felicities" was "a wise and frugal Government, which shall restrain men from injuring one another, shall leave them otherwise free to regulate their own pursuits of industry and improvement."

This prescription may have seemed at once too flabby for those craving above all else, "energy in the government," and too French for those living in terror of the people. Yet, as Jefferson soon showed (and as he had earlier shown during his governorship of Virginia), it did not preclude the application of great energy on the people's behalf, nor the people's own quiet exercise of self-reliance. Alexander Hamilton himself said of Jefferson: "It is not true that he is an enemy of the power of the Executive. . . . While we were in the administration together, he was generally for a large construction of the Executive authority and not backward to act upon it in cases which coincided with his views." His views, in turn, would coincide with those of the American people for generations.

Jefferson, to be sure, believed Americans in a special way to be a chosen people as well as their country a chosen land (see Document No. 21, below). His philosophy of government was framed for such a people, and for one so providentially endowed. For such a people, he said, among whom every man made sovereignty under law his personal concern, "I believe this the strongest Government on earth." For all others, it provided "the world's best hope."

*March 4, 1801*

Thomas Jefferson:

First Inaugural Address

*Friends and Fellow-Citizens:* Called upon to undertake the duties of the first executive office of our country, I avail myself of the presence of that portion of my fellow-citizens which is here assembled to express my grateful thanks for the favor with which they have been pleased to look toward me, to declare a sincere consciousness that the task is above my talents, and that I approach it with those anxious and awful presentments which the greatness of the charge and the weakness of my powers so justly inspire. A rising nation, spread over a wide and fruitful land, traversing all the seas with the rich productions of their industry, engaged in commerce with nations who feel power and forget right, advancing rapidly to destinies beyond the reach of mortal eye—when I contemplate these transcendent objects, and see the honor, the happiness and the hopes of this beloved country committed to the issue, and the auspices of this day, I shrink from the contemplation, and humble myself before the magnitude of the undertaking. Utterly, indeed, should I despair did not the presence of many whom I here see remind me that in the other high authorities provided by our Constitution I shall find resources of wisdom, of virtue, and of zeal on which to rely under all difficulties. To you, then, gentlemen, who are charged with the sovereign functions of legislation, and to those associated with you, I look with encouragement for that guidance and support which may enable us to steer with safety the vessel in which we are all embarked amidst the conflicting elements of a troubled world.

During the contest of opinion through which we have passed the animation of discussions and of exertions has sometimes worn an aspect which might impose on strangers unused to think freely and to speak and to write what they think; but this being now decided by the voice of the nation, announced according to the rules of the Constitution, all will, of course, arrange themselves under the will of the law, and united in common efforts for the common good. All, too, will bear in mind this sacred principle, that though the will of the majority is in all cases to prevail, that will to be rightful must be reasonable; that the minority possesses their equal rights, which equal law must protect, and to violate would be oppression. Let us, then fellow-citizens, unite with one heart and one mind. Let us restore to social intercourse that harmony and affection without which liberty and even life itself are but dreary things. And let us reflect that, having banished from our land that religious intolerance under which mankind so long bled and suffered, we have yet gained little if we countenance a political intolerance as despotic, as wicked, and capable of as bitter and bloody persecutions. During the throes and convulsions of the ancient world, during the agonizing spasms of infuriated man, seeking through blood and slaughter his long-lost liberty, it was not wonderful that the agitation of the billows should reach even this distant and peaceful shore; that this should be more felt and feared by some and less by others, and should divide opinions as to measures of safety. But every difference of opinion is not a difference of principle. We have called by different names brethren of the same principle. We are all Republicans, we are all Federalists. If there be any among us who would wish to dissolve this Union or to change its republican form, let them stand undisturbed as monuments of the safety with which error of opinion may be tolerated where reason is left free to combat it. I know, indeed, that some honest men fear that a republican government can not be strong, that this Government is not strong enough; but would the honest patriot, in the full tide of successful experiment, abandon a government which has so far kept us free and firm on the theoretic and visionary fear that this Government, the world's best hope, may by possibility want energy to preserve itself? I trust not. I believe this, on the contrary, the strongest Government on earth. I believe it the only one where every man, at the call of the law, would fly to the standard of the law, and would meet invasions of the public order as his own personal concern. Sometimes it is said that man can not be trusted with the government of himself. Can he, then, be trusted with the government of others? Or have we found angels in the forms of kings to govern him? Let history answer this question.

Let us, then, with courage and confidence pursue our own Federal and Republican principles, our attachment to union and representative government. Kindly separated by nature and a wide ocean from the exterminating havoc of one quarter of the globe; too high-minded to endure the degradations of the others; possessing a chosen country, with room enough for our descendants to the thousandth and thousandth generation; entertaining a due sense of our equal right to the use of our own faculties, to the acquisitions of our own industry, to honor and confidence from our fellow-citizens, resulting not from birth, but from our actions and their sense of them; enlightened by a benign religion, professed, indeed, and practiced in various forms, yet all of them inculcating honesty, truth, temperance, gratitude, and the love of man; acknowledging and adoring an overruling Providence, which by all its dispensations proves that it delights in the happiness of man here and his greater happiness hereafter—with all these blessings, what more is necessary to make us a happy and a prosperous people? Still one thing more, fellow-citizens —a wise and frugal Government, which shall restrain men from injuring one another, shall leave them otherwise free to regulate their own pursuits of industry and improvement, and shall not take from the mouth of labor the bread it has earned. This is the sum of good government, and this is necessary to close the circle of our felicities.

About to enter, fellow-citizens, on the exercise of duties which comprehend everything dear and valuable to you, it is proper you should understand what I deem the essential principles of our Government, and consequently those which ought to shape its Administration. I will compress them within the narrowest compass they will bear, stating the general principle, but not all its limitations. Equal and exact justice to all men, of whatever state or persuasion, religious or political; peace, commerce, and honest friendship with all nations, entangling alliances with none; the support of the State governments in all their rights, as the most competent administrations for our domestic concerns and the surest bulwarks against antirepublican tendencies; the preservation of the General Government in its whole constitutional vigor, as the sheet anchor of our peace at home and safety abroad; a jealous care of the right of election by the people—a mild and safe corrective of abuses which are lopped by the sword of revolution where peaceable remedies are unprovided; absolute acquiescence in the decisions of the majority, the vital principle of republics, from which is no appeal but to force, the vital principle and immediate parent of despotism; a well-disciplined militia, our best reliance in peace and for the first moments of war, till regulars may relieve them; the supremacy of the civil over the military authority; economy in the public expense, that labor may be lightly burthened; the honest payment of our debts and sacred preservation of the public faith; encouragement of agriculture, and of commerce as its handmaid; the diffusion of information and arraignment of all abuses at the bar of the public reason; freedom of religion; freedom of the press, and freedom of person under the protection of the habeas corpus, and trial by juries impartially selected. These principles form the bright constellation which has gone before us and guided our steps through an age of revolution and reformation. The wisdom of our sages and blood of our heroes have been devoted to their attainment. They should be the creed of our political faith, the text of civic instruction, the touchstone by which to try the services of those we trust; and should we wander from them in moments of error or of alarm, let us hasten to retrace our steps and to regain the road which alone leads to peace, liberty, and safety.

I repair, then, fellow-citizens, to the post you have assigned me. With experience enough in subordinate offices to have seen the difficulties of this the greatest of all, I have learnt to expect that it will rarely fall to the lot of imperfect man to retire from this station with the reputation and the favor which bring him into it. Without pretentions to that high confidence you reposed in our first and greatest revolutionary character, whose preeminent services had entitled him to the first place in his country's love and destined for him the fairest page in the volume of faithful history, I ask so much confidence only as may give firmness and effect to the legal administration of your affairs. I shall often go wrong through defect of judgment. When right, I shall often be thought wrong by those whose positions will not command a view of the whole ground. I ask your indulgence for my own errors, which will never be intentional, and your support against the errors of others, who may condemn what they would not if seen in all its parts. The approbation implied by your suffrage is a great consolation to me for the past, and my future solicitude will be to retain the good opinion of those who have bestowed it in advance, to conciliate that of others by doing them all the good in my power, and to be instrumental to the happiness and freedom of all.

Relying, then, on the patronage of your good will, I advance with obedience to the work, ready to retire from it whenever you become sensible how much better choice it is in your power to make. And may that Infinite Power which rules the destinies of the universe lead our councils to what is best, and give them a favorable issue for your peace and prosperity.

# 21

*"Nor can we contemplate with satisfaction
either blot or mixture on that surface"*

The most far reaching and in many respects the most characteristic of Jefferson's acts as President was the purchase of Louisiana from France, April 30, 1803. Spain, pacific and feeble, had held Louisiana from 1762 to October, 1800, when she was prevailed upon secretly to restore it to Napoleon. "Till our population can be sufficiently advanced [in numbers] to gain it from them piece by piece," Jefferson had said of Spanish possession of the territory, it could not have been "in better hands." Not so with France. "The impetuosity of her temper, the energy and restlessness of her character," confronting ourselves, "enterprising and energetic as any nation on earth," renders it "impossible that France and the U.S. can continue long friends when they meet in so irritable a position."

In April, 1802, when the secrecy of the transfer of Louisiana had been entirely dispelled, Jefferson, in an effort to reduce the points of friction with France, instructed Robert R. Livingston, the United States Minister there, to sound out Napoleon on ceding at least the island of New Orleans, so essential to American Mississippi River traffic, and the adjoining Floridas, which he mistakenly believed Spain had also yielded. With these instructions he sent a stern warning to be conveyed by Livingston, that "the day France takes possession of N. Orleans . . . we must marry ourselves to the British fleet and nation." Livingston's soundings on New Orleans got nowhere; and when, in October, 1802, the Spanish official still in charge there closed the port and in effect the Mississippi itself to American vessels, American frontiersmen prepared to fight.

As a "visible measure" to help quiet the frontier, Jefferson, in January, 1803, dispatched James Monroe, with a purse of $2 million voted by Congress, to assist Livingston in his negotiations. By the time Monroe reached France in mid-April, Napoleon had become so heavily occupied with preparations for the resumption of the wars in Europe, which in fact began again in May, that he ordered Talleyrand to sound out Livingston now on buying not only New Orleans but the whole of Louisiana. On April 30, Livingston and Monroe grasped the "noble bargain." In October, in a special session called by Jefferson, the Senate, after heated debate, approved the purchase treaty; and the House, also sharply divided on the issue, appropriated the purchase money, approximately

$15 million. "The territory acquired," wrote the elated President, "as it includes all the waters of the Missouri & Mississippi, has more than doubled the area of the U.S. and the new part is not inferior to the old in soil, climate, productions, & important communications."

In August, 1803, in preparation for the meeting of Congress in October, Jefferson wrote a letter to his friend, John Dickinson, in which he examined the constitutionality, boundaries and future use of the princely acquisition. In explanation of this letter, Jefferson said that "the subject being new, it is advantageous to interchange ideas on it and to get our notions all corrected before we are obliged to act on them." But the subject of Louisiana could have been new to Jefferson in August, 1803, only in the sense of the suddenness and the scale of the windfall.

During all the years of Spanish occupation, the limitless West—and Canada, and Mexico, and the southern hemisphere, Spanish, British, Portuguese, Indian, no matter whose—licked at Jefferson's ambition as sedulously as at any speculator's, but not for gain. This veritable universe was to encompass a society as open in spirit as it would be broad in expanse. Jefferson called it his "empire of liberty," a phrase he first used in December, 1780, when as Governor of Virginia he urged Colonel George Rogers Clark to hold at all cost the fertile Illinois country "against the dangerous extension of the British Province of Canada." Here, and infinitely beyond, would be seated men "habituated to think for themselves," American yeomen, in short, who would pursue the godly work of agriculture, with "commerce as its handmaid," and "domestic manufactures" to supply essentials from spinning wheel, loom, mill, kiln, and forge. In his land ordinance of 1785 (see p. 71), Jefferson had set forth how this seating should take place to forestall the speculator who would himself forestall the yeoman pioneer. In his ordinance of the year before on the government of the territory thus settled, he had prescribed how it might then enter the Union progressively, as states "on an equal footing with the . . . original states," a prescription followed in essence in the great Ordinance of 1787 (see Document No. 15, above).

And Jefferson had indeed done much more. In 1786 and again in 1792 he had given his blessing to two breathtaking schemes, the first to explore the farthermost western country by means of an approach across the Bering Straits from Siberia, the second to "cross the Stony Mountains" from the east and "descend down the nearest river to the Pacific." Both of these schemes failed. In February, 1803, however, by stretching the commerce clause to "place the principal object within the constitutional powers and care of Congress," Jefferson was able to report that "I have at length succeeded in procuring an essay to be made of exploring the Missouri & whatever river heading with that, runs into the western ocean. Congress by a secret authority enables me to do it." Such was the initiation of the Lewis and Clark expedition which, leaving the vicinity of St. Louis in the spring of 1804, came upon the Columbia River in

October, 1805, and on November 7, as Clark recorded in his Journal, reached "this great Pacific Ocean which we been so long anxious to See."

Spurred on rather than satiated by the acquisition of Louisiana and the success of Lewis and Clark, Jefferson thereafter wrung appropriation after appropriation from a laggard Congress to enlarge the breadth and the knowledge of the empire of liberty. "I know that the acquisition of Louisiana has been disapproved by some," he said in 1805 in his second inaugural address,

> from a candid apprehension that the enlargement of our territory would endanger its union. But who can limit the extent to which the federative principle may operate effectively? The larger our association the less will it be shaken by local passions; and in any view is it not better that the opposite bank of the Mississippi should be settled by our own brethren and children than by strangers of another family?

Items "a" and "b," below, disclose Jefferson's thinking during his first year as President on America's role in the world, and the West's role in America, once "just and solid republican government" had taken hold. Such government, he writes in item "a," but two days after his first inauguration, "is of all others the most energetic," and will make the United States "a standing monument and example for the aim and imitation of the people of other countries." In item "b," November 24, 1801, the Great West—that is to say, the limitless frontier generally—is seen as the guarantor of the kind of society that alone could support such government. It will come as a shock to find Jefferson's most expansive hopes to "cover the whole northern, if not the southern continent, with a people speaking the same language, governed in similar forms, & by similar laws," expressed in this item in terms of keeping Negroes out: "nor can we contemplate with satisfaction either blot or mixture on that surface." Nor, as the following items show, were red men much more warmly welcomed. Item "c" presents Jefferson's confidential message to Congress proposing the Lewis and Clark expedition, January 18, 1803. It is followed, in item "d," by Jefferson's comprehensive instructions on New Orleans to Robert R. Livingston in France, April 18, 1802; and in item "e," by Jefferson's letter to John Dickinson, August 9, 1803, on the immeasurable value of the Louisiana Purchase as justifying his decision to "rely on the nation to sanction an act done for its great good, without its previous authority."

1801-1803

# The Louisiana Purchase

# in the Empire of Liberty

(a)   "A *standing monument and example for . . . people of other countries*"
(Thomas Jefferson to John Dickinson, March 6, 1801)

DEAR SIR,— . . . The storm through which we have passed, has been tremendous indeed. The tough sides of our Argosy have been thoroughly tried. Her strength has stood the waves into which she was steered, with a view to sink her. We shall put her on her republican tack, and she will now show by the beauty of her motion the skill of her builders. . . .

A just and solid republican government maintained here, will be a standing monument and example for the aim and imitation of the people of other countries; and I join with you in the hope and belief that they will see, from our example, that a free government is of all others the most energetic; that the inquiry which has been excited among the mass of mankind by our revolution and its consequences, will ameliorate the condition of man over a great portion of the globe. What a satisfaction have we in the contemplation of the benevolent effects of our efforts, compared with those of the leaders on the other side, who have discountenanced all advances in science as dangerous innovations, have endeavored to render philosophy and republicanism terms of reproach, to persuade us that man cannot be governed but by the rod, etc. I shall have the happiness of living and dying in the contrary hope.

(b)   "*Nor can we contemplate . . . either blot or mixture on that surface*"
(Thomas Jefferson to James Monroe, November 24, 1801) *

DEAR SIR; I had not been unmindful of your letter of June 15, covering a resolution of the House of Representatives of Virginia. . . . The importance of the subject, and the belief that it gave us time for consideration till the next meeting of the Legislature, have induced me to defer the answer to this date. You will perceive that some circumstances connected with the subject, & necessarily presenting themselves to view, would be improper but for yours' & the legislative ear. Their publication might have an ill effect in more than

* One of the circumstances that deterred Napoleon from ever actually taking possession of Louisiana, which he had hoped to use as a granary for French West Indian sugar plantations, was the slave revolt led by Toussaint L'Ouverture in San Domingo from 1794 to its successful conclusion ten years later. Knowledge of Toussaint's uprising had created much unrest among American Negroes, and in particular had inspired perhaps a thousand Virginia slaves in the vicinity of Richmond, led by the slave Gabriel, to plan a revolt of their own which failed in the summer of 1800. Twenty to thirty Negroes were executed for their part in this misadventure. Governor Monroe's concern for the rest had elicited his letter to Jefferson to which Jefferson here replies.

one quarter. In conndence of attention to this, I shall indulge greater freedom in writing.

Common malefactors, I presume, make no part of the object of that resolution. . . . Conspiracy, insurgency, treason, rebellion, among that description of persons who brought on us the alarm, and on themselves the tragedy, of 1800, were doubtless within the view of every one. . . .

The idea seems to be to provide for these people by a purchase of lands; and it is asked whether such a purchase can be made of the U S in their western territory? A very great extent of country, north of the Ohio, has been laid off into townships, and is now at market, according to the provisions of the acts of Congress, with which you are acquainted. There is nothing which would restrain the State of Virginia either in the purchase or the application of these lands; but a purchase, by the acre, might perhaps be a more expensive provision than the H of Representatives contemplated. Questions would also arise whether the establishment of such a colony within our limits, and to become a part of our union, would be desirable to the State of Virginia itself, or to the other States— especially those who would be in its vicinity?

Could we procure lands beyond the limits of the U S to form a receptacle for these people? . . . It is hardly to be believed that either Great Britain or the Indian proprietors . . . on the north-

em boundary . . . have so disinterested a regard for us, as to be willing to relieve us, by receiving such a colony themselves; and as much to be doubted whether that race of men could long exist in so rigorous a climate. On our western & southern frontiers, Spain holds an immense country, the occupancy of which, however, is in the Indian natives, except a few insolated spots possessed by Spanish subjects. It is very questionable, indeed, whether the Indians would sell? whether Spain would be willing to receive these people? and nearly certain that she would not alienate the sovereignty. The same question to ourselves would recur here also, as did in the first case: should we be willing to have such a colony in contact with us? However our present interests may restrain us within our own limits, it is impossible not to look forward to distant times, when our rapid multiplication will expand itself beyond those limits, & cover the whole northern, if not the southern continent, with a people speaking the same language, governed in similar forms, & by similar laws; nor can we contemplate with satisfaction either blot or mixture on that surface. . . .

The West Indies offer a more probable & practicable retreat for them. Inhabited already by a people of their own race & color; climates congenial with their natural constitution; insulated from the other descriptions of men; nature seems to have formed these islands to become the receptacle of the blacks transplanted into this hemisphere. Whether we could obtain from the European sovereigns of those islands leave to send thither the persons under consideration, I cannot say; but I think it more probable than the former propositions, because of their being already inhabited more or less by the same race. The most promising portion of them is the island of St. Domingo, where the blacks are established into a sovereignty *de facto*, & have organized themselves under regular laws & government. I should conjecture that their

---

In a later letter to Rufus King, United States Minister to Great Britain, July 13, 1802, Jefferson sought British cooperation in settling the rebellious slaves in Sierre Leone, in Africa. "It is material to observe," he wrote King, "that they are not felons, or common malefactors, but persons guilty of what the safety of society, under actual circumstances, obliges us to treat as a crime, but which their feelings may represent in a far different shape. They are such as will be a valuable acquisition to the settlement already existing there and well calculated to cooperate in the plan of civilization."

present ruler might be willing, on many considerations, to receive even that description which would be exiled for acts deemed criminal by us, but meritorious, perhaps, by him. The possibility that these exiles might stimulate & conduct vindicative or predatory descents on our coasts, & facilitate concert with their brethren remaining here, looks to a state of things between that island & us not probable on a contemplation of our relative strength, and of the disproportion daily growing; and it is overweighed by the humanity of the measures proposed, & the advantages of disembarrassing ourselves of such dangerous characters. Africa would offer a last & undoubted resort, if all others more desirable should fail us.

### (c)　Thomas Jefferson's Confidential Message to Congress on the Lewis and Clark Expedition, January 18, 1803

*Gentlemen of the Senate, and of the House of Representatives:* The Indian tribes residing within the limits of the United States, have, for a considerable time, been growing more and more uneasy at the constant diminution of the territory they occupy, although effected by their own voluntary sales: and the policy has long been gaining strength with them, of refusing absolutely all further sale, on any conditions; . . .

In order peaceably to counteract this policy of theirs, and to provide an extension of territory which the rapid increase of our numbers will call for, two measures are deemed expedient. First: to encourage them to abandon hunting, to apply to the raising stock, to agriculture and domestic manufacture, and thereby prove to themselves that less land and labor will maintain them in this, better than in their former mode of living. The extensive forests necessary in the hunting life, will then become useless, and they will see advantage in exchanging them for the means of improving their farms, and of increasing their domestic comforts. Secondly: to multiply trading houses among them and place within their reach those things which will contribute more to their domestic comfort, than the possession of extensive, but uncultivated wilds. Experience and reflection will develop to them the wisdom of exchanging what they can spare and we want, for what we can spare and they want. In leading them to agriculture, to manufactures, and civilization; in bringing together their and our settlements, and in preparing them ultimately to participate in the benefits of our governments, I trust and believe we are acting for their greatest good. . . .

While the extension of the public commerce among the Indian tribes, may deprive of that source of profit such of our citizens as are engaged in it, it might be worthy the attention of Congress, in their care of individual as well of the general interest, to point, in another direction, the enterprise of these citizens, as profitably for themselves, and more usefully for the public.

The river Missouri, and the Indians inhabiting it, are not as well known as is rendered desirable by their connexion with the Mississippi, and consequently with us. It is, however, understood, that the country on that river is inhabited by numerous tribes, who furnish great supplies of furs and peltry to the trade of another nation, carried on in a high latitude, through an infinite number of portages and lakes, shut up by ice through a long season. The commerce on that line could bear no competition with that of the Missouri, traversing a moderate climate, offering according to the best accounts, a continued navigation from its source, and possibly with a single portage, from the Western Ocean, and finding to the Atlantic a choice of channels through the Illinois or Wabash, the lakes and Hudson, through the Ohio and Susquehanna, or Potomac or James rivers, and through the Tennessee and Savannah, rivers.

An intelligent officer, with ten or twelve chosen men, fit for the enterprise, and willing to undertake it, taken from our posts, where they may be spared without inconvenience, might explore the whole line, even to the Western Ocean, have conferences with the natives on the subject of commercial intercourse, get admission among them for our traders, as others are admitted, agree on convenient deposits for an interchange of articles, and return with the information acquired, in the course of two summers. Their arms and accoutrements, some instruments of observation, and light and cheap presents for the Indians, would be all the apparatus they could carry, and with an expectation of a soldier's portion of land on their return, would constitute the whole expense. Their pay would be going on, whether here or there. While other civilized nations have encountered great expense to enlarge the boundaries of knowledge by undertaking voyages of discovery, and for other literary purposes, in various parts and directions, our nation seems to owe to the same object, as well as to its own interests, to explore this, the only line of easy communication across the continent, and so directly traversing our own part of it.

The interests of commerce place the principal object within the constitutional powers and care of Congress, and that it should incidentally advance the geographical knowledge of our own continent, cannot be but an additional gratification. The nation claiming the territory, regarding this as a literary pursuit, which it is in the habit of permitting within its dominions, would not be disposed to view it with jealousy, even if the expiring state of its interests there did not render it a matter of indifference. The appropriation of two thousand five hundred dollars, 'for the purpose of extending the external commerce of the United States,' while understood and considered by the Executive as giving the legislative sanction, would cover the undertaking from notice, and prevent the obstructions which interested individuals might otherwise previously prepare in its way.

(d) *Thomas Jefferson to Robert R. Livingston,*
*United States Minister to France,*
*on French possession of Louisiana, April 18, 1802*

DEAR SIR— . . . The cession of Louisiana and the Floridas by Spain to France works most sorely on the U. S. . . . It compleatly reverses all the political relations of the U. S. and will form a new epoch in our political course. Of all nations of any consideration France is the one which hitherto has offered the fewest points on which we could have any conflict of right, and the most points of a communion of interests. From these causes we have ever looked to her as our *natural friend.* . . .

There is on the globe one single spot, the possessor of which is our natural and habitual enemy. It is New Orleans, through which the produce of three-eighths of our territory must pass to market, and from its fertility it will ere long yield more than half of our whole produce and contain more than half our inhabitants. France placing herself in that door assumes to us the attitude of defiance. Spain might have retained it quietly for years. Her pacific dispositions, her feeble state, would induce her to increase our facilities there, so that her possession of the place would be hardly felt by us, and it would not perhaps be very long before some circumstance might arise which might make the cession of it to us the price of something of more worth to her. Not so can it ever be in the hands of France. The impetuosity of her temper, the energy and restlessness of her character, placed in a point of eternal friction with us, and our character, which though quiet, and loving peace and the pursuit of wealth, is high-minded, despising wealth in competition with insult or injury, enterprising and energetic as any nation on earth, these circumstances render it impossible that France and the U. S. can continue long friends when they meet in so irritable a position. . . .

The day that France takes possession of N. Orleans . . . seals the union of two nations who in conjunction can maintain exclusive possession of the ocean. From that moment we must marry ourselves to the British fleet and nation. . . . In that case France will have held possession of New Orleans during the interval of a peace, long or short, at the end of which it will be wrested from her. Will this short-lived possession have been an equivalent to her for the transfer of such a weight into the scale of her enemy? Will not the amalgamation of a young, thriving nation continue to that enemy the health and force which are at present so evidently on the decline? And will a few years possession of N. Orleans add equally to the strength of France? She may say she needs Louisiana for the supply of her West Indies. She does not need it in time of peace. And in war she could not depend on them because they would be so easily intercepted. I should suppose that all these considerations might in some proper

form be brought into view of the government of France. . . .

If France considers Louisiana however as indispensable for her views she might perhaps be willing to look about for arrangements which might reconcile it to our interests. If anything could do this it would be the ceding to us the island of New Orleans and the Floridas. This would certainly in a great degree remove the causes of jarring and irritation between us, and perhaps for such a length of time as might produce other means of making the measure permanently conciliatory to our interests and friendships. It would at any rate relieve us from the necessity of taking immediate measures for countervailing such an operation by arrangements in another quarter. Still we should consider N. Orleans and the Floridas as equivalent for the risk of a quarrel with France produced by her vicinage.

I have no doubt you have urged these considerations on every proper occasion with the government where you are. They are such as must have effect if you can find the means of producing thorough reflection on them by that government. The idea here is that the troops sent to St. Domingo, were to proceed to Louisiana after finishing their work in that island. If this were the arrangement, it will give you time to return again and again to the charge, for the conquest of St. Domingo will not be a short work.

(e)   *"We must . . . rely on the nation to sanction an act
done for its great good, without its previous authority"*
(Thomas Jefferson to John Dickinson on the Louisiana purchase, August 9, 1803)

DEAR SIR,—Your friendly favor of the 1st inst. is received with that welcome which always accompanies the approbation of the wise & good. The acquisition of New Orleans would of itself have been a great thing, as it would have ensured to our western brethren the means of exporting their produce: but that of Louisiana is in-

appreciable, because, giving us the sole dominion of the Mississippi, it excludes those bickerings with foreign powers, which we know of a certainty would have put us at war with France immediately: and it secures to us the course of a peaceable nation.

The *unquestioned* bounds of Louisiana are the Iberville & Mississippi on the east, the Mexicana, or the Highlands east of it, on the west; then from the head of the Mexicana gaining the highlands which include the waters of the Mississippi, and following those highlands round the head springs of the western waters of the Mississippi to its source where we join the English or perhaps to the Lake of the Woods. This may be considered as a triangle, one leg of which is the length of the Missouri, the other of the Mississippi, and the hypothenuse running from the source of the Missouri to the mouth of the Mississippi. I should be averse to exchanging any part of this for the Floridas, because it would let Spain into the Mississippi on the principle of natural right, we have always urged & are now urging to her, that a nation inhabiting the upper part of a stream has a right of innocent passage down that stream to the ocean; and because the Floridas will fall to us peaceably the first war Spain is engaged in.

We have some pretensions to extend the western territory of Louisiana to the Rio Norte, or Bravo; and still stronger the eastern boundary to the Rio Perdido between the rivers Mobile & Pensacola. These last are so strong that France had not relinquished them & our negotiator expressly declared we should claim them, by properly availing ourselves of these with offers of a price, and our peace, we shall get the Floridas in good time. But in the meantime we shall enter on the exercise of the right of passing down all the rivers which rising in our territory, run thro' the Floridas. Spain will not oppose it by force.

But there is a difficulty in this acquisition which presents a handle to the malcontents among us, though they have not yet discovered it. Our confederation is certainly confined to the limits established by the revolution. The general government has no powers but such as the constitution has given it; and it has not given it a power of holding foreign territory, & still less of incorporating it into the Union. An amendment of the Constitution seems necessary for this. In the meantime we must ratify & pay our money, as we have treated, for a thing beyond the constitution, and rely on the nation to sanction an act done for its great good, without its previous authority. With respect to the disposal of the country, we must take the island of New Orleans and west side of the river as high up as Point Coupee, containing nearly the whole inhabitants, say about 50,000, and erect it into a state or annex it to the Mississippi territory: and shut up all the rest from settlement for a long time to come, endeavoring to exchange some of the country there unoccupied by Indians for the lands held by the Indians on this side the Mississippi, who will be glad to cede us their country here for an equivalent there: and we may sell out our lands here & pay the whole debt contracted before it comes due. . . . I have indulged myself in these details because the subject being new, it is advantageous to interchange ideas on it and to get our notions all corrected before we are obliged to act on them. In this idea I receive & shall receive with pleasure anything which may occur to you.

## 22

*"It is emphatically the province and duty of
the judicial department to say what the law is"*

In November, 1790, when the Virginia Legislature resolved that Hamilton's funding system "demands the marked disapproval of the General Government," and that assumption of state debts in particular was "repugnant to the Constitution of the United States," Hamilton himself asked John Jay, the first Chief Justice of the Supreme Court: "Ought not the collective weight of the different parts of the Government to be employed in exploding the principles" the Virginians espoused? Jay replied coldly that, whatever other parts of the government might do, the judiciary would respect the constitutional provisions limiting its own pronouncements to "cases" properly brought before it.

Jay's stand, with certain recent technical exceptions, has been uniformly followed ever since. Jay, his five associates on the Supreme Court, and most of their successors during the Court's first decade, were even stricter than this. In the few cases that did come before them, they wrote decisions that stuck closely to the facts at issue, abhorring political and even legal *obiter dicta*. Moreover, although a majority of the Court was required in making decisions, each justice wrote his own opinion to support his vote, and no one spoke authoritatively for the Court itself or undertook to give consistency to the Court's reasoning and conclusions.

Such modesty and maundering was intolerable to John Marshall, and soon after he took the oath of office as Chief Justice on February 4, 1801, the Court underwent a sea change. The transfer of political leadership at this time from the Federalists to the Republicans no doubt strengthened the Federalist Marshall's determination to plant a powerful judiciary athwart the path of the "turbulent democracy" he saw on the threshold. But Marshall had leveled his sights long before this on his two principal targets, state rights and legislative autonomy. In the prime of life at forty-five on donning the judicial robes, Marshall was a political veteran who had long since learned from their sorry performance during the Revolution to scorn the pretensions of the states to sovereignty. The pretensions of legislatures to omnipotence, in turn, he had dealt with as early as 1788 when defending the judiciary article of the Constitution at the Virginia ratifying convention:

If they were to make a law not warranted by any of the powers enumerated, it would be considered by the judges as an infringement of the Constitution which they are to guard. They would not consider such a law as coming under their jurisdiction. They would declare it void.

On becoming Chief Justice, Marshall found in President Jefferson, his cousin whom he hated, a worthy antagonist who as recently as 1798 had championed state rights in the Kentucky Resolutions (Document No. 19, above). Jefferson would also soon prod his followers in the Congress to assert their independence of the judiciary where, as he said, the Federalists, having been repudiated at the polls, had "retired . . . as a stronghold . . . and from that battery all the works of Republicanism are to be beaten down and erased." Thus was the issue joined.

Jefferson and the Republican Congress enjoyed the initial advantage of being able to speak and legislate at will. In his first annual message to Congress in December, 1801, Jefferson had simply stated that "the judiciary system of the United States, and especially that portion of it recently erected, will of course present itself to the contemplation of Congress." That portion of it "recently erected" was the large number of new federal judgeships which the lame duck Federalists had set up in the Judiciary Act of February, 1801, and which President Adams had hastily filled with party-proven men. By March, 1802, Congress's contemplation of this measure had hatched its repeal, and the new judges were unceremoniously dislodged.

Marshall viewed these goings on with misgiving, but in keeping with Jay's sound dictum, he had to find the appropriate case for his riposte. In vain he tried to get some of the dislodged judges to sue for their jobs on the ground that they had been appointed in effect for life and were not removable by the legislature or any one else except for cause. When this and other stratagems failed, Marshall turned in desperation to the case of William Marbury which had been put over from December, 1801, to the 1803 term of his Court.

Marbury, among the last of Adams's "midnight appointments," had been named to a five-year term as justice of the peace in the District of Columbia, but his commission had not been delivered to him before Jefferson took office. Jefferson ordered Marbury's commission withheld; and the appointee, under the terms of the Judiciary Act of 1789 giving the Supreme Court original jurisdiction in such matters, promptly pressed for a writ of mandamus requiring Secretary of State Madison (whose duty it then was) to install him. No case could have been more inconspicuous in substance, but Marshall by sheer bravado bent it to his purpose. Moreover, when he delivered his opinion on February 24, 1803, he explicitly spoke for a unanimous Court which he had bent to his will.

The burden of the Court's finding was that Marbury had a right to his job, that he merited the writ by which he sought to obtain it, but that the Supreme Court could not issue the writ because the provision in the Judiciary Act of

1789 granting it the power to do so was unconstitutional. In 1792, a United States circuit court in Pennsylvania, without fanfare, had declared a federal statute unconstitutional, so Marshall's decision did not set a precedent. What made the decision memorable was Marshall's direct confrontation of the administration with grand *ex cathedra* proclamations which have stood the test of time: that the Constitution was law, to be painstakingly consulted in *cases* and enforced by *courts*; that it was the *supreme law* to which even federal legislation must conform if it was to stand; and that in conflicts over the meaning of the Constitution or the validity of legislation, "it is emphatically the province and duty of the judicial department"—and not of the states or the popularly elected legislature—"to say what the law is." Marshall's decision in *Marbury* v. *Madison* is presented in part below, as item "a."

So great was Marshall's anxiety by 1803 to proclaim the supremacy of the courts, and to brook no further delay in doing so, that he was driven, in *Marbury* v. *Madison,* to employ a case which required for his purposes the strictest interpretation of the Constitution and especially of legislative powers under it. So strong was Marshall's leaning on most other occasions toward the broadest interpretation of the Constitution and the widest legislative latitude, that this point is often neglected.

Marshall's earliest opportunity to expand on the breadth of national legislative power, and on the limitations of the legislative powers of the states, came in 1819 in the case of *McCulloch* v. *Maryland.* This case arose from the efforts of the state of Maryland, prompted by the state bankers, to tax out of existence the Baltimore branch of the Second Bank of the United States, whose competition they feared. In defense of the state tax, Maryland's attorneys reopened the issue of the constitutionality of national incorporation acts, and particularly of the incorporation of banks (see Document No. 17, above). But, said Marshall, national corporations are only means to legitimate national ends; and he added his famous dictum: "Let the end be legitimate, let it be within the scope of the constitution, and all means which are appropriate, which are plainly adopted to that end, which are not prohibited, but consist with the letter and spirit of the constitution, are constitutional." Marshall's decision in *McCulloch* v. *Maryland* is presented in part below as item "b."

It is often said that while the Republicans dominated national politics for more than a generation following Jefferson's election in 1800, Marshall, from his empyrean in the Supreme Court where he reigned for thirty-four years, was handing down Federalist law. It is far closer to the truth to say that, once his war with Jefferson himself had ended, Marshall gave all his great abilities to extending national power, just as Jefferson had given his to extending the national domain. Both were expansionists; the work of one complemented that of the other; together they afforded Americans of the oncoming Jacksonian era the unrivaled space and legal spaciousness within which, unencumbered by local monopolists, to seek out their individual destinies.

# John Marshall and the Constitution

## (a)  *Marbury v. Madison, February 24, 1803*

OPINION OF THE COURT

At the last term . . . a rule was granted in this case requiring the secretary of state to show cause why a mandamus should not issue, directing him to deliver to William Marbury his commission as a justice of the peace for the county of Washington, in the District of Columbia.

No cause has been shown, and the present motion is for a mandamus. . . .

The first object of enquiry is, Has the applicant a right to the commission he demands? . . .

Mr. Marbury, . . . since his commission was signed by the President, and sealed by the secretary of state, was appointed; and as the law creating the office, gave the officer a right to hold for five years, independent of the executive, the appointment was no revocable; but vested in the officer legal rights, which are protected by the laws of his country.

To withhold his commission, therefore, is an act deemed by the court not warranted by law, but violative of a vested legal right.

2d. This brings us to the second enquiry: which is, if he has a right, and that right has been violated, do the laws of his country afford him a remedy?

The very essence of civil liberty certainly consists in the right of every individual to claim the protection of the laws, whenever he receives an injury. One of the first duties of government is to afford that protection. . . . It is, then, the opinion of the Court that . . . refusal to deliver [the commission] is a plain violation . . . for which the laws of his country afford him a remedy. . . .

It remains to be inquired whether, 3d. He is entitled to the remedy for which he applies. This depends on, 1st. The nature of the writ applied for, and 2d., The power of this court.

1st. The nature of the writ. . . . To render the mandamus a proper remedy, the officer to whom it is to be directed, must be one to whom, on legal principles, such writ may be directed; and the person applying for it must be without any other specific and legal remedy. . . . Where the head of a department acts in a case, in which executive discretion is to be exercised; in which he is the mere organ of executive will; it is again repeated, that any application to a court to control, in any respect, his conduct would be rejected without hesitation.

But where he is directed by law to do a certain act affecting the absolute rights of individuals, in the performance of which he is not placed under the particular direction of the President, . . . it is not perceived on what ground the courts of the country are further excused from the duty of giving judgement that right be done to an injured individual, than if the same services were to be performed by a person not the head of a department. . . . [Since] the applicant has a right to the office or to nothing, . . . this, then, is a plain case for a mandamus, either to deliver the commission, or a copy of it from the record; and it only remains to be inquired,

Whether it can issue from this court.

The act to establish the judicial courts of the United States authorizes the Supreme Court "to issue writs of mandamus, in cases warranted by the principles and usages of law, to any courts appointed, or persons holding office, under the authority of the United States."

The secretary of state, being a person holding an office under the authority of the United States is precisely within the letter of the description; and if this court is not authorized to issue a writ of mandamus to such an officer, it must be because the law is unconstitutional, and therefore absolutely incapable of conferring the authority and assigning the duties which its words purport to confer and assign.

The constitution vests the whole judicial power of the United States in one supreme court, and such inferior courts as congress shall, from time to time, ordain and establish. This power is expressly extended to all cases arising under the laws of the United States; and consequently, in some form, may be exercised over the present case; because the right claimed is given by a law of the United States.

In the distribution of this power it is declared, that "the supreme court shall have original jurisdiction in all cases affecting ambassadors, other public ministers and consuls, and those in which a state shall be a party. In all other cases, the supreme court shall have appellate jurisdiction.". . .

If it had been intended to leave it in the discretion of the legislature to apportion the judicial power between the supreme and inferior courts according to the will of that body, it would certainly have been useless to have proceeded further than to have defined the judicial power, and the tribunals in which it should be vested. The subsequent part of the section is mere surplusage, is entirely without meaning, if such is to be the construction. If congress remains at liberty to give this court appellate jurisdiction, where the constitution has declared their juris-diction shall be original; and original jurisdiction where the constitution has declared it shall be appellate; the distribution of jurisdiction, made in the constitution, is form without substance.

Affirmative words are often, in their operation, negative of other objects than those affirmed; and in this case, a negative or exclusive sense must be given to them or they have no operation at all. . . .

The authority, therefore, given to the supreme court, by the act establishing the judicial courts of the United States, to issue writs of mandamus to public officers, appears not to be warranted by the constitution; and it becomes necessary to inquire whether a jurisdiction so conferred can be exercised.

The question whether an act repugnant to the constitution can become the law of the land, is a question deeply interesting to the United States; but, happily not of an intricacy proportioned to its interest. It seems only necessary to recognize certain principles supposed to have been long and well established, to decide it.

That the people have an original right to establish for their future government such principles as, in their opinion, shall most conduce to their own happiness, is the basis on which the whole American fabric has been erected. The exercise of this original right is a very great exertion, nor can it nor ought it to be frequently repeated. The principles therefore so established are deemed fundamental. And as the authority from which they proceed is supreme and can seldom act, they are designed to be permanent.

This original and supreme will organizes the government, and assigns to different departments their respective powers. It may either stop here or establish certain limits not to be transcended by those departments.

The government of the United States is of the latter description. The powers of the legislature are defined and limited; and that those limits may not be mistaken or forgotten, the constitution is written. . . . The constitution is either a superior paramount law, unchangeable by ordinary means, or it is on a level with ordinary legislative acts, and, like other acts, is alterable when the legislature shall please to alter it. If the former part of the alternative be true, then a legislative act contrary to the constitution is not law; if the latter part be true, then written constitutions are absurd attempts, on the part of the people, to limit a power in its own nature illimitable.

Certainly all those who have framed written constitutions contemplate them as forming the fundamental and paramount law of the nation, and, consequently, the theory of every such government must be, that an act of the legislature repugnant to the Constitution, is void. . . .

If an act of the legislature repugnant to the constitution is void, does it, notwithstanding its invalidity, bind the courts and oblige them to give it effect? Or, in other words, though it be not law, does it constitute a rule as operative as if it was a law? This would be to overthrow in fact what was established in theory, and would seem, at first view, an absurdity too gross to be insisted on. It shall, however, receive a more attentive consideration.

It is emphatically the province and duty of the judicial department to say what the law is. Those who apply the rule to particular cases must of necessity expound and interpret that rule. If two laws conflict with each other, the courts must decide on the operation of each.

So if a law be in opposition to the constitution; if both the law and the constitution apply to a particular case, so that the court must either decide that case conformably to the law, disregarding the constitution, or conformably to the constitution, disregarding the law, the court must determine which of these conflicting rules governs the case. This is of the very essence of judicial duty.

If, then, the courts are to regard the constitution, and the constitution is superior to any ordinary act of the legislature, the constitution, and not such ordinary act, must govern the case to which they both apply.

Those, then, who controvert the principle that the constitution is to be considered in court as a paramount law, are reduced to the necessary of maintaining that courts must close their eyes on the constitution and see only the law.

This doctrine would subvert the very foundation of all written constitutions. It would declare that an act which, according to the principles and theory of our government, is entirely void, is yet, in practice, completely obligatory. It would declare that if the legislature shall do what is expressly forbidden, such act, notwithstanding the express prohibition, is in reality effectual. It would be giving to the legislature a practical and real omnipotence with the same breath which professes to restrict their powers within narrow limits. It is prescribing limits and declaring that those limits may be passed at pleasure.

That it thus reduces to nothing what we have deemed the greatest improvement on political institutions, a written constitution, would of itself be sufficient, in America, where written constitutions have been viewed with so much reverence, for rejecting the construction. But the peculiar expressions of the constitution of the United States furnish additional arguments in favor of its rejection.

The judicial power of the United States is extended to all cases arising under the constitution.

Could it be the intention of those who gave this power to say that in using it the constitution should not be looked into? That a case arising under the constitution should be decided without examining the instrument under which it arises?

This is too extravagant to be maintained. . . .

It is also not entirely unworthy of observation, that in declaring what shall be the supreme law of the land, the constitution itself is first mentioned; and not the laws of the United States generally, but those only which shall be made in pursuance of the constitution, have that rank.

Thus, the particular phraseology of the constitution of the United States confirms and strengthens the principle,

supposed to be essential to all written constitutions, that a law repugnant to the constitution is void, and that courts, as well as other departments, are bound by that instrument.

[Mandamus denied because power to issue it is unconstitutional]

## (b)  McCulloch v. Maryland, March 6, 1819

MARSHALL, C.J.— . . . The first question made in this cause is, has Congress power to incorporate a bank? . . .

In discussing this question, the counsel for the State of Maryland have deemed it of some importance, in the construction of the constitution, to consider that instrument not as emanating from the people, but as the act of sovereign and independent States. The powers of the general government, it has been said, are delegated by the States, who alone are truly sovereign; and must be exercised in subordination to the States, who alone possess supreme dominion.

It would be difficult to sustain this proposition. The convention which framed the constitution was indeed elected by the State legislatures. But the instrument, when it came from their hands, was a mere proposal, without obligation, or pretensions to it. It was reported to the then existing Congress of the United States, with a request that it might "be submitted to a convention of Delegates, chosen in each State, by the people thereof, under the recommendation of its legislature, for their assent and ratification." This mode of proceeding was adopted; and by the Convention, by Congress, and by the State Legislatures, the instrument was submitted to the people. They acted upon it, in the only manner in which they can act safely, effectively, and wisely, on such a subject, by assembling in Convention. . . . From these Conventions the constitution derives its whole authority. The govern-

ment proceeds directly from the people; is "ordained and established" in the name of the people. . . . The assent of the States, in their sovereign capacity, is implied in calling a Convention, and thus submitting that instrument to the people. But the people were at perfect liberty to accept or reject it; and their act was final. It required not the affirmance, and could not be negatived, by the State governments. . . .

The government of the Union, then (whatever may be the influence of this fact on the case), is emphatically and truly a government of the people. In form and in substance it emanates from them, its powers are granted by them, and are to be exercised directly on them, and for their benefit.

This government is acknowledged by all to be one of enumerated powers. . . . But the question respecting the extent of the powers actually granted, is perpetually arising, and will probably continue to arise, as long as our system shall exist. In discussing these questions, the conflicting powers of the State and general governments must be brought into view, and the supremacy of their respective laws, when they are in opposition, must be settled.

If any one proposition could command the universal assent of mankind, we might expect it would be this: that the government of the Union, though limited in its powers, is supreme within its sphere of action. This would seem to result necessarily from its nature. It is the government of all; its powers are delegated by all; it represents all, and acts for all. . . . But this question is not left to mere reason: the people have, in express terms, decided it, by saying, "this constitution, and the laws of the United States, which shall be made in pursuance thereof," "shall be the supreme law of the land," and by requiring that the members of the State legislatures, and the officers of the executive and judicial departments of the States, shall take the oath of fidelity to it. . . .

Among the enumerated powers, we do not find that of establishing a bank or creating a corporation. But there is no phrase in the instrument which, like the articles of confederation, excludes incidental or implied powers; and which requires that everything granted shall be expressly and minutely described. . . . A constitution, to contain an accurate detail of all the subdivisions of which its great powers will admit, and of all the means by which they may be carried into execution, would partake of the prolixity of a legal code, and could scarcely be embraced by the human mind. It would probably never be understood by the public. Its nature, therefore, requires that only its great outlines should be marked, its impor-tant objects designated, and the minor ingredients which compose those objects be deduced from the nature of the objects themselves. . . .

Although, among the enumerated powers of government, we do not find the word "bank," or "incorporation," we find the great powers to lay and collect taxes; to borrow money; to regulate commerce; to declare and conduct a war; and to raise and support armies and navies. . . . A goverment, intrusted with such ample powers, on the due execution of which the happiness and prosperity of the nation so vitally depends, must also be intrusted with ample means for their execution. . . .

The creation of a corporation, it is said, appertains to sovereignty. This is admitted. But to what portion of sovereignty does it appertain? Does it belong to one more than to another? In America, the powers of sovereignty are divided between the government of the Union, and those of the States. They are each sovereign, with respect to the objects committed to it, and neither sovereign with respect to the objects committed to the other. . . . The power of creating a corporation, though appertaining to sovereignty, is not, like the power of making war, or levying taxes, or of regulating commerce, a great substantive and independent power, which cannot be implied as incidental to other powers, or used as a means of executing them. It is never the end for which other powers are exercised, but a means by which other objects are accomplished. . . . No suffi-cient reason is, therefore, perceived, why it may not pass as incidental to those powers which are expressly given, if it be a direct mode of executing them.

But the constitution of the United States has not left the right of Congress to employ the necessary means, for the execution of the powers conferred on the government, to general reasoning. To its enumeration of powers is added that of making "all laws which shall be necessary and proper, for carrying into execution the foregoing powers, and all other powers vested by this constitu-tion, in the government of the United States, or in any department thereof."

The counsel for the State of Mary-land have urged various arguments, to prove that this clause, though in terms a grant of power, is not so in effect; but is really restrictive of the general right, which might otherwise be im-plied, of selecting means of executing the enumerated powers. . . . But the argument on which most reliance is placed, is drawn from the peculiar lan-guage of this clause. . . . The word *"necessary"* is considered as controlling the whole sentence, and as limiting the right to pass laws for the execution of the granted powers, to such as are in-dispensable, and without which the power would be nugatory. . . . Is it true, that this is the sense in which the word *"necessary"* is always used? Does it always import an absolute physical necessity, so strong, that one thing, to which another may be termed necessary cannot exist without that other? We think it does not. . . . To employ the means necessary to an end, is generally understood as employing any means calculated to produce the end, and not as being confined to those single means, without which the end would be entirely unattainable. . . .

We think the sound construction of the constitution must allow to the national legislature that discretion, with respect to the means by which the powers it confers are to be carried into execution, which will enable that body to perform the high duties assigned to it, in the manner most beneficial to the people. Let the end be legitimate, let it be within the scope of the constitution, and all means which are appropriate, which are plainly adapted to that end, which are not prohibited, but consist with the letter and spirit of the constitution, are constitutional. . . .

If a corporation may be employed indiscriminately with other means to carry into execution the powers of the government, no particular reason can be assigned for excluding the use of a bank, if required for its fiscal operations. . . . After the most deliberate consideration, it is the unanimous and decided opinion of this court, that the act to incorporate the Bank of the United States is a law made in pursuance of the constitution, and is a part of the supreme law of the land. . . .

It being the opinion of the Court, that the act incorporating the bank is constitutional; and that the power of establishing a branch in the State of Maryland might be properly exercised by the bank itself, we proceed to inquire—whether the State of Maryland may, without violating the constitution, tax that branch?

That the power of taxation is one of vital importance; that it is retained by the States; that it is not abridged by the grant of a similar power to the government of the Union; that it is to be concurrently exercised by the two governments; are truths which have never been denied. But, such is the paramount character of the constitution that its capacity to withdraw any subject from the action of even this power, is admitted. The States are expressly forbidden to lay any duties on imports or exports, except what may be absolutely necessary for executing their inspection laws. If the obligation of this prohibition must be conceded—if it may restrain a state from the exercise of its taxing power on imports and exports, the same paramount character would seem to restrain, as it certainly may restrain, a state from such other exercise of this power, as is in its nature incompatible with, and repugnant to, the constitutional laws of the Union. A law, absolutely repugnant to another, as entirely repeals that other as if express terms of repeal were used.

On this ground the counsel for the bank place its claim to be exempted from the power of a State to tax its operations. There is no express provision for the case, but the claim has been sustained on a principle which so entirely pervades the constitution, is so intermixed with the materials which compose it, so interwoven with its web, so blended with its texture, as to be incapable of being separated from it, without rending it into shreds.

This great principle is, that the constitution and the laws made in pursuance thereof are supreme; that they control the constitution and laws of the respective States, and cannot be controlled by them. From this, which may be almost termed an axiom, other propositions are deduced as corollaries, on the truth or error of which, and on their application to this case, the cause has been supposed to depend. These are, 1. That a power to create implies a power to preserve. 2. That a power to destroy, if wielded by a different hand, is hostile to, and incompatible with, these powers to create and preserve. 3. That where this repugnancy exists, that authority which is supreme must control, not yield to that over which it is supreme. . . .

The power of Congress to create, and of course to continue, the bank, was the subject of the preceding part of this opinion; and is no longer to be considered as questionable.

That the power of taxing it by the States may be exercised so as to destroy it, is too obvious to be denied. . . . That the power to tax involves the power to destroy; that the power to destroy may defeat and render useless the power to create; that there is a plain repugnance, in conferring on one government a power to control the constitutional measures of another, which other, with respect to those very measures, is declared to be supreme over that which exerts the control, are propositions not to be denied.

If we apply the principle for which the State of Maryland contends, to the constitution generally, we shall find it capable of . . . arresting all the measures of the government, and of prostrating it at the foot of the States. . . .

If the States may tax one instrument, employed by the government in the execution of its powers, they may tax any and every other instrument. . . . They may tax all the means employed by the government, to an excess which would defeat all the ends of government. This was not intended by the American people. They did not design to make their government dependent on the States. . . .

The Court has bestowed on this subject its most deliberate consideration. The result is a conviction that the States have no power, by taxation or otherwise, to retard, impede, burden, or in any manner control, the operations of the constitutional laws enacted by Congress to carry into execution the powers vested in the general government. This is, we think, the unavoidable consequence of that supremacy which the constitution has declared. We are unanimously of opinion, that the law passed by the legislature of Maryland, imposing a tax on the Bank of the United States, is unconstitutional and void.

# 23

*"The American continents . . . are henceforth not to be considered as subjects for future colonization by any European powers"*

The systematic suppression of popular uprisings in Europe and the restoration of "legitimate" rulers to many thrones, following the end of the Napoleonic Wars in 1815, made all the clearer to Americans the growing differences between what they more and more frequently referred to as their "system"—free, republican, expansive—and the reactionary system of the Old World—orthodox, monarchist, repressive.

The main instrument of suppression in Europe was the Holy Alliance, promoted by Russia, Austria, and Prussia, but eventually subscribed to by the whole "concert of Europe," except Great Britain. When the Holy Alliance threatened to move against the liberals in Spain in 1822, both the British and the Americans believed that the Latin-American nations which had recently made good their independence of Spain (and Brazil, which had declared her independence of Portugal) were also in danger of invasion. As early as 1810 the British had been among the first to assist the Latin-American rebels, and in return had gained valuable commercial concessions once their freedom had been won. When France, as the instrument of the Holy Alliance, did invade Spain in the spring of 1823, George Canning, the British Foreign Secretary, "unofficially and confidentially" proposed to Richard Rush, the United States Minister in London, that their two countries announce to the world, for the ears of France, that "we conceive the recovery of the [American] Colonies by Spain to be hopeless," and that "we could not see any portion of them transferred to any other Power, with indifference."

President Monroe, on learning of Canning's proposal, promptly consulted Jefferson in Monticello; and both yearned to adopt it. Secretary of State John Quincy Adams, however, had other ideas, which prevailed. Having trod lightly on Spain until the acquisition of Florida was completed in 1821, Adams would now neither surrender United States expectations of further grand accessions of Spanish, or for that matter, of British territory in North America, nor permit Britain in the meantime to share the credit for sustaining the American system in the former Spanish provinces. Adams succinctly set down in his diary his thoughts on the first of these subjects arising from a Cabinet discussion as early as November 16, 1819. This short entry is presented here in item "a," below, as an illuminating introduction to the Monroe Doctrine, America's independent declaration on the future of the New World, which follows it in full.

The Monroe Doctrine was addressed as much to the Russians as to the western European powers. After their harrowing experience with Napoleon in 1812, the Russians kept their gaze fixed sharply on the West, but their expansive activities in the Far East did not lag. These gradually carried them across Bering Sea and Bering Strait to the North American mainland. In 1821, the Russian government announced that "the pursuits of commerce, whaling, and fishery, and of all other industry on all islands, posts, and gulfs, including the whole of the northwest coast of America, beginning from Behring Straits to the 51° of northern latitude . . . is exclusively granted to Russian subjects." No declaration could have stirred Secretary Adams more deeply, and in July, 1823, he advised Henry Middleton, the American Minister in Russia, that "the United States can admit no part of these claims." The following December, in his annual message to Congress, President Monroe used the famous words quoted at the head of this Document to warn the Russians off. In April the next year, Middleton and the Russians agreed on 54° 40′ as their southernmost limit in North America.

What we know as the Monroe Doctrine is wholly contained in two sections of Monroe's December message, the first admonishing the Russians, the second the western powers, that vast as the New World was, there was no room in it for further European settlements or for the advance of the European system. Monroe's were brave, and to many, bombastic words. When, in 1824, the minister of the new country of Colombia asked Secretary Adams, "in what manner the Government of the United States intends to resist on its part any interference of the Holy Alliance for the purpose of subjugating the new Republics, or interfering in their political form?" Adams was forced to reply that "it is obvious that the United States could not undertake resistance to them by force of Arms, without a previous understanding with those European Powers, whose Interests and whose principles would secure them an active and efficient cooperation in the cause." Adams, in effect, was backtracking behind the screen of the British navy. Yet, if the Monroe Doctrine gave neighboring Latin America little ground for hope, it gave more distant Europe ample grounds for fear. Prince Metternich of Austria, the guiding genius of the Holy Alliance, wrote in January, 1824:

> These United States of America, which we have seen arise and grow, and which during their too short youth already meditated projects which they dared not then avow, have suddenly left a sphere too narrow for their ambition. . . . They have distinctly and clearly announced their intention to set not only power against power, but, to express it more exactly, altar against altar. In their indecent declarations they have cast blame and scorn on the institutions of Europe most worthy of respect. . . . In fostering revolutions wherever they show themselves, in regretting those which have failed, in extending a helping hand to those which seem to prosper, they lend new strength to the apostles of sedition, and reanimate the courage of every conspirator.

*December 2, 1823*

# The Monroe Doctrine

(a) *John Quincy Adams on "the gigantic grasp of our ambition" from his Diary, November 16, 1819*

[Mr. Crawford, Secretary of the Treasury] said he had been conversing with Mr. Lowndes, who told him that, both in England and France, everybody with whom he had conversed appeared to be profoundly impressed with the idea that we were an ambitious and encroaching people, and he thought we ought to be very guarded and moderate in our policy, to remove this impression.

I said I doubted whether we ought

to give ourselves any concern about it. Great Britain, after vilifying us twenty years as a mean, low-minded, peddling nation, having no generous ambitions and no God but gold, had now changed her tone, and was endeavoring to alarm the world at the gigantic grasp of our ambition. Spain was doing the same; and Europe . . . readily gave credit to the envious and jealous clamor. . . . Nothing that we could say or do would remove this impression until the world shall be familiarized with the idea of coonsidering our proper dominion to be the continent of North America.

From the time when we became an independent people it was as much a law of nature that this should become our pretension as that the Mississippi should flow to the sea. Spain had possessions upon our southern and Great Britain upon our northern border. It was impossible that centuries should elapse without finding them annexed to the United States; not that any spirit of encroachment or ambition on our part renders it necessary, but because it is a physical, moral, and political absurdity that such fragments of territory, with sovereigns at fifteen hundred miles beyond sea, worthless and burdensome to their owners, should exist permanently contiguous to a great, powerful, enterprising, and rapidly-growing nation. . . . But it is very lately that we have distinctly seen this ourselves; very lately that we have avowed the pretension of extending to the South Sea; and until Europe shall find it a settled geographical element that the United States and North America are identical, any effort on our part to reason the world out of a belief that we are ambitious will have no other effect than to convince them that we add to our ambition hypocrisy.

### (b) *The Monroe Doctrine, December 2, 1823*

At the proposal of the Russian Imperial Government, made through the minister of the Emperor residing here, a full power and instructions have been transmitted to the minister of the United States at St. Petersburg to arrange by amicable negotiation the respective rights and interests of the two nations on the northwest coast of this continent. A similar proposal had been made by His Imperial Majesty to the Government of Great Britain, which has likewise been acceded to. The Government of the United States has been desirous by this friendly proceeding of manifesting the great value which they have invariably attached to the friendship of the Emperor and their solicitude to cultivate the best understanding with his Government. In the discussions to which this interest has given rise and in the arrangements by which they may terminate the occasion has been judged proper for asserting, as a principle in which the rights and interests of the United States are involved, that the American continents, by the free and independent condition which they have assumed and maintain, are henceforth not to be considered as subjects for future colonization by any European powers. . . .

It was stated at the commencement of the last session that a great effort was then making in Spain and Portugal to improve the condition of the people of those countries, and that it appeared to be conducted with extraordinary moderation. It need scarcely be remarked that the result has been so far very different from what was then anticipated. Of events in that quarter of the globe, with which we have so much intercourse and from which we derive our origin, we have always been anxious and interested spectators. The citizens of the United States cherish sentiments the most friendly in favor of the liberty and happiness of their fellow-men on that side of the Atlantic. In the wars of the European powers in matters relating to themselves we have never taken any part, nor does it comport with our policy so to do. It is only when our rights are invaded or seriously menaced that we resent injuries or make preparation for our defense.

With the movements in this hemisphere we are of necessity more immediately connected, and by causes which must be obvious to all enlightened and impartial observers. The political system of the allied powers is essentially different in this respect from that of America. This difference proceeds from that which exists in their respective Governments; and to the defense of our own, which has been achieved by the loss of so much blood and treasure, and matured by the wisdom of their most enlightened citizens, and under which we have enjoyed unexampled felicity, this whole nation is devoted. We owe it, therefore, to candor and to the amicable relations existing between the United States and those powers to declare that we should consider any attempt on their part to extend their system to any portion of this hemisphere as dangerous to our peace and safety. With the existing colonies or dependencies of any European power we have not interfered and shall not interfere. But with the Governments who have declared their independence and maintained it, and whose independence we have, on great consideration and on just principles, acknowledged, we could not view any interposition for the purpose of oppressing them, or controlling in any other manner their destiny, by any European power in any other light than as the manifestation of an unfriendly disposition toward the United States.

In the war between those new Governments and Spain we declared our neutrality at the time of their recognition, and to this we have adhered, and shall continue to adhere, provided no change shall occur which, in the judgement of the competent authorities of this Government, shall make a corresponding change on the part of the United States indispensable to their security.

The late events in Spain and Portugal shew that Europe is still unsettled. Of this important fact no stronger proof can be adduced than that the allied powers should have thought it proper, on any principle satisfactory to themselves, to have interposed by force in the internal concerns of Spain. To what extent such interposition may be carried, on the same principle, is a question in which all independent powers whose governments differ from theirs are interested, even those most remote, and surely none more so than the United States. Our policy in regard to Europe, which was adopted at an early stage of the wars which have so long agitated that quarter of the globe, nevertheless remains the same, which is, not to interfere in the internal concerns of any of its powers; to consider the government de facto as the legitimate government for us; to cultivate friendly relations with it, and to preserve those realtions by a frank, firm, and manly policy, meeting in all instances the just claims of every power, submitting to injuries from none.

But in regard to those continents circumstances are eminently and conspicuously different. It is impossible that the allied powers should extend their political system to any portion of either continent without endangering our peace and happiness; nor can anyone believe that our southern brethren, if left to themselves, would adopt it of their own accord. It is equally impossible, therefore, that we should behold such interposition in any form with indifference. If we look to the comparative strength and resources of Spain and those new governments, and their distance from each other, it must be obvious that she can never subdue them. It is still the true policy of the United States to leave the parties to themselves, in the hope that other powers will pursue the same course.

# 24

*"All white male inhabitants above the age of twenty-one years . . . shall enjoy the right of an elector"*

At the New York State constitutional convention in 1821, Dr. John Z. Ross of the committee on the right of suffrage offered the following justification for a committee proposal:

> That all men are free and equal, according to the usual declarations, applies to them only in a state of nature, and not after the institution of civil government; for then many rights, flowing from a natural equality, are necessarily abridged, with a view to produce the greatest amount of security and happiness to the whole community. On this principle the right of suffrage is extended to white men only.

The convention debated the committee proposal off and on for well over a month before accepting it. In the New York constitution of 1821, a handful of free Negroes who could meet the most onerous residence and property qualifications retained the right to vote; by the same instrument, virtually all adult white males were enfranchised, and those omitted were brought in by an amendment to the constitution in 1826 (see item "b," below).

By law, as late as 1821, free Negroes still were permitted to vote equally with whites in northern New England, where they were very few; in Pennsylvania, where they were more numerous than in any other northern state; and even in such southern states as Tennessee and North Carolina. In other states where they once enjoyed the franchise they had already been deprived of it (or, where past Negro voters still could vote, newly freed ones were disfranchised), usually by the same article which for the first time provided full or virtually full white manhood suffrage—in Kentucky in 1799, in New Jersey in 1807, in Maryland in 1810, and in Connecticut in 1818. Tennessee disfranchised Negroes in 1834, North Carolina in 1835, Pennsylvania in 1838.

No state entering the Union after 1819, moreover, permitted free Negroes to vote before the Civil War. In 1819, in elections of delegates from Michigan Territory, Congress itself restricted the franchise to adult white males. When in 1825 certain Michigan Indians voted in such elections, the canvassers, in throwing out their ballots, declared ". . . that it was as foreign from the intention of the general government to admit Indians to the privilege of voting as to ex-

134

tend the franchise to the descendants of African parents: both are excluded, for neither of them form component parts of the great North American family." In neighboring Wisconsin, nevertheless, the first constitution in 1848 did specifically enfranchise "civilized persons of Indian descent not members of any tribe." In 1849, Wisconsin voters approved a law giving free Negroes as well as Indians the vote, but the state supreme court delayed until 1866 to acknowledge this law's validity, and not until then could Wisconsin Negroes exercise the privilege.

In 1821, there were, all told, about 225,000 free Negroes in the United States, or approximately 2.5 per cent of the entire population. No more than 50,000 of these Negroes were males over 21. Had all of them been permitted to vote, they would have made up, at most, but 4 per cent of the electorate. Thereafter, the number of free Negroes grew far less rapidly than the rest of the population, and by the time Wisconsin entered the Union the free Negro electorate survived only in New England, north of Connecticut. Loss of the franchise, of course, was only one of the lengthening list of disabilities of the free Negro in free as well as slave states. Where he legally could vote, moreover, his right usually had arisen only from omissions in the law and was subject to every sort of abuse until the law was corrected. As a delegate to the Pennsylvania constitutional convention of 1837 said on his way to the disfranchising meeting, "the people of this state are for continuing this commonwealth, what it always has been, a political community of white persons."

Many explanations were offered in the expansive Jacksonian era itself for the cruel and comprehensive attention then given to so infinitesimal a class of persons as the free Negro. These ranged from his alleged congenital biological deficiencies to the necessity of protecting him from the even greater wrath of rampaging whites whom the cruel law might constrain. Such explanations, as far as the franchise was concerned, buttressed the argument most frequently advanced by reformers, that for manhood suffrage to be made palatable to conservatives it had to be restricted to whites alone, and preferably to white farmers. Many reformers, however, proved even more sensitive than conservatives on this point, and the latter often advocated free Negro suffrage in order to defeat reform by contamination. But this stratagem failed.

In the Jacksonian era, the breakup of vast landed estates in the older sections, the establishment of small family farms in the West, the growth of commerce and the spread of manufacturing in the cities, all supplied strong material reasons in addition to the prevailing philosophical ones for enlarging the franchise to include the restive thousands who could not meet the typical old freehold qualifications. In the New York constitutional convention of 1821, the force of these reasons was most clearly conveyed by no less a personage than Martin Van Buren, already a powerful Democratic leader, who also disclosed the close connection between the attainment of broad white suffrage and the disfranchisement of the blacks.

Van Buren fought universal manhood suffrage for whites or Negroes, just as he fought the $250 freehold requirement for electors of New York senators and governors. His goal was to extend the franchise for all elective officers to adult white male taxpayers only; and this goal he reached. Selections from his remarks in the convention are presented below in item "a," in the third person, as reported, along with an extension of the remarks of the Democratic Dr. Ross, wherein the free Negro's biological and social limitations are expanded upon. Peter A. Jay, as conservative as his father, John, and as honorable, asserted even this early that the Doctor's allegations were "now so universally exploded" that they need not be dignified by disproof. Jay's defense of Negro suffrage follows Dr. Ross's attack upon it.

In item "b" are presented sections from a number of state constitutions or constitutional amendments of what we more or less freely call the Jacksonian era showing the hand-in-hand advance in the free states of white manhood suffrage and free Negro disfranchisement.

*1818-1848*

# The Spirit of the Jacksonian Franchise

(a)  *Martin Van Buren, Dr. John Z. Ross, and Peter A. Jay*
 *on the suffrage, in the New York State Constitutional Convention, 1821*

MR. VAN BUREN

In the constitution of the Union, too, which has been in operation long enough to test the correctness and soundness of its principles, there was no excessive freehold representation. That constitution was now the boast and pride of the American people, and the admiration of the world. He presumed there was not an individual in that committee, who would question the sufficiency of the general government, for the protection of life, liberty, and property. . . .

By the census of 1814, it appeared that of 163,000 electors in this state, upwards of 75,000 were freeholders, under $250 [then required to vote for state senators], and all of them householders, who may possess any amount of personal property. . . . And the question was, whether, in addition to those

who might, by this Convention, be clothed with the right of suffrage, this class of men, composed of mechanics, professional men, and small landholders, and constituting the bone, pith, and muscle of the population of the state, should be excluded entirely from all representation in that branch of the legislature [the Senate] which had equal power to originate all bills, and a complete negative upon the passage of all bills. This, said he, is, in sober truth, the question under discussion; and it would seem to be only necessary, that it should be fairly stated, and correctly understood, to secure its rejection. . . .

In whose name, and for whose benefit, he inquired, were they called upon to disappoint the just expectation of their constituents? . . . It was in the name, and for the security of '*farmers*,' that they were called upon to adopt this measure. This, he said, was, indeed, acting in an imposing name. . . . But how did this matter stand? . . . Who, he asked, had hitherto constituted a majority of the voters of the state? The *farmers*—who had called for, and insisted upon the Convention. *Farmers and freeholders!* . . . The farmers of this state had, he said, by an overwhelming majority, admitted those who were not freeholders, to a full participation with themselves in every stage of this great effort to amend our constitution, and to ameliorate the condition of the people. Could he, then, ought he to be told, that they would be disappointed in their expectations? . . . He did not believe it. . . .

Mr. V.B. [also] did not believe that there were twenty members . . . who, were the bare naked question of universal suffrage put to them, would vote in its favor; and he was very sure that its adoption was not expected, and would not meet the views of their constituents. . . . We had already reached the verge of universal suffrage. There was but one step beyond. And are gentlemen prepared to take that step? We were cheapening this invaluable right. He was disposed to go as far as any man in the extension of rational liberty; but he could not consent to undervalue this precious privilege, so far as to confer it with an undiscriminating hand upon every one, black or white, who would be kind enough to condescend to accept it. . . .

He knew that he would be able to convince every member of this committee of the dangerous and alarming tendency of that precipitate and unexpected prostration of all qualifications. . . .

First. It would give the city of New-York about twenty-five thousand votes; whilst, under the liberal extension of the right on the choice of delegates to this convention, she had but about thirteen or fourteen thousand. That the character of the increased number of votes would be such as would render their elections rather a curse than a blessing; which would drive from the polls all sober minded people. . . .

Secondly. . . . that injury would work an equally great one to the western and northern parts of the state. It was the present consolation of our hardy sons of the west, that, for their toils and their sufferings in reducing the wilderness to cultivation, they were cheered by the conviction, not only that they would be secure in the enjoyment of their dear bought improvements, in consequence of their representation in the legislature, but that any increase of that representation gave them a still greater influence there. That as far as it respected this state, their march, and the march of empire kept pace. . . . [But] under the vote the other day . . . the direct consequence would be, that the additional representation of fourteen members . . . would, instead of going principally to the west, be surrendered to the worst population of the old counties and cities.

DR. ROSS

That all men are free and equal, according to the usual declarations, applies to them only in a state of nature, and not after the institution of civil government; for then many rights, flowing from a natural equality, are necessarily abridged, with a view to produce the greatest amount of security and happiness to the whole community. On this principle the right of suffrage is extended to white men only. But why, it will probably be asked, are blacks to be excluded? I answer, because they are seldom, if ever, required to share in the common burthens or defence of the state. There are also additional reasons; they are a peculiar people, incapable, in my judgment, of exercising that privilege with any sort of discretion, prudence, or independence. They have no just conceptions of civil liberty. They know not how to appreciate it, and are consequently indifferent to its preservation.

Under such circumstances, it would hardly be compatible with the safety of the state, to entrust such a people with this right. It is not thought advisable to permit aliens to vote, neither would it be safe to extend it to the blacks. We deny to minors this right, and why? Because they are deemed incapable of exercising it discreetly, and therefore not safely, for the good of the whole community.—Even the better part of creation, as my honourable friend from Oneida stiles them, are not permitted to participate in this right. No sympathies seemed to be awakened in their behalf, nor in behalf of the aborigines, the original and only rightful proprietors of our soil—a people altogether more acute and discerning, and in whose judicious exercise of the right I should repose far more confidence, than in the African race. . . . And, sir, I fear that an extension to the blacks would serve to invite that kind of population to this state, an occurrence which I should most sincerely deplore. The petition presented in their behalf, now on your table, in all probability has been instigated by gentlemen of a different colour, who expect to control their votes. But whether this be so or not, next the blacks will claim to be represented by persons of their own colour, in your halls of legislation. And can you consistently refuse them? It would be well to be prepared for such a claim.

MR. JAY

[Dr. Ross has] informed us that all who were not white ought to be excluded from political rights. . . . When this Convention was first assembled, it was generally understood that provisions would be made to extend the right of suffrage, and some were apprehensive that it might be extended to a degree which they could not approve. But, sir, it was not expected that this right was in any instance to be restricted, much less was it anticipated, or desired, that a single person was to be disfranchised. Why, sir, are these men to be excluded from rights which they possess in common with their countrymen? What crime have they committed for which they are to be punished? Why are they, who were born as free as ourselves, natives of the same country, and deriving from nature and our political institutions, the same rights and privileges which we have, now to be deprived of all those rights, and doomed to remain forever as aliens among us? . . .

We are told by one of the select committee, that people of colour are incapable of exercising the right of suffrage. I may have misunderstood that gentleman; but I thought he meant to say, that they laboured under a physical disability. It is true that some philosophers have held that the intellect of a black man, is naturally inferior to that of a white one; but this idea has been so completely refuted, and is now so universally exploded, that I did not expect to have heard it in an assembly so enlightened as this, nor do I now think it necessary to disprove it. That in general the people of colour are inferior to the whites in knowledge and in industry, I shall not deny. You made them slaves, and nothing is more true than the ancient saying, "The day you make a man a slave takes half his worth away." Unaccustomed to provide for themselves, and habituated to regard labour as an evil, it is no wonder that when set free, they should be improvident and idle, and that their children should be brought up without education, and without prudence or forethought. But will you punish the children for your own crimes; for the injuries which you have inflicted upon their parents? Besides, sir, this state of things is fast passing away. Schools have been opened for them, and it will, I am sure, give pleasure to this committee to know, that in these schools there is discovered a thirst for instruction, and a progress in learning, seldom to be seen in the other schools of the state. They also have churches of their own, and clergymen of their own colour, who conduct their public worship with perfect decency and order, and not without ability.

This state, Mr. Chairman, has taken high ground against slavery, and all its degrading consequences and accompaniments. . . . Adopt the amendment now proposed, and you will hear a shout of triumph and a hiss of scorn from the southern part of the union, which I confess will mortify me—I shall shrink at the sound, because I fear it will be deserved. But it has been said that this measure is necessary to preserve the purity of your elections. . . . But where is the necessity in the present instance? The whole number of coloured people in the state, whether free or in bondage, amounts to less than a fortieth part of the whole population. When your numbers are to theirs as forty to one, do you still fear them? . . . But there are a greater number in the city of New-York. How many? Sir, in even that city, the whites are to the blacks as ten to one. And even of the tenth which is composed of the black population, how few are there that are entitled to vote? . . . Will you, then, without necessity, and merely to gratify an unreasonable prejudice, stain the constitution you are about to form, with a provision equally odious and unjust, and in direct violation of the principles which you profess, and upon which you intend to form it? I trust, I am sure, you will not.

(b) *Enfranchising adult white males and disfranchising free Negroes in selected free state constitutions, 1818-1848*

FIRST CONSTITUTION
OF ILLINOIS, 1818,
ARTICLE II, SECTION 27.

In all elections, all white male inhabitants above the age of twenty-one years, having resided in the State six months next preceding the election, shall enjoy the right of an elector.

CONSTITUTION
OF CONNECTICUT, 1818,
ARTICLE SIXTH

*Section 1.* All persons who have been, or shall hereafter, *previous* to the ratification of this Constitution, be admitted freemen, according to the existing laws of this State, shall be electors.

*Sec. 2.* Every white male citizen of the United States, who shall have gained a settlement in this State, attained the age of twenty-one years, and resided in the town in which he may offer himself to be admitted to the privilege of an elector, at least six months preceding; and have a freehold estate of the yearly value of seven dollars in this State; or, having been enrolled in the militia, shall have performed military duty therein for the term of one year next preceding the time he shall offer himself for admission, or being liable thereto shall have been, by authority of law, excused therefrom; or shall have paid a State tax within the year next preceding the time he shall present himself for such admission; and shall sustain a good moral character, shall, on his taking such oath as may be prescribed by law, be an elector.

CONSTITUTION
OF NEW YORK STATE, 1821,
ARTICLE II

*Section 1.* Every male citizen of the age of twenty-one years, who shall have been an inhabitant of this State one year preceding any election, and for the last six months a resident of the town or county where he may offer his vote; and shall have, within the year next preceding the election, paid a tax to the State or county, assessed upon his real or personal property; or shall by law be exempted from taxation; or being armed and equipped according to law, shall have performed within that year military duty in the militia of this State; or who shall be exempted from performing militia duty in consequence of being a fireman in any city, town, or village in this State; and also every male citizen of the age of twenty-one years, who shall have been, for three years next preceding such election, an inhabitant of this State; and for the last year a resident in the town or county where he may offer his vote; and shall have been, within the last year, assessed to labor upon the public highways, and shall have performed the labor, or paid an equivalent therefor, according to law, shall be entitled to vote in the town or ward where he actually resides, and not elsewhere, for all officers that now are, or hereafter may be, elective by the people; *but no man of color*, unless he shall have been for three years a citizen of this State, and for one year next preceding any election shall be seized and possessed of a freehold estate of the value of two hundred and fifty dollars, over and above all debts and incumbrances charged thereon, and shall have been actually rated, and paid a tax thereon, shall be entitled to vote at any such election. And no person of color shall be subject to direct taxation unless he shall be seized or possessed of such real estate as aforesaid.

AMENDMENT TO 1821 CONSTITUTION OF NEW YORK STATE, 1826

II.   That so much of the first section of the second article of the constitution as prescribes the qualifications of voters, other than persons of color [as above], be, and the same is hereby, abolished, and that the following be substituted in place thereof: "Every male citizen of the age of twenty-one years, who shall have been an inhabitant of this State one year next preceding any election, and for the last six months a resident of the county where he may offer his vote, shall be entitled to vote in the town or ward where he actually resides, and not elsewhere, for all officers that now are or hereafter may be elective by the people."

FIRST CONSTITUTION OF WISCONSIN, 1848, ARTICLE III

Section 1. Every male person of the age of twenty-one years or upwards, belonging to either of the following classes, who shall have resided in the State for one year next preceding any election, shall be deemed a qualified elector at such election:

*First.*—White citizens of the United States.

*Second.*—White persons of foreign birth who shall have declared their intention to become citizens, conformably to the laws of the United States on the subject of naturalization.

*Third.*—Persons of Indian blood who have once been declared by law of Congress to be citizens of the United States, any subsequent law of Congress to the contrary notwithstanding.

*Fourth.*—Civilized persons of Indian descent, not members of any tribe: PROVIDED, that the legislature may at any time extend, by law, the right of suffrage to persons not herein enumerated, but no such law shall be in force until the same shall have been submitted to a vote of the people at a general election, and approved by a majority of all the votes cast at such election.

# 25

*"To create this home market, to lay the foundations of a genuine American policy"*

The Treaty of Ghent ending the War of 1812 between the United States and Great Britain settled nothing, and on that account the war itself was often said to have been a futile venture. Not so, however, to Henry Clay and his fellow "War Hawks," whom the war had launched on national careers. They felt that simply by having taken on the mistress of the seas, our own hostile states and sections had become fused into one great and happy land. Recently returned from Ghent and London, and glad of it, Clay, early in 1816, challenged the House of Representatives: "Let any man look at the degraded condition of this country before the war—the scorn of the universe, the contempt of ourselves—and tell me, if we have gained nothing by the war. What is our present situation? Respectability and character abroad; security and confidence at home; . . . our Constitution placed on a solid basis, never to be shaken. . . . Is there a man," Clay asked, "who could not desire participation in the national glory acquired by the war?"

And yet Clay nursed profound misgivings. Early in 1812, he had said, "the real cause of British aggression was not to distress an enemy, but to destroy a rival." In 1816, once more, he told the House, "That man must be blind to the indications of the future, who can not see that we are destined to have war after war with Great Britain until, if one of the two nations be not crushed, all grounds of collision shall have ceased between us." By 1824, although eight years had gone by and the peace remained unbroken, Clay still felt that we had been engaged, and to our discredit, in the Carthaginian struggle he had foretold—in a war of trade right in our home ports and around the world, whose object as the enemy British themselves acknowledged, was "to stifle in the cradle those rising manufactures in the United States, which the war [of 1812] had forced into existence, contrary to the natural course of things."

In 1816, on his part, Clay had helped push through Congress, largely against British textiles and iron ware, the first avowedly protective tariff in United States history. This tariff failed utterly to protect, not, according to Clay, because of its deficiencies, which were many, nor, as he said later, because of smuggling, "which has something bold, daring, and enterprising in it," but because of Britain's "mean, barefaced, cheating, by fraudulent invoices and false denominations." When a worldwide financial panic in 1819 marked the

141

end of the postwar boom, Clay was shocked by the evidence everywhere around him of decay in the mere infancy of development, of helplessness among hardy "self-made men" (a phrase he coined later on), and by what he felt was the dastardly cause of it all, "the overwhelming pressure of foreign competition." The defeat of new tariff proposals in 1820, 1821, and 1823 by commercial and agricultural opposition at last drove Clay to broaden his own ideas of America's destiny; to formulate a single grand plan to embrace these ideas, with something for every interest; and to seek the presidency for the power to practice what he preached.

The hub of Clay's program remained the protective tariff. By promoting the growth of American factories and factory towns, protection would provide both the South and the West with secure and growing *home markets* for their food crops and fibers, and the whole nation with an independent *supply* of manufactures, something especially desirable in case of war. The tariff, together with the sale (as against the free settlement) of the public lands, would also provide revenue to help pay for federal aid to "internal improvements"—that is, the construction of roads and canals—another part of Clay's plan. Such improvements, by reducing oppressive carrying costs, would give farmers of the South and West at once higher net prices for their own produce and lower prices for the American manufactures they needed. Finally, to provide adequate credit facilities for agricultural as well as industrial expansion, and a stable currency for the security of investment, Clay would have all sections rally to the support of the national bank.

Clay gave his plan the effective name, the "American System." The opening gun in his campaign was his two-day speech in the House, March 30-31, 1824, in support of a new protective tariff bill, which was enacted the following May. In this speech, Clay argued that it was nothing less than the "solemn duty" of the national government, not merely its right (as John Marshall had said), to employ its constitutional powers to the limit in furthering proper national purposes. One of the most legitimate of these was the guarding of its citizens from virtual foreign invasion by means of trade, by assisting them in developing their own economic strength. Clay's speeches often gained greater weight from their great length. This speech, the subject of this Document, was no exception. It is presented only in part below.

Clay never did win the presidency, partly because he alienated the West by his public-land policy, the South by his tariff policy, and the West and the South by his endorsement of Biddle's bank. He also had the misfortune, just when his enemies were seeking a likely candidate of their own, to have awakened both the ire and the ambition of Andrew Jackson. But Clay did have the satisfaction of seeing parts of the "American System" adopted during his lifetime. Had he lived past the Civil War, he would have seen it enacted virtually in full once the South was out of the Union, and sustained for generations while the Jacksonian party languished.

**March 30-31, 1824**

# Henry Clay: The "American System"

Two classes of politicians divide the people of the United States. According to the system of one, the produce of foreign industry should be subjected to no other impost than such as may be necessary to provide a public revenue; and the produce of American industry should be left to sustain itself, if it can, with no other than that incidental protection, in its competition, at home as well as abroad, with rival foreign articles. According to the system of the other class, while they agree that the imposts should be mainly, and may under any modification be safely, relied on as a fit and convenient source of public revenue, they would so adjust and arrange the duties on foreign fabrics as to afford a gradual but adequate protection to American industry, and lessen our dependence on foreign nations, by securing a certain and ultimately a cheaper and better supply of our own wants from our own abundant resources. . . . In our deliberations on this great question, we should look fearlessly and truly at the actual condition of the country, retrace the causes which have brought us into it, and snatch, if possible, a view of the future. . . .

In casting our eyes around us, the most prominent circumstance which fixes our attention, and challenges our deepest regret, is the general distress which pervades the whole country. . . . What, . . . I would ask, is the CAUSE of [our] unhappy condition? . . . It is to be found in the fact that during almost the whole existence of this government, we have shaped our industry, our navigation, and our commerce, in reference to an extraordinary war in

Europe, and to foreign markets, which no longer exist. . . . The consequence of the termination of the war of Europe has been, the resumption of European commerce, European navigation, and the extension of European agriculture and European industry, in all its branches. Europe, therefore, has no longer occasion, to any thing like the same extent as that she had during her wars, for American commerce, American navigation, the produce of American industry. Europe, in commotion, and convulsed through all her members, is to America no longer the same Europe as she is now, tranquil, and watching with the most vigilant attention all her own peculiar interests, without regard to the operation of her policy upon us. . . .

The greatest want of civilized society is, a market for the sale and exchange of the surplus of the produce of the labor of its members. This market may exist at home or abroad, or both; but it must exist somewhere, if society prospers; and, wherever it does exist, it should be competent to the absorption of the entire surplus of production. It is most desirable that there should be both a home and a foreign market. But, with respect to their relative superiority, I can not entertain a doubt. The home market is first in order, and paramount in importance. The object of the bill under consideration, is, to create this home market, and to lay the foundations of a genuine American policy. . . .

Our agriculture is our greatest interest. It ought ever to be predominant. . . . The creation of a home market is not only necessary to procure for our agriculture a just reward for its labors, but it is indispensable to obtain a supply for our necessary wants. If we can not sell, we can not buy. That portion of our population (and we have seen that it is not less than four fifths), which makes comparatively nothing that foreigners will buy, has nothing to make purchases with from foreigners. It is in vain that we are told of the amount of our exports supplied by the planting interest. They may enable the planting interest to supply all its wants; but they bring no ability to the interests not planting. . . . Even if it were true that the American manufacturer would supply consumption at dearer rates, it is better to have his fabrics than the unattainable foreign fabrics; because it is better to be ill supplied than not supplied at all. A coarse coat, which will communicate warmth and cover nakedness, is better than no coat. The superiority of the home market results, first, from its steadiness and comparative certainty at all times; secondly, from the creation of reciprocal interest; thirdly, from its greater security; and, lastly, from an ultimate and not distant augmentation of consumption (and consequently of comfort), from increased quantity and reduced prices. But this home market, highly desirable as it is, can only be created and cherished by the PROTECTION of our own legislation against the inevitable prostration of our industry, which must ensue from the action of FOREIGN policy and legislation. . . .

Having called the attention of the committee to the present adverse state of our country, and endeavored to point out the causes which have led to it; having shown that similar causes, wherever they exist in other countries, lead to the same adversity in their condition; and having shown that, wherever we find opposite causes prevailing, a high and animating state of national prosperity exists, the committee will agree with me in thinking that it is the solemn duty of government to apply a remedy to the evils which afflict our country, if it can apply one. Is there no remedy within the reach of the government? Are we doomed to behold our industry languish and decay yet more and more? But there is a remedy, and that remedy consists in modifying our foreign policy, and in adopting a genuine AMERICAN SYTEM. We must naturalize the arts in our country; and we must naturalize them by the only means which the wisdom of nations has yet discovered to be effectual; by adequate protection against the otherwise overwhelming influence of foreigners. This is only to be accomplished by the establishment of a tariff, to the consideration of which I am now brought.

And what is this tariff? . . . The sole object of the tariff is to tax the produce of a foreign industry, with the view of promoting American industry. The tax . . . has been treated as an imposition of burdens upon one part of the community by design, for the benefit of another; as if, in fact, money were taken from the pockets of one portion of the people and put into the pockets of another. But is that a fair representation of it? No man pays the duty assessed on the foreign article by compulsion, but voluntarily; and this voluntary duty, if paid, goes into the common exchequer, for the common benefit of all.

Consumption has four objects of choice. First, it may abstain from the use of the foreign article, and thus avoid the payment of the tax. Second, it may employ the rival American fabric. Third, it may engage in the business of manufacturing, which this bill is designed to foster. Fourth, or it may supply itself from the household manufactures. But it is said by the honorable gentleman from Virginia, that the South, owing to the character of a certain portion of its population, can not engage in the business of manufacturing. Now I do not agree in that opinion to the extent in which it is asserted. . . . But if the gentleman's premises were true, could his conclusion be admitted? According to him, a certain part of our population, happily much the smallest, is peculiarly situated. The circumstance of its degradation unfits it for the manufacturing arts. The well-being of the other, and the larger part of our population, requires the introduction of those arts. What is to be done in this conflict? The gentleman would have us abstain from adopting a policy called for by the interest of the greater and freer part of our population. But is that reasonable? Can it be expected that the interests of the greater part should be made to bend to the condition of the servile part of our population? That, in effect, would be to make us the slaves of slaves. . . .

The existing state of things, indeed, presents a sort of tacit compact between the cotton-grower and the British manufacturer, the stipulations of which are, on the part of the cotton-grower, that the whole of the United States, the other portions as well as the cotton-growing, shall remain open and unrestricted in the consumption of British manufactures; and, on the part of the British manufacturer, that in consideration thereof, he will continue to purchase the cotton of the South. . . . Supposing the South to be actually incompetent, or disinclined, to embark at all in the business of manufacturing, is not its interest, nevertheless, likely to be promoted by creating a new and an American source of supply for its consumption? Now foreign powers, and Great Britain principally, have the monopoly of the supply of southern consumption. If this bill should pass, an American competitor, in the supply of the South, would be raised up, and ultimately, I can not doubt, that it will be supplied more cheaply and better. . . .

But it is said that, wherever there is a concurrence of favorable circumstances, manufactures will arise of themselves, without protection; and that we should not disturb the natural progress of industry, but leave things to themselves. If all nations would

modify their policy on this axiom, perhaps it would be better for the common good of the whole. Even then, in consequence of natural advantages and a greater advance in civilization and in the arts, some nations would enjoy a state of much higher prosperity than others. But there is no universal legislation. . . . If I were to attempt to particularize the causes which prevent the success of the manufacturing arts, without protection, I should say that they are, first, the obduracy of fixed habits. No nation, no individual, will easily change an established course of business, even if it be unprofitable; and least of all is an agricultural people prone to innovation. . . . Secondly, the uncertainty, fluctuation, and unsteadiness, of the home market, when liable to an unrestricted influx of fabrics from all foreign nations; and, thirdly, the superior advance of skill, and amount of capital, which foreign nations have obtained, by the protection of their own industry. From the latter or from other causes, the unprotected manufactures of a country are exposed to the danger of being crushed in their infancy, either by the design or from the necessities of foreign manufacturers. . . .

The next objection of the honorable gentleman from Virginia which I shall briefly notice is, that the manufacturing system is adverse to the genius of our government, in its tendency to the accumulation of large capitals in a few hands; in the corruption of the public morals, which is alleged to be incident to it; and in the consequent danger to the public liberty. . . . If his principle be correct, it should be extended to any and every vocation which had a similar tendency. The enormous fortunes in our country—the nabobs of the land—have been chiefly made by the profitable pursuit of that foreign commerce, in more propitious times, which the honorable gentleman would so carefully cherish. Immense estates have also been made in the South. . . . The best security against the demoralization of society is the constant and profitable employment of its members. The greatest danger to public liberty is from idleness and vice. If manufactures form cities, so does commerce. And the disorders and violence which proceed from the contagion of the passions, are as frequent in one description of those communities as in the other. There is no doubt but that the yeomanry of a country is the safest depository of public liberty. In all time to come, and under any probable direction of the labor of our population, the agricultural class must be much the most numerous and powerful, and will ever retain, as it ought to retain, a preponderating influence in our councils. The extent and the fertility of our lands constitute an adequate security against an excess in manufactures, and also against oppression, on the part of capitalists, toward the laboring portions of the community.

The last objection, with a notice of which I shall trouble the committee, is, that the Constitution does not authorize the passage of the bill. The gentleman from Virginia does not assert, indeed, that it is inconsistent with the express provisions of that instrument, but he thinks it incompatible with the spirit of the Constitution. If we attempt to provide for the internal improvement of the country, the Constitution, according to some gentlemen, stands in our way. If we attempt to protect American industry against foreign policy and the rivalry of foreign industry, the Constitution presents an insuperable obstacle. This Constitution must be a most singular instrument! It seems to be made for any other people than our own. Its action is altogether foreign. Congress has power to lay duties and imposts, under no other limitation whatever than that of their being uniform throughout the United States. But they can only be imposed, according to the honorable gentleman, for the sole purpose of revenue. This is a restriction which we do not find in the Constitution. . . . The gentleman from Virginia has, however, entirely mistaken the clause of the Constitution on which we rely. It is that which gives to Congress the power to regulate commerce with foreign nations. The grant is plenary, without any limitation whatever, and includes the whole power of regulation, of which the subject to be regulated is susceptible. It is as full and complete a grant of the power as that is to declare war. . . .

Mr. Chairman, our confederacy comprehends, within its vast limits, great diversity of interests: agricultural, planting, farming, commercial, navigating, fishing, manufacturing. No one of these interests is felt in the same degree, and cherished with the same solicitude, throughout all parts of the Union. Some of them are peculiar to particular sections of our common country. But all these great interests are confided to the protection of one government—to the fate of one ship—and a most gallant ship it is, with a noble crew. If we prosper, and are happy, protection must be extended to all; it is due to all. It is the great principle on which obedience is demanded from all. If our essential interests can not find protection from our own government against the policy of foreign powers, where are they to get it? We did not unite for sacrifice, but for preservation. . . . The South entertains one opinion, and imagines that a modification of the existing policy of the country, for the protection of American industry, involves the ruin of the South. The North, the East, the West, hold the opposite opinion, and feel and contemplate, in a longer adherence to the foreign policy, as it now exists, their utter destruction. Is it true, that the interests of these great sections of our country are irreconcilable with each other? Are we reduced to the sad and afflicting dilemma of determining which shall fall a victim to the prosperity of the other? Happily, I think, there is no such distressing alternative. . . .

Other and animating considerations invite us to adopt the policy of this system. Its importance, in connection with the general defense in time of war, can not fail to be duly estimated. . . . Its importance, in reference to the stability of our Union, that paramount and greatest of all our interests, can not fail warmly to recommend it, or at least to conciliate the forbearance of every patriot bosom. Now our people present the spectacle of a vast assemblage of jealous rivals, all eagerly rushing to the sea-board, jostling each other in their way, to hurry off to glutted foreign markets the perishable produce of their labor. The tendency of that policy, in conformity to which this bill is prepared, is to transform these competitors into friends and mutual customers; and, by the reciprocal exchanges of their respective productions, to place the confederacy upon the most solid of all foundations, the basis of common interest. And is not government called upon, by every stimulating motive, to adapt its policy to the actual condition and extended growth of our great republic? . . . An interior has sprung up, as it were by enchantment, and along with it new interests and

new relations, requiring the parental protection of government. Our policy should be modified accordingly, so as to comprehend all, and sacrifice none. . . .

We have had great difficulties to encounter. First, the splendid talents which are arrayed in this House against us. Second, we are opposed by the rich and powerful in the land. Third, the executive government, if any, affords us but a cold and equivocal, support. Fourth, the importing and navigating interest, I verily believe from misconception, are adverse to us. Fifth, the British factors and the British influence are inimical to our success. Sixth, long-established habits and prejudices oppose us. Seventh, the reviewers and literary speculators, foreign and domestic. And, lastly, the leading presses of the country, including the influence of that which is established in this city, and sustained by the public purse.

From some of these, or other causes, the bill may be postponed, thwarted, defeated. But the cause is the cause of the country, and it must and will prevail.

**26**

*"Most of the dangers which impend over our Union have sprung from an abandonment of the legitimate objects of Government by our national legislation"*

His soldiers in the War of 1812 nicknamed Andrew Jackson "Old Hickory" out of respect for his toughness. His backers for the presidency in the 1820's nicknamed him the "Old Hero" out of respect for his age. On becoming President in March, 1829, Jackson, just ten days short of 62, was ten years older than Clay, fifteen years older than Webster, Calhoun, and Van Buren, almost twenty years older than Nicholas Biddle. He alone, among these men, had grown to manhood by the time of the Great Convention of 1787; and he was not long in the White House before he considered himself the only oracle on what was and was not constitutional. "Never for a moment," said President Jackson," believe that the great body of citizens of any state can deliberately intend to do wrong." If, by some accident, they, or their duly elected representatives, nevertheless did wrong, as President of *all* the people, he was the man to set things right again.

For all his respect for the people and the virtue of their representatives, Jackson vetoed more legislation than all his predecessors combined, often on constitutional grounds, and usually on the specific point of an unwarranted invasion of state rights by the national government. This record is all the more remarkable in view of Jackson's peculiar opinion of the makeup of the national legislature and the sources of its power. Few, if any, of the Framers, whose apostle he thought himself, would ever have referred to Congress, as Jackson did in his famous "Maysville veto" (item "a," below), as "the representatives of the several states," or to acts of Congress as acts "authorized by the States." The whole motivation for assembling the Great Convention of 1787 (see Documents No. 16 and 22, above) was to free the nation from the dominion of the states; and the main strength of the Constitution written there lay in its authorization by "We, the people." And yet Congress could not say it had not been warned by the new President. In his first annual message to both houses, December 8, 1829, Jackson declared:

> Nothing is clearer, in my view, than that we are chiefly indebted for the success of the Constitution under which we are now acting to the watchful and auxiliary operation of the State authorities. This is not the reflection of a day, but belongs to the most deeply rooted coonvictions of my mind. I can not, therefore, too strongly or too earnestly, for my own sense of its importance, warn you against all encroachments upon the legitimate sphere of State sovereignty.

Despite the watchfulness of the states, it was Jackson's belief that every president and every federal legislature since 1800 had trampled on state rights by adopting "a more enlarged construction" of "the enumerated authorities vested in Congress." They had been especially culpable in approving appropriations for internal improvements, and their guilt was evident "in its most imposing aspect" in the building of the National, or Cumberland, Road. "No less than twenty-three different laws," said Old Hickory in his Maysville veto, "have been passed through all the forms of the Constitution appropriating upward of $2,500,000 out of the National Treasury in support of that improvement, with the approbation of every President of the United States, including my predecessor, since its commencement, . . . thus giving an admonitory proof of the force of implication and the necessity of guarding the Constitution with sleepless vigilance against the authority of precedents which have not the sanction of its most plainly defined powers."

Jackson himself could not resist approving additional federal funds for the National Road; but he destroyed its national character by handing over the completed sections to the states in which they lay. Since his administration also voted unprecedented amounts for the dredging of rivers and harbors and similar pork-barrel items, a case has been made for the exceptional nature of the Maysville veto and Jackson's genuine sympathy for federal aid to internal improvements. But Old Hickory was at pains to disavow any such interpretation. At the very start of his administration, as his biographer, Marquis James, writes, he told "Van Buren to watch Congress and bring to the White House the first vulnerable [internal improvement] bill to meet his eye." In May, 1830, Van Buren pounced on the Maysville bill proposing federal investment in road-building in Kentucky, and together he and Jackson killed it.

When warned, "you will crush your friends in Kentucky if you veto that [Maysville] bill," Old Hickory retorted, "There is no money to be expended as my friends desire. I stand committed before the Country to pay off the National Debt. This pledge I am determined to redeem." When Jackson's first annual message was being written a few months earlier, his advisors urged him to say nothing about the Second Bank of the United States. "My friend," Jackson reminded one of them, "I am pledged against the Bank." Jackson's pledges, made in his distant youth and early manhood, were the undoing of his younger friends and enemies alike.

Back in 1816, when the Second Bank was first chartered after delays on constitutional grounds, Alexander J. Dallas, then Secretary of the Treasury, wondered whether at last it might not be deemed proper "to consider the constitutionality of a national bank as a question forever settled and at rest." In 1831, George McDuffie of South Carolina, Chairman of the House Ways and Means Committee and a more zealous state-rights man even than Jackson on everything but the Bank, recalled with favor Dallas's observation. He added on his own that "the solemn and unanimous opinion of the Supreme Court, in a case [*McCulloch* v. *Maryland*: see Document No. 22, above] which fully and distinctly submitted the constitutional question to their cognizance," had subsequently buttressed the Bank's position. Jackson himself could not care less: "I have read the opinion of John Marshall, . . . and could not agree with him." The Bank, Jackson said, was manifestly unconstitutional: "I do not think that Congress has a right to create a corporation out of the ten mile square"—that is, the District of Columbia.

Jackson's politics were so little known before he entered the White House that Biddle himself voted for him in 1824 and 1828. In his first annual message in December, 1829, Jackson did commend the Bank for its "early anticipation" and "judicious arrangements" in helping to pay off close to $9 million of the national debt the preceding July. Biddle thus felt he had reason to believe the prospects for a new charter to be brighter than ever under this administration. Despite much talk of Jackson's standing by his old pledges, McDuffie and others among Old Hickory's congressional lieutenants egged Biddle on, and by July 3, 1832, both the Senate and the House had passed the recharter bill Biddle sought.

When Jackson's decision to veto was seen to be final, his closest confidants in the White House "prayed, begged, and entreated" him to make his rejection "soft," so that the 3 million people included in the census of 1830 but as yet unrepresented in Congress might have a chance to ballot on the issue in the impending national election. But Jackson dissented. He did not need the vote to know the people's mind. He would crush the "monster" once and for all. Jackson's veto of the Bank bill, as narrowly state rights in its philosophy as the Maysville veto, is presented below in item "b."

Jackson's Bank veto is famous for its opening attack on the foreign stock-holders; but it may be said that the only consequence of their subscription to Bank shares was the salutary one of increasing the young nation's supply of capital funds. The veto is even more famous for its closing attack on "the rich and powerful" who "too often bend the acts of government to their selfish purposes." Against their pretensions, the Old Hero particularly set his face. What he closed his eyes to were the "nabobs of the land" in the states, not least in the slave states, against whose real monopoly of wealth and power Clay's American System in all its national scope and variety, including the national bank, was directly aimed.

*May 27, 1830*     *July 10, 1832*

# Andrew Jackson:

# The Maysville Veto and Bank Veto

### (a) *The Maysville Veto, May 27, 1830*

*To the House of Representatives.* I have maturely considered the bill proposing to authorize "a subscription of stock in the Maysville, Washington, Paris, and Lexington Turnpike Road Company," and now return the same . . . with my objections. . . .

The constitutional power of the Federal Government to construct or promote works of internal improve-ment presents itself in two points of view—the first as bearing upon the sovereignty of the States within whose limits their execution is contemplated, if jurisdiction of the territory which they may occupy be claimed as neces-sary to their preservation and use; the second as asserting the simple right to appropriate money from the National Treasury in aid of such works when undertaken by State authority, surrendering the claim of jurisdiction. In the first view the question of power is an open one. . . . Although frequently and strenuously attempted, the power to this extent has never been exercised by the Government in a single instance. It does not, in my opinion, possess it; and no bill, therefore, which admits it can receive my official sanction.

But in the other view of the power the question is differently situated. The ground taken at an early period of the Government was "that whenever money has been raised by the general authority and is to be applied to a particular measure, a question arises whether the particular measure be within the enumerated authorities vested in Congress. If it be, the money requisite for it may be applied to it; if not, no such application can be made." . . . The symmetry and purity of the Government would doubtless have been better preserved if this restriction of the power of appropriation could have been maintained without weakening its ability to fulfill the general objects of its institution, an effect so likely to attend its admission, notwithstanding its apparent fitness, that every subsequent Administration of the Government, embracing a period of thirty out of the forty-two years of its existence, has adopted a more enlarged construction of the power. . . .

In the Administration of Mr. Jefferson we have two examples of the exercise of the right of appropriation, which in the considerations that led to their adoption and in their effects upon the public mind have had a greater agency in marking the character of the power than any subsequent events. I allude to the payment of $15,000,000 for the purchase of Louisiana and to the original appropriation for the construction of the Cumberland road, the latter act deriving much weight from the acquiescence and approbation of three of the most powerful of the original members of the Confederacy, expressed through their respective legislatures. . . . No

less than twenty-three different laws have been passed, through all the forms of the Constitution, appropriating upward of $2,500,000 out of the National Treasury in support of that improvement, with the approbation of every President of the United States, including my predecessor, since its commencement, . . . thus giving an admonitory proof of the force of implication and the necessity of guarding the Constitution with sleepless vigilance against the authority of precedents which have not the sanction of its most plainly defined powers. . . .

The bill before me does not call for a more definite opinion upon the particular circumstances which will warrant appropriations of money by Congress to aid works of internal improvement, for although the extension of the power to apply money beyond that of carrying into effect the object for which it is appropriated has, as we have seen, been long claimed and exercised by the Federal Government, yet such grants have always been professedly under the control of the general principle that the works which might be thus aided should be "of a general, not local, national, not State," character. A disregard of this distinction would of necessity lead to the subversion of the federal system. . . . I am not able to view . . . [the present bill] in any other light than as a measure of purely local character; . . . It has no connection with any established system of improvements; is exclusively within the limits of a State, starting at a point on the Ohio River and running out 60 miles to an interior town, and even as far as the State is interested conferring partial instead of general advantages. . . . No aid can be derived from the intervention of corporations. The question regards the character of the work, not that of those by whom it is to be accomplished. Notwithstanding the union of the Government with the corporation by whose immediate agency any work of internal improvement is carried on, the inquiry will still remain, Is it national and conducive to the benefit of the whole, or local and operating only to the advantage of a portion of the Union?

But although I might not feel it to be my official duty to interpose the Executive veto to the passage of a bill appropriating money for the construction of such works as are authorized by the States and are national in their character, I do not wish to be understood as expressing an opinion that it is expedient at this time for the General Government to embark in a system of this kind. . . . The appropriations for internal improvement are increasing beyond the available means of the Treasury, and . . . it may be safely affirmed that $10,000,000 would not make up the excess over the Treasury receipts, unless the payment of the national debt be postponed and the means now pledged to that object applied to those enumerated in these bills. Without a well-regulated system of internal improvement this exhausting mode of appropriation is not likely to be avoided, and the plain consequence must be either a continuance of the national debt or a resort to additional taxes.

Although many of the States, with a laudable zeal and under the influence of an enlightened policy, are successfully applying their separate efforts to works of this character, the desire to enlist the aid of the General Government in the construction of such as from their nature ought to devolve upon it, and to which the means of the individual States are inadequate, is both rational and patriotic, and if that desire is not gratified now it does not follow that it never will be. . . . But great as this object undoubtedly is, it is not the only one which demands the fostering care of the Govern-

ment. The preservation and success of the republican principle rest with us. To elevate its character and extend its influence rank among our most important duties, and the best means to accomplish this desirable end are those which will rivet the attachment of our citizens to the Government of their choice by the comparative lightness of their public burthens and by the attraction which the superior success of its operations will present to the admiration and respect of the world. . . .

If it be the wish of the people that the construction of roads and canals should be conducted by the Federal Government, it is not only highly expedient, but indispensably necessary, that a previous amendment of the Constitution, delegating the necessary power and defining and restricting its exercise with reference to the sovereignty of the States should be made. Without it nothing extensively useful can be effected. . . . No good motive can be assigned for the exercise of power by the constituted authorities, while those for whose benefit it is to be exercised have not conferred it and may not be willing to confer it. . . . The difficulty and supposed impracticability of obtaining an amendment of the Constitution in this respect is, I firmly believe, in a great degree unfounded. The time has never yet been when the patriotism and intelligence of the American people were not fully equal to the greatest exigency, and it never will when the subject calling forth their interposition is plainly presented to them. To do so with the questions involved in this bill, and to urge them to an early, zealous, and full consideration of their deep importance, is, in my estimation, among the highest of our duties.

### (b)  The Bank Veto, July 10, 1832

*To the Senate*: The bill "to modify and continue" the act entitled "An act

to incorporate the subscribers to the Bank of the United States" was presented to me on the 4th July instant. Having considered it with that solemn regard to the principles of the Constitution which the day was calculated to inspire, and come to the conclusion that it ought not to become a law, I herewith return it . . . with my objections.

A bank of the United States is in many respects convenient for the Government and useful to the people. Entertaining this opinion, and deeply impressed with the belief that some of the powers and privileges possessed by the existing bank are unauthorized by the Constitution, subversive of the rights of the States, and dangerous to the liberties of the people, I felt it my duty at an early period in my Administration to call the attention of Congress to the practicability of organizing an institution combining all its advantages and obviating these objections. I sincerely regret that in the act before me I can perceive none of those modifications. . . .

The present corporate body, denominated the president, directors, and company of the Bank of the United States, will have existed at the time this act is intended to take effect twenty years. It enjoys an exclusive privilege of banking under the authority of the General Government, a monopoly of its favor and support, and, as a necessary consequence, almost a monopoly of the foreign and domestic exchange. The powers, privileges, and favors bestowed upon it in the original charter, by increasing the value of the stock far above its par value, operated as a gratuity of many millions to the stockholders.

An apology may be found for the failure to guard against this result in the consideration that the effect of the original act of incorporation could not be certainly foreseen at the time of its passage. The act before me proposes another gratuity to the holders of the same stock, and in many cases to the same men, of at least seven millions more. . . . It is not our own citizens only who are to receive the bounty of our Government. More than eight millions of the stock of this bank are held by foreigners. By this act the American Republic proposes virtually to make them a present of some millions of dollars. For these gratuities to foreigners and to some of our own opulent citizens the act secures no equivalent whatever. . . .

The modifications of the existing charter proposed by this act are not such, in my view, as make it consistent with the rights of the States or the liberties of the people. . . . All the objectionable principles of the existing corporation, and most of its odious features, are retained without alleviation. The fourth section provides "that the notes or bills of the said corporation, although the same be, on the faces thereof, respectively made payable at one place only, shall nevertheless be received by the said corporation at the bank or at any of the offices of discount and deposit thereof if tendered in liquidation or payment of any balance or balances due to said corporation or to such office of discount and deposit from any other incorporated bank." This provision secures to the State banks a legal privilege in the Bank of the United States which is withheld from all private citizens. . . . This boon conceded to the State banks, though not unjust in itself, is most odious because it does not measure out equal justice to the high and the low, the rich and the poor. To the extent of its practical effect it is a bond of union among the banking establishments of the nation, erecting them into an interest separate from that of the people, and its necessary tendency is to unite the Bank of the United States and the State banks in any measure which may be thought conducive to their common interest.

The ninth section of the act recognizes principles of worse tendency than any provision of the present charter. It enacts that "the cashier of the bank shall annually report to the Secretary of the Treasury the names of all stockholders who are not resident citizens of the United States, and on the application of the treasurer of any State shall make out and transmit to such treasurer a list of stockholders residing in or citizens of such State, with the amount of stock owned by each." Although this provision, taken in connection with a decision of the Supreme Court, surrenders, by its silence, the right of the States to tax the banking institutions created by this corporation under the name of branches throughout the Union, it is evidently intended to be construed as a concession of their right to tax that portion of the stock which may be held by their own citizens and residents. . . . As it is only the stock *held* in the States and not that *employed* within them which would be subject to taxation, and as the names of foreign stockholders are not to be reported to the treasurers of the States, it is obvious that the stock held by them will be exempt from this burden. . . . When by a tax on resident stockholders the stock of this bank is made worth 10 or 15 per cent more to foreigners than to residents, most of it will inevitably leave the country. . . .

Is there no danger to our liberty and independence in a bank that in its nature has so little to bind it to our country? The president of the bank has told us that most of the State banks exist by its forbearance. Should its influence become concentrated, as it may under the operation of such an act as this, in the hands of a self-elected directory whose interests are identified with those of the foreign stockholders, will there not be cause to tremble for the purity of our elections in peace and for the independence of our country in war? . . . If we must have a bank with private stockholders, every consideration of sound policy and every impulse of American feeling admonishes that it should be *purely American.* . . .

It is maintained by the advocates of the bank that its constitutionality in all its features ought to be considered as settled by precedent and by the decision of the Supreme Court. To this conclusion I can not assent. Mere precedent is a dangerous source of authority, and should not be regarded as deciding questions of constitutional power except where the acquiescence of the people and the States can be considered as well settled. . . . If the opinion of the Supreme Court covered the whole ground of this act, it ought not to control the coordinate authorities of this Government. . . . It is as much the duty of the House of Representatives, of the Senate, and of the President to decide upon the constitutionality of any bill or resolution which may be presented to them for passage or approval as it is of the supreme judges when it may be brought before them for judicial decision. The opinion of the judges has no more authority over Congress than the opinion of Congress has over the judges, and on that point the President is independent of both. The authority of the Supreme Court must not, therefore, be permitted to control the Congress or the Executive when acting in their legislative capacities, but to have only such influence as the force of their reasoning may deserve.

But in the case relied upon [*McCulloch* v. *Maryland:* see Document No. 22] the Supreme Court have not decided that all the features of this corporation are compatible with the Constitution. . . . The principle here affirmed is that the "degree of its necessity," involving all the details of a banking institution, is a question exclusively for legislative consideration. A bank is constitutional, but it is the province of the Legislature to determine whether this or that particular power, privilege, or exemption is "necessary and proper" to enable the bank to discharge its duties to the Government, and from their decision there is no appeal to the courts of justice. Under the decision of the Supreme

Court, therefore, it is the exclusive province of Congress and the President to decide whether the particular features of this act are *necessary* and *proper* in order to enable the bank to perform conveniently and efficiently the public duties assigned to it as a fiscal agent, and therefore, constitutional, or *unnecessary* and *improper*, and therefore unconstitutional. . . .

It is maintained by some that the bank is a means of executing the constitutional power "to coin money and regulate the value thereof." Congress have established a mint to coin money and passed laws to regulate the value thereof. The money so coined, with its value so regulated, and such foreign coins as Congress may adopt are the only currency known to the Constitution. But if they have other power to regulate the currency, it was conferred to be exercised by themselves, and not to be transferred to a corporation. If the bank be established for that purpose, with a charter unalterable without its consent, Congress have parted with their power for a term of years, during which the Constitution is a dead letter. It is neither necessary nor proper to transfer its legislative power to such a bank, and therefore unconstitutional.

By its silence, considered in connection with the decision of the Supreme Court in the case of McCulloch against the State of Maryland, this act takes from the States the power to tax a portion of the banking business carried on within their limits, in subversion of one of the strongest barriers which secured them against Federal encroachments. . . . Upon the formation of the Constitution the States guarded their taxing power with peculiar jealousy. They surrendered it only as its regards imports and exports. In relation to every other object within their jurisdiction, whether persons, property, business, or professions, it was secured in as ample a manner as it was before possessed. . . . Every private business, whether carried on by an officer of the General Government or not, whether it be mixed with public concerns or not, even if it be carried on by the Government of the United States itself, separately or in partnership, falls within the scope of the taxing power of the State. Nothing comes more fully within it than banks and the business of banking, by whomsoever instituted and carried on. . . .

The principle is conceded that the States can not rightfully tax the operations of the General Government. They can not tax the money of the Government deposited in the State banks, nor the agency of those banks in remitting it; but will any man maintain that their mere selection to perform this public service for the General Government would exempt the State banks and their ordinary business from State taxation? Had the United States, instead of establishing a bank at Philadelphia, employed a private banker to keep and transmit their funds, would it have deprived Pennsylvania of the right to tax his bank and his usual banking operations? It will not be pretended. . . . It can not be *necessary* to the character of the bank as a fiscal agent of the Government that its private business should be exempted from that taxation to which all the State banks are liable, nor can I conceive it "*proper*" that the substantive and most essential powers reserved by the States shall be thus attacked and annihilated as a means of executing the powers delegated to the General Government. . . .

It is to be regretted that the rich and powerful too often bend the acts of government to their selfish purposes. Distinctions in society will always exist under every just government. Equality of talents, of education, or of wealth can not be produced by human institutions. In the full enjoyment of the gifts of Heaven and the fruits of superior industry, economy, and virtue, every man is equally entitled to protection by law; but when the laws undertake to add to these natural and just advantages artificial distinctions, to grant titles, gratuities, and exclusive privileges, to make the rich richer and the potent more powerful, the humble members of society—the farmers, mechanics, and laborers—who have neither the time nor the means of securing like favors to themselves, have a right to complain of the injustice of their Government. There are no necessary evils in government. Its evils exist only in its abuses. If it would confine itself to equal protection, and, as Heaven does its rains, shower its favors alike on the high and the low, the rich and the poor, it would be an unqualified blessing. In the act before me there seems to be a wide and ununecessary departure from these just principles.

Nor is our Government to be maintained or our Union preserved by invasions of the rights and powers of the several States. In thus attempting to make our General Government strong we make it weak. Its true strength consists in leaving individuals and States as much as possible to themselves—in making itself felt, not in its power, but in its beneficence; not in its control,

but in its protection; not in binding the States more closely to the center, but leaving each to move unobstructed in its proper orbit.

Experience should teach us wisdom. Most of the difficulties our Government now encounters and most of the dangers which impend over our Union have sprung from an abandonment of the legitimate objects of Government by our national legislation, and the adoption of such principles as are embodied in this act. Many of our rich men have not been content with equal protection and equal benefits, but have besought us to make them richer by act of Congress. By attempting to gratify their desires we have in the results of our legislation arrayed section against section, interest against interest, and man against man, in a fearful commotion which threatens to shake the foundations of our Union. It is time to pause in our career to review our principles, and if possible revive that devoted patriotism and spirit of compromise which distinguished the sages of the Revolution and the fathers of our Union.

# 27

*"If they can be induced to educate their children, even from inferior motives, the children, when educated, will feel its higher and nobler affinities"*

The phrase, "a liberal education," is no doubt one of the vaguest and most threadbare in the language. In the Greek city-states, where democracy rested on a large slave population, a liberal education was one suitable for the full development of the talents and personalities of free men. In imperial Rome, authority and conformity were more highly valued than in Greece, but Roman youths marked for rulership nevertheless were educated in the Greek spirit and in the Greek language as well as their native Latin. By the time of the Italian Renaissance, slavery had virtually disappeared from Europe and feudal serfdom had also long been on the wane. Many "new men" held land of their own in the country, and in the cities they enjoyed broader if not absolute liberty of movement and choice of occupation, and even the opportunity to accumulate income-producing capital. While freedom itself thereafter gradually became more common, the idea of a free man—that is, one permitted to participate formally in political decisions—narrowed. Few but aristocrats and members of certain less clearly defined elites were included within the pale. Their education, in turn, in imitation of that of the free men of antiquity, and possibly in attempts at emulation of the glory and the grandeur of Greece and Rome, was confined to the classical tradition.

Once the exhilaration arising from the discovery of the cultural riches of antiquity had run its course in Europe, and political participation had become largely a hereditary right, a liberal education, even in colleges, sank to little more than rote learning of the dead languages as an adornment rather than an enlivener of gentlemanly minds. On the preparatory level, such education was available at high cost in Latin and grammar schools such as Eton and St. Paul's in England, where little of any other kind of schooling was offered the young before the nineteenth century. This classical or liberal system found its way to America in 1635 with the establishment of the Latin grammar school in Boston, the prototype of many other American preparatory schools. The tradition of the Reformation—the idea that every Protestant youth must be made literate enough at public expense if need be to read the Bible in vernacular translations —had also been carried early to Massachusetts Bay, whence it spread to the other New England colonies (see "Children," in Document No. 4, above).

In the general history of education, and in America itself, the family, the church, and the employer all participated in the training of oncoming generations, often without the intervention of schools at all. The motives for establishing schools, in turn, grew far more numerous than the nurture of rulers or of the individual soul. The school was looked to as the keeper and purveyor of the established values of society. It was the instrument of conversion from one faith to another, the guardian of sectarianism, the rod of the watchful and avenging God. When men like Jefferson and Madison discarded what they viewed as the superstition of the fall of man and accepted his innate goodness, they looked to the school to supplant the church, to knowledge to supplant fear, as youth's moral guide. Early in the nineteenth century, as participation in politics broadened in America, political leaders looked to the schools as the fountainheads of good citizenship. By the middle of the century, when democracy also came to mean provision of equality of opportunity by the state, the schools were to be the upward levelers. In all past ages, moreover, and nowhere more confidently than in the United States, the school was enlisted for vocational training.

What is often overlooked is that schools, and especially free public schools, always had pertinacious and effective enemies—among the rich who thought they soured the poor on their station in life, among the poor themselves who thought schools spoiled the children and were too costly in taxes and their offspring's working time, among the godly who thought them too worldly, among the practical who thought them too bookish, and, notoriously, among the students, who with disheartening frequency assaulted teachers, smashed desks, defaced buildings, and then stayed home. The average American in 1800 had received no more than four months of formal schooling in his lifetime. This figure had risen to ten months by 1840, but with the thinning out of population and the growing parsimony and parochialism of school management, the quality of American education had by then almost certainly declined.

In 1826 a great revival of the public school system of Massachusetts had begun, which culminated in the creation, in 1837, of the first state Board of Education in the country, and the momentous appointment of Horace Mann as its first full-time secretary. On taking his new post, Mann wrote in his diary:

> I have faith in the improvability of the race—in their accelerating improvability. This effort may do, apparently, little. But mere beginning a good cause is never little. If we can get this vast wheel into any perceptible motion, we shall have accomplished much.

That a mere beginning might indeed do much was evident from Mann's first annual report to the Board. Here he observed that in Massachusetts, the topmost state in educational progress, and after ten years of improvement, from one-third to two-fifths of those children between the ages of four to sixteen who were wholly dependent upon the free schools for their education never attended. Those that did attend were in class no more than four widely separated months of the year. What struck Mann even more forcibly was the inequality of educational opportunity from town to town. In money appropriated for the public schools, "the difference between the foremost and the hindmost towns in the State is more than *seven to one!*" Besides Boston, the forty-three largest Massachusetts towns were required by law to maintain higher schools for "bookkeeping, surveying, geometry and algebra," and still higher ones "competent to instruct in the Latin and Greek languages and general history, rhetoric and logic." In no less than twenty-nine of these towns, "this provision of the law is wholly disregarded." Believing that "this subject," Mann told his superiors, "bears very nearly the same relation to the healthfulness of our republican institutions, that air does to animal life, I must solicit for it in some detail, the consideration of the Board."

The vagueness of the phrase, "a liberal education," arises from changing conceptions of the nature of man and the nature of mind. The centuries-long debate over these conceptions and the curricula by which man and his mind might best be improved, and for what ends, is what has made this phrase so threadbare.

Horace Mann himself was dedicated to the *goals* of a liberal education in the ennobling Greek sense. He believed in the highest cultivation of the individual mind as the surest guarantee of social wisdom and virtue. His higher schools would offer "an equal welcome to each one . . . whom a peculiar destination, or an impelling spirit of genius, shall send to its open doors—especially to the children of the poor." The education of those below the level of genius would proceed on the same exalted plane. He made this clear in his first report, when, with classic simplicity, he told the Board:

> The object of the common school system of Massachusetts was to give every child in the Commonwealth a free, straight, solid path-way, by which he could walk directly up from the ignorance of an infant to a knowledge of the primary duties of a man; and could acquire a power and an invincible will to discharge them.

Mann knew, however, that he had first to awaken parents, public, and politicians in order to get his "vast wheel into any perceptible motion." To this thankless labor he gave all his energy without losing sight of his transcendent goal, indeed always inspired by it. His principal instrument was publicity. He traveled constantly throughout Massachusetts and in other states and abroad. He promoted frequent County Common School Conventions for the special edification of local school committeemen. In 1838 he started *The Common School Journal,* a semi-monthly organ covering every aspect of school business, and he edited it himself for ten years. By far his most influential promotional materials, however, were his annual reports to the Massachusetts Board, each a comprehensive examination, based on thorough study, of some grave school problem, along with a review of progress on other consuming if elementary issues—school buildings, textbooks, apparatus, registers of attendance, and so forth. And progress there was. During his twelve-year administration, Mann could point to significant annual increases in Massachusetts in school appropriations, school attendance, length of school terms, the number of school libraries. He took most pride, perhaps, in the normal schools he created and the vast improvement in teacher training they effected. He could point, moreover, to the influence of his reports throughout the land, where they were read by school administrators with absorption and put to almost instantaneous use.

Yet midway in his tenure, Mann felt he had not yet truly hit the mark. In his fifth annual report, January, 1842, he wrote: "The best minds in our community have been reached. What is now wanted is to reach another class of persons, numerically greater, but having less appreciation of the value of education, and less knowledge of the means by which it should be conducted." To capture them, Mann devoted his fifth annual report, from which the quotation at the head of this document is taken, and which is reproduced in part below, to "showing the effect of education upon *The Worldly Fortunes or Estates* of men." This view, he wrote, "so far from being the highest which can be taken of the beneficent influence of education, may, perhaps, be justly regarded as the lowest. But . . . it will meet the case of thousands, who are now indifferent about the education of their offspring, because they foresee . . . no return in money, or in money's worth, for money expended." Catching them thus, he hoped "those loftier . . . attributes of the cause, which have the power of converting material wealth into spiritual well-being," would at least be caught by their children. Mann's fifth report was perhaps his most famous one; New York State alone ordered 18,000 copies. Public education in America still lay deep in the pit of darkness; but because of Horace Mann, its rise was sharply speeded up.

*January 1, 1842*

# Horace Mann's Fifth Annual Report
# to the Massachusetts Board of Education

Having now established, beyond the possibility of denial or doubt, the extraordinary and heretofore unrecognized inequalities existing between different towns in the Commonwealth, as it respects the educational advantages they bestow upon their children, the natural course of the argument would lead, at once, to an exposition or development of the consequences which must grow out of this wide departure, on each hand, from a common standard. To follow out the premises here established, to their legitimate conclusions, it should be shown what effect these different educational advantages will produce upon

1. The Worldly Fortunes,
2. The Health and Length of Life,
3. The Manners and Tastes, and
4. The Intellectual and Moral Character,

of the rising generation. This could be easily done, for the declination of the sun towards the southern tropic, is not more certainly followed by winter, with all its blankness and sterility, nor does the ascension of that luminary towards our own part of the heavens, more certainly bring on summer, with all its beauty and abundance, than does the want of enjoyment of education degrade or elevate the condition of a people. But such an undertaking would be incompatible with the limits of a document like this. The most that can be ventured upon, is a brief reference to a single branch of the manifold subject.

For this end, I will occupy the short space which propriety allows to me, in concluding this report, by showing the effect of education upon *the Worldly Fortunes or Estates* of men,—its influence upon property, upon human comfort and competence, upon the outward, visible, material interests or well-being of individuals and communities.

This view, so far from being the highest which can be taken of the beneficent influences of education, may, perhaps, be justly regarded as the lowest. But it is a palpable view. It presents an aspect of the subject susceptible of being made intelligible to all; and, therefore, it will meet the case of thousands, who are now indifferent about the education of their offspring, because they foresee no reimbursement in kind,—no return in money, or in money's worth, for money expended. The coöperation of this numerous class is indispensable, in order to carry out the system; and if they can be induced to educate their children, even from inferior motives, the children, when educated, will feel its higher and nobler affinities. So, too, in regard to towns. . . .

I am the more induced to take this view of the subject, because the advocates and eulogists of education have, rarely if ever, descended to so humble a duty as to demonstrate its pecuniary value, both to individuals and to society. They have expended their strength in portraying its loftier attributes, its gladdening, refining, humanizing tendencies. They have not deigned to show how it can raise more abundant harvests, and multiply the conveniences of domestic life; how it can build, transport, manufacture, mine, navigate, fortify; how, in fine, a single new idea is often worth more to an individual than a hundred workmen, —and to a nation, than the addition of provinces to its territory. I have novel and striking evidence to prove that education is convertible into houses and lands, as well as into power and virtue. . . .

During the past year I have opened a correspondence, and availed myself of all opportunities to hold personal interviews with many of the most practical, sagacious and intelligent business men amongst us, who for many years have had large numbers of persons in their employment. My object has been to ascertain the difference in the productive ability,—where natural capacities have been equal,—between the educated and the uneducated,—between a man or woman whose mind has been awakened to thought and supplied with the rudiments of knowledge, by a good Common School education, and one whose faculties have never been developed, or aided in emerging from their original darkness and torpor by such a privilege. For this purpose I have conferred and coresponded with manufacturers of all kinds, with machinists, engineers, rail-road contractors, officers

in the army, &c. These various classes of persons have means of determining the effects of education on individuals, equal in their natural abilities, which other classes do not possess. . . .

When hundreds of men or women work side by side, in the same factory, at the same machinery, in making the same fabrics, and, by a fixed rule of the establishment, labor the same number of hours each day; and when, also, the products of each operative can be counted in number, weighed by the pound, or measured by the yard or cubic foot,—then it is perfectly practicable to determine with arithmetical exactness, the productions of one individual and one class as compared with those of another individual and another class.

So where there are different kinds of labor, some simple, others complicated, and of course requiring different degrees of intelligence and skill, it is easy to observe what class of persons rise from a lower to a higher grade of employment.

This too is not to be forgotten, that in a manufacturing or mechanical establishment, or among a set of hands engaged in filling up a valley or cutting down a hill, where scores of people are working together, the absurd and adventitious distinctions of society do not intrude. The capitalist and his agents are looking for the greatest amount of labor, or the largest income in money from their investments; and they do not promote a dunce to a station, where he will destroy raw material, or slacken industry, because of his name, or birth, or family connections. The obscurest and humblest person has an open and fair field for competition. That he proves himself capable of earning more money for his employer, is a testimonial, better than a diploma from all the colleges.

Now many of the most intelligent and valuable men in our community, in compliance with my request,—for which I tender them my public and grateful acknowledgements,—have examined their books for a series of years, and have ascertained both the quality and the amount of work performed by persons in their employment; and the result of the investigation is a most astonishing superiority in productive power, on the part of the educated over the uneducated laborer. The hand is found to be another hand, when guided by an intelligent mind. Processes are performed, not only more rapidly, but better, when faculties which have been exercised in early life, furnish their assistance. Individuals who, without the aid of knowledge, would have been condemned to perpetual inferiority of condition, and subjected to all the evils of want and poverty, rise to competence and independence, by the uplifting power of education. In great establishments, and among large bodies of laboring men, where all services are rated according to their pecuniary value, where there are no extrinsic circumstances to bind a man down to a fixed position, after he has shown a capacity to rise above it;—where, indeed, men pass by each other, ascending or descending in their grades of labor, just as easily and certainly as particles of water of different degrees glide by each other,—there is found as an almost invariable fact,—other things being equal,—that those who have been blessed with a good Common School education, rise to a higher and a higher point, in the kinds of labor performed, and also in the rate of wages paid, while the ignorant sink, like dregs, and are always found at the bottom. . . .

Education is not only a moral renovator, and a multiplier of intellectual power, but . . . it is also the most prolific parent of material riches. It has a right, therefore, not only to be included in the grand inventory of a nation's resources, but to be placed at the very head of that inventory. It is not only the most honest and honorable, but the surest means of amassing property. A trespasser or a knave may forcibly or fraudulently appropriate the earnings of others to himself; but education has

the prerogative of originating or generating property, more certainly and more rapidly than it was ever accumulated by force or fraud. . . . As it enjoys an immunity from common casualties, it incurs no cost for insurance or defence. It is above the reach of changes in administration, or in administrational policy; and it is free from those fluctuations of trade which agitate the market, and make it so frequent an occurrence, that a merchant who goes to bed a man of wealth at night, rises a pauper in the morning. Possessing these qualities, it . . . is more powerful in the production and gainful employment of the total wealth of a country, than all other things mentioned in the books of the political economist. . . .

Perhaps there is no spot in the world of such limited extent, where there is a greater variety of agricultural productions than in Massachusetts. This brings into requisition all that chemical and experimental knowledge which pertains to the rotation of crops, and the enrichment of soils. . . . Without further exposition, it may be remarked generally, that the spread of intelligence, through the instrumentality of good books, and the cultivation in our children of the faculties of observing, comparing and reasoning, through the medium of good schools, would add millions to the agricultural products of the Commonwealth, without imposing upon the husbandman an additional hour of labor. . . .

Now for the successful prosecution, —it may almost be said, for the very existence amongst us of the manufacturing and mechanic arts, there must be, not only the exactness of science, but also exactness or skill in the application of scientific principles, throughout the whole processes, either of constructing machinery, or of transforming raw materials into finished fabrics. This ability to make exact and skilful applications of science to an unlimited variety of materials, and especially to the subtile but most energetic agencies of nature, is one of the latest attainments of the human mind. . . . It is in ways similar to this,—that is, by accomplishing greater results with less means; by creating products, at once cheaper, better, and by more expeditious methods; and by doing a vast variety of things, otherwise impossible, that the cultivation of mind may be truly said to yield the highest pecuniary requital. Intelligence is the greatest money-maker,—not by extortion, but by production. There are ten thousand things in every department of life, which, if done in season, can be done in a minute, but which, if not seasonably done, will require hours, perhaps days or weeks, for their performance. An awakened mind will see and seize the critical juncture; the perceptions of a sluggish one will come too late, if they come at all. . . .

And why is it that, so far as this Union is concerned, four-fifths of all the improvements, inventions and discoveries in regard to machinery, to agricultural implements, to superior models in ship-building, and to the manufacture of those refined instruments on which accuracy in scientific observations depends, have originated in New England. I believe no adequate reason can be assigned, but the early awakening and training of the power of thought in our children. . . .

Amongst a people, then, who must gain their subsistence by their labor, what can be so economical, so provident and far-sighted, and even so wise,—in a lawful and laudable, though not in the highest sense of that word,

—as to estabish, and, with open heart and hand, to endow and sustain the most efficient system of Universal Education for their children; and, where the material bounties of nature are comparatively narrow and stinted, to explore, in their stead, those exhaustless and illimitable resources of comfort and competency and independence, which lie hidden in the yet dormant powers of the human intellect?

But notwithstanding all I have said of the value of education, in a pecuniary sense, and of its power to improve and elevate the outward domestic and social condition of all men, yet, in closing this report, I should do injustice to my feelings, did I abstain from declaring that to my own mind, this tribute to its worth, however well deserved, is still the faintest note of praise which can be uttered, in honor of so noble a theme;—and that, however deserving of attention may be the *economical* view of the subject which I have endeavored to present, yet it is one that dwindles into insignficance when compared with those loftier and more sacred attributes of the cause, which have the power of converting material wealth into spiritual well-being, and of giving to its possessor lordship and sovereignty, alike over the temptations of adversity, and the still more danger-ous seducements of prosperity,—and which,—so far as human agency is concerned,—must be looked to for the establishment of peace and righteousness upon earth, and for the enjoyment of glory and happiness in heaven.

## 28

*"The only channel for the commerce of all the western coast of Mexico and South America, . . . of all China . . . Australia, Java, Singapore, Calcutta, and Bombay"*

On January 28, 1845, Asa Whitney, of the City of New York, as he styled himself, presented simultaneously to the House and Senate his Memorial for "A grant of land to enable him to construct a railroad from Lake Michigan to the Pacific Ocean." A House committee, during the following congressional session, rejected Whitney's plan as "too gigantic and, at least for the present, entirely impracticable." The Senate Committee on Public Lands, on the other hand, reporting in July, 1846, was enthusiastic about the present as the right time, and Whitney's plan as the right one:

> A few years since, in the then existing state of the arts and sciences, a committee of this body would have been excused for treating [Whitney's proposal] as a visionary speculation. . . . But the advances made in science, combining the active and formidable power of steam with the concentrating properties of machinery, and adapting this combination to the propulsion of vehicles by land and on water, . . . have so familiarized the public mind to the contemplation of the wonderful achievements of the age, that it would seem to be the part only of benighted prejudice to avoid due consideration of any proposition . . . resting upon established principles of mechanical philosophy, tested by the experience of civilized nations, and intended to benefit in the highest degree the whole country, and to elevate its character.

The Senate Committee acknowledged that there might be unknown obstacles on the proposed route, but "what obstacle cannot American ingenuity and energy overcome!" The committee was "by no means perfectly satisfied" with other details, but, "as at least twenty years will be consumed in constructing it, it becomes important that the earliest moment should be seized in which to commence operations."

As modern and forward looking as the Senate Committee was, it could not refrain from referring to Whitney's project as establishing "a short route to the riches and marvels of the Indies," and from writing at greatest length, in a vein remarkably reminiscent of Columbus himself, about the access it would afford to the glittering wonders of the golden cities of Cathay. And indeed

Whitney was proposing nothing less than a mechanized northwest passage *across* the continent that had proved such a frustrating barrier to generations of intrepid mariners trying to sail around it. Whitney's goals, nevertheless, were more comprehensive than the mere enlargement of the China trade, in which he himself had long been engaged and which in fact had given birth to his grand conception. The American system, he said, "diffusing so much intelligence, dispensing equal justice, and insuring safety to all, and producing so much general comfort and prosperity, . . . must, like a mighty flood, sweep away all other systems." From his Pacific railroad scheme, said Whitney, "your memorialist expects all this, and more."

The notion of crossing from the Atlantic to the Pacific by rail had first been proposed in 1832, when railroads themselves were in their infancy. In 1835, one Samuel Parker outlined the first explicit route based on his own travels from Buffalo to the Columbia River. Thereafter, as Americans pushed westward to Oregon, and as China was forced to open new ports for trading, and as Pacific whaling and other fisheries expanded, and as nations competed for strategic Pacific islands to protect their ships, and for strategic Pacific ports to harbor them, many more Pacific railroad proposals were offered in Congress and the press. Whitney's was the most specific, the most inspiring, and certainly the boldest. When Congressman Stephen A. Douglas, who had grand railroad ideas of his own, learned of Whitney's request that Congress grant to him personally a lordly strip "sixty miles in width from . . . Lake Michigan . . . to the Pacific Ocean," with which to pay for construction, he exclaimed: "This grant would amount to 144,000 square miles, . . . a quantity greater than is contained in the entire states of New York, New Jersey, Pennsylvania, and Ohio, collectively; . . . more extensive than England, Ireland, Scotland, and half a dozen of the German states, combined." Whitney was not checked by such calculations. When Congress failed to act on his proposal, he took it to the people in a vast publicity campaign. Largely through his work, the idea of a Pacific railroad gained irreversible momentum.

Whitney's project lost out because of the doubts about his land scheme, uncertainties about its timeliness, and ultimately because of the shift of interest from Oregon to California following the Mexican War in 1846 and the discovery of gold at Sutter's Fort in 1848. The whole Pacific railroad idea thereafter was held back by sectional conflicts over alternative routes and local conflicts over eastern terminals. But when the Union Pacific, the first transcontinental, at last was chartered by Congress in 1862 (Document No. 33, below) and completed (with the Central Pacific) from Omaha to Sacramento in 1869, Whitney could with pardonable pride congratulate himself on the nation's achievement. His first Memorial, aglow with the idealization of material progress so characteristic of his age, is presented in part below.

*January 28, 1845*

# Asa Whitney's Memorial
## for a Land Grant for a Pacific Railroad

*To the honorable the Senate and House of Representatives of the United States in Congress assembled:* Your memorialist begs respectfully to represent to your honorable body, that, by rivers, railroads, and canals, all the States east and north of the Potomac connect directly with the waters of the great lakes.

That there is a chain of railroads in projection, and being built, from New York to the southern shore of Lake Michigan, which, crossing all the veins of communication to the ocean through all the States south and east of the Ohio river, will produce commercial, political, and national results and benefits, which must be seen and felt through all our vast Confederacy. Your memorialist would further represent to your honorable body, that he has devoted much time and attention to the subject of a railroad from Lake Michigan, through the Rocky mountains, to the Pacific ocean, and that he finds such a route practicable, the results from which would be incalculable, far beyond the imagination of man to estimate. . . . Such easy and rapid communication, with such facilities for exchanging the different products of the different parts, would bring all our immensely wide-spread population together as one vast city, the moral and social effects of which must harmonize all together as one family, with but one interest—the general good of all.

Your memorialist respectfully represents to your honorable body, that the roads from New York to Lake Michigan, a distance of 840 miles, will no

doubt be completed by the States through which they pass, or by individuals; that from Lake Michigan to the mouth of the Columbia river is 2,160 miles, making from New York to the Pacific ocean 3,000 miles; from the Columbia river to the Sandwich Islands is 2,100 miles, making from New York to the Sandwich Islands 5,100 miles; from the Columbia river to Japan is 5,600 miles, making from New York to Japan 8,600 miles; from the Columbia river to Amoy, in China, (the port nearest the tea and silk provinces,) is 6,200 miles, making from New York to Amoy only 9,200 miles, which, with a railroad to the Pacific, thence to China by steam, can be performed in 30 days, now being a sailing distance of nearly 17,000 miles, requiring from 100 to 150 days for its performance. Then the drills and sheetings of Connecticut, Rhode Island, and Massachusetts, can be transported to China in thirty days, and the teas and rich silks of China in exchange come back to New Orleans, to Charleston, to Washington, to Baltimore, to Philadelphia, to New York, and to Boston, in thirty days more. Comment is unnecessary.

Your honorable body will readily see the revolution by this to be wrought in the entire commerce of the world, and that this must inevitably be its channel, when the rich freights from the waters of the Mississippi and the Hudson will fill to overflowing, with the products of all the earth, the storehouses of New York and New Orleans, the great marts dividing the commerce of the world, while each State and every town in our vast Confederacy would receive its just proportion of influence and benefits, compared with its vicinity to or facility to communicate with any of the rivers, canals, or railroads, crossed by this great road. Your memorialist would respectfully represent to your honorable body its political importance, that, affording a communication from Washington to the Columbia river in less than eight days, a naval depot, with a comparatively small navy, would command the Pacific, the South Atlantic, and the Indian oceans, and the Chinese seas, . . . thus at once giving us the power of dictation to those who will not long remain satisfied without an attempt to dictate to us.

Our system of free government works so well, diffusing so much intelligence, dispensing equal justice, and insuring safety to all, and producing so much general comfort and prosperity, that its influence must, like a mighty flood, sweep away all other systems. Then let us not flatter ourselves that this overwhelming current is not to meet resistance, for to us directly will that resistance be applied; and your memorialist believes that we must yet meet that desperate and final struggle which shall perpetuate our system and religious and civil liberty.

Your honorable body are aware of the over population of Europe; and your memorialist would respectfully represent that, by the application of machinery, and its substitution for manual labor, the latter no longer receives its just or sufficient reward; and thousands, in the fear of starvation at home, are driven to our shores, hoping, from our wide-spread and fertile soil, to find a rich reward for their labor—most of them ignorant, and all inexperienced. Having been herded together in large numbers at home, they dread separation even from misery; they fear the wilderness or prairie; they refuse to leave the city; their small means are soon exhausted; they see abundance around them, almost without price, but

that small price they can no longer pay; necessity plunges them into vice, and often crime, and they become burdensome to our citizens—and which evil is increasing to an alarming extent; and your memorialist believes it must increase, unless there can be some great and important point in our interior to which they can be attracted immediately on their landing, where their little means, with their labor, can purchase lands, where they will escape the tempting vices of our cities, where they will have a home with their associates, and where their labor from their own soil will not only produce their daily bread, but in time an affluence of which they could never have dreamed in their native land.

Your memorialist believes that this road will be the great and desirable point of attraction; that it will relieve our cities from a vast amount of misery, crime, and taxation; that it will take the poor unfortunates to a land where they will not be compelled to labor for a subsistence; and as they will soon find that their labor and efforts receive a just reward—finding themselves and their little ones surrounded with comfort and plenty, the recompense for their own toil—their energies will kindle into a flame of ambition and desire; and we shall be enabled to educate them to our system—to industry, prosperity, and virtue. Your memorialist confidently expects all this, and more.

Your memorialist would respectfully represent, further, . . . that, . . . the total estimated cost of said road, when completed, [will be] $65,000,000, . . . that after a period of ——— years, and at the very lowest possible rates of tolls, it must earn more than ample for its repairs and expenses. It would be the only channel for the commerce of all the western coast of Mexico and South America, of the Sandwich islands, of Japan, of all China, Manilla, Australia, Java, Singapore, Calcutta, and Bombay—not only all ours, but the commerce of all Europe. To the most of these places must pass this road —your memorialist says *must* because the saving of time, (so all-important to the merchant) from the long and hazardous voyage around either of the capes, would force it; and in a few years would be built up cities, towns, and villages, from the lake to the ocean, which would alone support the road.

Being built from the public lands, the road should be free, except so far as sufficient for the necessary expenses of operation, repairs, &c.; and your memorialist believes that, at a very low rate of tolls, a sum would be gained, after all current expenses, sufficient to make a handsome distribution for public education. . . .

Your memorialist respectfully represents, further, to your honorable body, that, from the knowledge he can procure, he finds that the lands, for a long distance east of the mountains, are bad, of little or no value for culture; that through and for some distance beyond the mountains would also be of but little if any value; therefore, your memorialist is satisfied that it will require an entire tract of sixty miles in width, from as near to Lake Michigan as the unappropriated lands commence, to the Pacific ocean.

Therefore, in view of all the important considerations here set forth, your memorialist is induced to pray that your honorable body will grant to himself, his heirs, and assigns, such tract of land, the proceeds of which to be strictly and faithfully applied to the building and completing the said road, always with such checks and guaranties to your honorable body as shall secure a faithful performance of all the obligations and duties of your memorialist; and that, after the faithful completion of this great work, should any lands remain unsold, or any moneys due for lands, or any balance of moneys received for lands sold, which have not been required for the building of said road, then all and every of them shall belong to your memorialist, his heirs and assigns, forever. . . .

Your memorialist would respectfully represent one further consideration to your honorable body: that, in his opinion, Oregon must fast fill up with an industrious, enterprising people from our States; that they will soon attract and draw to them large numbers from the States of Europe—all expecting to share in the benefits from our free Government—claiming its care and protection; but the difficulty of access to them either by land or water will forbid such a hope.

And your memorialist believes that the time is not far distant when Oregon will become a State of such magnitude and importance as to compel the establishment of a separate Government—a separate nation, which will have cities, ports, and harbors, all free, inviting all the nations of the earth to a free trade with them; when they will control and monopolize the valuable fisheries of the Pacific; control the coast trade of Mexico and South America, of the Sandwich islands, Japan, and all China, and be our most dangerous and successful rivals in the commerce of the world.

But your memorialist believes that this road will unite them to us, enabling them to receive the protecting care of our Government, sharing in its blessings, benefits, and prosperity, and imparting to us our share of the great benefits from their local position, enterprise, and industry; but your honorable body will see all this, and more.

# 29

## *"We want almost unlimited power of expansion. That is our safety valve."*

The phrase "safety valve," a famous one in American history, is ordinarily used to dramatize the role of the ever-receding West in drawing off the excess population of the older sections and thereby preserving the whole nation's Jeffersonian way of life (see Document No. 21, above). In this sense, were it not still a foreign land, it may be said that Texas offered a safety valve to Moses and Stephen Austin and their fellow *empresarios* of the 1820's, once the Panic of 1819 had got them into serious financial difficulties in then neighboring Missouri; and that Oregon served the same salutary purpose once the Panic of 1837 had ruined the prospects of yeoman pioneers on the edge of "The Great American Desert."

The movement of American slaveholders into Texas, however, soon fed the hope of its early annexation to the United States, against the wishes of Mexico and of those many Americans who doubted the place of the South's "peculiar institution" in the Jeffersonian "empire of liberty." The progress of the Oregon pioneers, in turn, brought the United States face to face with hated Britain's claims to the ill-defined northwestern territory on "our continent."

Active British interest in Texas, moreover, linked the two issues in a way that was particularly challenging to the South. In December, 1843, the British Foreign Secretary wrote officially to Washington, through the British Minister there, Sir Richard Pakenham, that "it must be and is well known to the United States and to the whole world, that Great Britain desires, and is constantly exerting herself to procure the general abolition of slavery throughout the world," and "with regard to Texas, we avow that we wish to see slavery abolished there, as elsewhere." Britain in Oregon appeared as well to offer at least as grave a challenge to the free states, especially the maritime states of the Northeast. These states envied her suzerainty of the seas, coveted her commercial leadership, and yearned particularly for good Pacific harbors from which to capture once and for all the whole beckoning Oriental trade.

It was in this connection with Texas and Oregon—as handmaiden to that other famous phrase of the time, "manifest destiny"—that the idea of the "safety valve" first took on the more wishful and hence more ominous meaning with which it is used at the head of this Document and in certain items reproduced below. No longer an expression merely for the desirability of expansion as an outlet for excess population, "safety valve" became an expression also for the desirability of conquest as therapy for the sectional lesions that expansion made worse. The morbid depths of this line of thought were plumbed in April, 1861, by no less a person than Lincoln's Secretary of State, William H. Seward, who proposed that the Cabinet "change the question before the public from one upon slavery or about slavery, . . . to one of patriotism or union," by fomenting war with all the European nations at once, who still possessed New World land or land hunger.

The safety valve failed to work, then and earlier. In 1845, Senator Edward A. Hannegan of Indiana, a leader of the expansionist "ultras," offered this bellicose toast: "Oregon—Every foot or not an inch; 54 degrees 40 minutes or delenda est Britain." Yet President James K. Polk was soon to back down to 49 degrees north latitude as the line at which he gladly made permanent peace with Britain over Oregon's boundary. Oregon, a Whig editor had said a year earlier, was "wrapped around" Texas, "just as the nurse disguises a nauseous dose in honey to cheat the palate of a rebellious patient." Texas soon was swallowed, to be followed by even larger doses of Mexican territory, including California. But the war with Mexico by which we made good our "manifest destiny" in these vast lands only aggravated the slavery issue and thereby quickened rather than quieted disunion talk.

Thereafter, as the stress of slavery grew, expansionists in both sections grasped at all other likely straws of Union sentiment. One of the most appealing of these (as in Document No. 28, above) was the grand promise of the new technological wonders—of the steam railroad, the steamship, the telegraph—"to bind still closer," as Lewis Cass said in 1847, "the portions of this empire, as they recede from its capital." As late as 1853, in seeking the organization of Nebraska Territory in anticipation of his own plans for a Pacific railroad, Stephen A. Douglas, now Senator, rallied laggard colleagues: "If they are opposed to open a communication between the Atlantic and Pacific, if they are in favor of disunion, let them declare it."

History, geography, and oceanography also were enlisted by the "safety valve," "manifest destiny," school. Yet, no matter what Providence may seem to have ordained, the sectional issue, after all, was not to be met by seeking ascendancy in India and China, nor authority in Central and South America, nor territorial accessions even in the nearby Caribbean or in adjacent Canada. By 1850 it was to be met most imminently in California. And having failed of settlement there (only a month after California had been admitted as a free state under the compromise of 1850, Senator Douglas observed that, "the agitation on the subject of slavery [is] now raging through the breadth of the land . . . with renewed vigor and increased violence") it had soon to be met even closer to home, in Nebraska. And having failed of settlement there by means of Douglas's vaunted "popular sovereignty," it had soon to be met once more in "bleeding Kansas." And having failed of settlement there by means of the first confrontation of armed bands, it had to be met at last no farther away from Washington than Fort Sumter in Charleston harbor.

In item "a," below, we present in part the letter Senator Robert J. Walker of Mississippi addressed on January 8, 1844, to the Democratic leaders of Carroll County, Kentucky, on the subject of Texas, "the only safety valve for the whole Union." Tens of thousands of copies of this letter were circulated across the country as the opening volley in the campaign which carried James K. Polk to the Presidency later that year, and Walker to the position of power behind the throne. Their platform, in Walker's words, called for "the reannexation of Texas," on the fanciful ground that it had once been our own, and for "the reoccupation of Oregon," on the ground that no one else could more rightfully claim it.

On March 4, 1845, in his inaugural address (item "b"), President Polk urged foreign powers to keep out of the Texas controversy and warned Britain in particular not to contest the right of the United States to all of Oregon. In his first annual message to Congress, December 2, 1845, (item "c"), Polk beefed up his warning: "should . . . any European interference on the North American continent . . . be attempted," the United States "will be ready to resist it at any and all hazards." Polk then went on to assert what has become known as his corollary to the Monroe Doctrine (Document No. 23, above): "Should any portion . . . of the people of this continent . . . constituting an independent state, propose to unite themselves with our Confederacy, this will be a question for them and us to determine without any foreign interposition."

In his inaugural, Polk pointed out that "Our Union is a confederation of independent States, whose policy is peace with each other and all the world. To enlarge its limits is to extend the dominions of peace over additional territories and increasing millions." If the process of enlargement itself nevertheless required breaking the peace, as it soon did with Mexico for the purpose of acquiring California, that had to be faced. In item "d" we present in part then Congressman Stephen A. Douglas's speech in the House, May 13, 1846, in support of the Mexican War. "American blood has been shed on American soil by a treacherous foe," said Douglas. In these circumstances, "I know no sections, no divisions."

On August 8, 1846, as an amendment to a bill for an appropriation to purchase additional territory from Mexico at the war's end, David Wilmot of Pennsylvania offered his famous "proviso":

> As an express and fundamental condition to the acquisition of any territory from the Republic of Mexico by the United States, by virtue of any treaty that may be negotiated between them, and to the use by the Executive of the moneys herein appropriated, neither slavery nor involuntary servitude shall ever exist in any part of said territory, except for crime, whereof the party shall first be duly convicted.

This "mischievous and foolish amendment," as Polk characterized it, never was adopted. In item "e" we present a portion of the speech of Senator Lewis Cass, February 10, 1847, in defense of the appropriation without the proviso, from which the quotation at the head of this Document is taken.

The suppression of widespread popular revolts in Europe in 1848, especially that of the Hungarians against the Austrian Empire of which they were a part, aroused stronger anti-European feelings than ever in the United States. Such feelings were strongest in the North, which was taking more and more pride in its own strength and in the institutions of liberty to which it attributed its astonishing recent growth. The classic statement of the deepening consciousness of the manifest destiny of "Young America" to spread democracy and republicanism around the world, is Secretary of State Daniel Webster's formal letter to the Austrian Chargé d'Affaires in Washington, Chevalier J. G. Hülsemann, December 21, 1850. This letter, contrasting remarkably with Polk's corollary and Monroe's doctrine warning Europe out of America, is presented in part in item "f." In explaining its "boastful" tone, Webster wrote to a friend in January, 1851: "I wished to write a paper which would touch the national pride, and make a man feel *sheepish* and look *silly* who would speak of disunion."

*1844-1850*

## Manifest Destiny and Disunion

(a) *From Robert J. Walker's letter on Texas
as "the only safety valve for the whole Union," January 8, 1844*

Is it expedient to reannex Texas to the American Union? This is the greatest question, since the adoption of the constitution, ever presented for the decision of the American people. . . .

If the Creator had separated Texas from the Union by mountain barriers, the Alps or the Andes, there might be plausible objections; but he has planed down the whole [Mississippi] valley, including Texas, and united every atom of the soil and every drop of the waters of the mighty whole. He has linked their rivers with the great Mississippi, and marked and united the whole for the dominion of one government and the residence of one people; and it is impious in man to attempt to dissolve this great and glorious union. . . . The treaty which struck Texas from the Union, inflicted a blow upon this mighty valley. And who will say that the West shall remain dismembered and mutilated, and that the ancient boundaries of the republic shall never be restored? Who will desire to check the young eagle of America, now refixing her gaze upon our former limits, and repluming her pinions for her returning flight? . . . To refuse to accept the reannexation . . . is to lower the flag of the Union before the red cross of St. George, and to surrender the Florida pass, the mouth of the Mississippi, the command of the Mexican gulf, and finally Texas itself, into the hands of England. . . .

Of all the forms of government, our confederacy is most specially adapted for an extended territory, and might, without the least danger, but with increased security, and vastly augmented benefits, embrace a continent. . . . Has the Union been endangered by the advance in the number of States from thirteen to twenty-six? Look also at all the new States that have been added to the Union since the adoption of the constitution. . . . No rebellion or insurrection has ever raised its banner within their limits, nor have traitorous or union-dissolving conventions, in war or peace, ever been assembled within the boundary of any of the new States of the West; but in peace, they have nobly and faithfully performed all their duties to the Union; and in war, the spirit of party has fled before an ardent patriotism, and all have rushed to the standard of their common country. . . .

The greater the extent of territory, the more enlarged is the power, and the more augmented the blessings of such a government. . . . Especially is this important to the great manufacturing interest, that its home market, which is almost its only market, should be enlarged and extended by the accession of new territory, and an augmented population. . . .

Nor is it only the mining and manufacturing interests that would feel the influence of such a new and rapidly augmenting home market; but agriculture, commerce, and navigation, the products of the forest and fisheries, the freighting and shipbuilding interests, would all feel a new impulse; and the great internal communications, by railroads and canals, engaged in transporting our own exchangeable products, would find a great enlargement of their business and profits, . . . bringing nearer and nearer to each other the remotest portions of the mighty whole, multiplying their trade and intercourse, breaking down the barriers of local and

sectional prejudice, and scouting the thought of disunion from the American heart, and leaving the very term obsolete. . . . He who, under such circumstances, would still say that Texas was too large or distant for reannexation to the Union, must have been sleeping since the application of steam to locomotion.

But if Texas is too large for incorporation into the Union, why is not Oregon also, which is nearly double the size of Texas? . . . There, upon the shores of the distant Pacific, if my vote can accomplish it, shall be planted the banner of the Union; and, with my consent, never shall be surrendered a single point of its coast, an atom of its soil, or a drop of all its waters. . . . Let not those, then, who advocate the occupation of Oregon, tell us that Texas is too distant, or too inaccessible, or too extensive for American occupancy. . . .

The only remaining objection is the question of slavery. And have we a question which is to curtail the limits of the republic—to threaten its existence—to aim a deadly blow at all its great and vital interests—to court alliances with foreign and with hostile powers—to recall our commerce, and expel our manufactures from bays and rivers that once were all our own—to strike down the flag of the Union, as it advances towards our ancient boundary —to resurrender a mighty territory, and invite to its occupancy the deadliest (in truth the only) foes this government has ever encountered? Is antislavery to do all this? . . . The avowed object of this party is the immediate abolition of slavery. For this, . . . they hold conventions in the capital of England; and there they . . . join in denunciations of their countrymen, until their hearts are filled with treason . . . . Let us all, then, feel and know, whether we live North or South, that this party, if not vanquished, must overthrow the government, and dissolve the Union. . . .

If slavery be considered by the States of the North as an evil, why should they prefer that its location should be continued in States on their border, rather than in the more distant portions of the Union? It is clear that, as slavery advanced in Texas, it would recede from the States bordering on the free States of the North and West. . . . As regards the slaves, the African being from a tropical climate, and from the region of the burning sands and sun, his comfort and condition would be greatly improved, by a transfer from northern latitudes to the genial and most salubrious climate of Texas. . . . Nor can it be disguised that, by the reannexation, as the number of free blacks augmented in the slave-holding States, they would be diffused gradually through Texas into Mexico, and Central and Southern America, where nine-tenths of their present population are already of the colored races. . . .

The process will be gradual and progressive, without a shock, and without a convulsion; whereas, by the loss of Texas, and the imprisonment of the slave population of the Union within its present limits, slavery would *increase* in nearly all the slaveholding States, and a change in their condition would become impossible; or if it did take place by sudden or gradual abolition, the result would as certainly be the sudden or gradual introduction of hundreds of thousands of free blacks into the States of the North; and if their condition there is already deplorable, how would it be when their number there should be augmented tenfold, and the burden become intolerable? . . . There is but one way in which the North can escape these evils; and that is the reannexation of Texas, which is the only safety-valve for the whole Union.

### (b)  *From James K. Polk's inaugural address, March 4, 1845*

The Republic of Texas has made known her desire to come into our Union, to form a part of our Confederacy and enjoy with us the blessings of liberty secured and guaranteed by our Constitution. Texas was once a part of our country—was unwisely ceded away to a foreign power. . . . I congratulate my country that by an act of the late Congress of the United States the assent of this Government has been given to the reunion, and it only remains for the two countries to agree upon the terms to consummate an object so important to both.

I regard the question of annexation as belonging exclusively to the United States and Texas. . . . Foreign nations have no right to interfere with them or to take exceptions to their reunion. Foreign powers do not seem to appreciate the true character of our Government. Our Union is a confederation of independent States, whose policy is peace with each other and all the world. To enlarge its limits is to extend the dominions of peace over additional territories and increasing millions. The world has nothing to fear from military ambition in our Goverment. While the Chief Magistrate and the popular branch of Congress are elected for short terms by the suffrages of those millions who must in their own persons bear all the burdens and miseries of war, our Government can not be otherwise than pacific. Foreign powers should therefore look on the annexation of Texas to the United States not as the conquest of a nation seeking to extend her dominions by arms and violence, but as the peaceful acquisition of a territory once her own, by adding another member to our confederation, with the consent of that member, thereby diminishing the chances of war and opening to them new and ever-increasing markets for their products. . . .

Nor will it become in a less degree my duty to assert and maintain by all constitutional means the right of the United States to that portion of our territory which lies beyond the Rocky Mountains. Our title to the country of the Oregon is "clear and unquestion- able," and already are our people pre- paring to perfect that title by occupying it with their wives and children.

### (c) Polk's corollary to the Monroe Doctrine: from his first annual message to Congress, December 2, 1845

The rapid extension of our settlements over our territories heretofore unoccupied, the addition of new States to our Confederacy, the expansion of free principles, and our rising greatness as a nation are attracting the attention of the powers of Europe, and lately the doctrine has been broached in some of them of a "balance of power" on this continent to check our advancement. The United States, sincerely desirous of preserving relations of good understanding with all nations, can not in silence permit any European interference on the North American continent, and should any such interference be attempted will be ready to resist it at any and all hazards. . . .

The nations of America are equally sovereign and independent with those of Europe. They possess the same rights, independent of all foreign interposition, to make war, to conclude peace, and to regulate their internal affairs. The people of the United States can not, therefore, view with indifference attempts of European powers to interfere with the independent action of the nations on this continent. The American system of government is entirely different from that of Europe. Jealousy among the different sovereigns of Europe, lest any one of them might become too powerful for the rest, has caused them anxiously to desire the establishment of what they term the "balance of power." It can not be per-

mitted to have any application on the North American continent, and especially to the United States. We must ever maintain the principle that the people of this continent alone have the right to decide their own destiny. Should any portion of them, constituting an independent state, propose to unite themselves with our Confederacy, this will be a question for them and us to determine without any foreign interposition. . . . Near a quarter of a century ago the principle was distinctly announced to the world, in the annual message of one of my predecessors, that—

The American continents, by the free and independent condition which they have assumed and maintained, are henceforth not to be considered as subject for future colonization by any European powers.

This principle will apply with greatly increased force should any European power attempt to establish any new colony in North America. . . . Existing rights of every European nation should be respected, but it is due alike to our safety and our interests that the efficient protection of our laws should be extended over our whole territorial limits, and that it should be distinctly announced to the world as our settled policy that no future European colony or dominion shall with our consent be planted or established on any part of the North American continent.

### (d) Stephen A. Douglas on the war with Mexico, in the House of Representatives, May 13, 1846

My object is to vindicate our government and country from the aspersions and calumnies which have been cast upon them by several gentlemen

in the course of this debate, in connection with the causes which have led to the existing war with Mexico. . . . I commend the patriotism, if not the morality of the sentiment, . . . "I go for my country, right or wrong." I fear, however, that this sentiment, once so much applauded by our countrymen is about to be brought into ridicule and contempt. . . . They tell us that they go for their country, right or wrong; but they insist that their country is and has been all the time in the wrong. They profess to support the war, but they vote against the law which recognizes its existence and provides the means—the money and the men—to expel a hostile army that has invaded our country and butchered our citizens. They profess great anxiety for the triumph of our arms, but they denounce the war—the cause in which our country is engaged—as "unholy, unrighteous, and damnable." . . .

Sir, I tell these gentlemen it requires more charity than falls to the lot of frail men to believe that the expression of such sentiments is consistent with the sincerity of their professions—with patriotism, honor, and duty to their country. Patriotism emanates from the heart; it fills the soul; inspires the whole man with a devotion to his country's cause, and speaks and acts the same language. America wants no friends, acknowledges the fidelity of no citizen who, after war is declared, condemns the justice of her cause and sympathizes with the enemy. All such are traitors in their hearts, and it only remains for them to commit some overt act for which they may be dealt with according to their deserts. . . .

Patriots may differ as to the expediency of a declaration of war, or the wisdom of a course of policy which may probably lead to such a result, but honor and duty forbid divided counsels after our country has been invaded, and American blood has been shed on American soil by a treacherous foe. Party strife and political conflicts should then cease. One sentiment should animate every heart; one object control every movement—the triumph of our country. . . .

We are at war with Mexico. Our armies will soon march into the heart of that country. I trust they will penetrate as far as the capital, and capture not only the army, but the government itself in the halls of the Montezumas, that we may make them all prisoners of war, and keep them in duress until they shall make a treaty of peace and boundary with us, by which they shall recognize not only the Rio del Norte, [Rio Grande], but such other line as we shall choose to dictate or accept. . . .

I had hoped and trusted that there would be no anti-war party after war was declared. In this I have been sadly disappointed. I have been particularly mortified to see one with whom I have acted on the Oregon question, who was ready to plunge the country into immediate war, if necessary, to maintain the rights and honor of the country in that direction, now arraying himself on the side of the enemy when our country is invaded by another portion of the Union. To me, our country and all its parts are one and indivisible.

(e)    *Lewis Cass on the "safety valve"*
       *of "unlimited expansion," in the Senate, February 10, 1847*

I do not rise sir, with the emotions so visibly felt and so eloquently described by the distinguished Senator from South Carolina [Calhoun, who had spoken the day before]. I do not consider this country, or its institutions in the slightest danger. Never was it more free, powerful, or prosperous, than at the present moment, when untimely warnings come to assail us. . . .

Mr. President, it gives me great pain to hear any allusions to the dissolution of this Confederacy; and of all the places in this republic, this high place is the last, in which they should be expressed. The Constitution is in no danger. It has survived many a shock, and it will survive many more. . . . It is at this moment stronger in the affections of the American people, than at any other period of its existence. . . . If we are not struck with judicial blindness, as were God's chosen people of old, and punished for national offences by national punishments, we shall cling to this Constitution, as the mariner clings to the last plank, when night and the tempest close around him; and we shall cling to it the stronger, as the danger is greater.

Mr. President, I shall not touch any of the topics before us, as a sectional man. I view them, and shall present them, as an American citizen, looking to the honor and interests of his country, and of his whole country. In these great questions of national bearing, I acknowledge no geographical claims. . . .

A strong desire pervades this country, that a region, extending west of our present possessions to the Pacific ocean, should be acquired and become part of our Confederacy. The attempt to purchase it was made during the administration of General Jackson, and the hope of succeeding has never since been wholly abandoned. I will not detain the Senate by spreading out the reasons, which render such a measure desirable. It would give us a large territory, a great deal of it calculated for American settlement and cultivation, and it would connect us with the great western ocean, giving us a front along its shores in connexion with Oregon of, perhaps, thirteen or fourteen degrees of latitude. It would give us also the magnificent bay of St. Francisco, one of the noblest anchorages in the world, capable of holding all the navies of the earth; and from its commanding position, controlling, in some measure, the trade of the northern Pacific. But, sir, besides these advantages, commercial and geographical, there are important political considerations, which point to extension as one of the great measures of safety for our institutions.

In Europe, . . . men are brought too much and kept too much in contact. There is not room for expansion. Minds of the highest order are pressed down by adverse circumstances, without the power of free exertion. . . . Hence the *emeutes*, which disturb and alarm the Governments of the Old World, and which must one day or other shake them to their centre. . . . I trust we are far removed from all this; but to remove us further yet, we want almost unlimited power of expansion. That is our safety valve. The mightiest intellects which when compressed in thronged cities, and hopeless of their future, are ready to break the barriers around them the moment they enter the new world of the West, feel their freedom, and turn their energies to contend with the works of creation; converting the woods and the forests into towns, and villages, and cultivated fields, and extending the dominion of civilization and improvement over the domain of nature. This process has been going on since the first settlement of our country; and while it continues, whatever other evils betide us, we shall be free from the evils of a dense population, with scanty means of subsistence, and with no hope of advancement.

The Senator from South Carolina has presented some views of our augmenting population as true as they are striking. . . . There are those yet living, who will live to see our Confederacy numbering a population, equal to the Chinese empire. This stupendous progress outstrips the imagination. The mind cannot keep up with the fact. *It toils after it in vain*; and as we increase in numbers and extend in space, our power of communication is still more augmented. The telegraph has come with its wonderful process to bind still closer the portions of this empire, as these recede from its capital. . . . Who can tell where future improvements may conduct it, or what sway it may hereafter exercise over the social and political condition of the world? What people it may bring together and keep together by the power of instantaneous communication? . . . I shall not pursue these investigations; they are sufficiently obvious in their general bearing, though the practical result of this great measure is beyond the reach of human vision.

We are at war with Mexico, brought on by her injustice. Before peace is established, we have a right to require a reasonable indemnity. . . . In the condition of Mexico, there is no disposition in this country to ask of her an unreasonable sacrifice. . . . But there are certain territorial acquisitions, which are important to us, and whose cession cannot injure Mexico, as she never can hold them permanently. We are willing, after settling the indemnity satisfactorily, to pay for the excess in money.

(f)   *Daniel Webster to J. G. Hülsemann, on Americans' "lively interest in the fortunes of nations struggling for institutions like their own," December 21, 1850*

If it had been the pleasure of his Majesty, the Emperor of Austria, during the struggles in Hungary, to have admonished the provisional government or the people of that country against involving themselves in disaster, by following the evil and dangerous example of the United States of America in making efforts for the establishment of independent governments, such an admonition from that sovereign to his Hungarian subjects would not have originated here a diplomatic correspondence. . . . But, out of proper respect for the Austrian government, it has been thought better to answer the note at length; and the more especially, as the . . . undersigned . . . freely admits that, in proportion as these extraordinary events appeared to have their origin in these great ideas of responsible and popular government, on which the American constitutions themselves are wholly founded, they could not but command the warm sympathy of the people of this country.

Well-known circumstances in their history, indeed their whole history, have made them the representatives of purely popular principles of government. In this light they now stand before the world. They could not, if they would, conceal their character, their condition, or their destiny. They could not, if they so desired, shut out from the view of mankind the causes which have placed them, in so short a national career, in the station which they now hold among the civilized states of the world. They could not, if they desired it, suppress either the thoughts or the hopes which arise in men's minds, in other countries, from contemplating their successful example of free government. . . .

The position thus belonging to the United States is a fact as inseparable from their history, their constitutional organization, and their character, as the opposite position of the powers composing the European alliance is from the history and constitutional organization of the government of those powers. The sovereigns who form that alliance have not infrequently felt it their right to interfere with the political movements of foreign states; and have, in their manifestoes and declarations, denounced the popular ideas of the age in terms so comprehensive as of necessity to include the United States, and their forms of government. . . . These declarations amount to nothing less than a denial of the lawfulness of the origin of the government of the United States, since it is certain that that government was established in consequence of a change which did not proceed from thrones, or the permission of crowned heads. But the government of the United States heard these denunciations of its fundamental principles without remonstrance, or the disturbance of its equanimity. This was thirty years ago.

The power of this republic, at the present moment, is spread over a region one of the richest and most fertile on the globe, and of an extent in comparison with which the possessions of the house of Hapsburg are but as a patch on the earth's surface. Its population, already twenty-five millions, will exceed that of the Austrian empire within the period during which it may be hoped that Mr. Hülsemann may yet remain in the honorable discharge of his duties to his government. Its navigation and commerce are hardly exceeded by the oldest and most commercial nations; its maritime means and its maritime power may be seen by Austria herself, in all seas where she has ports, as well as they may be seen, also, in all other quarters of the globe. Life, liberty, property, and all personal rights, are amply secured to all citizens, and portected by just and stable laws; and credit, public and private, is as well established as in any government of Continental Europe. . . .

Certainly, the United States may be pardoned, even by those who profess adherence to the principles of absolute government, if they entertain an ardent affection for those popular forms of political organization which have . . . enabled them, in so short a period, to bring their country, and the hemisphere to which it belongs, to the notice and respectful regard of the civilized world. Nevertheless, the United States have abstained, at all times, from acts of interference with the political changes of Europe. They cannot, however, fail to cherish always a lively interest in the fortunes of nations struggling for institutions like their own; . . . and if the United States wish success to countries contending for popular constitutions and national independence, it is only because they regard such constitutions and such national independence, not as imaginary, but as real blessings.

They claim no right, however, to take part in the struggles of foreign powers in order to promote these ends. It is only in defence of his own government, and its principles and character, that the undersigned has now expressed himself on this subject. But when the people of the United States behold the people of foreign countries, without any such interference, spontaneously moving toward the adoption of institutions like their own, it surely cannot be expected of them to remain wholly indifferent spectators. . . . and, while performing with strict and exact fidelity all their natural duties, nothing will deter either the government or the people of the United States from exercising, at their own discretion, the rights belonging to them as an independent nation. . . . Their own institutions stand upon the broadest principles of civil liberty; and believing those principles . . . to be, in fact, the only principles of government which meet the demands of the present enlightened age, the President . . . cherishes a sincere wish that they may produce the same happy effects throughout his Austrian Majesty's extensive dominions that they have done in the United States.

## 30

*"If the negro is a man, is it not . . . a total destruction of self-government to say that he too shall not govern himself?"*

During his great contest with Stephen A. Douglas in the summer and fall of 1858 for United States Senator from Illinois, in which Lincoln acknowledged that "I am, in a certain sense, made the standard-bearer of the Republicans," Honest Abe drew "tremendous cheering and laughter" with the following explanation of "still another disadvantage under which we labor":

> It arises out of the relative positions of the two persons who stand before the State as candidates for the Senate. Senator Douglas is of world wide renown. All the anxious politicians of his party, or who have been of his party for years past, have been looking upon him as certainly, at no distant day, to be the President of the United States. They have seen in his round, jolly, fruitful face, postoffices, landoffices, marshalships, and cabinet appointments, chargeships and foreign missions, bursting and sprouting out in wonderful exuberance ready to be laid hold of by their greedy hands. . . . On the contrary nobody has ever expected me to be President. In my poor, lean, lank, face, nobody has ever seen that any cabbages were sprouting out.

Two years earlier, Lincoln had written down for some unknown purpose:

> Twenty-two years ago Judge Douglas and I first became acquainted. We were both young then; he a trifle younger than I. Even then, we were both ambitious; I, perhaps quite as much so as he. With *me*, the race of ambition has been a failure—a flat failure; with *him* it has been one of splendid success. His name fills the nation; and is not unknown, even, in foreign lands.

Yet, as the world goes, Lincoln was not perhaps even then quite the failure he made himself out to be. Perhaps, too, he was aware of this, and of his own potential; and of the fact that his own star might at last be rising. To this note on Douglas he added these sentences:

> I affect no contempt for the high eminence he has reached. So reached, that the oppressed of my species might have shared with me in the elevation, I would rather stand on that eminence, than wear the richest crown that ever pressed a monarch's brow.

In 1832, as a jobless young man of twenty-three, Lincoln had signed up with a volunteer company in the Black Hawk War, fought to speed the removal beyond the Mississippi River of the Indians of northern Illinois. "To his own sur-prize," he recalled in his third-person autobiographical sketch penned in 1860, he "was elected captain of it. He says he has not since had any success in life which gave him so much satisfaction." Lincoln, indeed, had been so bucked up by this early recognition that "he, the same year, ran for the legislature and was beaten." Even so, he was proud enough to add in 1860 that "this was the only time I was ever beaten on a direct vote of the people."

Lincoln was elected to the state legislature in 1834, 1836, 1838, and 1840. In 1837, he and a fellow Whig took the trouble to register a formal protest against the legislature's ruthless rejection of certain anti-slavery petitions. In 1846, Lincoln was elected to Congress, the only Whig to win in Illinois. During his single term, the Wilmot Proviso proposing to ban slavery in new territory (see Document No. 29, above), "was constantly coming up in some shape or other," Lincoln said, "and I think I . . . voted for it at least forty times."

In 1836, although by his own estimate he had had no more than one year's schooling his entire life, Lincoln had obtained his license to practice law. By the time he entered Congress, he was acknowledged as the best jury trial lawyer in Illinois. "Upon his return from Congress," he writes in his autobiographical sketch, "he went to the practice of law with greater earnestness than ever before," and in the opinion of his partner, William Herndon, he soon "got to be a No. 1 Supreme Court lawyer." But he still campaigned actively for the Whig ticket, served as a presidential elector, and was much in demand as a speaker.

By 1854, "his profession," Lincoln writes, "had almost superseded the thought of politics in his mind, when the repeal of the Missouri Compromise aroused him as he had never been before." Repeal had been effected in May, that year, by Douglas's Kansas-Nebraska Act organizing the two new territories on the prin-ciple of deciding by "popular sovereignty" whether they should be slave or free. Northern Democrats of Douglas's own party as well as northern Whigs like Lincoln were so incensed by this stratagem for smuggling slavery into free territory that when Douglas appeared in Chicago early in September to defend his Act was hooted off the platform and menaced by mobs in the streets.

Repeal of the Kansas-Nebraska Act itself quickly became the leading issue in the congressional elections of 1854, and Douglas was obliged to come to the rescue of "Nebraska men" by speaking everywhere he could. Lincoln, in his own words, also "took the stump," but "with no broader practical aim or object than to secure, if possible, the reelection of Hon. Richard Yates [a stern "anti-Nebraska" Whig] to Congress." But Lincoln found that "his speeches at once attracted a more marked attention than they had ever before done," and that, "as the canvass proceeded, he was drawn to different parts of the state, outside Mr. Yates' district."

As Lincoln's range widened, his study deepened. Lincoln, Herndon wrote, "was in no sense, except in politics, a general reader; he read specially for a special object and applied it. . . . He hated study except for the practical to be applied right off. In other words, he had an end in view always." On October 3, 1854, Douglas was to appear at the State Fair in Springfield, once more to defend his bitter pill. Lincoln was present to listen and to reply. As the opposition press noted, "he had been nosing for weeks in the State Library, pumping his brain and imagination for points and arguments." On October 4, tieless, in shirt sleeves, his rumpled trousers too short for his six-four frame, Lincoln delivered his rebuttal. Twelve days later, after Douglas had once again offered his familiar harangue in Peoria, Lincoln again replied with his Springfield argument, which was here first reported verbatim and on that account has become famous as the "great Peoria speech." Many think it was Lincoln's greatest and it is reproduced in part in this Document.

However he may subsequently have deprecated his standing or his renown (and drawn only laughter for his pains), Lincoln with this speech, had taken direct aim at a seat in the United States Senate, and by way of that seat, in the opinion of Douglas himself, on nothing short of the Presidency. Lincoln failed to gain the Senate seat in 1854 and again in 1858, when he defeated Douglas in the popular vote but lost once more in the legislature. But Lincoln, as Herndon said, when "the Kansas-Nebraska Bill was introduced into Congress in 1854 by Senator Douglas, . . . saw his opportunity and Douglas's downfall." And Lincoln was "a long-headed strong man" inured to biding his time. Whatever he meant by "the oppressed of my species"—the Negro in slavery, or the white by slavery dragged down—by separating Douglas from both and attaching abolitionists and free soilers to himself, Lincoln, by 1860, attained that eminence for which Douglas may long have been marked but of which he would forever be deprived.

In one variation of a story Herndon often told, Lincoln said to him,

> Billy, I am like a long strong jackknife doubled up in the handle. The extreme point of the blade has to move through a wider space before it is open than your little short woman's knife which you hold in your hand, but when the jackknife is open, it cuts wider and *deeper* than your little thing. I am six feet four inches high and it takes me a good while to open and to act, . . . but when I do throw off a thought it seems to me, though it comes with some effort, it has force enough to cut its own way and travel a greater distance.

By the time of his October, 1854, speech, Lincoln at long last had become fully "open," and ready to cut deeply on all questions but one, which for all his study he was never to resolve: "If all earthly power were given to me," he said in that speech, "I should not know what to do as to the existing institution" in the slave states. Lincoln was haunted by what he understood to be the misfortune of his own prejudices. But as with Jefferson, whom he most admired (see Document No. 21, above), his very ambiguities counseled charity not chains, tolerance not abuse, patience not proscription. "It does seem to me that systems of gradual emancipation might be adopted, but for their tardiness in this I will not undertake to judge our brethren of the South."

On all other questions raised by the repeal of the Missouri Compromise,

Lincoln had become and was to remain clear enough. On slavery: "I hate it because of the monstrous injustice of slavery itself." "The thing is hid away in the Constitution, just as an afflicted man hides away a wen or cancer which he dares not cut out at once, lest he bleed to death,—with the promise, nevertheless, that the cutting may begin at a certain time." On popular sovereignty: "This declared indifference, but, as I must think, covert real zeal for the spread of slavery, I cannot but hate." On the territories: "The whole nation is interested that the best use shall be made of these Territories. We want them for homes of free white people. . . . Slave states are places for poor white people to remove from, not to remove to." On self-government: "What I do say is that no man is good enough to govern another man without that other's consent. I say this is the leading principle, the sheet-anchor of American republicanism." And on the Negro himself in the "empire of liberty": "But if the negro is a man, is it not to that extent a total destruction of self-government to say that he too shall not govern himself?"

*October 16, 1854*

# Abraham Lincoln:

# Speech at Peoria, Illinois, in Reply

# to Senator Douglas

The repeal of the Missouri Compromise, and the propriety of its restoration, constitute the subject of what I am about to say. . . . And as this subject is no other than part and parcel of the larger general question of domestic slavery, I wish to make and to keep the distinction between the existing institution and the extension of it, so broad and so clear that no honest man can misunderstand me, and no dishonest one successfully misrepresent me. . . .

When we established our independence, . . . Virginia . . . owned the Northwestern Territory—the country out of which the principal part of Ohio, all Indiana, all Illinois, all Michigan, and all Wisconsin have since been formed. . . . The question of ceding the territories to the General Government

was set on foot. Mr. Jefferson, the author of the Declaration of Independence, . . . a Virginian by birth and continued residence, and withal a slaveholder, conceived the idea of taking that occasion to prevent slavery ever going into the Northwestern Territory. He prevailed on the Virginia legislature to adopt his views, . . . and the first ordinance (which the acts of Congress were then called) for the government of the Territory provided that slavery should never be permitted therein. This is the famed "Ordinance of '87," so often spoken of.

Thenceforward for sixty-one years, and until, in 1848, the last scrap of this Territory came into the Union as the State of Wisconsin, all parties acted in quiet obedience to this ordinance.

It is now what Jefferson foresaw and intended—the happy home of teeming millions of free, white, prosperous people, and no slave among them.

Thus, with the author of the Declaration of Independence, the policy of prohibiting slavery in new territory, originated. . . . And thus, in those five States, and in five millions of free, enterprising people, we have before us the rich fruits of this policy.

But now new light breaks upon us. Now Congress declares this ought never to have been, and the like of it must never be again. The sacred right of self-government is grossly violated by it. We even find some men who drew their first breath—and every other breath of their lives—under this very restriction, now live in dread of absolute suffocation if they should be restricted in the "sacred right" of taking slaves to Nebraska. That perfect liberty they sigh for—the liberty of making slaves of other people—Jefferson never thought of, their own fathers never thought of, they never thought of themselves, a year ago. How fortunate for them they did not sooner become sensible of their great misery! Oh, how difficult it is to treat with respect such assaults upon all we have ever really held sacred! . . .

During this long period of time, Nebraska had remained substantially an uninhabited country, but now emigration to and settlement within it began to take place. It is about one third as large as the present United States, and its importance, so long overlooked, begins to come into view. The restriction of slavery by the Missouri Compromise directly applies to it—in fact was first made, and has since been maintained, expressly for it. In 1853, a bill to give it a territorial government passed the House of Representatives, and, in the hands of Judge Douglas, failed of passing [the Senate] only for want of time. This bill contained no repeal of the Missouri Compromise. . . . On January 4, 1854, Judge Douglas introduces a new bill to give Nebraska territorial government. . . . Before long the bill is so modified as to make two territories instead of one, calling the southern one Kansas. Also, about a month after the introduction of the bill, on the judge's own motion it is so amended as to declare the Missouri Compromise inoperative and void; and, substantially, that the people who go and settle there may establish slavery, or exclude it, as they may see fit. In this shape the bill passed both branches of Congress and became a law.

This is the repeal of the Missouri Compromise. . . . I think, and shall try to show, that it is wrong—wrong in its direct effect, letting slavery into Kansas and Nebraska, and wrong in its prospective principle, allowing it to spread to every other part of the wide world where men can be found inclined to take it.

This declared indifference, but, as I must think, covert real zeal, for the spread of slavery, I cannot but hate. I hate it because of the monstrous injustice of slavery itself. I hate it because it deprives our republican example of its just influence in the world; enables the enemies of free institutions with plausibility to taunt us as hypocrites; causes the real friends of freedom to doubt our sincerity; and especially because it forces so many good men among ourselves into an open war with the very fundamental principles of civil liberty, criticizing the Declaration of Independence, and insisting that there is no right principle of action but self-interest.

Before proceeding let me say that I think I have no prejudice against the Southern people. They are just what we would be in their situation. . . . If all earthly power were given me, I should not know what to do as to the existing institution. My first impulse would be to free all the slaves, and send them to Liberia, to their own native land. But a moment's reflection would convince me that whatever of high hope (as I think there is) there may be in this in the long run, its sudden execution is impossible. . . . What then? Free them all, and keep them among us as underlings? Is it quite certain that this betters their condition? . . . What next? Free them, and make them politically and socially our equals. My own feelings will not admit of this, and if mine would, we well know that those of the great mass of whites will not. Whether this feeling accords with justice and sound judgment is not the sole question, if indeed it is any part of it. A universal feeling, whether well or ill founded, cannot be safely disregarded. We cannot then make them equals. It does seem to me that systems of gradual emancipation might be adopted, but for their tardiness in this I will not undertake to judge our brethren of the South. . . .

But all this, to my judgment, furnishes no more excuse for permitting slavery to go into our own free territory than it would for reviving the African slave-trade by law. . . . It is argued that slavery will not go to Kansas and Nebraska, in any event. This is a palliation, a lullaby. I have some hope that it will not; but let us not be too confident. As to climate, a glance at the map shows that there are five slave states—Delaware, Maryland, Virginia, Kentucky, and Missouri, and also the District of Columbia, all north of the Missouri Compromise line. The census returns of 1850 show that within these there are eight hundred and sixty seven thousand two hundred and seventy-six slaves, being more than one fourth of all the slaves in the nation.

It is not climate then, that will keep slavery out of these Territories. . . . But it is said, there now is no law in Nebraska on the subject of slavery, and that, in such case, taking a slave there operates his freedom. That is good book-law, but is not the rule of actual practice. Wherever slavery is it has been first introduced without law. The oldest laws we find concerning it are not laws introducing it, but regulating it as an already existing thing. A white man takes his slave to Nebraska now. Who will inform the negro that he is free? Who will take him before court to test the question of his freedom? . . . Keep [slavery] out until a vote is taken, and a vote in favor of it cannot be got in any population of forty thousand on earth, who have been drawn together by the ordinary motives of emigration and settlement. To get slaves into the Territory simultaneously with the whites in the incipient stages of settlement is the precise stake played for and won in this Nebraska measure. . . .

Another lullaby argument is that taking slaves to new countries does not increase their number, does not make any one slave who would otherwise be free. There is some truth in this, and I am glad of it; but it is not wholly true. . . . We know the opening of new countries to slavery tends to the perpetuation of the institution, and so does keep men in slavery who would otherwise be free. This result we do not feel like favoring, and we are under no legal obligation to suppress our feelings in this respect.

Equal justice to the South, it is said, requires us to consent to the extension of slavery to new countries. That is to say, inasmuch as you do not object to my taking my hog to Nebraska, therefore I must not object to you taking your slave. Now, I admit that this is perfectly logical, if there is no difference between hogs and negroes. But while you thus require me to deny the humanity of the negro, I wish to ask whether you of the South, yourselves, have ever been willing to do as much? . . . The great majority South, as well as North, have human sympathies, of which they can no more divest themselves than they can of their sensibility to physical pain. . . . In 1820 you joined the North, almost unanimously, in declaring the African slave-trade piracy, and in annexing to it the punishment of death. . . . Again, you have among you a sneaking individual of the class of native tyrants known as the "Slave-Dealer." He watches your necessities, and crawls up to buy your slave, at a speculating price. If you cannot help it, you sell to him; but if you can help it, you drive him from your door. You despise him utterly. You do not recognize him as a friend, or even as an honest man. Your children must not play with his; they may rollick freely with the little negroes, but not with the slave-dealer's children. . . .

And now why will you ask us to deny the humanity of the slave, and estimate him as only the equal of the hog? Why ask us to do what you will not do yourselves? . . .

But one great argument in support of the repeal of the Missouri Compromise is still to come. That argument is "the sacred right of self-government." . . . I trust I understand and truly estimate the right of self-government. . . . I extend the principle to communities of men as well as to individuals. . . . The doctrine of self-government is right,—absolutely and eternally right,—but it has no just application as here attempted. Or perhaps I should rather say that whether it has such application depends upon whether a negro is not or is a man. If he is not a man, in that case he who is a man may as a matter of self-government do just what he pleases with him. But if the negro is a man, is it not to that extent a total destruction of self-government to say that he too shall not govern himself? When the white man governs himself, that is self-government; but when he governs himself and also governs another man, that is more than self-government—that is despotism. If the negro is a man, why then my ancient faith teaches me that "all men are created equal," and that there can be no moral right in connection with one man's making a slave of another.

Judge Douglas frequently, with bitter irony and sarcasm, paraphrases our argument by saying: "The white people of Nebraska are good enough to govern themselves, but they are not good enough to govern a few miserable negroes!"

Well! I doubt not that the people of Nebraska are and will continue to be as good as the average of people elsewhere. I do not say the contrary. What I do say is that no man is good enough to govern another without that other's consent. I say this is the leading principle, the sheet-anchor of American republicanism. . . . The master not only governs the slave without his consent, but he governs him by a set of rules altogether different from those which he prescribes for himself. Allow all the governed an equal voice in the government, and that, and that only, is self-government.

In support of his application of the doctrine of self-government, Senator Douglas has sought to bring to his aid the opinions and examples of our Revolutionary fathers. I am glad he has done this. I love the sentiments of those old-time men, and shall be most happy to abide by their opinion. . . . This . . . generation of men, and mostly the same individuals who . . . declared independence, who fought the war of the Revolution through, who afterward made the Constitution under which we still live—these same men passed the ordinance of '87, declaring that slavery should never go to the Northwest Territory. . . . There is not an inch of ground left for his claiming that their opinions, their example, their authority are on his side in the controversy. . . .

Whether slavery shall go into Nebraska, or other new Territories, is not a matter of exclusive concern to the people who may go there. The whole nation is interested that the best use be made of these Territories. We want them for homes of free white people. . . . Slave States are places for poor white people to remove from, not to remove to. New free States are the places for poor people to go to, and better their condition. For this use the nation needs these Territories.

Still further: there are constitutional relations between the slave and free States which are degrading to the latter. We are under legal obligations to catch and return their runaway slaves to them: a sort of dirty, disagreeable job, which, I believe, as a general rule, the slaveholders will not perform for one another. Then again, . . . by the Constitution each State has two senators, each has a number of representatives in proportion to the number of its people, and each has a number of presidential electors equal to the whole number of its senators and representatives together. But in ascertaining the number of the people for this purpose, five slaves are counted as being equal to three whites. The slaves do not vote; they are only counted and so used as to swell the influence of the white people's votes. . . .

Now all this is manifestly unfair; yet I do not mention it to complain of it, in so far as it is already settled. . . . But when I am told I must leave it altogether to other people to say whether new partners are to be bred up and brought into the firm, on the same degrading terms against me, I respectfully demur. . . .

Finally, I insist that if there is anything which it is the duty of the whole people to never intrust to any hands but their own, that thing is the preservation and perpetuity of their own liberties and institutions. And if they shall think, as I do, that the extension of slavery endangers them more than any or all other causes, how recreant to themselves if they submit the question, and with it the fate of their country, to a mere handful of men bent only on self-interest. If this question of slavery extension were an insignificant one—one having no power to do harm —it might be shuffled aside in this way; and being, as it is, the great

Behemoth of danger, shall the strong grip of the nation be loosened upon him, to intrust him to the hands of such feeble keepers?

I have done with this mighty argument of self-government. Go, sacred thing! Go in peace.

But Nebraska is urged as a great Union-saving measure. Well, I too go for saving the Union. Much as I hate slavery, I would consent to the extension of it rather than see the Union dissolved, just as I would consent to any great evil to avoid a greater one. But when I go to Union-saving, I must believe, at least, that the means I employ have some adaptation to the end. To my mind, Nebraska has no such adaptation. "It hath no relish of salvation in it." It is an aggravation, rather, of the only one thing which ever endangers the Union. . . . In the whole range of possibility, there scarcely appears to me to have been anything out of which the slavery agitation could have been revived, except the very project of repealing the Missouri Compromise. . . .

The Missouri Compromise was repealed; and here we are in the midst of a new slavery agitation, such, I think, as we have never seen before. Who is responsible for this? Is it those who resist the measure, or those who causelessly brought it forward and pressed it through, having reason to know, and in fact knowing, it must and would be so resisted? It could not but be expected by its author that it would be looked upon as a measure for the extension of slavery, aggravated by a gross breach of faith.

Argue as you will and long as you will, this is the naked front and aspect of the measure. And in this aspect it could not but produce agitation. Slavery is founded in the selfishness of man's nature—opposition to it in his love of justice. These principles are an eternal antagonism, and when brought into collision so fiercely as slavery extension brings them, shocks and throes and convulsions must ceaselessly follow. Repeal the Missouri Compromise, repeal all compromises, repeal the Declaration of Independence, repeal all past history, you still cannot repeal human nature. It still will be the abundance of man's heart that slavery extension is wrong, and out of the abundance of his heart his mouth will continue to speak.

The structure, too, of the Nebraska bill is very peculiar. The people are to decide the question of slavery for themselves; but when they are to decide, or how they are to decide, or whether, when the question is once decided, it is to remain so or is to be subject to an indefinite succession of new trials, the law does not say. . . . Some Yankees in the East are sending emigrants to Nebraska to exclude slavery from it; and, so far as I can judge, they expect the question to be decided by voting in some way or other. But the Missourians are awake, too. They are within a stone's-throw of the contested ground. They hold meetings and pass resolutions, in which not the slightest allusion to voting is made. They resolve that slavery already exists in the Territory; that more shall go there; that they, remaining in Missouri, will protect it, and that Abolitionists shall be hung or driven away. Through all this bowie-knives and six-shooters are seen plainly enough, but never a glimpse of the ballot-box. . . . And if this fight should begin, is it likely to take a very peaceful, Union-saving turn? Will not the first drop of blood so shed be the real knell of the Union?

The Missouri Compromise ought to be restored. For the sake of the Union, it ought to be restored. We ought to elect a House of Representatives which will vote its restoration. If by any means we omit to do this, what follows? . . . One side will provoke, the other resent. The one will taunt, the other defy; one aggresses, the other retaliates. Already a few in the North defy all constitutional restraints, resist the execution of the fugitive-slave law, and even menace the institution of slavery in the States where it exists. Already a few in the South claim the constitutional right to take and to hold slaves in the free States—demand the revival of the slave-trade—and demand a treaty with Great Britain by which fugitive slaves may be reclaimed from Canada. . . .

But restore the compromise, and what then? We thereby restore the national faith, the national confidence, the national feeling of brotherhood. . . . The South ought to join in doing this. The peace of the nation is as dear to them as to us. In memories of the past and hopes of the future, they share as largely as we. . . .

Some men, mostly Whigs, who condemn the repeal of the Missouri Compromise, nevertheless hesitate to go for its restoration, lest they be thrown in company with the Abolitionists. Will they allow me, as an old Whig, to tell them, good-humoredly, that I think this is very silly? Stand with anybody that stands right. Stand with him while he is right, and part with him when he goes wrong. . . . In both cases you expose the dangerous extremes. In both you stand on middle ground, and hold the ship level and steady. In both you are national, and nothing less than national. . . .

I particularly object to the new position which the avowed principle of this Nebraska law gives to slavery in the body politic. I object to it because it assumes that there can be moral right in the enslaving of one man by another. I object to it as a dangerous dalliance for a free people—a sad evidence that, feeling prosperity, we forget right; that liberty, as a principle, we have ceased to revere. I object to it because the fathers of the republic eschewed and rejected it. The argument of "necessity" was the only argument they ever admitted in favor of slavery; . . . At the framing and adoption of the Constitution they forbore to so much as mention the word "slave" or "slavery" in the whole instrument. . . . Thus the thing is hid away in the

Constitution, just as an afflicted man hides away a wen or cancer which he dares not cut out at once, lest he bleed to death,—with the promise, nevertheless, that the cutting may begin at a certain time. . . .

But now it is to be transformed into a "sacred right." . . . Henceforth it is to be the chief jewel of the nation— the very figurehead of the ship of state. Little by little, but steadily as man's march to the grave, we have been giving up the old for the new faith. Near eighty years ago we began by declaring that all men are created equal; but now from that beginning we have run down to the other declaration, that for some men to enslave others is a "sacred right of self-government." These principles cannot stand together. They are as opposite as God and Mammon; and who ever holds to the one must despise the other. When Pettit, in connection with his support of the Nebraska bill, called the Declaration of Independence "a self-evident lie," he only did what consistency and candor require all other Nebraska men to do. Of the forty-odd Nebraska senators who sat present and heard him, no one rebuked him. . . . If this . . . had been said in old Independence Hall seventy-eight years ago, the very doorkeeper would have throttled the man and thrust him into the street. Let no one be deceived. The spirit of seventy-six and the spirit of Nebraska are utter antagonisms; and the former is being rapidly displaced by the latter.

Fellow-countrymen, Americans, South as well as North, shall we make no effort to arrest this? Already the liberal party throughout the world express the apprehension "that the one retrograde institution in America is undermining the principles of progress, and fatally violating the noblest political system the world ever saw." This is not the taunt of enemies, but the warning of friends. Is it quite safe to disregard it—to despise it? Is there no danger to liberty itself in discarding the earliest practice and first precept of our ancient faith? In our greedy chase to make profit of the negro, let us beware lest we "cancel and tear in pieces" even the white man's charter of freedom.

Our republican robe is soiled and trailed in the dust. Let us repurify it. Let us turn and wash it white in the spirit, if not the blood, of the Revolution. Let us turn slavery from its claims of "moral right" back upon its existing legal rights and its arguments of "necessity." Let us return it to the position our fathers gave it, and there let it rest in peace. Let us readopt the Declaration of Independence, and with it the practices and policy which harmonize with it. Let North and South— let all Americans—let all lovers of liberty everywhere join in the great and good work. If we do this, we shall not only have saved the Union, but we shall have so saved it as to make and to keep it forever worthy of the saving. We shall have so saved it that the succeeding millions of free happy people, the world over, shall rise up and call us blessed to the latest generations.

## 31

## *"Can a negro . . . become a member of the political community?"*

The United States Supreme Court has led a much more troubled life than historians ordinarily acknowledge. Strong executives such as Jefferson and Jackson might have been expected to bridle, as they did, at the pretensions of the judicial branch, especially when advanced by so combative a judge as John Marshall (see Documents No. 22 and 26, above). But weak executives, and weak legislatures, have also got the Court into ill repute, largely by vacillation on political issues.

The Supreme Court never stood so well with the country as it did around 1850, midway in the twenty-eight-year reign of Chief Justice Taney of Maryland. At about that time, Martin Van Buren wrote in his autobiography that "We might, perhaps, have expected that in such a calm even Mr. Jefferson's alarm, if he had lived to see it, would at least in some degree have subsided." Van Buren, however, was not himself taken in. He continues:

> This state of things can only be expected to last until a . . . strong interest is brought under discussion of a character to excite the whole country, and to enlist the sympathies of a majority of the Court and requiring the intervention of that high tribunal to sustain its unconstitutional assumptions by unauthorized and unrestrained construction. Whether the institution of domestic slavery is destined to be such an interest remains to be seen.

Little Van's clairvoyance was somewhat less than magical. The case of *Dred Scott* v. *Sandford*, decided by Taney's court on March 6, 1857, and the subject of this Document, was only the last of a long series of cases on slavery in the 1850's which sent public confidence in the federal judiciary plummeting. The Supreme Court itself remained predominantly southern in composition in this period, and its decisions and those of its members on circuit, however strictly constitutional, were predominantly pro-slavery in character. It was in the North, therefore, that the Court fell farthest in public esteem. Decisions arising out of enforcement of the despised fugitive slave laws in particular were greeted there not only with talk of nullification but with demonstrations so violent that public prosecutors began to demand indictments for treason against agitators, and the death penalty on conviction.

Yet eventually most costly to the standing and self-respect of the Court was its involvement in the seething issue of free soil. As early as 1848, John M.

Clayton of Delaware introduced a bill in the Senate providing for appeals on the issue of slavery in the territories from territorial courts to the supreme bench. "This bill," Clayton boasted, "leaves the entire question in dispute to . . . that Court which occupies the highest place in the [people's] confidence." The Senate unthinkingly adopted Clayton's measure. In the House, however, there was less willingness to burden the Court with responsibilities certain to undermine it, and the bill failed. During the House debate, Congressman George P. Marsh of Vermont asked, "Is that Court a fit tribunal for the determination of a great political question like this?" Marsh answered his own query:

> It is precisely because of my reverence for that Court . . . that I would not impose upon it the painful and dangerous obligation . . . of determining so weighty and delicate a question as this. We should hazard not its impartiality and its high moral influence only, but its constitution and even its existence. During the long period of the pendency of this question, it would be incessantly exposed to every adverse influence. Local sympathies, long cherished prejudices, the predilections of party, the known wishes of the Administration and of the National Legislature, would all conspire to bias the decision; intervening vacancies would be filled with reference to the supposed, perhaps even pledged, opinion of the candidate upon this one question, and when, finally, the decision should be promulgated, the Court itself would become, with the defeated party, the object of a hostility, as deep-rooted, as persevering, as widely diffused, and as rancorous as are at this moment the feelings and prejudices of the parties now arrayed against each other upon this great issue.

By 1857, the Court had indeed fallen into the disreputable condition Marsh had foreseen, and for the reasons he had put forward. It had been pummeled in the press, castigated in Congress, mocked at in state legislatures, and defied with impunity by state tribunals. The corrosive effects of this experience are nowhere more evident than in the Court's performance in the *Dred Scott* case itself from the time it first came up for argument in February, 1856, until it was decided by the most "tangled and obscure set of opinions," as Allan Nevins calls them, after reargument more than a year later.

The *Dred Scott* case hinged on these questions: did Scott, a slave in Missouri, gain his freedom by having been taken by his master as early as 1834 to the free state of Illinois, and to the free Territory of Louisiana where slavery was prohibited by the Missouri Compromise; and, if so, did he remain free on his return once more to the slave state? If he remained a slave, naturally he could not sue for his freedom. But could he sue if he were indeed free?

Of the nine justices, no fewer than eight wrote opinions on all or some of these issues. In speaking for the Court for almost two hours, the Chief Justice spent half his time arguing that even if free, a former slave or a descendant of a slave *never* could become a citizen of the United States, and thus could in no circumstances sue in a United States court. Only two justices would subscribe to Taney's rank racial animadversions and *ex parte* perversions of history. Six justices, however, joined the Chief Justice in finding that Scott, even had he become free, had reverted to slavery on his return to the slave state. On this finding, he had no legitimate access to free tribunals; and on this ground the Court majority could simply have thrown out his case.

Five justices, nevertheless, joined the Chief Justice in plunging farther. The slave, Taney said, is property, pure and simple. Nothing in the Constitution gives Congress the right to legislate differently on this kind of property than on any other kind. Legislation forbidding a slave owner to hold his slave in any part of the Union, by depriving him of his property without due process of law, is in direct violation of the Fifth Amendment. The Missouri Compromise was such legislation, and was null and void.

Before Taney had spoken thus for the Court, the Kansas-Nebraska Act had already repealed the Missouri Compromise and ordered that the question of slavery in the territories be decided on the principle of popular sovereignty. On the other hand, in the recent presidential election of 1856, the new Republican party had made an eye-opening showing on the principle that the territories be kept forever free. In that election, the Democrat, James Buchanan of Pennsylvania, had won; and as his inauguration neared, the clash of these opposing principles in "bleeding Kansas" seemed about to grow into a larger if not a limitless war.

Buchanan was a "doughface," or northern man with southern leanings. Could he look to the sympathetic Supreme Court to pull him and the country out of the hole? Could he, in his inaugural address, tell the people that the Court would do it? These remarkable questions Buchanan had addressed to one of his friends among the justices on February 3, 1857. Two weeks later he had his answer. Certain justices realized "how good an opportunity" they had in the *Dred Scott* case to act. They were convinced, wrote one, "that it was practicable for the Court to quiet all agitation on the question of slavery in the Territories by affirming that Congress had no constitutional power to prohibit its introduction." Thus reassured, in his inaugural Buchanan said: The issue of slavery in Kansas "is a judicial question, which legitimately belongs to the Supreme Court of the United States before whom it is now pending, and will, it is understood, be speedily and finally settled."

When the Court spoke at long last two days after the inauguration, it was found that two justices still dissented from the whole of Taney's argument. A third would have no part of Taney's Missouri Compromise foray. But worse still, even within Taney's majority of six there was no consensus on the law. As Edward S. Corwin writes: "When the student finds six judges arriving at precisely the same result by three distinct processes of reasoning, he is naturally disposed to surmise that the result may have induced the processes rather than that the processes compelled the reasoning."

So confident was Buchanan of the "result," that he had gone on to say of the Court: "To their decision, in common with all good citizens, I shall cheerfully submit." But what the President and the justices, so concerned over the predicament of the country, unfortunately failed to concern themselves with was the predicament of the Court itself. "You may 'cheerfully submit,' of course, you will, to whatever the five slaveholders and two or three doughfaces on the bench of the Supreme Court may be ready to utter on this subject," cried the New York *Tribune* the day after Buchanan's address. "But not one man who really desires the triumph of Freedom over Slavery in the Territories will do so. . . . Happily this is a country in which the People make both laws and Judges, and they will try their strength on the issue here presented." The following June, in one of his continuing attacks on Douglas, Lincoln said of the *Dred Scott* case:

> If this important decision had been made by the unanimous concurrence of the judges, and without any partisan bias, and . . . had been in no part, based on assumed historical facts which are not really true; or, if wanting in some of these, it had been before the court more than once, and had there been affirmed and re-affirmed through a course of years, it then might be, perhaps would be, factious, nay, even revolutionary, to not acquiesce in it as a precedent.
>
> But when, as it is true we find it wanting in all these claims to the public confidence, it is not resistance, it is not factious, it is not even disrespectful, to treat it as not having yet quite established a settled doctrine for the country.

*March 6, 1857*

# Dred Scott *v.* Sandford

Mr. Chief Justice Taney. This case has been twice argued. After the argument at the last term, differences of opinion were found to exist among the members of the court; and as the questions in controversy are of the highest importance, . . . it was deemed advisable to direct a reargument on some of the points. . . . I now proceed to deliver its opinion.

There are two leading questions presented by the record:

1. Had the Circuit Court of the United States jurisdiction to hear and determine the case between these parties? And

2. If it had jurisdiction, is the judgment it has given erroneous or not? . . .

Before we speak of the pleas in bar, it will be proper to dispose of the questions which have arisen on the plea in abatement. . . .

The question is simply this: Can a negro, whose ancestors were imported into this country, and sold as slaves, become a member of the political community formed and brought into existence by the Constitution of the United States, and as such become entitled to all the rights, and privileges, and immunities, guaranteed by that instrument to the citizen? One of which rights is the privilege of suing in a court of the United States in the cases specified in the Constitution.

It will be observed, that the . . . only matter in issue before the court, therefore, is, whether the descendants of such slaves, when they shall be emancipated, or who are born of parents who had become free before their birth, are citizens of a State, in the sense in which the word citizen is used in the Constitution of the United States. . . .

The words "people of the United

States" and "citizens" are synonymous terms, and mean the same thing. They both describe the political body who, according to our republican institutions, form the sovereignty, and who hold the power and conduct the government through their representatives. They are what we familiarly call the "sovereign people," and every citizen is one of this people, and a constituent member of this sovereignty. The question before us is, whether the class of persons described in the plea in abatement compose a portion of this people, and are constituent members of this sovereignty? We think they are not, and that they are not included, and were not intended to be included, under the word "citizens" in the Constitution, and can, therefore, claim none of the rights and privileges which that instrument provides for and secures to citizens of the United States. On the contrary, they were at that time considered as a subordinate and inferior class of beings, who had been subjugated by the dominant race, and whether emancipated or not, yet remained subject to their authority, and had no rights or privileges but such as those who held the power and the government might choose to grant them. . . .

In discussing this question, we must not confound the rights of citizenship which a state may confer within its own limits, and the rights of citizenship as a member of the Union. It does not by any means follow, because he has all the rights and privileges of a citizen of a State, that he must be a citizen of the United States. He may have all of the rights and privileges of the citizen of a State, and yet not be . . . a citizen in the sense in which that word is used in the Constitution of the United States, nor entitled to sue as such in one of its courts, nor to the privileges and immunities of a citizen in the other States. . . . No State can, by any Act or law of its own, passed since the adoption of the Constitution, introduce a new member into the political community created by the Constitution of the United States. It cannot make him a member of this community by making him a member of its own. . . .

The question then arises, whether the provisions of the Constitution, in relation to the personal rights and privileges to which the citizen of a State should be entitled, embraced the negro African race, at that time in this country, or who might afterwards be imported, who had then or should afterwards be made free in any State; and to put it in the power of a single State to make him a citizen of the United States, and endue him with the full rights of citizenship in every other State without their consent. Does the Constitution of the United States act upon him whenever he shall be made free under the laws of a State, and raised there to the rank of a citizen, and immediately clothe him with all the privileges of a citizen in every other State, and in its own courts?

The court thinks the affirmative of these propositions cannot be maintained. And if it cannot, the plaintiff in error could not be a citizen of the State of Missouri, within the meaning of the Constitution of the United States, and, consequently, was not entitled to sue in its courts.

It is true, every person, and every class and description of persons, who were at the time of the adoption of the Constitution recognized as citizens in the several States, became also citizens of this new political body; but none other; it was formed by them, and for them and their posterity, but for no one else. . . .

It becomes necessary, therefore, to determine who were citizens of the several States when the Constitution was adopted. . . . In the opinion of the court, the legislation and histories of the times, and the language used in the Declaration of Independence, show, that neither the class of persons who had been imported as slaves, nor their descendants, whether they had become free or not, were then acknowledged as a part of the people, nor intended to be included in the general words used in that memorable instrument.

It is difficult at this day to realize the state of public opinion in relation to that unfortunate race, which prevailed in the civilized and enlightened portions of the world at the time of the Declaration of Independence, and when the Constitution of the United States was framed and adopted. But the public history of every European nation displays it in a manner too plain to be mistaken.

They had for more than a century before been regarded as beings of an inferior order; and altogether unfit to associate with the white race, either in social or political relations; and so far inferior that they had no rights which the white man was bound to respect; and that the negro might justly and lawfully be reduced to slavery for his benefit. He was bought and sold, and treated as an ordinary article of merchandise. . . . This opinion was at that time fixed and universal in the civilized portion of the white race . . . and men in every grade and position in society daily and habitually acted upon it in their private pursuits, as well as in matters of public concern, without doubting for a moment the correctness of this opinion.

And in no nation was this opinion more firmly fixed or more uniformly acted upon than by the English government and English people. . . . The opinion thus entertained . . . was naturally impressed upon the colonies. . . . And accordingly, a negro of the African race was regarded by them as an article of property. . . . The legislation of the different Colonies furnishes positive and indisputable proof of this fact. . . . The language of the Declaration of Independence is equally conclusive. . . .

This state of public opinion had undergone no change when the Constitution was adopted, as is equally evident from its provisions and language. . . . Indeed, when we look to the con-

dition of this race in the several States at the time, it is impossible to believe that these rights and privileges were intended to be extended to them. . . . More especially, it cannot be believed that the large slave-holding States regarded them as included in the word "citizens," or would have consented to a constitution which might compel them to receive them in that character from another State. . . .

A person may be entitled to vote by the law of the State, who is not a citizen even of the State itself. And in some of the States of the Union foreigners not naturalized are allowed to vote. And the State may give the right to free negroes and mulattoes, but that does not make them citizens of the State, and still less of the United States. And the provision in the Constitution giving privileges and immunities in other States, does not apply to them.

Neither does it apply to a person who, being the citizen of a State, migrates to another State. For then he becomes subject to the laws of the State in which he lives, and he is no longer a citizen of the State from which he removed. And the State in which he resides may then, unquestionably, determine his *status* or condition, and place him among the class of persons who are not recognized as citizens, but belong to an inferior and subject race; and may deny him the privileges and immunities enjoyed by its citizens. . . .

If persons of the African race are citizens of a state, and of the United States, they would be entitled to all of these privileges and immunities in every State, and the State could not restrict them; for they would hold these privileges and immunities, under the paramount authority of the Federal Government, and its courts would be bound to maintain and enforce them, the Constitution and laws of the State to the contrary notwithstanding. . . . This is evidently not the construction or meaning of the clause in question. It guarantees rights to the citizen, and the State cannot withhold them. And these rights are of a character and would lead to consequences which make it absolutely certain that the African race were not included under the name of citizens of a State, and were not in the contemplation of the framers of the Constitution when these privileges and immunities were provided for the protection of the citizens in other States. . . .

The court is of opinion that, upon the facts stated in the plea in abatement, Dred Scott was not a citizen of Missouri within the meaning of the Constitution of the United States, and not entitled as such to sue in its courts; and, consequently, that the Circuit Court had no jurisdiction of the case, and that the judgment on the plea in abatement is erroneous. . . .

It has been said, that as this court has decided against the jurisdiction of the Circuit Court . . . anything it may say upon . . . any other material error . . . will be extra-judicial, and mere *obiter dicta*. This is manifestly a mistake. . . . We proceed, therefore, to inquire whether the facts relied on by the plaintiff entitled him to his freedom.

In considering this part of the controversy, two questions arise: 1st. Was he, together with his family, free in Missouri by reason of the stay in the territory of the United States hereinbefore mentioned? And 2d, if they were not, is Scott himself free by reason of his removal to Rock Island, in the State of Illinois, as stated in the above admissions?

We proceed to examine the first question.

The Act of Congress, upon which the plaintiff relies, declares that slavery and involuntary servitude, except as a punishment for crime, shall be forever prohibited in all that part of the territory ceded by France, under the name of Louisiana, which lies north of thirty-six degrees thirty minutes north latitude, and not included within the limits of Missouri. And the difficulty which meets us at the threshold of this part of the inquiry is, whether Congress was authorized to pass this law under any of the powers granted to it by the Constitution; for if the authority is not given by that instrument, it is the duty of this court to declare it void and inoperative, and incapable of conferring freedom upon any one who is held as a slave under the laws of any one of the States.

The counsel for the plaintiff has laid much stress upon that article in the Constitution which confers on Congress the power "to dispose of and make all needful rules and regulations respecting the territory or other property belonging to the United States"; but, in the judgment of the court, that provision has no bearing on the present controversy, and the power there given, whatever it may be, is confined, and was intended to be confined, to the territory which at that time belonged to, or was claimed by, the United States, and . . . can have no influence upon a territory afterwards acquired from a foreign Government. . . .

When . . . [such] Territory becomes a part of the United States, the Federal Government enters into possession in the character impressed upon it by those who created it. It enters upon it with its powers over the citizen strictly defined, and limited by the Constitution, from which it derives its own existence, and by virtue of which alone it continues to exist and act as a Governnment and sovereignty. It has no power of any kind beyond it; and it cannot, when it enters a Territory of the United States, put off its character, and assume discretionary or despotic powers which the Constitution has denied to it. . . . The rights of property are united with the rights of person, and placed on the same ground by the fifth amendment to the Constitution, which provides that no person shall be deprived of life, liberty, and property, without due process of law. An Act of Congress which deprives a person of the United States of his liberty or property merely because he came himself or brought his property into a particular Territory of the United States, and who had committed no offense against the laws, could hardly be dignified with the name of due process of law. . . .

The powers over persons and property of which we speak are not only not granted to Congress, but are in express terms denied, and they are forbidden to exercise them. . . . It is a total absence of power everywhere within the dominion of the United States, and places the citizens of a territory, so far as these rights are concerned, on the same footing with citizens of the States, and guards them as firmly and plainly against any inroads which the general government might attempt, under the plea of implied or incidental powers. And if Congress itself cannot do this—if it is beyond the powers conferred on the Federal Government—it will be admited, we presume, that it could not authorize a territorial government to exercise them. . . .

It seems, however, to be supposed, that there is a difference between property in a slave and other property, and that different rules may be applied to it in expounding the Constitution of the United States. . . . But . . . if the Constitution . . . makes no distinction between that description of property and other property owned by a citizen, no tribunal, acting under the authority of the United States, whether it be legislative, executive, or judicial, has a right to draw such a distinction, or deny to it the benefit of the provisions and guarantees which have been provided for the protection of private property against the encroachments of the Government. . . .

The right of property in a slave is distinctly and expressly affirmed in the Constitution. The right to traffic in it, like an ordinary article of merchandise and property, was guaranted to the citizens of the United States, in every State that might desire it, for twenty years. And the Government in express terms is pledged to protect it in all future time, if the slave escapes from his owner. . . . And no word can be found in the Constitution which gives Congress a greater power over slave property, or which entitles property of that kind to less protection than property of any other description. The only power conferred is the power coupled with the duty of guarding and protecting the owner in his rights.

Upon these considerations, it is the opinion of the court that the Act of Congress which prohibited a citizen from holding and owning property of this kind in the territory of the United States north of the line therein mentioned, is not warranted by the Constitution, and is therefore void; and that neither Dred Scott himself, nor any of his family, were made free by being carried into this territory; even if they had been carried there by the owner, with the intention of becoming a permanent resident. . . .

Upon the whole, therefore, it is the judgment of this court, that . . . the Circuit Court of the United States . . . had no jurisdiction in the case. . . . Its judgment for the defendant must, consequently, be reversed, and a mandate issued directing the suit to be dismissed.

# 32

## *"To those . . . who really love the Union may I not speak?"*

On May 18, 1860, at the Republican National Convention in Chicago, Abraham Lincoln was nominated for the presidency on a platform which stated that "the normal condition of all the territory of the United States is that of freedom; . . . and we deny the authority of Congress, of a territorial legislature, or of any individuals, to give legal existence to slavery in any territory of the United States." Early the following October, Governor William H. Gist of South Carolina wrote to the governors of other cotton states to find out who would take the lead in the secession movement. "If a single state secedes," the Governor promised, South Carolina "will follow her. If no other state takes the lead South Carolina will secede . . . alone if she has any assurance that she will be followed by another or other states."

By November 7, 1860, it was known that Lincoln was elected. Within three days, both South Carolina senators resigned from Congress. "The prospect before us in regard to our Slave Property, if we continue . . . in the Union," wrote a South Carolina planter on December 17, "is nothing less than utter ruin." South Carolina was less willing to acknowledge the likelihood of ruin through disunion, and on December 20, a special convention in the state

> . . . solemnly declared that the union heretofore existing between this state and the other states of North America is dissolved, and that the state of South Carolina has resumed her position among the nations of the world as a free, sovereign, and independent state, with full powers to levy war, conclude peace, contract alliances, establish commerce, and to do all other acts and things which independent states may, of right, do.

By February 1, 1861, six sister states, although with manifest misgivings, had followed South Carolina's lead, and three days later, at Montgomery, Alabama, together they formed the Confederate States of America, adopted a new flag, and prepared to write a new constitution. By the time President-elect Lincoln stood up, on March 4, 1861, to take his oath of office and deliver his anxiously awaited inaugural address, Confederate machinery of government was in operation and federal property in Confederate states had fallen to rebel hands.

"I need address no word to them," said the new President of those "persons in one section or another who seek to destroy the Union at all events and are

198

glad of any pretext to do it." But "to those . . . who really love the Union may I not speak?" Disunion had already moved almost irretrievably far along. Yet, said Lincoln, "nothing valuable can be lost by taking time. If there be an object to *hurry* any of you in hot haste to a step which you would never take *deliberately*, that object can be frustrated by taking time; but no good object can be frustrated by it."

Lincoln's inaugural is not overly long, and is presented here in full. Yet as it proceeds with augmented eloquence, it appears as though Lincoln might have hoped to heal the nation's wound by talking timelessly into the night. In his last paragraph he says as much: "I am loath to close." And when he does, it is with this most wistful of pleas:

> We are not enemies, but friends. We must not be enemies. Though passion may have strained it must not break our bonds of affection. The mystic chords of memory, stretching from every battlefield and patriot grave to every living heart and hearthstone all over the broad land, will yet swell the chorus of the Union, when again touched, as surely they will be, by the better angels of our nature.

But withal, there was to be no surrender. "No State upon its own mere motion can lawfully get out of the Union; . . . *resolves* and *ordinances* to that effect are legally void, and . . . acts of violence within any State or States against the authority of the United States are insurrectionary or revolutionary, according to circumstances. . . . To the extent of my ability, I shall take care, as the Constitution expressly enjoins me, that the laws of the Union be faithfully executed in all the States." You, "my dissatisfied fellow-countrymen, . . . have no oath registered in heaven to destroy the Government, while I shall have the most solemn one to 'preserve, protect, and defend it.' "

**March 4, 1861**

# Abraham Lincoln:

# First Inaugural Address

*Fellow-Citizens of the United States:* In compliance with a custom as old as the Government itself, I appear before you to address you briefly and to take in your presence the oath prescribed by the Constitution of the United States to be taken by the President "before he enters on the execution of this office."

I do not consider it necessary at present for me to discuss those matters of administration about which there is no special anxiety or excitement.

Apprehension seems to exist among the people of the Southern States that by the accession of a Republican Administration their property and their peace and personal security are to be endangered. There has never been any reasonable cause for such apprehension. Indeed, the most ample evidence to the contrary has all the while existed and been open to their inspection. It is found in nearly all the published speeches of him who now addresses you. I do but quote from one of those speeches when I declare that—

I have no purpose, directly or indirectly, to interfere with the institution of slavery in the States where it exists. I believe I have no lawful right to do so, and I have no inclination to do so.

Those who nominated and elected me did so with full knowledge that I had made this and many similar declarations and had never recanted them; and more than this, they placed in the platform for my acceptance, and as a law to themselves and to me, the clear and emphatic resolution which I now read:

Resolved, That the maintenance inviolate of the rights of the States, and especially the right of each State to order and control its own domestic institutions according to its own judgment exclusively, is essential to that balance of power on which the perfection and endurance of our political fabric depend; and we denounce the lawless invasion by armed force of the soil of any State or Territory, no matter what pretext, as among the gravest of crimes.

I now reiterate these sentiments, and in doing so I only press upon the public attention the most conclusive evidence of which the case is susceptible that the property, peace, and security of no section are to be in any wise endangered by the now incoming Administration. I add, too, that all the protection which, consistently with the Constitution and the laws, can be given will be cheerfully given to all the States when lawfully demanded, for whatever cause—as cheerfully to one section as to another.

There is much controversy about the delivering up of fugitives from service or labor. The clause I now read is as plainly written in the Constitution as any other of its provisions:

No person held to service or labor in one State, under the laws thereof, escaping into another, shall in consequence of any law or regulation therein be discharged from such service or labor, but shall be delivered up on claim of the party to whom such service or labor may be due.

It is scarcely questioned that this provision was intended by those who made it for the reclaiming of what we call fugitive slaves; and the intention of the lawgiver is the law. All members of Congress swear their support to the whole Constitution—to this provision as much as to any other. To the proposition, then, that slaves whose cases come within the terms of this clause "shall be delivered up" their oaths are unanimous. Now, if they would make the effort in good temper, could they not with nearly equal unanimity frame and pass a law by means of which to keep good that unanimous oath?

There is some difference of opinion whether this clause should be enforced by national or by State authority, but surely that difference is not a very material one. If the slave is to be surrendered, it can be of but little consequence to him or to others by which authority it is done. And should anyone in any case be content that his oath shall go unkept on a merely unsubstantial controversy as to *how* it shall be kept?

Again: In any law upon this subject ought not all the safeguards of liberty known in civilized and humane jurisprudence to be introduced, so that a free man be not in any case surrendered as a slave? And might it not be well at the same time to provide by law for the enforcement of that clause in the Constitution which guarantees that "the citizens of each State shall be entitled to all privileges and immunities of citizens in the several States"?

I take the official oath to-day with

no mental reservations and with no purpose to construe the Constitution or laws by any hypercritical rules; and while I do not choose now to specify particular acts of Congress as proper to be enforced, I do suggest that it will be much safer for all, both in official and private stations, to conform to and abide by all those acts which stand unrepealed than to violate any of them trusting to find impunity in having them held to be unconstitutional.

It is seventy-two years since the first inauguration of a President under our National Constitution. During that period fifteen different and greatly distinguished citizens have in succession administered the executive branch of the Government. They have conducted it through many perils, and generally with great success. Yet, with all this scope of precedent, I now enter upon the same task for the brief constitutional term of four years under great and peculiar difficulty. A disruption of the Federal Union, heretofore only menaced, is now formidably attempted.

I hold that in contemplation of universal law and of the Constitution the Union of these States is perpetual. Perpetuity is implied, if not expressed, in the fundamental law of all national governments. It is safe to assert that no government proper ever had a provision in its organic law for its own termination. Continue to execute all the express provisions of our National Constitution, and the Union will endure forever, it being impossible to destroy it except by some action not provided for in the instrument itself.

Again: If the United States be not a government proper, but an association of States in the nature of contract merely, can it, as a contract, be peaceably unmade by less than all the parties who made it? One party to a contract may violate it—break it, so to speak—but does it not require all to lawfully rescind it?

Descending from these general principles, we find the proposition that in legal contemplation the Union is perpetual confirmed by the history of the Union itself. The Union is much older than the Constitution. It was formed, in fact, by the Articles of Association in 1774. It was matured and continued by the Declaration of Independence in 1776. It was further matured, and the faith of all the then thirteen States expressly plighted and engaged that it should be perpetual, by the Articles of Confederation in 1778. And finally, in 1787, one of the declared objects for ordaining and establishing the Constitution was *"to form a more perfect Union."*

But if destruction of the Union by one or by a part only of the States be lawfully possible, the Union is *less* perfect than before the Constitution, having lost the vital element of perpetuity.

It follows from these views that no State upon its own mere motion can lawfully get out of the Union; that *resolves* and *ordinances* to that effect are legally void, and that acts of violence within any State or States against the authority of the United States are insurrectionary or revolutionary, according to circumstances.

I therefore consider that in view of the Constitution and the laws the Union is unbroken, and to the extent of my ability, I shall take care, as the Constitution itself expressly enjoins upon me, that the laws of the Union be faithfully executed in all the States. Doing this I deem to be only a simple duty on my part, and I shall perform it so far as practicable unless my rightful masters, the American people, shall withhold the requisite means or in some authoritative manner direct the contrary. I trust this will not be regarded as a menace, but only as the declared purpose of the Union that it *will* constitutionally defend and maintain itself.

In doing this there needs to be no bloodshed or violence, and there shall be none unless it be forced upon the national authority. The power confided to me will be used to hold, occupy, and possess the property and places belonging to the Government and to collect the duties and imposts; but beyond what may be necessary for these objects, there will be no invasion, no using of force against or among the people anywhere. Where hostility to the United States in any interior locality shall be so great and universal as to prevent competent resident citizens from holding the Federal offices, there will be no attempt to force obnoxious strangers among the people for that object. While the strict legal right may exist in the Government to enforce the exercise of these offices, the attempt to do so would be so irritating and so nearly impracticable withal that I deem it better to forego for the time the uses of such offices.

The mails, unless repelled, will continue to be furnished in all parts of the Union. So far as possible the people everywhere shall have that sense of perfect security which is most favorable to calm thought and reflection. The course here indicated will be followed unless current events and experience shall show a modification or change to be proper, and in every case and exigency my best discretion will be exercised, according to circumstances actually existing and with a view and a hope of a peaceful solution of the national troubles and the restoration of fraternal sympathies and affections.

That there are persons in one section or another who seek to destroy the Union at all events and are glad of any pretext to do it I will neither affirm nor deny; but if there be such, I need address no word to them. To those, however, who really love the Union may I not speak?

Before entering upon so grave a matter as the destruction of our national fabric, with all its benefits, its memories, and its hopes, would it not be wise to ascertain precisely why we do it? Will you hazard so desperate a step while there is any possibility that any portion of the ills you fly from have no real existence? Will you, while the certain ills you fly to are greater than all the real ones you fly from, will you risk the commission of so fearful a mistake?

All profess to be content in the Union if all constitutional rights can be maintained. Is it true, then, that any right plainly written in the Constitution has been denied? I think not. Happily, the human mind is so constituted that no party can reach to the audacity of doing this. Think if you can, of a single instance in which a plainly written provision of the Constitution has ever been denied. If by the mere force of numbers a majority should deprive a minority of any clearly written constitutional right, it might in a moral point of view justify revolution; certainly would if such right were a vital one. But such is not our case. All the vital rights of minorities and of individuals are so plainly assured to them by affirmations and negations, guaranties and prohibitions, in the Constitution that controversies never arise concerning them. But no organic law can ever be framed with a provision specifically applicable to every question which may occur in practical administration. No foresight can anticipate nor any document of reasonable length contain express provisions for all possible questions. Shall fugitives from labor be surrendered by national or by State authority? The Constitution does not expressly say. *May* Congress prohibit slavery in the Territories? The Constitution does not expressly say. *Must* Congress protect slavery in the Territories? The Constitution does not expressly say.

From questions of this class spring all our constitutional controversies, and we divide upon them into majorities and minorities. If the minority will not acquiesce, the majority must, or the Government will cease. There is no other alternative, for continuing the Government is acquiescence on one side or the other. If a minority in such case will secede rather than acquiesce, they make a precedent which in turn will divide and ruin them, for a minority of their own will secede from them whenever a majority refuses to be controlled by such minority. For instance, why may not any portion of a new confederacy a year or two hence arbitrarily secede again, precisely as portions of the present Union now claim to secede from it? All who cherish disunion sentiments are now being educated to the exact temper of doing this.

Is there such perfect identity of interests among the States to compose a new union as to produce harmony only and prevent renewed secession?

Plainly the central idea of secession is the essence of anarchy. A majority held in restraint by constitutional checks and limitations, and always changing easily with deliberate changes of popular opinions and sentiments, is the only true sovereign of a free people. Whoever rejects it does of necessity fly to anarchy or to despotism. Unanimity is impossible. The rule of a minority, as a permanent arrangement, is wholly inadmissible; so that, rejecting the majority principle, anarchy or despotism in some form is all that is left.

I do not forget the position assumed by some that constitutional questions are to be decided by the Supreme Court, nor do I deny that such decisions must be binding in any case upon the parties to a suit as to the object of that suit, while they are also entitled to very high respect and consideration in all parallel cases by all other departments of the Government. And while it is obviously possible that such decision may be erroneous in any given case, still the evil effect following it, being limited to that particular case, with the chance that it may be overruled and never become a precedent for other cases, can better be borne than could the evils of a different practice. At the same time, the candid citizen must confess that if the policy of the Government upon vital questions affecting the whole people is to be irrevocably fixed by decisions of the Supreme Court, the instant they are

made in ordinary litigation between parties in personal actions the people will have ceased to be their own rulers, having to that extent practically resigned their Government into the hands of that eminent tribunal. Nor is there in this view any assault upon the court or the judges. It is a duty from which they may not shrink to decide cases properly brought before them, and it is no fault of theirs if others seek to turn their decisions to political purposes.

One section of our country believes slavery is *right* and ought to be extended, while the other believes it is *wrong* and ought not to be extended. This is the only substantial dispute. The fugitive-slave clause of the Constitution and the law for the suppression of the foreign slave trade are each as well enforced, perhaps, as any law can ever be in a community where the moral sense of the people imperfectly supports the law itself. The great body of the people abide by the dry legal obligation in both cases, and a few break over in each. This, I think, can not be perfectly cured, and it would be worse in both cases *after* the separation of the sections than before. The foreign slave trade, now imperfectly suppressed, would be ultimately revived without restriction in one section, while fugitive slaves, now only partially surrendered, would not be surrendered at all by the other.

Physically speaking, we can not separate. We can not remove our respective sections from each other nor build an impassable wall between them. A husband and wife may be divorced and go out of the presence and beyond the reach of each other, but the different parts of our country can not do this. They can not but remain face to face, and intercourse, either amicable or hostile, must continue between them. Is it possible, then, to make that intercourse more advantageous or more satisfactory *after* separation than *before*? Can aliens make treaties easier than friends can make laws? Can treaties be more faithfully enforced between aliens than laws can among friends? Suppose you go to war, you can not fight always; and when, after much loss on both sides and no gain on either, you cease fighting, the identical old questions, as to terms of intercourse, are again upon you.

This country, with its institutions, belongs to the people who inhabit it. Whenever they shall grow weary of the existing Government, they can exercise their *constitutional* right of amending it or their *revolutionary* right to dismember or overthrow it. I can not be ignorant of the fact that many worthy and patriotic citizens are desirous of having the National Constitution amended. While I make no recommendation of amendments, I fully recognize the rightful authority of the people over the whole subject, to be exercised in either of the modes prescribed in the instrument itself; and I should, under existing circumstances, favor rather than oppose a fair opportunity being afforded the people to act upon it. I will venture to add that to me the convention mode seems preferable, in that it allows amendments to originate with the people themselves, instead of only permitting them to take or reject propositions originated by others, not especially chosen for the purpose, and which might not be precisely such as they would wish to either accept or refuse. I understand a proposed amendment to the Constitution—which amendment, however, I have not seen —has passed Congress, to the effect that the Federal Government shall never interfere with the domestic institutions of the States, including that of persons held to service. To avoid misconstruction of what I have said, I depart from my purpose not to speak of particular amendments so far as to say that, holding such a provision to now be implied constitutional law, I have no objection to its being made express and irrevocable.

The Chief Magistrate derives all his authority from the people, and they have conferred none upon him to fix terms for the separation of the States. The people themselves can do this if also they choose, but the Executive as such has nothing to do with it. His duty is to administer the present Government as it came to this hands and to transmit it unimpaired by him to his successor.

Why should there not be a patient confidence in the ultimate justice of the people? Is there any better or equal hope in the world? In our present differences, is either party without faith of being in the right? If the Almighty Ruler of Nations, with His eternal truth and justice, be on your side of the North, or on yours of the South, that truth and that Justice will surely prevail by the judgment of this great tribunal of the American people.

By the frame of the Government under which we live this same people have wisely given their public servants but little power for mischief, and have with equal wisdom provided for the return of that little to their own hands at very short intervals. While the people retain their virtue and vigilance no Administration by any extreme of wickedness or folly can very seriously injure the Government in the short space of four years.

My countrymen, one and all, think calmly and *well* upon this whole subject. Nothing valuable can be lost by taking time. If there be an object to *hurry* any of you in hot haste to a step which you would never take *deliberately*, that object can be frustrated by taking time; but no good object can be frustrated by it. Such of you as are now dissatisfied still have the old Constitution unimpaired, and, on the sensitive point, the laws of your own framing under it; while the new Administration will have no immediate power, if it would, to change either. If it were admitted that you who are dissatisfied hold the right side in the dispute, there still is no single good reason for precipitate action. Intelligence, patriotism, Christianity, and a firm reliance on Him who has never yet forsaken this favored land are still competent to adjust in the best way all our present difficulty.

In *your* hands, my dissatisfied fellow-countrymen, and not in *mine*, is the momentous issue of civil war. The Government will not assail *you*. You can have no conflict without yourselves being the aggressors. *You* have no oath registered in heaven to destroy the Government, while *I* shall have the most solemn one to "preserve, protect, and defend it."

I am loath to close. We are not enemies, but friends. We must not be enemies. Though passion may have strained it must not break our bonds of affection. The mystic chords of memory, stretching from every battlefield and patriot grave to every living heart and hearthstone all over the broad land, will yet swell the chorus of the Union, when again touched, as surely they will be, by the better angels of our nature.

# 33

## *"That there be granted . . . an amount of public land"*

The great sectional issue of the 1850's, which the nation failed to resolve, was not whether the Negro should remain a slave, but whether the public land should remain free. The secession of the slave states was itself a resounding acknowledgment of the strength of the free land forces and might have been cheered by them as a signal triumph were it not for the shock of disunion and the defeat *it* signalized for those very values— government of the people, by the people, for the people—the free land itself was rightfully expected to sustain.

Few in the free states cheered secession; yet when the war for the Union neared its darkest stage, the Union Congress passed and the Union President approved three fateful land measures which secessionists earlier had rejected or opposed—as though victory for the Union and for free land were indeed at hand or unmistakably on the horizon. These measures were, first, on May 20, 1862, "An Act to secure Homesteads to actual Settlers on the Public Domain"; second, on July 1, 1862, "An Act to aid in the Construction of a Railroad and Telegraph Line from the Missouri River to the Pacific Ocean"; and third, on July 2, 1862 "An Act donating Public Lands to the several States and Territories which may provide Colleges for the Benefit of Agriculture and the Mechanic Arts." These measures familiarly known as the Homestead Act, the Pacific Railroad Act, and the Morrill Act, are presented in part in items "a," "b," and "c," below.

The Homestead Act marked the culmination of the half-century-long agitation for free grants of the public domain to "actual settlers," in recognition of their own contribution to the national welfare in taming, cultivating, and guarding the ever-receding frontier. Such an act had at last passed Congress early in 1860, only to be vetoed by President Buchanan. The Pacific Railroad Act, in turn, was the fruit of thirty years of aspiration first brought into practical focus by Asa Whitney in 1845 (see Document No. 28, above), but long delayed by the sectional controversy over the route. The demand for donations of portions of the public domain to the states for the support of agricultural and mechanical colleges first reached Congress in the form of a resolution of the Illinois Legislature in 1853. An act for this purpose was passed in 1859, but was also vetoed by Buchanan. The history of the Morrill Act, however, goes back at least another generation, when agrarian spokesmen in particular began to urge equal educational opportunities even at the university level for American boys. At the same time, many educators themselves were becoming discontented with the classical curriculum of moribund American colleges. They wanted to shift the whole orientation of higher education toward the teaching of science, technology, and the forces of modern life in general, of which they hoped to make the United States the most advanced exemplar.

Each of these three acts was to disappoint its sponsors. Much more of the public domain was settled by the land-grant railroads than by free homesteads which proved to be available in the main on poorer land distant from transportation. The Union Pacific Railroad, in turn, found its land grant inadequate to attract investors to its stock, which had been counted upon to bring in the actual funds for early construction costs. In 1864, The Union Pacific was saved only by liberal revisions of its charter by Congress. Both the Homestead Act and the Pacific Railroad Act, by throwing open almost unlimited acreage in the West, tended to depress the price of other holdings, such as those set aside to support college education under the Morrill Act. The cost of administering their land on the one hand, and the offers of speculators to relieve them of their apparently lavish endowments for nominal cash payments on the other, also combined drastically to diminish the returns to the colleges.

Nevertheless, the Homestead Act drew many settlers westward even if they took up non-homestead land; the Union Pacific Act got the long-sought transcontinentals under way; and the Morrill Act led to the establishment of some of the leading agricultural and engineering schools in the world. Each act is a landmark in American history, and together they symbolize the continuing great moral expectations from America's unmatched material heritage.

*1862*

# The Homestead Act,
# the Pacific Railroad Act, and the Morrill Act

(a) *An Act to secure Homesteads to actual Settlers*
  *on the Public Domain, May 20, 1862*

Any person who is the head of a family, or who has arrived at the age of twenty-one years, and is a citizen of the United States, or who shall have filed his declaration of intention to become such, . . . and who has never borne arms against the United States Government or given aid and comfort to its enemies, shall, from and after the first January, eighteen hundred and sixty-three, be entitled to enter one quarter section or a less quantity of unappropriated public lands, upon which said person may have filed a preëmption claim, or which may, at the time the application is made, be subject to preëmption at one dollar and twenty-five cents or less, per acre; or eighty acres or less of such unappropriated lands, at two dollars and fifty cents per acre, to be located in a body, in conformity to the legal subdivisions of the public lands, and after the same shall have been surveyed. . . .

SEC. 2. The person applying for the benefit of this act shall, upon application to the register of the land office in which he or she is about to make such entry, make affidavit . . . that such application is made for his or her exclusive use and benefit, and that said entry is made for the purpose of actual settlement and cultivation, and not either directly or indirectly for the use or benefit of any other person

or persons whomsoever; . . . *Provided, however,* That no certificate shall be given or patent issued therefor until the expiration of five years from the date of such entry; and if, at the expiration of such time, or at any time within two years thereafter, the person making such entry;—or . . . his widow . . . heirs or devisee . . . shall prove by two credible witnesses that he, she, or they have resided upon or cultivated the same for the term of five years immediately succeeding the time of filing the affidavit aforesaid, and shall make affidavit that no part of said land has been alienated, and that he has borne true allegiance to the Government of the United States; then, in such case, he, she or they, if at that time a citizen of the United States, shall be entitled to a patent. . . .

SEC. 5. If, at any time after the filing of the affidavit, as required in the second section of this act, and before the expiration of the five years aforesaid, it shall be proven, after due notice to the settler, to the satisfaction of the register of the land office, that the person having filed such affidavit shall have actually changed his or her residence, or abandoned the said land for more than six months at any time, then and in that event the land so entered shall revert to the government. . . .

(b)    *An Act to aid in the Construction of a Railroad and Telegraph Line from the Missouri River to the Pacific Ocean, July 1, 1862*

Walter S. Burgess [and 157 other named men], together with five commissioners to be appointed by the Secretary of the Interior, and all persons who shall or may be associated with them, and their successors, are hereby created and erected into a body corporate and politic in deed and in law, by the name, style, and title of "The Union Pacific Railroad Company"; . . . and the said corporation is hereby authorized and empowered to lay out, locate, construct, furnish, maintain, and enjoy a continuous railroad and telegraph, with the appurtenances, from a point on the one hundredth meridian of longitude west from Greenwich, between the south margin of the valley of the Republican River and the north margin of the valley of the Platte River, in the Territory of Nebraska, to the western boundary of Nevada Territory, upon the route and terms hereinafter provided, . . .

The capital stock of said company shall consist of one hundred thousand shares of one thousand dollars each, which shall be subscribed for and held in not more than two hundred shares by any one person. . . . The persons hereinbefore named, together with those to be appointed by the Secretary of the Interior, are hereby constituted and appointed . . . the Board of Commissioners of the Union Pacific Railroad and Telegraph Company. . . . It shall be the duty of said board of commissioners to open books . . . at such times and in such principal cities in the United States as they or a quorum of them shall determine, to receive subscriptions to the capital stock of said corporation, and a cash payment of ten per centum on all subscriptions, and to receipt therefor. So soon as two thousand shares shall be in good faith suscribed for, and ten dollars per share actually paid into the treasury of the company, the said president and secretary of said board of commissioners shall appoint a time and place for the first meeting of the subscribers to the stock of said company . . . and such subscribers as shall attend the meeting so called, either in person or by proxy, shall then and there elect by ballot not less than thirteen directors for said corporation. . . . At the time of the first and each triennial election of directors by the stockholders two additional directors shall be appointed by the President of the United States. . . . The directors to be appointed by the President shall not be stockholders in the Union Pacific Railroad Company. . . .

SEC. 2. The right of way through the public lands . . . is hereby, granted to said company for the construction of said railroad and telegraph line; and the right, power, and authority is hereby given to said company to take from the public lands adjacent to the line of said road, earth, stone, timber, and other materials for the construction thereof; said right of way is granted . . . to the extent of two hundred feet in width on each side of said railroad where it may pass over the public lands, . . . The United States shall extinguish as rapidly as may be the Indian titles to all lands falling under the operation of this act and required for the said right of way and grants hereinafter made.

SEC. 3. There be, and is hereby, granted to the said company, for the purpose of aiding in the construction of said railroad and telegraph line, and to secure the safe and speedy transportation of the mails, troops, munitions of war, and public stores thereon, every alternate section of public land, designated by odd numbers, to the amount of five alternate sections per mile on each side of said railroad, on the line thereof, and within the limits of ten miles on each side of said road, not sold, reserved or otherwise disposed of by the United States, and to which a preëmption or homestead claim may not have attached, at the time the line of said road is definitely fixed: *Provided,* That all mineral lands shall be excepted from the operation of this act; but where the same shall contain timber, the timber thereon is hereby granted to said company. And all such lands, so granted by this section, which shall not be sold or disposed of by said company within three years after the entire road shall have been completed, shall be subject to settlement and preëmption, like other lands, at a price not exceeding one dollar and twenty-five cents per acre, to be paid to said company.

SEC. 4. Whenever said company shall have completed forty consecutive miles of any portion of said railroad and telegraph line, ready for the service contemplated by this act, . . . and all other appurtenances of a first class railroad, the rails and all the other iron used in the construction and equipment of said road to be American manufacture of the best quality, . . . then, . . . patents shall issue conveying the right and title to said lands to said company, on each side of the road as far as the same is completed; . . . and patents shall in like manner issue as each forty miles of said railroad and telegraph line are completed. . . .

SEC. 5. For the purposes herein mentioned the Secretary of the Treasury shall, upon the certificate in writing of said commissioners of the completion and equipment of forty consecutive miles of said railroad and telegraph, . . . issue to said company bonds of the United States of one thousand dollars each, payable in thirty years after date, bearing six per centum per annum interest, (said interest payable semi-annually), . . . to the amount of sixteen of said bonds per mile for such section of forty miles; and to secure the repayment to the United States . . . of the amount of said bonds . . . together with all interest thereon which shall have been paid by the United States, the issue of said bonds and delivery to the company shall ipso facto constitute a first mortgage on the whole line of the railroad and telegraph, together with the rolling stock, fixtures and property of every kind and decription, and in consideration of which said bonds may be issued; and on the refusal or failure of said company to redeem said bonds, or any part of them, when required so to do by the Secretary of the Treasury, . . . the said road, with all its rights, functions, immunities, and appurtenances thereunto belonging, and also all lands granted to the said company by the United States, which, at the time of said default, shall remain in the ownership of the said company, may be taken possession of by the Secretary of the Treasury, for the use and benefit of the United States: . . .

SEC. 6. The grants aforesaid are made upon condition that said company . . . shall at all times transmit despatches over said telegraph line, and transport mails, troops and munitions of war, supplies, and public stores upon said railroad for the government, . . . (at fair and reasonable rates of compensation, not to exceed the amounts paid by private parties for the same kind of service); . . .

SEC. 7. Said company . . . shall complete said railroad and telegraph . . . before the first day of July, one thousand eight hundred and seventy-four. . . .

SEC. 9. . . . The Central Pacific Railroad Company of California, a corporation existing under the laws of the State of California, are hereby authorized to construct a railroad and telegraph line from the Pacific coast, at or near San Francisco, or the navigable waters of the Sacramento River, to the eastern boundary of California, upon the same terms and conditions, in all respects, as are contained in this act for the construction of said railroad and telegraph line first mentioned, and to meet and connect with the first mentioned railroad and telegraph line on the eastern boundary of California. . . .

SEC. 18. Whenever it appears that the net earnings of the entire road and telegraph . . . shall exceed ten per centum upon its cost, . . . Congress may reduce the rates of fare thereon, if unreasonable in amount, and may fix and establish the same by law.

## (c)  An Act donating Public Lands to the several States and Territories which may provide Colleges for the Benefit of Agriculture and the Mechanic Arts, July 2, 1862

Be it enacted . . . That there be granted to the several States, for the purposes hereinafter mentioned, an amount of public land, to be apportioned to each State a quantity equal to thirty thousand acres for each senator and representative in Congress to which the States are respectively entitled by the apportionment under the census of eighteen hundred and sixty: Provided, That no mineral lands shall be selected or purchased under the provisions of this act.

SEC. 2. The land aforesaid, after being surveyed, shall be apportioned to the several States in sections or subdivisions of sections, not less than one quarter of a section; and whenever there are public lands in a State subject to sale at private entry at one dollar and twenty-five cents per acre, the quantity to which said State shall be entitled shall be selected from such lands within the limits of such State, and the Secretary of the Interior is hereby directed to issue to each of the States in which there is not the quantity of public lands subject to sale at private entry at one dollar and twenty-five cents per acre, to which said State may be entitled under the provisions of this act, land scrip to the amount in acres for the deficiency of its distributive share: said scrip to be sold by said States and the proceeds thereof applied to the uses and purposes prescribed in this act. . . .

SEC. 4. All moneys derived from the sale of the lands aforesaid by the States . . . and from the sales of land scrip . . . shall be invested in stocks of the United States, or of the States, or some other safe stocks, yielding not less than five per centum upon the par value of said stocks; and that the moneys so invested shall constitute a perpetual fund, the capital of which shall remain forever undiminished, (except so far as may be provided in section fifth of this act), and the interest of which shall be inviolably appropriated, by each State which may take and claim the benefit of this act, to the endowment, support, and maintenance of at least one college where the leading object shall be, without excluding other scientific and classical studies, and including military tactics, to teach such branches of learning as are related to agriculture and the mechanic arts, . . . in order to promote the liberal and practical education of the industrial classes in the several pursuits and professions in life.

SEC. 5. . . . No portion of said fund, nor the interest thereon, shall be applied, directly or indirectly, under any pretence whatever, to the purchase, erection, preservation, or repair of any building or buildings.

Any State which may take and claim the benefit of the provisions of this act shall provide, within five years, at least not less than one college, . . . or the grant to such State shall cease; and said State shall be bound to pay the United States the amount received of any lands previously sold, and that the title to purchasers under the State shall be valid. . . .

No State while in a condition of rebellion or insurrection against the government of the United States shall be entitled to the benefit of this act.

No State shall be entitled to the benefits of this act unless it shall express its acceptance thereof by its legislature within two years from the date of its approval by the President.

**34**

*"All persons held as slaves within any State,*
*. . . the people whereof shall then be in rebel-*
*lion against the United States, shall be . . .*
*forever free"*

On January 8, 1863, Abraham Lincoln wrote to Major-General John A. McClernand, who had complained of the Emancipation Proclamation the President had issued seven days before:

> After the commencement of hostilities I struggled nearly a year and a half to get along without touching the "institution"; and when finally I conditionally determined to touch it, I gave a hundred days fair notice of my purpose, to all the States and people, within which time they could have turned it wholly aside, by simply again becoming good citizens of the United States. They chose to disregard it, and I made the peremptory proclamation on what appeared to me to be a military necessity. And being made, it must stand.

Lincoln's "struggles" had been real enough, against every sort of pressure—religious, journalistic, political, and personal. More formal pressure also had not been lacking. During the early months of the war, stern anti-slavery generals such as Benjamin F. Butler, John C. Frémont, and David Hunter had interpreted their own "military necessity" as requiring the emancipation of many slaves in the areas of their commands. Lincoln instantly countermanded their orders, repudiated their actions, and punished them for their precipitancy. During the same and succeeding months, Congress passed two so-called "confiscation" acts, the first requiring only the seizure of all property used "in aid of the rebellion," the second a far more severe measure providing, among other penalties against those in any way supporting the rebellion, that their slaves shall be "forever free of their servitude." Lincoln felt obliged to sign both measures (the second only after having drafted a veto message), but not to undertake to enforce them with vigor. His principal fears were for the continuing allegiance of the loyal border states where slavery remained entrenched, and for the Negro himself, whom he still preferred to see ready to be deported and colonized in a more congenial climate before being set free here.

In an attempt to weaken the border states' attachment to the "institution," Lincoln, in March, 1862, sent a special message to Congress proposing that both houses adopt a joint resolution offering the cooperation of the United States "with any State which may adopt gradual abolishment of slavery, giving to such State pecuniary aid . . . to compensate for the inconveniences, public and private, produced by such a change of system." Lincoln went on to explain his purpose:

> The leaders of the existing insurrection entertain the hope that this government will ultimately be forced to acknowledge the independence of some part of the disaffected region, and that all the slave States north of such part will then say "the Union for which we have struggled being already gone, we now choose to go with the Southern section." To deprive them of this hope substantially ends the rebellion, and the initiation of emancipation completely deprives them of it as to all the States initiating it.

Congress, with border-state votes, rejected Lincoln's proposal, and on July 12, 1862, five days before the end of the session, the President invited border state representatives to the White House where he told them, "if you had all voted for the resolution . . . the war would now be substantially ended." He urged them to reconsider during the congressional recess; but they replied within 48 hours that in the opinion of the majority among them, "emancipation in the Border States would not, as the President supposed, lessen the pressure for 'unconstitutional' emancipation by proclamation of the remaining three million slaves in the seceded states, which [they] were unwilling to approve."

Rebuffed here, Lincoln dramatically shifted his target. Having lost his appeal to the border states to free their slaves and save the Union, he turned to the slave states and admonished them to return to the Union or see their slaves freed. On September 22, 1862, in his so-called preliminary emancipation proclamation, he gave them those hundred days he referred to in writing to General McClernand to restore their "constitutional relation" with the United States. To hurry them along he promised to propose to Congress (which he did in his second annual message on December 1, 1862) that it adopt an amendment to the Constitution providing that each slave state which would abolish slavery "any time before the 1st day of January, A.D. 1900, shall receive compensation from the United States," if it wished to accept it. Only states not in rebellion against the United States might participate in his offer; and those that remained in rebellion after January 1, 1863, would find all their slaves "peremptorily" freed with no compensation whatever to their former owners.

When Lincoln said "military necessity" forced his hand, he may indeed have been offering the best constitutional justification for a step his heart desired. But he certainly meant, as well, that the dreary reports from the battlefield had impressed him with the idea that only a political act could soon end the war in the Union's favor. His political appeal to the border states had failed. His preliminary proclamation of September, with its carrot of compensation in one hand and its stick of immediate and unrecompensed emancipation in the other, proved no more successful. On January 1, 1863, his hundred days of grace gone by with no takers among the Confederate commonwealths, Lincoln, "as a fit and necessary war measure," pointed the inevitable finger at those "States and parts of States, wherein the people thereof respectively" remained "in rebellion against the United States." There, but nowhere else, he declared that "all persons held as slaves . . . are, and henceforward shall be free; and that the Executive government of the United States, including the military and naval authorities thereof, will recognize and maintain the freedom of such persons."

Such was the burden of the great Proclamation which is presented below in full. No more than Lincoln's other political efforts did it shorten the awful war. But forever after the war, as Lincoln said to Congress in December, 1862, "in *giving* freedom to the *slave*, we *assure* freedom to the *free*."

*January 1, 1863*

# The Emancipation Proclamation

Whereas, on the twenty second day of September, in the year of our Lord one thousand eight hundred and sixty two, a proclamation was issued by the President of the United States, containing, among other things, the following, to wit:

That on the first day of January, in the year of our Lord one thousand eight hundred and sixty-three, all persons held as slaves within any State or designated part of a State, the people whereof shall then be in rebellion against the United States, shall be then, thenceforward, and forever free; and the Executive Government of the United States, including the military and naval authority thereof, will recognize and maintain the freedom of such persons, and will do no act or acts to repress such persons, or any of them, in any efforts they may make for their actual freedom.

That the Executive will, on the nrst day of January aforesaid, by proclamation, desig-

nate the States and parts of States, if any, in which the people thereof, respectively, shall then be in rebellion against the United States; and the fact that any State, or the people thereof, shall on that day be, in good faith, represented in the Congress of the United States by members chosen thereto at elections wherein a majority of the qualified voters of such State shall have participated, shall, in the absence of strong countervailing testimony, be deemed conclusive evidence that such State, and the people thereof, are not then in rebellion against the United States.

Now, therefore I, Abraham Lincoln, President of the United States, by virtue of the power in me vested as Commander-in-Chief, of the Army and Navy of the United States in time of actual armed rebellion against the authority and government of the United States, and as a fit and necessary war measure for suppressing said rebellion, do, on this first day of January, in the year of our Lord one thousand eight hundred and sixty three, and in accordance with my purpose so to do publicly proclaimed for the full period of one hundred days, from the day first above mentioned, order and designate as the States and parts of States wherein the people thereof respectively, are this day in rebellion against the United States, the following, to wit:

Arkansas, Texas, Louisiana, (except the Parishes of St. Bernard, Plaquemines, Jefferson, St. Johns, St. Charles, St. James [,] Ascension, Assumption, Terrebonne, Lafourche, St. Mary, St. Martin, and Orleans, including the City of New-Orleans) Mississippi, Alabama, Florida, Georgia, South-Carolina, North-Carolina, and Virginia, (except the forty eight counties designated as West Virginia, and also the counties of Berkley, Accomac, Northampton, Elizabeth-City, York, Princess Ann, and Norfolk, including the cities of Norfolk & Portsmouth [)]; and which excepted parts are, for the present, left precisely as if this proclamation were not issued.

And by virtue of the power, and for the purpose aforesaid, I do order and declare that all persons held as slaves within said designated States, and parts of States, are, and henceforward shall be free; and that the Executive government of the United States, including the military and naval authorities thereof, will recognize and maintain the freedom of said persons.

And I hereby enjoin upon the people so declared to be free to abstain from all violence, unless in necessary self-defence; and I recommend to them that, in all cases when allowed, they labor faithfully for reasonable wages.

And I further declare and make known, that such persons of suitable condition, will be received into the armed service of the United States to garrison forts, positions, stations, and other places, and to man vessels of all sorts in said service.

And upon this act, sincerely believed to be an act of justice, warranted by the Constitution, upon military necessity, I invoke the considerate judgment of mankind, and the gracious favor of Almighty God.

In witness whereof, I have hereunto set my hand and caused the seal of the United States to be affixed.

# 35

## "That these dead shall not have died in vain"

In an "Emancipation Memorial" presented to Lincoln by "Chicago Christians of all Denominations," September 13, 1862, the signers had argued that by making the war one for liberating the slaves, the Union would have the greatest principle around which to rally. Lincoln rejected the Memorial and demurred from its argument: "Let me say one thing more: I think you should admit that we already have an important principle to rally and unite the people in the fact that constitutional government is at stake. This is a fundamental idea, going down about as deep as anything."

Such was Lincoln's inspiration; and when he came to help dedicate the military cemetery at Gettysburg in November the following year with a "few appropriate remarks," such was the heart and soul of his message.

The Union victory at Gettysburg, July 3, 1863, had been the turning point of the war. Thousands who there "gave their lives" that this nation might live still remained unburied many months later, and the degrading sight led to a call for a national cemetery in their honor. At the dedication ceremony, November 19, 1863, Edward Everett of Massachusetts, one of the leading orators of the day, gave the long main speech, to prolonged applause. Lincoln's remarks followed. Everett, not least of all, was impressed by the President's "eloquent simplicity and appropriateness," as he wrote Lincoln the following day. "I should be glad, if I could flatter myself that I came as near to the central idea of the occasion in two hours, as you did in two minutes. My son . . . & my daughter, concur in this sentiment."

So many versions of Lincoln's few hundred words at Gettysburg exist that entire books are written about them and their composition. Lincoln's Gettysburg address is presented in full below in the final version he himself edited for posterity, with but few verbal changes, some months after the event.

*November 19, 1863*

# Lincoln's Gettysburg Address

Four score and seven years ago our fathers brought forth on this continent, a new nation, conceived in Liberty, and dedicated to the proposition that all men are created equal.

Now we are engaged in a great civil war, testing whether that nation, or any nation so conceived and so dedicated, can long endure. We are met on a great battle-field of that war. We have come to dedicate a portion of that field, as a final resting place for those who here gave their lives that that nation might live. It is altogether fitting and proper that we should do this.

But, in a larger sense, we cannot dedicate—we cannot consecrate—we cannot hallow—this ground. The brave men, living and dead, who struggled here, have consecrated it, far above our poor power to add or detract. The world will little note, nor long remember, what we say here, but it can never forget what they did here. It is for us the living, rather, to be dedicated here to the unfinished work which they who fought here have thus far so nobly advanced. It is rather for us to be here dedicated to the great task remaining before us—that from these honored dead we take increased devotion to that cause for which they gave the last full measure of devotion—that we here highly resolve that these dead shall not have died in vain—that this nation, under God, shall have a new birth of freedom—and that government of the people, by the people, for the people, shall not perish from the earth.

## 36

*"Shall not be construed as to allow any freed-
man, free negro or mulatto to rent or lease any
lands or tenements"*

The confiscation acts and other meas-
ures relating to slavery passed by Congress in the early years of the Civil War
did not affect the property of loyal southerners. Lincoln's Emancipation
Proclamation, in turn (Document No. 34, above), did not affect the property
of slaveholders in loyal states. The so-called Radicals in Congress thus had
reason to continue pressing for more comprehensive action to set the Negro free.

The Thirteenth Amendment to the Constitution, providing for the abolition
of slavery "within the United States or any place subject to their jurisdiction,"
was first proposed in Congress in December, 1863, and passed the Senate the
following April, 38 to 6. In the House, although the vote stood 93 for and 65
against the amendment, with 23 members abstaining, it failed to gain the
needed two-thirds majority. The amendment thus became a leading issue in the
presidential campaign of 1864, and Lincoln himself interpreted his re-election
that year as a mandate for the "utter and complete extirpation" of slavery, as
the Republican platform put it, at the earliest possible moment. At Lincoln's
urging, the lame duck Congress which met in December, 1864, soon took up
the measure; but only Lincoln's effective log rolling among House Democrats
won over enough votes to squeeze out the two-thirds margin by which it barely
passed on February 1, 1865. By December 18, 1865, the required three-fourths
of the states had approved the amendment and it was proclaimed the law of
the land.

The second section of the Thirteenth Amendment—"Congress shall have
power to enforce [abolition] . . . by appropriate legislation"—is often neglected.
It was the opinion of Charles Sumner of Massachusetts, the leading Radical
in the Senate, that this section meant that Congress had the right to enfranchise
the ex-slave if, in its judgment, the Negro required the right to vote in order to
protect his freedom. Few others even in the North subscribed to Sumner's view
of the Thirteenth Amendment. But many more soon were prepared to endorse
his stand that the Negro must be granted the suffrage, and to support those later
amendments, the Fourteenth and Fifteenth, by which he nominally gained it.

Much of the spirit of Radical Reconstruction is evident in the Thirteenth,
Fourteenth and Fifteenth amendments, which may be found above in Document

No. 16. But certain Radicals, sometimes known as Vindictives, with Congress-man Thaddeus Stevens of Pennsylvania at their head, had hoped to move farther along. No one backed Negro suffrage with more fervor than Stevens. Yet in speaking for the Fourteenth Amendment in Congress in May, 1866, Stevens said:

> In my judgement, we shall not approach the measure of justice until we have given every adult freedman a homestead on the land where he was born and toiled and suffered. Forty acres of land and a hut would be more valuable to him than the immediate right to vote. Unless we give them this we shall receive the censure of mankind and the curse of Heaven.

But Stevens himself acknowledged even of the indirect suffrage provisions of the Fourteenth Amendment, let alone of its failure to venture into the economic sphere, "I believe it is all that can be obtained in the present state of public opinion. . . . Upon a careful survey of the whole ground, we did not believe that nineteen of the loyal States [let alone any of the rebel states, whose right to vote on the amendment he scorned] could be induced to ratify any proposition more stringent than this."

Far less, indeed, could have been obtained from the loyal states had not the defeated section itself at the very earliest opportunity displayed a degree of intransigence that convinced many of the victors that the war had been waged in vain. Before the year 1865 was over, all but Texas of the eleven Confederate commonwealths had been "reconstructed" under President Johnson's magnani-mous terms. They proceeded, then, to elect Confederate generals as governors, Confederate solons as United States Senators, Confederate officers and enlisted men as local legislators. Other candidates, as a correspondent wrote President Johnson from Alabama, were denounced as "traitors to the South," and "over-whelmingly defeated." In some states, the secession ordinances simply were repealed rather than repudiated, as the President had required. In others, there was not only a reluctance to renounce the Confederate debt but also an avowed determination not to be taxed for the redemption of the national debt. At the same time, persistence was promised in pressing claims for compensation as the price for "acquiescence," to quote the Georgia constitutional convention, in this "war measure," the Emancipation Proclamation.

Once the Thirteenth Amendment had been enacted, moreover, the South almost as a unit warned Congress, as the South Carolina legislature put it, to keep hands off "the political status of former slaves, or their civil relations." It was the manner in which the South itself then proceeded to handle these matters that ultimately rekindled the militancy of the war-weary North, where the earlier intransigent acts had been merely disquieting.

The South's principal instruments were the so-called "Black Codes," which all the reconstructed governments enacted among their earliest measures. The Mississippi Code of November, 1865, the first to be adopted, is presented in large part in item "b," below, following the opening message to the Mississippi

Legislature, November 20, 1865, by Governor Benjamin G. Humphreys (item "a"). Humphreys had become a general in the Confederate army; but he was an ante-bellum Whig who had opposed secession and after the war supported the right of the freedman to testify in court. Although the Black Codes tended to be most comprehensive and most severe where freedmen were most numerous, the code in Mississippi, where freedmen indeed outnumbered whites, was not quite the harshest in the South; and Humphreys' message (the italics in it are his) itself reflects the spirit, such as it was, of Mississippi's own less extreme party.

Obviously, once the slave system was destroyed, revisions were called for in state laws. Those who wrote the Black Codes consulted British practice following emancipation in the West Indies as well as northern practice in legislating for the free Negro (see Document No. 24, above). But they naturally consulted as well their own slave codes, relevant parts of which, as in Mississippi, were re-enacted. In the new Codes, the "political status" of the freedman was nullified simply by being systematically ignored; but he did gain certain civil rights forbidden to slaves. The main objective of the Black Codes, however, like that of the defeated section's other intransigent acts, was to restore southern society, and especially its freedman sector, as nearly as feasible to its prewar condition. As a parish code in Louisiana stipulated: "Every negro is required to be in the regular service of some white person, or former owner, who shall be held responsible for the conduct of said negro." The comprehensive code of South Carolina stated:

> No person of color shall pursue or practice the art, trade or business of an artisan, mechanic or shop-keeper, or any other trade, employment or business (besides that of husbandry, or that of a servant under contract for service or labor) on his own account . . . or in partnership with a white person, . . . until he shall have obtained a license therefor, . . . which license shall be good for one year only.

The Mississippi Code, in turn, as in the quotation at the head of this Document, forbade the freedman's renting or leasing farm land.

The North, and especially the Radicals in the North, rightly interpreted the intention of the Black Codes, and the South reaped the whirlwind of Radical Reconstruction for its pains. The "carpetbag" governments in the South repealed the Black Codes, enlarged and protected the Negro's political as well as his civil rights, and broadened his social prerogatives. But when Radical Reconstruction was brought to an end in the 1870's and southern self-determination was largely regained, the spirit of the Codes revived and persisted (see Document No. 42, below). As the moderate Judge Henry D. Clayton, an Alabama Whig, said in 1866, by "the enactment of just and humane laws, . . . we secure the services of the negroes, teach them their places, and how to keep them, and convince them at last that we are indeed their best friends."

*1865*

# The Black Code of Mississippi

(a) *Governor Benjamin G. Humphreys to the Senate
and House of Representatives of Mississippi, November 20, 1865*

By the sudden emancipation of over three hundred thousand slaves, Mississippi has imposed upon her a problem of vast magnitude, upon the proper solution of which depend the hopes and future prosperity and welfare of ourselves and of our children.

*Under the pressure of federal bayonets, urged on by the misdirected sympathies of the world in behalf of the enslaved African,* the people of Mississippi have abolished the institution of slavery. . . . We must now meet the question as it is, and not as we would like to have it. The rule must be justice. The negro is free, whether we like it or not; we must realize that fact now and forever. *To be free, however, does not make him a citizen, or entitle him to social or political equality with the white man.* But the constitution and justice do entitle him to protection and security in his person and property, both real and personal.

In my humble judgment, no person, bond or free, under any form of government, can be assured of protection or security in either person or property, except through an independent and enlightened judiciary. The courts, then, should be open to the negro. . . . As a measure of domestic policy, whether for the protection of the person or the property of the freedman, or for the protection of society, the negro should be allowed and required to testify for or against the white and black according to the truth. There are few men living in the south who have not known many white criminals to go "un-whipped of justice" because negro testimony was not permitted in the courts. And now that the negro is no longer under the restraints and protection of his master, he will become the dupe and the "cat's-paw" of the vile and vicious white man who seeks his association, and will plunder our lands with entire security from punishment, unless he can be reached through negro testimony. It is an insult to the intelligence and virtue of our courts, and juries of white men, to say or suspect that they can not or will not protect the innocent, whether white or black, against the falsehood and perjury of black witnesses.

The question of admitting negro testimony for the protection of their person and property sinks into insignificance by the side of the other great question of *guarding them and the State* against the evils that may arise from their sudden emancipation. What are the evils that have already arisen, against which we are to guard the negro and the State? The answer is patent to all—vagrancy and pauperism, and their inevitable concomitant, crime and misery, hang like a dark pall over a once prosperous and happy, but now desolated land. . . .

Our rich and productive fields have been deserted for the filthy garrets and sickly cellars of our towns and cities. From producers they are converted into consumers, and, as winter approaches, their only salvation from starvation and want is federal rations, plunder, and pillage. *Four years of cruel war, con-*

*ducted on principles of vandalism disgraceful to the civilization of the age, were scarcely more blighting and destructive to the homes of the white man, and impoverishing and degrading to the negro, than has resulted in the last six or eight months from the administration of this black incubus.* . . .

How long this *hideous curse,* permitted of Heaven, is to be allowed to rule and ruin our unhappy people, I regret it is not in my power to give any assurance, . . . In this uncertainty . . . our duty to the State, and to the freedmen, seems to me to be clear, and I respectfully recommend—1st. That negro testimony should be admitted in our courts, not only for the protection of the person and property of the freedmen, but for the protection of society against the crimes of both races. 2d. That the freedman be encouraged at once to engage in some pursuit of industry for the support of his family and the education of his children, by laws assuring him of friendship and protection. Tax the freedman for the support of the indigent and helpless freedmen, and *then with an iron will and the strong hand of power take hold of the idler and the vagrant and force him to some profitable employment.* 3d. Pass a militia law that will enable the militia to protect our people against the insurrection, or any possible combination of vicious white men and negroes.

## (b) *From the Black Code of Mississippi, November, 1865*

AN ACT TO CONFER CIVIL RIGHTS
ON FREEDMEN,
AND FOR OTHER PURPOSES.

SECTION 1. All freedmen, free negroes and mulattoes may sue and be sued, implead and be impleaded in all the courts of law and equity of this State, and may acquire personal property and choses in action, by descent or purchase, and may dispose of the same, in the same manner, and to the same extent that white persons may: Provided that the provisions of this section shall not be so construed as to allow any freedman, free negro or mulatto, to rent or lease any lands or tenements, except in incorporated towns or cities in which places the corporate authorities shall control the same.

SEC. 2. Be it further enacted, That all freedmen, free negroes and mulattoes may intermarry with each other, in the same manner and under the same regulations that are provided by law for white persons. . . .

SEC. 3. . . . . That it shall not be lawful for any freedman, free negro or mulatto to intermarry with any white person, nor for any white person to intermarry with any freedman, free negro or mulatto; and any person who shall so intermarry shall be deemed guilty of felony, and on conviction thereof, shall be confined in the State Penitentiary for life. . . .

SEC. 4. In addition to cases in which freedmen, free negroes and mulattoes are now by law competent witnesses, freedmen, free negroes or mulattoes shall be competent in civil cases when a party or parties to the suit, either plaintiff or plaintiffs, defendant or defendants, also in cases where freedmen, free negroes and mulattoes is or are either plaintiff or plaintiffs, defendant or defendants, and a white person or white persons is or are the opposing party or parties, plaintiff or plaintiffs, defendant or defendants. They shall also be competent witnesses in all criminal prosecutions where the crime charged is alleged to have been committed by a white person upon or against the person or property of a freedman, free negro or mulatto. . . .

SEC. 5. Every freedman, free negro and mulatto, shall, on the second Monday of January, one thousand eight hundred and sixty-six, and annually thereafter, have a lawful home or employment, and shall have written evidence thereof, as follows, to-wit: if living in any incorporated city, town or village, a license from the mayor thereof; and if living outside of any incorporated city, town or village, from the member of the board of police of his beat, authorizing him or her to do irregular and job work, or a written contract, as provided in section sixth of this act, which licenses may be revoked for cause, at any time, by the authority granting the same.

SEC. 6. All contracts for labor made with freedmen, free negroes and mulattoes, for a longer period than one month shall be in writing and in duplicate, . . . and if the laborer shall quit the service of the employer, before expiration of his term of service, without good cause, he shall forfeit his wages for that year, up to the time of quitting.

SEC. 7. Every civil officer shall, and every person may arrest and carry back to his or her legal employer any freedman, free negro or mulatto, who shall have quit the service of his or her employer before the expiration of his or her term of service without good cause, and said officer and person shall be entitled to receive for arresting and carrying back every deserting employee aforesaid, the sum of five dollars, and ten cents per mile from the place of arrest to the place of delivery, and the same shall be paid by the employer, and held as a set-off for so much against the wages of said deserting employee: . . .

SEC. 9. If any person shall persuade or attempt to persuade, entice or cause any freedman, free negro or mulatto, to desert from the legal employment of any person, before the expiration of his or her term of service, or shall knowingly employ any such deserting freedman, free negro or mulatto, or shall knowingly give or sell to any such deserting freedman, free negro or mulatto, any food, rayment or other thing, he or she shall be guilty of a misdemeanor, and upon conviction, shall be fined not less than twenty-five dollars and not

more than two hundred dollars and the costs. . . .

SEC. 10. It shall be lawful for any freedman, free negro or mulatto, to charge any white person, freedman, free negro or mulatto, by affidavit, with any criminal offence against his or her person or property and upon such affidavit the proper process shall be issued and executed as if said affidavit was made by a white person. . . .

AN ACT TO BE ENTITLED
"AN ACT TO REGULATE THE RELATION
OF MASTER AND APPRENTICE,
AS RELATES TO FREEDMEN,
FREE NEGROES, AND MULATTOES."

SECTION 1. It shall be the duty of all sheriffs, justices of the peace, and other civil officers . . . to report to the probate courts of their respective counties, semi-annually, . . . all freedmen, free negroes and mulattoes, under the age of eighteen, . . . who are orphans, or whose parent or parents have not the means, or who refuse to provide for and support said minors, and thereupon it shall be the duty of said probate court, to order the clerk of said court to apprentice said minors to some competent and suitable person, . . . Provided, that the former owner of said minors shall have the preference, when in the opinion of the court, he or she shall be a suitable person for that purpose.

SEC. 2. . . . The said court shall require the said master or mistress to . . . furnish said minor with sufficient food and clothing, to treat said minor humanely, furnish medical attention in case of sickeness; teach or cause to be taught him or her to read and write, if under fifteen years old. . . . Said apprentice shall be bound by indenture, in case of males until they are twenty-one years old, and in case of females until they are eighteen years old. . . .

AN ACT TO AMEND
THE VAGRANT LAWS OF THE STATE.

SECTION 1. All rogues and vagabonds, idle and dissipated persons, beggars, jugglers, or persons practicing unlawful games or plays, runaways, common drunkards, common night-walkers, pilferers, lewd, wanton, or lascivious persons, in speech or behavior, common railers and brawlers, persons who neglect their calling or employment, misspend what they earn, or do not provide for the support of themselves or their families, or dependants, and all other idle and disorderly persons, including all who neglect all lawful business, or habitually misspend their time by frequenting houses of ill-fame, gaming-houses or tippling shops, shall be deemed and considered vagrants under the provisions of this act, and on conviction thereof shall be fined not exceeding one hundred dollars, with all accruing costs, and be imprisoned at the discretion of the court not exceeding ten days.

Sec. 2. All freedmen, free negroes and mulattoes in this State, over the age of eighteen years, found on the second Monday in January, 1866, or thereafter, with no lawful employment or business, or found unlawfully assembling themselves together either in the day or night time, and all white persons so assembling with freedmen, free negroes or mulattoes, or usually associating with freedmen, free negroes or mulattoes on terms of equality, or living in adultery or fornication with a freed-woman, free negro, or mulatto, shall be deemed vagrants, and on conviction thereof, shall be fined in the sum of not exceeding, in the case of a freed-man, free negro or mulatto, fifty dollars, and a white man two hundred dollars, and imprisoned at the discretion of the court, the free negro not exceeding ten days, and the white man not exceeding six months. . . .

SEC. 5. . . . In case any freedman, free negro or mulatto, shall fail for five days after the imposition of any fine or forfeiture upon him or her for violation of any of the provisions of this act, to pay the same, it shall be, and is hereby made the duty of the sheriff of the proper county to hire out said freed-man, free negro or mulatto, to any person who will, for the shortest period of service, pay said fine or forfeiture and all costs: . . .

SEC. 6. The same duties and liabilities existing among white persons of this State shall attach to freedmen, free negroes and mulattoes, to support their indigent families, and all colored paupers; and that in order to secure a support for such indigent freedmen, free negroes and mulattoes, it shall be lawful, and it is hereby made the duty of the boards of county police of each county in this State, to levy a poll or capitation tax on each and every freed-man, free negro or mulatto, between the ages of eighteen and sixty years, not to exceed the sum of one dollar annually, to each person so taxed, . . .

SEC. 7. If any freedman, free negro or mulatto shall fail, or refuse to pay any tax levied according to the provisions of the sixth section of this act, it shall be *prima facie* evidence of vagrancy, and it shall be the duty of the sheriff to arrest such freedman, free negro or mulatto, or such person refusing or neglecting to pay such tax, and proceed at once to hire, for the shortest time, such delinquent tax payer to any one who will pay the said tax, with accruing costs, giving preference to the employer, if there be one. . . .

AN ACT TO PUNISH
CERTAIN OFFENCES THEREIN NAMED,
AND FOR OTHER PURPOSES.

SEC. 4. All the penal and criminal laws now in force in this State, defining offences and prescribing the mode of punishment for crimes and misdemeanors committed by slaves, free negroes or mulattoes, be and the same are hereby re-enacted, and declared to be in full force and effect, against freedmen, free negroes and mulattoes. . . .

SEC. 5. If any freedman, free negro or mulatto, convicted of any of the misdemeanors provided against in this act, shall fail or refuse, for the space of five days after conviction, to pay the fine and costs imposed, such person shall be hired out by the sheriff or other officer, at public outcry, to any white person who will pay said fine and all costs, and take such convict for the shortest time.

# 37

*"If they stand up against the progress of civilization and industry, they must be relentlessly crushed"*

Although it was not until 1890 that the United States Census Office made the momentous pronouncement that there can hardly any longer "be said to be a frontier line," the rapid filling up of America's vast continental expanse was clearly foreshadowed a full generation earlier. In November, 1872, in his first and only Annual Report as Commissioner of Indian Affairs (the subject of this Document), General Francis A. Walker observed: "The westward course of population is neither to be denied nor delayed for the sake of all the Indians that ever called this country home. They must yield or perish; and there is something that savors of providential mercy in the rapidity with which their fate advances upon them."

General Walker's Report gives eloquent evidence of the demoralization of the red men under the fatal pressure of the westward movement following the outbreak of the Civil War. Within a decade, the "one great reservation" that had long been promised the aborigines as their eternal "Canaan" beyond the Father of Waters had been inundated by resolute whites. In this period, by scores of treaties; the horse Indians of the plains and the woods Indians of the forests who had been forcibly moved amongst them were terrorized or tempted into yielding territories, as General Walker puts it, "as large as some of the kingdoms of Europe."

By 1870, all but the most implacable braves were corraled on reservations. In March the next year, only a few months before Walker had been confirmed as Commissioner, Congress itself signalized the final annihilation of tribal autonomy when it passed the historic act declaring that, "hereafter no Indian nation or tribe within the territory of the United States shall be acknowledged or recognized as an independent nation, tribe, or power, with whom the United States may contract by treaty." Henceforth, as Walker said, the red men must become "suppliants for charity," and "brought distinctly to the realization of the law that if they would eat they must also work. . . . Such of them as went right," the General added, "should be protected and fed, and such as went wrong should be harassed and scourged without intermission."

Walker's Report also gives eloquent evidence of the demoralization of the Commissioner's office under the push and pull of aggression and guilt that characterized American attitudes toward the red men from the beginning of settlement, but which became most acute when settlement was almost complete.

The total confinement of the Indians on closed-in reservations had been one phase of the so-called "peace policy" which the United States adopted toward them in 1867 for reasons of economy as well as humanitarianism. The Indian's hot resentment against confinement, however, soon made it necessary to resume the costly wars against those who were constantly breaking out as well as against "implacables," who had never been subdued. Since the Indians were acting out of desperation and the army retaliated in kind, the Indian wars grew ever more savage. The Indian administration thus was bombarded by demands, on the one hand, that it abandon the butchery, and on the other that it speed it up.

The humanitarians, however, presented no alternative to the discredited policy of converting horse and blanket Indians to farming by allotting them individual pieces of land such as white men were satisfied with. The exterminators, in turn, offered no answer to General Sherman's complaint in 1868, that "the country is so large, and the advantage of the Indians so great, that we cannot make a single war end it."

Walker's office embraced both horns of the dilemma without success, permitting the red men on the reservations to fall "hopelessly into the condition of pauperism and petty crime," and white men to treat those off the reservation as "wild beasts" to be hunted. Walker also pointed out that Indians being "expressly excluded by the Constitution from citizenship, the Government is only bound in its treatment of them by considerations of present policy and justice." "Present policy," throughout American history, clearly overruled justice in Indian relations—whatever justice may have required, however often it was put forth in vindication of "present policy," and however little "present policy" at any time fully satisfied the conscience of the country.

*November 1, 1872*

# Annual Report

# of the Commissioner of Indian Affairs

Sir: . . . It has seemed desirable, in recognition of the wide popular interest taken in the dealings of the Government with the Indians, . . . to present at this time a pretty full statement of the situation of Indian affairs, and of the policy of the Government in view of that situation. . . . What shall be done with the Indian as an obstacle to the progress of settlement and industry? What shall be done with him as a dependent and pensioner on our civilization, when, and so far as, he ceases to oppose or obstruct the extension of railways and of settlement?

## THE INDIAN POLICY

The Indian policy, so called, of the Government, is a policy, and it is not a policy, or rather it consists of two policies, entirely distinct, seeming, indeed, to be mutually inconsistent and to reflect each upon the other; the one regulating the treatment of the tribes which are potentially hostile, that is, whose hostility is only repressed just so long as, and so far as, they are supported in idleness by the Government; the other regulating the treatment of those tribes which, from traditional friendship, from numerical weakness, or by the force of their location, are either indisposed toward, or incapable of, resistance to the demands of the Government. . . . This want of completeness and consistency in the treatment of the Indian tribes by the Government has been made the occasion of much ridicule and partisan abuse; and it is indeed calculated to provoke criticism and to afford scope for satire; . . . And yet, for all this, the Government is right and its critics wrong. . . .

It is not, of course, to be understood that the Government of the United States is at the mercy of Indians; but thousands of its citizens are, even thousands of families. Their exposed situation on the extreme verge of settlement affords a sufficient justification to the Government for buying off the hostility of the savages, excited and exasperated as they are, and most naturally so, by the invasion of their hunting-grounds and the threatened extinction of game. It would require one hundred thousand troops at least to form a *cordon* behind which our settlements could advance with the extent of range, the unrestrained choice of location, the security

of feeling, and the freedom of movement which have characterized the growth of the past three or four years. Indeed, the presence of no military force could give that confidence to pioneer enterprise which the general cessation of Indian hostilities has engendered. . . .

There are innumerable little rifts of agricultural or mining settlements all over the western country which, if unmolested, will in a few years become self-protecting communities, but which, in the event of a general Indian war occurring at the present time, would utterly and instantly disappear, either by abandonment or massacre. . . . Such would be the result even with the most favorable issue of military operations. It is right that those who criticize the policy of the Government toward the Indians, and ridicule it as undignified in its concessions and unstatesman-like in its temporizing with a recognized evil, should fairly face the one alternative which is presented. There is no question of national dignity, be it remembered, involved in the treatment of savages by a civilized power. With wild men, as with wild beasts, the question whether in a given situation one shall fight, coax, or run, is a question merely of what is easiest and safest.

## THE USE OF THE MILITARY ARM

The system now pursued in dealing with the roving tribes dangerous to our frontier population and obstructing our industrial progress, is entirely consistent with, and, indeed, requires the occasional use of the military arm, in restraining or chastising refractory individuals and bands. Such a use of the military constitutes no abandonment of the "peace policy," and involves no disparagement of it. . . . In the first announcement made of the reservation system, it was expressly declared that the Indians should be made as comfortable on, and as uncomfortable off, their reservations as it was in the power of the Government to make them; that such of them as went right should be protected and fed, and such as went wrong should be harassed and scourged without intermission. . . . Such a use of the strong arm of the Government is not war, but discipline. . . .

### THE FORBEARANCE OF THE GOVERNMENT

It is unquestionably true that the Government has seemed somewhat tardy in proceeding under the second half of the reservation policy, and in applying the scourge to individuals and bands leaving their prescribed limits without authority, or for hostile purposes. This has been partly from a legitimate deference to the conviction of the great body of citizens that the Indians have been in the past unjustly and cruelly treated, . . . and partly from the knowledge on the part of the officers of the Government charged with administering Indian affairs, that, from the natural jealousy of these people, their sense of wrongs suffered in the past, and their suspiciousness arising from repeated acts of treachery on the part of the whites; . . . from the efforts of abandoned and degraded whites, living among the Indians and exerting much influence over them, to misrepresent the policy of the Government, and to keep alive the hostility and suspicion of the savages; and, lastly, from the extreme untrustworthiness of many of the interpreters on whom the Government is obliged to rely for bringing its intentions to the knowledge of the Indians; that by the joint effect of all these obstacles, many tribes and bands could come very slowly to hear, comprehend, and trust the professions and promises of the Government.

Such being the sentiment of the general community, that forbearance was due to the Indians on account of past wrongs; and such the knowledge on the part of the Government of difficulties to be encountered in fully acquainting these people with its benevolent intentions, all the resources of expostulation

and conciliation have been exhausted before the aid of the military arm has been invoked. . . . The patience and forbearance exercised have been fully justified in their fruits. The main body of the roving Indians have, with good grace or with ill grace, submitted to the reservation system. . . .

### THE IMPLACABLES

There is a residue whose disposition and behaviour certainly give little encouragement to further forbearance. The numbers of the actually hostile and depredating bands of to-day probably do not exceed in the aggregate eight thousand. Among these are several bands of Apaches in Arizona, principally the Tonto Apaches, the Quahada Comanches and their confederates of the Staked Plains, west of the Indian Country, and the greater portion of the Kiowa nation. It would be impossible from the large number of tribes, great and small, known to the annals of the country, to select three which have so little in the way of past wrongs to justify present hostility as these three tribes, which commit, practically, all the outrages properly to be charged against the Indians. . . . A continuance in their present course will involve, as it ought, their extirpation. . . .

### THE POLICY OF TEMPORIZING

It is saying nothing against the course of the Government toward the semi-hostile tribes, to allege, as is often done, that it is merely temporizing with an evil. . . . When an evil is in its nature self-limited, and tends to expire by the very conditions of its existence; when time itself fights against it, and the whole progress of the physical, social, and industrial order by steady degrees circumscribes its field, reduces its dimensions, and saps its strength, then temporizing may be the highest statesmanship.

Such an evil is that which the United States Government at present encounters in the resistance, more or less suppressed, of the Indian tribes of this continent to the progress of railways and settlements, growing out of the reasonable apprehension that their own existence as nations, and even their own individual means of subsistence within the duration of their own lives, will be destroyed thereby. This case differs from others recorded in history only in this—that never was an evil so gigantic environed, invaded, devoured by forces so tremendous, so appalling in the celerity and the certainty of their advance. . . .

SUBMISSION THE ONLY HOPE
OF THE INDIANS

No one certainly will rejoice more heartily than the present Commissioner when . . . the last hostile tribe becomes reduced to the condition of suppliants for charity. This is, indeed, the only hope of salvation for the aborigines of the continent. If they stand up against the progress of civilization and industry, they must be relentlessly crushed. The westward course of population is neither to be denied nor delayed for the sake of all the Indians that ever called this country their home. They must yield or perish; and there is something that savors of providential mercy in the rapidity with which their fate advances upon them, leaving them scarcely the chance to resist before they shall be surrounded and disarmed. It is not feebly and futilely to attempt to stay this tide, whose depth and strength can hardly be measured, but to snatch the remnants of the Indian race from destruction before it, that the friends of humanity should exert themselves in this juncture, and lose no time. . . .

THE CLAIMS OF THE INDIANS

Had the settlements of the United States not been extended beyond the frontier of 1867, all the Indians of the continent would to the end of time have found upon the plains an inexhaustible supply of food and clothing. Were the westward course of population to be stayed at the barriers of today, notwithstanding the tremendous inroads made upon their hunting-grounds since 1867, the Indians would still have hope of life. But another such five years will see the Indians of Dakota and Montana as poor as the Indians of Nevada and Southern California; that is, reduced to an habitual condition of suffering from want of food.

The freedom of expansion which is working these results is to us of incalculable value. To the Indian it is of incalculable cost. Every year's advance of our frontier takes in a territory as large as some of the kingdoms of Europe. We are richer by hundreds of millions; the Indian is poorer by a large part of the little that he has. This growth is bringing imperial greatness to the nation; to the Indian it brings wretchedness, destitution, beggary. Surely there is obligation found in considerations like these, requiring us in some way, and in the best way, to make good to these original owners of the soil the loss by which we so greatly gain, . . . by . . . helping them over the first rough places on "the white man's road," and, meanwhile, supplying such subsistence as is absolutely necessary during the period of initiation and experiment.

A LEGALIZED REFORMATORY
CONTROL NECESSARY

The assistance due to the Indians from the Government in the discharge of those obligations which have been adverted to should not much longer be irrespective of their own efforts. Just so soon as these tribes cease to be formidable, they should be brought distinctly to the realization of the law that if they would eat they must also work. . . . The Government should extend over them a rigid reformatory discipline, to save them from falling hopelessly into the condition of pauperism and petty crime, . . . the men resorting for a living to basket-making and hog-stealing; the women to fortune-telling and harlotry. . . . Unused to manual labor, and physically disqualified for it by the habits of the chase, unprovided with tools and implements, without forethought and without self-control, singularly susceptible to evil influences, with strong animal appetites and no intellectual tastes or aspirations to hold those appetites in check, it would be to assume more than would be taken for granted of any white race under the same conditions, to expect that the wild Indians will become industrious and frugal except through a severe course of industrial instruction and exercise, under restraint. The reservation system affords the place for thus dealing with tribes and bands, without the access of influences inimical to peace and virtue. . . .

Especially is it essential that the right of the Government to keep Indians upon the reservations assigned to them, and to arrest and return them whenever they wander away, should be placed beyond dispute. . . . The right of the Government to do this cannot be seriously questioned. Expressly excluded by the Constitution from citizenship, the Government is only bound in its treatment of them by considerations of present policy and justice. Even . . . were there nothing in the history of the dealings of the United States with them to form a precedent for their being placed under arbitrary control, still, the manifest necessity of self-protection would amply justify the Government in any and all measures required to prevent the miserable conclusion I have indicated. . . .

THE ENDOWMENT
OF INDIAN TRIBES

I cannot admit that there is any reason for the apprehensions which many persons feel, that when the Indians cease to be formidable, they will be neglected. . . . The proceeds arising from sales, as their reservations are from time to time diminished by authority of law, for the sake of securing a higher culture of the portions remaining, ought, if the Indians are honestly treated in the transaction, to be sufficient to provide for all ordinary beneficial expenditures in behalf of tribes and bands having lands secured to them by treaty.

The reservations granted heretofore have generally been proportioned, and rightly so, to the needs of the Indians in a roving state, with hunting and fishing as their chief means of subsistence, which condition implies the occupation of a territory far exceeding what could possibly be cultivated. As they change to agriculture, however rude and primitive at first, they tend to contract the limits of actual occupation. . . . Where this change has taken place, there can be no question of the expediency of such sale or cession. . . .

For those tribes and bands which have no reservations secured to them by treaty, from which they can hope in the course of time to realize a civilization and improvement fund, provision will still require to be made by law. Their right to endowment is none the less clear than the right of other tribes whose fortune it was to deal with the United States by treaty, before Congress put an end to the treaty system, with its many abuses and absurdities. We have received the soil from them, and we have extinguished their only means of subsistence. Nothing in the history of the United States justifies the belief that either Congress or the country will be wanting in justice or generosity in dealing with the necessities of a people who have been impoverished that we might be rich.

# 38

*"I don't believe that by any legislative enact-
ment or anything else . . . you can keep such
men as them down"*

By the 1870's the American people
had long since established their attachment to the supremacy of written law, to
representative government, democratic elections, and the liberties and immunities inscribed in state and federal bills of rights. They had formed and preserved
their Union, extended its territory from sea to sea, bound it the more firmly
together by steamship, road, railroad, and telegraph, and opened its rich lands
as an asylum and offered them as a stake to the oppressed of Europe if not to
black and red men nearer home. Most recently, by means of the most advanced
technology, they had begun that tooth and claw competition for the incredible
metallic and mineral wealth stored for centuries for them to claim.

In 1872, commenting on the new spirit in Jefferson's old "empire of liberty,"
which Andrew Carnegie, his own efforts contributing no small part to the transformation, was soon to rechristen the "empire of business," Walt Whitman said:

> I may as well distinctly specify, as cheerfully included in the model and
> standard of these [Democratic] Vistas, a practical, stirring, worldly, money-
> making even materialistic character. . . . I perceive clearly that the extreme
> business energy, and this almost maniacal appetite for wealth in the United
> States, are parts of amelioration and progress, indispensably needed to prepare
> the very results I demand. My theory includes riches and the getting of riches.

For some time the supreme representatives of the new spirit were the creators
of what the perceptive James Bryce was to call "that prodigy of labour, wealth,
and skill—the American railway system." Bryce went on to say of American
railroad presidents: "No talents of the practical order can be too high for such a
position as this. . . . Probably no career draws to it or unfolds and develops so
much of the characteristic ability of the nation." Yet when Bryce first wrote
these words in 1888, the American railway system had, in fact, long been under
attack by urban shippers, farmers, stockholders, state railroad commissions, and
others especially fearful of its political as well as its economic power (see Document No. 39, below). Railroad managers themselves, moreover, had already met
their match in newer spheres of business enterprise.

The most dramatic as well as the most profitable of the new business spheres was the refining of petroleum; and the unmistakable lords of creation in it were the masters of the Standard Oil "trust," the prototype of all other such bogeys that were soon to appear on the modern business scene. As early as 1879, Standard Oil had gained control of 90 to 95 per cent of the refining capacity of the United States; and one of the principal instrumentalities in its success was its ability to exact special rates, rebates, and drawbacks from the railroads which coveted the vast business of carrying their crude and kerosene. Railroad rates, like those of other "common carriers," were supposed by law to be publicly posted and nondiscriminatory. But competing businessmen in other fields had learned how to tighten the screws on competing railroads in order to obtain secret rate and service concessions. In but a few months in the one year of 1879, the great New York Central alone had made more than 6,000 special contracts with more or less favored shippers. None fared better than Standard Oil had for many years past.

In 1879, in response to mounting public clamor against the railroads, the New York State Legislature set up the special committee known popularly, after its chairman, as the Hepburn Committee, to conduct an investigation of railroad practices. The Hepburn Committee placed in charge of its staff Simon Sterne, a New York lawyer exceedingly knowledgeable in railroad matters and wholly unawed by railroad power. Sterne made the Hepburn investigation the most complete and illuminating examination of American business up to that time, including the business of the railroad's best customers.

In this Document we present Sterne's interrogation of William K. Vanderbilt, President of the New York Central Railroad, on his relations with Standard Oil. Vanderbilt's squirming reluctance to acknowledge the principle of favoritism underscores all the more Standard's extraordinary ability to exact special treatment.

*August 29, 1879*

Simon Sterne

Interrogates William K. Vanderbilt

for the Hepburn Committee

Q. I understood you to say yesterday, that you were disposed, and meant to treat the producers of oil upon an equal basis? A. I did, if we had come to any terms; yes, sir.

Q. If you had come to any terms? A. Yes, sir.

Q. You heard me read the agreement, as arrived at in 1872; the agreement of March 25, 1872, is this: "That all arrangements for the transportation of oil after this date shall be upon a basis of perfect equality to all shippers, producers and refiners, and that no rebates, drawbacks or other arrangements of any character shall be made or allowed, that will give any party the slightest difference in rates or discrimination of any character whatever. . . . In the distribution of cars for shipment, it shall be done without discrimination;" now, do you consider that position of the New York Central, then taken, still in force? A. Under the same circumstances, yes.

Q. What do you mean by under the same circumstances? A. Circumstances have changed very largely since 1872; in 1872 there were probably fifty men in the oil business, where there is but one to-day, or two, but they were all on a perfect equality so far as I know now, so far as I can remember, at that time, but we have drifted along and got to where we are.

Q. Your getting where you are is because of the enormous growth of the Standard Oil Company, isn't it, and its affiliations? A. That is one of the causes; yes; one line, if you please, buying up all the others.

Q. In all candor, without going into the causes of it, does not that one great shipper dictate terms, practically to the railways? A. That is all owing to the railroads—what their relations are at the time that he comes to them; if the railways are at war with each other you may say, yes; if not, no.

Q. But the railways agree to give to the Standard—each railway in its turn has agreed, and between each other substantially they have agreed, have they not, to give to the Standard Company the lowest rate that the Standard Company obtains upon any other road. A. No, we never agreed to that: let me explain right here; the construction that the Standard put upon that and that others have put upon that, too—upon the contract that they had with us, would probably bear that construction, but that never was our intention and has

been distinctly repudiated by me time and time again; I said, "Gentlemen, you cannot walk into this office and say we are bound by any contract to do business with you at any price that any other road does that is in competition with us; it is only on a fair competitive basis, a fair competition for business at a price that I consider will pay the company to do it;" I am not going to put it in any man's power on cattle, or anything else; while we may do it, we are not going to put it in his power to come to us and make that claim upon us to do it; they did put that construction upon that contract early and I repudiated it distinctly to them, and if you put those gentlemen on the stand I guess they will all say I did; I am aware that it did bear that construction.

Q. Independently of that, substantially don't you carry out that construction of the agreement: I mean the construction that the Standard people put upon the agreement? A. No; we may carry it out so far as our action goes, but we don't carry out any such principle; in ordinary competion we do; we say we will do their business the same as any other company does, but we are not going to say if they do it for nothing that we will do it for nothing; we always base it upon a price that we consider is paying for the business that we do for them.

Q. As a matter of fact, are you not carrying oil now at a price far below any paying price? A. I don't know, for I don't know what the price is.

Q. When you last heard of the price were you not even then carrying it at a price far below a price that paid for carriage? A. No; I have heard that we were carrying it very low, but I have not heard prior to my coming here now (this few days' talk in this matter), that we have done that business at what may be called less than cost, except it may be for a few days.

Q. If your price is now ten cents a barrel, would you consider that a paying price? A. From where?

Q. From the oil regions to New York—on crude? A. No.

Q. Four hundred and fifty pounds carried a distance of five hundred miles, on which you must pro-rate with the Lake Shore Road? A. I should not think it was a paying price, if you do not take other things into consideration—take it by itself.

Q. Unless you do it for war purposes? A. Yes; for some ulterior object.

Q. Can you attribute, or do you attribute, in your own mind, the fact of there being one refiner instead of fifty, now, to any other cause except the larger capital of the Standard Oil Company? A. There are a great many causes; it is not from their capital alone that they have built up this business; there is no question about it but that these men—and if you come in contact with them, I guess you will come to the same conclusion I have long ago—I think they are smarter fellows than I am, a good deal; they are very enterprising and smart men; never came in contact with any class of men as smart and able as they are in their business, and I think a great deal is to be attributed to that.

Q. Would that alone monopolize a business of that sort? A. It would go a great ways toward building it up; they never could have got in the position they are in now, without a great deal of ability, and one man would hardly have been able to do it; it is a combination of men.

Q. Wasn't it a combination that embraced the smart men in the railways, as well as the smart men in the Standard Company? A. I think those gentlemen from their shrewdness have been able to take advantage of the competition that existed between the railroads for their business, as it grew, and that they have availed themselves of that there is not a question of doubt. . . .

Q. And that is the only way you can account for the enormous monopoly that has thus grown up? A. Yes; they are very shrewd men; I don't believe that by any legislative enactment or anything else through any of the States or all of the States, you can keep such men as them down; you can't do it; they will be up on top all the time; you see if they are not.

Q. You think they get on top of the railways? A. Yes; and on top of everybody that comes in contact with them; too smart for me.

Q. Then you want the power of the legislature to help you? A. No; I think the business is gone.

Q. What caused it to be gone? A. A multitude of causes; it came from the canal to us, and now it is going from us to other means of transportation. . . .

Q. Do you think it is a wholesome condition of affairs that a great business like that should be monopolized in a few hands? A. It is all owing to how they use it; they are very foolish men if they are going to use it so that it is going to ruin their business; I don't believe those people are so foolish by any means; I think they are very shrewd men.

# 39

*"Upon no public question are the people so nearly unanimous as upon the proposition that Congress should undertake in some way the regulation of interstate commerce"*

"During what may be termed the era of construction," said the Cullom Committee Report to the United States Senate in January, 1886 (the subject of this Document), "the chief consideration that influenced the people and the legislators . . . was how to secure railroads, not how to control them." By 1886, railroad rights of way, rolling stock, roundhouses, terminals, and other assets represented approximately 20 per cent of "the estimated actual wealth" of the entire nation. Almost two-thirds of all the mainline track ever to carry passengers and freight in the United States had by then been laid, and no fewer than 33,000 American communities enjoyed regular train service. To lure the iron horse, towns, cities, counties, and states in this era had mortgaged themselves for generations; and on the whole, as the Cullom Committee handsomely acknowledged, their glittering hopes had been fulfilled and more than fulfilled.

And yet cries of anguish over railroad practices had been heard across the land for almost a quarter of a century before 1886. At first they arose largely from those communities the rails forgot. But before long the wails from points remembered drowned out those of the disappointed.

The fundamental need of a successful railroad was paying territory; and once a great road entered a promising region its overweening goal was to keep other roads out. To accomplish this, it would extend feeder lines in every likely direction, often with money borrowed at high interest rates and before profitable traffic was available. It was largely on this account that of the 33,000 communities served by railroads in 1886, all but 2,700 were served by but one line. At many of these 2,700 points, railroad competition became so keen that rates, in order for the roads to secure some cash income with which to meet interest charges, often were reduced far below the cost of service, usually by secret contracts with shippers (see Document No. 38, above). To recoup losses here, individual roads were forced to charge "all the traffic would bear" at the many monopoly points they might control. Shippers at monopoly points on roads that terminated at competitive points were likely to fare worst of all since they often paid more for short hauls to one of the terminals than others paid for far longer hauls from one competitive terminal to another. As the Cullom Report says, "unjust discrimination is the chief cause of complaint against the management of railroads in the conduct of their business, and gives rise to much pressure upon Congress for regulative legislation."

Discriminatory charges themselves often had ancillary effects which swelled the chorus of complaint. It might reasonably have been expected, for example, that the availability of a modern transportation facility able to carry bulky or perishable produce speedily to markets would have raised land values in rural areas the railroads served. And so it did. But in areas where the roads could charge monopoly rates, land values usually soon fell again, often severely. In business areas where railroads might be forced to charge sacrificial competitive rates, in turn, the general consequences might be no less harsh. As the Cullom Committee reported:

> Whenever rates are fluctuating and not alike to all, it is the rule that some portions of the commercial community obtain secret advantages over the remainder. When unjust discrimination is practiced by the carrier, success in business depends more upon favoritism (if nothing worse) than upon intelligence, integrity, and enterprise. The effect is demoralizing in the extreme. Business is conducted upon a false basis, false standards of commercial honor are erected, and a premium is offered to corruption. Worst of all, the advantages of unjust discrimination are, as a rule, enjoyed by those who least need outside aid, and the inevitable effect of this indefensible practice is to build up the larger dealer and crush out the smaller, to foster monopoly, and, in short, to encourage the existing tendency already too strong, towards the concentration of capital and the control of commerce in the hands of the few.

Favoritism toward powerful shippers at competitive points often helped push even the largest railroads themselves toward bankruptcy. To preserve their assets, such roads would enter jointly into "pools" and similar arrangements by which they agreed to keep their respective rates up to profitable levels. When this happened, shippers at competitive points piled their protests on those arising from monopoly points; and before long the pools broke apart. In such cases, and "in the absence of national legislation," as the Cullom Committee put it, the railroads "naturally resorted to the only methods by which they could unaided secure any degree of stability and uniformity in their charges—consolidation and confederation." Between 1880 and 1886, nearly one-fourth of all American railroad corporations were brought under the control of other roads. "The final outcome of continued consolidation," the Committee Report warned, "would be the creation of an organization more powerful than the Government itself and perhaps beyond its control."

If "unjust discrimination" on rates was the source of most complaints against the railroads "in the conduct of their business," in the conduct of their finances the "pernicious practice . . . popularly known as stock watering," said the Committee, "has unquestionably done more to create and keep alive a popular feeling of hostility against the railroads of the United States than any other one cause." Stock watering diluted the dividends on legitimate railroad shares and in other ways tended sharply to reduce their value. Shareholders, moreover, could find many other causes of complaint, which the Cullom Committee recited in detail, in "the reckless manner in which the railroads are often managed." In periods of depression especially, as in the mid-'seventies and mid-'eighties, when share prices shrank in Wall Street and railroads all over the country fell into receivership with disheartening frequency, shareholders let themselves be heard as loudly as shippers. The voice of the general public was added to the hue and cry after the railroads by the mounting fear of their political as well as of their strategic and consolidated economic power.

The first state railroad regulatory commission was set up by Massachusetts in 1869. In the following decade, more than a dozen other states had followed Massachusetts's lead. Most of these were "Granger" states in the Middle West where farmers were the principal shippers. Granger railroad-rate regulation, even on interstate commerce passing through particular states, was upheld by the Supreme Court in 1877 in the famous case of *Munn* v. *Illinois*. But interstate railroads remained very hard to control. As the Cullom Report said, "in the controversies that naturally arose . . . in different States, . . . the railroad companies have not hesitated at every opportunity to insist upon . . . the exclusive power of Congress to regulate interstate commerce. And, on the other hand, . . . they have been equally swift to maintain and deprecate interference with the rights of the States whenever national regulation has been proposed."

The formation of a national railroad commission had been suggested in Congress as early as 1871, but nothing came of it for seventeen years. In October, 1886, in the *Wabash* case, the Supreme Court withdrew from the states the power acknowledged by the *Munn* decision to regulate rates within their borders on traffic originating outside or destined beyond them. By then the Cullom Bill, backed by the Cullom Report, for the establishment of a federal regulatory commission had already passed the Senate, while another bill proposing to regulate railroads directly without establishing a commission had still earlier passed the House. The *Wabash* decision seemed to make some national step mandatory, and the Cullom Report was eventually accepted as its guide. The Interstate Commerce Act, establishing the first federal regulatory agency, the Interstate Commerce Commission, was adopted by both houses on January 21, 1887, and signed by President Cleveland on February 4.

The Interstate Commerce Act proved vague enough, and the powers of the Commission it established certainly were ill-defined. The Cullom Committee itself, moreover, had felt obliged near the end of its Report to face up to the persistent question of whether the legislation it fathered was to be nothing more than a sop to the "nearly unanimous" public. This the Committee vehemently denied: "In undertaking the regulation of inter-State commerce Congress is entering upon a new and untried field. . . . Every consideration of prudence and justice demand[s] . . . precaution," especially in view of "the vast and varied interests to be affected."

Many in Congress, perhaps, used the need for caution as a shield for cynicism. But President Cleveland manned the first Commission with the most able men he could find; and it was largely their zeal at the outset, and a certain amount of success they achieved, that led the railroads to plumb the weaknesses of this "experimental legislation" in self-defense. The railroads were to prove more adept in evading the act than the Commission in applying it. Not until the Progressive era, when the yearning for information about the transformed society and the urgency for action to bend its creativity to the general welfare had grown stronger than in the 1880's, would federal regulation of trusts as well as railroads be outfitted with teeth (see Document No. 48, below). Nevertheless, the Cullom Committee, as its Report attests, was sincere in its representations; and the Report itself, like the earlier report of the Hepburn Committee, provided materials for informed action by the people, then and later.

*January 18, 1886*

# Report of the Committee
# on Interstate Commerce,
# Senator Shelby M. Cullom, Chairman

THE LEGAL STATUS
OF THE COMMON CARRIER.

Railroads are everywhere recognized as common carriers. . . . A common carrier must be able to carry for all alike, and cannot show any preferences without making himself liable for damages. Much is heard among the people about the giving of undue preferences to one man or one community as against another. Under the common law a common carrier has no right to give preferences, and is liable in an action for damages for accepting for transportation the goods of one man in preference to another, or for granting favors to one over another in the amount charged for similar service. . . .

Unjust discrimination is the chief cause of complaint against the management of railroads in the conduct of business, and gives rise to much of the pressure upon Congress for regulative legislation. . . . If the law as it now stands, and as it has over and over again been interpreted by the courts, in relation to the legal status and duties of railroads toward the public, were enforced, there would be no occasion for either the States or the National Government to take any action with a view to the regulation of commerce, either State or interstate. But the law is not enforced, for reasons which will hereafter be explained, and the experience of all States and nations where railroads have been built shows that the people cannot with safety rely upon the ordinary common law remedies to protect them against unjust discrimination and extortion. . . .

THE OBLIGATIONS
IMPOSED BY ITS PUBLIC NATURE
AND ITS EXERCISE
OF A PUBLIC FUNCTION.

As the State itself, in this country, has not deemed it advisable to construct and operate this class of highways, that work has been left to private enterprise, and it has been the universal policy, first as a matter of necessity, and since of convenience, to place the construction and management of the railroad in the hands of an artificial person, which assumed the duties of the State in this respect, and in return was authorized to collect tolls to meet the expenses of operation and maintenance, and to yield a reasonable return upon the capital invested. . . .

By granting railroad corporations authority to thus levy a tax upon commerce, even with the expressed or implied reservation that their charges should be reasonable, they were necessarily given a monopoly of this right, at least, so far as their own highways were concerned, and the fact that such a corporation is in the nature of a monopoly is a stronger and broader reason why it should be subject to the control and regulation of the State, and widely extends the jurisdiction and rights of the State in that respect. . . .

But when we consider the imperial influence which these most mighty engines of civilization can exercise upon the development, progress, and commerce of the country, making possible the ruin or prosperity of cities, States, or even larger areas of our territory by the exercise of their power, it becomes evident that the State possesses the right to supervise and regulate the administration of such imperial power upon the broad ground of public policy, in addition to the fact that a railroad

corporation manages a public highway, exercises a public function, and is in the nature of a monopoly. . . . Railroad corporations have been organized and manipulated by speculators; rings within rings have controlled their operations and fattened on their revenues; "railroad wrecking" has become a fine art; values have been made to fluctuate wildly, without due cause; panics have been occasioned by the magnitude of these operations, and the whole railroad system, as well as the commerce of the country, will suffer for years from the effects of those eras of mad speculation which are yet fresh in the memory of all. . . .

SOME OF THE DIFFICULTIES
OF EFFECTIVE
STATE REGULATION.

The States have chartered the railroads of the United States, and there can be no assurance of concert of action among them, or of any degree of uniformity in their legislation with respect to the granting of charters or the control of the financial operations of such corporations when organized. It was also urged by . . . [Mr. Simon Sterne] that the concentrated powers of these great instrumentalities of commerce had in various States proved too powerful for the State Government. His words were:

You get an . . . institution like the Burlington and Quincy Railroad, or the Northwestern Railroad, running through several States, and you concentrate that power at any State capital, the temptations are almost irresistible to bow to the powers that be, even if not corruptly, for the purpose of gaining its favor, on the part of an ambitious young legislator who is a lawyer and who desires to be appointed as counsel for the company in a particular district, and thus to make himself a member of like instruments of commerce and of influence. They have, like every other great agency, means of corruption that are not merely pecuniary. Then, the press is under their influence to a considerable extent; they are large advertisers; and it becomes a serious consideration in this country whether, independent of the question of freight charges and passenger traffic and individual rates, for the purpose of protecting the general weal it is not essential that these instrumentalities should be subordinated to the General Government. . . .

The essence of the effective regulation of business transactions is equality and uniformity, and this is impossible as to two transactions alike in every other respect when one reaches across a State line and the other does not. In the controversies that naturally arose over these questions in different States, as the records of the courts demonstrate, the railroad companies have not hesitated at every opportunity to insist upon and take advantage of the exclusive power of Congress to regulate interstate commerce. And, on the other hand, the records of Congress show that they have been equally swift to maintain and to deprecate interference with the rights of the States whenever national regulation has been proposed. . . .

THE PROTECTION
OF STOCKHOLDERS.

It is a singular feature of the existing condition of affairs that legislation is now asked of Congress for the protection of the interests of stockholders almost as urgently as for years past it has been sought for the protection of the people who use, but do not own, the railroads. . . .
The committee has been impressed by the unanimity with which the witnesses examined agreed in attributing the evils most complained of to transactions which have been made possible by the lax general legislation of the several States, such as the construction of unnecessary railroads for speculative purposes, fictitious capitalization, and all the fraudulent financial schemes by which such enterprises have been notably characterized. . . .
If a thorough investigation could be made into the history of the various

enterprises which are denounced as unnecessary and as speculative ventures, with a view to ascertaining the causes which influenced the construction of such new lines, the committee is satisfied that it would be made clear that, while some of these projects were inspired by the personal self-interest of the promoters, who counted upon gaining handsome profits at the expense of a confiding public, in every case these operations were made possible by the misconduct of the lines they were intended to injure, and in most cases they were actively aided or entirely engineered by rival lines.
It has been the settled policy of the stronger corporations to secure, by all means within their power, the absolute control of all the traffic possible. To accomplish this purpose, they have endeavored to obtain possession of the roads tributary to them, especially at competing points, in order to divert traffic away from their competitors. These in turn, animated by the predominating spirit of rivalry, and guided by the same policy, have in many instances constructed new feeders through territory already supplied with all the transportation facilities the traffic would legitimately support. In this way great wrongs have manifestly been committed, for which the railroads themselves have been directly responsible. Not only have the expenditures upon such uncalled-for lines robbed investors of their legitimate profits upon investments previously made in the lines pursuing this policy of reckless extension, but the addition of every unnecessary road has imposed an unjust burden upon the public. . . .

FICTITIOUS CAPITALIZATION.

Another serious evil incident to the prevailing methods of railroad management, and one which is especially conspicuous in connection with the construction of unnecessary roads, is fictitious capitalization, popularly known as stock watering. This pernicious practice has unquestionably done more to create and keep alive a popular feeling of hostility against the railroads of the United States than any other one cause. It has been the favorite device adopted to illegitimately increase the profits of these corporations and their speculative manipulators, and has been made use of to cover up and conceal from the knowledge of the public the returns really received from the capital actually invested. It has encouraged extravagance and corruption; has been made the means of swindling innocent investors out of millions of dollars; has promoted stock gambling, and, worst of all, has imposed a serious and continuous illegitimate burden upon commerce. . . .

As the committee is not prepared to suggest any method by which Congress can directly regulate such financial operations on the part of railroads chartered by the States, it is only deemed necessary at this time to call attention to the need of State legislation calculated to effectively check such speculative transactions.

The committee is, however, of the opinion that Congress can aid materially in bringing about this much to be desired result by causing the financial operations of all interstate roads to be thoroughly investigated and by requiring of them such detailed reports as will accurately exhibit their actual condition and the net results of their business. There is no uniformity in their methods of book-keeping or any guarantee that the reports published honestly represent their financial condition, nor can there be until they are required to adopt a uniform system of accounts, and provision is made for a thorough investigation and analysis of their accounts by trained experts representing the public.

The committee further believe that such investigations should be conducted under the direction of a national railroad commission, and that the importance of this work furnishes a strong argument in favor of the creation of such a commission. . . .

THE NECESSITY
OF NATIONAL REGULATION
OF INTERSTATE COMMERCE.

The two propositions which the committee has kept prominently in view throughout the entire investigation have been whether any legislation for the regulation of interstate transportation is necessary or expedient, and, if so, in what manner can the public interest be best subserved by legislation on that subject.

The consideration of the first proposition may seem to be a work of supererogation, for it is the deliberate judgment of the committee that upon no public question are the people so nearly unanimous as upon the proposition that Congress should undertake in some way the regulation of interstate commerce. . . .

Through the absence of national legislation the railroads of the United States have been left to work out their own salvation. The practical results of their efforts have been by no means encouraging. . . . It is true that . . . the railroads have accomplished wonders in reducing the cost of transportation, in removing the limitations of distance from trade between remote localities, and in building up and widely extending the general commerce of the country. But, notwithstanding all these marvelous achievements, for which due credit should be given, the solid fact still claims consideration, that the inequalities and discriminations which characterize the operations of the system in its entirety are now as pronounced as in the earlier stages of its development.

In the recognized existence of these evils and in the failure of the national authority to offer any remedy, railroad managers have found their justification for seeking a remedy through methods which have not commended themselves to the public judgment and which have threatened even greater dangers to the body-politic. In the absence of national legislation, the railroads have naturally resorted to the only methods by which they could unaided secure any degree of stability and uniformity in their charges —consolidation and confederation. The final outcome of continued consolidations would be the creation of an organization more powerful than the Government itself and perhaps beyond its control. . . .

When unjust discrimination is practiced by the carrier, success in business depends more upon favoritism (if nothing worse) than upon intelligence, integrity, and enterprise. The effect is demoralizing in the extreme. Business is conducted upon a false basis, false standards of commercial honor are erected, and a premium is offered to corruption. Worst of all, the advantages of unjust discrimination are, as a rule, enjoyed by those who least need outside aid, and the inevitable effect of this indefensible practice is to build up the larger dealer and crush out the smaller, to foster monopoly, and, in short, to encourage the existing tendency, already too strong, towards the concentration of capital and the control of commerce in the hands of the few. . . . If the publicity of rates and the prevention of unjust discrimination can be secured, a long step forward will have been taken, and the people will wait patiently until evils of less importance can be remedied.

A NATIONAL COMMISSION—
ITS ESTABLISHMENT RECOMMENDED
FOR THE ENFORCEMENT
OF THE LEGISLATION PROPOSED.

In the prosecution of the inquiry with which the committee was charged the following question was included in the interrogatories propounded by circular to those invited to express their views in writing, and was also in substance asked those who were examined in person:

In what manner can legislation for the regulation of inter-State commerce be best enforced? Should a commission or other special tribunal be established to carry out

the provisions of any law Congress may enact?

An examination of the testimony and written statements accompanying this report will show that nearly all of those who expressed an opinion on the subject favored the creation of a national commission or other special tribunal, or of a governmental department, to be charged with the duty of carrying out and enforcing whatever legislation may be enacted for the regulation of inter-State commerce. . . .

One of the favorite arguments of the opponents of a special tribunal has been that the contemplated commission is a mere subterfuge, intended as a harmless concession to the popular demand for legislation, designed to be of no advantage to the citizen with a complaint and no disadvantage to the corporations concerned, and that the commission scheme is simply a procrastinating device invented by the railroads, which if adopted would leave the people more completely at their mercy than they are now.

No such proposition could receive the approval or indorsement of this committee. . . . In the light of all the evidence . . . before it, the committee has become satisfied that no statutory regulations which may be enacted can be made fully effective without providing adequate and suitable machinery for carrying them into execution. . . . The value of the proposed commission must not be measured solely by its probable success, or want of success, in adjusting differences between shipper and carrier. Other wide fields of usefulness would lie open before it. In undertaking the regulation of inter-State commerce Congress is entering upon a new and untried field. Its legislation must be based upon theory instead of experience, and human wisdom is incapable of accurately forecasting its effect upon the vast and varied interests to be affected. The magnitude of these interests and every consideration of prudence and justice demand that provision should be made for an intelligent investigation of the operation of the regulations prescribed, in order that Congress may be kept advised as to the results of its action. Without such a precaution experimental legislation of this character would hardly be justified.

The proposed commission would also serve a useful purpose in collecting and giving publicity to accurate information concerning the affairs and transactions of corporations engaged in inter-State commerce. . . . This work intelligently performed would year by year remove "the railroad problem" farther from the realm of conjecture and speculation and would make it possible to gradually build a system of regulation upon the safe and enduring foundation of certain knowledge.

# 40

*"In the ever-growing desire of mankind for new worlds of comfort and luxury to conquer is the blazing promise of the unhasting, unresting march of civilization"*

When Henry Clay made his great speech on the "American System" in March, 1824 (Document No. 25, above), the Industrial Revolution still was largely confined to Great Britain. The United States at that time, because of the nature and success of her *political* revolution, cast a disquieting shadow over monarchical Europe, which grew longer as European unrest spread (see Document No. 23). Economically, however, the United States remained a minor power. Her people were scattered, her communications poor, her methods backward even in agriculture, her leading occupation, her manufactures indeed in their infancy. As the target of European antipathy she needed "protection" in more ways than one. Given the broad expanse of her territory, the rich variety of her virgin resources, the freedom of movement, enterprise, and thought of her people, tariffs high enough to encourage industrial expansion might well be defended as the most rewarding mode of protection possible, one all the more gratifying since its immediate target would be industrial Britain, the United States' natural and strongest enemy.

Clay won his protective tariff in 1824; but within a decade duties began to be significantly lowered and their downward tendency persisted until the outbreak not of any European assault but of the Civil War at home. To help finance this war in its early stages, Lincoln's government levied heavy internal taxes, many of them on manufactures in their different stages of production. To protect themselves now against an influx of untaxed foreign goods, northern manufacturers once more demanded a tariff wall. Without tariff protection in the prewar decades, their factories had in fact grown with marvelous rapidity and they themselves had become a powerful political interest. Under the pressure of wartime needs, their demands were readily met; and as the war progressed, protection spread to more and more commodities, and duties constantly rose.

Within seven years after the Civil War virtually all the internal taxes had been repealed; but the taste of protection had become too sweet for favored manufacturers to surrender it. The war debt, moreover, remained to be paid off; and on the theory that reductions in tariffs would endanger the debt incurred in the sacred cause (and open American markets once more to hated Britain who for so long had leaned toward the rebel side) the protectionists managed to gain strong support even among those whose interests, at least as consumers, the tariff actually harmed.

By the time Grover Cleveland was elected President in 1884, the war debt had disappeared; and within three years a surplus of more than $50 million had accumulated in the Treasury, largely from tariff income. Tariff-making, moreover, had sunk to one of the most sordid of all government activities, with industry agents familiarly stalking the very floors of Congress and browbeating committee sessions. Much of their power, in turn, derived from the noisome begging for party funds with which congressmen, or their party bosses, especially in election years, plied the protected interests. "I would put the manufacturers of Pennsylvania under the fire and fry all the fat out of them," advised James P. Foster of the protectionist Republican League on the eve of the 1888 election; and throughout that campaign, the cry of "fat" rang through the business community.

By the time of the election of 1888, protection probably had outlived such usefulness as it may have had in nursing infant industry to manly vigor. President Cleveland made downward revision of the tariff the great issue of the campaign that year by devoting his third annual message to Congress, in December, 1887, entirely to this subject. This message is presented in part below, as item "a."

In response to Cleveland's message, the mildly revisionist Mills Bill was introduced in the House early in 1888 and passed in July. Many protectionist congressmen (for home consumption in an election year) voted for it with the knowledge that it had no chance in the Senate. In the upper chamber, the "Allison substitute" was debated right up to election time, without result. With Cleveland's defeat by the Republican, Benjamin Harrison, in the unusually corrupt 1888 election, the drive for downward revision faltered.

During the debate on the Mills Bill in the House, Congressman Thomas B. Reed, according to his biographer in the *Dictionary of American Biography*, made "one of the greatest speeches on the subject [of protection] in congressional annals." This speech is presented in part below, as item "b."

The economic arguments for protection in Reed's speech even then were so hackneyed that in his message of December, 1887, half a year before Reed spoke, Cleveland had effectively answered all of them. Reed, no doubt, was aware of this. The greatness of his speech, in any case the greatness ascribed to it, stems rather from the flourish and the philosophical breadth of view with which its author transmutes special favors for the few into forwarders of the general welfare. Even this theme had been stressed by earlier protagonists of protection; but none, heretofore, had held civilization itself to be at stake in the American race for wealth. For Reed, man's "tremendous mission" lay just here: "to get . . . out of the earth all the wealth there is in . . . it." And "what concerns the nation is how to utilize all the work there is in men."

> In the ever-growing desire of mankind for new worlds of comfort and luxury to conquer is the blazing promise of the unhasting, unresting march of civilization. In that column of march the whole nation must be ranged.

In his well-known book, *Mechanization Takes Command*, Siegfried Giedion points out that the eighteenth century's faith in progress started from science, the nineteenth century's from mechanization. Giedion goes on to say: "With the waning of faith in progress, . . . there entered that faith in production as an end in itself. Fanaticism for production as such was heretofore confined to the manufacturing group. In the time of full mechanization, faith in production penetrated every class and ramification of life, thrusting all other considerations into the background." No doubt, Reed's America was entering "the time of full mechanization." Reed may have been wholly unaware of what was being lost in this process. But others, aware of the cost, nevertheless were able to discover even more good in it than he.

No one could have been more keenly aware of the cost than Charles Eliot Norton, aesthete, intermittent expatriate, and Professor of Fine Arts at Harvard, who wrote from Cambridge, Massachusetts, in 1883:

> In Europe I could not but feel, with pain, the ill wrought by the progress of democracy—the destruction of old shrines, the disregard of beauty, the decline in personal distinction, the falling off in manners. Here, as we have less to lose, we have less to regret, and the spread of comfort, the superb and unexampled spectacle of fifty millions of human beings living in peace and plenty, compensates in a certain measure for the absence of high culture, of generous ideals and of imaginative life.

Norton may have been a bit more optimistic than Reed himself about the spread of comfort and universality of plenty; but in the Progressive era ahead, the values of a high general standard of living were to become more widely embraced, and a more even distribution of opportunity, if not immediately of wealth, was to become more urgently sought.

# President Cleveland and Congressman Reed

## on the Protective Tariff

(a)   *President Cleveland's Third Annual Message to Congress, December 6, 1887*

*To the Congress of the United States:*
. . . The amount of money annually exacted, through the operation of present laws, from the industries and necessities of the people largely exceeds the sum necessary to meet the expenses of the Government.

When we consider that the theory of our institutions guarantees to every citizen the full enjoyment of all the fruits of his industry and enterprise, with only such deduction as may be his share toward the careful and economical maintenance of the Government which protects him, it is plain that the exaction of more than this is indefensible extortion and a culpable betrayal of American fairness and justice. . . .

Our scheme of taxation, by means of which this needless surplus is taken from the people and put into the public Treasury, consists of a tariff or duty levied upon importations from abroad and internal-revenue taxes levied upon the consumption of tobacco and spirituous and malt liquors. It must be conceded that none of the things subjected to internal-revenue taxation are, strictly speaking, necessaries. There appears to be no just complaint of this taxation by the consumers of these articles, and there seems to be nothing so well able to bear the burden without hardship to any portion of the people.

But our present tariff laws, the vicious, inequitable, and illogical source of unnecessary taxation, ought to be at once revised and amended. These laws, as their primary and plain effect, raise the price to consumers of all articles imported and subject to duty by precisely the sum paid for such duties. Thus the amount of the duty measures the tax paid by those who purchase for use these imported articles. Many of these things, however, are raised or manufactured in our own country, and the duties now levied upon foreign goods and products are called protection to these home manufactures, because they render it possible for those of our people who are manufacturers to make these taxed articles and sell them for a price equal to that demanded for the imported goods that have paid customs duty. So it happens that while comparatively a few use the imported articles, millions of our people, who never used and never saw any of the foreign products, purchase and use things of the same kind made in this country, and pay therefor nearly or quite the same enhanced price which the duty adds to the imported articles. Those who buy imports pay the duty charged thereon into the public Treasury, but the great majority of our citizens, who buy domestic articles of the same class, pay a sum at least approximately equal to this duty to the home manufacturer.

This reference to the operation of our tariff laws is not made by way of instruction, but in order that we may be constantly reminded of the manner in which they impose a burden upon those who consume domestic products as well as those who consume imported articles, and thus create a tax upon all our people. . . . Relief from the hardships and dangers of our present tariff laws should be devised with especial precaution against imperiling the existence of our manufacturing interests. But this existence should not mean a condition which, without regard to the public welfare or a national exigency, must always insure the realization of immense profits instead of moderately profitable returns.

We are in the midst of centennial celebrations, and with becoming pride we rejoice in American skill and ingenuity, in American energy and enterprise, and in the wonderful natural advantages and resources developed by a century's national growth. Yet when an attempt is made to justify a scheme which permits a tax to be laid upon every consumer in the land for the benefit of our manufacturers, quite beyond a reasonable demand for governmental regard, it suits the purposes of advocacy to call our maunfactures infant industries still needing the highest and greatest degree of favor and fostering care that can be wrung from Federal legislation.

It is also said that the increase in the price of domestic manufactures resulting from the present tariff is necessary in order that higher wages may be paid to our workingmen employed in manufactories than are paid for what is called the pauper labor of Europe. . . . [But] of the 17,392,099 of our population engaged in all kinds of industries, . . . [only] 2,623,089 persons [are] employed in such manufacturing industries as are claimed to be benefited by a high tariff. . . . Nor can the worker in manufactures fail to understand that while a high tariff is claimed to be necessary to allow the payment of remunerative wages, it certainly results in a very large increase in the price of nearly all sorts of manufactures, which, in almost countless forms, he needs for the use of himself and his family. . . .

In speaking of the increased cost to the consumer of our home manufactures resulting from a duty laid upon imported articles of the same description, the fact is not overlooked that competition among our domestic producers sometimes has the effect of keeping the price of their products below the highest limit allowed by such duty. But it is notorious that this competition is too often strangled by combinations quite prevalent at this time, and frequently called trusts, which have for their object the regulation of the supply and price of commodities made and sold by members of the combination. The people can hardly hope for any consideration in the operation of these selfish schemes. . . .

The necessity of combination to maintain the price of any commodity to the tariff point furnishes proof that someone is willing to accept lower prices for such commodity and that such prices are remunerative; and lower prices produced by competition prove the same thing. Thus where either of these conditions exists a case would seem to be presented for an easy reduction of taxation. . . .

Under our present laws more than 4,000 articles are subject to duty. Many of these do not in any way compete with our own manufactures, and many are hardly worth attention as subjects of revenue. A considerable reduction can be made in the aggregate by adding them to the free list. . . .

The radical reduction of the duties imposed upon raw material used in manufactures, or its free importation, is of course an important factor in any effort to reduce the price of these necessaries. . . . Such reduction or free importation would serve besides to largely reduce the revenue. It is not apparent how such a change can have any injurious effect upon our manufacturers. On the contrary, it would appear to give them a better chance in foreign markets with the manufacturers of other countries, who cheapen their wares by free material. Thus our people might have the opportunity of extending their sales beyond the limits of home consumption, saving them from the depression, interruption in business, and loss caused by a glutted domestic market, and affording their employees more certain and steady labor, with its resulting quiet and contentment.

### (b)  Congressman Thomas B. Reed's speech on the Mills Bill, in the House, May 19, 1888

The system we believe in is called protection, and is founded upon the doctrine that a great nation like ours, having all varieties of climate and soil, will be richer, more independent, and more thrifty, and that its people will be better fitted to enjoy the comforts and luxuries of peace, and better situated to endure the calamities of war, if its own people supply its own wants.

I do not purpose to defend protection. Its vast growth within the last quarter of a century defends it better even than eloquent orations. It was born with the Republic. It is the faith and practice of every civilized nation under the sun save one. It has survived the assaults of all the professors of the "dismal science" called political economy. It has stood up against all the half knowledge of learned men who never had sense enough to transmute their learning into wisdom.

On the face of the earth to-day there are but two sets of people who believe in free trade, whether pure and simple or disguised as revenue reform, and those two are the masked majority of the Committee on Ways and Means and their followers, and the United Kingdom of Great Britain and Ireland, with Ireland suppressed.

Russia, the granary of Europe, has abandoned free trade; . . . Austria, Germany, Italy, Mexico, and the Dominion of Canada, that child of Britain herself, have all joined the army of protection. It is the instinct of humanity against the assumptions of the book men. It is the wisdom of the race against the wisdom of the few.

Perhaps the best argument I can make for protection is to state what it is and the principles on which it is founded.

Man derives his greatest power from his association with other men, his union with his fellows. Whoever considers the human being as a creature alone, by himself, isolated and separated, and tries to comprehend mankind by mathematically adding these atoms together, has utterly failed to comprehend the human race and its tremendous mission.

Sixty millions even of such creatures without association are only so many beasts that perish. But sixty millions of men welded together by national brotherhood, each supporting, sustaining, and buttressing the other, are the sure conquerors of all those mighty powers of nature which alone constitute the wealth of this world. The great blunder of the Herr Professor of political economy is that he treats human beings as if every man were so many foot-pounds, such and such a fraction of a horse-power. All the soul of man he leaves out. . . . To grasp the full powers of nature, to reap the richest wealth of the world, we must utilize the full power of man, not merely muscles and brains, but those intangible qualities which we call energy, vigor, ambition, confidence, and courage. . . .

For a nation to get out of itself or out of the earth all the wealth there is in both, it is not necessary for the nation to buy cheap or sell dear. That concerns individuals alone. What concerns the nation is how to utilize all the work there is in men, both of muscle and brain, of body and of soul, in the great enterprise of setting in motion the ever-gratuitous forces of nature.

How shall you get out of the people of a nation their full powers. Right here is precisely the dividing line. The let-alone school say leave individual man to his own devices. The protectionist school say let us stimulate combined and aggregated man to united endeavor. What made men work before governments? Was it an intellectual belief that work was good for the muscles? Not the least in the world. It was hunger and desire. Hunger has ceased to play the greater part, but desire will never pass away.

In the ever-growing desire of mankind for new worlds of comfort and luxury to conquer is the blazing promise of the unhasting, unresting march of civilization. In that column of march the whole nation must be ranged. Association is the instinct of humanity which grows with its growth. First the family, then the tribe, and then the nation. The race will come by and by. Faithfulness to each in their order is the true route to the next.

Here in the United States are 60,-000,000 people with all the varied characters their numbers indicate. Some have faculties fit for farming, some for the management of machinery, some for invention. The problem before you is what system will get from all these creatures, so different from each other, the maximum of work and wealth and wisdom. . . .

There is only one way to get the best work out of men, and that is to give each the work he can do best. You can only accomplish this by diversifying industry. To diversify industry completely in a country such as ours, there is but one way given under Heaven among men. To enable the American people themselves to supply all their wants, you must give and assure to the American people the American markets. What does this phrase mean in practical life? It means that we, the nation, say to capital, "Embark yourself in the manufacture of such and such articles, and you shall have a market to the extent of the wants of the American people."

Capital then says to labor, "Go with me into this new field, all of you who like this work best, and we will share the results." Then begins a new industry. Multiply this by hundreds and you have a community where every man honestly minded will get what on the whole suits him best, and the nation will get the greatest amount of work from the greatest number.

To this system so far sketched, no human being can find reasonable objections. But it is averred that there are some drawbacks. . . . You tell us, they say, that protection is for the purpose of enhancing prices to enable high wages to be paid, and yet you say that protection lowers prices. This is flat contradiction. So it is as you state it. But your statement, like all revenue-reform statements, flourishes only by assumption.

In order to make yourself clear, you have utterly omitted the element of time. You assume that we say that both our statements of higher prices for higher wages and lower prices for consumers are for the same instant of time. Not so. When you begin there are higher prices for higher wages, but when you establish your manufactories, at once the universal law of competition begins to work. The manufactories abroad, urged upon by the lower prices which the tariff forces them to offer in order to compete with us, cause every element of economy in manufacture to be set in motion. Every intellect is put to work to devise new machinery which will produce at lower cost, to seek out new methods of utilizing waste, to consolidation of effort to lessen general expenses, and the thousand and one devices every year invented to get more work out of the powers of nature.

At home the same causes are at work, and with redoubled energy, because on account of higher wages there are greater inducements to substitute labor-saving devices for costly labor. And this colossal struggle between two great empires of industry, the foreign and the domestic, results everywhere in the cheapness of commodities, in which progress of cheapness the world has marched on in one unbroken undeviating line, until to-day the citizens of the United States, the sovereigns of to-day, as we call them in moments of patriotic exaltation, the poorest citizens have for the commonest necessities of life the luxuries of the sovereigns of old days. . . .

Perhaps some gentleman will say to me that this is all a dream; that the very fact of a barrier raised by our tariff prevents competition. Every manufacturer knows better. England must work or starve. She has piled up her capital, and if she can not get large profits she will take small. Let me not confine myself to theory. . . . I have here the report of the Royal Commission to inquire into the causes of the depression of British trade, . . . where you will find that the exports in 1883 were £240,-000,000, but that the value of those same exports at the prices of ten years before were £349,000,000.

The difference is £109,000,000—$545,000,000. If you want it in percentage, you will find that you must add more than 45 per cent to the price of 1883 to get the richly profitable prices of 1873. To what does the world owe this gain of $545,000,000 in a single year? Who was the fruitful mother of all this gain?

She whom in your short-sighted wisdom you have always called barren, tariff taxes; and facing your most opprobrious phrase, the one you roll most lovingly under your tongue, I dare to asseverate that if the whole world will repeal its tariff taxes, England will reap in the next ten years not only ten times these five hundred and forty-five millions, but a thousand millions more every year. Tariff taxes! How men like to fool themselves with phrases! Because the taxing power is used not only for revenue but as the barrier, and taxes are odious, therefore the barrier must be odious also. . . .

Let my poor scared friend who covers his head with the bed-clothes at night lest he should be devoured by monopolies take courage. . . . Now, which is the richest, Europe or America? We are all agreed on that. We say America because our eyes behold it. You say so because your eyes behold it, and you see one thousand millions wasted besides. What do you mean to do? I will tell you what we mean to do. We mean to keep this wealth here. We mean to do it even if we build a "Chinese" wall of tariff taxes around this country.

# 41

*"You are hereby restrained, commanded, and enjoined . . . from attempting to compel or induce, by threats, persuasion, or violence, any of the employees to refuse to perform their duties"*

In his philosophic speech on protection, May 19, 1888 (Document No. 40, above), Congressman Reed attacked the advocates of *laissez faire*. "The let-alone school say leave individual man to his own devices. The protectionist school say let us stimulate combined and aggregated man to united endeavor. . . . Man derives his greatest power from his association with other men, his union with his fellows."

Although much was made in Reed's day, and indeed by Reed himself, of the great social value of "the struggle for existence" among individuals in assuring "the survival of the fittest" among their leaders, those already at the peaks of power were more likely to have followed Reed's associative principle. In politics and business, especially, united parties and combined corporations called the tune. One advance on this principle at this time was the formation of regional and national employers' associations whose objective, in part, was further to mitigate the competitive struggle among the survivors in the different industries. Their main objective soon became the throttling of the associative principle among employees.

One of the first of these groups was the General Managers' Association of Chicago, organized early in 1886 by the operating heads of the railroads converging on this greatest of railroad terminals. Among its first victims was Eugene V. Debs's American Railway Union, formed just after the panic of 1893, "for the purpose of including railway employees born of white parents in one great brotherhood," the better to combat the "brotherhood" of the Managers' Association. The foreboding legal instrumentalities enlisted by the Association for preserving the precious individuality of the employees confronting it are presented in this Document.

Other associative activities in this period included those of western and southern farmers, who formed many state and regional "alliances" in the 1880's, and in 1892 even brought forth a national political party, the People's party, which, with little tradition, organization, or funds, won an extraordinary 8.6 per cent of the popular vote and 22 electoral votes in the presidential campaign that year. Thereafter, largely as a result of conflicts among its members, the Populist movement fell to pieces, even though its program penetrated the platforms of the two major parties.

It is often said that farmer organizations failed because of the scattered membership, dispersed leadership, and poor communications characteristic of rural areas. Yet at their peak the alliances boasted more than 4 million members, a figure nearly half that for all the farm households in the nation. In industrial towns and cities, by contrast, workers mobilized in factories and congregated in slums usually were in stiflingly close communication with one another. Yet the number in labor unions at the end of the 1880's hardly exceeded 400,000, but one-tenth of those in farm organizations, even though the pool of industrial labor had grown to nearly twice the size of that of farmers. Even white workers in the swarming slums were segregated by national origin and by religion. Within the factories and other industrial enterprises, they might also be segregated by age, sex, and skills. Often illiterate, at least in English, they tended to follow the conservative instincts of their particular clerical fathers, who would do their reading and writing for them. If their worker leaders, in turn, were in easy reach of one another, they were on that account only the more likely to splinter off over ideological differences brought over from Europe than to cooperate in policies and programs relevant to worker advancement in the United States.

Many union members themselves opposed strikes and feared violence. The broadest and most turbulent American labor conflicts in the latter part of the nineteenth century grew largely from spontaneous uprisings against the harshest of working and living conditions, aggravated by unemployment and related burdens during the frequent depression years. And even then such conflicts often were provoked only by thoughtless or incendiary official action. Public opinion appears to have been sympathetic to labor at the outset of many strikes. Once strikes grew riotous and destructive of life and property, public opinion altered and suppression became easier. As a contemporary wrote of Debs's involvement in the Pullman strike of 1894, once the mobilization of federal troops touched off violence where there had been little or none to justify their use: "With its leaders in jail, its forces disorganized, and the whole power of the Federal, State, and city authority ranged against it, the American Railway Union was hopelessly beaten—and with it the cause of the striking Pullman employees." The same observer added: "If, at the beginning of the strike, the United States government had placed itself under orders of the General Managers' Association, the cooperation could scarcely have been more perfect."

The Pullman strike began on May 10, 1894, after many months of company pigheadedness and provocation over wages and rents on company houses. A few weeks earlier, Pullman workers had begun to join Debs's union; and when, in June, the company rejected renewed union offers to arbitrate, the union itself ordered a boycott of Pullman cars on the railroads across the land. Other cars and trains were manned as usual, and interference with the mail (one of the excuses for federal troop intervention), where it occurred, was minimal. On the eve of the boycott, the chairman of the General Managers' Association had declared, "We cannot handle Debs. We have got to wipe him out." At the instigation of Cleveland's Attorney-General, Richard Olney, a former railroad lawyer himself and one wholly sympathetic with the Association's goals, the steps by which Debs's obliteration was accomplished, at least for the time being, were set in motion.

These steps were, (1) the issuance by federal courts on July 2 and 3, 1894, of "blanket injunctions" against the union and "all other persons whomsoever," enjoining virtually any activity, including "persuasion," against railroad service; (2) the mobilization in the Chicago area, between July 3 and July 9, first of thousands of federal marshals and then of thousands of federal troops, to see that the injunctions were obeyed; (3) the indictment on July 10 of Debs and three other American Railway Union officers for conspiracy in restraint of trade under the Sherman Anti-trust Act and on other grounds, and their arrest and release on bail; (4) their re-arrest on July 17, this time for contempt of court under the original injunction, partly in connection with their movement for a general strike in Chicago, which came to naught; (5) the collapse of the railroad boycott and Pullman strike in August and September; (6) the conviction and sentencing of Debs to six months in jail by the United States Circuit Court on the contempt charge in December; (7) the affirmation of this conviction and sentence by the United States Supreme Court in the case of *in re Debs*, in May, 1895.

These steps reflect the pervasive application of the philosophy of individualism to those in conflict with the associative powers. The "blanket injunction" of July 3, 1894, issued, as one of many identical ones, by the United States Circuit Court, District of Indiana, is presented in item "a," below, with the deletion only of its repeated identical phrases. It is followed, in item "b," by Judge Peter S. Grosscup's instructive charge to the grand jury in seeking the indictment of Debs under the Sherman Anti-trust Act, July 10. "I recognize the right of labor to organize," Judge Grosscup stated at one point; "and in their meetings to discuss perhaps 'the origin of man',," scoffed Samuel Gompers in a rejoinder to Grosscup's widely praised and publicized remarks. Following Judge Grosscup's charge (trial under this indictment was never pressed to a conclusion), we present in part in item "c," the Supreme Court's decision denying Debs's plea for release on *habeas corpus* proceedings, and thereby affirming his conviction for defying the injunction, in contempt of the court that had issued it.

Injunctions had been issued and sustained in labor cases before *in re Debs*, usually in connection with employer efforts to break up unions by tarring them as criminal conspiracies against the public under the common law. From the employer's point of view, however, such injunctions were only locking the stable after the horse had been stolen; moreover, they required long, cumbersome, and uncertain jury trials for punishment of the alleged criminal conspirators. In the case of *in re Debs*, the Supreme Court placed labor injunctions firmly within the context of equity rather than criminal proceedings. It thereby confirmed the power of civil courts to issue them in order to *forestall* a public nuisance or *prevent* unrecoverable damage to property, both traditional equity categories. The court based its action on the broadest possible definition of federal power.

This novel doctrine afforded employers a remedy against strikes and boycotts at their very outset. Even if an equity injunction were indefensible or merely temporary, it would usually check organized labor action long enough to kill it. If, on the other hand, union officials rashly chose to defy such an injunction, they became subject to the full penalties for contempt of court regardless of the legality of their related acts. As immigrant workers in particular became Americanized and overcame their traditional reserve in relation to labor unions, and as such unions themselves grew larger, more numerous, and more aggressive, blanket injunctions issued by courts friendly to employers remained one of the most effective weapons against them until specifically outlawed by the Norris-LaGuardia anti-injunction act of 1932. *In re Debs* was the case from which they spawned (see also Documents No. 47 and 48 below).

*1894      1895*

# The Labor Injunction in the Pullman Strike

(a)  *The "Blanket Injunction" against Debs and others, July 3, 1894*

The President of the United States of America to Eugene V. Debs, . . . , and the American Railway Union. And all other persons combining and conspiring with them, and to all other persons whomsoever:

You are hereby restrained, commanded, and enjoined absolutely to desist and refrain from in any way or manner interfering with, hindering, obstructing, or stopping any of the business of any of the following-named railroads: . . . [Twenty-three railroads are listed by name] as common carriers of passengers and freight between or among any States of the United States, and from in any way interfering with, [etc.] . . . any mail trains, express trains, whether freight or passenger, engaged in interstate commerce; . . . and from in any manner interfering with, . . . any trains carrying the mail, and from in any manner interfering with, . . . any engines, cars, or rolling stock of any of said companies engaged in interstate commerce; . . . and from in any manner interfering with, injuring, or destroying any of the property of any of said railroads engaged in or for the purposes of, or in connection with, interstate commerce, or the carriage of the mails of the United States; . . . and from entering upon the grounds or premises of any of said railroads for the purpose of interfering with, . . . any of said mail trains, passenger or freight trains engaged in interstate commerce;

. . . or for the purpose of interfering with, injuring, or destroying any of said property so engaged in or used in connection with interstate commerce; . . . and from injuring or destroying any part of the tracks, roadbed or road, or permanent structures of said railroads; and from injuring, destroying, or in any way interfering with any of the signals or switches of any of said railroads; and from displacing or extinguishing any of the signals of any of said railroads, and from spiking, locking, or in any manner fastening any of the switches of any of said railroads, and from uncoupling or in any way hampering or obstructing the control by any of said railroads of any of the cars, engines, or parts of train . . . ; and from compelling or inducing, or attempting to compel or induce, by threats, intimidation, persuasion, force, or violence, any of the employees of any of said railroads to refuse or fail to perform any of their duties as employees of any of said railroads in connection with the interstate business or commerce of such railroads, or the carriage of the United States mail by such railroads; . . . and from compelling or inducing, or attempting to compel or induce, by threats, intimidation, force, or violence, any of the employees of said railroads . . . to leave the service of such railroads, and from preventing any persons whatever, by threats, intimidation, force, or violence from entering the service of any of said railroads and doing the work thereof; . . . and from doing any act whatever in furtherance of any conspiracy or combination to restrain either of said railroad companies in the free and unhindered control and handling of interstate commerce over the lines of said railroads; . . . and from ordering, directing, aiding, assisting, or abetting, in any manner whatever, any person or persons to commit any or either of the acts aforesaid.

And Eugene V. Debs and all other persons are hereby enjoined and restrained from sending out any letters, messages, or communications directing, inciting, encouraging, or instructing any persons whatsoever to interfere with the business or affairs, directly or indirectly, of any of the railway companies hereinabove named, or from persuading any of the employees of said railway companies while in the employment of their respective companies to fail or refuse to perform the duties of their employment.

And it is further ordered, that the aforesaid injunction and writ of injunction shall be in force and binding upon such of said defendants as are named in said bill from and after the service upon them severally of said writ, . . . and shall be binding upon said defendants whose names are alleged to be unknown, from and after the service of such writ upon them respectively, by the reading of the same to them, or by the publication thereof by posting or printing, and after service of subpoena on any of said defendants herein named shall be binding upon said defendants and upon all other persons whatsoever who are not named herein from and after the time when they shall severally have knowledge of the entry of such order and the existence of said injunction.

(b) *U.S. Circuit Court Judge Peter S. Grosscup's charge to the grand jury seeking indictment of Debs for conspiracy, July 10, 1894*

Gentlemen of the Grand Jury: You have been summoned here to inquire whether any of the laws of the United States within this judicial district have been violated. You have come in an atmosphere and amid occurrences that may well cause reasonable men to question whether the government and laws of the United States are yet supreme. . . .

You doubtless feel, as I do, that the opportunities of life, under present conditions, are not entirely equal, and that changes are needed to forestall some of the dangerous tendencies of current industrial tendencies. But neither the torch of the incendiary, nor the weapon of the insurrectionist, nor the inflamed tongue of him who incites to fire and sword is the instrument to bring about reforms. . . . Men who appear as the champions of great changes must first submit them to discussion, discussion that reaches, not simply the parties interested, but the outer circles of society, and must be patient as well as persevering until the public intelligence has been reached, and a public judgment made up. An appeal to force before that hour is a crime, not only against government of existing laws, but against the cause itself. . . .

With the questions behind present occurrences, therefore, we have, as ministers of the law and citizens of the republic, nothing now to do. . . . Government by law is imperiled, and that issue is paramount.

The government of the United States has enacted laws designed, first, to protect itself and its authority as a government, and, secondly, its control over those agencies to which, under the constitution and laws, it extends governmental regulation. For the former purpose,—namely, to protect itself and its authority as a government,—it has enacted that every person who incites, sets on foot, assists, or engages in, any rebellion or insurrection against the authority of the United States or the laws thereof, or gives aid or comfort thereto, "and any two or more persons in any state or territory who conspire to overthrow, put down, or destroy by force the government of the United States, or to levy war against them, or to oppose by force the authority thereof; or by force to prevent, hinder or delay the execution of any law of the United States contrary to the authority thereof," shall be visited with certain penalties therein named.

Insurrection is a rising against civil or political authority,—the open and active opposition of a number of persons to the execution of law in a city or state. Now, the laws of the United States forbid, under penalty, any person from obstructing or retarding the passage of the mail, and make it the duty of the officers to arrest such offenders, and bring them before the court. If, therefore, it shall appear to you that any person or persons have wilfully obstructed or retarded the mails, and that their attempted arrest for such offense has been opposed by such a number of persons as would constitute a general uprising in that particular locality, and as threatens for the time being the civil and political authority, then the fact of an insurrection, within the meaning of the law, has been established; and he who by speech, writing, or other inducement assists in setting it on foot, or carrying it along, or gives it aid or comfort, is guilty of a violation of law.

It is not necessary that there should be bloodshed; it is not necessary that its dimensions should be so portentous as to insure probable success, to constitute an insurrection. . . . When men gather to resist the civil or political power of the United States, or to oppose the execution of its laws, and are in such force that the civil authorities are in-adequate to put them down, and a considerable military force is needed to accomplish that result, they become insurgents; and every person who knowingly incites, aids, or abets them, no matter what his motives may be, is likewise an insurgent. The penalty for the offense is severe, and, as I have said, is designed to protect the government and its authority against direct attack. There are other provisions of law designed to protect those particular agencies which come within governmental control. To these I will now call your attention.

The mails are in the special keeping of the government and laws of the United States. To insure their unhindered transmission, it is made an offense to knowingly and wilfully obstruct or retard the passage of the mail, or any carriage, horse, driver, or carrier carrying the same. It is also provided that "if two or more persons conspire together to commit any offense against the United States and one or more of such parties do any act to effect the object of the conspiracy," all the parties thereto shall be subject to a penalty. . . .

The constitution places the regulation of commerce between the several states, and between the states and foreign nations, within the keeping of the United States government; . . . and any conspiracy in restraint of such . . . commerce is an offense against the United States. . . . The restraint may be permanent or temporary. It may be intended to prohibit, limit, or abridge for all time, or for a day only. The law draws no distinction in this respect. . . . Temporary restraint is therefore as intolerable as permanent, and practical restraint by actual physical interference, as criminal as that which flows from the arrangements of business and organization. . . . But to complete this offense, as also that of conspiracy to obstruct the mails, there must exist, in addition to the overt act and purpose, the element of criminal conspiracy.

What is criminal conspiracy? If it shall appear to you that any two or more persons corruptly or wrongfully agreed with each other that the trains carrying the mails and interstate commerce should be forcibly arrested, obstructed, and restrained, such would clearly constitute a conspiracy. If it shall appear to you that two or more persons corruptly or wrongfully agreed with each other that the employés of the several railroads carrying the mails and interstate commerce should quit, and that successors should, by threats, intimidation, or violence, be prevented from taking their places, such would constitute a conspiracy.

I recognize, however, the right of labor to organize. Each man in America is a freeman, and, so long as he does not interfere with the rights of others, has the right to do with that which is his what he pleases. In the highest sense, a man's arm is his own, and, aside from contract relations, no one but he can direct when it shall be raised to work, or shall be dropped to rest. The individual option to work or to quit is the imperishable right of a freeman. But the raising and dropping of the arm is the result of a will that resides in the brain, and, much as we may desire that such wills should remain entirely independent, there is no mandate of law which prevents their association with others, and response to a higher will. The individual may feel himself, alone, unequal to cope with the conditions that confront him, or unable to comprehend the myriad of considerations that ought to control his conduct. . . . His right to choose a leader, one who observes, thinks, and wills for him,—a brain skilled to observe his interest,—is no greater pretension than that which is recognized in every other department of industry. So far, and within reasonable limits, associations of this character are not only not unlawful, but are, in my judgment, beneficial, when they do not restrain individual liberty, and are under enlightened and conscientious leadership.

But they are subject to the same laws as other associations. The leaders to whom are given the vast power of judging and acting for the members are simply, in that respect, their trustees. . . . No man, in his individual right, can lawfully demand and insist upon conduct by others which will lead to an injury to a third person's lawful rights. The railroads carrying the mails and interstate commerce have a right to the service of each of their employés until each lawfully chooses to quit; and any concerted action upon the part of others to demand or insist, under any effective penalty or threat, upon their quitting, to the injury of the mail service or the prompt transportation of interstate commerce, is a conspiracy, unless such demand or insistence is in pursuance of a lawful authority conferred upon them by the employés themselves, and is made in good faith in the execution of such authority. . . .

If it appears to you, therefore, . . . that any two or more persons, by concert, insisted or demanded, under effective penalties and threats, upon men quitting the employment of the railways, to the obstruction of the mails or interstate commerce, you may inquire whether they did these acts as strangers to these men, or whether they did them under the pretension of trustees or leaders of an association to which these men belong. And, if the latter appears, you may inquire whether their acts and conduct in that respect were in faithful and conscientious execution of their supposed authority, or were simply a use of that authority as a guise to advance personal ambition or satisfy private malice. . . . You should not brand any act of leadership as done dishonestly or in bad faith unless it clearly so appears. But if it does so appear,— if any person is shown to have betrayed the trust of these toiling men, and their acts fall within the definition of crime, as I have given it to you,—it is alike the interest, the pleasure, and the duty of every citizen to bring them to swift and heavy punishment.

(c)  *Justice David J. Brewer speaking*
*for the United States Supreme Court in* in re Debs, *May 27, 1895*

The case presented by the bill is this: The United States, finding that the interstate transportation of persons and property, as well as the carriage of the mails, is forcibly obstructed, and that a combination and conspiracy exists to subject the control of such transportation to the will of the conspirators, applied to one of their courts, sitting as a court of equity, for an injunction to restrain such obstruction and prevent carrying into effect such conspiracy. Two questions of importance are presented: First. Are the relations of the general government to interstate commerce and the transportation of the mails such as authorize a direct interference to prevent a forcible obstruction thereof? Second: If authority exists, as authority in governmental affairs implies both power and duty, has a court of equity jurisdiction to issue an injunction in aid of the performance of such duty? . . .

As, under the Constitution, power over interstate commerce and the transportation of the mails is vested in the national government, and Congress by virtue of such grant has assumed actual and direct control, it follows that the national government may prevent any unlawful and forcible interference therewith. But how shall this be accomplished? Doubtless, it is within the competency of Congress to prescribe by legislation that any interference with these matters shall be offences against the United States, and prosecuted and punished by indictment in the proper courts. But is that the only remedy? Have the vast interests of the nation in interstate commerce, and in the transportation of the mails, no other protection than lies in the possible punishment of those who interfere with it? To ask the question is to answer it. . . . There is no such impotency in the national government. The entire strength of the nation may be used to enforce in any part of the land the full and free exercise of all national powers and the security of all rights entrusted by the Constitution to its care. . . .

But passing to the second question, is there no other alternative than the use of force on the part of the executive authorities whenever obstructions arise to the freedom of interstate commerce or the transportation of the mails? Is the army the only instrument by which rights of the public can be enforced and the peace of the nation preserved? . . .

The right to use force does not exclude the right of appeal to the courts for a judicial determination and for the exercise of all their powers of prevention. Indeed, it is more to the praise than to the blame of the government, that, instead of determining for itself questions of right and wrong on the part of these petitioners and their associates and enforcing that determination by the club of the policeman and the bayonet of the soldier, it submitted all those questions to the peaceful determination of judicial tribunals. . . .

It is said that equity only interferes for the protection of property, and that the government has no property interest. A sufficient reply is that the United States have a property in the mails, the protection of which was one of the purposes of this bill. . . .

We do not care to place our decision upon this ground alone. Every government, entrusted, by the very terms of its being, with powers and duties to be exercised and discharged for the general welfare, has a right to apply to its own courts for any proper assistance in the exercise of the one and the discharge of the other, and it is no sufficient answer to its appeal to one of those courts that it has no pecuniary interest in the matter. The obligation which it is under to promote the interest of all, and to prevent the wrongdoing of one resulting in injury to the general welfare, is often of itself sufficient to give it a standing in court. . . .

Again, it is objected that it is outside of the jurisdiction of a court of equity to enjoin the commission of crimes. This, as a general proposition, is unquestioned. A chancellor has no criminal jurisdiction. . . . There must be some interferences, actual or threatened, with property or rights of a pecuniary nature, but when such interferences appear the jurisdiction of a court of equity arises, and is not destroyed by the fact that they are accompanied by or are themselves violations of the criminal law. . . .

The law is full of instances in which the same act may give rise to a civil action and a criminal prosecution. . . . So here, the acts of the defendants may or may not have been violations of the criminal law. If they were, that matter is for inquiry in other proceedings. The complaint made against them in this is of disobedience to an order of a civil court, made for the protection of property and the security of rights. . . .

Nor is there in this any invasion of the constitutional right of trial by jury. . . . The power of a court to make an order carries with it the equal power to punish for a disobedience of that order, and the inquiry as to the question of disobedience has been, from time immemorial, the special function of the court. . . .

In brief, a court, enforcing obedience to its orders by proceedings for contempt, is not executing the criminal laws of the land, but only securing to suitors the rights which it has adjudged them entitled to. . . .

Summing up our conclusions, we hold that the government of the United States is one having jurisdiction over every foot of soil within its territory, and acting directly upon each citizen; that while it is a government of enumerated powers, it has within the limits of those powers all the attributes of

sovereignty; that to it is committed power over interstate commerce and the transmission of the mail; that the powers thus conferred upon the national government are not dormant, but have been assumed and put into practical exercise by the legislation of Congress; that in the exercise of those powers it is competent for the nation to remove all obstructions upon highways, natural or artificial, to the passage of interstate commerce or the carrying of the mail; that while it may be competent for the government (through the executive branch and in the use of the entire executive power of the nation) to forcibly remove all such obstructions, it is equally within its competency to appeal to the civil courts for an inquiry and determination as to the existence and character of any alleged obstructions, and if such are found to exist, or threaten to occur, to invoke the powers of those courts to remove or restrain such obstructions; that the jurisdiction of courts to interfere in such matters by injunction is one recognized from ancient times and by indubitable authority; that such jurisdiction is not ousted by the fact that the obstructions are accompanied by or consist of acts in themselves violations of the criminal law; that the proceeding by injunction is of a civil character, and may be enforced by proceedings in contempt; that such proceedings are not in execution of the criminal laws of the land; that the penalty for a violation of injunction is no substitute for and no defence to a prosecution for any criminal offences committed in the course of such violation; that the complaint filed in this case clearly showed an existing obstruction of artificial highways for the passage of interstate commerce and the transmission of the mail—an obstruction not only temporarily existing, but threatening to continue; that under such complaint the Circuit Court had power to issue its process of injunction; that it having been issued and served on these defendants, the Circuit Court had authority to inquire whether its orders had been disobeyed, and when it found that they had been, then to . . . enter the order of punishment complained of; and, finally, that the Circuit Court, having full jurisdiction in the premises, its finding of the fact of dis-

obedience is not open in review on *habeas corpus* in this or any other court. . . .

The petition for a writ of *habeas corpus* is *Denied*.

# 42

*"Our mission was . . . to establish the supremacy of the white race . . . to the extent to which it could be legally and constitutionally done"*

The victory of Grover Cleveland in the presidential election of 1884 by a popular plurality of less than 25,000 votes was the first effective gift of the "solid South" to the national Democratic party. The South's reward was two seats in Cleveland's cabinet, the speakership of the House, and the chairmanship of the Ways and Means Committee. A greatly enlarged share in federal patronage followed as a matter of course.

Within the South itself, Cleveland's victory and Cleveland's largess strengthened the hand of the Bourbon, or conservative, Democrats who had taken the leadership in "redeeming" the rebel states from Republican carpetbag and scalawag rule. But at the same time, just as Cleveland's administration in the nation sharpened the farm revolt against conservative business leadership, which Cleveland himself represented, so in the South, the Bourbon participation in Cleveland's regime sharpened the traditional small farmer antagonism toward the inheritors of the power of the old planter caste. When farm discontent across the nation culminated in the Populist revolt of the late 1880's and early 1890's, some small southern farmers joined the army of westerners in the new People's party; but most of them, fearful of dividing white strength in their own section, remained in the Democratic ranks where, by their numbers, they became an ever greater menace to the Bourbon oligarchy.

In North Carolina alone, among the southern states, the Populists, by joining forces with rump Republicans still to be found there, defeated the Democrats in the elections of 1894 and 1896. In 1894 they won control of the state legislature, captured a majority of the state's congressional seats, and elected both United States senators. In 1896, while retaining control of the legislature and the congressional delegation, they also won the governorship. In these years they had the support of most colored voters and they appointed and elected hundreds of Negroes to office. They thereby became the target of the entire South which rallied to the support of the North Carolina Democratic party and helped it violently dislodge the heretic combination in the elections of 1898.

In many other southern states, and in certain counties in almost all of them, the Negroes, where they did not actually represent a majority of the voting population, were sufficiently numerous to hold the balance of power when the white voters split, as they often did on important local issues. The heaviest concentrations of Negroes were likely to be in the old plantation districts; and even though their own interests might be closer to those of the small farmers, when splits among white voters occurred the Negroes usually were counted on the Bourbon side. Perhaps the heirs of the old masters indeed knew how to manage the colored hands. In any case, their tactics, when they wanted the Negro vote, also included economic intimidation in the form of threats of loss of jobs, land, or credit; and economic and other inducements such as bribes and fiery libations. When intimidation and inducement failed, open resort was had to crude election frauds. All these expedients came to be used against susceptible whites as well.

Negro support of the hated Bourbons only intensified the small farmers' antipathy to the Negro himself. As Populism spread, these farmers sometimes overcame their prejudices and openly welcomed Negro assistance in seeking to unseat the Bourbon rulers. When, even at the peak of Populism's highly emotional appeal, Negro help proved insufficiently forthcoming, the small farmers' racism and their resentment of Bourbonism both ran amuck.

In order to restore some stability to white unity after they had thwarted the Populist challenge, the Bourbons displayed a growing willingness to sacrifice what remained of those Negro prerogatives which had served themselves so well. They were the more strongly motivated to do this by their own profound revulsion from the corruption and violence and even the sheer high cost of bribery that increasingly marred southern elections as differences among white voters widened. By appealing, at the same time, to the small farmers' deepened commitment to white supremacy, the Bourbons hoped to induce them to sacrifice some of their own prerogatives for the cause, and thereby offset Bourbon losses in Negro voting strength.

The small farmers proved very reluctant to be induced; yet, after making some genuine concessions, sometimes simply by legislation, sometimes by constitutional amendments, but most frequently by wholly new constitutions, the Bourbons carried the day after all. Their concessions included such Populist demands as railroad regulatory commissions, and paid public appraisers of corporation property so that it might more rewardingly be taxed. But the stormiest issue was the central one of the suffrage, and the broadest concessions were made here. These took such forms as the notorious "understanding" tests, "grandfather" clauses, "veterans" privileges, and "good character" provisos, all to be administered by Democratic registration boards and similarly "discreet" election officials. As the Chairman of the Judiciary Committee of the Louisiana Constitutional Convention of 1898, Thomas J. Semmes, said of the grandfather clause adopted there, by this means "every white man . . . although he may not be able to read and write, although he does not possess the property qualifications, may, notwithstanding, if he register himself pursuant to this ordinance of the Constitution, be thereafter entitled to vote."

Such were the sieves—and there were others, such as long residence requirements and disqualifications for the pettiest of crimes, that were especially effective against peripatetic and sufficiently provoked Negroes—that were to trap the Negro aspirant but let the white man through. Because they "did not on their face discriminate between the races," as they were forbidden to do by the Fifteenth Amendment, but rather "swept the circle of expedients" remaining, the Supreme Court itself, in the case of *Williams* v. *Mississippi*, April 25, 1898, held them to be "within the field of permissible action under the limitations imposed by the Federal Constitution."

Nevertheless, there were catches for the whites as well. One of them was the time limit often placed on the escape provisions. As Semmes said of the white man's grandfather clause, "If he doesn't choose to register between now and the 1st of September next, he loses the privilege conferred upon him, and thereafter he can only vote provided he possesses the qualifications which I have just mentioned—the property or education. That is the temporary clause." The property qualifications, in turn, were uniformly high, while the education clauses could be enforced stringently enough to discourage respectable illiterates from exposing their limitations in schooling to their neighbors. Another effective catch was the poll tax usually imposed by the new regulations. This tax was cumulative from year to year. Since little effort would be made to collect it, it often mounted up. Moreover, the only penalty for non-payment might be the loss of the right to vote, a loss the more stoically borne as the amount soared beyond reach.

The small farmers had been so certain that any means of disfranchising the Negro under the Fourteenth and Fifteenth amendments would necessarily disfranchise themselves that they vigorously fought even the calling of the new constitutional conventions. So certain were the Bourbons, in turn, that the escape clauses for the whites would prove unsatisfactory to these farmers that, except in Alabama, they declared the new fundamental laws adopted without submitting them to referendums. Both groups were proved right. In state after state, following Mississippi's example of 1890, as the new suffrage laws were adopted, Negro voting virtually ceased; and white voting also fell off. Throughout the South, small Democratic oligarchies gained control of election machinery. By returning their friends to Congress year after year, they also gained extraordinary power in major congressional committees. This was especially true during Democratic administrations which they themselves, by delivering the solid South to the party, helped to make more frequent. But these men also were in sympathy with conservative Republican administrations, which had long since lost their "Radical" tinge and welcomed Bourbon support.

In conformity with the Fourteenth and Fifteenth amendments, the northern states had uniformly repealed their anti-Negro franchise provisions (see Document No. 24, above), but as little northern sympathy as ever remained for northern as well as southern blacks. A long series of discriminatory Supreme Court decisions, the most famous being that of *Plessy* v. *Ferguson* (1896) which approved separate black and white facilities including public schools (see Document No. 55, below), reflected the national mood. After 1898, moreover, when the United States acquired new island territories with non-white populations, southern suffrage practice, regardless of its disqualification of whites as well as Negroes, was commended throughout the nation as the model for the new empire. Speaking of the Supreme Court's decision that year in *Williams* v. *Mississippi*, for example, the *Nation* of New York declared it "an interesting coincidence that this important decision is rendered at a time when we are considering the idea of taking in a varied assortment of inferior races in different parts of the world," races "which, of course, could not be allowed to vote." At the same time, The Boston *Evening Transcript* acknowledged that the southern way was "now the policy of the Administration of the very party which carried the country into and through a civil war to free the slave."

The national temper is also reflected in the fact that Thomas J. Semmes, the Chairman of the Judiciary Committee of the Louisiana Constitutional Convention of 1898, quoted above, had also been president of the American Bar Association. Semmes's commendatory speech to this Convention at the conclusion of its work is presented in part below in item "a." This speech is followed, in item "b," by extracts from the suffrage provisions of four new southern constitutions, that of Mississippi in 1890, South Carolina in 1895, Louisiana in 1898, and Alabama in 1901. The first is best known for its "understanding" qualification in its "literacy" provision; the second for making passing of the "understanding" test before a given date a lifetime qualification; the third for its hereditary "grandfather" clause; the fourth for its admission of veterans and others of "good character." But all four, and the others, became most effective through the "discreet" enforcement of the quoted provisions which, as C. Vann Woodward says, transformed into "the poor man's 'eye of the needle' . . . the wide gate to the franchise" that these famous concessions were "represented to be."

# The Spirit of the Southern Franchise

(a)  *The commendatory address of Thomas J. Semmes,*
*Chairman of the Judiciary Committee of the Louisiana*
*Constitutional Convention, May 12, 1898*

Mr. President and Gentlemen of the Convention: I have seconded the motion to approve and adopt by your signatures, the Constitution which has been the result of ninety-four days of labor on the part of this Convention. . . . I have no apologies to make, either for the Convention or for myself. . . .

This is the work of the Democratic party of the State, represented by its selected agents appointed to do that work. If we have done anything wrong, anything which will [further] the dissolution or disintegration or defeat of the Democratic party, then we ought to be condemned. It has been stated in some quarters that we have been actuated to a certain extent by party spirit. Grant it. What of it? What is the State? It is the Democratic party. (Applause.) What are the people of the State? They are the Democracy of the State, and when you eliminate the Democratic party or the Democracy of the State from the State, what is there left but that which we came here to suppress? I don't allude to the fragments of what is called the Republican party. We met here to establish the supremacy of the white race, and the white race constitutes the Democratic party of this State. . . .

Now then, what have we done? is the question. Our mission was, in the first place, to establish the supremacy of the white race in this State to the extent to which it could be legally and constitutionally done, and what has our ordinance on suffrage, the constitutional means by which we propose to maintain that ascendency, done? We have established throughout the State white manhood suffrage. A great cry went out that there should be a poll tax; that there should be an educational test; that as a qualification for the voter, he should be an owner of property. We have in the ordinance established those qualifications which are necessary to be passed in order to entitle these citizens to vote. . . . But a hue and cry has been raised by people . . . against what is called section 5 of the ordinance on suffrage. Now, what is section 5? Very few people know anything about it. Very few people understand its effects. They have taken their ideas from outside criticism, and suppose that we have committed some very great wrong.

I repeat, what is section 5? It is a declaration upon the part of this Convention, that no white man in this State . . . who has heretofore exercised the right of suffrage shall be deprived of it, whether or not he can read or write, or whether he possesses the property qualification. That is the meaning of it, nothing more and nothing less. It declares that every white man between now and the 1st day of September next, although he may not be able to read and write, although he does not possess the property qualification, may, notwithstanding, if he register himself pursuant to this ordinance of the Constitution, be thereafter entitled to vote. . . . If he doesn't choose to register between now and the 1st of September next, he loses the privilege conferred upon him, and, thereafter, he can only vote provided he possesses the qualifications which I have just mentioned—the property or education. That is the temporary clause. However ill-advised it might be; however, if you choose, unconstitutional it might be; its effect expires on the 1st of September next, and, thereafter, no man will be entitled to vote who has not registered, as provided by this fifth section, between now and the 1st of September next. No man can thereafter vote unless he possesses the property qualification or the educational qualification.

Now, why was this exception made? Because, and I am ashamed to say it, Louisiana is one of the most illiterate States in the Union. It is more illiterate than any other State except North Carolina. We, therefore, have in this State a large white population whose right to vote would have been stricken down but for the operation of section 5. And all of these men had aided the white people of the State to wrest from the hands of the Republican party, composed almost exclusively of negroes, the power which, backed by Federal bayonets, they had exercised for many years. How can we go to them, these men who stood side by side with us in the dark days of reconstruction, and say to them that a convention of Louisianians has deprived them of the right to vote? Could we face these men who have always been Democrats; who have always aided us in achieving the as-

cendancy of the Democratic party in this State, with such a record as that?

And where do these people principally reside? Not in New Orleans, but in . . . Southwestern Louisiana. That ancient Creole population; that ancient Acadian population; . . . these simple, good people, whose ancestors have been living there for a hundred and fifty years, surrounded by circumstances which debarred them from all the advantages of education, could any man with a heart in his breast be willing to strike them down and reduce them to the condition of the black race that we are proscribing? (Cries of "No," and applause.) Now there's our sin; that the fault we have committed, and God knows, if we had it to do over again, I would repeat the sin. (Great Applause.) . . . The favor that we have conceded them was this. You have been kept in this condition for centuries, by circumstances beyond your control, and for that reason we allow you to continue to exercise the right of suffrage without possessing a property or an educational qualification. But the circumstances and the times have changed. Your children must go to school; you must acquire property if you would exercise the right to vote, and not claim hereafter the benefit of the concessions which are now made. Was not this politic legislation? Was it not proper legislation, and was it not essential and necessary in justice to these people?

(b) *Suffrage provisions in selected southern constitutions, 1890-1901*

CONSTITUTION
OF MISSISSIPPI, 1890.

SEC. 241. Every male inhabitant of this State, except idiots, insane persons and Indians not taxed, who is a citizen of the United States, twenty-one years old and upwards, who has resided in this State two years, and one year in the election district, or in the incor-

porated city or town, in which he offers to vote, and who is duly registered as provided in this article, and who has never been convicted of bribery, burglary, theft, arson, obtaining money or goods under false pretenses, perjury, forgery, imbezzlement or bigamy, and who has paid, on or before the first day of February, of the year in which he shall offer to vote, all taxes which may have been legally required of him, and which he has had an opporunity of paying according to law, for the two preceding years, and who shall produce to the officers holding the election satisfactory evidence that he has paid said taxes, is declared to be a qualified elector. . . .

SEC. 243. A uniform poll tax of two dollars, to be used in aid of the common schools, and for no other purpose, is hereby imposed on every male inhabitant of this State between the ages of twenty-one and sixty years. . . . No criminal proceedings shall be allowed to enforce the collection of the poll tax.

SEC. 244. On and after the first day of January, A.D., 1892, every elector shall, in addition to the foregoing qualifications, be able to read any section of the constitution of this State; or he shall be able to understand the same when read to him, or give a reasonable interpretation thereof. A new registration shall be made before the next ensuing election after January the first, A.D., 1892.

CONSTITUTION
OF SOUTH CAROLINA, 1895.

SEC. 3. Every male citizen of this State and of the United States twenty-one years of age and upwards, not laboring under the disabilities named in this Constitution and possessing the qualifications required by it, shall be an elector.

SEC. 4. The qualifications for suffrage shall be as follows:

(a) Residence in the State for two years, in the County one year, in the polling precinct in which the elector offers to vote four months, and the payment six months before any election of any poll tax then due and payable . . .

(b) Registration, which shall provide for the enrollment of every elector once in ten years, and also an enrollment during each and every year of every elector not previously registered under the provisions of this Article.

(c) Up to January 1st, 1898, all male persons of voting age applying for registration who can read any Section in this Constitution submitted to them by the registration officer, or understand and explain it when read to them . . . shall be entitled to register and become electors. A separate record of all persons registered before January 1st, 1898, . . . shall be filed, . . . on or before February 1st, 1898, and such persons shall remain during life qualified electors unless disqualified by the other provisions of this Article. . . .

(d) Any person who shall apply for registration after January 1st, 1898, if otherwise qualified, shall be registered: *Provided,* That he can both read and write any Section of this Constitution submitted to him by the registration officer or can show that he owns, and has paid all taxes collectible during the previous year on property in this State assessed at three hundred dollars ($300) or more. . . .

SEC. 6. The following persons are disqualified from being registered or voting:

*First.* Persons convicted of burglary, arson, obtaining goods or money under false pretenses, perjury, forgery, robbery, bribery, adultery, bigamy, wife-beating, house-breaking, receiving stolen goods, breach of trust with fraudulent intent, fornication, sodomy, incest, assault with intent to ravish, miscegenation, larceny, or crimes against the election laws. . . .

SEC. 8. The General Assembly shall provide by law for the registration of all qualified electors, and shall prescribe the manner of holding elections and of ascertaining the results of the same: *Provided,* At the first registration under this Constitution, and until the first of January, 1898, the registration shall be conducted by a Board of three discreet persons in each County, to be appointed by the Governor. . . .

CONSTITUTION
OF LOUISIANA, 1898.

ART. 197. Every male citizen of this State and of the United States, native born or naturalized, not less than twenty-one years of age, and possessing the following qualifications, shall be an elector. . . .

SEC. 1. He shall have been an actual bona-fide resident of this State for two years, of the parish one year and of the precinct in which he offers to vote six months next preceding the election; . . .

SEC. 2. He shall have been at the time he offers to vote, legally enrolled as a registered voter on his personal application, . . .

SEC. 3. He shall be able to read and write, and shall demonstrate his ability to do so when he applies for registration, by making, under oath administered by the registration officer or his deputy, written application therefor, in the English language, or in his mother tongue, which application shall contain the essential facts necessary to show that he is entitled to register and vote, and shall be entirely written, dated and signed by him, in the presence of the registration officer or his deputy, without assistance or suggestion from any person or any memorandum whatever, except the form of application hereinafter set forth. . . .

SEC. 4. If he be not able to read and write, as provided by Section three of this article, then he shall be entitled to register and vote if he shall, at the time he offers to register, be the bona-fide owner of property assessed to him in this State at a valuation of not less than three hundred dollars. . . .

SEC. 5. No male person who was on January 1st, 1867, or at any date prior thereto, entitled to vote under the Constitution or statutes of any State of the United States, wherein he then resided, and no son or grandson of any such person not less than twenty-one years of age at the date of the adoption of this Constitution, and no male person of foreign birth, who was naturalized prior to the first day of January, 1898, shall be denied the right to register and vote in this State by reason of his failure to possess the educational or property qualifications prescribed by this Constitution; provided, he shall have resided in this State for five years next preceding the date at which he shall apply for registration, and shall have registered in accordance with the terms of this article prior to September 1, 1898, and no person shall be entitled to register under this section after said date. . . .

ART. 198. No person less than sixty years of age shall be permitted to vote at any election in the State who shall not, in addition to the qualifications above prescribed, have paid on or before the 31st day of December, of each year, for the two years preceding the year in which he offers to vote, a poll tax of one dollar per annum, to be used exclusively in aid of the public schools of the parish in which such tax shall have been collected; which tax is hereby imposed on every male resident of this State between the age of twenty-one and sixty years. Poll taxes shall be a lien only upon assessed property, and no process shall issue to enforce the collection of the same except against assessed property. . . .

Any person who shall pay the poll tax of another or advance him money for that purpose, in order to influence his vote, shall be guilty of bribery and punished accordingly.

CONSTITUTION
OF ALABAMA, 1901.

178. To entitle a person to vote at any election by the people, he shall have resided in the State at least two years, in the county one year, and in the precinct or ward three months, immediately preceding the election at which he offers to vote, and he shall have been duly registered as an elector, and shall have paid on or before the first day of February next preceding the date of the election at which he offers to vote, all poll taxes due from him for the year nineteen hundred and one, and for each subsequent year. . . .

180. The following male citizens of this State, who are citizens of the United States, and every male resident

of foreign birth, who, before the ratification of this Constitution, shall have legally declared his intention to become a citizen of the United States, . . . shall, upon application be entitled to register as electors prior to the twentieth day of December, nineteen hundred and two, namely:

First—All who have honorably served in the land or naval forces of the United States in the war of 1812, or in the war with Mexico, or in any war with the Indians, or in the war between the States, or in the war with Spain, or who honorably served in the land or naval forces of the Confederate States, or of the State of Alabama in the war between the States; or,

Second—The lawful descendants of [such] persons . . . or,

Third—All persons who are of good character and who understand the duties and obligations of citizenship under a republican form of government.

181. After the first day of January, nineteen hundred and three, the following persons, and no others, . . . shall be qualified to register as electors, provided, they shall not be disqualified under Section 182 of this Constitution.

First—Those who can read and write any article of the Constitution of the United States in the English language, and who are physically unable to work; and those who can read and write any article of the Constitution of the United States in the English language, and who have worked or been regularly engaged in some lawful employment, business or occupation, trade or calling for the greater part of the twelve months next preceding the time they offer to register. . . .

Second—The owner in good faith, in his own right, or the husband of a woman who is the owner in good faith, in her own right, of forty acres of land situate in this State, upon which they reside; or . . . of real estate, situate in this State, assessed for taxation at the value of three hundred dollars or more or . . . of personal property in this State assessed for taxation at three hundred dollars or more; . . .

182. The following persons shall be disqualified both from registering and from voting, namely:

All idiots and insane persons; those who shall by reason of conviction of crime be disqualified from voting at the time of the ratification of this Constitution; those who shall be convicted of treason, murder, arson, embezzlement, malfeasance in office, larceny, receiving stolen property, obtaining property or money under false pretenses, perjury, subornation of perjury, robbery, assault with intent to rob, burglary, forgery, bribery, assault and battery on the wife, bigamy, living in adultery, sodomy, incest, rape, miscegenation, crime against nature, or any crime punishable by imprisonment in the penitentiary, or of any infamous crime or crime involving moral turpitude; also any person who shall be convicted as a vagrant or tramp, or of selling or offering to sell his vote or the vote of another, or of making or offering to make false return in any election by the people or in any primary election to procure the nomination or election of any person to any office, or of suborning any witness or registrar to secure the registration of any person as an elector. . . .

194. The poll tax mentioned in this article shall be one dollar and fifty cents . . . but no legal process, nor any fee or commission shall be allowed for the collection thereof. . . .

# 43

*". . . issues wholly external to our body politic engross attention and stand in the way of the close devotion to domestic advancement that becomes a self-contained commonwealth."*

In his first Annual Report as United States Commissioner of Labor, in March, 1886, Carroll D. Wright devoted himself entirely to "the depressions with which the present generation is familiar." In the whole "family of manufacturing states," led by Great Britain, France, Belgium and Germany, and the United States, Wright said, "prices have been greatly reduced, . . . and profits carried to the minimum range. Over-production seems to prevail in all alike." These depressions, Wright observed, "belong to the age of invention and of organized industry." His "remedies," at least for the United States, were based solely on getting "a healthy public opinion" behind those restrictive, stabilizing, and self-regulatory measures which American as well as European industry, in self-defense, had in fact already begun to adopt.

Wright was not optimistic about the efficacy of his proposals. American public opinion in his time still plumped for opportunity not closure, for enterprise not restraint, for expansion not restriction. Much closer to the prevailing spirit was Chauncey M. Depew's advice to the Yale alumni: "The South is the Bonanza of the future. We have developed all the great and sudden opportunities for wealth . . . in the Northwest States and on the Pacific Slope." In the South lay "vast forests untouched; with enormous veins of coal and iron. . . . Go South, Young Man!"

A few other Americans cherished still larger ideas even more in keeping with the old venturesomeness of the people, although such ideas seemed to have gone out of fashion with the completion of transcontinental settlement. The public official who pressed these ideas most pertinaciously was James G. ("Jingo Jim") Blaine, especially after he became Secretary of State under President Garfield in 1881. Blaine was one of the first to advocate a navy second to none, an isthmian canal solely under American control, and the acquisition of strategic island bases to forestall foreign domination of the world's seas, the world's commerce, and the world's markets. Speaking of the same Northwest and Pacific slope as Depew, Blaine, in December, 1881, advised his subordinate, the American minister in Hawaii:

When we survey the stupendous progress made by the western coast during the thirty years of its national life as part of our dominion, its enormous increase of population, its vast resources of agriculture and mines, and its boundless enterprise, it is not easy to set a limit to its commercial activity or foresee a check to its maritime supremacy in the waters of the Orient. . . . In thirty years the United States has acquired a legitimately dominant influence in the North Pacific, which it can never consent to see decreased by the intrusion therein of any element of influence hostile to its own. . . . Hawaii, although much farther from the Californian coast than is Cuba from the Floridian peninsula, holds in the western sea the same position as Cuba in the Atlantic. It is the key to the maritime dominion of the Pacific states, as Cuba is the key to the Gulf trade. . . . The Hawaiian Islands cannot be joined to the Asiatic system. If they drift from their independent station it must be toward assimilation and identification with the American system, to which they belong by the operation of natural laws and must belong by the operation of political necessity.

As late as 1889, Henry Cabot Lodge, then an impatient young congressman of the Blaine school, lamented his countrymen's tenacious isolationism fed by their pride in the apparent self-sufficiency of their continental domain. "We have separated ourselves so completely from the affairs of other people," Lodge complained, "that it is difficult to realize how large a place they occupied when the government was founded." No one accepted this separation more serenely than Lodge's fellow congressman, William McKinley of Ohio. McKinley's "patriotic solution" for the recurrent gluts of goods in American markets was a tariff wall so high that foreign commodities would be barred altogether. The McKinley tariff of 1890 fully met its sponsor's requirements, and his isolationist credo—"Protection, Patriotism, and Prosperity"—soon carried him to the presidency on the strongest surge of popular sentiment since the re-election of Grant in 1872. But McKinley's and the people's test lay ahead.

When McKinley entered the White House in March, 1897, a new insurrection against Spain had been raging in Cuba for more than two years with the same ferocity that had reduced both sides to impotence after a full decade of combat in Grant's day. Grant had successfully withstood pressure to intervene in the early 1870's. Cleveland, McKinley's immediate predecessor, had withstood even greater pressure in the mid-1890's. The peaceable McKinley, supported by many of the "protected" industrialists who had backed him for the presidency with the expectation that he would not hare off on costly foreign adventures, strove to profit from Grant's and Cleveland's example. He failed utterly.

McKinley's capitulation to the Blaine school offers the best measure of those forces which, largely unknown to him and largely underestimated by men like Wright, had been remaking the whole world since Grant's time. Among these forces were the old expansive drives of western culture which had led to the discovery of America itself. The spread of the industrial revolution in the nineteenth century had given these drives massive momentum. As Wright pointed out in 1886, "each great manufacturing nation of the world is struggling for industrial existence against the fierce competition of every other nation engaged in like pursuits." The recurrent depressions which so absorbed Wright's interest intensified the quest for markets abroad. The rising and often retaliatory tariffs in industrial lands helped bend this quest toward the undeveloped regions of the world. These regions became the more alluring because, through the cultivation of exotic raw materials increasingly sought by manufacturers at home, they also seemed to offer such energizing "great and sudden opportunities for wealth" as Depew had held aloft.

The partition of Africa and the dismemberment of Southeast Asia by the industrial nations of Europe followed hard upon America's own reconquest of the cotton South in the Civil War. Soon the push for spheres of influence, territorial concessions, and financial domination reached ever more deeply into China, so long a loadstone of American ambition, and Latin America, so restive a ward of American policy. In this stirring renewal of the old competition for empire, History, Destiny, Race, the idea of Civilization itself, again were enlisted by each of "the Christian nations," as an American missionary said, "who are subduing the world in order to make mankind free." By 1898, having just emerged from the severest of nineteenth-century depressions with agrarian unrest quieted, labor violence quelled, and monetary heretics quashed at the polls, the United States, the darling of Destiny, the crown of Civilization, the Palladium of freedom, once more was spoiling for the fray.

During the previous decade, the burgeoning "yellow press," and strident young politicos of the Lodge and Teddy Roosevelt stamp, had whipped up each new imperial confrontation, especially in the western hemisphere, with tribal ululations for war. Renewed naval construction at home in that decade provided a fillip to America's soaring sense of power, while Europe's own headlong rush, seemingly to encompass the last remaining land on earth, gave an unwonted urgency to this power's prompt employment. The often recounted events in Cuba early in 1898, "right at our door," as McKinley at last was forced to concede, culminating in the blowing up of the new American battleship, *Maine*, on February 15, brought the full force of these tendencies sharply into focus in Washington. The stay-at-home President sought to blunt them by inaction. But "time," as Margaret Leech writes in her biography of McKinley, "was a license Congress denied." Early in his message to Congress, April 11, 1898, virtually asking for war with Spain over provocations to Americans in Cuba (presented in part in this Document, along with Congress's own joint resolution of April 20 on Cuban independence, which the Chief Executive grudgingly signed), McKinley summarized his submission to the surge of misplaced popular feeling:

> The temper and forbearance of our people have been so sorely tried as to beget a perilous unrest among its own citizens, which has inevitably found its expression from time to time in the National Legislature, so that issues wholly external to our own body politic engross attention and stand in the way of that close devotion to domestic advancement that becomes a self-contained

commonwealth whose primal maxim has been the avoidance of all foreign entanglements.

"By our code of morality," McKinley reminded the war pack, "forcible annexation" of Cuba "would be criminal aggression." To forestall the aggressors in Congress, the President proposed only "neutral intervention" to "enforce a truce" and "guide the eventual settlement."

Two days before McKinley's message Spain had in fact finally yielded to American demands that Cuba be granted self-government. A peaceful settlement with Spain was to follow; but Lodge, called to the White House to discuss this apparent Spanish concession, convinced McKinley that it was only a "humbug armistice." The President was constrained from altering his message, but he did add a face-saving paragraph at the end expressing the fond hope that if Spain's capitulation found support in Congress during its "solemn deliberations," then "our aspirations as a Christian, peace-loving people will be realized."

As McKinley knew it would, Congress sided with Lodge. In its resolution of April 20, Congress went beyond the Chief Executive in asserting Cuba's right not only to self-government but also to independence, even though—thoughtlessly, without debate and without a roll call—it adopted the soon lamented Teller Amendment disclaiming any intention of subjecting Cuba to American sovereignty. In response to Congress's resolution, Spain formally declared war on the United States on April 24. The next day, Congress made its own formal declaration, effective officially as of April 21.

Thus did the United States embark on her imperialist adventure which carried the flag to Puerto Rico, the Philippines, Guam, and Hawaii, as well as Cuba, and eventually carried the United States into World War I and the subsequent age of global violence. But more than once thereafter Americans sought to return to McKinleyism—to Xenophobia, Protectionism, and Isolationism—the program Warren G. Harding, for example, called "normalcy," and on which he rode to victory in the presidential election of 1920 with an unprecedented 60 per cent of the popular vote.

*April, 1898*

# McKinley's War Message and Congress's
# Joint Resolution on Cuban Independence

(a)  *McKinley's message to Congress on war with Spain, April 11, 1898*

To the Congress of the United States:
    Obedient to that precept of the Constitution which commands the Presi-

dent to give from time to time to the Congress information of the state of the Union and to recommend to their consideration such measures as he shall judge necessary and expedient, it becomes my duty to now address your body with regard to the grave crisis that has arisen in the relations of the United States to Spain by reason of the warfare that for more than three years has raged in the neighboring island of Cuba. . . .

The present revolution is but the successor of other similar insurrections which have occurred in Cuba against the dominion of Spain, extending over a period of nearly half a century, each of which during its progress has subjected the United States to great effort and expense in enforcing its neutrality laws, caused enormous losses to American trade and commerce, caused irritation, annoyance, and disturbance among our citizens, and, by the exercise of cruel, barbarous, and uncivilized practices of warfare, shocked the sensibilities and offended the human sympathies of our people. . . .

The temper and forbearance of our people have been so sorely tried as to beget a perilous unrest among our own citizens, which has inevitably found its expression from time to time in the National Legislature, so that issues wholly external to our own body politic engross attention and stand in the way of that close devotion to domestic advancement that becomes a self-contained commonwealth whose primal maxim has been the avoidance of all foreign entanglements. All this must needs awaken, and has, indeed, aroused, the utmost concern on the part of this Government, as well during my predecessor's term as in my own.

In April, 1896, the evils from which our country suffered through the Cuban war became so onerous that my predecessor made an effort to bring about a peace . . . on the basis of some effective scheme of self-government for Cuba under the flag and sovereignty of Spain. It failed through the refusal of the Spanish government then in power to consider any form of mediation or, indeed, any plan of settlement which did not begin with the actual submission of the insurgents to the mother country, and then only on such terms as Spain herself might see fit to grant. . . .

The war in Cuba is of such a nature that, short of subjugation or extermination, a final military victory for either side seems impracticable. The alternative lies in the physical exhaustion of the one or the other party, or perhaps of both—a condition which in effect ended the ten years' war by the truce of Zanjon. The prospect of such a protraction and conclusion of the present strife is a contingency hardly to be contemplated with equanimity by the civilized world, and least of all by the United States. . . .

Realizing this, it appeared to be my duty, in a spirit of true friendliness, no less to Spain than to the Cubans, . . . to seek to bring about an immediate termination of the war. To this end I submitted on the 27th ultimo, . . . propositions to the Spanish Government looking to an armistice until October 1 for the negotiation of peace with the good offices of the President. . . .

The reply of the Spanish cabinet was received on the night of the 31st ultimo. It offered, as the means to bring about peace in Cuba, to confide the preparation thereof to the insular parliament, . . . it being, however, understood that the powers reserved by the constitution to the central Government are not lessened or diminished. As the Cuban parliament does not meet until the 4th of May next, the Spanish Government would not object for its part to accept at once a suspension of hostilities if asked for by the insurgents from the general-in-chief, to whom it would pertain in such case to determine the duration and conditions of the armistice. . . .

With this last overture in the direction of immediate peace, and its disappointing reception by Spain, the Executive is brought to the end of his effort.

In my annual message of December last I said:

Of the untried measures there remain only: recognition of the insurgents as belligerents; recognition of the independence of Cuba; neutral intervention to end the war by imposing a rational compromise between the contestants, and intervention in favor of one or the other party. I speak not of forcible annexation, for that cannot be thought of. That, by our code of morality, would be criminal aggression.

Thereupon I reviewed these alternatives, . . . pointing out the inconveniences and positive dangers of a recognition of belligerence, which while adding to the already onerous burdens of neutrality within our own jurisdiction, could not in any way extend our influence or effective offices in the territory of hostilities.

Nothing has since occurred to change my view in this regard. . . .

There remain the alternative forms of intervention to end the war, either as an impartial neutral, by imposing a rational compromise between the contestants, or as the active ally of the one party or the other. . . .

The forcible intervention of the United States as a neutral to stop the war, according to the large dictates of humanity and following many historical precedents where neighboring states have interfered to check the hopeless sacrifices of life by internecine conflicts beyond their borders, is justifiable on rational grounds. It involves, however, hostile constraint upon both the parties to the contest, as well to enforce a truce as to guide the eventual settlement.

The grounds for such intervention may be briefly summarized as follows:

First. In the cause of humanity and to put an end to the barbarities, bloodshed, starvation, and horrible miseries now existing there, and which the parties to the conflict are either unable or unwilling to stop or mitigate. It is no answer to say this is all in another country, belonging to another nation, and is therefore none of our business. It is specially our duty, for it is right at our door.

Second. We owe it to our citizens in Cuba to afford them that protection and indemnity for life and property which no government there can or will afford, and to that end to terminate the conditions that deprive them of legal protection.

Third. The right to intervene may be justified by the very serious injury to the commerce, trade, and business of our people and by the wanton destruction of property and devastation of the island.

Fourth, and which is of the utmost importance. The present condition of affairs in Cuba is a constant menace to our peace and entails upon this Government an enormous expense. With such a conflict waged for years in an island so near us and with which our people have such trade and business relations; when the lives and liberty of our citizens are in constant danger and their property destroyed and themselves ruined; where our trading vessels are liable to seizure and are seized at our very door by war ships of a foreign nation; the expeditions of filibustering that we are powerless to prevent altogether, and the irritating questions and entanglements thus arising—all these and others that I need not mention, with the resulting strained relations, are a constant menace to our peace and compel us to keep on a semi-war footing with a nation with which we are at peace.

These elements of danger and disorder already pointed out have been strikingly illustrated by a tragic event which has deeply and justly moved the American people. I have already transmitted to Congress the report of the naval court of inquiry on the destruction of the battle ship *Maine* in the harbor of Havana during the night of the 15th of February. The destruction of that noble vessel has filled the national heart with inexpressible horror. . . .

The naval court of inquiry, which, it is needless to say, commands the unqualified confidence of the Government, was unanimous in its conclusion that the destruction of the *Maine* was caused by an exterior explosion—that of a submarine mine. It did not assume to place the responsibility. That remains to be fixed.

In any event, the destruction of the *Maine,* by whatever exterior cause, is a patent and impressive proof of a state of things in Cuba that is intolerable. . . . The only hope of relief and repose from a condition which can no longer be endured is the enforced pacification of Cuba. In the name of humanity, in the name of civilization, in behalf of endangered American interests which give us the right and the duty to speak and to act, the war in Cuba must stop.

In view of these facts and of these considerations I ask the Congress to authorize and empower the President to take measures to secure a full and final termination of hostilities between the Government of Spain and the people of Cuba, and to secure in the island the establishment of a stable government, capable of maintaining order and observing its international obligations, insuring peace and tranquillity and the security of its citizens as well as our own, and to use the military and naval forces of the United States as may be necessary for these purposes. . . . I await your action. . . .

Yesterday, and since the preparation of the foregoing message, official information was received by me that the latest decree of the Queen Regent of Spain directs General Blanco, in order to prepare and facilitate peace, to proclaim a suspension of hostilities, the duration and details of which have not yet been communicated to me.

This fact, with every other pertinent consideration, will, I am sure, have your just and careful attention in the solemn deliberations upon which you are about to enter. If this measure attains a successful result, then our aspirations as a Christian, peace-loving people will be realized. If it fails, it will be only another justification for our contemplated action.

## (b) *The Joint Resolution of Congress on Cuban Independence, April 20, 1898*

Whereas the abhorrent conditions which have existed for more than three years in the Island of Cuba, so near our own borders, have shocked the moral sense of the people of the United States, have been a disgrace to Christian civilization, culminating as they have, in the destruction of a United States battleship, with two hundred and sixty-six of its officers and crew, while on a friendly visit in the harbor of Havana, and cannot longer be endured, as has been set forth by the President of the United States in his message to Congress of April eleventh, eighteen hundred and ninety-eight, upon which the action of Congress was invited: Therefore,

*Resolved,* First. That the people of the Island of Cuba are, and of right ought to be, free and independent.

Second. That it is the duty of the United States to demand, and the Government of the United States does hereby demand, that the Government of Spain at once relinquish its authority and government in the Island of Cuba and withdraw its land and naval forces from Cuba and Cuban waters.

Third. That the President of the United States be, and he hereby is, directed and empowered to use the entire land and naval forces of the United States, and to call into the actual service of the United States the militia of the several States, to such extent as may be necessary to carry these resolutions into effect.

Fourth. That the United States hereby disclaims any disposition or intention to exercise sovereignty, jurisdiction, or control over said Island except for the pacification thereof, and asserts its determination, when that is accomplished, to leave the government and control of the Island to its people.

## 44

*"We will not abandon our opportunity in the Orient. We will not renounce our part in the mission of our race, trustee, under God, of the civilization of the world."*

On February 4, 1899, two days before the United States Senate narrowly approved the Treaty of Paris ending the Spanish-American War, an armed revolt broke out in the Philippines against American military rule. By the end of the year all formal opposition had been suppressed, but a brutal guerrilla war was to be fought eighteen months longer before Filipino resistance ended. The most controversial issue over the treaty in the Senate had been the acquisition of the archipelago, a distant land with a colored population "not of a self-governing race." After the approval of the treaty, the Filipino insurrection kept the islands so prominently in the public eye that their retention became the leading issue in the presidential election of 1900.

In this election, the Republicans, on the whole, supported McKinley's administration in taking and holding the islands. The Democrats, by and large, for partisan as well as substantial reasons, opposed. In order to satisfy the public demand for a clear stand on the issue, the Republican leadership of the Senate Philippines Committee, shortly after the convening of Congress in December, 1899, brought out the following resolution: "Resolved, that the Philippine Islands are territory belonging to the United States; that it is the intention of the United States to retain them as such, and to establish and maintain such governmental control throughout the archipelago as the situation may demand."

The Democrats denounced the resolution. As they said later in their platform, "The Filipinos cannot be citizens without endangering our civilization; they cannot be subjects without imperiling our form of government." The Democrats demanded "an immediate declaration of the nation's purpose to give the Filipinos . . . independence," with "protection from outside interference." The Republicans replied that we are our brothers' keeper: "God has made . . . the English-speaking and Teutonic peoples . . . the master organizers of the world to establish system where chaos reigns. . . . He has made us adepts in government that we may administer government among savage and senile peoples." The Democrats deplored "the greedy commercialism which dictated the Philippine policy of the Republican administration." The Republicans declared, "we will not retreat from China's illimitable markets. . . . The Pacific is our ocean. . . . This island empire is the last land left."

That the Republicans would carry the election was clearly foreshadowed in the debate over the Philippine Resolution. The most remarkable speech during this debate, from which the Republican quotations above are taken, was the maiden effort, on January 9, 1900, of Albert J. Beveridge of Indiana, the thirty-six-year-old lawyer who, on his election to the Senate the previous November, promptly took off for a tour of the Philippines whence he had returned with enhanced authority. Beveridge's speech is presented in part in this Document.

Only one sour note marred the new Senator's success. When his two-hour oration ended, Republican Senator George Frisbie Hoar of Massachusetts, who had entered Congress when Beveridge was six years old, "could not mutely acquiesce in the general approval." As Claude G. Bowers, Beveridge's biographer, writes, "face flushed, voice trembling with sincere emotion," Hoar caught the eye of the presiding officer and stood up to speak:

> I have listened delighted, as I suppose all the members of the Senate did, to the eloquence of my honorable friend from Indiana. I am glad to welcome to the public service his enthusiasm, his patriotism, his silver speech. . . . Yet, Mr. President, as I heard his eloquent description of wealth and glory and commerce and trade, . . . I could think of this brave young Republic of ours listening to what he had to say, of but one occurrence: "The devil taketh him up into an exceeding high mountain, and showeth him all the kingdoms of the world, and the glory of them; and saith unto him, All these things will I give thee, if thou wilt fall down and worship me. Then saith Jesus unto him, Get thee behind me, Satan."

It is difficult, as a leading scholar of this period writes, to "quite convey the atmosphere" of the times. Beveridge's amazing pastiche of pomposity and pride, racism and righteousness, commercialism and credulity clearly caught the prevailing mood and conveys the nature of the pressure McKinley faced. Old men like Hoar might think "the sentiments of the speech were treason to the Republic of the Fathers." But as a correspondent wrote to McKinley two years earlier, "If what I hear and what I read is true there is a tremendous party growing up for expansion of territory, especially by the younger and more active elements in the country." Beveridge, like Roosevelt and Lodge, caught youth's fancy. Broader experience was to bring misgivings. In 1907, for example, T.R., as President, advised his Secretary of War, William Howard Taft, under whose jurisdiction the Philippines remained:

> The Philippines form our heel of Achilles. They are all that makes the present situation with Japan dangerous. . . . I think that to have some pretty clear avowal of our intention not to permanently keep them and to give them independence would remove a temptation from Japan's way.

But in 1900, Beveridge's self-righteous certainties carried the day.

*January 9, 1900*

# Senator Albert J. Beveridge's Speech
# on Retaining the Philippine Islands

Mr. President, the times call for candor. The Philippines are ours forever, "territory belonging to the United States," as the Constitution calls them. And just beyond the Philippines are China's illimitable markets. We will not retreat from either. We will not repudiate our duty in the archipelago. We will not abandon our opportunity in the Orient. We will not renounce our part in the mission of our race, trustee, under God, of the civilization of the world. And we will move forward to our work, not howling out regrets like slaves whipped to their burdens, but with gratitude for a task worthy of our strength, and thanksgiving to Almighty God that He has marked us as His chosen people, henceforth to lead in the regeneration of the world.

This island empire is the last land left in all the oceans. . . . Our largest trade henceforth must be with Asia. The Pacific is our ocean. . . . China is our natural customer. She is nearer to us than to England, Germany, or Russia, the commercial powers of the present and the future. They have moved nearer to China by securing permanent bases on her borders. The Philippines give us a base at the door of all the East. . . . They are a self-supporting, dividend-paying fleet, permanently anchored at a spot selected by the strategy of Providence, commanding the Pacific. And the Pacific is the ocean of the commerce of the future. Most future wars will be conflicts for commerce. The power that rules the Pacific, therefore, is the power that rules the world. And with the Philippines, that power is and will forever be the American Republic.

China's trade is the mightiest commercial fact in our future. Her foreign commerce was $285,738,300 in 1897, of which we, her neighbor, had less than 9 per cent, of which only a little more than half was merchandise sold to China by us. We ought to have 50 per cent, and we will. And China's foreign commerce is only beginning. . . .

And yet American statesmen plan to surrender this commercial throne of the Orient where Providence and our soldiers' lives have placed us. When history comes to write the story of that suggested treason to American supremacy and therefore to the spread of American civilization, let her in mercy write that those who so proposed were merely blind and nothing more.

But if they did not command China, India, the Orient, the whole Pacific for purposes of offense, defense, and trade, the Philippines are so valuable in themselves that we should hold them. I have cruised more than 2,000 miles through the archipelago, every moment a surprise at its loveliness and wealth. I have ridden hundreds of miles on the islands, every foot of the way a revelation of vegetable and mineral riches. . . . The wood of the Philippines can supply the furniture of the world for a century to come. At Cebu the best informed man in the island told me that 40 miles of Cebu's mountain chain are practically mountains of coal. . . . I have a nugget of pure gold picked up in its present form on the banks of a Philippine creek. I have gold dust washed out by crude processes of careless natives from the sands of a Philippine stream. Both indicate great deposits at the source from which they come. In one of the islands great deposits of copper exist untouched. The mineral wealth of this empire of the ocean will one day surprise the world. . . .

The Philippines are beautiful and rich, with the healing seas pouring round and through them and fanned by a thousand winds. Even in the hottest season, under severest conditions, I found the weather tolerable and often delightful. . . . The European business men of Cebu, Iloilo, and Manila work as hard and as many hours a day as those of New York, and a finer body of physical manhood cannot be gathered at random in America. This proves that this garden of the seas is not the sweltering, steaming, miasmatic swamp it has been described.

It will be hard for Americans who have not studied them to understand the people. They are a barbarous race, modified by three centuries of contact with a decadent race. The Filipino is the South Sea Malay, put through a process of three hundred years of superstition in religion, dishonesty in dealing, disorder in habits of industry, and cruelty, caprice, and corruption in government. It is barely possible that 1,000 men in all the archipelago are capable of self-government in the Anglo-Saxon sense. My own belief is that there are not 100 men among them who comprehend what Anglo-Saxon self-government even means, and there are over 5,000,-000 people to be governed. . . .

Here, then, Senators, is the situation. Two years ago there was no land in all the world which we could occupy for any purpose. Our commerce was daily turning toward the Orient, and geography and trade developments made necessary our commercial empire over the Pacific. And in that ocean we had no commercial, naval, or military base. Today we have one of the three great ocean possessions of the globe, located at the most commanding commercial, naval, and military points in the eastern seas, within hail of India, shoulder to shoulder with China, richer in its own resources than any equal body of land on the entire globe, and peopled by a race which civilization demands shall be improved. Shall we abandon it? That man little knows the common people of the Republic, little understands the instincts of our race, who thinks we will not hold it fast and hold it forever, administering just government by simplest methods. . . .

But, Senators, it would be better to abandon this combined garden and Gibraltar of the Pacific, and count our blood and treasure already spent a profitable loss, than to apply any academic arrangement of self-government to these children. They are not capable of self-government. How could they be? They are not of a self-governing race. They are Orientals, Malays, instructed by Spaniards in the latter's worst estate.

They know nothing of practical government except as they have witnessed the weak, corrupt, cruel, and capricious rule of Spain. What magic will anyone employ to dissolve in their minds and characters those impressions of governors and governed which three centuries of misrule has created? What alchemy will change the oriental quality of their blood and set the self-governing currents of the American pouring through their Malay veins? How shall they, in the twinkling of an eye, be exalted to the heights of self-governing peoples which required a thousand years for us to reach, Anglo-Saxons though we are? . . . Self-government is no base and common thing, to be bestowed on the merely audacious. It is the degree which crowns the graduate of liberty, not the name of liberty's infant class, who have not yet mastered the alphabet of freedom. Savage blood, oriental blood, Malay blood, Spanish example—are those the elements of self-government?

We must act on the situation as it exists, not as we would wish it. . . .

Example for decades will be necessary to instruct them in American ideas and methods of administration. Example, example, always example—this alone will teach them. As a race, their general ability is not excellent. Educators, both men and women, to whom I have talked in Cebu and Luzon, were unanimous in the opinion that in all solid and useful education they are, as a people, dull and stupid. . . .

No one need fear their competition with our labor. No reward could beguile, no force compel, these children of indolence to leave their trifling lives for the fierce and fervid industry of high-wrought America. The very reverse is the fact. One great problem is the necessary labor to develop these islands. . . . Ultimately, when the real truth of the climate and human conditions is known, it is barely possible that our labor will go there. Even now young men with the right moral fiber and a little capital can make fortunes there as planters.

But the natives will not come here. Let all men dismiss that fear. . . .

Mr. President, self-government and internal development have been the dominant notes of our first century; administration and the development of other lands will be the dominant notes of our second century. . . . The Declaration of Independence does not forbid us to do our part in the regeneration of the world. If it did, the Declaration would be wrong, just as the Articles of Confederation, drafted by the very same men who signed the Declaration, was found to be wrong. The Declaration has no application to the present situation. It was written by self-governing men for self-governing men.

It was written by men who, for a century and a half, had been experimenting in self-government on this continent, and whose ancestors for hundreds of years before had been gradually developing toward that high and holy estate. The Declaration applies only to people capable of self-government. How dare any man prostitute this expression of the very elect of self-governing peoples to a race of Malay children of barbarism, schooled in Spanish methods and ideas? And you, who say the Declaration applies to all men, how dare you deny its application to the American Indian? And if you deny it to the Indians at home, how dare you grant it to the Malay abroad? . . .

Senators in opposition are estopped from denying our constitutional power to govern the Philippines as circumstances may demand, for such power is admitted in the case of Florida, Louisiana, Alaska. How, then, is it denied in the Philippines? Is there a geographical interpretation to the Constitution? Do degrees of longitude fix constitutional limitations? Does a thousand miles of ocean diminish constitutional power more than a thousand miles of land?

The ocean does not separate us from the field of our duty and endeavor—it joins us, an established highway needing no repair, and landing us at any point desired. . . . No; the oceans are not limitations of the power which the Constitution expressly gives Congress to govern all territory the nation may acquire. . . . The founders of the nation were not provincial. Theirs was the geography of the world. They were soldiers as well as landsmen, and they knew that where our ships should go our flag might follow. They had the logic of progress, and they knew that the Republic they were planting must, in obedience to the laws of our expanding race, necessarily develop into the greater Republic which the world beholds to-day, and into the still mightier Republic which the world will finally acknowledge as the arbiter, under God, of the destinies of mankind. And so our fathers wrote into the Constitution these words of growth, of expansion, of empire, if you will, unlimited by geography or climate or by anything but the vitality and possibilities of the American people: "Congress shall have power to dispose of and make all needful rules and regulations respecting the territory belonging to the United States." . . .

Power to administer government anywhere and in any manner the situation demands would have been in Congress if the Constitution had been silent; not merely because it is a power inherent in and an attribute of nationality; not even because it might be inferred from other specific provisions of the Constitution; but because it is the power most necessary for the ruling tendency of our race—the tendency to explore, expand, and grow, to sail new seas and seek new lands, subdue the wilderness, revitalize decaying peoples, and plant civilized and civilizing governments over all the globe. . . . You cannot interpret a constitution without understanding the race that wrote it. And if our fathers had intended a reversal of the very nature and being of their race, they would have so declared in the most emphatic words our language holds. But they did not. . . .

Mr. President, this question is deeper than any question of party politics; deeper than any question of the isolated policy of our country even; deeper even than any question of constitutional power. It is elemental. It is racial. God has not been preparing the English-speaking and Teutonic peoples for a thousand years for nothing but vain and idle self-contemplation and self-admiration. No! He has made us the master organizers of the world to establish system where chaos reigns. He has given us the spirit of progress to overwhelm the forces of reaction throughout the earth. He has made us adepts in government that we may administer government among savage and senile peoples. Were it not for such a force as this the world would relapse into barbarism and night. And of all our race He has marked the American people as His chosen nation to finally lead in the regeneration of the world. This is the divine mission of America, and it holds for us all the profit, all the glory, all the happiness possible to man. We are trustees of the world's progress, guardians of its righteous peace. The judgment of the Master is upon us: "Ye have been faithful over a few things; I will make you ruler over many things."

What shall history say of us? Shall it say that we renounced that holy trust, left the savage to his base condition, the wilderness to the reign of waste, deserted duty, abandoned glory, forgot our sordid profit even, because we feared our strength and read the charter of our powers with the doubter's eye and the quibbler's mind? Shall it say that, called by events to captain and command the proudest, ablest, purest race of history in history's noblest work, we declined that great commission? Our fathers would not have had it so. No! They founded no paralytic government, incapable of the simplest acts of administration. They planted no sluggard people, passive while the world's work calls them. They established no reactionary nation. They unfurled no retreating flag.

That flag has never paused in its onward march. Who dares halt it now —now, when history's largest events are carrying it forward; now, when we are at last one people, strong enough for any task, great enough for any glory destiny can bestow? How comes it that our first century closed with the process of consolidating the American people into a unit just accomplished, and quick upon the stroke of that great hour presses upon us our world opportunity, world duty, and world glory, which none but a people welded into an indivisible nation can achieve or perform?

Blind indeed is he who sees not the hand of God in events so vast, so harmonious, so benign. Reactionary indeed is the mind that perceives not that this vital people is the strongest of the saving forces of the world; that our place, therefore, is at the head of the constructing and redeeming nations of the earth; and that to stand aside while events march on is a surrender of our interests, a betrayal of our duty as blind as it is base. . . .

Mr. President and Senators, adopt the resolution offered, that peace may quickly come and that we may begin our saving, regenerating, and uplifting work. . . . How dare we delay when our soldiers' blood is flowing?

## 45

*"Chronic wrongdoing, or an impotence which results in a general loosening of the ties of civilized society, may in America, as elsewhere, ultimately require intervention by some civilized nation"*

Had Senator Beveridge given as much attention to Cuba as he had to the Philippines in the months preceding his speech on the Pacific archipelago in January, 1900 (see Document No. 44, above), he may have been less certain that the Lord had endowed Americans in particular with the divine talent of administration. In an article entitled, "American Misgovernment in Cuba," which appeared in the *North American Review* in February, 1900, Major James E. Runcie, an aide to General Leonard Wood on the island, wrote that no one in the McKinley coterie had really thought through any program for Cuba's care. As a result, for more than a year after the war with Spain, everything had to be done "as if the island had been captured the previous day." General John R. Brooke, the first United States Military Governor in Cuba, took a strictly military view of his position and waited upon Washington for political instructions which never came. His subordinate generals, the most influential of whom were Wood and James H. Wilson, had broader but conflicting concepts of their duty; and each sought primarily to unseat Brooke and impose his own ideas. The better to accomplish this, each also curried favor with receptive elements in Congress and the Cabinet, where discordant voices only added to the confusion, which McKinley himself did nothing to abate.

A fundamental source of difficulty in formulating a Cuban policy was the so-called "self-denying" Teller Amendment of April 20, 1898 (see Document No. 43, above), wherein the United States "disclaimed any disposition or intention to exercise sovereignty, jurisdiction, or control over said Island." In his annual message to Congress, December 5, 1899, McKinley declared that "the pledge contained in this resolution is of the highest honorable obligation and must be sacredly kept." But Cuba, he added, must nevertheless "be bound to us by ties of singular intimacy and strength." The Teller Amendment had gone on to say that when Cuban "pacification . . . is accomplished," the United States "asserts its determination . . . to leave the government and control of the

Island to its people." But McKinley, in his message, also added, "the destinies of Cuba are in some rightful form and manner irrevocably linked with our own." And he continued with frustrating indecisiveness: "but how and how far is for the future to determine in the ripeness of events."

From the American point of view, the United States having "captured" the island, as Major Runcie unthinkingly put it, annexation would have been the most clear-cut policy; and General Wood, who succeeded Brooke as Military Governor on December 13, 1899, was for it despite the Teller Amendment. Wood also proposed to follow annexation with "a firm and stable military government" of indefinite duration, "in the hands of men who would not hesitate to use severe measures should occasion arise." He was confident such occasions would be few. The Cubans, he said, "are a quiet people, without enough force of character to be seriously troublesome if we can only keep them moderately busy."

Orville H. Platt, Chairman of the Senate Committee on Relations with Cuba, concurred with Wood. Platt particularly regretted Congress's hasty adoption in March, 1899, of the "Foraker Amendment" to an army appropriation bill, declaring that "no property franchises or concessions of any kind whatever shall be granted . . . in the Island of Cuba during the occupation thereof by the United States." This amendment had been called forth by the speed with which speculative adventurers, eyes peeled on the high profits that might accompany the high risks in Cuba, organized to extract railroad, streetcar, electric lighting and similar monopolies from War Department officials in Washington before Cubans might resume control of their own resources. A governor of Wood's temper would have postponed such resumption and minimized the business risks. "If we had made no promises" in the Foraker Amendment, Platt said, "there would be, I think, a strong annexation sentiment among the business people of the United States."

Many of Wood's opponents, sharing the almost universal contempt in the United States for the "mongrel races" of Latin America, agreed with him that "the establishment of another Haitian Republic in the West Indies would be a serious mistake." More than he, however, they feared that annexation would quickly lead to an undesirable influx of the members of such "races" into the Anglo-Saxon mainland itself. They were also less certain of Cuban docility; and among additional reasons, they rejected annexation as likely to arouse in "Cuba libre" embarrassingly violent resistance similar to Aguinaldo's in the Philippines, and to the killing by Americans of those very people they went to war with Spain avowedly to save.

General Wilson was among the first to point the way toward the policy finally adopted, by which the United States was to have its cake of morality under the Teller commitment (which Wilson deplored as much as Wood), while at the same time enjoying the cake of control, which Wilson felt must lead to annexation in the long run.

Wilson grasped the opportunity to set forth his program when Elihu Root, on becoming McKinley's Secretary of War in August, 1899, asked the different generals in Cuba to write to him in detail on civil affairs on the island. The nub of Wilson's proposal lay in his assertion to Root that, "we have made no promises either to the Cubans or to the world at large" on the terms of a treaty which we might demand of Cuba once we fulfilled the promises we had made of independence and self-government. Wilson went on to detail his treaty terms, which were very similar to those ultimately imposed by the famous Platt Amendment (to another army appropriation bill) adopted by Congress March 1, 1901, signed by McKinley March 2, and presented in full in item "a" below. "I have not felt it necessary," Wilson wrote to Root, "to explain to you or anybody else that such a treaty as I have proposed would practically bind Cuba, hand and foot, and put her destinies absolutely within our control."

General Wood had called for a constitutional convention in Cuba, to convene in November, 1900, not only to formulate the island's basic law but at the same time, "to provide for and agree with the Government of the United States upon the relations to exist between that Government and the Government of Cuba." The convention, untrammeled, promptly went about its business of framing a constitution; but it demurred from settling relations with the United States until its own sovereign constitutional government should be seated. This stand upset Wood and Root, who almost plaintively instructed the General in February, 1900, that "the people of Cuba should desire to have incorporated in her fundamental law, provisions in substance" amounting to Wilson's proposals.

The Cuban convention had objected most strenuously to Article III of the Platt Amendment, permitting the United States to intervene in Cuban affairs at its own discretion; but pressure from Root, enhanced by economic threats, at last made the Cubans see the light. In June, 1902, the Platt Amendment was "annexed" to the Cuban constitution; and in May, 1903, it was incorporated into the permanent treaty between the United States and the island, which remained in force until May, 1934.

President McKinley was shot by an assassin on September 6, 1901, and died on September 14, when he was succeeded by the hero of San Juan Hill, Theodore Roosevelt. One of T.R.'s earliest acts was to "take Panama" from the Republic of Colombia and push forward the construction of the great canal across the isthmus which was opened to the world's commerce in August, 1914.

United States concern for control of Cuba naturally had been very much deepened by concern over the lasting safety of the canal. Similar considerations prompted the establishment of United States protectorates over Panama itself in 1903, over the Dominican Republic in 1905, over Nicaragua in 1911, and over Haiti in 1916. But Roosevelt's concern extended beyond these neighboring Caribbean lands to all of Latin America where, in the language of the day, he feared that "uncivilized" governments offered intriguing lures to the imperialist nations of Europe. The Monroe Doctrine might deter such nations from actually grasping territory in "our hemisphere"; but "uncivilized" finance might never-theless impel them to grasp control of Latin American customs receipts if the United States did not police Latin American interest and debt payments. T.R. was willing to recognize the validity of frequent European complaints against Latin American nations which did not know how to behave toward foreign financiers. To keep these complaints from snowballing into aggression, he de-cided that the United States must itself accept responsibility for "civilized" Latin American conduct. To let the Latin Americans and the world know of his willingness to accept this responsibility, Roosevelt, after unfortunate experi-ence in Venezuela and in Santo Domingo, set forth his famous corollary to the Monroe Doctrine, first in his annual message to Congress in December, 1904, and again a year later. These statements are presented below in item "b."

Roosevelt was perhaps more aware than the philosopher, William James, of the reality of international competition and the thoughtless surge of imperialist conquest. But his language in these statements, his cocksureness about right and wrong, his oozing certainty of the universality of his own values, left him as vulnerable as Beveridge to James's condemnation. In a letter to the *Boston Evening Transcript*, March 1, 1899, called forth by the war against Aguinaldo in the Philippines, James set down his own "damning indictment" of "that whole bloated idol termed 'modern civilization'," and his full estimate of the whole imperial adventure of his day:

> We gave the fighting instinct and the passion of mastery their outing . . .
> because we thought that . . . we could resume our permanent ideals and
> character when the fighting fit was done. We now see how we reckoned with-
> out our host. We see . . . what an absolute savage . . . the passion of military
> conquest always is, and how the only safeguard against the crimes to which it
> will infallibly drag the nation that gives way to it is to keep it chained
> forever. . . . Civilization is, then, the big, hollow, resounding, corrupting,
> sophisticating, confusing torrent of mere brutal momentum and irrationaliy
> that brings forth fruits like this.

**1901      1904      1905**

# The Platt Amendment
# and the Roosevelt Corollary

(a)  *The Platt Amendment, March 2, 1901*

Provided further, That in fulfillment of the declaration contained in the joint resolution approved April twen-tieth, eighteen hundred and ninety-eight, entitled, "For the recognition of the independence of the people of

Cuba . . . ," the President is hereby authorized to "leave the government and control of the island of Cuba to its people" so soon as a government shall have been established in said island under a constitution which, either as a part thereof or in an ordinance appended thereto, shall define the future relations of the United States with Cuba, substantially as follows:

I. That the Government of Cuba shall never enter into any treaty or other compact with any foreign power or powers which will impair or tend to impair the independence of Cuba, nor in any manner authorize or permit any foreign power or powers to obtain by colonization or for military or naval purposes or otherwise, lodgement in or control over any portion of said island.

II. That said Government shall not assume or contract any public debt, to pay the interest upon which, and to make reasonable sinking-fund provision for the ultimate discharge of which, the ordinary revenues of the island, after defraying the current expenses of Government shall be inadequate.

III. That the Government of Cuba consents that the United States may exercise the right to intervene for the preservation of Cuban independence, the maintenance of a government adequate for the protection of life, property, and individual liberty, and for discharging the obligations with respect to Cuba imposed by the treaty of Paris on the United States, now to be assumed and undertaken by the Government of Cuba.

IV. That all acts of the United States in Cuba during its military occupancy thereof are ratified and validated, and all lawful rights acquired thereunder shall be maintained and protected.

V. That the Government of Cuba will execute, and as far as necessary, extend, the plans already devised or other plans to be mutually agreed upon, for the sanitation of the cities of the island, to the end that a recurrence of epidemic and infectious diseases may be prevented thereby assuring protection to the people and commerce of Cuba, as well as the commerce of the Southern ports of the United States and the people residing therein.

VI. That the Isle of Pines shall be omitted from the proposed constitutional boundaries of Cuba, the title thereto being left to future adjustment by treaty.

VII. That to enable the United States to maintain the independence of Cuba, and to protect the people thereof, as well as for its own defense, the Government of Cuba will sell or lease to the United States lands necessary for coaling or naval stations at certain specified points, to be agreed upon with the President of the United States.

VIII. That by way of further assurance the Government of Cuba will embody the foregoing provisions in a permanent treaty with the United States.

## (b)  *The Roosevelt Corollary to the Monroe Doctrine, 1904, 1905*

FROM ROOSEVELT'S ANNUAL MESSAGE, DECEMBER 6, 1904

It is not true that the United States feels any land hunger or entertains any projects as regards the other nations of the Western Hemisphere save such as are for their welfare. All that this country desires is to see the neighboring countries stable, orderly, and prosperous. Any country whose people conduct themselves well can count upon our hearty friendship. If a nation shows that it knows how to act with reasonable efficiency and decency in social and political matters, if it keeps order and pays its obligations, it need fear no interference from the United States. Chronic wrongdoing, or an impotence which results in a general loosening of the ties of civilized society, may in

America, as elsewhere, ultimately require intervention by some civilized nation, and in the Western Hemisphere the adherence of the United States to the Monroe Doctrine may force the United States, however reluctantly, in flagrant cases of such wrongdoing or impotence, to the exercise of an international police power. If every country washed by the Caribbean Sea would show the progress in stable and just civilization which with the aid of the Platt amendment Cuba has shown since our troops left the island, and which so many of the republics in both Americas are constantly and brilliantly showing, all question of interference by this Nation with their affairs would be at an end.

Our interests and those of our southern neighbors are in reality identical. They have great natural riches, and if within their borders the reign of law and justice obtains, prosperity is sure to come to them. While they thus obey the primary laws of civilized society they may rest assured that they will be treated by us in a spirit of cordial and helpful sympathy. We would interfere with them only in the last resort, and then only if it became evident that their inability or unwillingness to do justice at home and abroad had violated the rights of the United States or had invited foreign aggression to the detriment of the entire body of American nations. It is a mere truism to say that every nation, whether in America or anywhere else, which desires to maintain its freedom, its independence, must ultimately realize that the right of such independence cannot be separated from the responsibility of making good use of it.

In asserting the Monroe Doctrine, in taking such steps as we have taken in regard to Cuba, Venezuela, and Panama, and in endeavoring to circumscribe the theater of war in the Far East, and to secure the open door in China, we have acted in our own interest as well as in the interest of humanity at large. There are, however, cases in which, while our own interests are not greatly involved, strong appeal is made to our sympathies. Ordinarily it is very much wiser and more useful for us to concern ourselves with striving for our own moral and material betterment here at home than to concern ourselves with trying to better the condition of things in other nations. We have plenty of sins of our own to war against, and under ordinary circumstances we can do more for the general uplifting of humanity by striving with heart and soul to put a stop to civic corruption, to brutal lawlessness and violent race prejudices here at home than by passing resolutions about wrongdoing elsewhere. Nevertheless there are occasional crimes committed on so vast a scale and of such peculiar horror as to make us doubt whether it is not our manifest duty to endeavor at least to show our disapproval of the deed and our sympathy with those who have suffered by it.

The cases must be extreme in which such a course is justifiable. There must be no effort made to remove the mote from our brother's eye if we refuse to remove the beam from our own. But in extreme cases action may be justifiable and proper. What form the action shall take must depend upon the circumstances of the case; that is, upon the degree of the atrocity and upon our power to remedy it. The cases in which we could interfere by force of arms as we interfered to put a stop to intolerable conditions in Cuba are necessarily very few.

FROM ROOSEVELT'S ANNUAL MESSAGE, DECEMBER 5, 1905

One of the most effective instruments for peace is the Monroe Doctrine as it has been and is being gradually developed by this Nation and accepted by other nations. No other policy could have been as efficient in promoting peace in the Western Hemisphere and in giving to each nation therein the chance to develop along its own lines.

If we had refused to apply the doctrine to changing conditions it would now be completely outworn, would not meet any of the needs of the present day, and, indeed, would probably by this time have sunk into complete oblivion. . . .

There are certain essential points which must never be forgotten as regards the Monroe Doctrine. In the first place we must as a Nation make it evident that we do not intend to treat it in any shape or way as an excuse for aggrandizement on our part at the expense of the republics to the south. . . . It must be understood that under no circumstances will the United States use the Monroe Doctrine as a cloak for territorial aggression. We desire peace with all the world, but perhaps most of all with the other peoples of the American Continent. There are, of course, limits to the wrongs which any self-respecting nation can endure. It is always possible that wrong actions toward this Nation, or toward citizens of this Nation, in some State unable to keep order among its own people, unable to secure justice from outsiders, and unwilling to do justice to those outsiders who treat it well, may result in our having to take action to protect our rights; but such action will not be taken with a view to territorial aggression, and it will be taken at all only with extreme reluctance and when it has become evident that every other resource has been exhausted.

Moreover, we must make it evident that we do not intend to permit the Monroe Doctrine to be used by any nation on this Continent as a shield to protect it from the consequences of its own misdeeds against foreign nations. If a republic to the south of us commits a tort against a foreign nation, such as an outrage against a citizen of that nation, then the Monroe Doctrine does not force us to interfere to prevent punishment of the tort, save to see that the punishment does not assume the form of territorial occupation in any shape. The case is more difficult when it refers to a contractual obligation. Our own Government has always refused to enforce such contractual obligations on behalf of its citizens by an appeal to arms. It is much to be wished that all foreign governments would take the same view. But they do not; and in consequence we are liable at any time to be brought to face with disagreeable alternatives. On the one hand, this country would certainly decline to go to war to prevent a foreign government from collecting a just debt; on the other hand, it is very inadvisable to permit any foreign power to take possession, even temporarily, of the custom houses of an American Republic in order to enforce the payment of its obligations; for such temporary occupation might turn into a permanent occupation. The only escape from these alternatives may at any time be that we must ourselves undertake to bring about some arrangement by which so much as possible of a just obligation shall be paid. It is far better that this country should put through such an arrangement, rather than allow any foreign country to undertake it. To do so insures the defaulting republic from having to pay debt of an improper character under duress, while it also insures honest creditors of the republic from being passed by in the interest of dishonest or grasping creditors. Moreover, for the United States to take such a position offers the only possible way of insuring us against a clash with some foreign power. The position is, therefore, in the interest of peace as well as in the interest of justice. It is of benefit to our people; it is of benefit to foreign peoples; and most of all it is really of benefit to the people of the country concerned.

# 46

## *"We take judicial cognizance of all matters of general knowledge"*

In February, 1903, the State of Oregon passed a law providing that, "no female (shall) be employed in any mechanical establishment, or factory, or laundry in this State more than ten hours during any one day." This law, as Louis D. Brandeis pointed out to the United States Supreme Court in defending its constitutionality in 1908, was one of twenty on the subject of women's hours passed by different states in all sections of the country during the previous thirty years, and one of eight also passed by the leading industrial nations of Europe over a longer period. None of these laws had ever been repealed; and when amended on the basis of experience, such action had always been taken to strengthen rather than weaken existing legislation. Only one such act in the United States, moreover, had been declared unconstitutional by a state supreme court as an indefensible infringement by state police power of the liberty of workers freely to contract for their labor under the "privileges and immunities," "due process" and "equal opportunity" clauses of section one of the Fourteenth Amendment. This was the eight-hour act for women in manufacturing enterprises passed by Illinois in 1893 and thrown out by its highest tribunal in the case of *Ritchie* v. *People* in 1895.

As the federal Judicial Code stood at the time of the *Ritchie* decision (and continued to stand until 1914), cases in which the constitutionality of state legislation was *denied* by the highest state tribunals could not be appealed to the United States Supreme Court. Such cases ended where the *Ritchie* case did— in the highest state courts; yet they did serve as minatory examples if not as formal precedents to legislatures and courts in other states. Decisions in which the constitutionality of state laws was *upheld* by the highest state tribunals could be appealed to the United States Supreme Court whose pronouncements decided the law of the land.

The conviction of a steam laundry operator in Portland, Oregon, Curt Muller, under the Oregon law of 1903 was upheld by the Oregon Supreme Court in 1905, and Muller promptly appealed the ruling to the United States Supreme Court. Until then, this Court had had occasion only in two cases to pass upon the voluminous "hours" legislation of the Progressive era. Neither of these cases concerned women's hours. The Court's decisions, while technically irrelevant to one another because of special circumstances in each instance, also appeared to be contradictory. Thus the standing of the widespread legislation on women's hours and on hours legislation in general were at issue in *Muller* v. *Oregon*, the subject of this Document.

Special consideration for women was sustained in *Muller* v. *Oregon* largely because of Brandeis's extraordinary brief for the State, for which the Court took the unusual step of commending counsel by name. The grounds supplied by Brandeis for sustaining women's hours legislation also helped clarify the conditions on which hours legislation for men might also be upheld.

In the first of the two cases decided earlier by the Court, *Holden* v. *Hardy* in 1898, the Justices (with but two dissenters) affirmed the decision of the Utah Supreme Court in sustaining, for the first time in the United States, a state law limiting to eight per day the hours men might work in "underground mines and in smelters and ore reduction works." Such legislation, the United States Supreme Court held, because of exceptional hazards in the jobs covered, was a proper exercise of state police power, "for the purpose of preserving the public health, safety, or morals." But the Court moved remarkably farther ahead, noting as an additional justification for state intervention on the worker's behalf the exceptional strength of his employers. "In passing upon the validity of state legislation under the Fourteenth Amendment," the majority said, "this court has not failed to recognize the fact that the law is to a certain extent a progressive science." As such, it may look to life as well as to law. In law, contracting parties are deemed to be equal and unfettered. In life, in the modern industrial age,

> The legislature has also recognized the fact, which the experience of legislators in many other states has corroborated, that the proprietors of these establishments and their operators do not stand upon an equality, and that their interests are, to a certain extent, conflicting. The former naturally desire to obtain as much labor as possible from their employees, while the latter are often induced by the fear of discharge to conform to regulations which their judgement, fairly exercised, would pronounce to be detrimental to their health or strength. In other words, the proprietors lay down the rules and the laborers are practically constrained to obey them. In such cases self-interest is often an unsafe guide, and the legislature may properly interpose its authority.

The spirit of the *Holden* decision did not carry over to 1905, when the Supreme Court handed down its second hours decision. By a 5 to 4 margin in the case of *Lochner* v. *New York* that year, the Court overruled the state Court of Appeals which had sustained a 10-hour law for bakers. "There is nothing in *Holden* v. *Hardy*," said the Supreme Court majority, "which covers the case now before us. . . . We think the limit of the police power has been reached and passed in this case."

The disabilities of the New York bakers were not as manifest to the justices as those of the Utah miners. Had they been, the Court acknowledged that it might have ruled differently. Had there been "some fair ground, reasonable in and of itself, to say that there is material danger to the public health, or to the health of the employees, if the hours of labor are not curtailed," then the New York law and the Court of Appeals' finding might have survived.

In offering his brief in *Muller* v. *Oregon*, Brandeis seized upon the realism of the *Holden* decision and this loophole in the *Lochner* decision to carry his case. In his 112-page presentation to the Court, he gave a scant two pages to the usual legal "argument" and "authorities." The rest of his brief consisted of historical, sociological, economic, and medical "facts" providing "some fair ground, reasonable in and of itself," on which the Court might find excessively long working hours for women sufficiently injurious to "the public health, safety, or welfare" to warrant limitation by the states. These "facts" swayed even the most conservative justices. As Justice David J. Brewer, who had dissented from the *Holden* decision and who had supported the *Lochner* ruling, said for the Court, "the legislation and opinions" offered by Brandeis,

> . . . may not be, technically speaking, authorities, and in them is little or no discussion of the constitutional question presented to us for determination. . . . At the same time, when a question of fact is debated and debatable, and the extent to which a special constitutional limitation goes is affected by the truth in respect to that fact, a widespread and long continued belief concerning it is worthy of consideration. We take judicial cognizance of all matters of general knowledge.

Following the decision in *Muller* v. *Oregon* the Supreme Court of Illinois, in the so-called second *Ritchie* case of 1910, reversed its earlier finding. In the next few years, 39 states either enacted new legislation governing women's work or strengthened existing laws. In the famous case of *Bunting* v. *Oregon* in 1917, on the basis of a brief almost a thousand pages long modeled on Brandeis's earlier one, the Supreme Court also upheld a 10-hour law for men. On the basis of similar briefs it also sustained legislation on minimum wages and other labor problems. But there were setbacks ahead.

The *Muller* case did not inaugurate a lasting liberal tradition in the United States Supreme Court; much that was not done was pointed out by Theodore Roosevelt himself in his equivalent of a farewell address presented below in Document No. 47. But Brandeis's revolutionary brief offered a method by which liberal counsel might sway even the most illiberal of judges from time to time and thereby keep open what Brandeis, in his brilliant essay on "The Living Law" (1916) called "the natural vent of legislation." When this vent was closed, respect for law waned. The men of the Progressive era had a profound respect for law; one of their weaknesses was their expectation that reform would follow hard upon the enactment of social legislation; one source of their disenchantment was the recalcitrance of the courts. Brandeis, in *Muller* v. *Oregon*, showed how such recalcitrance might be overcome. Beyond that, he looked to the education of lawyers in economics and other social sciences, as well as in the "logic of precedents," to enlarge counsels' grasp of reality and thereby enlarge that of the highest tribunals themselves.

*February 24, 1908*

# Muller *v.* Oregon

MR. JUSTICE BREWER delivered the opinion of the Court.

On February 19, 1903, the legislature of the State of Oregon passed an act (Session Laws, 1908, p. 148) the first section of which is in these words:

"Sec. 1. That no female (shall) be employed in any mechanical establishment, or factory, or laundry in this State more than ten hours during any one day. The hours of work may be so arranged as to permit the employment of females at any time so that they shall not work more than ten hours during the twenty-four hours of any one day."
. . .

The single question is the constitutionality of the statute under which the defendant was convicted so far as it affects the work of a female in a laundry. That it does not conflict with any provisions of the State constitution is settled by the decision of the Supreme Court of the State. The contentions of the defendant, now plaintiff in error, are thus stated in his brief:

"(1) Because the statute attempts to prevent persons, *sui juris*, from making their own contracts, and thus violates the provisions of the Fourteenth Amendment, as follows;

" 'No State shall make or enforce any law which shall abridge the privileges or immunities of citizens of the United States; nor shall any State deprive any person of life, liberty, or property, without due process of law; nor deny to any person within its jurisdiction the equal protection of the laws.'

"(2) Because the statute does not apply equally to all persons similarly situated, and is class legislation.

"(3) The statute is not a valid exercise of the police power. The kinds of work prescribed are not unlawful, nor are they declared to be immoral or dangerous to the public health; nor can such a law be sustained on the ground that it is designed to protect women on account of their sex. There is no necessary or reasonable connection between the limitation prescribed by the act and the public health, safety, or welfare."

It is the law of Oregon that women, whether married or single, have equal contractual and personal rights with men. . . . Their rights in these respects can no more be infringed than the equal rights of their brothers. We held in *Lochner* v. *New York*, 198 U.S. 45, that a law providing that no laborer shall be required or permitted to work in bakeries more than sixty hours in a week or ten hours in a day was not as to men a legitimate exercise of the police power of the State, but an unreasonable, unnecessary, and arbitrary interference with the right and liberty of the individual to contract in relation to his labor, and as such was in conflict with, and void under the Federal Constitution. That decision is invoked by plaintiff in error as decisive of the question before us. But this assumes that the difference between the sexes does not justify a different rule respecting a restriction of the hours of labor.

In patent cases counsel are apt to open the argument with a discussion of the state of the art. It may not be amiss, in the present case, before examining the constitutional question, to notice the course of legislation as well as expressions of opinion from other than judicial sources. In the brief filed by Mr. Louis D. Brandeis, for the defendant in error, is a very copious collection of all these matters, an epitome of which is found in the margin. . . .

The legislation and opinions referred to in the margin may not be, technically speaking, authorities, and in them is little or no discussion of the constitutional question presented to us for determination, yet they are significant of a widespread belief that woman's physical structure, and the functions she performs in consequence thereof, justify special legislation restricting or qualifying the conditions under which she should be permitted to toil. Constitutional questions, it is true, are not settled by even a consensus of present public opinion, for it is the peculiar value of a written constitution that it places in unchanging form limitations upon legislative action, and thus gives a permanence and stability to popular government which otherwise would be lacking. At the same time, when a question of fact is debated and debatable, and the extent to which a special constitutional limitation goes is affected by the truth in respect to that fact, a widespread and long continued belief concerning it is worthy of consideration. We take judicial cognizance of all matters of general knowledge.

It is undoubtedly true, as more than once declared by this court, that the general right to contract in relation to one's business is part of the liberty of the individual, protected by the Fourteenth Amendment to the Federal Constitution; yet it is equally well settled that this liberty is not absolute and extending to all contracts, and that a State may, without conflicting with the provisions of the Fourteenth Amendment, restrict in many respects the individual's power of contract. Without stopping to discuss at length the extent to which a State may act in this respect, we refer to the following cases in which the question has been considered: *Allgeyer v. Louisiana,* 165 U.S. 578; *Holden v. Hardy,* 169 U.S. 366; *Lochner v. New York, supra.*

That woman's physical structure and the performance of maternal functions place her at a disadvantage in the struggle for subsistence is obvious. This is especially true when the burdens of motherhood are upon her. Even when they are not, by abundant testimony of the medical fraternity continuance for a long time on her feet at work, repeating this from day to day, tends to injurious effects upon the body, and as healthy mothers are essential to vigorous offspring, the physical well-being of woman becomes an object of public interest and care in order to preserve the strength and vigor of the race.

Still again, history discloses the fact that woman has always been dependent upon man. He established his control at the outset by superior physical strength, and this control in various forms, with diminishing intensity, has continued to the present. As minors, though not to the same extent, she has been looked upon in the courts as needing especial care that her rights may be preserved. Education was long denied her, and while now the doors of the school-room are opened and her opportunities for acquiring knowledge are great, yet even with that and the consequent increase of capacity for business affairs it is still true that in the struggle for subsistence she is not an equal competitor with her brother.

Though limitations upon personal and contractual rights may be removed by legislation, there is that in her disposition and habits of life which will operate against a full assertion of those rights. She will still be where some legislation to protect her seems necessary to secure a real equality of right. Doubtless there are individual exceptions, and there are many respects in which she has an advantage over him; but looking at it from the viewpoint of the effort to maintain an independent position in life, she is not upon an equality. Differentiated by these matters from the other sex, she is properly placed in a class by herself, and legislation designed for her protection may be sustained, even when like legislation is not necessary for men and could not be sustained. It is impossible to close one's eyes to the fact that she still looks to her brother and depends upon him. Even though all restrictions on political, personal, and contractual rights were taken away, and she stood, so far as statutes are concerned, upon an absolutely equal plane with him, it would still be true that she is so constituted that she will rest upon and look to him for protection; that her physical structure and a proper discharge of her maternal functions—having in view not merely her own health, but the well-being of the race—justify legislation to protect her from the greed as well as the passion of man.

The limitations which this statute places upon her contractual powers, upon her right to agree with her employer as to the time she shall labor, are not imposed solely for her benefit, but also largely for the benefit of all. Many words cannot make this plainer.

The two sexes differ in structure of body, in the functions to be performed by each, in the amount of physical strength, in the capacity for long-continued labor, particularly when done standing, the influence of vigorous health upon the future well-being of the race, the self-reliance which enables one to assert full rights, and in the capacity to maintain the struggle for subsistence. This difference justifies a difference in legislation and upholds that which is designed to compensate for some of the burdens which rest upon her. . . .

For these reasons, and without questioning in any respect the decision in *Lochner* v. *New York*, we are of the opinion that it cannot be adjudged that the act in question is in conflict with the Federal Constitution, so far as it respects the work of a female in a laundry, and the judgment of the Supreme Court of Oregon is *Affirmed*.

47

*"For the peaceful progress of our people during the twentieth century we shall owe most to those judges who hold a twentieth century economic and social philosophy"*

In the presidential election of 1904, Theodore Roosevelt won by a popular majority of more than two and a half million votes, "by far the largest popular majority" he noted in his *Autobiography*, "ever hitherto given any Presidential candidate." Awed, for once, by this stunning show of confidence on the part of the common man in the (then) youngest president in history, T.R., but one day after the election, made an impulsive purifying commitment he was promptly to regret:

On the fourth of March next I shall have served three and a half years, and this three and a half years constitutes my first term. The wise custom which limits the President to two terms regards the substance not the form. Under no circumstances will I be a candidate for or accept another nomination.

Just because he so obviously thrived on power and so openly acknowledged its attractions, T.R. felt obliged, at the very moment of his triumph, to deny the Democratic assertions that his "supposed personal ambition" would lead him to perpetuate himself in office. He had withheld his renunciation during the campaign, he added, because he did not wish to blemish it by having it "construed into a promise offered as a consideration in order to secure votes."

Almost from the start of his second administration, T.R. and his well-wishers were preoccupied with what he was to do when, barely fifty, he would be obliged to leave the White House in March, 1909. Only a year after T.R.'s inauguration, Nicholas Murray Butler, the President of Columbia University who fancied himself a "real friend" and a force in politics, urged Roosevelt, like a true Roman, to run for the Senate. Senators at this time still were elected by state legislatures (a situation Roosevelt himself deplored) and did not have to truckle to the mob in order to gain their seats. For this reason, Butler, like certain other respectable progressives who cared as little for the people as they did for the plutocrats, held the aloof upper house in higher esteem than the presidency. On joining it, Butler said, T.R. would provide, "on March 4, 1909, the unprecedented and dramatic spectacle of the outgoing President taking the oath of office as Senator before proceeding with his successor . . . to hear the inaugural address."

Nothing came of this proposal, nor of many others. "I do not think I can undertake reminiscences," Roosevelt told the editor of *Century* magazine in February, 1908, " and I do not want to go around the world; and I won't be Mayor or Senator!" A few months later, after he had decided on his African big-game safari, he thought, if there were to be a war on his return, he would "certainly try to raise a brigade, and if possible a division of cavalry," like the Rough Riders. If the war he clearly foresaw were still a few years off, he would go on "fighting for political, social and industrial reforms." The substance of these he spelled out in what amounted to his farewell address, his last annual message to Congress, December 8, 1908. This message, as the Washington *Post* said, "looks forward and not back." It is presented in part in this Document.

T.R.'s well-wishers were especially concerned about his future because they feared for his judgment, "coupled with such enormous energy," when he was released from the constraints of office and the discipline of having to deal with recalcitrant Congresses. Their direst apprehensions soon were confirmed. T.R. returned to New York from his African trip in June, 1910. Within ten weeks, when the congressional election campaigns had begun to boil, he set out on his swing through the West where he gave the rousing series of speeches on the "welfare state" known as the *New Nationalism*: "The object of government is the welfare of the people." "This New Nationalism regards the executive power as the steward of the public welfare. It demands of the judiciary that it shall be interested primarily in human welfare rather than in property." "Property shall be the servant and not the master of the commonwealth." "The essence of any struggle for healthy liberty has always been, and must always be, to take from some one man or class of men the right to enjoy power, or wealth, or position, or immunity, which has not been earned by service to his or their fellows." "When I say that I am for the square deal, I mean not merely that I stand for fair play under the present rules of the game, but that I stand for having those rules changed so as to work for a more substantial equality of opportunity." "Our country—this great republic—means nothing unless it means the triumph of a real democracy, the triumph of popular government, and, in the long run of an economic system under which each man shall be guaranteed the opportunity to show the best that there is in him."

These statements are from T.R.'s early speech at Osawatomie, Kansas, August 31, 1910. Thereafter, as more and more of the sacred cows of McKinleyism and materialism fell before him, his respectable friends slunk away. Butler was shocked by T.R.'s assaults on business, Henry Cabot Lodge by his advocacy of majoritarianism, Elihu Root by his temerity to question the value of "judicial review," President Taft, his hand-picked successor, by his "ego," "swell-headedness," and "wild ideas" in general. "In most of his speeches he utterly ignored me," Taft complained to his brother. "He is at the head of the insurgents, and for the time being the insurgents are at the top of the way, . . . and they may carry Washington."

Henry Adams observed at this time that, "even so clear-headed a man as Root thinks that Theodore has not the Presidency in his mind, but that he aims at a leadership far in the future, as a sort of Moses and Messiah for a vast progressive tide of a rising humanity." Root was at least half right. For every eastern "respectable" who fled the zealot, a genuine western "progressive" rallied to his cause. "Taft," said Roosevelt a few months after his triumphant tour, "is a flubdub with a streak of the second-rate and the common in him, and he has not the slightest idea of what is necessary if this country is to make social and industrial progress." As the administration floundered, the progressive tide gained the momentum of a crusade, the New Nationalism on its banners, T.R. at its head.

And yet it was without a doubt a yearning for the presidency once again and not some vague evangelism that directed T.R.'s course once he felt he had honorably fulfilled his early, too earnest abjuration. In his *Autobiography* he deemed it "a duty to add this comment" on that hasty step:

> An ex-President stands precisely in the position of any other private citizen, and has not one particle more power to secure a nomination or election than if he had never held office at all. . . . Therefore the reasoning on which the

anti-third term custom is based has no application whatever to anything except consecutive terms.

When the National Progressive Republican League was formed in January, 1911, to promote the candidacy of Senator Robert M. LaFollette, T.R. found reasons not to join. Later in the year, he "did not wish to put myself in the position where, if it became my plain duty to accept [the nomination] I shall be obliged to shirk it." Early the following year, "if the people as a whole desire me, not for my sake, but for their own sake, to undertake the job, I would feel honor bound to do so."

When T.R. did make his bid in 1912, first for the Republican nomination, and when denied that by the Old Guard, as a vengeful third-party candidate, it was not on any program of irresponsible iconoclasm, but on the substantial reforms laid out in his annual message of 1908 and his earlier messages to Congress.

As Root also said in 1910, "the only real objection" to the New Nationalism was Roosevelt's calling it "new!" Few presidents had written or spoken so much as T.R. None, in his annual messages to Congress, quoted his earlier messages at such length, or repeated his own earlier thoughts so often. Roosevelt, of course, was aware of this. Much as he accomplished in office in foreign affairs, he always put domestic reform first. Much as he accomplished in such domestic matters as railroad regulation, consumer protection, and conservation, almost everything in righting the wrongs of wealth and promoting the welfare of the underprivileged remained still to be done. And nothing would be done, unless the nation's leaders—and especially the judiciary, "the chief law makers in our country"—accepted the new reality of twentieth-century economic and social life. What this meant in substance as well as in spirit he was determined at last to hammer home in his final message, and in his subsequent campaign.

*December 8, 1908*

# Theodore Roosevelt on Liberty and Property

## in an Industrial Society

*(From his last Annual Message to Congress)*

CORPORATIONS.

As regards the great corporations engaged in interstate business, and especially the railroad, I can only repeat what I have already again and again said in my messages to the Congress. I believe that under the interstate clause of the Constitution the United States has complete and paramount right to control all agencies of interstate commerce, and I believe that the National Government alone can exercise this right with wisdom and effectiveness so as both to secure justice from, and to do justice to, the great corporations which are the most important factors in modern business. I believe that it is worse than folly to attempt to prohibit all combinations as is done by the Sherman anti-trust law, because such a law can be enforced only imperfectly and unequally, and its enforcement works almost as much hardship as good. I strongly advocate that instead of an unwise effort to prohibit all combinations there shall be substituted a law which shall expressly permit combinations which are in the interest of the public, but shall at the same time give to some agency of the National Government full power of control and supervision over them, . . . not by judicial but by executive action. . . .

To permit every lawless capitalist, every law-defying corporation, to take any action, no matter how iniquitous, in the effort to secure an improper profit and to build up privilege, would be ruinous to the Republic and would mark the abandonment of the effort to secure in the industrial world the spirit of democratic fair dealing. On the other hand, to attack these wrongs in that spirit of demagogy which can see wrong only when committed by the man of wealth, and is dumb and blind in the presence of wrong committed against men of property or by men of no property, is exactly as evil as corruptly to defend the wrongdoing of men of wealth. The war we wage must be waged against misconduct, against wrongdoing wherever it is found. . . .

The effective fight against adequate Government control and supervision of individual, and especially of corporate, wealth engaged in interstate business is chiefly done under cover; and especially under cover of an appeal to State's rights. . . . The chief reason, among the many sound and compelling reasons, that led to the formation of the National Government was the absolute need that the Union, and not the several States, should deal with interstate and foreign commerce; and the power to deal with interstate commerce was granted absolutely and plenarily to the Central Government and was exercised completely as regards the only instruments of interstate commerce known in those days—the waterways, the highroads, as well as the partnerships of individuals who then conducted all of what business there was. Interstate commerce is now chiefly conducted by railroads; and the great corporation has supplanted the mass of small partnerships or individuals. The proposal to make the National Government supreme over, and therefore to give it complete control over, the railroads and other instruments of interstate commerce is merely a proposal to carry out to the letter one of the prime purposes, if not the prime purpose, for which the Constitution was founded. It does not represent centralization. It represents merely the acknowledgment of the patent fact that centralization has already come in business. . . .

Those who believe in efficient national control . . . do not in the least object to combinations; do not in the least object to concentration in business administration. On the contrary, they favor both, with the all important proviso that there shall be such publicity about their workings, and such thoroughgoing control over them, as to insure their being in the interest, and not against the interest, of the general public. . . . We believe that the administration should be for the benefit of the many; and that greed and rascality, practiced on a large scale, should be punished as relentlessly as if practiced on a small scale. . . .

We no more believe in that empiricism which demands absolutely unrestrained individualism than we do in that empiricism which clamors for a deadening socialism which would destroy all individual initiative and would ruin the country with a completeness that not even an unrestrained individualism itself could achieve. The danger to American democracy lies not in the least in the concentration of administrative power in responsible and accountable hands. It lies in having the power insufficiently concentrated, so that no one can be held responsible to the people for its use. . . . Democracy is in peril wherever the administration of political power is scattered among a variety of men who work in secret, whose very names are unknown to the common people. It is not in peril from any man who derives authority from the people, who exercises it in sight of the people, and who is from time to time compelled to give an account of its exercise to the people.

LABOR.

I believe in a steady effort, or perhaps it would be more accurate to say in steady efforts in many different directions, to bring about a condition of affairs under which the men who work with hand or with brain, the laborers, the superintendents, the men who produce for the market and the men who find a market for the articles produced, shall own a far greater share than at present of the wealth they produce, and be enabled to invest it in the tools and instruments by which all work is carried on. . . . There must be prohibition of child labor, diminution of woman labor, shortening of hours of all mechanical labor. . . . There should be a progressive inheritance tax on large fortunes. . . . It is eminently right that the Nation should fix the terms upon which the great fortunes are inherited. They rarely do good and they often do harm to those who inherit them. . . .

PROTECTION FOR WAGEWORKERS.

The above is the merest sketch, hardly even a sketch in outline, of the reforms for which we should work. But there is one matter with which the

Congress should deal at this session. There should no longer be any paltering with the question of taking care of the wageworkers who, under our present industrial system, become killed, crippled, or worn out as part of the regular incidents of a given business. . . . The object sought for could be achieved to a measurable degree, as far as those killed or crippled are concerned, by proper employers' liability laws. As far as concerns those who have been worn out, I call your attention to the fact that definite steps toward providing old-age pensions have been taken in many of our private industries. . . . To strengthen these practical measures should be our immediate duty. . . .

When a workman is injured what he needs is not an expensive and doubtful lawsuit, but the certainty of relief through immediate administrative action. The number of accidents which result in the death or crippling of wageworkers, in the Union at large, is simply appalling; in a very few years it runs up a total far in excess of the aggregate of the dead and wounded in any modern war. No academic theory about "freedom of contract" or "constitutional liberty to contract" should be permitted to interfere with this and similar movements. Progress in civilization has everywhere meant a limitation and regulation of contract. . . .

There is no good ground for the distinction made in the law between those engaged in hazardous occupations and those not so engaged. If a man is injured or killed in any line of work, it was hazardous in his case. . . . The terms of the act providing compensation should be made more liberal than in the present act. . . . In this respect the generosity of the United States towards its employees compares most unfavorably with that of every country in Europe—even the poorest.

The terms of the act are also a hardship in prohibiting payment in cases where the accident is in any way due to the negligence of the employee. It is inevitable that daily familiarity with danger will lead men to take chances that can be construed into negligence. So well is this recognized that in practically all countries in the civilized world, except the United States, only a great degree of negligence acts as a bar to securing compensation. Probably in no other respect is our legislation, both State and National, so far behind practically the entire civilized world as in the matter of liability and compensation for accidents in industry. . . .

I also renew my recommendation that the principle of the eight-hour day should as rapidly and as far as practicable be extended to the entire work being carried on by the Government; the present law should be amended to embrace contracts on those public works which the present wording of the act seems to exclude.

### THE COURTS.

At the last election certain leaders of organized labor made a violent and sweeping attack upon the entire judiciary of the country, an attack couched in such terms as to include the most upright, honest and broad-minded judges, no less than those of narrower mind and more restricted outlook. . . .

The violence of the crusade . . . and its complete failure, illustrate two truths which it is essential our people should learn. . . . "Class consciousness," where it is merely another name for the odious vice of class selfishness, is equally noxious whether in an employer's association or in a workingman's association. The movement in question was one in which the appeal was made to all workingmen to vote primarily, not as American citizens, but as individuals of a certain class in society. Such an appeal in the first place revolts the more high-minded and far-sighted among the persons to whom it is addressed, and in the second place tends to arouse a strong antagonism among all other classes of citizens, whom it therefore tends to unite against the very organization on whose behalf it is issued. The result is

therefore unfortunate from every standpoint.

The wageworkers, the workingmen, the laboring men of the country, by the way in which they repudiated the effort to get them to cast their votes in response to an appeal to class hatred, have emphasized their sound patriotism and Americanism. . . . Such an attitude is an object-lesson in good citizenship to the entire nation.

But the extreme reactionaries, the persons who blind themselves to the wrongs now and then committed by the courts on laboring men, should also think seriously as to what such a movement as this portends. The judges who have shown themselves able and willing effectively to check the dishonest activity of the very rich man who works iniquity by the mismanagement of corporations, who have shown themselves alert to do justice to the wageworker, and sympathetic with the needs of the mass of our people, so that the dweller in the tenement houses, the man who practices a dangerous trade, the man who is crushed by excessive hours of labor, feel that their needs are understood by the courts—these judges are the real bulwark of the courts. . . . The courts are jeopardized primarily by the action of those Federal and State judges who show inability or unwillingness to put a stop to the wrongdoing of very rich men under modern industrial conditions, and inability or unwillingness to give relief to men of small means or wageworkers who are crushed down by these modern industrial conditions; who, in other words, fail to understand and apply the needed remedies for the new wrongs produced by the new and highly complex social and industrial civilization which has grown up in the last half century.

The rapid changes in our social and industrial life which have attended this rapid growth have made it necessary that, in applying to concrete cases the great rule of right laid down in our Constitution, there should be a full understanding and appreciation of the new conditions to which the rules are to be applied. What would have been an infringement upon liberty half a century ago may be the necessary safeguard of liberty to-day. What would have been an injury to property then may be necessary to the enjoyment of property now.

Every judicial decision involves two terms—one, as interpretation of the law; the other, the understanding of the facts to which it is to be applied. The great mass of our judicial officers are, I believe, alive to those changes of conditions which so materially affect the performance of their judicial duties. . . . There are, however, some members of the judicial body who have lagged behind in their understanding of these great and vital changes in the body politic, whose minds have never been opened to the new applications of the old principles made necessary by the new conditions. Judges of this stamp do lasting harm by their decisions, because they convince poor men in need of protection that the courts of the land are profoundly ignorant of and out of sympathy with their needs, and profoundly indifferent or hostile to any proposed remedy. To such men it seems a cruel mockery to have any court decide against them on the ground that it desires to preserve "liberty" in a purely technical form, by withholding liberty in any real and constructive sense.

It is desirable that the legislative body should possess, and wherever necessary exercise, the power to determine whether in a given case employers and employees are not on an equal footing, so that the necessities of the latter compel them to submit to such exactions as to hours and conditions of labor as unduly tax their strength; and only mischief can result when such determination is upset on the ground that there must be no "interference with the liberty to contract"—often a merely academic "liberty," the exercise of which is the negation of real liberty.

There are certain decisions by various courts which have been exceedingly detrimental to the rights of wagework-

ers. This is true of all the decisions that decide that men and women are, by the Constitution, "guaranteed their liberty" to contract to enter a dangerous occupation, or to work an undesirable or improper number of hours, or to work in unhealthy surroundings; and therefore cannot recover damages when maimed in that occupation and cannot be forbidden to work what the legislature decides is an excessive number of hours, or to carry on the work under conditions which the legislature decides to be unhealthy. The most dangerous occupations are often the poorest paid and those where the hours of work are longest; and in many cases those who go into them are driven by necessity so great that they have practically no alternative. Decisions such as those alluded to above nullify the legislative effort to protect the wageworkers who most need protection from those employers who take advantage of their grinding need. They halt or hamper the movement for securing better and more equitable conditions of labor. The talk about preserving to the misery-hunted beings who make contracts for such service their "liberty" to make them, is either to speak in a spirit of heartless irony or else to show an utter lack of knowledge of the conditions of life among the great masses of our fellow-countrymen, a lack which unfits a judge to do good service just as it would unfit any executive or legislative officer.

There is also, I think, ground for the belief that substantial injustice is often suffered by employees in consequence of the custom of courts issuing temporary injunctions without notice to them, and punishing them for contempt of court in instances where, as a matter of fact, they have no knowledge of any proceedings. Outside of organized labor there is a widespread feeling that this system often works great injustice to wageworkers when their efforts to better their working condition result in industrial disputes. A temporary injunction procured ex parte may as a matter of fact have all the effect of a permanent injunction in causing disaster to the wageworkers' side in such a dispute. Organized labor is chafing under the unjust restraint which comes from repeated resort to this plan of procedure. Its discontent has been unwisely expressed, and often improperly expressed, but there is a sound basis for it, and the orderly and law-abiding people of a community would be in a far stronger position for upholding the courts if the undoubtedly existing abuses could be provided against. . . .

The chief lawmakers in our country may be, and often are, the judges, because they are the final seat of authority. Every time they interpret contract, property, vested rights, due process of law, liberty, they necessarily enact into law parts of a system of social philosophy; and as such interpretation is fundamental, they give direction to all law-making. The decisions of the courts on economic and social questions depend upon their economic and social

philosophy; and for the peaceful progress of our people during the twentieth century we shall owe most to those judges who hold to a twentieth century economic and social philosophy and not to a long outgrown philosophy, which was itself the product of primitive economic conditions. . . . A law may be unwise and improper; but it should not for these reasons be declared unconstitutional by a strained interpretation, for the result of such action is to take away from the people at large their sense of responsibility and ultimately to destroy their capacity for orderly self restraint and self government. Under such a popular government as ours, founded on the theory that in the long run the will of the people is supreme, the ultimate safety of the Nation can only rest in training and guiding the people so that what they will shall be right, and not in devising means to defeat their will by the technicalities of strained construction.

## 48

*"It will bring new men, new energies, a new spirit of initiative, new blood, into the management of our great business enterprises"*

Starting in mid-October, 1912, when the presidential campaign was nearing its climax, Theodore Roosevelt repeatedly reproached his Democratic opponent, Woodrow Wilson, the Governor of New Jersey, for attacking the unprecedented growth of "trusts" under recent Republican administrations. "Almost all the big trusts against which there is complaint," T.R. said, "are organized and now hold their charters in New Jersey. This is true of the Standard Oil Trust, the Tobacco Trust, the Steel Trust, the Beef Trust, and practically every other trust of importance."

Wilson retorted that "the Republican majority in the Legislature" of New Jersey had alone frustrated his trust-busting efforts.

Wilson's victory at the polls in November, 1912, carried a Democratic legislature into power in his state, and he promptly called a special session in January, 1913, to adopt his famous "Seven Sister Acts." These seven acts so curtailed business combinations that New Jersey's income from corporate franchise taxes and related sources (which was simply lost to more congenial commonwealths) fell within five years from an annual average of $2,600,000 to barely more than $1 million. When the last of the Sister Acts was repealed in 1920 for the purpose of regaining corporation income, no more noticeable impact had been made by New Jersey (or any other single state, for that matter) on the "monopoly" problem in the country than had been made by the Sherman Anti-trust Act of 1890.

There is no denying that the multiplication of trusts and the misfiring of regulatory measures made the monopoly issue a formidable one in the Progressive era. Even when preoccupied with America's new imperial relations following his rise to the presidency in 1901, T.R., in virtually all his annual messages to Congress, put it at the head of the topics discussed. In his very first annual message, he sounded his persistent theme: "The creation of these great corporate fortunes has not been due to the tariff nor to any other government action, but to natural causes in the business world, operating in other countries as they operate in our own." And he added:

> An additional reason for caution in dealing with corporations is to be found in the international commercial conditions of today. The same business conditions which have produced the great aggregations of corporate and individual wealth have made them very potent factors in international commercial competition. . . . America has only just begun to assume that commanding position in the international business world which we believe will more and more be hers. . . . Under such conditions it would be most unwise to cramp or fetter the youthful strength of our Nation.

In 1904, in the *Northern Securities Case*, the Supreme Court of the United States, in the first such decision under the Sherman Act, ordered the dissolution of the vast Morgan-Rockefeller Northern Securities Company. T.R. hailed this decision as "one of the greatest achievements of my administration." He followed it up with orders to prosecute such other evil giants as the Oil and Tobacco trusts. When the dissolution decrees also won in these cases (like that in the *Northern Securities Case*, as well) were in effect instantly nullified by the persistence of those "natural causes in the business world" which had fostered combination in the first place. T.R. did not hesitate to call it lamentable. "Surely, miscarriage of justice is not too strong a term to apply to such a result," he said. At the same time, his loyalty to his old views (see also Document No. 47, above) was only strengthened. In November, 1911, after the Oil and Tobacco decisions that year, he wrote in the *Outlook*, in one of his early volleys in the approaching presidential campaign:

We should not strive for a policy of unregulated competition and of the destruction of all big corporations, that is, of all the most efficient business industries in the land. Nor should we persevere in the hopeless experiment of trying to regulate these industries by means only of lawsuits, each lasting several years, and of uncertain result.

What was required, T.R. said, was a government agency which, on application, would give "anyone engaged in big business . . . in advance full information as to just what he can and what he cannot legally and properly do." Such an agency would also "enter upon a course of supervision, control, and regulation of these great corporations."

Wilson, in turn, was most willing to lock horns on the trust issue. In an early campaign speech, in September, 1912, he said:

There is one proposition upon which this campaign turns. . . . That proposition is this: that monopoly is inevitable, . . . and that is what I deny. If monopoly is inevitable, then the thing to do is for the government to take hold of monopoly and regulate it. If monopoly is not inevitable, then the thing for law to do is to break it up and prevent its forming again. I believe that monopoly can be broken up. If I didn't believe it, I would know that all the roads of free development were shut in this country.

Wilson continued: "The leaders of the third party [say] . . . that the best we can do is to establish an industrial commission which will take charge of . . . the big combinations which now control business in this country . . . and see to it that they are good to us." And he added:

If the President of the United States can through a commission guide the business of the United States, soon the businessmen of the United States who are interested in these combinations will put forth greater ingenuity and endeavor than ever to capture the Presidency of the United States. Ah, gentlemen, don't deceive yourselves. If men control business, then business will seek to control men. The only salvation for this country is that law shall control business. Now here is the parting of the ways.

And yet, earlier still, on August 7, 1912, in his speech accepting the Democratic nomination, Wilson had said, "I am not one of those who think that competition can be established by law against the drift of a world-wide economic tendency." He also said, "Power in the hands of great business men does not make me apprehensive." He also tendered this olive branch: "Let me say again that what we are seeking is not destruction of any kind nor the disruption of any sound or honest thing."

Once elected, moreover, and having salved his conscience with the Seven Sister Acts, Wilson held out the olive branch to the full extent of his reach. In his message to Congress on the trust problem on January 20, 1914 (presented in part in item "a" below), he declared, "The antagonism between business and Government is over." In the legislation he proposed, there will be "nothing essential disturbed, nothing torn up by the roots, no parts rent asunder which can be left in wholesome combination." And he added, "The business men of the country desire . . . the advice, the definite guidance, and information which can be supplied by an administrative body, an interstate trade commission. The opinion of the country would instantly approve of such a commission," and it shall therefore be supplied.

There always remained a profound difference between Roosevelt and Wilson on the "trust" issue: T.R. wanted to preserve the power of big business in order to promote the power of the nation in relations with other nations. Federal social justice would look after the welfare of the people. Wilson wanted to limit the power of big business in order to promote the liberty of the people so that they might the more readily look after themselves. Yet little was made of this distinction during the campaign, largely because Wilson cared little about relations with other nations, and T.R. had made much of his own vast reputation, whatever he said of big business, in promoting the very democratic principles which Wilson himself only belatedly embraced.

When the campaigning was done, moreover, Wilson capitulated wholly to the Roosevelt position. In his trust message to Congress he proposed five new regulatory measures, which promptly were popularized as the Five Brother Acts. One of these, as promised, proposed the establishment of the Federal Trade Commission, "to prevent persons, partnerships, or corporations" only from "using *unfair* methods of competition in commerce." This commission was established by law on September 26, 1914. Wilson's other proposals were gathered together into a single measure known as the Clayton Anti-trust Act, which was adopted October 15, 1914, and is presented in large part in item "b" below. Section 11 of the Clayton Act repeats much of the language of the law establishing the Federal Trade Commission, so we have not presented the FTC Act itself.

"Nothing hampers business like uncertainty," Wilson said. The Clayton Act, like the FTC Act, was designed to make "explicit and intelligible" in advance, just as T.R. had demanded, those practices big business should avoid. The Clayton Act left the more comprehensive Sherman Act intact, but offered *reasonable* qualifications of the Sherman Act's general prohibitions. Wilson, in his trust message, moreover, said not a word about the relation of the anti-trust acts to labor, a very sore point since the Pullman strike of 1894 (see Document No. 41, above). Yet the Clayton Act (Sec. 6) made this resounding declaration: "The labor of a human being is not a commodity or article of commerce." As T.R. had demanded in his annual message of 1908 (Document No. 47, above), the Clayton Act also explicitly exempted labor organizations from anti-trust prosecutions. In the same message, T.R. had urged tough restrictions on the use of injunctions in labor disputes; and the Clayton Act (Sec. 20) advanced the cause of labor in that direction as well. As time passed, Wilson's capitulation became all the more comprehensive. In 1918, with his approval, Congress adopted the Webb-Pomerene Act exempting, as T.R. had always wished, combinations engaged in the export trade from the anti-trust acts. By then, Wilson had also approved a number of social welfare measures on hours, wages, accident liability, and even on the distribution of wealth.

Unlike the Sherman Act, which was meant to punish trusts and monopolists, the Clayton Act was meant to forestall monopoly where it could. This approach led to many complaints. Senator James A. Reed of Missouri declared that the Act established "Peace on earth, good will toward trusts." Many economists and historians have since adopted Reed's view that the combined Five Brother Acts were no more effective nationally than the Seven Sister Acts had been in New Jersey. Businessmen, however, demur; and prosecutions have been frequent enough and penalties stern enough to make it clear to them that the anti-trust laws are meant to be enforced. The Clayton Act, like the Sherman Act, was especially intended, by restraints on *unfair* competitive practices, to broaden business opportunity. Again, many believe that the acts have been ineffective in this respect. Others (see, for example, Edith T. Penrose, *The Theory of the Growth of the Firm*, published in 1959) believe that opportunity has become greater than ever *within* large firms, and indeed that many modern mergers are motivated by the quest for talent and not to put a quietus upon it.

## 1914

# Regulating Trusts and Monopolies

(a) *President Wilson's Special Message to Congress on Trusts and Monopolies, January 20, 1914*

Mr. Speaker, Mr. President, gentlemen of the Congress, in my report "on the state of the Union," . . . I ventured to reserve for discussion at a later date the subject of additional legislation regarding the very difficult and intricate matter of trusts and monopolies. The time now seems opportune to turn to that great question. . . .

Legislation has its atmosphere like everything else, and the atmosphere of accommodation and mutual understanding which we now breathe with so much refreshment is a matter of sincere congratulation. . . . Legislation is a business of interpretation, not of origi-

nation; and it is now plain what the opinion is to which we must give effect in this matter. It is not recent or hasty opinion. It springs out of the experience of a whole generation. . . .

The great business men who organized and financed monopoly and those who administered it in actual everyday transactions have, year after year until now, either denied its existence or justified it as necessary for the effective maintenance and development of the vast business processes of the country in the modern circumstances of trade and manufacture and finance; but all the while opinion has made head against them; and at last the masters of business on the great scale have begun to yield their preference and purpose, perhaps their judgment also, in honorable surrender.

What we are purposing to do, therefore, is, happily, not to hamper or interfere with business as enlightened business men prefer to do it, or in any sense to put it under the ban. The antagonism between business and Government is over. . . .

When serious contest ends, when men unite in opinion and purpose, those who are to change their ways of business joining with those who ask for the change, it is possible to effect it . . . with as few, as slight, as easy and simple business readjustments as possible in the circumstances, nothing essential disturbed, nothing torn up by the roots, no parts rent asunder which can be left in wholesome combination. . . .

We are all agreed that "private monopoly is indefensible and intolerable," and our program is founded upon that conviction. It will be a comprehensive but not a radical or unacceptable program and these are its items, the changes which opinion deliberately sanctions and for which business waits:

It waits with acquiescence, in the first place, for laws which will effectually prohibit and prevent . . . interlockings of the *personnel* of the directorates of great corporations. . . . Such a prohibition will work much more than a mere negative good by correcting the serious evils which have arisen because, for example, the men who have been the directing spirits of the great investment banks have usurped the place which belongs to independent industrial management working in its own behoof. It will bring new men, new energies, a new spirit of initiative, new blood, into the management of our great business enterprises. It will open the field of industrial development and origination to scores of men who have been obliged to serve when their abilities entitled them to direct. It will immensely

hearten the young men coming on and will greatly enrich the business activities of the whole country. . . .

The business of the country awaits also, has long awaited and has suffered because it could not obtain, further and more explicit legislative definition of the policy and meaning of the existing antitrust law. Nothing hampers business like uncertainty. Nothing daunts or discourages it like the necessity to take chances, to run the risk of falling under the condemnation of the law before it can make sure just what the law is. . . .

And the business men of the country desire something more than that the menace of legal process in these matters be made explicit and intelligible. They desire the advice, the definite guidance, and information which can be supplied by an administrative body, an interstate trade commission. . . . Producing industries, for example, which have passed the point up to which combination may be consistent with the public interest and the freedom of trade, cannot always be dissected into their component units as readily as railroad companies or similar organizations can be. Their dissolution by ordinary legal process may oftentimes involve financial consequences likely to overwhelm the security market and bring upon it breakdown and confusion. There ought to be an administrative commission capable of directing and shaping such corrective processes . . . not only in aid of the courts but also by independent suggestion, if necessary.

Inasmuch as our object and the spirit of our action in these matters is to meet business half way in its processes of self-correction and disturb its legitimate course as little as possible, we ought to see to it . . . that penalties and punishments should fall not upon business itself, to its confusion and interruption, but upon the individuals who use the instrumentalities of business to do things which public policy and sound business practice condemn. Every act of business is done at the command or upon the initiative of some ascertainable person or group of persons. These should be held individually responsible and the punishment should fall upon them. . . .

Enterprises in these modern days of great individual fortunes are oftentimes interlocked, not by being under the control of the same directors but by the fact that the greater part of their corporate stock is owned by a single person or group of persons who are in some way intimately related in interest. We are agreed, I take it, that holding *companies* should be prohibited, but what of the controlling private ownership of individuals or actually co-operative groups of individuals? . . . Shall we require the owners of stock, when their voting power in several companies which ought to be independent of one another would constitute actual control, to make election in which of them they will exercise their right to vote? This question I venture for your consideration. . . .

I have laid the case before you, no doubt, as it lies in your own mind, as it lies in the thought of the country.

(b) *"An Act to supplement existing laws against unlawful restraints and monopolies, and for other purposes," known as the Clayton Anti-trust Act, October 15, 1914*

*Be it enacted* . . . That . . . "Commerce," as used herein, means trade or commerce among the several states and with foreign nations, or between the District of Columbia or any Territory of the United States and any State, Territory, or foreign nation, or between any insular possessions or other places under the jurisdiction of the United States, or between any such possession or place and any State or Territory of the United States or the District of Columbia or any foreign nation, or within the District of Columbia or any Territory or any insular possession or other place under the jurisdiction of the United States: *Provided,* That nothing in this Act contained shall apply to the Philippine Islands.

The word "person" or "persons" wherever used in this Act shall be deemed to include corporations and associations existing under or authorized by the laws of either the United States, the laws of any of the Territories, the laws of any State, or the laws of any foreign country.

SEC. 2. That it shall be unlawful for any person engaged in commerce, in the course of such commerce, either directly or indirectly to discriminate in price between different purchasers of commodities which commodities are sold for use, consumption, or resale within the United States or any . . . place under the jurisdiction of the United States, where the effect of such discrimination may be to substantially lessen competition or tend to create a monopoly in any line of commerce: *Provided,* That nothing herein contained shall prevent discrimination in price between purchasers of commodities on account of differences in the grade, quality, or quantity of the commodity sold, or that makes only due allowance for difference in the cost of selling or transportation, or discrimination in price in the same or different communities made in good faith to meet competition: *And provided further,* That nothing herein contained shall prevent persons engaged in selling goods, wares, or merchandise in commerce from selecting their own customers in bona fide transactions and not in restraint of trade.

SEC. 3. That it shall be unlawful for any person engaged in commerce, in the course of such commerce, to lease or make a sale or contract for sale of goods, wares, merchandise, machinery, supplies or other commodities, whether patented or unpatented, for use, consumption or resale within the United States or any . . . place under the jurisdiction of the United States, or fix a price charged therefor, or discount from, or rebate upon, such price, on the condition, agreement or understanding that the lessee or purchaser thereof shall not use or deal in the goods, wares, merchandise, machinery, supplies or other commodities of a competitor or competitors of the lessor or seller, where the effect of such lease, sale, or contract for sale or such condition, agreement or understanding may be to substantially lessen competition or tend to create a monopoly in any line of commerce.

SEC. 4. That any person who shall be injured in his business or property by reason of anything forbidden in the antitrust laws may sue therefor in any district court of the United States in the district in which the defendant resides or is found or has an agent, without respect to the amount in controversy, and shall recover threefold the damages by him sustained, and the cost of suit, including a reasonable attorney's fee. . . .

SEC. 6. That the labor of a human being is not a commodity or article of commerce. Nothing contained in the antitrust laws shall be construed to forbid the existence and operation of labor, agricultural, or horticultural organizations, instituted for the purposes of mutual help, and not having capital stock or conducted for profit, or to forbid or restrain individual members of such organizations from lawfully carrying out the legitimate objects thereof; nor shall such organizations, or the members thereof, be held or construed to be illegal combinations or conspiracies in restraint of trade, under the antitrust laws.

SEC. 7. That no corporation engaged in commerce shall acquire, directly or indirectly, the whole or any part of the stock or other share capital of another corporation engaged also in commerce, where the effect of such acquisition may be to substantially lessen competition between the corporation whose stock is so acquired and the corporation making the acquisition, or to restrain such commerce in any section or community, or tend to create a monopoly of any line of commerce.

No corporation shall acquire, directly or indirectly, the whole or any part of the stock or other share capital of two or more corporations engaged in commerce where the effect of such acquisition, or the use of such stock by the voting or granting of proxies or otherwise, may be to substantially lessen competition between such corporations, or any of them, whose stock or other share capital is so acquired, or to restrain such commerce in any section or community, or tend to create a monopoly of any line of commerce.

This section shall not apply to corporations purchasing such stock solely for investment and not using the same by voting or otherwise to bring about, or in attempting to bring about, the substantial lessening of competition. Nor shall anything contained in this section prevent a corporation engaged in commerce from causing the formation of subsidiary corporations for the actual carrying on of their immediate lawful business, or the natural and legitimate branches or extensions thereof, or from owning and holding all or a part of the stock of such subsidiary corporations, when the effect of such formation is not to substantially lessen competition. . . .

SEC. 8. That from and after two years from the date of the approval of this Act no person shall at the same time be a director or other officer or employee of more than one bank, banking association or trust company, organized or operating under the laws of the United States, either of which has deposits, capital, surplus, and undivided profits aggregating more than $5,000,-000; and no private banker or person who is a director in any bank or trust company, organized and operating under the laws of a State, having deposits, capital, surplus, and undivided profits aggregating more than $5,000,-000, shall be eligible to be a director in any bank or banking association organized or operating under the laws of the United States. . . .

No bank, banking association or trust company, organized or operating under the laws of the United States, in any city or incorporated town or village of more than two hundred thousand inhabitants, as shown by the last preceding decennial census of the United States, shall have as a director or other officer or employee any private banker or any director or other officer or employee of any other bank, banking association or trust company located in the same place: *Provided,* That nothing in this section shall apply to mutual savings banks not having a capital stock represented by shares: *Provided further,* That a director or other officer or employee of such bank, banking association, or trust company may be a director or other officer or employee of not more than one other bank or trust company organized under the laws of the United States or any State where the entire capital stock of one is owned by stockholders in the other; *And provided further,* That nothing contained in this section shall forbid a director of class A of a Federal reserve bank, as defined in the Federal Reserve Act, from being an officer or director or both an officer and director in one member bank.

That from and after two years from the date of the approval of this Act no person at the same time shall be a director in any two or more corporations, any one of which has capital, surplus, and undivided profits aggregating more than $1,000,000, engaged in whole or in part in commerce, other than banks, banking associations, trust companies and common carriers subject to the Act to regulate commerce, approved February fourth, eighteen hundred and eighty-seven, if such corporations are or shall have been theretofore, by virtue of their business and location of operation, competitors, so that the elimination of competition by agreement between them would constitute a violation of any of the provisions of any of the antitrust laws. . . .

SEC. 11. That authority to enforce compliance with sections two, three, seven and eight of this Act by the persons respectively subject thereto is hereby vested: in the Interstate Commerce Commission where applicable to common carriers, in the Federal Reserve Board where applicable to banks, banking associations and trust companies, and in the Federal Trade Commission where applicable to all other character of commerce, to be exercised as follows:

Whenever the commission or board vested with jurisdiction thereof shall have reason to believe that any person is violating or has violated any of the provisions of sections two, three, seven and eight of this Act, it shall issue and serve upon such person a complaint stating its charges in that respect, and containing a notice of a hearing upon a day and at a place therein fixed at least thirty days after the service of said complaint. The person so complained of shall have the right to appear at the place and time so fixed and show cause why an order should not be entered by the commission or board requiring such person to cease and desist from the violation of the law so charged in said complaint.

Any person may make application, and upon good cause shown may be allowed by the commission or board, to intervene and appear in said proceeding by counsel or in person. The testimony in any such proceeding shall be reduced to writing and filed in the office of the commission or board. If upon such hearing the commission or board, as the case may be, shall be of the opinion that any of the provisions of said sections have been or are being violated, it shall make a report in writing in which it shall state its findings as to the facts, and shall issue and cause to be served on such person an order requiring such person to cease and desist from such violations, and divest itself of the stock held or rid itself of the directors chosen contrary to the provisions of sections seven and eight of this Act, if any there be, in the manner and within the time fixed by said order. . . .

If such person fails or neglects to obey such order of the commission or board while the same is in effect, the commission or board may apply to the circuit court of appeals of the United States, within any circuit where the violation complained of was or is being committed or where such person resides or carries on business, for the enforcement of its order, and shall certify and file with its application a transcript of the entire record in the proceeding, including all the testimony taken and the report and order of the commission or board.

Upon such filing of the application and transcript the court shall cause notice thereof to be served upon such person and thereupon shall have jurisdiction of the proceeding and of the question determined therein, and shall have power to make and enter upon the pleadings, testimony, and proceedings set forth in such transcript a decree affirming, modifying, or setting aside the order of the commission or board.

The findings of the commission or board as to the facts, if supported by testimony, shall be conclusive. If either party shall apply to the court for leave to adduce additional evidence, and shall show to the satisfaction of the court that such additional evidence is material and that there were reasonable grounds for the failure to adduce such evidence in the proceeding before the commission or board, the court may order such additional evidence to be taken before the commission or board and to be adduced upon the hearing in such manner and upon such terms and conditions as to the court may seem proper. The commission or board may modify the findings as to the facts, or make new findings, by reason of the additional evidence so taken, and it shall file such modified or new findings,

which, if supported by testimony, shall be conclusive, and its recommendation, if any, for the modification or setting aside of its original order, with the return of such additional evidence. The judgment and decree of the court shall be final, except that the same shall be subject to review by the Supreme Court upon certiorari as provided in section two hundred and forty of the Judicial Code.

Any party required by such order of the commission or board to cease and desist from a violation charged may obtain a review of such order in said circuit court of appeals by filing in the court a written petition praying that the order of the commission or board be set aside. A copy of such petition shall be forthwith served upon the commission or board, and thereupon the commission or board forthwith shall certify and file in the court a transcript of the record as hereinbefore provided. Upon the filing of the transcript the court shall have the same jurisdiction to affirm, set aside, or modify the order of the commission or board as in the case of an application by the commission or board for the enforcement of its order, and the findings of the commission or board as to the facts, if supported by testimony, shall in like manner be conclusive. . . .

Such proceedings in the circuit court of appeals shall be given precedence over other cases pending therein, and shall be in every way expedited. No order of the commissioner or board or the judgment of the court to enforce the same shall in any wise relieve or absolve any person from any liability under the antitrust Acts. . . .

SEC. 14. That whenever a corporation shall violate any of the penal provisions of the antitrust laws, such violation shall be deemed to be also that of the individual directors, officers, or agents of such corporation who shall have authorized, ordered, or done any of the acts constituting in whole or in part such violation, and such violation shall be deemed a misdemeanor, and upon conviction therefor of any such director, officer, or agent he shall be punished by a fine of not exceeding $5,000 or by imprisonment for not exceeding one year, or by both, in the discretion of the court. . . .

SEC. 20. That no restraining order or injunction shall be granted by any court of the United States, or a judge or the judges thereof, in any case between an employer and employees, or between employers and employees, or between employees, or between persons employed and persons seeking employment, involving, or growing out of, a dispute concerning terms or conditions of employment, unless necessary to prevent irreparable injury to property, or to a property right, of the party making the application, for which injury there is no adequate remedy at law, and such property or property right must be described with particularity in the application, which must be in writing and sworn to by the applicant or by his agent or attorney.

And no such restraining order or injunction shall prohibit any person or persons, whether singly or in concert, from terminating any relation of employment, or from ceasing to perform any work or labor, or from recommending, advising, or persuading others by peaceful means so to do; or from attending at any place where any such person or persons may lawfully be, for the purpose of peacefully obtaining or communicating information, or from peacefully persuading any person to work or to abstain from working; or from

ceasing to patronize or to employ any party to such dispute, or from recommending, advising, or persuading others by peaceful and lawful means so to do; or from paying or giving to, or withholding from, any person engaged in such dispute, any strike benefits or other moneys or things of value; or from peaceably assembling in a lawful manner, and for lawful purposes; or from doing any act or thing which might lawfully be done in the absence of such dispute by any party thereto; nor shall any of the acts specified in this paragraph be considered or held to be violations of any law of the United States.

SEC. 21. That any person who shall willfully disobey any lawful writ, process, order, rule, decree, or command of any district court of the United States or any court of the District of Columbia by doing any act or thing therein, or thereby forbidden to be done by him, if the act or thing so done by him be of such character as to constitute also a criminal offense under any statute of the United States, or under the laws of any State in which the act was committed, shall be proceeded against for his said contempt as hereinafter provided. . . .

SEC. 22 . . . In all cases within the purview of this Act such trial may be by the court, or, upon demand of the accused, by a jury; . . . and such trial shall conform as near as may be, to the practice in criminal cases prosecuted by indictment or upon information.

# 49

*"What we demand in this war . . . is that the world be made fit and safe to live in"*

Although Woodrow Wilson has been described by his principal biographers as the most contradictory of men and the most idealistic of presidents, it is perfectly clear where he stood on many subjects and that his idealism was, and was meant to be, a force for realists to stand up to if they could.

Wilson believed that all peoples were capable of self-government. He believed it to be the divine mission of the American people, the best governed of all, to foster democracy around the world. He believed that world-wide democracy offered the best chance permanently to end war. He would even fight to make the world safe for democracy, so that henceforth it might be "fit and safe to live in."

To remain fit and safe, Wilson believed the world must yield to the rule of law, openly arrived at and declared. If all nations became democratic, a league of nations, the capstone of his thinking, would be the more likely to succeed. In such a league, as in the American Congress, even the most divisive international issues would be freely debated and lawfully resolved. Conflicts over league decisions would themselves be adjudicated in a world court, whose judgments, as those of the United States Supreme Court became the law of the land, would then become the law of the universe. Such law would also include independent treaties between nations in which nothing would be binding that did not appear "in the final covenant made public to the world." To insure obedience to such law Wilson believed a force must be created "so much greater than the force of any nation . . . or any alliance, . . . that no nation, no probable combination of nations could face or withstand it."

Wilson was in office but two weeks when, on March 19, 1913, he withdrew the support Taft had given, following the precepts of "dollar diplomacy," to the participation of American bankers in a huge international loan to China. "The conditions of the loan," he said, "seem to us to touch very nearly the administrative independence of China," and thus are "obnoxious to the principles upon which the government of our people rests." Referring to the abdication of the Manchu emperor in 1912 and the establishment of the Chinese Republic under the leadership of Sun Yat-sen, Wilson added:

The awakening of the people of China to a consciousness of their possibilities under free government is the most significant, if not the most momentous event of our generation. With this movement and aspiration the American people are in profound sympathy.

He would not make the United States a party to this movement's disturbance or defeat, and the offending international loan fell through.

Hands off in distant China was followed only a few months later by Wilson's laying on of hands in neighboring Mexico—again for the extension of the democratic principle. Early in 1913 the Mexican reform government of Francisco I. Madero was overthrown by Victoriano Huerta, with Madero himself shot dead. Wilson alone among the leaders of the great powers refused to recognize Huerta's "government of butchers." When the followers of the "constitutionalist," Venustiano Carranza, seemed to have a chance to unseat Huerta, Wilson gave them every encouragement, and eventually decided to intervene on their behalf. On August 27, 1913, he told Congress:

> The peace, prosperity, and contentment of Mexico mean more, much more, to us than merely an enlarged field for our commerce and enterprise. They mean an enlargement of the field of self-government, . . . and the whole world is interested as never before.

To further such enlargement for Mexico's benefit and the world's edification, Wilson, in April, 1914, sent the fleet to occupy Vera Cruz. For his pains he was castigated by humanitarians at home and by Mexicans of all political persuasions who resented American officiousness in their land as much as the Chinese had wanted American aid in theirs.

Wilson found his greatest opportunity in one of democracy's greatest catastrophes—the Russian revolutions of March and November, 1917, which eventually freed the Germans on the eastern front in World War I and permitted them to press France and Britain almost to the breaking point in the West.

When World War I started in Europe in August, 1914, Wilson shared the widespread illusion that it would soon be over. As the war lengthened and grew more heartless, his shock on finding the most civilized of nations on both sides of the conflict embarked on such a barbaric course deepened. At the same time, his awareness of the imperfections of European democracy, even in Britain, and especially in international relations, grew sharper. Germany's decision early in 1917 to make all neutral as well as enemy vessels victims of unlimited submarine warfare exhausted his tolerance. "The challenge is to all mankind," he told Congress in his war message of April 2, 1917.

> I was for a little while unable to believe that such things would in fact be done by any government that had hitherto subscribed to the humane practices of civilized nations. . . . The wrongs against which we now array ourselves are no common wrongs; they cut to the very roots of human life.

The news of the Russian revolution in March, however, had more than compensated Wilson for the news of German depravity. On March 18, 1917, Ambassador David R. Francis reported from Petrograd:

> This revolution is the practical realization of that principle of government which we have championed and advocated. I mean government by consent of the governed. Our recognition will have a stupendous moral effect especially if given first.

Wilson accepted at face value this and similar optimistic reports, and in the same message in which he asked for war on the German government he welcomed the allegiance of the Russian people:

> Does not every American feel that assurance has been added to our hope for the future peace of the world by the wonderful and heartening things that have been happening within the last few weeks in Russia? Russia was known by those who knew it best to have been always in fact democratic at heart. . . . The great, generous Russian people have been added in all their naive majesty and might to the forces that are fighting for freedom in the world, for justice and for peace. Here is a fit partner for a League of Honor.

Wilson's satisfaction with his purified Russian partner was enhanced by his being made privy, soon after his entry into the war, to the secret treaties among the allies for dividing up the spoils of the German empire and merchant marine and for the imposition of vengeful indemnities upon the German people. These treaties so sullied the avowed civilized aims of the allies that Wilson attempted to fight his part of the war independently of them. The November Revolution in Russia, which brought the Bolsheviks into power, hardly shook Wilson's faith in Russian democracy at all; and the Bolsheviks' closing down of the eastern front he viewed largely as a test of Germany's own peace program. This proved to be as vindictive as that of the allies.

The refusal of the allies to accede to Bolshevik demands that they try to bring the entire war to a halt before Russia was forced to make monstrous concessions to German power further alienated Wilson from his partners. When the Bolsheviks next threatened to publish the allies' vengeful treaties (to which the deposed Czar had been a party) and thereby expose allied hypocrisy to all the world, Wilson, after failing to gain allied agreement on his own peace plans, felt impelled to attempt to diminish the impact of the Bolshevik revelation with a resounding statement of the full fruition of his own humane thought. This he did in his message to Congress, January 8, 1918, in which he set forth as the famous Fourteen Points the ideas he had been presenting for foreign as well as domestic consumption at every opportunity during the past two years. This message went far beyond Wilson's enthusiasm for democracy as he thought he found it in newly awakened China, Mexico, and Russia. It encompassed all his hopes for an entire world of democratic governments, representative of the spirit of their people, stable, prosperous, and at peace. This message is presented in full in this Document.

The idea of democracy, of course, had been fermenting in Europe at least since the American and French Revolutions. With monarchical Europe in ashes in 1918, its economies bankrupt, its leadership discredited, the morale of its people undermined even in victory, Wilson's pronouncements, coming as they did with eloquence and simplicity from the leader of the unscathed United States, must indeed have appeared to many as brilliant illuminations from on high. Their sequel is too well known to require elaboration. Wilson's faith in ill-defined words, his simplistic constructs, his hasty and often mischievous interference in affairs of other nations, his ignorance or evasions of Europe's bitter historical legacy, his underestimation of the force of centuries of hate and rivalry, his refusal to acknowledge the existence even of his most manifest enemies at home—all, indeed, made it easier for the realists of his day to stand up to and thwart the purposes of his idealism.

When one forgets the soured alternatives at hand in 1918, one finds it easier to blame Wilson for the tragic consequences of his own limitations and failures. And yet (as certain of the remaining documents below testify) both the United States and a large part of the world, after a decade of flirtation with the "normalcy" of nationalism and isolation, have since accepted the spirit of his ideals and have altered their institutions to accommodate them. If progress has been faltering, Wilson's vision itself has not been supplanted and remains heartening, clear and operative.

*January 8, 1918*

# Woodrow Wilson: The Fourteen Points

*Gentlemen of the Congress:*

Once more, as repeatedly before, the spokesmen of the Central Empires have indicated their desire to discuss the objects of the war and the possible basis of a general peace. Parleys have been in progress at Brest-Litovsk between Russian representatives and representatives of the Central Powers, to which the attention of all the belligerents has been invited for the purpose of ascertaining whether it may be possible to extend these parleys into a general conference with regard to terms of peace and settlement.

The Russian representatives presented not only a perfectly definite statement of the principles upon which they would be willing to conclude peace but also an equally definite program for the concrete application of those principles. The representatives of the Central Powers, on their part, presented an outline of settlement which, if much less definite, seemed susceptible of liberal interpretation until their specific program of practical terms was added. That program proposed no concessions at all either to the sovereignty of Russia or to the preferences of the populations with whose fortunes it dealt, but meant, in a word, that the Central Empires were to keep every foot of territory their armed forces had occupied—every province, every city, every point of vantage—as a permanent addition to their territories and their power.

It is a reasonable conjecture that the general principles of settlement which they at first suggested originated with the more liberal statesmen of Germany and Austria, the men who have begun to feel the force of their own peoples' thought and purpose, while the concrete terms of actual settlement came from the military leaders who have no thought but to keep what they have got. The negotiations have been broken off. The Russian representatives were sincere and in earnest. They cannot entertain such proposals of conquest and domination.

The whole incident is full of significance. It is also full of perplexity. With whom are the Russian representatives dealing? For whom are the representatives of the Central Empires speaking? Are they speaking for the majorities of their respective Parliaments or for the minority parties, that military and imperialistic minority which has so far dominated their whole policy and controlled the affairs of Turkey and of the Balkan States which have felt obliged to become their associates in this war?

The Russian representatives have insisted, very justly, very wisely, and in the true spirit of modern democracy, that the conferences they have been holding with the Teutonic and Turkish statesmen should be held with open, not closed, doors, and all the world has been audience, as was desired. To whom have we been listening, then? To those who speak the spirit and intention of the resolutions of the German Reichstag of the 9th of July last, the spirit and intention of the Liberal leaders and parties of Germany, or to those who resist and defy that spirit and intention and insist upon conquest and subjugation? Or are we listening, in fact, to both, unreconciled and in open and hopeless contradiction? These are very serious and pregnant questions. Upon the answer to them depends the peace of the world.

But whatever the results of the parleys at Brest-Litovsk, whatever the confusions of counsel and of purpose in the utterances of the spokesmen of the Central Empires, they have again attempted to acquaint the world with their objects in the war and have again challenged their adversaries to say what their objects are and what sort of settlement they would deem just and satisfactory. There is no good reason why that challenge should not be responded to, and responded to with the utmost candor. We did not wait for it. Not once, but again and again, we have laid our whole thought and purpose before the world, not in general terms only, but each time with sufficient definition to make it clear what sort of definite terms of settlement must necessarily spring out of them. Within the last week Mr. Lloyd George has spoken with admirable candor and in admirable spirit for the people and Government of Great Britain.

There is no confusion of counsel among the adversaries of the Central Powers, no uncertainty of principle, no vagueness of detail. The only secrecy of counsel, the only lack of fearless frankness, the only failure to make definite statement of the objects of the war, lies with Germany and her allies. The issues of life and death hang upon these definitions. No statesman who has the least conception of his responsibility ought for a moment to permit himself to continue this tragical and appalling outpouring of blood and treasure unless he is sure beyond a peradventure that the objects of the vital sacrifice are part and parcel of the very life of Society and that the people for whom he speaks think them right and imperative as he does.

There is, moreover, a voice calling for these definitions of principle and of purpose which is, it seems to me, more thrilling and more compelling than any of the many moving voices with which the troubled air of the world is filled. It is the voice of the Russian people. They are prostrate and all but helpless, it would seem, before the grim power of Germany, which has hitherto known no relenting and no pity. Their power, apparently, is shattered. And yet their soul is not subservient. They will not yield either in principle or in action. Their conception of what is right, of what is humane and honorable for them to accept, has been stated with a frankness, a largeness of view, a generosity of spirit, and a universal human sympathy which must challenge the admiration of every friend of mankind; and they have refused to compound their ideals or desert others that they themselves may be safe.

They call to us to say what it is that we desire, in what, if in anything, our purpose and our spirit differ from theirs; and I believe that the people of the United States would wish me to respond with utter simplicity and frankness. Whether their present leaders believe it or not, it is our heartfelt desire and hope that some way may be opened whereby we may be privileged to assist the people of Russia to attain their utmost hope of liberty and ordered peace.

It will be our wish and purpose that the processes of peace, when they are begun, shall be absolutely open, and that they shall involve and permit henceforth no secret understandings of any kind. The day of conquest and aggrandizement is gone by; so is also the day of secret covenants entered into in the interest of particular governments and likely at some unlooked for moment to upset the peace of the world. It is this happy fact, now clear to the view of every public man whose thoughts do not still linger in an age that is dead and gone, which makes it possible for every nation whose purposes are consistent with justice and the peace of the world to avow now or at any other time the objects it has in view.

We entered this war because violations of right had occurred which touched us to the quick and made the life of our own people impossible unless they were corrected and the world secured once for all against their recurrence.

What we demand in this war, therefore, is nothing peculiar to ourselves. It is that the world be made fit and safe to live in; and particularly that it be made safe for every peace-loving nation which, like our own, wishes to live its own life, determine its own institutions, be assured of justice and fair dealing by the other peoples of the world as against force and selfish aggression.

All the peoples of the world are in effect partners in this interest, and for our own part we see very clearly that unless justice be done to others it will not be done to us. The program of the world's peace, therefore, is our program, and that program, the only possible program, as we see it, is this:

1.—Open covenants of peace, openly arrived at, after which there shall be no private international understandings of any kind, but diplomacy shall proceed always frankly and in the public view.

2.—Absolute freedom of navigation upon the seas, outside territorial waters, alike in peace and in war, except as the seas may be closed in whole or in part by international action for the enforcement of international covenants.

3.—The removal, so far as possible, of all economic barriers and the establishment of an equality of trade conditions among all the nations consenting to the peace and associating themselves for its maintenance.

4.—Adequate guarantees given and taken that national armaments will be reduced to the lowest point consistent with domestic safety.

5.—A free, open-minded, and absolutely impartial adjustment of all colonial claims, based upon a strict observance of the principle that in determining all such questions of sovereignty the interests of the populations concerned must have equal weight with the equitable claims of the government whose title is to be determined.

6.—The evacuation of all Russian territory and such a settlement of all questions affecting Russia as will secure the best and freest cooperation of the other nations of the world in obtaining for her an unhampered and unembarrassed opportunity for the independent determination of her own political development and national policy and assure her of a sincere welcome into the society of free nations under institutions of her own choosing; and, more than a welcome, assistance also of every kind that she may need and may herself desire. The treatment accorded Russia by her sister nations in the months to come will be the acid test of their goodwill, of their comprehension of her needs as distinguished from their own interests, and of their intelligent and unselfish sympathy.

7.—Belgium, the whole world will agree, must be evacuated and restored, without any attempt to limit the sovereignty which she enjoys in common with all other free nations. No other single act will serve as this will serve to restore confidence among the nations in the laws which they have themselves set and determined for the government of their relations with one another. Without this healing act the whole structure and validity of international law is forever impaired.

8.—All French territory should be freed and the invaded portions restored, and the wrong done to France by Prussia in 1871 in the matter of Alsace-Lorraine, which has unsettled the peace of the world for nearly fifty years, should be righted, in order that peace may once more be made secure in the interest of all.

9.—A readjustment of the frontiers of Italy should be effected along clearly recognizable lines of nationality.

10.—The peoples of Austria-Hun-gary, whose place among the nations we wish to see safeguarded and assured, should be accorded the freest opportunity of autonomous development.

11.—Rumania, Serbia, and Montenegro should be evacuated; occupied territories restored; Serbia accorded free and secure access to the sea; and the relations of the several Balkan States to one another determined by friendly counsel along historically established lines of allegiance and nationality; and international guarantees of the political and economic independence and territorial integrity of the several Balkan States should be entered into.

12.—The Turkish portions of the present Ottoman Empire should be assured a secure sovereignty, but the other nationalities which are now under Turkish rule should be assured an undoubted security of life and an absolutely unmolested opportunity of autonomous development, and the Dardanelles should be permanently opened as a free passage to the ships and commerce of all nations under international guarantees.

13.—An independent Polish State should be erected which should include the territories inhabited by indisputably Polish populations, which should be assured a free and secure access to the sea, and whose political and economic independence and territorial integrity should be guaranteed by international covenant.

14.—A general association of nations must be formed under specific covenants for the purpose of affording mutual guarantees of political independence and territorial integrity to great and small states alike.

In regard to these essential rectifications of wrong and assertions of right, we feel ourselves to be intimate partners of all the governments and peoples associated together against the imperialists. We cannot be separated in interest or divided in purpose. We stand together until the end.

For such arrangements and covenants we are willing to fight and to continue to fight until they are achieved; but only because we wish the right to prevail and desire a just and stable peace, such as can be secured only by removing the chief provocations to war, which this program does remove.

We have no jealousy of German greatness, and there is nothing in this program that impairs it. We grudge her no achievement or distinction of learning or of pacific enterprise such as have made her record very bright and very enviable. We do not wish to injure her or to block in any way her legitimate influence or power. We do not wish to fight her either with arms or with hostile arrangements of trade, if she is willing to associate herself with us and the other peace-loving nations of the world in covenants of justice and law and fair dealing.

We wish her only to accept a place of equality among the peoples of the world—the new world in which we now live—instead of a place of mastery.

Neither do we presume to suggest to her any alteration or modification of her institutions. But it is necessary, we must frankly say, and necessary as a preliminary to any intelligent dealings with her on our part, that we should know whom her spokesmen speak for when they speak to us, whether for the Reichstag majority or for the military party and the men whose creed is imperial domination.

We have spoken, now, surely, in terms too concrete to admit of any further doubt or question. An evident principle runs through the whole program I have outlined. It is the principle of justice to all peoples and nationalities, and their right to live on equal terms of liberty and safety with one another, whether they be strong or weak.

Unless this principle be made its foundation no part of the structure of international justice can stand. The people of the United States could act upon no other principle; and to the vindication of this principle they are ready to devote their lives, their honor, and everything that they possess. The moral climax of this the culminating and final war for human liberty has come, and they are ready to put their own strength, their own highest purpose, their own integrity and devotion to the test.

# 50

*"I shall ask the Congress for . . . power to wage a war against the emergency, as great as the power that would be given me if we were in fact invaded by a foreign foe"*

When Franklin D. Roosevelt, on March 4, 1933, took office as the thirty-second President of the United States, three and a half years had passed since the Great Crash of October, 1929. No peacetime period in American history, and no wartime period unless it be

Washington's winter at Valley Forge or the Confederacy's last spring, rivals these three and a half years in drawing from contemporaries and historians alike the bleakest language parched by fear. During these years, Roosevelt said in his inaugural address (presented in full in this Document), "values have shrunken to fantastic levels." Among other "dark realities of the moment," he noted that

> . . . the means of exchange are frozen in the currents of trade, the withered leaves of industrial enterprise lie on every side; farmers find no markets for their produce; the savings of many years in thousands of families are gone. More important, a host of unemployed citizens face the grim problem of existence, and an equally great number toil with little return.

The vaunted "American system" had quivered to a standstill in a wilderness. "The American system," Herbert Hoover had said in his redoubtable "Rugged Individualism" speech of October 22, 1928, only two weeks before his own election to the presidency, "is just as definite and positive a political and social system as has ever been developed on earth. It is founded upon a particular conception of self-government in which decentralized local responsibility is the very base." Decentralized local responsibility faltered and folded up in the tragic test of the months soon at hand; and Hoover, although in fact he took more far-reaching steps than any earlier depression president, was disqualified by his philosophy from dispelling the people's sick sense of being lost. "The history of H's administration," Agnes Meyer, the future Washington publisher, wrote in her diary in February, 1933, "is Greek in its fatality." Midway in the following month she wrote of the new regime: "The people trust this admin. as they distrusted the other. This is the secret of the whole situation."

Roosevelt had earned the people's trust. New York, while he was Governor and Hoover was President, had done more than any other state, on the local level Hoover leaned upon, to mitigate the heartbreak of the country's collapse. In preparation for his presidential campaign, Roosevelt called for "the building of plans . . . that put their faith once more in the forgotten man at the bottom of the economic pyramid." In accepting the Democratic nomination, he pledged himself, in the tradition of his cousin Teddy (see Document No. 47, above), to "a new deal for the American people." In his inaugural in the same tradition, he declared that "the measure of the restoration lies in the extent to which we apply social values more noble than mere monetary profit." And he added: "Restoration calls, however, not for changes in ethics alone. This nation asks for action, and action now." Our Constitution, he said, "is so simple and practical that it is possible always to meet extraordinary needs by changes in emphasis and arrangement without loss of essential form." And he promised to take all "measures that a stricken nation . . . may require."

Lincoln, at the hour of his inaugural address, faced the terrors of disunion and civil war and pled for time to calm them. His deliberate dawdling in his early months in office frightened his best friends. FDR, in March, 1933, faced the greater terrors of social decomposition and individual inertness. And he promised instant mobilization to rouse and reunite the people. In his first hundred days his sweeping action frightened only his diehard enemies.

FDR's storm of activity centered on reform, relief, retrenchment, restoration. But it was all accompanied by such militant concern for the welfare of all the people that it was easy even for the lowliest to believe that they were on the way to a better life. In fact, FDR had no program for the growth of the economy, the broadening of opportunity, the advancement of the mind and spirit. But he talked as though he had, which was just as effective under the circumstances. "In one week," wrote Walter Lippmann following the assembling of the special session of Congress called by Roosevelt for March 8, "the nation, which had lost confidence in everything and everybody, has regained confidence in the government and in itself." "Capitalism was saved in eight days," Raymond Moley wrote of the same period in his *After Seven Years*.

After seven years, in fact, the New Deal was a manifest failure. As *Fortune* magazine wrote in its brilliant February, 1940, issue, there remained "some nine million American citizens who were, as the term is, 'unemployed.' " With their dependents these "members of the dispossessed . . . total about thirty millions." For this "nearly one-fourth of the population there is no economic system—and from the rest there is no answer." An answer was on the horizon; another real war whose cost only measured the conservatism of the New Deal's eventual pump-priming efforts, and whose demands at last met "our greatest primary task," as FDR said in his first inaugural, "to put the people to work."

And yet to deny FDR's great role in restoring the health of the nation is to underestimate the depth of the social crisis he inherited. To point only to the inconclusiveness and even the failure of the New Deal is to misjudge how much in spirit and even in substance it afforded. Many of its specific acts, moreover, such as those presented in Document No. 51, below, initiated policies and programs that a generation later continue to advance the general welfare.

**March 4, 1933**

# Franklin D. Roosevelt:
# First Inaugural Address

I am certain that my fellow Americans expect that on my induction into the Presidency I will address them with a candor and a decision which the present situation of our Nation impels. This is preeminently the time to speak the truth, the whole truth, frankly and boldly. Nor need we shrink from honestly facing conditions in our country to-day. This great Nation will endure as it has endured, will revive and will prosper. So, first of all, let me assert my firm belief that the only thing we have to fear is fear itself—nameless, unreasoning, unjustified terror which paralyzes needed efforts to convert retreat into advance. In every dark hour of our national life a leadership of frankness and vigor has met with that understanding and support of the people themselves which is essential to victory. I am convinced that you will again give that support to leadership in these critical days.

In such a spirit on my part and on yours we face our common difficulties. They concern, thank God, only material things. Values have shrunken to fantastic levels; taxes have risen; our ability to pay has fallen; government of all kinds is faced by serious curtailment of income; the means of exchange are frozen in the currents of trade; the withered leaves of industrial enterprise lie on every side; farmers find no markets for their produce; the savings of many years in thousands of families are gone.

More important, a host of unemployed citizens face the grim problem of existence, and an equally great number toil with little return. Only a foolish optimist can deny the dark realities of the moment.

Yet our distress comes from no failure of substance. We are stricken by no plague of locusts. Compared with the perils which our forefathers conquered because they believed and were not afraid, we have still much to be thankful for. Nature still offers her bounty and human efforts have multiplied it. Plenty is at our doorstep, but a generous use of it languishes in the very sight of the supply. Primarily this is because the rulers of the exchange of mankind's goods have failed, through their own stubbornness and their own incompetence, have admitted their failure, and abdicated. Practices of the unscrupulous money changers stand indicted in the court of public opinion, rejected by the hearts and minds of men.

True they have tried, but their efforts have been cast in the pattern of an outworn tradition. Faced by failure of credit they have proposed only the lending of more money. Stripped of the lure of profit by which to induce our people to follow their false leadership, they have resorted to exhortations, pleading tearfully for restored confidence. They know only the rules of a generation of self-seekers. They have no vision, and when there is no vision the people perish.

The money changers have fled from their high seats in the temple of our civilization. We may now restore that temple to the ancient truths. The measure of the restoration lies in the extent to which we apply social values more noble than mere monetary profit.

Happiness lies not in the mere possession of money; it lies in the joy of achievement, in the thrill of creative effort. The joy and moral stimulation of work no longer must be forgotten in the mad chase of evanescent profits. These dark days will be worth all they cost us if they teach us that our true destiny is not to be ministered unto but to minister to ourselves and to our fellow men.

Recognition of the falsity of material wealth as the standard of success goes hand in hand with the abandonment of the false belief that public office and high political position are to be valued only by the standards of pride of place and personal profit; and there must be an end to a conduct in banking and in business which too often has given to a sacred trust the likeness of callous and selfish wrongdoing. Small wonder that confidence languishes, for it thrives only on honesty, on honor, on the sacredness of obligations, on faithful protection, on unselfish performance; without them it can not live.

Restoration calls, however, not for changes in ethics alone. This Nation asks for action, and action now.

Our greatest primary task is to put people to work. This is no unsolvable problem if we face it wisely and courageously. It can be accomplished in part by direct recruiting by the Government itself, treating the task as we would treat the emergency of a war, but at the same time, through this employment, accomplishing greatly needed projects to stimulate and reorganize the use of our natural resources.

Hand in hand with this we must frankly recognize the overbalance of population in our industrial centers and, by engaging on a national scale in a redistribution, endeavor to provide a better use of the land for those best fitted for the land. The task can be helped by definite efforts to raise the values of agricultural products and with this the power to purchase the output of our cities. It can be helped by preventing realistically the tragedy of the growing loss through foreclosure of our small homes and our farms. It can be helped by insistence that the Federal, State, and local governments act forthwith on the demand that their cost be drastically reduced. It can be helped by the unifying of relief activities which to-day are often scattered, uneconomical, and unequal. It can be helped by national planning for and supervision of all forms of transportation and of communications and other utilities which have a definitely public character. There are many ways in which it can be helped, but it can never be helped merely by talking about it. We must act and act quickly.

Finally, in our progress toward a resumption of work we require two safeguards against a return of the evils of the old order; there must be a strict supervision of all banking and credits and investments; there must be an end to speculation with other people's money, and there must be provision for an adequate but sound currency.

There are the lines of attack. I shall presently urge upon a new Congress in special session detailed measures for their fulfillment, and I shall seek the immediate assistance of the several States.

Through this program of action we address ourselves to putting our own national house in order and making income balance outgo. Our international trade relations, though vastly important, are in point of time and necessity secondary to the establishment of a sound national economy. I favor as a practical policy the putting of first things first. I shall spare no effort to restore world trade by international economic readjustment, but the emergency at home can not wait on that accomplishment.

The basic thought that guides these specific means of national recovery is not narrowly nationalistic. It is the insistence, as a first consideration, upon the interdependence of the various elements in all parts of the United States —a recognition of the old and permanently important manifestation of the American spirit of the pioneer. It is the way to recovery. It is the immediate way. It is the strongest assurance that the recovery will endure.

In the field of world policy I would dedicate this Nation to the policy of the good neighbor—the neighbor who resolutely respects himself and, because he does so, respects the rights of others —the neighbor who respects his obligations and respects the sanctity of his agreements in and with a world of neighbors.

If I read the temper of our people correctly, we now realize as we have never realized before our interdependence on each other; that we can not merely take but we must give as well; that if we are to go forward, we must move as a trained and loyal army willing to sacrifice for the good of a common discipline, because without such discipline no progress is made, no leadership becomes effective. We are, I know, ready and willing to submit our lives and property to such discipline, because it makes possible a leadership which aims at a larger good. This I propose to offer, pledging that the larger purposes will bind upon us all as a sacred obligation with a unity of duty hitherto evoked only in time of armed strife.

With this pledge taken, I assume unhesitatingly the leadership of this great army of our people dedicated to a disciplined attack upon our common problems.

Action in this image and to this end is feasible under the form of government which we have inherited from our ancestors. Our Constitution is so simple and practical that it is possible always to meet extraordinary needs by changes in emphasis and arrangement without loss of essential form. That is why our constitutional system has proved itself the most superbly enduring political mechanism the modern world has produced. It has met every stress of vast expansion of territory, of foreign wars, of bitter internal strife, of world relations.

It is to be hoped that the normal balance of executive and legislative authority may be wholly adequate to meet the unprecedented task before us. But it may be that an unprecedented demand and need for undelayed action may call for temporary departure from that normal balance of public procedure.

I am prepared under my constitutional duty to recommend the measures that a stricken nation in the midst of a stricken world may require. These measures, or such other measures as the Congress may build out of its experience and wisdom, I shall seek, within my constitutional authority, to bring to speedy adoption.

But in the event that the Congress shall fail to take one of these two courses, and in the event that the national emergency is still critical, I shall not evade the clear course of duty that will then confront me. I shall ask the Congress for the one remaining instrument to meet the crisis—broad Executive power to wage a war against the emergency, as great as the power that would be given to me if we were in fact invaded by a foreign foe.

For the trust reposed in me I will return the courage and the devotion that befit the time. I can do no less.

We face the arduous days that lie before us in the warm courage of the national unity; with the clear consciousness of seeking old and precious moral values; with the clean satisfaction that comes from the stern performance of duty by old and young alike. We aim at the assurance of a rounded and permanent national life.

We do not distrust the future of essential democracy. The people of the United States have not failed. In their need they have registered a mandate that they want direct, vigorous action. They have asked for discipline and direction under leadership. They have made me the present instrument of their wishes. In the spirit of the gift I take it.

In this dedication of a Nation we humbly ask the blessing of God. May He protect each and every one of us. May He guide me in the days to come.

## 51

*"It is . . . the policy of the United States . . .*
*to balance . . . the production and consump-*
*tion of agricultural commodities; . . . to . . .*
*encourage . . . collective bargaining; . . . to*
*make more adequate provision for aged per-*
*sons, . . . and unemployment compensation"*

In commenting on Theodore Roosevelt's last annual message to Congress in December, 1908 (Document No. 47, above), the New York *Tribune* observed that the enduring service of the Square Deal lay in its "calling public attention to social problems and bringing them into politics." The enduring service of the New Deal lay in its transforming political debate over social justice into far-reaching legislation and administration—as in the three epochal acts presented in this Document.

By its manifest contributions to winning the Great War in 1918, Big Business had regained much of the prestige it had lost during the Square Deal era; and the social backsliding in the politics of the 'twenties reflected the popular belief in Big Business assertions that it could again be trusted to preserve prosperity and public well-being forever. The Great Crash of 1929 made Big Business spokesmen eat their words; and the mounting wrathfulness of social comment and social action as the business depression deepened, disclosed the shallowness of the popular belief in them.

Speaking for the cities, Father John A. Ryan of the National Catholic Welfare Council declared in 1932: "I wish we might double the number of Communists in this country, to put the fear, if not of God, then the fear of something else, into the hearts of our leaders." Speaking for the farmers that same summer, Milo Reno of the Farmers' Holiday Association said:

> We have issued an ultimatum to the other groups of society. If you continue to confiscate our property and demand that we feed your stomachs and clothe your bodies, we will refuse to function. We don't ask people to make implements, cloth, or houses at the price of degradation, bankruptcy, dissolution, and despair.

Speaking to the cities a few months later about violence in the country against foreclosing judges, the New York *World-Telegram* remarked:

Americans are slow to understand that actual revolution already exists in the farm belt. . . . When the local revolt springs from old native stock, conservatives fighting for the right to hold their homesteads, there is the warning of a larger explosion.

The crack-up of conservatism under the pressures evident in such statements carried men of many shades of opinion on to the New Deal bandwagon. And New Deal legislation, especially in the early years, reflected the many voices that clamored to be heard. Yet underlying all but the most superficial measures for immediate relief lay certain generally accepted ideas: The depression in the United States was mainly an American not a foreign phenomenon. The disaster in the United States must be met largely by domestic measures. Similar disasters in the future must be mitigated by domestic reforms. Modern American business enterprise was essentially national not local in scope. The failure of modern business enterprise required national, not simply local, public, not simply private, action. Modern business enterprise swept away individual self-sufficiency, even on family farms. National government action must recognize the interdependency of the whole population and make enduring economic and social plans for the welfare of all the people.

FDR summed up the prevailing spirit of the New Deal when he told the Federal Council of Churches of Christ in December, 1933: "If I were asked to state the great objective which Church and State are both demanding for the sake of every man and woman and child in this country, I would say, that great objective is 'a more abundant life.' " In a "Fireside Chat" in September, 1934, FDR was more specific:

I am not for a return to that definition of liberty under which for many years a free people were being gradually regimented into the service of the privileged few. I prefer and I am sure you prefer that broader definition of liberty under which we are moving forward to greater freedom, to greater security for the average man than he has ever known in the history of America.

Three basic weaknesses in the American economy in the 'twenties were disastrously intensified by the depression: (1) the downward tendency in farm population and farm family purchasing power; (2) the low wages, long hours, and recurrent layoffs in the new mass-production industries where union membership was small and union militancy weak; (3) the maldistribution of national income which in 1929 found 40 per cent of American families with little savings "in our richest year for the hard times that were coming."

From the unprecedented torrent of New Deal legislation we present below excerpts from three enduring New Deal measures aimed at offsetting and eliminating these weaknesses: "a" the Agricultural Adjustment Act of May 12, 1933; "b" the National Labor Relations Act of July 5, 1935; and "c" the Social Security Act of August 14, 1935. Each of these acts has since been amended. But each was a striking success in its own terms; and its specific objective—"to reestablish prices to farmers"; to reduce "the inequality of bargaining power between employees . . . and employers"; and to secure "the men, women, and children of the Nation against certain hazards and vicissitudes of life"—continue under Republican and Democratic administrations alike to animate the spirit and illuminate the goals of government.

These three measures share other features characteristic of New Deal actions and aspirations. They were adventurous. As FDR said to Congress on March 16, 1933, in proposing the farm bill: "I tell you frankly that it is a new and untrod path, but I tell you with equal frankness that an unprecedented condition calls for the trial of new means to rescue agriculture." They were experimental. As FDR told Congress on January 1, 1935, in proposing the Social Security Bill: "It is overwhelmingly important to avoid any danger of permanently discrediting the sound and necessary policy of Federal legislation for economic security by attempting to apply it on too ambitious a scale before actual experience has provided guidance for the permanently safe direction of such efforts." And they were pragmatic in promise. As FDR stated on signing the National Labor Relations Act on July 5, 1935: "It may eventually eliminate one major cause of labor disputes, but it will not stop all labor disputes."

These three acts had other significant New Deal features in common: The Agricultural Adjustment Act and the Social Security Act, and the National Industrial Recovery Act of 1933 from which the National Labor Relations Act stems, were all omnibus acts, veritable Rube Goldbergs in their intricacy. As such they reflected the difficulties in attempting by legislation to plan for an economy as complex as that of the United States. To make such planning more flexible, and more responsive to the myriad details of economic reality, each of these acts set up a federal administrative board with quasi-judicial powers. While national in scope, however, each act also looked to local governments and economic groups for grass-roots implementation.

New Deal measures such as the three presented here vastly enlarged government intervention and government costs. They also greatly advanced the general welfare. Even more important, for all their bureaucratic tendencies, by greatly broadened the participation of the people in decisions critical to their well-being, they revitalized and extended the whole democratic process.

Thousands of Negro cotton farmers in the South who had never voted before took part equally with others in the referendums by which regional crop controls under the AAA were voted up and down. Millions of aged and incapacitated workers in the cities as well as on the farms found a new interest in state governments made responsible by the Social Security Act for state contributions to pension and other funds. "Yes ma'am," said a destitute old woman after a week of publicity for "human security" in her state, "we all know about it. We learned about it because we were going to vote about it . . . Now that we know all the facts the legislators just can't rightly afford not to find the money." The National Labor Relations Act, in turn, undertook explicitly to protect "the exercise by workers of full freedom of association, self-organization, and designation of representatives of their own choosing, for the purpose of negotiating the terms and conditions of their employment or other mutual aid or protection."

The tumult and taxation that accompanied the New Deal's social and economic legislation embittered middlemen, management, and the well-to-do in general. The "hate Roosevelt" hysteria proved as lasting as it was deep. Yet much of this legislation, however much altered in detail, has survived in spirit and function. The excerpts that follow, from extraordinarily lengthy acts, have been selected to convey the spirit of these acts rather than their specific operational terms.

**1933      1935**

# General Welfare Legislation
## under the New Deal

### (a)   *The Agricultural Adjustment Act, May 12, 1933*

AN ACT *to relieve the existing national economic emergency by increasing agricultural purchasing power . . . to provide emergency relief with respect to agricultural indebtedness, . . . and for other purposes.*

TITLE I—AGRICULTURAL ADJUSTMENT

*Declaration of Emergency*

That the present acute economic emergency being in part the consequence of a severe and increasing disparity between the prices of agricultural and other commodities, which disparity has largely destroyed the purchasing power of farmers for industrial products, has broken down the orderly exchange of commodities, and has seriously impaired the agricultural assets supporting the national credit structure, it is hereby declared that these conditions in the basic industry of agriculture have affected transactions in agricultural com-

modities with a national public interest, have burdened and obstructed the normal currents of commerce in such commodities, and render imperative the immediate enactment of title I of this Act.

*Declaration of Policy*

SEC. 2. It is hereby declared to be the policy of Congress—

(1) To establish and maintain such balance between the production and consumption of agricultural commodities, and such marketing conditions therefor, as will reestablish prices to farmers at a level that will give agricultural commodities a purchasing power with respect to articles that farmers buy, equivalent to the purchasing power of agricultural commodities in the base period. The base period in the case of all agricultural commodities except tobacco shall be the prewar period, August 1909-July 1914. In the case of tobacco,

the base period shall be the postwar period, August 1919-July 1929.

(2) To approach such equality of purchasing power by gradual correction of the present inequalities therein at as rapid a rate as is deemed feasible in view of the current consumptive demand in domestic and foreign markets.

(3) To protect the consumers' interest by readjusting farm production at such level as will not increase the percentage of the consumers' retail expenditures for agricultural commodities, or products derived therefrom, which is returned to the farmer, above the percentage which was returned to the farmer in the prewar period, August 1909-July 1914.

### PART 1—COTTON OPTION CONTRACTS

SEC. 6. (a) The Secretary of Agriculture is hereby authorized to enter into option contracts with the producers of cotton to sell to any such producer an amount of cotton to be agreed upon not in excess of the amount of reduction in production of cotton by such producer below the amount produced by him in the preceding crop year, in all cases where such producer agrees in writing to reduce the amount of cotton produced by him in 1933, below his production in the previous year, by not less than 30 per centum, without increase in commercial fertilization per acre. . . . *Provided further*, That such agreement to curtail cotton production shall contain a further provision that such cotton producer shall not use the land taken out of cotton production for the production for sale, directly or indirectly, of any other nationally produced agricultural commodity or product. . . .

### PART 2—COMMODITY BENEFITS

#### General Powers

SEC. 8. In order to effectuate the declared policy, the Secretary of Agriculture shall have power—

(1) To provide for reduction in the acreage or reduction in the production for market, or both, of any basic agricultural commodity, through agreements with producers or by other voluntary methods, and to provide for rental or benefit payments in connection therewith or upon that part of the production of any basic agricultural commodity required for domestic consumption, in such amounts as the Secretary deems fair and reasonable, to be paid out of any moneys available for such payments. . . .

(2) To enter into marketing agreements with processors, associations of producers, and others engaged in the handling, in the current of interstate or foreign commerce of any agricultural commodity or product thereof, after due notice and opportunity for hearing to interested parties. The making of any such agreement shall not be held to be in violation of any of the antitrust laws of the United States. . . .

#### Processing Tax

SEC. 9. (a) To obtain revenue for extraordinary expenses incurred by reason of the national economic emergency, there shall be levied processing taxes as hereinafter provided. . . . The processing tax shall be levied, assessed, and collected upon the first domestic processing of the commodity, whether of domestic production or imported, and shall be paid by the processor. . . .

(b) The processing tax shall be at such rate as equals the difference between the current average farm price for the commodity and the fair exchange value of the commodity; except that if the Secretary has reason to believe that the tax at such rate will cause such reduction in the quantity of the commodity or products thereof domestically consumed as to result in the accumulation of surplus stocks of the commodity or products thereof or in the depression of the farm price of the commodity, then he shall cause an appropriate investigation to be made and afford due notice and opportunity for hearing to interested parties. If thereupon the Secretary finds that such result will occur, then the processing tax shall be at such rate as will prevent such accumulation of surplus stocks and depression of the farm price of the commodity. . . .

(c) For the purposes of part 2 of this title, the fair exchange value of a commodity shall be the price therefor that will give the commodity the same purchasing power, with respect to articles farmers buy, as such commodity had during the base period specified in section 2; . . .

SEC. 10. . . . (b) The Secretary of Agriculture is authorized to establish, for the more effective administration of the functions vested in him by this title, State and local committees, or associations of producers, and to permit cooperative associations of producers, when in his judgment they are qualified to do so, to act as agents of their members and patrons in connection with the distribution of rental or benefit payments. . . .

SEC. 11. As used in this title, the term "basic agricultural commodity" means wheat, cotton, field corn, hogs, rice, tobacco, and milk and its products, and any regional or market classification, type, or grade thereof; . . .

TITLE II—AGRICULTURAL CREDITS

*Purchase, Reduction,
and Refinancing of Farm Mortgages*

SEC. 22. . . . the Federal Farm Loan Act, . . . is amended by adding at the end thereof the following new sentence:

"In order to reduce and/or refinance farm mortgages, [a Federal land-bank may] . . . invest . . . in the purchase of first mortgages on farm lands situated within the Federal land-bank dis-

trict within which it is organized or for which it is acting, or . . . exchange farm-loan bonds for any duly recorded first mortgages on farm lands executed prior to the date this paragraph, as amended, takes effect, at a price which shall not exceed in each individual case the amount of the unpaid principal of the mortgage on the date of such purchase or exchange, or 50 per centum of the normal value of the land mortgaged and 20 per centum of the value of the permanent insured improvements thereon as determined upon an appraisal made pursuant to this Act, whichever is the smaller: . . ."

*Reduction of Interest on Loans
and Deferment of Principal*

SEC. 24. . . . the Federal Farm Loan Act, . . . is amended by adding at the end thereof the following new paragraph:

"Twelfth. Notwithstanding the provisions of paragraph 'Second,' the rate of interest on any loans on mortgage made through national farm-loan associations or through agents . . . or purchased from joint-stock land banks, by any Federal land bank, outstanding on the date this paragraph takes effect or made through national farm-loan associations within two years after such date, shall not exceed 4½ per centum per annum of all interest payable on installment dates occurring within a period of five years commencing sixty days after the date this paragraph takes effect; and no payment of the principal portion of any installment of any such loan shall be required during such five-year period if the borrower shall not be in default with respect to any other condition or covenant of his mortgage."

## (b) The National Labor Relations Act, July 5, 1935

*An Act to diminish the causes of labor disputes burdening or obstructing interstate and foreign commerce, to create a National Labor Relations Board, and for other purposes.*

*Findings and Policy*

SECTION 1. The denial by employers of the right of employees to organize and the refusal by employers to accept the procedure of collective bargaining lead to strikes and other forms of industrial strife or unrest, which have the intent or the necessary effect of burdening or obstructing commerce by (a) impairing the efficiency, safety, or operation of the instrumentalities of commerce; (b) occurring in the current of commerce; (c) materially affecting, restraining, or controlling the flow of raw materials or manufactured or processed goods from or into the channels of commerce, or the prices of such materials or goods in commerce; or (d) causing diminution of employment and wages in such volume as substantially to impair or disrupt the market for goods flowing from or into the channels of commerce.

The inequality of bargaining power between employees who do not possess full freedom of association or actual liberty of contract, and employers who are organized in the corporate or other forms of ownership association substantially burdens and affects the flow of commerce, and tends to aggravate recurrent business depressions, by depressing wage rates and the purchasing power of wage earners in industry and by preventing the stabilization of competitive wage rates and working conditions within and between industries.

Experience has proved that protection by law of the right of employees to organize and bargain collectively safeguards commerce from injury, impairment, or interruption, and promotes the flow of commerce by removing certain recognized sources of industrial strife and unrest, by encouraging practices fundamental to the friendly adjustment of industrial disputes arising out of differences as to wages, hours, or other working conditions, and by restoring equality of bargaining power between employers and employees.

It is hereby declared to be the policy of the United States to eliminate the causes of certain substantial obstructions to the free flow of commerce and to mitigate and eliminate these obstructions when they have occurred by encouraging the practice and procedure of collective bargaining and by protecting the exercise by workers of full freedom of association, self-organization, and designation of representatives of their own choosing, for the purpose of negotiating the terms and conditions of their employment or other mutual aid or protection.

### Definitions

SEC. 2. When used in this Act— . . .

The term "employer" includes any person acting in the interest of an employer, directly or indirectly, but shall not include the United States, or any State or political subdivision thereof . . .

The term "employee" shall include any employee, and shall not be limited to the employees of a particular employer, unless the Act explicitly states otherwise, and shall include any individual whose work has ceased as a consequence of, or in connection with, any current labor dispute or because of any unfair labor practice, and who has not obtained any other regular and substantially equivalent employment . . .

The term "labor organization" means any organization of any kind, or any agency or employee representation committee or plan, in which employees participate and which exists for the purpose, in whole or in part, of dealing with employers concerning grievances, labor disputes, wages, rates of pay, hours of employment, or conditions of work. . . .

The term "labor dispute" includes any controversy concerning terms, tenure or conditions of employment, or concerning the association or representation of persons in negotiating, fixing, maintaining, changing, or seeking to arrange terms or conditions of employment, regardless of whether the disputants stand in the proximate relation of employer and employee. . . .

### National Labor Relations Board

SEC. 3. (a) There is hereby created a board, to be known as the "National Labor Relations Board," which shall be composed of three members, who shall be appointed by the President, by and with the advice and consent of the Senate, . . . for terms of five years. . . .

### Rights of Employees

SEC. 7. Employees shall have the right of self-organization, to form, join, or assist labor organizations, to bargain collectively through representatives of their own choosing, and to engage in concerted activities, for the purpose of collective bargaining or other mutual aid or protection.

SEC. 8. It shall be unfair labor practice for an employer—

(1) To interfere with, restrain, or coerce employees in the exercise of the rights guaranteed in section 7.

(2) To dominate or interfere with the formation or administration of any labor organization or contribute financial or other support to it: *Provided*, That . . . an employer shall not be prohibited from permitting employees to confer with him during working hours without loss of time or pay.

(3) By discrimination in regard to hire or tenure of employment or any term or condition of employment to encourage or discourage membership in any labor organization: *Provided*, That nothing in this Act, . . . or in any other statute of the United States, shall preclude an employer from making an agreement with a labor organization (not established, maintained, or assisted by any action defined in this Act as an unfair labor practice) to require as a condition of employment membership therein, if such labor organization is the representative of the employees as provided in section 9 (a), in the appropriate collective bargaining unit covered by such agreement when made.

(4) To discharge or otherwise discriminate against an employee because he has filed charges or given testimony under this Act.

(5) To refuse to bargain collectively with the representatives of his employees, subject to the provisions of Section 9 (a).

### Representatives and Elections

SEC. 9. (a) Representatives designated . . . for the purposes of collective bargaining by the majority of the employees in a unit appropriate for such purposes, shall be the exclusive representatives of all the employees in such unit . . . : *Provided*, That any individual employee or a group of employees shall have the right at any time to present grievances to their employer.

(b) The Board shall decide in each case whether . . . the unit appropriate for the purposes of collective bargaining shall be the employer unit, craft unit, plant unit, or subdivision thereof.

(c) Whenever a question . . . arises concerning the representation of employees, the Board may investigate such controversy and certify to the parties, in writing, the name or names of the representatives that have been designated or selected. In any such investigation, the Board shall provide for an appropriate hearing upon due notice, . . . and may take a secret ballot of employees, or utilize any other suitable method to ascertain such representatives. . . .

### Prevention of Unfair Labor Practices

SEC. 10. (a) The Board is empowered, as hereinafter provided, to prevent any person from engaging in any unfair labor practice (listed in section 8). . . .

(b) Whenever it is charged that any person has engaged in or is engaging in any such unfair labor practice, the Board . . . shall have power to . . . cause to be served upon such person a complaint stating the charges. . . . The person so complained of shall have the right to file an answer . . . and give testimony at the place and time fixed in the complaint. In the discretion of the member, agent or agency conducting the hearing or the Board, any other person may be allowed to intervene in the said proceeding and to present testimony. In any such proceeding the rules of evidence prevailing in courts of law or equity shall not be controlling.

(c) . . . If upon all the testimony taken the Board shall be of the opinion that any person named in the complaint has engaged in or is engaging in any such unfair labor practice, then the Board shall state its findings of fact and shall issue and cause to be served on such person an order requiring such person to cease and desist from such unfair labor practice, and to take such affirmative action, including reinstatement of employees with or without back pay, as will effectuate the policies of this Act. Such order may further require such person to make reports from time to time showing the extent to which it has complied with the order. If . . . the Board shall be of the opinion that no person named in the complaint has engaged in or is engaging in any such unfair labor practice, then the Board shall . . . issue an order dismissing the said complaint. . . .

(e) The Board shall have power to petition any circuit court of appeals of the United States, or . . . any district court of the United States, . . . wherein the unfair labor practice in question occurred or wherein such person resides or transacts business, for the enforcement of such order and for appropriate temporary relief or restraining order, and shall certify and file in the court a transcript of the entire record in the proceeding. . . . Upon such filing, the court shall cause notice thereof to be served upon such person . . . and shall have power to grant such temporary relief or restraining order as it deems just and proper, and to . . . set forth in such transcript a decree enforcing, modifying, and enforcing as so modified, or setting aside in whole or in part the order of the Board. . . . The findings of the Board as to the facts, if supported by evidence, shall be conclusive. . . .

The jurisdiction of the court shall be exclusive and its judgment and decree shall be final except that the same shall be subject to review by the appropriate circuit court of appeals if application was made to the district court, . . . and by the Supreme Court of the United States. . . .

(f) Any person aggrieved by a final order of the Board granting or denying in whole or in part the relief sought may obtain a review of such order in any circuit court of appeals of the United States in the circuit wherein the unfair labor practice in question was alleged to have been engaged in or wherein such person resides or transacts business. . . .

(g) The commencement of proceedings under subsection (e) and (f) of this section shall not, unless specifically ordered by the court, operate as a stay of the Board's order. . . .

*Investigatory Powers*

SEC. 11. For the purpose of all hearings and investigations, . . . any member of the Board shall have power to issue subpenas requiring the attendance and testimony of witnesses and the production of any evidence that relates to any matter under investigation or in question. . . .

SEC. 12. Any person who shall willfully resist, prevent, impede, or interfere with any member of the Board or any of its agents or agencies in the performance of duties pursuant to this Act shall be punished by a fine of not more than $5,000 or by imprisonment for not more than one year, or both.

*Limitations*

SEC. 13. Nothing in this Act shall be construed so as to interfere with or impede or diminish in any way the right to strike.

(c)   *The Social Security Act, August 14, 1935*

*An Act to provide for the general welfare by establishing a system of Federal old-age benefits, and by enabling the several States to make more adequate provision for aged persons, blind persons, dependent and crippled children,* maternal and child welfare, public health, and the administration of their unemployment compensation laws; to establish a Social Security Board; to raise revenue; and for other purposes.

## TITLE I—GRANTS TO STATES FOR OLD AGE ASSISTANCE

### Appropriation

SECTION 1. For the purpose of enabling each State to furnish financial assistance, as far as practicable under the conditions in such State, to aged needy individuals, there is hereby authorized to be appropriated for the fiscal year ending June 30, 1936, the sum of $49,750,000, and there is hereby authorized to be appropriated for each fiscal year thereafter a sum sufficient to carry out the purposes of this title. The sums made available under this section shall be used for making payments to States which have submitted, and had approved by the Social Security Board established by Title VII, State plans for old-age assistance.

### State Old-Age Assistance Plans

SEC. 2. (a) A State plan for old-age assistance must (1) provide that it shall be in effect in all political subdivisions of the State, and, if administered by them, be mandatory upon them; (2) provide for financial participation by the State; (3) . . . provide for the establishment or designation of a single State agency to administer . . . or . . . to supervise the administration of the plan; (4) provide for granting to any individual, whose claim for old-age assistance is denied, an opportunity for a fair hearing before such State agency; (5) provide such methods of administration . . . as are found by the Board to be necessary for the efficient operation of the plan; (6) provide that the State agency will make such reports . . . as the Board may from time to time require. . . .

### Payment to States

SEC. 3. (a) . . . The Secretary of the Treasury shall pay to each State which has an approved plan for old-age assistance, for each quarter, . . . (1) an amount, which shall be used exclusively as old-age assistance, equal to one-half of the total of the sums expended during such quarter as old-age assistance under the State plan with respect to each individual who at the time of such expenditure is sixty-five years of age or older, and . . . (2) 5 per centum of such amount, which shall be used for paying the costs of administering the State plan. . . .

## TITLE II—FEDERAL OLD-AGE BENEFITS

### Old-Age Reserve Account

SECTION 201. (a) There is hereby created an account in the Treasury of the United States to be known as the "Old-Age Reserve Account." . . .

### Old-Age Benefit Payments

SEC. 202. (a) Every qualified individual shall be entitled to receive, with respect to the period beginning on the date he attains the age of sixty-five, or on January 1, 1942, whichever is the later, and ending on the date of his death, an old-age benefit (payable [with respect to employment] as nearly as practicable in equal monthly installments) as follows [details omitted]. . . .

(b) In no case shall the monthly rate . . . exceed $85. . . .

### Payments upon Death

SEC. 203. (a) If any individual dies before attaining the age of sixty-five, there shall be paid to his estate an amount equal to 3½ per centum of the total wages determined by the Board to have been paid to him, with respect to employment after December 31, 1936. . . .

### Payments to Aged Individuals Not Qualified for Benefits

SEC. 204. (a) There shall be paid in a lump sum to any individual who, upon attaining the age of sixty-five, is not a qualified individual, an amount equal to 3½ per centum of the total wages determined by the Board to have been paid to him, with respect to employment after December 31, 1936, and before he attained the age of sixty-five. . . .

SEC. 210. . . . (b) The term "employment" means any service, of whatever nature, performed within the United States by an employee for his employer, except—

(1) Agricultural labor;

(2) Domestic service in a private home;

(3) Casual labor not in the course of the employer's trade or business;

(4) Service performed as an officer or member of the crew of a vessel documented under the laws of the United States or of any foreign country;

(5) Service performed in the employ of the United States Government or of an instrumentality of the United States;

(6) Service performed in the employ of a State, a political subdivision thereof, or an instrumentality of one or more States or political subdivisions;

(7) Service performed in the employ of a corporation, community chest, fund, or foundation, organized and operated exclusively for religious, charitable, scientific, literary, or educational purposes. . . .

TITLE III—GRANTS TO STATES FOR UNEMPLOYMENT COMPENSATION ADMINISTRATION

. . . SEC. 302. (a) The Board shall from time to time certify to the Secretary of the Treasury for payment to each State which has an unemployment compensation law approved by the Board . . . such amounts as the Board determines to be necessary for the proper administration of such law during the fiscal year in which such payment is to be made. The Board's determination shall be based on (1) the population of the State; (2) an esti-

mate of the number of persons covered by the State law and of the cost of proper administration of such law; and (3) such other factors as the Board finds relevant [protective and administrative details omitted]. . . .

TITLE IV—GRANTS TO STATES FOR AID TO DEPENDENT CHILDREN

. . . SEC. 403. (a) From the sums appropriated therefor, the Secretary of the Treasury shall pay to each State which has an approved plan for aid to dependent children, for each quarter, . . . an amount . . . equal to one-third of the total of the sums expended during such quarter under such plan, not counting so much of such expenditure with respect to any dependent child for any month as exceeds $18, or if there is more than one dependent child in the same home, as exceeds $18 in any month with respect to one such dependent child and $12 for such month with respect to each of the other dependent children [other clauses omitted]. . . .

TITLE V—GRANTS TO STATES FOR MATERNAL AND CHILD WELFARE

Part 1—Maternal and Child Health Services

. . . SECTION 501. For the purpose of enabling each State to extend and improve, as far as practicable under the conditions in such State, services for promoting the health of mothers and children, especially in rural areas and in areas suffering from severe economic distress, there is hereby authorized to be appropriated for each fiscal year, beginning with the fiscal year ending June 30, 1936, the sum of $3,800,-000. The sums made available under this section shall be used for making payments to States which have submitted, and had approved by the Chief of the Children's Bureau, State plans for such services [other details omitted]. . . .

*Part 2—Services for
Crippled Children Appropriation*

SEC. 511. For the purpose of enabling each State to extend and improve, . . . as far as practicable under the conditions in such State, services for locating crippled children, and for providing medical, surgical, corrective, and other services and care, and facilities for diagnosis, hospitalization, and after-care, for children who are crippled or who are suffering from conditions which lead to crippling, there is hereby authorized to be appropriated for each fiscal year, beginning with the fiscal year ending June 30, 1936, the sum of $2,850,000. The sums made available under this section shall be used for making payments to States which have submitted, and had approved by the Chief of the Children's Bureau, State plans for such services [other details omitted]. . . .

*Part 3—Child-Welfare Services*

SEC. 521. (a) For the purpose of enabling the United States, through the Children's Bureau, to cooperate with State public-welfare agencies in establishing, extending, and strengthening, especially in predominantly rural areas, public-welfare services . . . for the protection and care of homeless, dependent, and neglected children, and children in danger of becoming delinquent, there is hereby authorized to be appropriated for each fiscal year, beginning with the fiscal year ending June 30, 1936, the sum of $1,500,000. Such amount shall be allotted by the Secretary of Labor for use by cooperating State public-welfare agencies [other details omitted]. . . .

*Part 4—Vocational Rehabilitation*

SEC. 531. (a) In order to enable the United States to cooperate with the States . . . in extending and strengthening their programs of vocational rehabilitation of the physically disabled, . . . there is hereby authorized [details omitted]. . . .

TITLE VI—PUBLIC HEALTH WORK

SECTION 601. For the purpose of assisting States, counties, health districts, and other political subdivisions of the States in establishing and maintaining adequate public-health services, including the training of personnel for State and local health work, there is hereby authorized to be appropriated for each fiscal year, beginning with the fiscal year ending June 30, 1936, the sum of $8,000,000 to be used as hereinafter provided [details omitted]. . . .

TITLE VII—SOCIAL SECURITY BOARD

SECTION 701. There is hereby established a Social Security Board to be composed of three members to be appointed by the President, by and with the advice and consent of the Senate. . . . Not more than two of the members of the Board shall be members of the same political party. Each member shall . . . hold office for a term of six years, . . .

SEC. 702. The Board shall perform the duties imposed upon it by this Act and shall also have the duty of studying and making recommendations as to the most effective methods of providing economic security through social insurance, and as to legislation and matters of administrative policy concerning old-age pensions, unemployment compensation, accident compenastion, and related subjects. . . .

TITLE X—GRANTS TO STATES
FOR AID TO THE BLIND

SECTION 1001. For the purpose of enabling each State to furnish financial assistance, as far as practicable under the conditions in such State, to needy individuals who are blind, there is hereby authorized to be appropriated [details omitted]. . . . The sums made available under this section shall be used for making payments to States which have submitted, and have approved by the Social Security Board, State plans for aid to the blind.

## 52

*"The future and the safety of our country and
of our democracy are overwhelmingly involved
in events beyond our borders "*

Although Wendell Willkie had been talked of as a dark-horse Republican candidate for the presidency as early as February, 1939, in April, 1940, he still counted no following whatever among Republican bosses or the Republican rank and file, both heavily isolationist in spirit. On April 9, 1940, the "phony war" in Europe came to a shocking end when Hitler, roused from the winter's apparent lethargy after his conquest of Poland the previous Fall, overran all of Denmark and the principal ports of Norway in 24 hours. In four days in mid-May the German blitzkrieg overwhelmed the Netherlands, and before the end of that month Belgium also had succumbed. When France capitulated in mid-June, Winston Churchill told a stunned House of Commons:

> I expect the Battle of Britain is about to begin. . . . Hitler knows that he will have to break us in this island or lose the war. If we can stand up to him, all Europe may be free. . . . But if we fail, then the whole world, including the United States, . . . will sink into the abyss of a new Dark Age, made more sinister, and perhaps more protracted, by the lights of perverted science.

With every advance of the Nazi terror in Europe that fateful Spring, isolationist ranks in the United States shrank back while Willkie's stock mounted. Willkie's startling triumph over Thomas E. Dewey and Robert A. Taft in the Republican convention in June, 1940, finished isolationism as a dominant force in American national politics. Roosevelt's triumph over Willkie in the elections in November, in turn, liberated from the constraints of domestic political concerns his own strong impulse to intervene on Britain's behalf.

Already, on September 3, 1940, Roosevelt had risked popular revulsion and congressional censure when, impatient of legislative delays and debates, he personally made the bold deal with Churchill in which the beleaguered British navy was augmented by fifty over-age American destroyers. Churchill's reaction to this virtual act of war had been that the United States and Britain henceforth would become "somewhat mixed up together." Churchill added:

> I do not view the process with any misgivings. I could not stop it if I wished; no one can stop it. Like the Mississippi, it just keeps rolling along. Let it roll.

Let it roll on—full flood, inexorable, irresistible, benignant, to broader lands and better days.

At home even Willkie denounced Roosevelt's daring as "the most dictatorial and arbitrary act of any President in the history of the United States." The recently formed America First Committee emitted harsher words. But the people apparently approved, for FDR, having also seen through Congress on September 16 the first peacetime compulsory military service act, went on to his decisive election victory only two months later.

It was in his first post-election "Fireside Chat" on December 29, 1940, that Roosevelt declared, "There will be no 'bottlenecks' in our determination to aid Great Britain." For more than a year American industry had been girding itself for "defense" production. "But," Roosevelt said now, "all our present efforts are not enough. We must have more ships, more guns, more planes—more of everything. . . . We must be the great arsenal of democracy."

In his first third-term annual message to Congress, January 6, 1941—presented in large part in this Document—Roosevelt went much farther:

> I shall ask this Congress for greatly increased new appropriations and authorizations to carry on what we have begun. . . . The time is near when . . . those nations which are now in actual war with aggressor nations . . . will not be able to pay . . . in ready cash. We cannot, and will not, tell them they must surrender, merely because of inability to pay for the weapons we know they must have.

On Roosevelt's recommendation in this message, Congress, on March 11, 1941, passed the "lend-lease" act under which, during the course of World War II, arms, equipment, and other supplies valued at more than $50 billion were made available to those nations whose defense was deemed vital to the survival of the United States.

Roosevelt knew that more than weapons were needed:

> As men do not live by bread alone, they do not fight by armaments alone. Those who man our defenses, and those behind them who build our defenses, must have the stamina and courage which come from an unshakeable belief in the manner of life which they are defending.

He proceeded to review those New Deal measures—parts of "the social revolution which is today the supreme factor in the world"—that "toughened the fibre of our people" and "strengthened their devotion to the institutions which we make ready to protect." And he looked forward, "in the future days, which we seek to make secure," to "a world founded upon four essential human freedoms, . . . a kind of world attainable in our own time and generation." Such a world was *our* only future guarantee: "We know that enduring peace cannot be bought at the cost of other people's freedom." World freedom, like our own, required eternal vigilance, not withdrawal: "I find it necessary to report that the future and the safety of our country and of our democracy are overwhelmingly involved in events far beyond our borders."

*January 6, 1941*

# Franklin D. Roosevelt

# and the End of Isolation

*(From his ninth State of the Union Message to Congress)*

I ADDRESS YOU, the Members of the Seventy-seventh Congress, at a moment unprecedented in the history of the Union. I use the word "unprecedented," because at no previous time has American security been as seriously threatened from without. . . .

It is true that prior to 1914 the United States often had been disturbed by events in other Continents. . . . In no case, however, had a serious threat been raised against our national safety or our independence.

What I seek to convey is the historic truth that the United States as a Nation has at all times maintained opposition to any attempt to lock us in behind an ancient Chinese wall while the procession of civilization went past. Today, thinking of our children and their children, we oppose enforced isolation for ourselves or for any part of the Americas. . . .

Even when the World War broke out in 1914, it seemed to contain only small threat of danger to our own American future. But, as time went on, the American people began to visualize what the downfall of democratic nations might mean to our own democracy.

We need not over-emphasize imperfections in the Peace of Versailles. We need not harp on failure of the democracies to deal with problems of world reconstruction. We should remember that the Peace of 1919 was far less unjust than the kind of "pacification" which began even before Munich, and which is being carried on under the new order of tyranny that seeks to spread over every continent today. The American people have unalterably set their faces against that tyranny.

Every realist knows that the democratic way of life is at this moment being directly assailed in every part of the world—assailed either by arms, or by secret spreading of poisonous propaganda by those who seek to destroy unity and promote discord in nations still at peace.

During sixteen months this assault has blotted out the whole pattern of democratic life in an appalling number of independent nations, great and small. The assailants are still on the march, threatening other nations, great and small.

Therefore, as your President, performing my constitutional duty to "give to the Congress information of the state of the Union," I find it necessary to report that the future and the safety of our country and of our democracy are overwhelmingly involved in events far beyond our borders.

Armed defense of democratic existence is now being gallantly waged in four continents. If that defense fails, all the population and all the resources of

Europe, Asia, Africa and Australasia will be dominated by the conquerors. The total of those populations and their resources greatly exceeds the sum total of the population and resources of the whole of the Western Hemisphere—many times over.

In times like these it is immature—and incidentally untrue—for anybody to brag that an unprepared America, single-handed, and with one hand tied behind its back, can hold off the whole world.

No realistic American can expect from a dictator's peace international generosity, or return of true independence, or world disarmament, or freedom of expression, or freedom of religion—or even good business.

Such a peace would bring no security for us or for our neighbors. "Those, who would give up essential liberty to purchase a little temporary safety, deserve neither liberty nor safety."

As a Nation we may take pride in the fact that we are soft-hearted; but we cannot afford to be soft-headed.

We must always be wary of those who with sounding brass and a tinkling cymbal preach the "ism" of appeasement.

We must especially beware of that small group of selfish men who would clip the wings of the American eagle in order to feather their own nests.

I have recently pointed out how quickly the tempo of modern warfare could bring into our very midst the physical attack which we must expect if the dictator nations win this war.

There is much loose talk of our immunity from immediate and direct invasion from across the seas. Obviously, as long as the British Navy retains its power, no such danger exists. Even if there were no British Navy, it is not probable that any enemy would be stupid enough to attack us by landing troops in the United States from across thousands of miles of ocean, until it had acquired strategic bases from which to operate.

But we learn much from the lessons of the past years in Europe—particularly the lesson of Norway, whose essential seaports were captured by treachery and surprise built up over a series of years.

The first phase of the invasion of this Hemisphere would not be the landing of regular troops. The necessary strategic points would be occupied by secret agents and their dupes—and great numbers of them are already here, and in Latin America.

As long as the aggressor nations maintain the offensive, they—not we—will choose the time and the place and the method of their attack.

That is why the future of all American Republics is today in serious danger.

That is why this Annual Message to the Congress is unique in our history.

That is why every member of the Executive Branch of the Government and every member of the Congress faces great responsibility—and great accountability.

The need of the moment is that our actions and our policy should be devoted primarily—almost exclusively—to meeting this foreign peril. For all our domestic problems are now a part of the great emergency.

Just as our national policy in internal affairs has been based upon a decent respect for the rights and dignity of all our fellowmen within our gates, so our national policy in foreign affairs has been based on a decent respect for the rights and dignity of all nations, large and small. And the justice of morality must and will win in the end.

Our national policy is this:

First, by an impressive expression of the public will and without regard to partisanship, we are committed to all-inclusive national defense.

Second, by an impressive expression of the public will and without regard to partisanship, we are committed to full support of all those resolute peoples, everywhere, who are resisting aggression and are thereby keeping war away from our Hemisphere. By this support, we express our determination that the democratic cause shall prevail; and we strengthen the defense and security of our own nation.

Third, by an impressive expression of the public will and without regard to partisanship we are committed to the proposition that principles of morality and considerations for our own security will never permit us to acquiesce in a peace dictated by aggressors and sponsored by appeasers. We know that enduring peace cannot be bought at the cost of other people's freedom.

In the recent national election there was no substantial difference between the two great parties in respect to that national policy. No issue was fought out on this line before the American electorate. Today, it is abundantly evident that American citizens everywhere are demanding and supporting speedy and complete action in recognition of obvious danger.

Therefore, the immediate need is a swift and driving increase in our armament production.

Leaders of industry and labor have responded to our summons. Goals of speed have been set. In some cases these goals are being reached ahead of time; in some cases we are on schedule; in other cases there are slight but not serious delays; and in some cases—and I am sorry to say very important cases— we are all concerned by the slowness of the accomplishment of our plans.

The Army and Navy, however, have made substantial progress during the past year. Actual experience is improving and speeding up our methods of production with every passing day. And today's best is not good enough for tomorrow.

I am not satisfied with the progress thus far made. The men in charge of the program represent the best in training, ability and patriotism. They are not satisfied with the progress thus far made. None of us will be satisfied until the job is done.

No matter whether the original goal was set too high or too low, our objective is quicker and better results.

To give two illustrations:

We are behind schedule in turning out finished airplanes; we are working day and night to solve the innumerable problems and to catch up.

We are ahead of schedule in building warships; but we are working to get even further ahead of schedule.

To change a whole nation from a basis of peacetime production of implements of peace to a basis of wartime production of implements of war is no small task. And the greatest difficulty comes at the beginning of the program, when new tools and plant facilities and new assembly lines and ship ways must first be constructed before the actual material begins to flow steadily and speedily from them. . . .

New circumstances are constantly begetting new needs for our safety. I shall ask this Congress for greatly increased new appropriations and authorizations to carry on what we have begun.

I also ask this Congress for authority and for funds sufficient to manufacture additional munitions and war supplies of many kinds, to be turned over to those nations which are now in actual war with aggressor nations.

Our most useful and immediate role is to act as an arsenal for them as well as for ourselves. They do not need man power. They do need billions of dollars worth of the weapons of defense.

The time is near when they will not be able to pay for them in ready cash. We cannot, and will not, tell them they must surrender, merely because of present inability to pay for the weapons which we know they must have.

I do not recommend that we make them a loan of dollars with which to pay for these weapons—a loan to be repaid in dollars.

I recommend that we make it possible for those nations to continue to obtain war materials in the United States, fitting their orders into our own program. Nearly all of their matériel would, if the time ever came, be useful for our own defense. . . .

For what we send abroad, we shall be repaid, within a reasonable time following the close of hostilities, in similar materials, or, at our option, in other goods of many kinds which they can produce and which we need.

Let us say to the democracies: "We Americans are vitally concerned in your defense of freedom. We are putting forth our energies, our resources and our organizing powers to give you the strength to regain and maintain a free world. We shall send you, in ever-increasing numbers, ships, planes, tanks, guns. This is our purpose and our pledge."

In fulfillment of this purpose we will not be intimidated by the threats of dictators that they will regard as a breach of international law and as an act of war our aid to the democracies which dare to resist their aggression. Such aid is not an act of war, even if a dictator should unilaterally proclaim it so to be.

When the dictators are ready to make war upon us, they will not wait for an act of war on our part. They did not wait for Norway or Belgium or the Netherlands to commit an act of war.

Their only interest is in a new one-way international law, which lacks mutuality in its observance, and, therefore, becomes an instrument of oppression.

The happiness of future generations of Americans may well depend upon how effective and how immediate we can make our aid felt. No one can tell the exact character of the emergency situations that we may be called upon to meet. The Nation's hands must not be tied when the Nation's life is in danger.

We must all prepare to make the sacrifices that the emergency—as serious as war itself—demands. Whatever stands in the way of speed and efficiency in defense preparations must give way to the national need.

A free nation has the right to expect full cooperation from all groups. A free nation has the right to look to the leaders of business, of labor, and of agriculture to take the lead in stimulating effort, not among other groups but within their own groups.

The best way of dealing with the few slackers or trouble makers in our midst is, first, to shame them by patriotic example, and, if that fails, to use the sovereignty of government to save government.

As men do not live by bread alone, they do not fight by armaments alone. Those who man our defenses, and those behind them who build our defenses, must have the stamina and courage which come from an unshakeable belief in the manner of life which they are defending. The mighty action which we are calling for, cannot be based on a disregard of all things worth fighting for.

The Nation takes great satisfaction and much strength from the things which have been done to make its people conscious of their individual stake in the preservation of democratic life in America. Those things have toughened the fibre of our people, have renewed their faith and strengthened their devotion to the institutions we make ready to protect.

Certainly this is no time to stop thinking about the social and economic problems which are the root cause of the social revolution which is today a supreme factor in the world.

There is nothing mysterious about the foundations of a healthy and strong democracy. The basic things expected by our people of their political and economic systems are simple. They are:

Equality of opportunity for youth and for others.

Jobs for those who can work.

Security for those who need it.

The ending of special privilege for the few.

The preservation of civil liberties for all.

The enjoyment of the fruits of scientific progress in a wider and constantly rising standard of living.

These are the simple and basic things that must never be lost sight of in the turmoil and unbelievable complexity of our modern world. The inner and abiding strength of our economic and political systems is dependent upon the degree to which they fulfill these expectations. . . .

I have called for personal sacrifice. I am assured of the willingness of almost all Americans to respond to that call.

A part of the sacrifice means the payment of more money in taxes. In my budget message I recommend that a greater portion of this great defense program be paid for from taxation than we are paying today. No person should try, or be allowed, to get rich out of this program; and the principle of tax payments in accordance with ability to pay should be constantly before our eyes to guide our legislation.

If the Congress maintains these principles, the voters, putting patriotism ahead of pocketbooks, will give you their applause.

In the future days, which we seek to make secure, we look forward to a world founded upon four essential human freedoms.

The first is freedom of speech and expression—everywhere in the world.

The second is freedom of every person to worship God in his own way—everywhere in the world.

The third is freedom from want—which, translated into world terms, means economic understandings which will secure to every nation a healthy peacetime life for its inhabitants—everywhere in the world.

The fourth is freedom from fear—which, translated into world terms, means a world-wide reduction of armaments to such a point and in such a thorough fashion that no nation will be in a position to commit an act of physical aggression against any neighbor—anywhere in the world.

That is no vision of a distant millennium. It is a definite basis for a kind of world attainable in our own time and generation. That kind of world is the very antithesis of the so-called new order of tyranny which the dictators seek to create with the crash of a bomb.

To that new order we oppose the greater conception—the moral order. A good society is able to face schemes of world domination and foreign revolutions alike without fear.

Since the beginning of our American history we have been engaged in change —in a perpetual peaceful revolution— a revolution which goes on steadily, quietly adjusting itself to changing conditions—without the concentration camp or the quick-lime in the ditch. The world order which we seek is the cooperation of free countries, working together in a friendly, civilized society.

This Nation has placed its destiny in the hands and heads and hearts of its millions of free men and women; and its faith in freedom under the guidance of God. Freedom means the supremacy of human rights everywhere. Our support goes to those who struggle to gain those rights or keep them. Our strength is in our unity of purpose.

To that high concept there can be no end save victory.

## 53

*"We the peoples of the United Nations, determined to save succeeding generations from the scourge of war"*

On June 26, 1945, delegates from 50 nations, after meeting in San Francisco for two months, signed the United Nations Charter, the subject of this Document. In June, 1964, the United Nations boasted 111 members.

The two decades of United Nations history are also the two decades which saw the sudden dissolution of the vast empires which the great Western powers had begun to build in the age of Columbus and which grew to immense proportions, especially in Asia and Africa, in the age of Queen Victoria. From this process of dissolution most of the new members of the United Nations had emerged as new states. Some had gained statehood peacefully, others violently. In either case, independence tended to breed narrow nationalism, costly pride, a passion for self-determination.

The birth traumas and the period of the new states' growing pains coincided not only with the birth and growth of the United Nations but also with the start and spread of the great confrontation of "east" and "west," of "communism" and "democracy," and more particularly of the U.S.S.R. and the United States, the Herculean nuclear powers of the postwar world. This confrontation took place in the arena of the United Nations as well as outside it. One of its principal prizes was influence if not suzerainty over the newly independent states and regions. The nuclear powers' pursuit of this prize often unbearably stretched the severe tensions within its innocent objects and within the great powers themselves. But the quest for predominance also took the form of competition in aid and assistance which, while offensive to the reigning spirit of nationalism and self-determination, sometimes strengthened the foundations and brightened the prospects of both (see Document No. 54, below).

The nuclear powers' confrontation heightened tensions all over the world, not only in new states, and presented the United Nations with the sturdiest challenges to its police power and its undertaking to end "the scourge of war." It also presented the United Nations with its broadest opportunities to conduct new and old nations alike along the most promising paths toward lasting peace. The United Nations' early and lasting failure to control armaments, especially nuclear armaments, made all the more terrible the easily imagined consequences of its weakness in "policing" possible collisions of the nuclear powers. Yet these powers' own apparent terror of one another may have made all the more successful the worldwide "politics of arrangement" by which the general peace has been kept under the canopy of the nuclear stalemate and in the halls and lobbies of the U.N.

In any case it has been suggested by knowledgeable observers of the world organization in action that "one of the most valuable functions of the United Nations is to integrate the new states into the world community." Such observers, as one of them said of his colleagues, "have also remarked upon the great speed with which representatives of the new states have adjusted themselves to the new environment." There is also the other side of the coin, which has not been neglected. As Joseph E. Johnson, President of the Carnegie Endowment for International Peace, said in 1961:

> Indeed, I wonder whether the greatest contribution of the United Nations will not be, ultimately, to smooth *our* adjustment to the fact of the new states, to help *us* accommodate ourselves to a world that is changing rapidly and will change even more drastically in the future.

The nuclear stalemate, at a time "when the forces of social and political action can be as explosive as an uncontrolled nuclear reaction," has put a premium, as Lester B. Pearson of Canada put it, upon "an understanding of the techniques necessary to effect political, social, economic and cultural change without recourse to force." The process of accommodation within the United Nations of the new states to the ways of the old, of the old states to the temperament of the new, hopefully has advanced this understanding and the prospects for peace it affords. As Pearson stated, "we have nothing more certain to guide our program than the politics of arrangement between nations and blocks of nations. . . . There is no other practical focus for our aspirations."

Time probably is on the side of understanding, and on the side of the U.N. Perhaps the U.N., as much as the nuclear stalemate in the great confrontation outside it, is to be credited with the general peace of the past generation. Perhaps it is only a symbol of the good intentions with which Hell is said to be paved. If so, it is not the paving that makes Hell what it is said to be; and even there good intentions may have smoothed out the pricks of existence. Nothing is as full of good intentions as the Charter of the U.N., which is the feature emphasized in the extensive excerpts below.

As late as August, 1941, still respectful of isolationist opinion and isolationist power, President Roosevelt, in the Atlantic Charter, felt obliged to repulse Churchill's proposal of an "effective international organization" to maintain peace in the postwar world. Roosevelt dared plead only for disarmament, "pending the establishment of a wider and permanent system of general security." Thereafter, however, Secretary of State Cordell Hull, with widening bipartisan support in Congress, placed the United States squarely in the lead in developing United Nations plans, which themselves became the foundation of Roosevelt's wartime diplomacy. The United States Senate had debated the Covenant of the League of Nations eight months before rejecting it. In July, 1945, the Senate approved United States membership in the U.N. in six days by a vote of 89 to 2. The resounding opening phrases of the charter, quoted in part at the head of this Document, disclose its debt to the United States Constitution and to the spirit of twentieth-century democracy in the United States.

*June 26, 1945*

# The Charter of the United Nations

WE THE PEOPLES of the United Nations, determined to save succeeding generations from the scourge of war, which twice in our life-time has brought untold sorrow to mankind, and to reaffirm faith in fundamental human rights, in the dignity and worth of the human person, in the equal rights of men and women and of nations large and small, and to establish conditions under which justice and respect for the obligations arising from treaties and other sources of international law can be maintained, and to promote social progress and better standards of life in larger freedom, and for these ends to practice tolerance and live together in peace with one another as good neighbors, and to unite our strength to maintain international peace and security, and to ensure, by the acceptance of principles and the institution of methods, that armed force shall not be used, save in the common interest, and to employ international machinery for the promotion of the economic and social advancement of all peoples, have resolved to combine our efforts to accomplish these aims.

Accordingly, our respective Governments, through representatives assembled in the city of San Francisco, who have exhibited their full powers found to be in good and due form, have agreed to the present Charter of the United Nations and do hereby establish an international organization to be known as the United Nations.

CHAPTER I.
PURPOSES AND PRINCIPLES

ARTICLE 1. The Purposes of the United Nations are:

1. To maintain international peace and security, and to that end: to take effective collective measures for the prevention and removal of threats to the peace, and for the suppression of acts of aggression or other breaches of the peace, and to bring about by peaceful means, and in conformity with the principles of justice and international law, adjustment or settlement of international disputes or situations which might lead to a breach of the peace;

2. To develop friendly relations among nations based on respect for the principle of equal rights and self-determination of peoples, and to take other appropriate measures to strengthen universal peace;

3. To achieve international cooperation in solving international problems of an economic, social, cultural, or humanitarian character, and in promoting and encouraging respect for human rights and for fundamental freedoms

for all without distinction as to race, sex, language, or religion, and

4. To be a center for harmonizing the actions of nations in the attainment of these common ends.

*Article 2.* The Organization and its Members, in pursuit of the Purposes stated in Article 1, shall act in accordance with the following Principles.

1. The Organization is based on the principle of the sovereign equality of all its Members.

2. All Members, in order to ensure to all of them the rights and benefits resulting from membership, shall fulfil in good faith the obligations assumed by them in accordance with the present Charter.

3. All Members shall settle their international disputes by peaceful means in such a manner that international peace and security, and justice, are not endangered.

4. All Members shall refrain in their international relations from the threat or use of force against the territorial integrity or political independence of any state, or in any other manner inconsistent with the Purposes of the United Nations.

5. All Members shall give the United Nations every assistance in any action it takes in accordance with the present Charter, and shall refrain from giving assistance to any state against which the United Nations is taking preventive or enforcement action.

6. The Organization shall ensure that states which are not Members of the United Nations act in accordance with those Principles so far as may be necessary for the maintenance of international peace and security.

7. Nothing contained in the present Charter shall authorize the United Nations to intervene in matters which are essentially within the domestic jurisdiction of any state or shall require the Members to submit such matters to settlement under the present Charter; but this principle shall not prejudice the application of enforcement measures under Chapter VII. . . .

CHAPTER III. ORGANS

*Article 7.* There are established as the principal organs of the United Nations: a General Assembly, a Security Council, an Economic and Social Council, a Trusteeship Council, an International Court of Justice, and a Secretariat. . . .

CHAPTER IV.
THE GENERAL ASSEMBLY
*Composition*

*Article 9.* The General Assembly shall consist of all the Members of the United Nations. . . .

*Functions and Powers*

*Article 10.* The General Assembly may discuss any questions or any matters within the scope of the present Charter . . . and, except as provided in Article 12, may make recommendations to the Members of the United Nations or to the Security Council or to both on any such questions or matters.

*Article 11.* 1. The General Assembly may consider the general principles of cooperation in the maintenance of international peace and security, including the principles governing disarmament and the regulation of armaments, and may make recommendations with regard to such principles to the Members or to the Security Council or to both. . . .

3. The General Assembly may call the attention of the Security Council to situations which are likely to endanger international peace and security. . . .

*Article 12.* 1. While the Security Council is exercising in respect of any dispute or situation the functions assigned to it in the present Charter, the General Assembly shall not make any recommendation with regard to that dispute or situation unless the Security Council so requests. . . .

*Article 13.* 1. The General Assembly shall initiate studies and make recommendations for the purpose of:

a. promoting international cooperation in the political field and encouraging the progressive development of international law and its codification;

b. promoting international cooperation in the economic, social, cultural, educational, and health fields, and assisting in the realization of human rights and fundamental freedoms for all without distinction as to race, sex, language, or religion. . . .

*Article 14.* Subject to the provisions of Article 12, the General Assembly may recommend measures for the peaceful adjustment of any situation, regardless of origin, which it deems likely to impair the general welfare or friendly relations among nations. . . .

*Voting*

*Article 18.* 1. Each member of the General Assembly shall have one vote.

2. Decisions of the General Assembly on important questions shall be made by a two-thirds majority of the members present and voting. . . .

3. Decisions on other questions, including the determination, of additional categories of questions to be decided by a two-thirds majority, shall be made by a majority of the members present and voting.

*Article 19.* A Member of the United Nations which is in arrears in the payment of its financial contributions to the Organization shall have no vote in the General Assembly if the amount of its arrears equals or exceeds the amount of the contributions due from it for the preceding two full years. . . .

CHAPTER V.

THE SECURITY COUNCIL

*Article 23.* 1. The Security Council shall consist of eleven Members of the United Nations. The Republic of China, France, the Union of Soviet Socialist Republics, the United Kingdom of Great Britain and Northern Ireland, and the United States of America shall be permanent members of the Security Council. The General Assembly shall elect six other Members of the United Nations to be non-per-

manent members of the Security Council, due regard being specially paid, in the first instance to the contribution of Members of the United Nations to the maintenance of international peace and security and to the other purposes of the Organization, and also to equitable geographical distribution.

2. The non-permanent members of the Security Council shall be elected for a term of two years. . . .

*Functions and Powers*

*Article 24.* 1. In order to ensure prompt and effective action by the United Nations, its Members confer on the Security Council primary responsibility for the maintenance of international peace and security, and agree that in carrying out its duties under this responsibility the Security Council acts on their behalf. . . .

*Article 25.* The Members of the United Nations agree to accept and carry out the decisions of the Security Council in accordance with the present Charter.

*Article 26.* In order to promote the establishment and maintenance of international peace and security with the least diversion for armaments of the world's human and economic resources, the Security Council shall be responsible for formulating, with the assistance of the Military Staff Committee referred to in Article 47, plans to be submitted to the Members of the United Nations for the establishment of a system for the regulation of armaments.

*Voting*

*Article 27.* 1. Each member of the Security Council shall have one vote.

2. Decisions of the Security Council on procedural matters shall be made by an affirmative vote of seven members.

3. Decisions of the Security Council on all other matters shall be made by an affirmative vote of seven members including the concurring votes of the permanent members. . . .

*Procedure*

*Article 28.* 1. The Security Council shall be so organized as to be able to function continuously. . . .

*Article 31.* Any Member of the United Nations which is not a member of the Security Council may participate, without vote, in the discussion of any question brought before the Security Council whenever the latter considers that the interests of that Member are specifically affected.

*Article 32.* Any Member of the United Nations which is not a member of the Security Council or any state which is not a Member of the United Nations, if it is a party to a dispute under consideration by the Security Council, shall be invited to participate, without vote, in the discussion relating to the dispute. . . .

CHAPTER VI.
PACIFIC SETTLEMENT OF DISPUTES

*Article 33.* 1. The parties to any dispute, the continuance of which is likely to endanger the maintenance of international peace and security, shall, first of all, seek a solution by negotiation, enquiry, mediation, conciliation, arbitration, judicial settlement, resort to regional agencies or arrangements, or other peaceful means of their own choice. . . .

*Article 36.* The Security Council may, at any stage of a dispute of the nature referred to in Article 33 or of a situation of like nature, recommend appropriate procedures or methods of adjustment. . . .

*Article 37.* Should the parties to a dispute of the nature referred to in Article 33 fail to settle it by the means indicated in that Article, they shall refer it to the Security Council.

CHAPTER VII.
ACTION WITH RESPECT TO THREATS
TO THE PEACE, BREACHES OF THE PEACE,
AND ACTS OF AGGRESSION

*Article 39.* The Security Council shall determine the existence of any threat to the peace, breach of the peace, or act of aggression and shall make recommendations, or decide what measures shall be taken . . . to maintain or restore international peace and security. . . .

*Article 41.* The Security Council may decide what measures not involving the use of armed force are to be employed to give effect to its decisions, and it may call upon the Members of the United Nations to apply such measures. These may include complete or partial interruption of economic relations and of rail, sea, air, postal, telegraphic, radio, and other means of communication, and the severance of diplomatic relations.

*Article 42.* Should the Security Council consider that measures provided for in Article 41 would be inadequate or have proved to be inadequate, it may take such action by air, sea, or land forces as may be necessary to maintain or restore international peace and security. Such action may include demonstrations, blockade, and other operations by air, sea, or land forces of Members of the United Nations.

*Article 43.* 1. All Members of the United Nations, in order to contribute to the maintenance of international peace and security, undertake to make available to the Security Council, on its call and in accordance with a special agreement or agreements, armed forces, assistance, and facilities, including rights of passage, necessary for the purpose of maintaining international peace and security. . . .

3. The agreement or agreements shall be negotiated as soon as possible on the initiative of the Security Council. They shall be concluded between the Security Council and Members or between the Security Council and groups of Members and shall be subject to ratification by the signatory states in accordance with their respective constitutional processes.

*Article 44.* When the Security Council has decided to use force it shall, before calling upon a Member not represented on it to provide armed forces in fulfillment of the obligations assumed under Article 43, invite that Member, if the Member so desires, to participate in the decisions of the Security Council concerning the employment of contingents of that Member's armed forces.

*Article 45.* In order to enable the United Nations to take urgent military measures, Members shall hold immediately available national air-force contingents for combined international enforcement action. . . .

*Article 47.* There shall be established a Military Staff Committee to advise and assist the Security Council on all questions relating to the Security Council's military requirements for the maintenance of international peace and security, the employment and command of forces placed at its disposal, the regulation of armaments, and possible disarmament. . . .

*Article 51.* Nothing in the present Charter shall impair the inherent right of individual or collective self-defense if an armed attack occurs against a member of the United Nations, until the Security Council has taken the measures necessary to maintain international peace and security. Measures taken by Members in the exercise of this right of self-defense shall be immediately reported to the Security Council and shall not in any way affect the authority and responsibility of the Security Council under the present Charter to take at any time such action as it deems necessary in order to maintain or restore international peace and security.

CHAPTER VIII.
REGIONAL ARRANGEMENTS

*Article 52.* Nothing in the present Charter precludes the existence of regional arrangements or agencies for dealing with such matters relating to the maintenance of international peace and security as are appropriate for regional action, provided that such arrangements . . . and their activities are consistent with the Purposes and Principles of the United Nations. . . .

*Article 53.* 1. The Security Council shall, where appropriate, utilize such regional arrangements or agencies for enforcement action under its authority. But no enforcement action shall be taken under regional arrangements or by regional agencies, without the authorization of the Security Council, with the exception of measures against any enemy state, as defined in paragraph 2 of this Article. . . .

2. The term enemy state as used in paragraph 1 of this Article applies to any state which during the Second World War has been an enemy of any signatory of the present Charter. . . .

CHAPTER IX.
INTERNATIONAL ECONOMIC
AND SOCIAL COOPERATION

*Article 55.* With a view to the creation of conditions of stability and well-being which are necessary for peaceful and friendly relations among nations based on respect for the principle of equal rights and self-determination of peoples, the United Nations shall promote:

a. higher standards of living, full employment, and conditions of economic and social progress and development;

b. solutions of international economic, social, health, and related problems; and international cultural and educational cooperation; and

c. universal respect for, and observance of, human rights and fundamental freedoms for all without distinction as to race, sex, language, or religion. . . .

## 54

## *"Our hemisphere's mission is not yet completed"*

On March 13, 1961, in addressing "the Ambassadorial Corps of Our Hemisphere," President John F. Kennedy presented to the nations of Latin America his proposal that they join with the United States "in a new Alliance for Progress—*Alianza para Progreso*—a vast cooperative effort . . . to satisfy the basic needs of the American people for homes, work and land, health and schools—*techo, trabajo y tierra, salud y escuela*." This vast effort, Kennedy said, with his characteristic largeness of view, was "unparalleled in magnitude and nobility of purpose." Yet he shortly referred to an earlier effort by which, as he said, we also "helped to provide, against equal odds, nearly, the resources adequate to help rebuild the economies of Western Europe." This was the Marshall Plan. Both Kennedy's proposal and Marshall's plan are presented below in this Document.

Our "purpose," said Secretary of State Marshall on June 5, 1947, at the Harvard commmencement in which he first set forth his program, "should be the revival of a working economy in the world so as to permit the emergence of political and social conditions in which free institutions can exist." Our "unfulfilled task," Kennedy told the assembled ambassadors in 1961, "is to demonstrate to the entire world that man's unsatisfied aspiration for economic progress and social justice can best be achieved by free men working within a framework of democratic institutions."

Since the United States shunned any responsibility for further dividing a Europe cleft by the Iron Curtain, Marshall invited *all* European nations to share American assistance. At the same time, he warned that "any government which maneuvers to block the recovery of other countries cannot expect help from us," and any which seeks "to perpetuate human misery in order to profit therefrom politically," will encounter American opposition. Russian denunciation of the Marshall Plan was received in the United States with vast relief. Among those participating in the Plan, on the other hand, the United States insisted on a common, not a national, effort to "provide a cure rather than a mere palliative" for Europe's crisis.

This crisis was massive and universal. As Secretary Marshall said, "The breakdown of the business structure of Europe during the war was complete." The winter of 1946-1947 after the war was one of the coldest in European history, and the prostrate economies froze to an absolute standstill. Britain, among the old allies, was much the worst off because of her virtually total dependence on outside food supplies and on world trade for the wherewithal to pay for them. But the situation in France appeared even more ominous because of the large Communist party there, a reflection of a century of deprivation among the working classes, which thwarted all efforts at revival and reform in order to hasten a general political collapse. In defeated Italy deprivation had a still longer history and communism an even stronger hold. In defeated Germany starvation had become common and chaos reigned.

"The rehabilitation of the economic structure of Europe," Marshall said, "quite evidently will require a much longer time and greater effort than had been foreseen." To speed and strengthen such rehabilitation, the United States Congress, in the Economic Cooperation Act of 1948 in which the first appropriations under the Marshall Plan were made, declared that in assisting Europe, Americans were "mindful of the advantage which the United States has enjoyed through the existence of a large-scale domestic market with no internal barriers." Congress believed "that similar advantages can accrue to the countries of Europe," if they would combine into a single economic unit. Western Europe was slow to respond to Congress's prod. Nevertheless, nation by nation, Europe's recovery, built on Marshall Plan aid, was startlingly swift.

Between 1948 and 1952 the Economic Cooperation Administration advanced about $12 billion, somewhat more than half of this sum to Britain, France and Germany. By 1952 the crisis was past; and by the early 1960's Western Europe had attained such levels of economic growth that representatives of the then more sluggish American economy journeyed overseas to find the secret. Moreover, the primary political goals of the program had been won. Communism had been contained on the Continent, and Communist parties in the West languished.

The Alliance for Progress in some respects faced problems similar to those faced by the Marshall Plan. Referring to the Castroist infection in Cuba, Kennedy said in his presentation "At this very moment . . . we confront the same forces which have imperiled America throughout its history—the alien forces which once again seek to impose the despotisms of the Old World on the people of the New." And his solution was similar—an economic revolution for salutary political purposes, one not nationally oriented but "consistent with the majestic concept of Operation Pan America." In recognition of endemic Latin American economic and social conditions that had endured for centuries, however, Kennedy proposed not a four-year program, but a ten-year one; not up to $20 billion in investment, but up to $100 billion, of which the Latin Americans themselves were to make up 80 per cent, a disciplinary as well as an economic goal.

The problems of poverty and population growth together present probably the sternest challenge to the spread and survival of free institutions. Many see the Alliance for Progress as the first stage of a Marshall Plan for the vast underdeveloped regions of the globe. They see it as consistent with America's traditional mission in the world, as a "must" for the perpetuation even at home of the institutions which alone make that mission worthwhile. In the decades since the end of World War II the United States committed itself to this mission to the tune of $95 billion in so-called foreign aid. "Probably no other nation in human history," Senator Paul H. Douglas said in 1957, "has ever exerted itself so intelligently to preserve its own safety or to be helpful to others." The persistence of such exertions since Douglas wrote belies, so far at least, the revival of isolationist power which he foresaw. Nor has the United States neglected its duty to the underprivileged among its own people (see Document No. 55, below).

*1947    1961*

# The Marshall Plan
# and the Alliance for Progress

(a)   *The Marshall Plan, June 5, 1947*
(Remarks by the Honorable George C. Marshall, Secretary of State, at Harvard University on June 5, 1947)

I need not tell you gentlemen that the world situation is very serious. That must be apparent to all intelligent people. I think one difficulty is that the people of this country are . . . distant from the troubled areas of the earth and it is hard for them to comprehend the plight and consequent reactions of the long-suffering peoples, and the effect of those reactions on their governments in connection with our efforts to promote peace in the world.

In considering the requirements for the rehabilitation of Europe the physical loss of life, the visible destruction of cities, factories, mines, and railroads was correctly estimated, but it has become obvious during recent months that this visible destruction was probably less serious than the dislocation of the entire fabric of European economy.

For the past 10 years conditions have been highly abnormal. The feverish preparation for war and the more feverish maintenance of the war effort engulfed all aspects of national economies. Machinery has fallen into disrepair or is entirely obsolete. Under the arbitrary and destructive Nazi rule, virtually every possible enterprise was geared into the German war machine. Long-standing commercial ties, private institutions, banks, insurance companies and shipping companies disappeared, through loss of capital, absorption through nationalization or by simple destruction. In many countries, confidence in the local currency has been severely shaken. The breakdown of the business structure of Europe during the war was complete. Recovery has been seriously retarded by the fact that 2 years after the close of hostilities a peace settlement with Germany and Austria has not been agreed upon. But even given a more prompt solution of these difficult problems, the rehabilitation of the economic structure of Europe quite evidently will require a much longer time and greater effort than had been foreseen.

There is a phase of this matter which is both interesting and serious. The farmer has always produced the foodstuffs to exchange with the city dweller for the other necessities of life. This division of labor is the basis of modern civilization. At the present time it is threatened with breakdown. . . . The farmer or the peasant cannot find the goods for sale which he desires to purchase. So the sale of his farm produce for money which he cannot use seems to him an unprofitable transaction. He, therefore, has withdrawn many fields from crop cultivation and is using them for grazing. He feeds more grain to stock and finds for himself and his family an ample supply of food, however short he may be on clothing and the other ordinary gadgets of civilization. Meanwhile people in the cities are short of food and fuel. So the government is forced to use their foreign money and credits to procure these necessities abroad. This process exhausts funds which are urgently needed for reconstruction. Thus a very serious situation is rapidly developing which bodes no good for the world. . . .

The truth of the matter is that Europe's requirements for the next 3 or 4 years of foreign food and other essential products—principally from America—are so much greater than her present ability to pay that she must have substantial additional help, or face economic, social, and political deterioration of a very grave character.

The remedy lies in breaking the vicious circle and restoring the confidence of the European people in the economic future of their own countries and of Europe as a whole. . . . It is logical that the United States should do whatever

it is able to do to assist in the return of normal economic health in the world, without which there can be no political stability and no assured peace. Our policy is directed not against any country or doctrine but against hunger, poverty, desperation, and chaos. Its purpose should be the revival of a working economy in the world so as to permit the emergence of political and social conditions in which free institutions can exist. Such assistance, I am convinced, must not be on a piecemeal basis as various crises develop. Any assistance that this Government may render in the future should provide a cure rather than a mere palliative. Any government that is willing to assist in the task of recovery will find full cooperation, I am sure, on the part of the United States Government. Any government which maneuvers to block the recovery of other countries cannot expect help from us. Furthermore, governments, political parties, or groups which seek to perpetuate human misery in order to profit therefrom politically or otherwise will encounter the opposition of the United States.

It is already evident that, before the United States Government can proceed much further in its efforts to alleviate the situation and help start the European world on its way to recovery, there must be some agreement among the countries of Europe as to the requirements of the situation and the part those countries themselves will take in order to give proper effect to whatever action might be undertaken by this Government. It would be neither fitting nor efficacious for this Government to undertake to draw up unilaterally a program designed to place Europe on its feet economically. This is the business of the Europeans. The initiative, I think, must come from Europe. The role of this country should consist of friendly aid in the drafting of a European program and of later support of such a program so far as it may be practical for us to do so. The program should be a joint one, agreed to by a

number, if not all European nations.
...

With foresight, and a willingness on the part of our people to face up to the vast responsibility which history has clearly placed upon our country, the difficulties I have outlined can and will be overcome.

(b) *John F. Kennedy:*
*On Establishing the Alliance for Progress, March 13, 1961*

(Address at a White House Reception for Members of Congress and for the Diplomatic Corps of the Latin American Republics)

One hundred and thirty-nine years ago this week the United States, stirred by the heroic struggle of its fellow Americans, urged the independence and recognition of the new Latin American Republics. It was then, at the dawn of freedom throughout this hemisphere, that Bolívar spoke of his desire to see the Americas fashioned into the greatest region in the world, "greatest," he said, "not so much by virtue of her area and her wealth, as by her freedom and her glory."

Never in the long history of our hemisphere has this dream been nearer to fulfillment, and never has it been in greater danger.

The genius of our scientists has given us the tools to bring abundance to our land, strength to our industry, and knowledge to our people. For the first time we have the capacity to strike off the remaining bonds of poverty and ignorance—to free our people for the spiritual and intellectual fulfillment which has always been the goal of our civilization.

Yet at this very moment of maximum opportunity, we confront the same forces which have imperiled America throughout its history—the alien forces which once again seek to impose the despotisms of the Old World on the people of the New.

I have asked you to come here today so that I might discuss these challenges and these dangers.

We meet together as firm and ancient friends, united by history and experience and by our determination to advance the values of American civilization. For this New World of ours is not a mere accident of geography. Our continents are bound together by a common history, the endless exploration of new frontiers. Our nations are the product of a common struggle, the revolt from colonial rule. And our people share a common heritage, the quest for the dignity and the freedom of man.

The revolutions which gave us birth ignited, in the words of Thomas Paine, "a spark never to be extinguished." And across vast, turbulent continents these American ideals still stir man's struggle for national independence and individual freedom. But as we welcome the spread of the American revolution to other lands, we must also remember that our own struggle—the revolution which began in Philadelphia in 1776, and in Caracas in 1811—is not yet finished. Our hemisphere's mission is not yet completed. For our unfulfilled task is to demonstrate to the entire world that man's unsatisfied aspiration for economic progress and social justice can best be achieved by free men working within a framework of democratic institutions. If we can do this in our own hemisphere, and for our own people, we may yet realize the prophecy of the great Mexican patriot, Benito Juarez, that "democracy is the destiny of future humanity."

As a citizen of the United States let me be the first to admit that we North Americans have not always grasped the significance of this common mission, just as it is also true that many in your own countries have not fully understood the urgency of the need to lift people from poverty and ignorance and despair. But we must turn from these mistakes—from the failures and the misunderstandings of the past to a future full of peril, but bright with hope.

Throughout Latin America, a continent rich in resources and in the spiritual and cultural achievements of its people, millions of men and women suffer the daily degradations of poverty and hunger. They lack decent shelter or protection from disease. Their children are deprived of the education or the jobs which are the gateway to a better life. And each day the problems grow more urgent. Population growth is outpacing economic growth—low living standards are further endangered—and discontent—the discontent of a people who know that abundance and the tools of progress are at last within their reach —that discontent is growing. In the words of José Figueres, "once dormant peoples are struggling upward toward the sun, toward a better life."

If we are to meet a problem so staggering in its dimensions, our approach must itself be equally bold—an approach consistent with the majestic concept of Operation Pan America. Therefore I have called on all people of the hemisphere to join in a new Alliance for Progress—*Alianza para Progreso*—a vast cooperative effort, unparalleled in magnitude and nobility of purpose, to satisfy the basic needs of the American people for homes, work and land, health and schools—*techo, trabajo y tierra, salud y escuela*.

*First*, I propose that the American Republics begin on a vast new Ten Year Plan for the Americas, a plan to transform the 1960's into a historic decade of democratic progress.

These 10 years will be the years of maximum progress-maximum effort, the years when the greatest obstacles must be overcome, the years when the need for assistance will be the greatest.

And if we are successful, if our effort is bold enough and determined enough,

then the close of this decade will mark the beginning of a new era in the American experience. The living standards of every American family will be on the rise, basic education will be available to all, hunger will be a forgotten experience, the need for massive outside help will have passed, most nations will have entered a period of self-sustaining growth, and though there will be still much to do, every American Republic will be the master of its own revolution and its own hope and progress.

Let me stress that only the most determined efforts of the American nations themselves can bring success to this effort. They, and they alone, can mobilize their resources, enlist the energies of their people, and modify their social patterns so that all, and not just a privileged few, share in the fruits of growth. If this effort is made, then outside assistance will give the vital impetus to progress; without it, no amount of help will advance the welfare of the people.

Thus if the countries of Latin America are ready to do their part, and I am sure they are, then I believe the United States, for its part, should help provide resources of a scope and magnitude sufficient to make this bold development plan a success—just as we helped to provide, against equal odds, nearly, the resources adequate to help rebuild the economies of Western Europe. For only an effort of towering dimensions can ensure fulfillment of our plan for a decade of progress.

*Secondly*, I will shortly request a ministerial meeting of the Inter-American Economic and Social Council, a meeting at which we can begin the massive planning effort which will be at the heart of the Alliance for Progress.

For if our Alliance is to succeed, each Latin nation must formulate long-range plans for its own development, plans which establish targets and priorities, ensure monetary stability, establish the machinery for vital social change, stimulate private activity and initiative, and provide for a maximum national effort. These plans will be the foundation of our development effort, and the basis for the allocation of outside resources.

A greatly strengthened IA-ECOSOC, working with the Economic Commission for Latin America and the Inter-American Development Bank, can assemble the leading economists and experts of the hemisphere to help each country develop its own development plan—and provide a continuing review of economic progress in this hemisphere.

*Third,* I have this evening signed a request to the Congress for $500 million as a first step in fulfilling the Act of Bogotá. This is the first large-scale Inter-American effort, instituted by my predecessor President Eisenhower, to attack the social barriers which block economic progress. The money will be used to combat illiteracy, improve the productivity and use of their land, wipe out disease, attack archaic tax and land tenure structures, provide educational opportunities, and offer a broad range of projects designed to make the benefits of increasing abundance available to all. We will begin to commit these funds as soon as they are appropriated.

*Fourth,* we must support all economic integration which is a genuine step toward larger markets and greater competitive opportunity. The fragmentation of Latin American economics is a serious barrier to industrial growth. Projects such as the Central American common market and free trade areas in South America can help to remove these obstacles.

*Fifth,* the United States is ready to cooperate in serious, case-by-case examinations of commodity market problems. Frequent violent change in commodity prices seriously injure the economies of many Latin American countries, draining their resources and stultifying their growth. Together we must find practical methods of bringing an end to this pattern.

*Sixth,* we will immediately step up our Food for Peace emergency program, help establish food reserves in areas of recurrent drought, help provide school lunches for children, and offer feed grains for use in rural development. For hungry men and women cannot wait for economic discussions or diplomatic meetings—their need is urgent—and their hunger rests heavily on the conscience of their fellow men.

*Seventh,* all the people of the hemisphere must be allowed to share in the expanding wonders of science—wonders which have captured man's imagination, challenged the powers of his mind, and given him the tools for rapid progress. I invite Latin American scientists to work with us in new projects in fields such as medicine and agriculture, physics and astronomy, and desalinazation, to help plan for regional research laboratories in these and other fields, and to strengthen cooperation between American universities and laboratories.

We also intend to expand our science teacher training programs to include Latin American instructors, to assist in establishing such programs in other American countries, and translate and make available revolutionary new teaching materials in physics, chemistry, biology, and mathematics, so that the young of all nations may contribute their skills to the advance of science.

*Eighth,* we must rapidly expand the training of those needed to man the economies of rapidly developing countries. This means expanded technical training programs, for which the Peace Corps, for example, will be available when needed. It also means assistance to Latin American universities, graduate schools, and research institutes.

We welcome proposals in Central America for intimate cooperation in higher education—cooperation which can achieve a regional effort of increased effectiveness and excellence. We are ready to help fill the gap in trained manpower, realizing that our ultimate goal must be a basic education for all who wish to learn.

*Ninth,* we reaffirm our pledge to come to the defense of any American nation whose independence is endangered. As its confidence in the collective security system of the OAS spreads, it will be possible to devote to constructive use a major share of those resources now spent on the instruments of war. Even now, as the government of Chile has said, the time has come to take the first steps toward sensible limitations of arms. And the new generation of military leaders has shown an increasing awareness that armies cannot only defend their countries—they can, as we have learned through our own Corps of Engineers, they can help to build them.

*Tenth*, we invite our friends in Latin America to contribute to the enrichment of life and culture in the United States. We need teachers of your literature and history and tradition, opportunities for our young people to study in your universities, access to your music, your art, and the thought of your great philosophers. For we know we have much to learn.

In this way you can help bring a fuller spiritual and intellectual life to the people of the United States—and contribute to understanding and mutual respect among the nations of the hemisphere.

With steps such as these, we propose to complete the revolution of the Americas, to build a hemisphere where all men can hope for a suitable standard of living, and all can live out their lives in dignity and in freedom.

To achieve this goal political freedom must accompany material progress. Our Alliance for Progress is an alliance of free governments, and it must work to eliminate tyranny from a hemisphere in which it has no rightful place. Therefore let us express our special friendship to the people of Cuba and the Dominican Republic—and the hope they will soon rejoin the society of free men, uniting with us in common effort.

This political freedom must be accompanied by social change. For unless necessary social reforms, including land and tax reform, are freely made—unless

we broaden the opportunity for all of our people—unless the great mass of Americans share in increasing prosperity—then our alliance, our revolution, our dream, and our freedom will fail. But we call for social change by free men—change in the spirit of Washington and Jefferson, of Bolívar and San Martín and Martí—not change which seeks to impose on men tyrannies which we cast out a century and a half ago. Our motto is what it has always been—progress yes, tyranny no—*progreso sí, tiranía no!*

But our greatest challenge comes from within—the task of creating an American civilization where spiritual and cultural values are strengthened by an ever-broadening base of material advance—where, within the rich diversity of its own traditions, each nation is free to follow its own path towards progress.

The completion of our task will, of course, require the efforts of all governments of our hemisphere. But the efforts of governments alone will never be enough. In the end, the people must choose and the people must help themselves.

And so I say to the men and women of the Americas—to the *campesino* in the fields, to the *obrero* in the cities, to the *estudiante* in the schools—prepare your mind and heart for the task ahead—call forth your strength and let each devote his energies to the betterment of all, so that your children and our children in this hemisphere can find an ever richer and a freer life.

Let us once again transform the American continent into a vast crucible of revolutionary ideas and efforts—a tribute to the power of the creative energies of free men and women—an example to all the world that liberty and progress walk hand in hand. Let us once again awaken our American revolution until it guides the struggle of people everywhere—not with an imperialism of force or fear—but the rule of courage and freedom and hope for the future of man.

## 55

*"Without discrimination or segregation on the ground of race, color, religion, or national origin"*

One of the snares of good intentions is that they are likely to be taken at face value. One of the burdens of a free society is that its shortcomings in performing up to its well-meaning pronouncements, its principles, its traditional values, must be fully exposed to public view. If it is true that the American mission in the Western Hemisphere, this Hemisphere's mission around the world, is not yet finished, or at least that our acknowledgment of this mission is not yet stilled, it is also true that our performance at home continues to leave much to be desired, and that our enemies abroad shout our conspicuous failures around the globe.

As much as our vision, in the twentieth century, must encompass the earth, so everywhere on earth eyes are focused on us. It is often recommended as an axiom in the conduct of "foreign affairs" that even great nations must limit their commitments to their physical ability to carry them out. Yet, in what may better be called "international relations," this "realistic" choice may not always be available; and in confronting unlimited moral challenges abroad, physical ability has often shown unanticipated and extraordinary elasticity. Such elasticity, no doubt, feeds on the severity of the foreign challenge; but it feeds best on the meeting of moral challenges at home.

In meeting such challenges the United States probably more closely approaches its pronouncements, more nearly fulfills its good intentions, than most other nations, partly because its people in fact do feel the eyes of the world upon them, partly because of their own magnificent endowment in physical resources and the good luck to have embarked on their development in an expansive age and in a virtually empty land.

Empty and beckoning to exploitation as the land may have seemed, however (see Document No. 1, for example), earlier arrivals continually, often violently, withstood the newcomers—the Indians the English, the Christians the Jews, the Protestants the Catholics, the old stock the new immigrants—and, lastly, the whites the colored, who of course are newcomers only in the political and moral sense. Assimilation probably has been America's oldest problem, one still with us on more grounds than color alone, as the quotation at the head of this Document from the Civil Rights Act of 1964 indicates. And yet, as history attests, it is a problem that has been met more successfully in this country than in many other places in the world. As President Lyndon B. Johnson said in his first state of the Union message to Congress, January 8, 1964, "Today, Americans of all races stand side by side in Berlin and Vietnam. They died side by side in Korea." He added, "Surely they can work and eat and travel side by side in their own country." And he pledged:

> As far as the writ of Federal law will run, we must abolish not some, but all racial discrimination. For this is not merely an economic issue, or a social, political or international issue. It is a moral issue, and it must be met by the passage this session of the bill now pending in the House.

The House in fact passed the Civil Rights bill of 1964 on February 10 by the resounding bipartisan margin of 290 to 130. The Senate, after an extraordinary invoking of cloture to terminate the southern bitter-ender filibuster, passed the bill on June 19 by an even broader margin, 73 to 27. After joint conferences over Senate amendments to the House version, the bill went to the President who signed it on July 2. The Civil Rights Act of 1964, a striking fulfillment of good intentions, is presented in part in item "b," below.

In his state of the Union message, President Johnson stressed another issue which Americans, probably because of their commitment to a blue-sky standard of living for all, have also been the more willing to face:

> Unfortunately, many Americans live on the outskirts of hope, some because of their poverty and some because of their color, and all too many because of both.

"Very often," Johnson said, "a lack of jobs and money is not the cause of poverty, but the symptom. The cause may be deeper." And he pointed especially to "a lack of education and training" as the source of "our failure to give our fellow citizens a fair chance to develop their own capacities."

No one has been more eloquent on the relationship between education and opportunity in modern society than the Chief Justice of the Supreme Court of the United States, Earl Warren. And nowhere was he more eloquent than in his short but momentous opinion, speaking for a unanimous Court, in *Brown* v. *Board of Education of Topeka*, May 17, 1954. This opinion is presented in full in item "a," below. Wholly meeting Theodore Roosevelt's qualifications for twentieth-century judges (see Document No. 47, above), Warren wrote a year after the desegregation decision: "Our judges are not monks or scientists, but participants in the living stream of our national life." In his opinion, he acted clearly on this philosophy:

> In approaching . . . the effect of segregation itself on public education . . . we cannot turn the clock back to 1868 when the [Fourteenth] Amendment was adopted, or even to 1896 when *Plessy* v. *Ferguson* [sanctioning separate but

equal facilities] was written. We must consider public education in the light of its full development and its present place in American life throughout the Nation. . . . Today, education is perhaps the most important function of state and local governments. . . . It is the very foundation of good citizenship. Today it is a principal instrument in awakening the child to cultural values, in preparing him for later professional training, and in helping him to adjust normally to his environment. . . . In the field of public education the doctrine of "separate but equal" has no place. Separate educational facilities are inherently unequal.

In the ten years since this memorable decision, despite the violence of Little Rock and Birmingham, much progress has been made, north and south, in enlarging the Negro's educational opportunties. But the full impact of this decision, like that of the Civil Rights Act, is still to be determined. Both acts, in the opinion of some commentators, have only broadened the gap between the races in America and hardened their differences. But with the Executive, Legislative, and Judicial departments so solidly behind desegregation, so urgently forwarding it as a moral imperative, it seems that the people of the United States will themselves adopt it, and the peoples of the world will commend them for it.

*1954      1964*

# The Desegregation Decision
# and the Civil Rights Act

(a)   *Brown* v. *Board of Education of Topeka, May 17, 1954*

WARREN, C. J., These cases come to us from the States of Kansas, South Carolina, Virginia, and Delaware. They are premised on different facts and different local conditions, but a common legal question justifies their consideration together in this consolidated opinion.

In each of the cases, minors of the Negro race, through their legal representatives, seek the aid of the courts in obtaining admission to the public schools of their community on a nonsegregated basis. In each instance, they had been denied admission to schools attended by white children under laws requiring or permitting segregation according to race. This segregation was alleged to deprive the plaintiffs of the equal protection of the laws under the Fourteenth Amendment. In each of the cases other than the Delaware case, a three-judge federal district court denied relief to the plaintiffs on the so-called "separate but equal" doctrine announced by this Court in *Plessy* v. *Ferguson,* 163 U.S. 537. Under that doctrine, equality of treatment is accorded when the races are provided substantially equal facilities, even though these facilities be separate. In the Delaware case, the Supreme Court of Delaware adhered to that doctrine, but ordered that the plaintiffs be admitted to the white schools because of their superiority to the Negro schools.

The plaintiffs contend that segregated public schools are not "equal" and cannot be made "equal," and that hence they are deprived of the equal protection of the laws. Because of the obvious importance of the question presented, the Court took jurisdiction. Argument was heard in the 1952 Term, and reargument was heard this Term on certain questions propounded by the Court.

Reargument was largely devoted to the circumstances surrounding the adoption of the Fourteenth Amendment in 1868. It covered exhaustively consideration of the Amendment in Congress, ratification by the states, then existing practices in racial segregation, and the views of proponents and opponents of the Amendment. This discussion and our own investigation convince us that, although these sources cast some light, it is not enough to resolve the problem with which we are faced. At best, they are inconclusive. The most avid proponents of the post-War Amendments undoubtedly intended them to remove all legal distinctions among "all persons born or naturalized in the United States." Their opponents, just as certainly, were antagonistic to both the letter and the spirit of the Amendments and wished them to have the most limited effect. What others in Congress and the state legislatures had in mind cannot be determined with any degree of certainty.

An additional reason for the inconclusive nature of the Amendment's history, with respect to segregated schools, is the status of public education at that time. In the South, the movement toward free common schools, supported by general taxation, had not yet taken hold. Education of white children was largely in the hands of private groups. Education of Negroes was almost nonexistent, and practically all of the race were illiterate. In fact, any education of Negroes was forbidden by law in some states. Today, in contrast, many Negroes have achieved outstanding success in the arts and sciences as well as in the business and professional world. It is true that public school education at the time of the Amendment had advanced further in the North, but the effect of the Amendment on Northern States was generally ignored in the congressional debates. Even in the North, the conditions of public education did not approximate those existing today. The curriculum was usually rudimentary; ungraded schools were common in rural areas; the school term was but three months a year in many states; and compulsory school attendance was virtually unknown. As a consequence, it is not surprising that there should be so little in the history of the Fourteenth Amendment relating to its intended effect on public education.

In the first cases in this Court construing the Fourteenth Amendment, decided shortly after its adoption, the Court interpreted it as proscribing all state-imposed discriminations against the Negro race. The doctrine of "separate but equal" did not make its appearance in this Court until 1896 in the case of *Plessy* v. *Ferguson, supra,* involving not education but transportation. American courts have since labored with the doctrine for over half a century. In this Court, there have been six cases involving the "separate but equal" doctrine in the field of public education. In *Cumming* v. *County Board of Education,* 175 U.S. 528, and *Gong Lum* v. *Rice,* 275 U.S. 78, the validity of the doctrine itself was not challenged. In more recent cases, all on the graduate school level, inequality was found in that specific benefits enjoyed by white students were denied to Negro students of the same educational qualifications. *Missouri ex rel. Gaines* v. *Canada,* 305 U.S. 337; *Sipuel* v. *Oklahoma,* 332 U.S. 631; *Sweatt* v. *Painter,* 339 U.S. 629; *McLaurin* v. *Oklahoma State Regents,* 339 U.S. 637. In none of these cases was it necessary to re-examine the doctrine to grant relief to the Negro plaintiff. And in *Sweatt* v. *Painter, supra,* the Court expressly reserved decision on the question whether

*Plessy* v. *Ferguson* should be held inapplicable to public education.

In the instant cases, that question is directly presented. Here, unlike *Sweatt* v. *Painter*, there are findings below that the Negro and white schools involved have been equalized, or are being equalized, with respect to buildings, curricula, qualifications and salaries of teachers, and other "tangible" factors. Our decision, therefore, cannot turn on merely a comparison of these tangible factors in the Negro and white schools involved in each of the cases. We must look instead to the effect of segregation itself on public education.

In approaching this problem, we cannot turn the clock back to 1868 when the Amendment was adopted, or even to 1896 when *Plessy* v. *Ferguson* was written. We must consider public education in the light of its full development and its present place in American life throughout the Nation. Only in this way can it be determined if segregation in public schools deprives these plaintiffs of the equal protection of the laws.

Today, education is perhaps the most important function of state and local governments. Compulsory school attendance laws and the great expenditures for education both demonstrate our recognition of the importance of education to our democratic society. It is required in the performance of most basic public responsibilities, even service in the armed forces. It is the very foundation of good citizenship. Today it is a principal instrument in awakening the child to cultural values, in preparing him for later professional training, and in helping him to adjust normally to his environment. In these days, it is doubtful that any child may reasonably be expected to succeed in life if he is denied the opportunity of an education. Such an opportunity, where the state has undertaken to provide it, is a right which must be made available to all on equal terms.

We come then to the question presented: Does segregation of children in public schools solely on the basis of race, even though the physical facilities and other "tangible" factors may be equal, deprive the children of the minority group of equal educational opportunities? We believe that it does.

In *Sweatt* v. *Painter*, *supra*, in finding that a segregated law school for Negroes could not provide them equal educational opportunities, this Court relied in large part on "those equalities which are incapable of objective measurement but which make for greatness in a law school." In *McLaurin* v. *Oklahoma State Regents*, *supra*, the Court, in requiring that a Negro admitted to a white graduate school be treated like all other students, again resorted to intangible considerations: ". . . his ability to study, to engage in discussions and exchange views with other students, and, in general, to learn his profession." Such considerations apply with added force to children in grade and high schools. To separate them from others of similar age and qualifications solely because of their race generates a feeling of inferiority as to their status in the community that may affect their hearts and minds in a way unlikely ever to be undone. The effect of this separation on their educational opportunities was well stated by a finding in the Kansas case by a court which nevertheless felt compelled to rule against the Negro plaintiffs:

"Segregation of white and colored children in public schools has a detrimental effect upon the colored children. The impact is greater when it has the sanction of the law; for the policy of separating the races is usually interpreted as denoting the inferiority of the negro group. A sense of inferiority affects the motivation of a child to learn. Segregation with the sanction of law, therefore, has a tendency to [retard] the educational and mental development of negro children and to deprive them of some of the benefits they would receive in a racial[ly] integrated school system."

Whatever may have been the extent of psychological knowledge at the time of *Plessy* v. *Ferguson*, this finding is amply supported by modern authority. Any language in *Plessy* v. *Ferguson* contrary to this finding is rejected. We conclude that in the field of public education the doctrine of "separate but equal" has no place. Separate educational facilities are inherently unequal. Therefore, we hold that the plaintiffs and others similarly situated for whom the actions have been brought are, by reason of the segregation complained of, deprived of the equal protection of the laws guaranteed by the Fourteenth Amendment. This disposition makes unnecessary any discussion whether such segregation also violates the Due Process Clause of the Fourteenth Amendment.

Because these are class actions, because of the wide applicability of this decision, and because of the great variety of local conditions, the formulation of decrees in these cases presents problems of considerable complexity. On reargument, the consideration of appropriate relief was necessarily subordinated to the primary question—the constitutionality of segregation in public education. We have now announced that such segregation is a denial of the equal protection of the laws. In order that we may have the full assistance of the parties in formulating decrees, the cases will be restored to the docket, and the parties are requested to present further argument on Questions 4 and 5 [dealing with detailed implementation of the decision] previously propounded by the Court for the reargument of this Term.

## (b) *The Civil Rights Act, July 2, 1964*

AN ACT to enforce the constitutional right to vote, to confer jurisdiction upon the district courts of the United States to provide injunctive relief against discrimination in public accommodations, to authorize the Attorney General to institute suits to protect constitutional rights in public facilities and public education, to extend the Commission on Civil Rights, to prevent discrimination in federally assisted programs, to establish a Commission on Equal Employment Opportunity, and for other purposes.

### TITLE I—VOTING RIGHTS

(2) No person acting under color of law shall—

(A) in determining whether any individual is qualified under State law or laws to vote in any Federal election, apply any standard, practice, or procedure different from the standards, practices, or procedures applied under such law or laws to other individuals within the same county, parish, or similar political subdivision who have been found by State officials to be qualified to vote:

(B) deny the right of any individual to vote in any Federal election because of an error or omission on any record or paper relating to any application, registration, or other act requisite to voting, if such error or omission is not material in determining whether such individual is qualified under State law to vote in such election; or

(C) employ any literacy test as a qualification for voting in any Federal election unless (i) such test is administered to each individual and is conducted wholly in writing, and (ii) a certified copy of the test and of the answers given by the individual is furnished to him within twenty-five days of the submission of his request. . . .

### TITLE II—
### INJUNCTIVE RELIEF AGAINST
### DISCRIMINATION IN PLACES
### OF PUBLIC ACCOMMODATION

SEC. 201. (a) All persons shall be entitled to the full and equal enjoyment of the goods, services, facilities, privileges, advantages, and accommodations of any place of public accommodation, as defined in this section, without discrimination or segregation on the ground of race, color, religion, or national origin.

(b) Each of the following establishments which serves the public is a place of public accommodation within the meaning of this title if its operations affect commerce, or if discrimination or segregation by it is supported by State action:

(1) any inn, hotel, motel or other establishment which provides lodging to transient guests, other than an establishment located within a building which contains not more than five rooms for rent or hire and which is actually occupied by the proprietor of such establishment as his residence;

(2) any restaurant, cafeteria, lunchroom, lunch counter, soda fountain, or other facility principally engaged in selling food for consumption on the premises, including, but not limited to, any such facility located on the premises of any retail establishment; or any gasoline station;

(3) any motion picture house, theater, concert hall, sports arena, stadium or other place of exhibition or entertainment; . . .

SEC. 202. All persons shall be entitled to be free, at any establishment or place, from discrimination or segregation of any kind on the ground of race, color, religion, or national origin, if such discrimination or segregation is or purports to be required by any law, statute, ordinance, regulation, rule, or order of a State or any agency or political subdivision thereof.

SEC. 203. No person shall (a) withhold, deny, or attempt to withhold or deny, or deprive or attempt to deprive, any person of any right or privilege secured by section 201 or 202, or (b) intimidate, threaten, or coerce, or attempt to intimidate, threaten, or coerce any person with the purpose of interfering with any right or privilege secured by section 201 or 202, or (c) punish or attempt to punish any person for exercising or attempting to exercise any right or privilege secured by section 201 or 202.

SEC. 204. (a) Whenever any person has engaged or there are reasonable grounds to believe that any person is about to engage in any act or practice prohibited by section 203, a civil action for preventive relief, including an application for a permanent or temporary injunction, restraining order, or other order, may be instituted by the person aggrieved and, upon timely application, the court may, in its discretion, permit the Attorney General to intervene in such civil action if he certifies that the case is of general public importance. . . .

SEC. 206. (a) Whenever the Attorney General has reasonable cause to believe that any person or group of persons is engaged in a pattern or practice of resistance to the full enjoyment of any of the rights secured by this title, and that the pattern or practice is of such a nature and is intended to deny the full exercise of the rights herein described, the Attorney General may bring a civil action in the appropriate district court of the United States. . . .

TITLE III—DESEGREGATION
OF PUBLIC FACILITIES

SEC. 301. (a) Whenever the Attorney General receives a complaint in writing signed by an individual to the effect that he is being deprived of or threatened with the loss of his right to the equal protection of the laws, on account of his race, color, religion, or national origin, by being denied equal utilization of any public facility which is owned, operated, or managed by or on behalf of any State or subdivision thereof, other than a public school or public college as defined in section 401 of title IV hereof, and the Attorney General believes the complaint is meritorious and certifies that the signer or signers of such complaint are unable, in his judgment, to initiate and maintain appropriate legal proceedings for relief and that the institution of an action will materially further the orderly progress of desegregation in public facilities, the Attorney General is authorized to institute for or in the name of the United States a civil action in any appropriate district court of the United States against such parties and for such relief as may be appropriate, and such court shall have and shall exercise jurisdiction of proceedings instituted pursuant to this section. The Attorney General may implead as defendants such additional parties as are or become necessary to the grant of effective relief hereunder. . . .

TITLE IV—DESEGREGATION
OF PUBLIC EDUCATION SUITS
BY THE ATTORNEY GENERAL

SEC. 407. (a) Whenever the Attorney General receives a complaint in writing—

(1) signed by a parent or group of parents to the effect that his or their minor children, as members of a class of persons similarly situated, are being deprived by a school board of the equal protection of the laws, or

(2) signed by an individual, or his parent, to the effect that he has been denied admission to or not permitted to continue in attendance at a public college by reason of race, color, religion, or national origin,

—and the Attorney General believes the complaint is meritorious and certifies that the signer or signers of such complaint are unable, in his judgment, to initiate and maintain appropriate legal proceedings for relief and that the institution of an action will materially further the orderly achievement of desegregation in public education, the Attorney General is authorized, after giving notice of such complaint to the appropriate school board or college authority and after certifying that he is satisfied that such board or authority has had a reasonable time to adjust the conditions alleged in such complaint, to institute for or in the name of the United States a civil action in any appropriate district court of the United States against such parties and for such relief as may be appropriate, and such

court shall have and shall exercise jurisdiction of proceedings instituted pursuant to this section, provided that nothing herein shall empower any official or court of the United States to issue any order seeking to achieve a racial balance in any school by requiring the transportation of pupils or students from one school to another or one school district to another in order to achieve such racial balance, or otherwise enlarge the existing power of the court to insure compliance with constitutional standards. . . .

TITLE VI—
NONDISCRIMINATION IN FEDERALLY
ASSISTED PROGRAMS

SEC. 601. No person in the United States shall, on the ground of race, color, or national origin, be excluded from participation in, be denied the benefits of, or be subjected to discrimination under any program or activity receiving Federal financial assistance.

SEC. 602. Each Federal department and agency which is empowered to extend Federal financial assistance to any program or activity, by way of grant, loan, or contract other than a contract of insurance or guaranty, is authorized and directed to effectuate the provisions of section 601 with respect to such program or activity by issuing rules, regulations, or orders of general applicability which shall be consistent with achievement of the objectives of the statute authorizing the financial assistance in connection with which the action is taken. No such rule, regulation, or order shall become effective unless and until approved by the President. Compliance with any requirement adopted pursuant to this section may be effected (1) by the termination of or refusal to grant or to continue assistance under such program or activity to any recipient as to whom there has been an express finding on the record, after opportunity for hearing, of a failure to comply with such requirement, but such termination or refusal shall be limited to the particular political entity, or part thereof, or other recipient as to whom such a finding has been made and, shall be limited in its effect to the particular program, or part thereof, in which non-compliance has been so found, or (2) by any other means authorized by law: Provided, however, That no such action shall be taken until the department or agency concerned has advised the appropriate person or persons of the failure to comply with the requirement and has determined that compliance cannot be secured by voluntary means. In the case of any action terminating, or refusing to grant or continue, assistance because of failure to comply with a requirement imposed pursuant to this section, the head of the Federal department or agency shall file with the committees of the House and Senate having legislative jurisdiction over the program or activity involved a full written report of the circumstances and the grounds for such action. No such action shall become effective until thirty days have elapsed after the filing of such report. . . .

TITLE VII—
EQUAL EMPLOYMENT OPPORTUNITY.
DISCRIMINATION
BECAUSE OF RACE, COLOR,
RELIGION, SEX,
OR NATIONAL ORIGIN

SEC. 703. (a) It shall be an unlawful employment practice for an employer—

(1) to fail or refuse to hire or to discharge any individual, or otherwise to discriminate against any individual with respect to his compensation, terms, conditions, or privileges of employment, because of such individual's race, color, religion, sex, or national origin; or

(2) to limit, segregate, or classify his employees in any way which would deprive or tend to deprive any individual of employment opportunities or otherwise adversely affect his status as an employee, because of such individual's race, color, religion, sex, or national origin.

(b) It shall be an unlawful employment practice for an employment agency to fail or refuse to refer for employment, or otherwise to discriminate against, any individual because of his race, color, religion, sex, or national origin, or to classify or refer for employment any individual on the basis of his race, color, religion, sex, or national origin.

(c) It shall be an unlawful employment practice for a labor organization—

(1) to exclude or to expel from its membership, or otherwise to discriminate against, any individual because of his race, color, religion, sex, or national origin;

(2) to limit, segregate, or classify its membership, or to classify or fail or refuse to refer for employment any individual, in any way which would deprive or tend to deprive any individual of employment opportunities, or would limit such employment opportunities or otherwise adversely affect his status as an employee or as an applicant for employment, because of such individual's race, color, religion, sex, or national origin; or

(3) to cause or attempt to cause an employer to discriminate against an individual in violation of this section.

(d) It shall be an unlawful employment practice for any employer, labor organization, or joint labor-management committee controlling apprenticeship or other training or retraining, including on-the-job training programs to discriminate against any individual because of his race, color, religion, sex, or national origin in admission to, or employment in, any program established to provide apprenticeship or other training. . . .

EFFECT ON STATE LAWS

SEC. 708. Nothing in this title shall be deemed to exempt or relieve any person from any liability, duty, penalty, or punishment provided by any present or future law of any State or political subdivision of a State, other than any such law which purports to require or permit the doing of any act which would be an unlawful employment practice under this title. . . .

SEC. 1104. Nothing contained in any title of this Act shall be construed as indicating an intent on the part of Congress to occupy the field in which any such title operates to the exclusion of State laws on the same subject matter, nor shall any provision of this Act be construed as invalidating any provision of State law unless such provision is inconsistent with any of the purposes of this Act, or any provision thereof.

## Selections and Sources

**Document 1:** William Symonds, *Virginia, A Sermon Preached at White-Chappel* (London, 1609). **2:** W. W. Hening, *The Statutes at Large: Being a Collection of All the Laws of Virginia* (13 vols., Richmond, Va., 1810-1823). All from Vol. I. (a) p. 64, (b) 68-69, (c) 74, (e) 110-113, (f) 319-320, (g) 371-372, (h) 372, (i) 499-503; (d) S. M. Kingsbury, *The Records of the Virginia Company of London* (4 vols., Washington, D.C., 1906-1935), III, 99-102. **3:** William Bradford, *Of Plimouth Plantation* (Boston, 1898), 109-110. **4:** Max Farrand, ed., *The Laws and Liberties of Massachusetts*, reprinted from the copy of the 1648 edition in the Henry E. Huntington Library, San Marino, Calif. (Cambridge, Mass., 1929). (a) p. A2, (b) 1-51. **5:** (a) Kingsbury, *Records*, II, 358-361. (b) Hening, *Statutes*, I, 227, 333-334, 403, 411-412; II, 280, 356-357, 380, 425-426; III, 172-173, 238; IV, 133-134, 475-476. **6:** Hening, *Statutes*, I, 146, 226; II, 26, 170, 260, 267, 283, 288, 481-482; III, 86, 86-87, 87-88. **7:** (a) George Staughton, B. M. Nead, Thomas McCamant, eds., *Charter to William Penn and Laws of the Province of Pennsylvania Between the Years 1682 and 1700* (Harrisburg, Pa., 1879), 268-272. (b) R. N. Toppan, A. T. S. Goodrick, eds., *Edward Randolph: Including His Letters and Official Papers . . . 1676-1703* (5 vols., Boston, 1898-1909), V, 189-190. (c) Toppan and Goodrick, *Randolph*, V, 263-268. **8:** *The Trial of John Peter Zenger . . . with a Narrative of His Case* (London, 1745). **9:** (a) E. B. O'Callaghan, ed., *Documents Relative to the Colonial History of the State of New York* (10 vols., Albany, N.Y., 1849-1858), VII, 17-28. (b) *Minutes of the Provincial Council of Pennsylvania* (Harrisburg, Pa., 1852), IX, 407-410. **10:** E. S. Morgan, ed., *Prologue to Revolution: Sources and Documents on the Stamp Act Crisis, 1764-1766* (Chapel Hill, No. Car., 1959), 62-63. **11:** Peter Force, ed., *American Archives* (9 vols., Washington, D.C., 1837-1853), I, 914-915. **12:** C. C. Tansill, ed., *Documents Illustrative of the Formation of the Union of the American States* (Washington, D.C., 1927), 22-26. **13:** (a) C. F. Adams, ed., *The Works of John Adams* (10 vols., Boston, 1850-1856), IV, 193-200. (b) Tansill, *Documents*, 27-37. **14:** Gaillard Hunt, ed., *The Writings of James Madison* (9 vols., New York, 1900-1910), II, 183-191. **15:** Tansill, *Documents*, 47-54. **16:** E. S. Corwin, ed., *The Constitution of the United States of America* (Washington, D.C., 1953), 19-54. **17:** J. C. Hamilton, ed., *The Works of Alexander Hamilton* (7 vols., New York, 1851), IV, 104-138. **18:** J. D. Richardson, ed., *A Compilation of the Messages and Papers of the Presidents,*

*1789-1897* (10 vols., Washington, D.C., 1896-1899), I, 213-224. **19:** Jonathan Elliot, *The Debates in the Several State Conventions on the Adoption of the Federal Constitution, etc.* (5 vols., Washington, D.C., 1836-1845), IV, 540-544. **20:** *Inaugural Addresses of the Presidents of the United States from George Washington 1789 to John F. Kennedy 1961* (Washington, D.C., 1961), 13-16. **21:** P. L. Ford, ed., *The Writings of Thomas Jefferson* (10 vols., New York, 1892-1899), VIII. (a) 7-8, (b) 103-106, (c) 192-202, (d) 144-147, (e) 261-263. **22:** *Supreme Court Reports.* (a) 1 Cranch 66. (b) 4 Wheaton 316. **23:** (a) C. Adams, ed., *Memoirs of John Quincy Adams* (4 vols., Philadelphia, 1875), IV, 438-439. (b) Richardson, *Messages*, II, 209, 217-219. **24:** (a) N. H. Carter, W. L. Stone, M. T. C. Gould, eds., *Reports of the Proceedings and Debates of the Convention of 1821 Assembled for the Purpose of Amending the Constitution of the State of New York* (Albany, N.Y., 1821), 180-181, 183-185, 256-258, 367-368. (b) F. N. Thorpe, *The Federal and State Constitutions, Colonial Charters, . . . (etc.),* (7 vols., Washington, D.C., 1909), I, 544; II, 975; V, 2642, 2652, 3108; VII, 4080. **25:** Calvin Colton, ed., *The Works of Henry Clay* (10 vols., New York, 1904), VI, 256-294. **26:** Richardson, *Messages*, II, 483-494, 576-591. **27:** *Fifth Annual Report of the Board of Education, Together with the Fifth Annual Report of the Secretary of the Board* (Boston, 1842), 80-120. **28:** *U.S. Senate, 28th Cong., 2nd Sess.: Senate Documents* v. III, 1844-1845, No. 69. **29:** (a) R. J. Walker, *Letter . . . Relative to the Annexation of Texas, in Reply to the Call of the People of Carroll County, Kentucky* (Washington, D.C., 1844). (b) Richardson, *Messages*, IV, 379-381. (c) Richardson, *Messages*, IV, 398-399. (d) James W. Sheahan, *The Life of Stephen A. Douglas* (New York, 1860), 75-90. (e) *Congressional Globe, 29th Cong., 2nd Sess., Appendix, 186-196.* (f) Edward Everett, ed., *The Works of Daniel Webster* (6 vols., 1851) VI, 492-497. **30:** R. P. Basler, ed., *The Collected Works of Abraham Lincoln* (9 vols., New Brunswick, N.J., 1953-1955), II, 247-283. **31:** B. C. Howard, *Report of the Decision of the Supreme Court of the United States and the Opinions of the Judges Thereof in the Case of Dred Scott Versus John F. A. Sandford* (Washington, D.C., 1857). **32:** *Inaugural Addresses* (as in 20), 119-126. **33:** *U.S. Statutes at Large,* 37th Cong., 2nd Sess., 1862, XII. (a) 392-393, (b) 489-497, (c) 503-505. **34:** Basler, *Lincoln,* VI, 28-30. **35:** Basler, *Lincoln,* VII, 23. **36:** (a) *Report of the Joint Committee on Reconstruction* (Washington, D.C., 1866), Part

III, 182-183. (b) *Laws of the State of Mississippi,* 1865 (Jackson, Miss., 1866), 82-93, 165-167. **37:** *Annual Report of the Commissioner of Indian Affairs* (Washington, D.C., 1872), 3-14. **38:** New York State, *Report of the Special (Hepburn) Committee on Railroads* (6 vols., Albany, N.Y., 1880), II, 1667-1670. **39:** *Report of the Select (Cullom) Committee . . . to Investigate the Subject . . . of the Regulation of . . . Transportation,* U.S. Senate, 49th Cong., 1st Sess., Report No. 46 (Washington, D.C., 1886), 37-215. **40:** (a) Richardson, *Messages,* VIII, 580-591. (b) *Congressional Record,* 50th Cong., 1st Sess., 4440-4446. **41:** (a) United States Strike Commission: *Report on the Chicago Strike* (Washington, D.C., 1895), 179-180. (b) 62 *Federal Reporter,* 828-833. (c) 158 *U.S. Supreme Court Reports,* 579. **42:** (a) *Official Journal of the Proceedings of the Constitutional Convention of the State of Louisiana* (New Orleans, 1898), 374-379. (b) Thorpe, *Constitutions,* I, 209-211, 215; III, 1562-1565; IV, 2120-2121; VI, 3310-3311. **43:** (a) Richardson, *Messages,* X. 139-150. (b) *U.S. Statutes at Large,* 55th Cong., 2nd Sess., XXX, 738-739. **44:** *Congressional Record,* 56th Cong., 1st Sess., 704-712. **45:** (a) *Congressional Record,* 56th Cong., 2nd Sess., 2954. (b) Richardson, *Messages,* enlarged and extended edition, XVI, 7053-7054, 7374-7376. **46:** *Women in Industry, Decision of the United States Supreme Court in Curt Muller vs. State of Oregon . . . and Brief for the State of Oregon by Louis D. Brandeis* (reprinted for National Consumers League), 1-8 (following p. 113). **47:** Richardson, *Messages,* extended ed., XVII, 7579-7598. **48:** (a) Albert Shaw, ed., *The Messages and Papers of Woodrow Wilson* (2 vols., New York, 1924), I, 48-55. (b) *U. S. Statutes at Large,* 63rd Cong., 2nd Sess., 1914, XXXVIII, 730-740. **49:** Shaw, *Wilson,* I, 464-472. **50:** *Inaugural Addresses* (as in 20), 235-239. **51:** *U.S. Statutes at Large.* (a) 73rd Cong., 1st Sess., 1933, XLVIII, 31-54. (b) 74th Cong., 1st Sess., 1935, XLIX, 449-457. (c) (as in 51b), 620-648. **52:** S. I. Rosenman, ed., *The Public Papers and Addresses of Franklin D. Roosevelt* (9 vols., New York, 1938-1941), 1940 vol., 663-672. **53:** *Congressional Record,* 79th Cong., 1st Sess., 7941-7946. **54:** (a) *Congressional Record,* 80th Cong., 1st Sess., Appendix, A 3248. (b) *Public Papers of the Presidents of the United States: 1961* (Washington, D.C., 1962), 170-175. **55:** (a) 347 *U.S. Supreme Court Reports,* 483. (b) *House Document 7152,* 88th Cong., 2nd Sess.

## DATE DUE

| DEC 5 1977 | | | |
|---|---|---|---|
| | | | |
| | | | |
| | | | |
| | | | |
| | | | |
| | | | |
| | | | |
| | | | |
| | | | |
| | | | |
| | | | |
| | | | |
| | | | |
| | | | |
| | | | PRINTED IN U.S.A. |